A History of Archaeological Thought

Second Edition

In its original edition, Bruce Trigger's book was the first ever to examine the history of archaeological thought from medieval times to the present in world-wide perspective. Now, in this new edition, he both updates the original work and introduces new archaeological perspectives and concerns. At once stimulating and even-handed, it places the development of archaeological thought and theory within a broad social and intellectual framework. The successive but interacting trends apparent in archaeological thought are defined and the author seeks to determine the extent to which these trends were a reflection of the personal and collective interests of archaeologists as these relate – in the West at least – to the fluctuating fortunes of the middle classes. Although subjective influences have been powerful, Professor Trigger argues that the gradual accumulation of archaeological data has exercised a growing constraint on interpretation. In turn, this use of data has increased the objectivity of archaeological research and enhanced its value for understanding the entire span of human history and the human condition in general.

Bruce G. Trigger is James McGill Professor in the Department of Anthropology at McGill University. He received his PhD from Yale University and has carried out archaeological research in Egypt and the Sudan. His interests include the comparative study of early civilizations, the history of archaeology, and archaeological and anthropological theory. He has received various scholarly awards, including the prestigious Prix Léon-Gérin from the Quebec government, for his sustained contributions to the social sciences. He is an honorary fellow of the Society of Antiquaries of Scotland and an honorary member of the Prehistoric Society (UK). His numerous books include the first edition of *A History of Archaeological Thought* (Cambridge 1989); *The Cambridge History of the Native Peoples of the Americas, Volume I* (Cambridge 1996), coedited with Wilcomb E. Washburn; and *Understanding Early Civilizations* (Cambridge 2003).

BRUCE G. TRIGGER

—

A History
of
Archaeological
Thought

Second Edition

CAMBRIDGE
UNIVERSITY PRESS

CAMBRIDGE UNIVERSITY PRESS
Cambridge, New York, Melbourne, Madrid, Cape Town, Singapore,
São Paulo, Delhi, Dubai, Tokyo

Cambridge University Press
32 Avenue of the Americas, New York, NY 10013-2473, USA

www.cambridge.org
Information on this title: www.cambridge.org/9780521600491

First edition 1989
Second edition 2006
Reprinted 2007 (twice), 2008, 2009 (twice), 2010

Printed in Great Britain by Clays Ltd, St Ives plc

A catalog record for this publication is available from the British Library.

Library of Congress Cataloging in Publication Data
Trigger, Bruce G.
A history of archaeological thought / Bruce G. Trigger. – 2nd ed.
p.   cm.
Includes bibliographical references and index.
ISBN-13: 978-0-521-84076-7 (hardback)
ISBN-10: 0-521-84076-7 (hardback)
ISBN-13: 978-0-521-60049-1 (pbk.)
ISBN-10: 0-521-60049-9 (pbk.)
1. Archaeology – History.   2. Archaeology – Philosophy – History.
I. Title.
CC100.T75   2006
930.1 – dc22   2006007559

ISBN 978-0-521-84076-7 Hardback
ISBN 978-0-521-60049-1 Paperback

To BARBARA

CONTENTS

Contents

Contents

ILLUSTRATIONS

Illustrations

Illustrations

PREFACE TO THE SECOND EDITION

Since the first edition of *A History of Archaeological Thought* was published in 1989, there has been a significant upsurge of interest in the history of archaeology and a vast increase in the publication of books and papers relating to this topic. As recently as the 1970s, one or two significant books and a handful of papers dealing with the history of archaeology were published each year. At the height of their influence in the 1970s, processual archaeologists proclaimed that the history of archaeology was irrelevant for understanding the development of the discipline, which they argued was shaped by the deployment of ever more rigorous forms of scientific method. This view reduced the history of archaeology to being little more than a form of entertainment or propaganda. Today, a growing number of archaeologists, who accept that what archaeologists believe influences not only the questions they ask but also the answers they find acceptable, maintain that all archaeological interpretations must be evaluated in relation to their historical context. This growing interest has transformed the history of archaeology into being an established subdiscipline of archaeology with its own international bulletin, symposia, encyclopedias, textbooks, and publication series. An increasing number of studies, often based on painstaking archival research and oral histories, are examining the archaeology practiced at specific times and in specific places from a variety of analytical perspectives. These works have made a new edition of *A History of Archaeological Thought* essential.

Archaeological theory and practice have also changed radically since the 1980s. The last fifteen years have witnessed the growing diversification of postprocessual archaeology and the spread of some of its key ideas throughout archaeology, as archaeologists have striven to understand better how human beliefs and behavior relate to material culture. At the same time, Darwinian and behavioral archaeology have been challenging processual archaeology's long-standing monopoly of materialist explanations of archaeological findings and there is growing interest in the possible constraints that psychological and biological factors exert on human behavior and beliefs. The collapse of the communist regimes of Eastern Europe and of the Soviet Union and the growing impact that an increasingly transnational economy has been having on regional, national, and supranational loyalties in various parts of the world have encouraged a renewed interest in culture-historical archaeology and its key concept, ethnicity. Under these conditions, the inadequacies of the processual/postprocessual dichotomy that arose in the 1980s and early 1990s are becoming ever more evident. Theoretical diversity is increasingly being appreciated as a source of enhanced understanding rather than regarded as a threat to archaeology. As a result, efforts are being made to produce broader theoretical frameworks within which diverse approaches can be synthesized and assigned mutually supportive roles.

Archaeologists also are becoming more aware of what is known about the nature of scientific enquiry. In the 1960s, the naive empiricism of many American archaeologists was challenged by a dogmatic positivism that stressed the need to create knowledge by formulating and testing deductive propositions about human behavior. More recently, a growing appreciation of relativism and a reviving interest in the role played by beliefs in influencing human behavior have promoted a growing appreciation of realist and idealist epistemologies. As a result, a growing number of archaeologists have come to view the positivism and ecological determinism of the 1960s as outmoded and erroneous. A second edition of *A History of Archaeological Thought* is needed not only to survey the theoretical developments of the last fifteen years but to take account of the important insights gained as a result of these developments as they relate to viewing the entire history of archaeological thought.

In this second edition, I also seek to rectify the shortcomings of my original work. In addition to correcting factual errors, I have tried to provide a more balanced coverage by paying more attention to classical and other forms of historical archaeology, as well as to prehistoric archaeology in continental Europe and other non-English speaking parts of the world. I also pay more attention to gender issues and discuss in some detail the work of R. G. Collingwood, André

Leroi-Gourhan, and other archaeological theorists who received little or no attention in the first edition.

To keep this edition about the same length as the first one, I have had to condense or omit sections of the original work that seem less important in the early 2000s than they did in the late 1980s. The material that appeared in the chapter on "Soviet Archaeology" has been broken up and now appears, often in abbreviated form, in the chapters dealing with culture-historical, early functional-processual, and recent archaeology. The amount of coverage devoted to Gordon Childe also has been reduced, and hindsight has permitted the treatment of processual and postprocessual archaeology to be simultaneously condensed and clarified.

The need for concision also has compelled me to recognize more clearly than I did in the first edition that I am writing an intellectual history of archaeology. The primary focus of this edition is on the development of the main ideas that have guided archaeological thought, not on great discoveries, the development of analytical techniques, or the accumulation of factual knowledge about the past, although I acknowledge that these are important and worthwhile topics. This book also does not attempt to provide a balanced coverage of archaeological research done in all countries or regions of the world, or to describe the networks of archaeological researchers that have played a key role in shaping archaeological thought. Likewise, although I recognize that social, political, economic, and institutional factors have played important roles in the development of archaeological thought, tracing these influences is not my primary goal. While these topics are discussed, insofar as they are necessary for understanding the development of archaeological theory, I have taken care that this book does not become primarily a social or institutional history. Finally, because I view archaeology from a world perspective, my primary emphasis is on comparison rather than providing detailed accounts of specific events, which are now being examined in a growing number of books and monographs.

After 1989, I spent twelve years researching and writing *Understanding Early Civilizations* (2003a), the goal of which was to develop a better understanding of archaeological and anthropological theory. My findings have been applied in the present work. As a result, my critiques of various theoretical positions are more specific and detailed than they were in the first edition. I am also prepared to project certain trends into the future, subject to the understanding that these are extrapolations, not predictions, which I do not believe are possible in the social sciences.

The original edition of *A History of Archaeological Thought* was based to a considerable extent on my previous writings, as detailed in my Preface to that work. In many respects, that edition betrays its piecemeal origins. Although the second edition is based on the first, it is also grounded on considerable original research and has been rewritten and reshaped from beginning to end. Scarcely a sentence has not been altered and much new material has been substituted for the original text. I hope that careful planning and thorough revision have resulted in a more unified as well as an updated work.

In the first edition, I thanked for their help Rosemarie Bernard, Chen Chun, Margaret Deith, Brian Fagan, Norman Hammond, Fumiko Ikawa-Smith, Jane Kelley, Philip Kohl, Isabel McBryde, Mary Mason, Valerie Pinsky, Neil Silberman, Peter Timmins, Robert Vogel, Alexander von Gernet, Michael Woloch, and Alison Wylie, as well as other colleagues who sent me reprints of their papers. For help with the second edition, I wish to thank especially Wakoh Anazawa for generously sharing with me his perspectives on the history of Japanese archaeology; Mario Bunge and Oscar Moro Abadía for their close reading of the first edition and their numerous helpful comments on it; Stephen Chrisomalis for his research on the concept of ethnicity and his summaries and evaluations of the many papers on the history of archaeology published between 1989 and 2002; Michael O'Brien and his coauthors for providing me in advance of publication with a copy of their trendsetting book *Archaeology as a Process*; and Peter Rowley-Conwy for sharing with me on an ongoing basis the findings of his important research on the development of prehistoric archaeology in Scandinavia from 1835 to 1843. I am most grateful to Randall McGuire for reading and commenting in detail on a preliminary draft of the entire book. I also thank for their help Brian Alters, Linda Beringhaus, André Costopoulos, Nicole Couture, Marguerita Díaz-Andreu, John Galaty, Heinrich Härke, Alice Kehoe, Kristian Kristiansen, Harry Lerner, Michael Lever, Tim Murray, Nadezhda Platinova, Jonathan Reyman, Ulrike Sommer, George Stocking, Thomas Patterson, and numerous undergraduates who since the 1970s have taken my courses, "The History of Archaeological Theory" and "Current Issues in Archaeology," as well as graduate students who have participated in various seminars. A detailed review of the original edition of my book by L. B. Vishnyatsky et al. (1992) was very helpful for revising my treatment of Soviet archaeology. It was translated for me from Russian by Natasha Pakhomova.

I further thank Petra Kalshoven for her skillful editorial work. She provided my manuscript with American spelling and grammar, as well as assiduously challenging how I expressed my ideas and not infrequently the ideas themselves. Her knowledge of both classical archaeology and sociocultural anthropology made her a most helpful and welcome critic and the result is a more accurate and reader-friendly book. I am also most grateful to Diane Mann for expertly turning my numerous index cards into a bibliography and for word-processing the final versions of the manuscript, Rose Marie Stano for keeping my accounts, and Cynthia Romanyk for her help with mailing and communications. Jenna Friedman and Rosalyn Trigger helped to verify the references and Rosalyn Trigger prepared the new illustrative material for submission to the publisher. I also thank Cathy Felgar (Cambridge University Press) and Mary Paden (TechBooks) for overseeing production of this book, Lindsey Smith for securing permission to use illustrations, Susan Stevenson for expert proofreading, and Catherine Fox for preparing the index. Last, but not least, I thank Frank Smith for his good advice at every stage in the production of this book.

As in the first edition, sources for specific facts and ideas are provided between brackets in the text, whereas the Bibliographical Essay at the end of the book supplies a more general guide to the sources that are relevant for each chapter.

Research for the first edition was greatly assisted by a sabbatical leave from McGill University and a Canada Council Leave Fellowship in 1976–1977 and a second sabbatical leave and a Social Sciences and Humanities Research Council of Canada Leave Fellowship in 1983. The second edition was largely drafted during a sabbatical leave in 2004 and work on it has been supported since 2002 by the stipend attached to my James McGill Professorship.

This book is written from the perspective of ontological materialism and epistemological realism. These are positions that I am convinced any social scientist who believes in the evolutionary origin of the human species must adopt. I also appreciate the value of relativist critiques of knowledge for promoting sound scientific practice.

I developed my understanding of relativism from traditional (materialist) Marxist philosophy. Although I accept the importance of theories of culture for understanding human behavior, I reject cultural determinism, just as I reject ecological determinism and unilinear evolutionism. Inspired by the work of Gordon Childe, I have long sought to reconcile a materialist approach with efforts to account for the cultural and historical diversity that characterizes both human behavior and the archaeological record.

This book goes to press at a time that should see archaeology consolidate its position as a mature social science devoted to the study of past human behavior, culture, and history by means of material culture. Much of this development will come about as the result of fractious theoretical confrontations being balanced by a growing emphasis on theoretical accommodation and synthesis. Archaeology also will establish its credentials as the only social science with a broad enough temporal perspective that the historical significance of all the other social sciences has to be established in relation to it.

Last but not least, I rededicate this second edition to my wife Barbara, with love and gratitude for all the happiness and purpose she brings to my life. I also thank her for providing Fisherman's Retreat, a haven where over three summers I was able to focus on this book. She also has read the entire manuscript and made valuable contributions to improving its clarity.

CHAPTER I

Studying the History of Archaeology

——

Though there exists one major academic industry... telling the
social scientists... how they can turn themselves into genuine
scientists, there exists another, with at least as flourishing an
output, putatively establishing that the study of man and society
cannot be scientific.

ERNEST GELLNER, *Relativism and the Social Sciences* (1985), p. 120

Since the 1950s archaeology, especially in North America and western Europe, has shifted from a seemingly complacent culture-historical orthodoxy to ambitious theoretical innovations. These innovations have led to growing disagreements about the goals of the discipline and how these goals can be achieved. Increasing numbers of archaeologists, following in the wake of historians and sociologists, have abandoned positivist certainty and begun to entertain doubts about the objectivity of their research. They see social factors as determining not only the questions they ask but also the answers they judge to be convincing. Extreme versions of this view deny that archaeologists can offer interpretations of their data that are other than a reflection of the transient values of the societies in which they live. Yet, if archaeology cannot produce some kind of cumulative understanding of the past and a commentary that is at least partially independent of specific historical contexts, what scientific – as opposed to political, psychological, or aesthetic – justification can be offered for doing archaeological research?

These concerns have encouraged studying the history of archaeological thought as a means by which problems of subjectivity, objectivity, and the gradual accumulation of knowledge can be assessed. A growing number of archaeologists have come to agree with the philosopher and archaeologist R. G. Collingwood (1939: 132) that "no historical problem should be studied without studying... the history of historical thought about it." The clear implication of

Collingwood's position is that archaeological interpretation and the history of archaeology are closely aligned. In recent decades, historical investigations of archaeological interpretation have multiplied and more advanced methodologies for carrying out such studies have been adopted from the history of science (Corbey and Roebroek 2001). Christopher Gosden (1999: 34) has argued that to be effective, disciplinary histories must not be purely intellectual or social but both.

This historical approach is not, however, without its critics. Michael Schiffer (1976: 193) once asserted that graduate courses should cease to be "histories of thought" and instead should systematically expound and articulate current theories, as, in a general sort of way, K. R. Dark has since done in his book *Theoretical Archaeology* (1995). Schiffer's position embodied the view that the truth or falseness of theoretical formulations is independent of social influences and hence of history but can be determined by applying scientifically valid procedures of evaluation to adequate bodies of data. Taken to an extreme, this view implies that the history and philosophy of archaeology are totally unrelated to each other.

The primary goal of this book is to survey the intellectual history of archaeology in an attempt to evaluate the claims of three alternative epistemologies that are currently being applied to archaeology. Positivist epistemologists maintain that society and culture exert no significant influence on the development of archaeology, which is shaped by explanations based on explicit theories being tested in the light of adequate evidence and according to proper scientific methods. Extreme relativists argue that the interpretation of archaeological data is so influenced by the intellectual persuasions, class interests, ethnic loyalties, gender prejudices, and personal self-interest of archaeologists that objectivity is impossible. There is no such thing as objective knowledge, and, therefore, no one truth but many possibly antithetical truths. Moderate relativists concede that archaeological interpretations are influenced by society, culture, and self-interest but maintain that archaeological evidence constrains speculation. The term relativism, as used here, embraces both relativism, in the strict sense of phenomena being perceived, valued, and understood differently as a result of cultural variation, and subjectivism, which refers to how phenomena are perceived, valued, and understood differently as a result of variations in individual comprehension. To address these questions, it is necessary to consider what archaeologists have learned about the past, how the methods they use to study the past have changed, what ideas have guided the development of archaeology at different periods, how these ideas relate to broader social, cultural, and intellectual trends, whether different societies produce different kinds of archaeology and, if so, what are the differences, and finally whether there is long-term convergence or divergence in the development of archaeology. It also cannot be assumed that the same factors necessarily influence archaeology to the same extent at every stage in its development.

Archaeology is not a universal or self-evident activity. In some countries, people debate whether foreign archaeologists are treasure hunters or spies. They cannot imagine that anyone would be interested in going to so much trouble and expense to study the past for its own sake. In Western civilization, despite the popularity of the Indiana Jones stereotype, it is generally accepted that archaeology is an esoteric discipline that has no relevance for the needs or concerns of the present. Ernest Hooton (1938: 218) once described archaeologists as "the senile playboys of science rooting in the rubbish heaps of antiquity." Yet for almost 200 years a widespread concern for the broader implications of archaeological discoveries has contradicted this image of archaeology. No one would deny the romantic fascination aroused by spectacular archaeological finds, such as those by Austen Layard at Nimrud or Heinrich Schliemann at Troy in the nineteenth century, and the more recent discoveries of the tomb of Tutankhamen, the Palace of Minos at Knossos, the life-size ceramic army of the Chinese Emperor Qin Shihuangdi, and numerous several-million-years-old remains of hominids in East Africa. This does not, however, explain the intense public interest in the controversies that have surrounded the interpretation of many more routine archaeological finds, the attention that diverse political, social, and religious movements throughout the world have paid to archaeological research, and rigorous efforts by various totalitarian regimes to control the interpretation of archaeological data. During the second half of the nineteenth century, archaeology was looked to for support by both sides in the debate about whether evolutionism or the book of Genesis provided a more reliable account of human origins. Later, W. M. F. Petrie, Leonard Woolley, and John Garstang claimed to have made finds in Egypt, Iraq, and Palestine that supported historical accounts in the Hebrew Bible. Elsewhere German and Polish archaeologists engaged in polemics about whether the Lusatian culture had been created by prehistoric Germans or Slavs. As recently as the 1970s, Peter Garlake, a government-employed archaeologist in Southern Rhodesia, found his position no longer tenable because he refused to cast doubt on conclusive archaeological evidence that stone ruins in that part of central Africa had been built by ancestors of the Bantu peoples who live in that region. Today, the findings of ecological archaeologists are being coopted both by conservationists and by those who are anxious to minimize legal restraints on environmental pollution and degradation.

My adoption of a historical perspective does not mean that I claim any privileged status with respect to objectivity for such an approach. Historical interpretations are notoriously conjectural and open-ended, to the extent that some historians have characterized them as merely expressions of personal opinion. It is also recognized that, because of the abundance of historical data, evidence can be selectively marshaled to "prove" almost anything. There may, however, be some truth in William McNeill's (1986: 164) argument that, even if historical interpretation is a form of myth-making, such myths help to guide public action and can be regarded as a human substitute for instinct. If this is so, it follows that they are subject to the operation of the social equivalent of natural selection and hence may more closely approximate reality over long periods of time. This, however, is a tenuous basis on which to base hopes for the objectivity of historical interpretations.

I therefore do not claim that the historical study presented here is any more objective than are the interpretations of archaeological or ethnological data that it examines. I believe, however, as do many others who study the history of archaeology, that a historical approach offers a special vantage point from which to examine the changing relations between archaeological interpretation and its social and cultural milieu. The time perspective provides a different basis for studying the ties between archaeology and society than do philosophical or sociological approaches. In particular, it permits the researcher to identify the influence of subjective factors by observing how and under what circumstances interpretations of the archaeological record have changed. Although this does not eliminate the bias of the observer, or the possibility that this bias will influence the interpretation of archaeological data, it increases the chances of gaining more rounded insights into what happened in the past.

Approaches to the History of Archaeology

The need for a more systematic study of the history of archaeological interpretation is indicated by serious disagreements about the nature and significance of that history. Much of the controversy centers on the role played by explanation in the study of archaeological data over the last two centuries.

Some historians of archaeology believe that the discipline has evolved in a predetermined manner through a series of stages (Schwartz 1967; Fitting 1973). In *A History of American Archaeology*, G. R. Willey and J. A. Sabloff (1974, 1980) posited an initial Speculative period (1492–1840) followed by Classificatory-Descriptive (1840–1914), Classificatory-Historical (1914–1960), and Explanatory (1960–) ones. This scheme was based in part on Douglas Schwartz's (1967) previous division of the history of American archaeology into three stages: Speculative, Empirical, and Explanatory. Only in the 1993 edition of *A History of American Archaeology* was the final period, which began in 1960, renamed the Modern one. Although this series of stages was applied only to New World archaeology, Willey and Sabloff (1974: 209–10) observed that their scheme was likely to apply everywhere. They proposed that over the course of 150 years archaeology had developed according to an inductive Baconian model of doing science, which involves first collecting data, then describing and classifying it, and finally trying to explain it. Yet this approach does not account for why archaeological findings were already highly controversial during the nineteenth century. Such debates were only possible because various conclusions about the past were already being drawn on the basis of available evidence and some of these conclusions were offending people. Also, if archaeologists could not draw any conclusions, what motivated them to continue to study the past or to collect artifacts? As the British historian E. H. Carr (1967: 3–35) has reminded us, the mere characterization of data as being relevant or irrelevant, that occurs even in the most descriptive historical studies, implies the existence of some kind of theoretical framework. It can further be argued in opposition to the idea of a neutral observational language that not even the simplest archaeological fact can be established independently of a theoretical context (Wylie 1982: 42). In the past, most of these frameworks were not formulated explicitly or even consciously by archaeologists. Today, especially in the context of American and British archaeology, many theoretical propositions are systematically elaborated. Explanation was an inherent aspect of archaeology from the beginning, even if much of the theory that was employed was left implicit rather than clearly spelled out.

David Clarke (1973) proposed a convergent model of archaeological development. He argued that until the 1960s archaeology had consisted of isolated regional traditions of research, each following its own idiosyncratic and largely uncritical practices and characterized by its own preferred forms of description, interpretation, and explanation. Because these sorts of archaeology were scientifically undisciplined, their modes of analysis tended to be highly subjective and produced the results that local archaeologists expected. According to Clarke, in the 1960s these prescientific approaches were replaced by a new, sophisticated, self-critical, universal, and objective scientific archaeology. This is a false, or at best partial, view of the history of archaeology. International contacts characterized archaeology from the earliest stages of its development. Therefore, if local forms of research have been radically different from one another, an explanation other than mutual isolation is required.

Many archaeologists have utilized the philosopher Thomas Kuhn's (1962, 1970) more relativistic concept of scientific revolutions to try to understand the development of archaeology. Kuhn formulated his ideas to explain the development of the physical sciences and, in the first edition of *The Structure of Scientific Revolutions* (1962), he spoke of a preparadigmatic period to which his concept of scientific revolutions did not apply. He also appears to have believed that all social sciences remained in that category. However, in the second edition, he accepted that immature disciplines might be described as having multiple research paradigms (Kuhn 1970). Kuhn described a research paradigm as having an accepted canon of scientific practice, including laws, theory, applications, and instrumentation, that provides a model for a "particular coherent tradition of scientific research." Such a tradition is sustained by a "scientific community," defined as a group of scholars working together in the same discipline. Kuhn argued that every scientific community develops a paradigm that influences the types of questions thought to be worth asking, the theories that are used to explain data, and the procedures that are employed to collect and analyze evidence. Scientists promote such paradigms through their control of teaching, journals, research grants, professional accreditation, hiring, tenure, and promotion. In normal times, scientists conduct their research within the context of the dominant paradigm, which they seek to elaborate. Paradigms are thus not merely scientific theories but also belief systems that constitute the culture of scientific communities. In adopting this view, Kuhn was building on the work of Ludwik Fleck ([1935], English translation 1979), who maintained that science was a collective creation within a social milieu.

According to Kuhn, paradigm shifts occur when an old paradigm is seen as not supported by accumulating data or when scientists working within it grow interested in problems that the existing paradigm is not equipped to answer. Kuhn maintained that this leads to the old paradigm's being replaced by a new one. He also argued that successive paradigms are incommensurate. This means that a scientist working in terms of one paradigm can never understand how matters are perceived by someone working in terms of an alternative one. Kuhn originally argued in extreme relativistic terms that a new paradigm was not necessarily more comprehensive or accurate than its predecessor. Eventually, he accepted that, at least in the physical sciences, later paradigms are more comprehensive and account for more than do antecedent ones (Kuhn 1970; Bird 2000). This represented a shift from an extreme to a more moderate relativist position. He also argued late in his career that without debates among scientists who hold different views, incorrect assumptions would go unchecked and improved scientific insights would be impossible (Kuhn 1977).

Some archaeologists, especially processual ones seeking to enhance the innovativeness of their movement, combined Kuhn's idea of scientific revolutions with a unilinear evolutionary view of the development of their discipline. They maintained that successive phases in the development of archaeological theory display enough internal consistency to qualify as paradigms and that the replacement of one paradigm by another constituted a scientific revolution (Sterud 1973). According to this view, successive innovators, such as Christian Thomsen, Oscar Montelius, Gordon Childe, and

Lewis Binford, recognized major anomalies and inadequacies in conventional interpretations of archaeological data and created new paradigms that significantly changed the direction of archaeological research. These paradigms not only altered the significance that was accorded to archaeological data but also determined what kinds of problems were and were not regarded as important. Clarke, however, regarded archaeology before 1960 as being in a preparadigmatic state.

Such unilinear views of the history of archaeology fail to account for why archaeologists or other social scientists, in part because of the emergent complexity of their subject matter, never agree about high-level theory. This disagreement has meant that several rival paradigms coexist at any one time. Currently, processual archaeology treats ideas as epiphenomenal, whereas postprocessual archaeology regards them as the principal determinants of behavior. Simultaneously, evolutionary archaeology is seeking to create a new paradigm by combining elements of culture-historical archaeology with a selectionist Darwinian explanation of changes in material culture. Although archaeologists often display considerable bias in their support for different schools, there is no evidence that they are trapped in noncommunicating discourses or that it is impossible for them to understand their opponents. On the contrary, their arguments often display considerable knowledge of such positions. Robert Chapman (2003: 14) argues that in archaeology rival positions are not only not hermetically sealed but also internally highly variable. Thus, they are not incommensurate with one another in the Kuhnian sense. Both Michael Schiffer (1996: 659) and Todd and Christine VanPool (2003) maintain that regarding theoretical orientations as paradigms radicalizes positions and encourages exclusion and polemic rather than the systematic comparison, testing, and synthesis of ideas.

The relevance of Kuhn's concept of revolutionary change also has been questioned. Most alterations in the theory and practice of archaeology appear to occur gradually and there are growing doubts that even what appear to be rapid shifts accord with his concept of revolutions. Kuhn also failed to account for the longevity of various positions and for why rival positions fluctuate in relative importance, often repeatedly, rather than one position definitively replacing another, or for why few positions are ever totally abandoned. Thus, the new cultural anthropology and postprocessual archaeology address many of the same issues that Boasian culture-historical anthropology and archaeology once did, and early neoevolutionary archaeology strongly resembled nineteenth-century unilinear archaeology. To accommodate the concept of paradigm to these realities, Margaret Masterman (1970) differentiated three main types of paradigm: metaphysical, relating to the worldview of a group of scientists; sociological, that define what is accepted; and construct, that supply the tools and methods for solving problems. No one of these types alone constitutes "the" paradigm of a particular era. Despite such efforts to modify Kuhn's ideas, there is a growing sense that the concept of paradigm may not be appropriate to describe changing trends in interpretation in archaeology or any of the social sciences, and perhaps not even in science in general (Gándara 1980, 1981). Finally, Jean Molino (1992: 19) argues that nothing is more dangerous than the belief that a scientific revolution allows a science to start again. Old questions, methods, and answers frequently remain valid. Once the principle of stratigraphy was established as a reliable technique for inferring chronology, it continued to be used by archaeologists regardless of what other views they might espouse (Dunnell 2001: 1298). The same is true of Ian Hodder's (1982b) demonstration that material culture can be used to distort or invert as well as to reflect social reality. The development of such broad agreements is another factor reducing the incommensurability of different bodies of theory. For all these reasons, I will avoid the term "paradigm" and speak simply of schools or theoretical positions.

Shaun Hides (1996) and, in a more nuanced and careful manner, Ian Morris (1994b) have attempted to understand the development of archaeology in relation to Michel Foucault's (1970, 1972) concept of four successive but radically different and in his view discontinuous *epistemes* or modes of knowledge: Renaissance (ca. 1400–1650), Classical (ca. 1650–1800), Modern (ca. 1800–1950), and Postmodern (ca. 1950–). Foucault understands these epistemes as general modes of thought, each of which in turn influenced all fields of knowledge and dominated an era of modern Western civilization. Each episteme is radically different from any other. No one could escape the episteme of the time in which they lived, which imposed a particular set of norms and postulates on all thinking. Thus, epistemes, as dominant cultural patterns, are very different from Kuhn's paradigms, although both have been used to characterize general stages in the development of scientific interpretation.

Although Foucault's views about epistemes have potentially valuable contributions to make to understanding the development of archaeological thought, they have been criticized because of his reluctance to study causation and how epistemes may have been influenced by changing social realities (Morris 1994b: 10; Gutting 1989). Foucault also appears to underestimate the extent to which epistemes have overlapped and mutually influenced people's thinking. Epistemes can contribute little to understanding the theoretical diversity that characterizes archaeology at any given point in time.

An alternative unilinear evolutionary view to those based on the ideas of Kuhn and Foucault, and that accords with Stephen Toulmin's (1970) thesis that sciences do not experience revolutions but, rather, gradual changes or progressions, holds that the history of archaeology has been characterized by a cumulative growth of knowledge about the past from early times to the present (Casson 1939; Heizer 1962a; Meltzer 1979). It is maintained that, although various phases in this development may be delineated arbitrarily, in reality archaeology changes in a gradual fashion, with no radical breaks or sudden transformations. Some archaeologists view the development of their discipline as following a course that is inevitable. Jaroslav Malina and Zdenek Vašíček (1990) document how an expanding database, with evidence increasingly being derived from settlement data and ecofacts as well as from artifacts and monuments, together with new theories from the other social sciences and biology has shaped the development of archaeology. Like other unilinear views, theirs does not take account of the variability of archaeological theories at any one time. Nor does it explain the frequent failure of archaeologists to develop their ideas in a systematic fashion. For example, although nineteenth-century naturalists with archaeological interests, such as Japetus Steenstrup (Morlot 1861: 300) and William Buckland (Dawkins 1874: 281–4), carried out experiments to determine how faunal remains were introduced into sites, research of this sort did not become routine in archaeology until the 1970s (Binford 1977, 1981).

Other historians of archaeology have rejected unilinear interpretations in favor of cyclical ones. This view began with Stuart Piggott (1935, 1950, 1968, 1976, 1985) and Glyn Daniel (1950). They argued that archaeological interpretations were influenced by the varying popularity of the opposing rationalist and romantic views of human behavior that had been constructed in France during the eighteenth century. The romantic view was seen as encouraging an interest in culture-history, ethnicity, and idealism in archaeology, whereas rationalism encouraged the adoption of evolutionary and material-ist approaches. Piggott and Daniel assumed that human behavior was too complex and unpredictable ever to be fully understood. They believed that archaeological interpretations therefore tended to reflect the dominant intellectual fashions of the time, which them-selves changed in an unpredictable manner. It was therefore con-cluded that little progress could be made in understanding the past apart from that facilitated by a growing database. Archaeologists often returned to studying the same problems after long gaps during which what had been learned previously had been forgotten. Another application of a cyclical view to studying the history of archaeology is Kristian Kristiansen's (2002) characterization of Danish archae-ology as consisting of alternating phases of interest in ecological and culture-historical problems. Although these shifts can be con-strued as alternations of rationalist and romantic approaches, they do not appear to have been produced by alterations in general intel-lectual fashions but by processes internal to Danish archaeology and society.

Some archaeologists doubt that the basic interests and concepts of their discipline change significantly from one period to another. Bryony Orme (1973: 490) has maintained that the archaeological interpretations offered in the past were more like those of the present than is commonly believed and that archaeological preoccupations have changed little. Jean-Claude Gardin (1980: 165–80) argues that it is wrong to believe that there is a great gap between the present and earlier times in the "small world" of archaeological interpretation. He suggests that there has been little change in what archaeologists do over time, that the same formulae have been used for site reports over a long period, and that there is no gulf between processual and post-processual approaches. Long-term continuities in interpretation have been shown to occur in studies of human evolution (Landau 1991; Stoczkowski 2002). A remarkable antiquity also can be demonstrated for some ideas that are commonly believed to be modern. Archaeol-ogists argued that growing population densities led to the adoption of more labor-intensive forms of food production long before they rediscovered this idea in the work of the economist Ester Boserup (Smith and Young 1972). As early as 1673, the British statesman William Temple had adumbrated this theory with his observation that high population densities force people to work hard (Slotkin 1965: 110–11). In 1843, the Swedish archaeologist Sven Nilsson (1868: lxvii) argued that increasing population had brought about a shift from pastoralism to agriculture in prehistoric Scandinavia. This concept also was implicit in the "oasis" theory of the origin of food production, as expounded by Raphael Pumpelly (1908: 65–6) and adopted by Harold Peake and H. J. Fleure (1927) and then by Gordon Childe (1928). They proposed that postglacial desiccation in the Middle East had compelled people to cluster around surviving sources of water, where they had to innovate in order to feed higher population densities. Yet, although ideas persist and recur in the history of archaeology, this does not mean that there is nothing new in the interpretation of archaeological data. Such ideas must be examined in relation to the different conceptual frameworks of which they were a part at each period. It is from these frameworks that these concepts derive their significance to the discipline and, as the frameworks change, their significance does as well. According undue importance to particular ideas and not paying enough attention to their changing context will lead archaeologists to underestimate the amount of change that has characterized the development of archaeological interpretation. It also has been argued that a major goal of the history of archaeology must be to study critically how archaeological concepts and understandings have altered over time, so that they are not accepted as natural and given in their current state (Trigger 1978b). Recent work along these lines has been inspired by Pierre Bourdieu's (1980) concept of the social history of the social sciences (Moro Abadía and González Morales 2003).

Many archaeologists note that one of the principal characteristics of archaeological interpretation has been its enduring regional diversity. Leo Klejn (1977, 1990) and Trigger and Glover (1981–1982) have examined the history of archaeology as one of regional schools. In her review of Japanese and North American studies of the Jomon culture, Junko Habu (2004: 5) has demonstrated how assumptions, goals, methods, and theoretical developments cannot be considered apart from one another in a single tradition of archaeological practice and hence the distinctive and often complementary findings of different research traditions cannot be sucessfully synthesized without an understanding of the specific circumstances in which these findings were produced. Nadia Abu El-Haj (2001) argues that specific expressions of archaeological practice must be examined independently in order to understand how each of them articulated with, and both transformed and was shaped by, local social and political conditions. She implies that little is to be gained by comparing such situations and trying to generalize about them. Yet, although Abu El-Haj is correct that every practice of archaeology has unique features, this does not mean that detailed comparisons may not help to understand better archaeological practice and the history of archaeology.

Robert Dunnell (2001: 1290–1) argues that the overall history of archaeology displays both a lack of linear development and much parochial diversity. This is because archaeology is not a science in the sense that it systematically uses theory to explain evidence. Dunnell regards archaeology as remaining in a preparadigmatic state. Only occasionally has something resembling a paradigm arisen and these have proved to be short-lived.

It is clear that there have been, and still are, regional traditions in archaeological interpretation and that each of them has its own unique features (Daniel 1981b; Evans et al. 1981: 11–70). What has not yet been studied adequately is the significance of their divergences. To what degree do they represent irreconcilable differences in the understanding of human behavior, differences in the questions being asked, or the same basic ideas being studied under the guise of different terminologies?

Over the past few decades, archaeologists have identified various types of approaches to doing archaeology, each of which is represented by various examples in different parts of the world. Although these began with geographical groupings, as the list has expanded it has come to include other types of social differences. Each type is distinguished by the cause whose interest it serves: national archaeology (Fleury-Ilett 1996: 200–1), nationalist archaeology, colonialist archaeology, imperialist archaeology (Trigger 1984a), third-world archaeology (Chakrabarti 2001: 1191–3), continentalist archaeology (Morris 1994b: 11), regional or proto-national archaeology (Díaz-Andreu 1996b: 86), community archaeology (Moser 1995a; Marshall 2002), indigenous archaeology (Watkins 2000), internalist archaeology (Yellowhorn 2002), working-class archaeology (McGuire and Reckner 2003), touristic archaeology, and the archaeologies of protest (Silberman 1995: 261), of the disenfranchised, and of cultural identity (Scham 2001). The list might technically include gender archaeology although this approach is different because, instead of simply representing an alternative focus of research, it has established itself as a necessary and integral part of all other archaeologies. Although no two examples of any one of these varied approaches to archaeology are identical, they share sufficient features to identify each approach as a distinctive type, the development and function of which are worthy of study.

Yet ideas diffuse and convergent as well as independent development characterize archaeology. Studies of archaeology, with a few notable exceptions (I. Bernal 1980; Chakrabarti 1982), have failed to take account of the vast intellectual exchange that characterized the development of archaeology in all parts of the world during the nineteenth and twentieth centuries. This is dramatically illustrated by the early study of shell mounds. Reports of the pioneering studies by Danish scholars, who began their work in the 1840s, stimulated a large number of investigations of shell heaps along the Atlantic and later the Pacific coasts of North America in the latter half of the nineteenth century (Trigger 1986a). When the American zoologist Edward Morse went to teach in Japan, after analyzing material from shell mounds along the coast of Maine for the Harvard University archaeologist Jeffries Wyman, he discovered and excavated in 1877 a large Mesolithic shell deposit at Omori, near Tokyo. Some of his students dug another shell mound by themselves and it was not long before Japanese archaeologists who had been educated in Europe established the study of the Mesolithic Jomon culture on a professional basis (Ikawa-Smith 1982). The Scandinavian studies also stimulated the early investigation of shell mounds in Brazil (Ihering 1895) and Southeast Asia (Earl 1863). Even the ideologically opposed archaeological traditions of Western Europe and the Soviet Union significantly influenced each other, despite decades when scientific contact of any sort was very difficult and politically dangerous for scholars on both sides of the Iron Curtain. For all these reasons it seems unwise to overestimate the historical independence or theoretical distinctiveness of these regional archaeologies. One of the important tasks for historians of archaeology is to determine to what extent developments in one region did or did not influence developments elsewhere. For early times, this is hard to do because archaeologists often failed to indicate the sources of their ideas.

Less attention has been paid to the effects of disciplinary specialization within archaeology on the ways in which archaeological data are interpreted (Rouse 1972: 1–25). Yet differing orientations along these lines may account for as many differences as do social and political orientations. Classical archaeology, Egyptology, and Assyriology have been strongly committed to studying epigraphy and art history within a historical framework (Bietak 1979). Medieval archaeology developed as an investigation of material remains that complements research based on written records (M. Thompson 1967; D. M. Wilson 1976; Barley 1977; Andrén 1998). Palaeolithic archaeology developed alongside historical geology and palaeontology and has maintained close ties with these disciplines, whereas the study of later prehistoric periods frequently combines information from numerous other disciplines, including linguistics, folklore, biological anthropology, and comparative ethnology, with archaeological findings (D. McCall 1964; Trigger 1968a; Jennings 1979).

Yet, although many of these types of archaeology have developed in considerable intellectual isolation from each other over long periods and have been further estranged as a result of the balkanization of their respective jargons, historical connections, sporadic interaction, and common methodological interests have been sufficient for all of them to share numerous interpretive concepts. Tim Murray (2001a: xix–xx) points out that, despite archaeology's great diversity, the common questions and fundamental activities, such as classification, that lie at the core of archaeology enable archaeologists to communicate with each other and exchange knowledge. Yet, although they share a general commitment to making the human past intelligible and to developing the intellectual tools required for this task, archaeologists have gone about doing their work in many different ways and have sought to use archaeology to serve many different political and cultural ends.

More narrowly focused studies of the history of archaeology examine the role played by institutions, such as archaeological societies and archaeological departments in museums or universities, in promoting the development of archaeology. Michael O'Brien, R. Lee

Lyman, and Michael Schiffer (2005) have traced the development of New Archaeology in terms of the contributions of individual archaeologists and of clusters of cooperating or competing archaeologists. Michael Balter (2005) has studied, again from the perspective of the individual participants, the interactive team that has been excavating at the early Neolithic site of Çatalhöyük, in Turkey, under the innovative leadership of Ian Hodder. This fine-grained type of approach reveals much about the social dynamics and academic strategies that have shaped broader trends in the development of archaeology.

Biography and autobiography have long been part of the history of archaeology, but they have generally been viewed as a means of celebrating or justifying the careers of individual archaeologists. Today, there is growing interest in using a biographical approach to investigate how archaeologists have interpreted the past. John Chapman (1998) explains the role that the real-life experiences of the Lithuanian-born archaeologist Marija Gimbutas played in shaping her interpretations of European prehistory, especially the distinction that she drew between what she believed had been a matriarchal and peaceful Early Europe and the patriarchal and warlike Indo-European societies that replaced it. Jean-Paul Sartre (1971–1972) explored in detail the problems of this sort of approach in his innovative "total biography" of the French novelist Gustave Flaubert. He showed how Flaubert was shaped by the culture in which he lived and the social class to which he belonged. He also demonstrated, however, that many aspects of Flaubert's life and writings could only be understood by means of a detailed psychological analysis of his childhood and family relations. Clearly, if we are to understand all aspects of what archaeologists do, we have to study them as individuals. Sartre's work makes it clear that because of psychological factors even archaeologists who share similar ethnic and class backgrounds and the same historical experiences are unlikely to interpret archaeological data in precisely the same manner. By contrast, analogous social and cultural contexts produce general similarities in the interpretation of archaeological data that are deserving of consideration.

Although biographical and sociopolitical perspectives on the history of archaeology are complementary, some of the specific approaches outlined above are contradictory and hence not all of them can be valid. Because this study attempts to trace the development of archaeological thought from a broad perspective, it is impossible for it to examine the contributions of all archaeologists or even to investigate systematically the developments that have taken place in each country and each branch of archaeology (Schuyler 1971). Instead, I will investigate a number of major interpretive trends in roughly the chronological order in which they came into prominence. These trends frequently overlapped and interacted with one another, both temporally and geographically, and the work of individual archaeologists often reflects several of these trends, either at different stages of their careers or in some combination at a single point in time. My thematic approach allows a historical study to take account of changing styles of archaeological interpretation that cannot be fitted into clearly defined chronological or geographical pigeonholes but that reflect waves of innovation that have transformed archaeology.

Social Context

No one denies that archaeological research is influenced by many different kinds of factors. The most controversial of these is the social context in which archaeologists live and work. Very few archaeologists, including those who favor a positivistic view of scientific research, would reject the proposal that the questions archaeologists ask are influenced at least to some degree by this milieu. Yet positivists maintain that, so long as adequate data are available and these data are analyzed using proper scientific methods, the validity of the resulting conclusions is independent of the prejudices or beliefs of the investigator. Other archaeologists believe that, because their discipline's findings concerning the past consciously or unconsciously are perceived to have implications for the present or about human nature generally, and because people easily accept what they want to believe but demand overwhelming evidence before they accept ideas that they find abhorrent, changing social conditions influence not only the questions archaeologists ask but also the answers that they are predisposed to find acceptable. Even statistical tests, because they employ arbitrary levels of confidence, are open to subjective interpretation. Strong positivists, who believe that a single exception invalidates a law, would theoretically have to examine all possible cases to prove that they are dealing with a universal generalization. Because such proof is normally impossible, faith is also involved there.

David Clarke (1979: 85) had these subjective factors in mind when he described archaeology as an adaptive system "related internally to its changing content and externally to the spirit of the times." Elsewhere he wrote: "Through exposure to life in general, to educational processes and to the changing contemporary systems of belief we acquire a general philosophy and an archaeological philosophy in particular – a partly conscious and partly subconscious system of beliefs, concepts, values and principles, both realistic and metaphysical" (Ibid.: 25). Still earlier, Collingwood (1939: 114) had observed that every archaeological problem "ultimately arises out of 'real' life . . . we study history in order to see more clearly into the situation in which we are called upon to act."

In recent decades archaeology has been powerfully influenced by the attacks that relativists have launched against the concept of science as a rational and objective enterprise. These attacks have their roots in the antipositivism of the para-Marxist Frankfurt School, as represented in the writings of Walter Benjamin (1969), Jürgen Habermas (1971), and Herbert Marcuse (1964). These philosophers stressed that social conditions influence both what data are regarded as important and how they are interpreted (Kolakowski 1978c: 341–95). Their views have been strengthened by Kuhn's paradigmatic concept, by the arguments of the sociologist Barry Barnes (1974, 1977) that scientific knowledge is not different in kind from any other forms of cultural belief, and by the anarchistic claims of the American philosopher of science Paul Feyerabend (1975) that, because objective criteria for evaluating theories do not exist, science should not be fettered by rigid rules and personal preferences and aesthetic tastes may be relied on when evaluating rival theories. Ideas of this sort have attracted a considerable following among self-styled critical archaeologists, especially in Britain and the United States.

Although some relativists argue that, in the long run, greater awareness of social biases will promote more objectivity (Leone 1982), others maintain that even basic archaeological data are mental constructs and, hence, are not independent of the social milieu in which they are created and utilized (Gallay 1986: 55–61). The more extreme relativists ignore the qualifications of Habermas and Barnes that "knowledge arises out of our encounters with reality and is continually subject to feedback-correction from these encounters" (B. Barnes 1977: 10). Instead, they conclude that archaeological interpretations are determined entirely by their social context rather than by any objective evidence. Thus statements about the past cannot be evaluated by any criteria other than the internal coherence of a particular study "which can only be criticised in terms of internal conceptual relations and not in terms of externally imposed standards or criteria for 'measuring' or 'determining' truth or falsety" (Miller and Tilley 1984b: 151). A broad spectrum of alternatives separates those hyperpositivistic archaeologists who believe that only the quality of archaeological data and of analytical techniques determines the value of archaeological interpretations and the hyperrelativists who are inclined to accord archaeological data no role, but instead explain archaeological interpretations entirely in terms of the social and cultural loyalties of researchers. Despite its extremes and inconsistencies, the relativist critique of science has played an important and on the whole a beneficial role in making social scientists more aware of the subjective biases that influence their findings.

Although the influences that societies exert on archaeological interpretations are potentially very diverse, the development of archaeology has corresponded temporally with the rise to power of the middle classes in Western society. Many of the early patrons of classical archaeology belonged to the aristocracy, but ever since the Italian trader Ciriaco de' Pizzicolli in the fifteenth century, those who have actively studied archaeological remains have come predominantly from the middle classes. They have been civil servants, clergymen, wealthy merchants, country squires, and, with increasing professionalization, university teachers and museologists. In addition, much of the public interest in archaeological findings has been associated with the educated members of the bourgeoisie.

All branches of scientific investigations that have developed since the seventeenth century have done so under the aegis of the middle classes. Because archaeology and history are readily intelligible disciplines, their findings have important implications for shaping views of human nature and how and why modern societies have come to be as they are (Levine 1986). This transparent relevance for current political, economic, and social issues has made relations between archaeology and society especially complex and important. It therefore seems reasonable to examine archaeology as an expression of the ideology of the middle classes and to try to discover to what extent changes in archaeological interpretation reflect the altering fortunes of that group. Yet, although it is reasonable to assume that archaeologists are always influenced by the circumstances in which they live, it does not necessarily follow that, as archaeological data accumulate and archaeology develops as a discipline, all archaeological interpretations will be influenced to the same extent by contemporary social biases.

Moreover, the middle classes have not been a homogeneous phenomenon, either over time or in any one society. Their interests and degree of development have varied greatly from one country to another and within each country they have been divided into various strata, with individuals who prefer either more radical or more conservative political options being present in each stratum. The bourgeoisie of the Ancien Régime in France, composed largely of clerics, professionals, and royal administrators, has to be distinguished from the entrepreneurial bourgeoisie and factory owners of the industrial era (Darnton 1984: 113; E. Wood 2000). It is also evident that archaeology has not been of equal interest to the whole middle class, but mainly to that part of it, largely composed of professionals, which is inclined to be interested in scholarship (Kristiansen 1981; Levine 1986). Karl Marx noted rather condescendingly that in many ways intellectuals were very different in outlook and interest from other members of the middle class. He argued that what made them "representatives of the lower-middle class is the fact that in their minds they do not get beyond the limits which the lower-middle class do not get beyond in life, and that they are consequently driven, theoretically, to the same problems and social positions to which material interest and social position drive the latter in practice" (Marx [1852] in Marx and Engels 1962, I: 275).

Relations between interests and ideas are contextually mediated by a large number of heterogeneous factors. Archaeologists therefore cannot expect to establish a one-to-one correspondence between specific archaeological interpretations and particular class interests. Instead, they must analyze the ideas influencing archaeological interpretations as tools with which social groups seek to achieve their goals in particular situations. Among these goals are to enhance a group's self-confidence by making its success appear natural, predestined, and inevitable; to inspire and justify collective action; and to disguise collective interests as altruism (B. Barnes 1974: 16); in short, to provide groups and whole societies with mythical charters (McNeill 1986). Without denying the significance of individual psychological traits and cultural traditions, such considerations provide an important focus for examining the relations between archaeology and society.

Most professional archaeologists also believe archaeological interpretation to be significantly influenced by a large number of other factors. All but the most radical relativists agree that one of these is the archaeological database. Archaeological data have been accumulating continuously over several centuries and new data are held to constitute a test of earlier interpretations. Yet what data are collected and by what methods are influenced by every archaeologist's sense of what is significant, which in turn reflects his or her theoretical presuppositions. This creates a reciprocal relation between data collection and interpretation that leaves both open to social influences. Moreover, the data recovered in the past are often neither adequate nor appropriate to solve the problems that are considered important at a later time. This is not simply because archaeologists were unfamiliar with techniques that became important later and therefore failed to preserve charcoal for radiocarbon dating or soil samples for phytolith analysis, although such gaps in documentation can be extremely limiting. New perspectives frequently open up whole new lines of investigation. For example, Grahame Clark's (1954) interest in the subsistence economy of the Mesolithic period led him to ask questions that could not be answered using data collected when the main interest of Mesolithic studies was typological (Clark 1932). Likewise, the development of an interest in settlement archaeology revolutionized archaeological site surveys (Willey 1953) and provided a stronger impetus for the recording and analysis of intrasite distributions of features and artifacts (Millon et al. 1973). Hence, although archaeological data are collected continuously, the results are not necessarily as cumulative as many archaeologists believe. Indeed, archaeologists often seem to build more readily on what their predecessors concluded about the past than on the actual evidence on which those conclusions were based.

What archaeologists can study is also influenced by the resources that are made available for archaeological research, the institutional and public contexts in which research is carried out, and the kinds of investigations societies or governments are prepared to let archaeologists undertake. To obtain support archaeologists must please their sponsors, whether these be wealthy patrons (Hinsley 1985), colleagues and politicians managing the allocation of public funds (Patterson 1986a, 1999), or the general public. There also may be social restrictions on excavating certain kinds of sites, such as cemeteries or religious localities. To protect cultural resources, governments frequently enact stringent controls over when and how archaeologists excavate and how they record their findings. They sometimes prevent archaeologists from sending even mundane finds, such as soil samples, abroad for analysis. There is also a growing tendency to assign responsibility for managing archaeological research to local or ethnic groups on the grounds that such resources are part of their heritage. Although many archaeologists accept these controls as appropriate, they may impose major constraints on the research archaeologists do and how they interpret their finds. Such constraints have given rise to considerable tensions between archaeologists and aboriginal resource managers (Moser 1995b; Nicholas and Andrews 1997; Swidler et al. 1997; D. Thomas 2000).

Until the twentieth century, few archaeologists were educated in the discipline. Instead they brought to archaeology a variety of skills and viewpoints acquired in many different fields and avocations. All of them had studied a general school curriculum in which classical and biblical material was emphasized. Basic principles derived from a widespread interest in numismatics played an important role in the development of typology and seriation by Christian Thomsen, John Evans, and other early archaeologists (McKay 1976). In the nineteenth century, a growing number who took up the study of archaeology had been further educated in the physical and biological sciences. Even now, it is claimed that significant differences can be noted between the work done by professional archaeologists whose undergraduate studies were in the humanities and in the natural sciences (R. Chapman 1979: 121). More recently, a large number of prehistoric archaeologists have been educated in anthropology or history departments, depending on local preferences. In general, archaeologists trained within the context of history remain interested in the pasts of specific countries or peoples, whereas archaeologists trained in anthropology are more likely to be interested in studying the past from a comparative perspective.

The roles played by particularly successful or charismatic archaeologists as exemplars in shaping the practice of archaeology on a national and an international scale also are significant, even if they probably developed their ideas in contexts that were fertile to those ideas. Younger archaeologists may strike off in new directions and pioneer novel techniques of analysis or interpretation in order to try to establish professional reputations for themselves.

Archaeological interpretation also has been influenced by technical developments in the physical and biological sciences. Until recent decades, when collaborative research involving archaeologists and natural scientists became routine, with rare exceptions the flow of information between these disciplines was unidirectional, with archaeologists being the recipients. Hence, research in the natural sciences was only fortuitously related to the needs of archaeologists, although from time to time discoveries were made that were of tremendous importance for archaeology. The development of radiocarbon and other geochronometric dating techniques after World War II provided archaeologists for the first time with a universally applicable chronology that allowed the approximate year as well as the relative order of archaeological manifestations to be determined. These dating techniques also constituted an independent test of chronologies that had been inferred by means of seriation alone or were based on limited textual data. Pollen analysis provided valuable new insights into prehistoric climatic and environmental changes and trace-element analyses added an important dimension to the study of the prehistoric movement of certain kinds of goods. While there is considerable variation in how quickly and insightfully archaeologists apply innovations derived from the physical and biological sciences to their work, once they have been incorporated into archaeological research such innovations tend to spread throughout the world rapidly and with little resistance. The main obstacle to their spread is lack of funds and trained scientific personnel, factors that probably create more disparity between the archaeology of rich and poor nations than any other. Yet even now, when more physical and biological research is being undertaken specifically to solve archaeological problems, discoveries in these fields remain among the least predictable factors influencing archaeological interpretation (Nash 2000a).

The proliferation of electronic forms of data processing has revolutionized archaeological analysis no less than did radiocarbon dating. It is now possible to correlate in a routine fashion vast amounts of data, which in the past only an exceptional archaeologist, such as W. M. F. Petrie, would have attempted to analyze (Kendall 1969, 1971). This allows archaeologists to use the abundant data at their disposal to search for more detailed patterning in the archaeological record (Hodson et al. 1971; Doran and Hodson 1975; Hodder 1978b; Orton 1980; Sabloff 1981) and to explore the test implications of ever more complex hypotheses about human behavior so that these findings can be compared with the archaeological record (Wobst 1974; Mithen 1993; Costopoulos 2002). New theoretical orientations have been encouraged by specific developments of a mathematical nature. General systems theory (Flannery 1968; Steiger 1971; Laszlo 1972a; Berlinski 1976) and catastrophe theory (Thom 1975; Renfrew 1978a; Renfrew and Cooke 1979; Saunders 1980) are both mathematical approaches to the study of change, even if their strictly mathematical aspects have been emphasized less than the underlying concepts in applying them to archaeological problems.

The interpretation of archaeological data also has been significantly affected by the changing theories of human behavior and cognition espoused by the social sciences. It has been especially influenced by concepts derived from ethnology and history, the two related disciplines with which archaeologists have maintained the closest ties. Theoretical concepts derived from geography, sociology, economics, and political science also have influenced archaeology, either directly or through anthropology and history. Yet, because all these disciplines have been shaped by many of the same social movements that have influenced archaeology, it is often difficult to distinguish social science influences on archaeology from those of society at large.

The interpretation of archaeological data is also influenced by established beliefs about what has been learned from the archaeological record. Often specific interpretations of the past are uncritically accommodated to changing general views, rather than carefully scrutinized and assessed, even when these interpretations were formulated in accordance with a general view that has been rejected. Because of this, specific views about the past can persist and influence archaeological interpretation long after the reasoning that led to their formulation has been discredited and abandoned. In their detailed study of research at the Neolithic site of Avebury in England, Peter Ucko et al. (1991) demonstrated how the uncritical acceptance of older findings has constrained more recent research. Various studies have traced how interpretive motifs derived from classical and medieval Europe have influenced the understanding of early human behavior and how Marcelin Boule's and Arthur Keith's contrasting portrayals of Neanderthals have continued to play a central role in constructing knowledge about them (Moser 1992; Trinkaus and Shipman 1993; Stringer and Gamble 1993). By contrast, David Wengrow (2003: 134) has argued that studying the history of archaeology can contribute to the better understanding of the past and present through reengagement in a new context with ideas long forgotten as a result of what Laura Nader (2001) calls the "collective amnesia" associated with changing research programs. It thus becomes obvious that, although archaeologists' understandings of the past are influenced by the social milieu in which they exist, they also are influenced by many factors that relate to the ongoing development of archaeology as a discipline or set of disciplines. A history of archaeological thought requires knowledge not only of the social setting in which archaeological research is carried out but also of the ongoing development of archaeology as a practice.

Like other studies of the history of science, the history of archaeology is characterized by two broad approaches: internalist and externalist or contextual (Kuhn 1977: 109–10; Bauer 1992: 110–14). Internalist studies trace the discoveries and intellectual debates that have shaped archaeological interpretation. An excellent example of such an endeavor is Donald Grayson's *The Establishment of Human Antiquity* (1983). Internalist approaches continue to be preferred by epistemological positivists and political conservatives. They also are generally accepted as a valid way to study the history of archaeology. Externalist approaches seek to relate changes in archaeological understanding to changes in the social, economic, and political milieus in which archaeology is practiced. Although there is growing interest in such studies in both Western and ex-colonial countries (Klindt-Jensen 1975; I. Bernal 1980; Robertshaw 1990; Patterson 1995; Marchand 1996), conservative archaeologists and historians of science often criticize such interpretations on the grounds that they are speculative and ideologically driven (Daniel and Renfrew 1988: 199). In recent years, however, this sort of approach has acquired new levels of respectability as a result of Adrian Desmond's (1982, 1989; Desmond and Moore 1992) studies of the social and political implications of biological evolutionism in Victorian England. Moreover, there is a large body of evidence that interpretations are influenced by social milieus. Although it would seem ideal for studies to combine both approaches, in practice few historians of archaeology attempt to do this. I will, however, apply both approaches in this book.

Histories of science also are expected to avoid presentism, which involves judging past developments in terms of the current practices and beliefs of the discipline. This sort of approach evaluates what happened in the past in terms of present concerns and treats the history of archaeology as a chronicle of its progress toward its present state. Presentism is generally regarded by historians of science as a common shortcoming of amateur historians, especially scientists writing about their own disciplines. More sophisticated studies are expected to try to understand past events on their own terms and in relation to past social and political, as well as disciplinary, contexts. Yet Tim Murray (1999b) embraces an "avowedly presentist" approach and Robert Dunnell (2001: 1291) objects that by avoiding presentism historians of archaeology fail to distinguish between scientific discoveries of lasting value and those that are of no importance for the development of the discipline. To be relevant, Dunnell argues, studies of the history of archaeology must be theoretically informed. Thus, his position appears to be an endorsement of presentism.

Archaeological Interpretation

Archaeologists debate whether their discipline, or any social science, can or should be scientific. In part, these debates arise from disagreements about what constitutes science and scientific behavior. Most historians and philosophers of science trace the origin of modern science back to the philosopher Francis Bacon and regard it as a method of knowing rather than a body of knowledge. Bacon sought to persuade scholars to cease relying on revealed or authoritative knowledge to understand the world and instead to employ observation, classification, comparison, and where possible experimentation to achieve this goal. In this way, scientific knowledge was made the ever-developing product of communities of researchers (Zimmerman 2001: 117).

It is a fundamental tenet of science that nothing is significant by itself but only in relation to hypotheses; hence only theories can explain phenomena (Dunnell 1982b; Bird 2000: 18). Scientists must search for order, most often in the form of systemic properties, that facilitates the construction of explanations, without subjecting themselves to any *a priori* limiting presuppositions about the general extent or nature of that order. Their goal is to discover mechanisms that account for how things work and have come to be as they find them (Bunge 1997).

A scientific viewpoint treats the idea of absolute, unchanging truth as a dangerous and absurd illusion. Although scientists seek the most comprehensible and enduring understanding that their data permit, they acknowledge that they are unable to transcend the limitations of their data and what they are capable of perceiving at any particular point in time. Hence, they expect that in due course every scientific theory will be altered and probably become outmoded. Scientists are professionally obligated to test every theory against new evidence and to ensure that no theory logically contradicts any other accepted ones (Klejn 2001a: 86). Contrary to Karl Popper's (1959) argument that theories can only be disproved rather than proved, the philosopher of science Mario Bunge (1996: 180–3) argues that, because even the refutation of a theory is not necessarily definitive, scientists are justified in supporting a likely theory until convincing evidence to the contrary emerges. It is also now widely accepted that the processes of recovering and analyzing data are generally no less biased than is their explanation.

There is no fundamental disagreement between this position and relativist claims that science is an ensemble of social practices that seek to make the world and human behavior meaningful and intelligible; that science is embedded in society; and that its claims are at best partial, negotiated, and contested positions about what is to be taken for granted (Shanks 1996: 103), provided that it is also recognized that archaeological data were created independently of archaeologists and therefore have the capacity to resist their interpretations (Wylie 1982, 1989b, 2002; Trigger 1989b, 1998b). Kristiansen (2002) argues that archaeologists must regard such observations not as invitations to cultivate subjectivity but as a challenge to try hard to be objective.

Science presupposes a commitment to use more than rhetoric, persuasion, and political power or academic authority to recruit support for a position.

Jean-Claude Gardin (1980: 4) identifies the goal of archaeology as being to create intellectual constructions relating to the study of objects of all sorts that originated in the past. Leo Klejn (2001a: 88) defines archaeology as a discipline constructed by theories related to the study of material culture and antiquity. Lynn Meskell (2002: 293) observes that what sets archaeology apart from history and anthropology is its materiality. Yet David Wengrow (2003: 134) identifies it with an improved understanding of human behavior and history, whereas others have suggested that its goal should be to generalize about processes of cultural change (Binford 1962, 1983b). These perspectives are not antithetical. Archaeology is based on recovering and studying material culture but that does not prevent archaeologists from trying to study past human behavior, any more than palaeontologists are precluded from trying to understand the behavior of prehistoric animals. Today, there is a growing tendency to view archaeological theory as a subset of anthropological (or social science) theory dealing with how human behavior and beliefs are related to material culture and how material culture influences human behavior.

Scientific theory is a form of generalization that addresses how things work and change. Theories generally promote an understanding of one realm or dimension of reality by ignoring others. They do not seek to analyze the world as it is observed but through what are judged to be appropriate categories (Hegmon 2003: 213). To account for a specific situation, it is necessary to combine various explanations of this sort to form an explanatory argument (Roberts 1996). As a result of increasing relativism, there is growing interest in how knowledge is constructed, including how archaeologists evaluate knowledge claims and reach conclusions. This has produced a growing concern with archaeological theory even if many archaeologists, including archaeological theorists, believe that the close relations between theories and practice cast doubt on the desirability of establishing a separate subdiscipline of theoretical archaeology.

Archaeology is a social science in the sense that it tries to explain what has happened to specific groups of human beings in the past. Yet, unlike ethnologists, geographers, sociologists, political scientists, and economists, archaeologists cannot observe the behavior of the people they are studying and, unlike historians, most of them do not have direct access to the thoughts of these people as recorded in written texts. Instead, archaeologists must conjecture human behavior and ideas from the material remains of what human beings have made and used and the lasting physical impact of their activities on the environment. The interpretation of archaeological data depends on an understanding of how human beings behave at the present time and particularly of how this behavior is reflected in material culture. Archaeologists also must invoke uniformitarian principles in order to use an understanding of geological and biological processes going on at the present time to infer how natural processes have helped to shape the archaeological record. Yet they are far from agreed how such understanding can be applied legitimately and comprehensively to derive an understanding of past human behavior from their data (Binford 1967a, 1981; Gibbon 1984; Gallay 1986).

For a long time, most archaeologists were naive empiricists, offering what appeared to be plausible explanations for the evidence they were recovering. Then, in the 1960s, processual archaeologists embraced a positivist epistemology that emphasized establishing general regularities between observable phenomena and explaining these regularities. They also treated explanation and prediction as equivalent. This approach favored studying behavior, as it privileged what can be witnessed instead of dealing with more elusive thoughts and motives. It also privileged methodological individualism and because it doubted the epistemological validity of emergent properties was reductionist. It therefore promoted a belief in a "unified science," which sought to apply methodologies derived from the physical sciences to study everything (Hempel and Oppenheim 1948; Hempel 1965). Postprocessualists, and still earlier archaeologists such as R. G. Collingwood, embraced an opposing idealist epistemology that maintains that perceptions only acquire meaning as a result of discriminations that occur in the observer's mind. Idealists therefore believe that concepts play an important role in determining perception: humans do not adjust to the world as it really is but to the world as they imagine it to be. Idealism thus emphasizes the value of a cultural rather than a behavioral approach to understanding human activities (Collingwood 1946; Barnes 1974; Laudan 1990). Postprocessualists object that positivists ignore the cognitively mediated nature of human behavior and hence downplay the importance of culture. Positivists maintain that, because of its wholly subjective nature, the hermeneutic method does not provide a scientific approach for the study of beliefs. Each of these approaches is the formalization of a way of gaining a type of knowledge that is vital for everyday human living. Positivism relates to the sort of knowledge that is necessary to adapt to the natural world and idealism to what is required to interact with other human beings.

The inadequacies of both positivism and idealism as epistemologies for the social sciences have promoted the popularity of a third option: realism (Bhaskar 1978; Harré 1970, 1972; Harré and Madden 1975; Bunge 2003). Mario Bunge (1996: 355–8) maintains that realism is the epistemology that all reasonable and productive scientists actually follow, whatever epistemology they advocate. Realists identify the object of scientific study as being not only what can be perceived with the senses or conceptualized in the brain but all that exists and happens. Thus, realists pay equal attention to all things, whether they can observe them or only their effects. Ideas are viewed as processes that occur in the human brain and hence can be studied from a materialist perspective. Realists maintain that some imperceptible entities are appropriate objects of study. Thus, they do not confine themselves to appearances, as positivists do, but they also do not make common cause with idealists in belittling the significance of appearances. Often they begin with appearances and try to explain them by postulating unobservable entities, as Gregor Mendel did when he proposed that what are now called genes were necessary to explain the results of his interbreeding of different varieties of garden peas. Because it accepts the validity of studying structures as well as entities, realism is antireductionist. As a result of acknowledging the complexity of the real world, it also rejects the positivist equating of explanation and prediction.

Generalizations, which can concern both patterns and the mechanisms that account for patterns, play a role in all scientific operations relating to the collection, description, classification, and interpretation of data. Archaeologists follow the example of philosophers of science (Nagel 1961) and other social science disciplines in classifying their generalizations into high, middle, and low categories (Klejn 1977; Raab and Goodyear 1984) (Figure 1.1). Only middle- and high-level generalizations count as hypotheses or theories, according to the extent of their confirmation, because they alone propose mechanisms

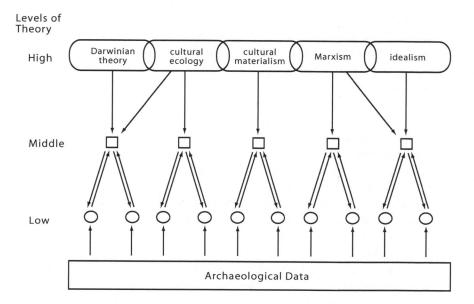

(length of arrow indicates relative importance of relationship)

Figure 1.1 Relations between levels of generalization

that account for why things are as they are and change as they do in multiple instances.

Low-level generalizations seek to discover patterns in archaeological data (Klejn 1977: 2). These patterns appear to be the same as Ernest Nagel's (1961: 79–105) experimental laws, of which he offers as an example the proposition that all female whales suckle their young. Such generalizations are normally based on regularities that are repeatedly observed and can be refuted by the observation of contrary cases. The vast majority of generalizations on which higher-level archaeological interpretations are based are empirical ones of this sort. They include most typological classifications of artifacts; the delineation of specific archaeological cultures; the demonstration by means of stratification, seriation, or radiocarbon dating that one archaeological manifestation dates earlier, or later, than another; and the observation that in an individual culture all humans are buried in a particular position accompanied by specific types of artifacts. These generalizations are based on observations that specific attributes or artifact types occur repeatedly in a particular association with each other, correlate with a specific geographical locality, or date to a certain period. The dimensions of such generalizations are the classical ones of space, time, and form (Spaulding 1960; Gardin 1980: 62–97). Archaeologists also may assume that specific types of projectile points served particular functions and that each archaeological culture was associated with a specific people. These inferences, which refer to human behavior, differ substantially from generalizations that are based on empirical observations of correlations between two or more categories of archaeologically tangible data and do not constitute examples of low-level generalizations. In many instances, the behavioral assumptions turn out to be incorrect, unproved, or misleading (Hodder and Hutson 2003: 173–5).

Because of the nature of archaeological data, low-level generalizations never refer to human behavior. They only reveal correlations between one sort of archaeological observation and another, thus providing evidence of hitherto unnoticed patterning or ordering in archaeological data. These empirical observations never provide explanations but constitute patterns that require explanation. Discovering generalizations of this sort is the most time-consuming and arguably the most productive activity in which archaeologists engage. Yet, from a theoretical perspective, it is the least studied of archaeological activities. Most historical work of this sort has been done by archaeologists interested in classification and seriation and by logicists (Gardin 1980: 10; Malina and Vašíček 1990: 149–209).

Middle-level theories have been defined as generalizations that attempt to explain the regularities that occur between two or more variables in multiple instances (Raab and Goodyear 1984). Such generalizations can be produced either by refining high-level theories so that they are applicable to specific data sets (such as archaeological data) or by seeking to provide an explanation for why certain low-level generalizations occur in multiple instances. All social science generalizations should have cross-cultural validity and also make some reference to human behavior. In addition, they must be sufficiently specific that they can be tested by applying them to particular sets of data. An example of a middle-level anthropological generalization is Ester Boserup's (1965) proposition that among agricultural economies increasing population pressure leads to situations that require more labor for each unit of food produced in order to derive more food from each available unit of arable land. This theory would be archaeologically testable if archaeologists could establish reliable measures of absolute or relative changes in population, the labor-intensiveness and productivity of specific agricultural regimes, and a sufficiently precise chronology to specify the temporal relationship between changes in population and food production. Doing this would require elaborating what Lewis Binford (1981) calls middle-range theory, which attempts to use ethnographic data to establish reliable correlations between archaeologically observable phenomena and archaeologically unobservable human behavior. Although "middle-level" and "middle-range" theories are not identical, in that middle-level theory can refer exclusively to human behavior, whereas middle-range theory must by definition refer to both human behavior and archaeologically observable traits, all Binford's middle-range theory can be regarded as a special type of middle-level theory. Middle-range theory is vital for testing all middle-level theory relating to archaeological data.

High-level, or general theories, which Marvin Harris (1979: 26–7) has called "research strategies" and David Clarke (1979: 25–30) labeled "controlling models," have been defined as abstract rules that explain relations among the theoretical propositions that are relevant for understanding a major field of knowledge. Darwinian evolutionism and more recently the synthetic theory of biological evolution, which combines Darwinian principles with genetics, are examples of general theories relating to the biological sciences. In the human domain, general theories exclusively relate propositions about human behavior to one another; hence, there are no theoretical formulations at this level that pertain specifically to archaeology rather than to the social sciences in general. This is true even of theories that relate human behavior to material culture. Examples of rival high-level theories that currently influence archaeological research are selectionism, cultural ecology, cultural materialism, and historical materialism (Marxism). These are all materialist approaches and overlap to varying degrees. In recent years, there has been a resurgence of interest in high-level theories that attempt to explain human behavior in terms of cultural beliefs or underlying cultural structures. Such theories share an idealist approach. Still other theories, such as neo-Marxism, bridge the gap between materialist and idealist high-level positions creating a broad spectrum of high-level social science theories.

Because high-level theories attempt to interrelate concepts about human behavior rather than to account for specific observations, they cannot be confirmed or falsified directly (M. Harris 1979: 76). In that respect, they resemble religious dogmas. Their credibility can, however, be influenced by the repeated success or failure of middle-level theories that are logically dependent on them. Yet such testing is anything but straightforward. Although many middle-range theories may have significance for distinguishing between materialist and idealist modes of explanation, the complexity of all human behavior and its symbolically mediated nature create much opportunity for obfuscation. Social scientists exhibit great ingenuity in dismissing results that do not agree with their presuppositions as exceptions or even reinterpreting them as likely confirmation of what they believe. As the result of a growing appreciation of the role played by ideas in influencing human behavior, many Marxists have shifted from a purely materialist to a more idealist view of human behavior. Sometimes this new position is distinguished as neo-Marxism, sometimes it is not (McGuire 1993; Trigger 1993). Likewise, in recent years, many cultural ecologists have shifted from a more deterministic to a less deterministic position. The overlapping nature of high-level theories of human behavior provides considerable opportunities for such intellectual gymnastics. It is still more difficult for archaeologists to assess the relative utility of the various materialist positions listed above. Tests of Boserup's middle-level theory have implications for both cultural materialism and cultural ecology and hence would be of little use for assessing the relative utility of one or the other. The failure of middle-level theories to confirm preferred high-level ones also can be dismissed as the result of inadequate or inappropriate data rather than accepted as casting doubt on high-level propositions.

Because of the indirectness of tests, the rise and fall in the popularity of specific high-level theories seems to be influenced more by social processes than by the scientific examination of logically related middle-level theories. Between 1850 and 1945, a strong emphasis was placed on biological, and more specifically racial, explanations of variation in human behavior. Scientific demonstrations that explanations of this sort did not hold in specific instances were inadequate to undermine the faith that many scholars had in the general validity of a racist approach (M. Harris 1968a: 80–107). Yet racial and, for a time, almost all biologically based theories were abandoned as scientific explanations of human behavior following the military defeat of Nazi Germany in 1945 and the consequent revelation of the full extent of its racist-inspired atrocities. It often has been observed that materialist theories tend to flourish in the social sciences when middle-class intellectuals feel secure, whereas idealist ones are espoused during periods when economic and social upheaval create uncertainty (Engels [1868] in Marx and Engels 1964: 263–8).

Archaeologists generally accept, mostly implicitly, that scientific explanations are subject to two types of verification (Lowther 1962; Kosso 2001). The first test is that of correspondence truth. This test seeks to determine if an explanation corresponds to the facts. It is useless to suggest that a drought accounts for the collapse of centralized political control in an early civilization if no evidence of a drought can be produced. The second test is that of coherence truth: whether or not an argument is logically consistent. Over two and a half millennia, rationalist philosophers have developed logic as a powerful tool for detecting flaws in explanations. Few archaeologists have studied formal logic, but they enjoy discovering logical flaws in one another's arguments as a way of discrediting both unwelcome theories and academic rivals. Complex arguments are needed to cope with phenomena relating to human behavior. Political collapse might result from a severe famine but only if a society lacks stored surpluses or access to alternative sources of food. Hence, monocausal explanations are rarely, if ever, adequate in the social sciences. Moreover, the same effect may result from a number of different causes: a breakdown in normal patterns of succession to high leadership also might result in political collapse. This is a situation known as equifinality.

Ideally, it should be possible to establish a logically coherent relationship among high, middle, and low levels of theory and a factual correspondence between middle- and low-level generalizations and observable evidence. Because low-level generalizations are empirical in nature, coherence tests do not apply to the relations between them and evidence, whereas, as we have already noted, factual correspondence rarely serves as a direct test of high-level theories. American archaeologists have fiercely debated whether middle-level theory ought to be derived deductively as a coherent set of interrelated concepts from high-level theories or whether it also can be constructed inductively from evidence and low-level generalizations. Those who support the deductive approach argue that explanations of human behavior, as opposed to empirical generalizations about it, should be based on covering laws stated as hypotheses and tested against independent sets of data (Watson et al. 1971: 3–19; Binford 1972: 111). They seek to establish explicit, logical connections between high- and middle-level theory. Generally, however, they underestimate the tenuous, complex, and intractable nature of the relations between these two levels. By contrast, because high-level theory is hard to verify, highly susceptible to subjective influence, and not absolutely required to create middle-level theories, many inductivists regard the creation of high-level theories as an ultimate goal that archaeologists should address only after they have established a large corpus of reliable generalizations at the middle level (M. Salmon 1982: 33–4; Gibbon 1984: 35–70; Gallay 1986: 117–21). In keeping with what they regard as the Baconian tradition of science, inductivists also maintain that, although deductive research cannot go beyond confirming or disproving existing theories, an inductive approach has the potential for making genuinely new discoveries about aspects of human behavior. They also believe that an inductive approach is superior because it is grounded on evidence collected without presuppositions. Yet it is evident that theories are not derived from evidence but imposed on it.

The debate whether explanations are better produced by induction or deduction poses a false dichotomy. Observations that Charles Darwin made in the course of a five-year voyage around the world led him to doubt whether creationism could best account for the geographical distributions of various species of plants and animals. For over two decades he collected vast amounts of information on variations within and between different species. Yet, according to his own account, the concept of natural selection occurred to him not as a direct result of his research but as a consequence of his reading the economist Thomas Malthus's (1798) theory that the main cause of human suffering is the natural tendency for human population increase to outrun the available food supply. Once the theory of natural selection had occurred to Darwin, he was able to use the data he had collected to present convincing arguments in support of his idea. Both induction and deduction played significant roles in the development of the theory of natural selection and continue to do so in the creation of all scientific theories. The credibility of all scientific theories depends on their maintaining logical coherence with other relevant theories and satisfactory correspondence with relevant evidence. Because numerous implicit assumptions about the nature of human behavior color what is believed to be any sound explanation of archaeological data, high-level concepts can be ignored only at the risk that implicit ones will unwittingly distort archaeological interpretations. Successful theory-building involves the combining of both approaches.

Archaeologists also disagree about the formal nature of the generalizations that they seek to elaborate. Processual archaeologists assumed that all laws must be universal in nature. They also believed these laws to be primarily ecological, although today archaeologists are deriving a growing number of such generalizations from evolutionary psychology, neuroscience, and biology. Such laws relate to variables that are assumed to hold true regardless of the temporal period, region of the world, or specific cultures that are being studied. These generalizations vary in scale from major assumptions about historical processes to regularities dealing with relatively trivial aspects of human behavior (M. Salmon 1982: 8–30). A good example of this sort of approach is formalist economics, which maintains that the rules used to explain the economic behavior of Western societies explain the behavior of all human beings. Such an approach accounts for significant variations in human behavior in different societies by viewing them as the results of novel combinations and permutations of a fixed set of interacting variables (Burling 1962; Cancian 1966; Cook 1966). Universal generalizations are frequently interpreted as reflecting an invariant human nature.

Other archaeologists maintain that universal laws concerning human nature are relatively few in number and that most cross-cultural generalizations apply only to societies that share the same or closely related modes of production. This position is similar in general orientation to that of the economic substantivists. In contrast to formalists, substantivists maintain that the rules, as well as the forms, of economic behavior are fundamentally transformed by evolutionary processes (Polanyi 1944, 1966; Polanyi et al. 1957; Dalton 1961).

The substantivist approach implies that novel properties can and do emerge as a result of sociocultural change (Childe 1947a). This distinction between universal generalizations and more restricted ones may not be as far-reaching or absolute as its proponents maintain. Generalizations that apply only to specific types of societies can be rewritten in the form of universal generalizations, whereas universal ones may be reformulated, usually in greater detail, so that they apply specifically to a particular class of society. Yet those who stress the importance of restricted generalizations argue that all or most of them cannot be transformed into universal generalizations without a severe loss in content and significance (Trigger 1982a).

The third type of generalization is specific to an individual culture or to a single group of historically related cultures. Examples would be the definitions of the canons that governed ancient Egyptian or classical Greek art (Childe 1947: 43–9; Montané 1980: 130–6). Such generalizations are potentially very important inasmuch as most cultural patterning is probably of this sort. Yet, where no culturally specific meanings can be applied to such patterns, they remain at the level of empirical generalizations.

Challenge

A final question is whether a historical study can measure progress in the interpretation of archaeological data. Are steady advances being made toward a more objective and comprehensive understanding of archaeological findings, as many archaeologists assume? Or is the interpretation of such data largely a matter of fashion and the accomplishments of a later period not necessarily more comprehensive or objective than those of an earlier one? Answering this question is vital for considering whether the development of archaeology does or does not promote greater objectivity in its findings.

In examining the patterns that have characterized the interpretation of archaeological data, I shall attempt to ascertain to what extent archaeological techniques as well as a general understanding of human history and behavior have been irreversibly altered as a result of archaeological activity. There is evidence of some linearity in the development of archaeology as, for example, with the continuing relevance of the principle of stratigraphy, of frequency seriation, and of Ian Hodder's (1982b) demonstration that material culture can play an active as well as an epiphenomenal role in social processes. Yet there is no evidence that archaeologists at any one period are less influenced by subjective beliefs and social circumstances than they are at any other. In addition, contingent factors, personalities, academic policies, sheer ignorance, professional biases, and funding all influence the acceptance and application of new ideas and techniques (Nash 2000b: 208). It is possible, however, that archaeological interpretation, although initially highly subjective, becomes less influenced by social biases and less susceptible to political manipulation as the archaeological database becomes more abundant, and, therefore, that an understanding of the past grows more objective as more archaeological research is carried out. That trend would accord with the claims of moderate relativists that archaeological evidence has the capacity to limit speculation about the past. If archaeological interpretations are wholly, or even largely, subjective, we should not be able to discover many significant long-term patterns but only random variations brought about by changes in the economic, social, and intellectual milieu. If evidence plays a role in limiting speculation, the development of archaeology should be increasingly constrained by knowledge that belongs to the discipline, even if subjective factors continue to influence significantly the answers to what are regarded at any given time as interesting questions. If archaeological evidence plays a significant role in shaping an understanding of the past, the study of ontology, in particular of the factors that constrain human behavior, will become as – if not more – important than learning about epistemology, or the nature of understanding, for the future development of our discipline. That would reverse a trend that has prevailed since the 1960s or even the 1930s. By learning more about how archaeological questions are answered over time, we may hope to gain additional insights into the objectivity or subjectivity of archaeological interpretations; to what extent archaeology can be more than the past relived in the present, in the sense Collingwood defined that process; and the degree to which any sort of understanding can be communicated from one age or culture to another.

CHAPTER 2

Classical and Other Text-Based Archaeologies

Everyone should be Greek in his own way! But he should be Greek!

JOHANN WOLFGANG VON GOETHE, "Antik und Modern"
trans. P. Marchand (1996), p. 16

Historians of archaeology used to assume that archaeology was a self-evident branch of human knowledge and that its development was inevitable. The growing popularity of relativism among archaeologists has heightened their awareness that archaeology is a field of investigation, or discourse, that has evolved only recently and been anticipated only a few times in human history. It is therefore worth enquiring what kinds of conditions give rise to archaeology and what sorts of archaeology may be the first to evolve.

Some histories of archaeology have traced its origins to any interest in what modern archaeologists identify as the material remains of the human past (Schnapp 1997). Others have restricted their focus to the deliberate use of material culture to learn more about the past (Trigger 1989a). These two approaches are obviously historically related and it is possible that the former interest was a prerequisite for the development of the latter. Yet an interest in material remains of the past does not inevitably lead to the development of archaeology, which to a significant degree seems to grow out of interests in the past that are not primarily associated with material culture. I will therefore limit the current study to tracing the use of material culture to study the past, either for its own sake or for some assumed practical purpose.

Interests in the Past

All human groups appear to be interested in their own past. Many social scientists believe that knowledge of sociocultural origins is fundamental for the development of individual and social identity. This assessment assumes that there is a past and, hence, that time, whether it is viewed as an attribute of the natural world or a form of perception embedded in the human brain, is invariably conceptualized as a linear, irreversible flow. This conclusion may be psychologically correct in the sense that, because of awareness of causality, everyone perceives time as they are experiencing it to be unidirectional. Yet it is known anthropologically that the imaging of time is culturally variable (Moro Abadía 2002; T. Murray 2004b). The Australian aborigine concept of dream-time posits that the supernatural time of creation continues to exist alongside the present world (J. Isaacs 1980). In many cultures, rituals are believed to renew the cosmos periodically by repeating the act of creation. Hunter-gatherers regard time differently from the way farmers do, not least because the two groups schedule their subsistence activities differently. The ancient Maya viewed time as cyclical and events as repeating themselves over intervals of varying lengths. Ancient Mesopotamians seem to have conceptualized time as something they viewed facing the past with their backs to the future (Schnapp 1997: 30–1). Chinese, Koreans, and Japanese talk of ascending to the past, which they associate with the sky realm, that is inhabited by the creator deities and the souls of their human ancestors (G. Barnes 1990a). Even different groups of archaeologists perceive time differently. British archaeologists usually place the oldest period at the top of their time charts, perhaps in keeping with the idea that time is a river and hence flows downward, whereas American archaeologists habitually put the oldest period at the bottom of their charts, either in imitation of stratigraphy or to symbolize their faith in evolutionary progress. Although the perception of time is psychologically shaped by a common experience of it as an irreversible sequence of cause and effect, there is no basis for assuming that all cultures have conceptualized time or the past in the same way.

For much of human history, interest in what we call the past was satisfied by myths and legends concerning the creation of the world and chronicling the origins and adventures of specific ethnic groups. Hence, high-level theories, in this case in the form of the basic religious beliefs underlying such stories about the past, long antedate the middle- and low-level generalizations of archaeologists. Ideas about the past were often contested by different political or ethnic groups as part of their efforts to legitimate rival political and economic claims

(Carassco 1982). The relations between material culture and such interests in the past are highly complex.

Projectile points, stone pipes, and native copper tools made millennia earlier are found in Iroquoian sites dating from the fifteenth and sixteenth centuries AD in eastern North America. Ethnographic evidence indicates that they were regarded as having been made by spirits who had lost them in the forest. Such objects were collected because they were credited with magical powers that would bring their human possessors various forms of good fortune (Thwaites 1896–1901, vol. 33: 211). In medieval Europe, peasants collected stone celts and projectile points that they discovered in the course of their agricultural work. They believed such finds to be produced by lightning or by supernatural creatures such as elves. Stone celts were kept as protection against lightning bolts or sold to goldsmiths who used them for burnishing metal (Heizer 1962a: 63). The Japanese believed stone arrowheads that appeared in fields after rainstorms to be the weapons of supernatural armies that had fallen to earth. Their discovery required the performance of special rituals (Ikawa-Smith 2001: 735). Upper-class Maya prized jade ornaments that had been passed from generation to generation as heirlooms or been recovered from old tombs (Joyce 2003) and the Aztecs included ancient Olmec figurines in the ritual deposits that they incorporated into their major temples (Matos Moctezuma 1984).

All peoples also seek to explain their landscapes, including the ancient monuments that are part of them. In early societies, such explanations took the form of historically transmitted knowledge, altered to varying degrees over time, or pure inventions, which were believed to varying degrees. In medieval Europe, burial mounds were associated with supernatural beings, prehistoric giants, or early historical peoples such as the Huns. In prehistoric Mexico, ancient cities were viewed as places of historical and supernatural significance (Hamann 2002). In the sixteenth century, the Aztecs regularly performed rituals amidst the ruins of Teotihuacán, which had been inhabited in the first millennium AD and was believed to be where the gods had reestablished the cosmic order at the beginning of the most recent cycle of existence. The Inkas regarded large rocks as deities or ancestors who had transformed themselves into stones. The ancient Egyptian priests at Heliopolis claimed that the remains of a fossilized forest nearby were the charred bones of a giant serpent that the sun god had slain in the course of creating the universe (Meeks and Favard Meeks 1996: 21). These explanations assigned both human and supernatural origins to features of the landscape that we understand to be human or natural creations. Because attributions of this sort are highly idiosyncratic, archaeologists require culturally specific data coded in verbal form to be able to assign original meanings to such data. These meanings are not inherent in material forms, nor can they be assumed to be universal. Richard Bradley (2003: 225) has proposed that the materiality of ancient remains would have posed problems to ancient communities that were similar in nature to those they posed to early antiquaries and that in each instance learning about these monuments might have taken a similar course. Yet there is little evidence of a desire in most human societies to use material remains to learn about the past. Instead, these remains were explained in terms of commonly held beliefs that in their specificity are usually unknown to us. Hence, to identify such interpretations as "indigenous archaeology," or even as precursors to archaeology, is to transgress the limits of inference.

In the earliest literate civilizations, written records provided a chronological framework (sometimes incorrectly interpreted) as well as sources of information about what had happened in the past that were independent of human memory and hence inhibited the revision of recollections of the past. Even so, the compiling of annals did not give rise to the writing of detailed histories or analytical narratives of current events either in the Middle East or in China until after 700 BC (Van Seters 1983; Redford 1986). Donald E. Brown (1988) has demonstrated that there is great variation in the extent to which civilizations that have been literate for equally long periods are interested in the study of history. There also is abundant evidence that the development of history as a literary genre does not ensure the concomitant growth of a disciplined interest in the material remains of earlier times.

In ancient Egypt and Mesopotamia, artifacts and ancient buildings came to be valued not only as relics of former rulers and periods of political greatness but as sources of information about the past. In Egypt, from the beginning of the Twelfth Dynasty (1991–1786 BC), royal craftsmen began to copy styles of art and architecture from the late Old Kingdom. In the course of the Twelfth Dynasty, features copied from still older and abandoned royal monuments, or perhaps

from their surviving plans, were incorporated into royal tombs
(I. Edwards 1985: 210–17; Dodson 1988). During the Eighteenth
Dynasty (1552–1305 BC), scribes left graffiti recording their visits to
ancient and abandoned monuments, studies were made of records
of ancient royal festivals in an effort to enhance the authenticity and
ritual power of their reenactments, and a predynastic palette was
inscribed with the name of Queen Tiye (1405–1367 BC), who was presumably its owner. In the Nineteenth Dynasty, a son of Ramesses II,
Khaemwese, whose fame as a sage and magician was to endure into
Greco-Roman times, cleared and studied the texts associated with
abandoned religious buildings near the capital city of Memphis in
order to repair those structures and revive their cults (Gomaa 1973;
J. P. Allen 1999). In Iraq, King Nabonidus (r. 556–539 BC) and other
Late Babylonian rulers excavated and studied the ruins of ancient
mudbrick temples so that they could rebuild them on their original
foundations and restore their cults. Collections also were made of
statues and ancient texts to help purify rituals. One of these collections, amassed by Bel-Shalti-Nannar, a daughter of Nabonidus, has
been described as the world's oldest known museum of antiquities
(Woolley 1950: 152–4). Great effort also went into cultivating the
skills needed to read the ancient texts associated with these finds
(Jonker 1995).

Both the Egyptians' and the Mesopotamians' interest in the material remains of the past had a strong religious component. It was
believed that the gods had established civilization in a perfect form
at the beginning of time. Although individual kings might strive to
outdo their predecessors, later generations had in general failed to
sustain the original divine perfection. The monuments, as well as the
written records of the past, therefore constituted tangible links to
eras that were closer to the time of creation and, hence, provided
the models by which the sacred prototypes of civilization could be
more nearly approximated. Because of their greater proximity to the
cosmic drama of creation, these artifacts also were probably believed
to be endowed with unusual divine power. Yet, although the purpose of much of this ancient Egyptian and Mesopotamian research
was to manipulate supernatural powers more effectively, it can be
regarded as constituting an early form of antiquarianism, as it used
material remains to enhance an understanding of the past. It was,
however, based on the idea that the past differed from the present

only to the extent that it had possessed superior knowledge that could enhance the supernatural power of those who possessed it. Although, in Egypt, ancient art continued to be carefully studied and copied, after 700 BC a growing awareness of differences between the present and the past seems to have stifled rather than encouraged the development of antiquarianism (Loprieno 2003).

The ancient Greeks used the terms history and archaeology to distinguish two historical genres, although at first neither term was employed in its modern sense. *Historia* was originally used to designate a form of enquiry that involved first posing a question, then looking for relevant information, and finally drawing a conclusion from the data. In the fifth century BC, Herodotus and others began to use it to signify the study of the recent past based on recollections of people who had participated in the events they described. This sort of chronicling began in the aftermath of the Persian Wars. Later, scholars began to synthesize chronicles of this sort to produce document-based histories in the modern sense. Henceforth, as it does now, history designated the study of the past based on written records. Until recently, the main focus of such histories was the study of political and military events.

The term *archaiologia* (Latin *antiquitates*) was first used in the fourth century BC to refer to the study of the more remote past (literally, "beginnings" *arche*) using myths, legends, oral traditions, and material remains. The main emphasis was on genealogies, the founding of cities, and the origins of peoples, institutions, and customs. The survival of traditions about the past was facilitated by hero cults that had persisted through the Early Iron Age (Antonaccio 1995). These traditions, for example, transmitted accurate memories of an age when bronze had been used but not iron (Momigliano 1966; Schnapp 1997: 60–5). Knowledge of this sort was incorporated into the broad range of speculative chronologies that largely replaced religious accounts of the origins of the universe and of human beings in classical Greece. These included cyclical and steady-state views of the universe as well as degenerationist accounts that posited successive ages of gold, silver, bronze, iron, and, in the future, lead, each characterized by harder work and greater human misery than the one before, and the evolutionary theories of Epicureans who posited that technological progress moved from the use of bare hands and then stones to the manufacture first of bronze and then of iron tools. Both the degenerationist and evolutionary theories incorporated memories that an age of bronze had preceded that of iron.

The ancient Greeks preserved as votive offerings in their temples artifacts that were said to have belonged to great men of the past and sometimes opened graves to recover what they believed were the relics of ancient heroes. The historian Thucydides noted that many of the graves dug up on the island of Delos, when that island was religiously purified in the fifth century BC, revealed weapons and a method of burial resembling those of the Carian people of his own day. He concluded that this confirmed a tradition that Carians had once lived on the island (Casson 1939: 71). Increasingly, ancient bronzes and pottery vessels that were accidentally unearthed or plundered by dealers were sold to wealthy art collectors (Wace 1949). One example of mass plunder occurred in the cemeteries of old Corinth, when that abandoned city was refounded by Julius Caesar in 44 BC. Wealthy Romans admired the works of talented Greek artists and sought to purchase the originals or good copies of them. This interest inspired the Roman author Pliny the Elder's (AD 23–79) historical account of Greek art and artists. Yet, despite a growing interest in ancient works of art, scholars made no effort to recover or collect such artifacts systematically, nor, with the notable exception of a few works, such as that of Pliny on art, did artifacts become a specialized focus of analysis. In his guide to Greece written in the second century AD, the physician Pausanias systematically described the public buildings, art works, rites, and customs of the different regions of southern Greece. He regarded it as significant that the blade of a spear attributed to Achilles, a hero of the Trojan War, which was kept in the temple of Athena at Phaselis, was made of bronze (Levi 1979, vol. 2: 17) and he briefly described the celebrated Bronze Age ruins at Tiryns and Mycenae. Yet for him and other writers of guide books ruined buildings were "hardly worth mentioning" (Levi 1979, vol. 1: 3). Inferences based on accurate historical and ethnographic knowledge, such as that of Thucydides, were likewise notable for their rarity. Educated Greeks and Romans were aware that the culture of the remote past was different from that of the present and valued the fine art works from earlier times as collectibles. Yet, they did not develop a sense that these objects could be used as a basis for learning more about the past, as written records and oral traditions were being used.

So far there has been no detailed study of why archaeology in the modern sense failed to develop in ancient Greece and Rome and why the investigation of the remote past remained a subject for philosophical speculation. Schnapp (1997: 70) attributes it to a general gap between theory and practice in Greek science, whereas Moses Finley (1975: 22) sees it as part of a more general lack of interest in material culture among Greek and Roman intellectuals. It also might relate to a strong dislike among intellectuals for studying mundane objects. The well-developed infrastructure of libraries, archives, and facilities for reproducing manuscripts also must have favored the study of the written word. *Historia*, by distinguishing itself for its methodological rigor, must have further reinforced its disciplinary credentials at the expense of a more discursive *archaiologia* and the study of material culture.

During the Eastern Zhou Dynasty (771–221 BC), the philosopher Han Feizu ascribed what we recognize as Neolithic painted and incised pottery to an early period in the development of Chinese civilization. In the third century BC, there was speculation about successive ages of stone, jade, bronze, and iron. Sima Qian (ca. 145–85 BC), the great Chinese historian, visited ancient ruins and examined relics from the past when he was collecting information for the *Shi Ji*, his influential history of ancient China. Confucian scholars valued the systematic study of the past as a guide to moral behavior and, by stressing a common heritage extending back at least to the Xia Dynasty (2205–1766 BC), they made historical studies perform a powerful role in unifying Chinese cultural and political life (G. Wang 1985). Sima Qian and other early Chinese historians seem to have been interested in inscribed ancient objects as direct sources of information about the past that might be used to supplement and correct errors in the available corpus of historical literature. Bronze vessels, jade carvings, and other ancient works of art were collected and treasured as prestige objects as statues and fancy vases were in the classical civilizations of the Mediterranean region.

Although some scholars in later antiquity occasionally used artifacts as other than a source of texts to supplement what could be learned about the past and scholars as a whole became aware that the material culture of the past had been markedly different from that of the present, they did not develop a specific corpus of techniques for recovering and studying such artifacts and utterly failed to establish any tradition of antiquarian research. Nothing resembling an enduring discipline of archaeology developed in any of these civilizations. Although in Greece and China, beginning in the first millennium BC, philosophers replaced fixed religious beliefs with various, contending explanations of the origins of human beings and civilizations, their proposals remained speculative.

The Medieval View of History

Recent research has demonstrated greater awareness of the material remains of Roman culture in medieval western Europe than was previously believed (Greenhalgh 1989). More buildings and sculpture surviving from the classical period were visible in medieval times than at any subsequent period before the nineteenth century, and such material is often mentioned briefly in written records. In a few Italian and French cities, some of the most impressive Roman monuments were officially protected as objects of civic pride. The medieval period also was a time of massive destruction of such remains, as Roman cemeteries and ruined buildings were plundered of material to erect churches, houses, and city walls. Marble was so easily obtained from classical sites that this stone ceased to be quarried. Such acts of destruction led to the discovery of ancient inscriptions and works of art, but few of these finds have survived. Roman sarcophagi continued to be emptied and reused for burials as late as the sixteenth century. Ancient gems, coins, and ivories that were recovered in the course of plundering Roman ruins were recycled or incorporated into new works of art. A limited and disorganized interest in what was being found was combined with the belief that these objects might possess supernatural powers. Because of this, classical statues were sometimes destroyed or mutilated (Sklenář 1983: 15).

As a result of these finds, medieval artists living within the borders of what had been the Roman Empire sometimes had opportunities to study classical art. Roman art was not continuously known, admired, or copied but encounters of this sort provided the basis for short bursts of interest in Roman iconography and style: a series of mini-renascences that preceded the Renaissance (Panofsky 1960). The Lombard kings of northern Italy (AD 568–774) imitated Roman epigraphy and coinage, whereas the Merovingian rulers of France

(476–750) plundered Roman burials for their own grave goods. Charlemagne (r. 768–814), in his efforts to substantiate his claim to be a successor to the Roman emperors, revived many aspects of Roman art including the making of bronze statues and laying mosaics in the Roman style. The great population expansion and the accompanying destruction of old buildings that took place in Europe from the twelfth to the thirteenth centuries once again intensified this process, especially in Italy. Some stone carvers adopted numerous classical motifs and depicted Roman soldiers dressed as legionaries. The Holy Roman Emperor Frederick II (r. 1220–1250) both dug for and purchased antiquities. He also imitated Roman coinage and built a Roman-style triumphal arch in Capua. At the same time, an awareness of classical culture had all but disappeared in France, where both prehistoric and Roman ruins were attributed to recent Saracen (Arab) invaders (Weiss 1969: 3–15; Geary 1986; Greenhalgh 1989; Schnapp 1997: 80–103).

Yet at no time during the medieval period was archaeological excavation seen as providing a source of history. Digging was reserved for recovering holy relics, which were associated with saints and required to consecrate churches. Discoveries of classical artifacts were sometimes noted and comments made about them but no effort was made to study such finds in a methodical fashion. Even if classical art was reused and copied, the dominant styles of art and architecture throughout Europe, Romanesque (AD 1075–1125) followed by Gothic (1125–1500), were new creations that over time exhibited ever fewer Roman features. Yet, despite these and many other striking changes, it did not occur to medieval scholars to regard classical antiquity as constituting a different civilization from their own, except in matters relating to religion. There was no significant awareness of a cultural break between the classical age and their own time (Weiss 1969: 3).

In the medieval period, the Roman Catholic Church monopolized and regulated learning, a situation very different from the contending philosophical schools of classical civilization. The only certain knowledge of ancient times was thought to be what was recorded in the Bible and the surviving histories of Greece and Rome. Moreover, it was believed that the Bible provided a complete history not only of humanity but also of the cosmos since the time of its creation. On this basis, a Christian view of the past was constructed that in various ways has continued to influence the interpretation of archaeological data to the present. This view can be summarized in terms of six propositions:

1. The world was thought to be of recent, supernatural origin and unlikely to last more than a few thousand years. Rabbinical authorities estimated that it had been created about 3700 BC, whereas Pope Clement VIII dated the creation to 5199 BC and as late as the seventeenth century Archbishop James Ussher was to set it at 4004 BC. These dates, which were computed using biblical genealogies, agreed that the world was only a few thousand years old. It also was believed that this world would cease to exist following the return of Christ. Although the precise timing of this event was unknown, the earth was generally thought to be in its last days (Slotkin 1965: 36–7; D. Wilcox 1987).

2. The physical world was believed to be in an advanced state of degeneration and most natural changes to represent the decay of God's original creation. Because the earth was intended to endure for only a few thousand years, there was little need for divine provision to counteract depletions resulting from natural processes and human exploitation of its resources. The biblical documentation of greater human longevity in ancient times provided a warrant for believing that human beings as well as the environment had been deteriorating physically and intellectually since their creation. The decay and impoverishment of the physical world also bore witness to humanity of the transience of all material things, confirming the Christian Church's emphasis on spiritual matters (Slotkin 1965: 37; Toulmin and Goodfield 1966: 75–6).

3. Humanity was affirmed to have been created by God in the Garden of Eden, which was located in the Middle East, and to have spread from that region to other parts of the world, first after the expulsion of the original humans from the Garden of Eden and again following Noah's flood, which was believed to have taken place about 2500 BC. The second dispersal was hastened by the differentiation of languages, which was imposed on humanity as divine retribution for their presumption in building the Tower of Babel. The center of world history long remained in the Middle East, where the Bible chronicled the development of Judaism and from where Christianity had been carried to Europe.

Scholars sought to link northern and western Europe to the recorded history of the Middle East and the classical world by constructing fanciful pedigrees that identified biblical personages or individuals known from other historical accounts as the founders of European nations or early kings in that region (Kendrick 1950: 3).

4. It was believed to be natural for standards of human conduct to decline over time, an idea that was reinforced by knowledge of classical theories of degeneration. The Bible affirmed that Adam, the earliest man, and his first descendants had been farmers and herdsmen and that iron working had been practiced in the Middle East only a few generations later. The earliest humans had shared in God's revelation of himself to Adam. Knowledge of God and his wishes was subsequently maintained and elaborated through successive divine revelations made to Hebrew patriarchs and prophets. These, together with the revelations contained in the New Testament, became the property of the Christian Church, which henceforth was responsible for upholding standards of human conduct. By contrast, it was believed that those groups who had moved away from the Middle East and failed to have their faith renewed by divine revelation or Christian teaching tended to degenerate into polytheism, idolatry, and immorality. The ultimate products of this process were the monsters that were believed to inhabit the most remote regions of the world. The theory of degeneration was also used to account for the primitive technologies of hunter-gatherers and tribal agriculturalists when they were encountered by Europeans. Yet, when applied to technology and material culture, the concept of degeneration conflicted with the alternative – but to Christians an equally attractive – view, promoted by ancient Roman historians such as Cornelius Tacitus (ca. AD 56–120), that material prosperity encouraged moral depravity. Another competing idea anchored in classical philosophy held that any non-Judaeo-Christian religious beliefs that vaguely resembled Christian ones had arisen from the study of the natural world, which Christian theologians maintained reflected God's own nature (MacCormack 1991: 214). Medieval scholars were primarily concerned with explaining moral and spiritual rather than technological progress and decay.

5. The history of the world was interpreted as a succession of unique events. Christianity encouraged a historical view of human affairs in the sense that world history was seen as a series of happenings that had cosmic significance. These events were interpreted as the results of God's predetermined interventions, the final one of which would terminate the ongoing struggle between good and evil. There was, therefore, no sense that change or progress was intrinsic in human history or that human beings, unaided by God, were capable of achieving anything of historical significance (Kendrick 1950: 3; Toulmin and Goodfield 1966: 56). Between God's interventions, human affairs proceeded in a static or cyclical fashion.

6. Finally, medieval scholars and artisans were even less aware of changes in material culture than ancient Greek and Roman ones had been. It was not widely realized that in biblical times human beings had worn clothes or lived in houses that were significantly different from those of the medieval period.

During the Middle Ages, interest in the material remains of the past was even more limited and transient than it had been in classical times, apart from the collection and preservation of holy relics. This did not encourage the development of a systematic study of the material remains of the past. Yet the understanding of the past that was created at this time from selected written records formed the conceptual basis out of which the study of archaeology was to develop in Europe as social conditions changed. Moreover, despite the strenuous efforts that many generations of prehistoric archaeologists have made to refute it, in most of its essentials the medieval view remains very much alive. A Gallup poll conducted in the United States in 2001 indicated that 45 percent of respondents believed that human beings had been created in more or less their present form and at one point in time within the last 10,000 years (Alters and Nelson 2002: 1892).

Renaissance Antiquarianism

As a consequence of increasing trade and other economic changes, during the fourteenth century a feudal organization in northern Italy gave way to mercantile cities. People also became aware for the first time of irreversible changes taking place in the course of their lifetimes. Scholars came to regard cities such as Verona, Padua, and Florence as revivals of the city-states of antiquity and began to search surviving classical writings to provide these cities with individual pedigrees that would enhance their reputations and with precedents that would sanction the political changes that were occurring in them, both of which would help them to resist the efforts of German and French kings to control them. The views of these scholars reflected the interests of the new urban nobility and upper-middle class on whose patronage they depended. This interest in origins also attracted attention among the free cities of the Holy Roman Empire. In the early fifteenth century, Sigismund Meisterlin's studies of the origin of such communities marked the beginning of a longstanding interest in Italian humanist studies in Germany (Schnapp 1997: 110–11).

This use of historical precedents to justify innovations had its roots in medieval thinking, which, at least with respect to secular matters, viewed the remote past as superior to the present and therefore as a source of information that could improve life. Yet in the Renaissance an expanding search for historical texts that would justify political innovations gradually led to the realization that contemporary social and cultural life did not significantly resemble that of classical antiquity. The Italian poet Petrarch (1304–1374) clearly realized that ancient Rome had long ago disappeared from the world and had been succeeded by an unworthy era of cultural deprivation, later to be called the Middle Ages or medieval period, from which he hoped his own age was finally emerging. Rejecting the more recent past, Petrarch believed that only the history of ancient Rome was worth studying (Rowe 1965; D. Wilcox 1987). The aim of Renaissance scholars was to emulate as best they could the glorious achievements of antiquity. At first, there was little hope that in their current degenerate condition human beings could ever hope to excel the greatest achievements of ancient Rome. Only in its possession of a religion based on divine revelation could the modern age be viewed as unambiguously superior to pagan antiquity.

The early Renaissance scholarship of the fourteenth century was focused on the recovery from monastic libraries and renewed study of surviving Latin texts, especially those dealing with historical, legal, and literary themes. In the fifteenth century, more attention was paid to Greek texts, which were then becoming available in Italy from abroad in larger numbers. Many of these texts, however, dealt with philosophy, theology, magic, and science and, hence, were of less specific interest to Italian scholars and their patrons. Attempts to work out the topography of ancient Rome were based on the general comparison of ancient descriptions of the city with the locations of its surviving monuments. Even the original appearance of major buildings was at first ascertained from how they were portrayed on Roman coins rather than by studying the buildings themselves (Jacks 1993).

A more disciplined interest in classical antiquity gradually spread from texts to architecture and art. The topographer Leon Battista Alberti (1404–1472) argued that it was necessary to study ancient architecture as well as to read about it (Andrén 1998: 108). Ancient art and architecture were of particular interest to the urban nobility and wealthy merchants who sought to manifest their newly achieved social status by becoming patrons of the arts. Interest also was being spurred by the unprecedented destruction of ancient buildings, which were being quarried for ready building materials for churches and the palaces of the rich as the city of Rome once again began to expand. The decrees of successive popes did little to safeguard Roman ruins, although they may have been more successful in preventing the unauthorized export of artworks from the papal domains (Weiss 1969: 99–100). The artist Raphael (1483–1520), who oversaw the supplying of stone for building the new St. Peter's Cathedral, recorded ancient buildings that were being destroyed, but only sought to preserve inscriptions and sculpture (Parslow 1995: 160).

There was a growing interest in creating new forms of art and architecture to replace the Gothic style that was now associated with the declining feudal upper class. Models were provided by works of art and architecture that had survived from classical times and which in the case of architecture often were studied as they were being demolished. By sponsoring the recovery of knowledge about classical art and architecture and the production of new work modeled on classical examples, the leaders of the new social order that was emerging in northern Italy stylistically identified themselves with the glories of ancient times and further distinguished themselves from the feudal society they were seeking to replace.

An early interest in both written texts and material objects surviving from the past is expressed in the work of Cyriacus of Ancona (Ciriaco de' Pizzicolli, AD 1391–1454). He was an Italian merchant who traveled extensively in Greece and the eastern Mediterranean over a period of twenty-five years, often specifically in order to collect information about ancient monuments. In the course of his travels, he copied hundreds of inscriptions, made drawings of monuments, and collected books, coins, and works of art. His chief interest, however, remained public inscriptions. Although his six volumes of commentaries on these texts were destroyed in a fire in 1514, some of his other works survive (Casson 1939: 93–9; Weiss 1969: 137–42).

By the late fifteenth century, popes such as Paul II and Alexander VI, cardinals, and other members of the Italian nobility were collecting and displaying ancient works of art. They also began to sponsor searching beneath the ground for such objects. For a long time, there were no systematic excavations but merely digging in likely places for objects that had historical, aesthetic, and commercial value. Nowhere were such objects recovered in greater abundance than in Rome. These works inspired contemporary sculptors and painters, such as Michelangelo and Baccio Bandinelli, who both eventually claimed that they could carve better statues than the ancient Romans had (L. Barkan 1999: 10). An interest in classical antiquities gradually spread throughout the rest of Europe. Classical inscriptions, monuments, and works of art found in England, France, parts of Germany, and other lands that had been part of the Roman Empire were studied by local antiquaries, such as William Camden, as early as the sixteenth century. In due course, members of the nobility became avid collectors of Roman and Greek art, which their agents purchased for them in Italy and Greece. Early in the seventeenth century, King Charles I, the Duke of Buckingham, and the Earl of Arundel were friendly rivals in importing such works into England (Parry 1995: 125; Scott 2003).

In the fourteenth century, the term *antiquitates* referred only to compilations of written texts. By 1600, the philological approach to studying the past seemed exhausted and those who studied classical antiquity had redefined their principal task as being to collect material evidence relating to the past (Jacks 1993: 9). The term antiquary or antiquarian was used as early as the fifteenth century, and by the next century sometimes designated an official appointment as well as amateurs studying ancient objects (Piggott 1989: 13–17).

Jacob Spon (1647–1685), an antiquary from Lyon who specialized in epigraphy (the study of ancient inscriptions), was the first person to use the term archaeology in its modern sense to designate the investigation of the material remains of former human societies. Both he and his contemporary, the numismatist Ezechiel Spanheim (1629–1710), regarded ancient inscriptions as more direct and reliable sources of information than surviving texts, which had been recopied many times. Near the end of the seventeenth century, Francesco Bianchini (1662–1729), who pioneered the study of classical iconography, began to specify the ways in which the study of images provided information that was different from, and complementary to, that provided by texts. In addition to establishing the significance of artifacts as objects of antiquarian study, Bianchini theorized what antiquaries had already been doing for some time when they compared ancient monuments with the principles of classical architecture as expounded in the writings of the ancient Roman architect Marcus Vitruvius Pollio (first century BC) or what numismatists did when they combined the study of images and texts.

The importance of artifacts was realized even more strongly by the French Benedictine monk Bernard de Montfaucon (1655–1741) and by the French aristocrat Anne Claude Philippe de Turbières, comte de Caylus (1692–1765). Their works provide early examples of the predilection of French academics for creating extensive compilations. Montfaucon's fifteen-volume *L'antiquité expliquée et représentée en figures* (1719–1724) consists of illustrations of artifacts topically arranged and accompanied by explanatory texts. Caylus's heavily illustrated seven-volume *Recueil d'antiquités égyptiennes, étrusques, grecques, romaines, et gauloises* (1752–1767) broke new ground by stressing the need to compare artifacts with one another as well as with texts. Caylus drew attention not only to how cultural differences were expressed in material culture but also to what could be learned from careful descriptions and classifications of artifacts and by studying how they had been manufactured. Yet, although Montfaucon and Caylus both realized that style changed over time as well as differing from one group to another, they failed to discover how to utilize stylistic criteria to date archaeological material (Laming-Emperaire 1964: 80–5).

Throughout the eighteenth century, antiquaries spent much time studying works of art from classical times. The British ambassador in Naples, Sir William Hamilton (1730–1803), lived there for almost forty years collecting and popularizing painted Greek ceramics as major works of art and models for modern artists. Stone and metal statues and painted pottery were described and aesthetically appreciated, and efforts were made to ascertain the meaning of their decoration. Unfortunately, such works could be dated only by historical texts and few bore inscriptions, had been found in a context that dated them, or could be identified as a specific work described in ancient historical records. This problem was resolved by the German antiquary Johann Winckelmann (1717–1768). Winckelmann believed that because of their great love of liberty the ancient Greeks had produced the greatest art the world has ever seen, most evident in their anthropomorphic images. He devoted his career to studying the Greek and Roman sculpture that was on display in Italy; much of the best Greek art being available only in the form of Roman copies. Inspired by the philologist Julius Caesar Scaliger's (1484–1558) division of Greek literature into four successive periods, Winckelmann sought to date as many sculptures as possible from the inscriptions they bore or by identifying them with dated works described in classical literature. Then, by carefully noting the stylistic traits of these dated works, he determined the styles that were characteristic of different periods. In this manner, he divided classical sculpture into four successive types: an old or primitive style; a high style associated with the work of Phidias; a refined style inspired by the sculptor Praxiteles; and a period of "imitation" and "decay" characteristic of the Roman age. Using these styles, it was possible to assign statues about which no written information was available to one of these four periods of classical antiquity.

Although this sequence depended on written texts for its creation, once the stylistic trends were recognized, it was possible for art historians to date ancient sculpture without reference to textual data. Winckelmann's *Geschichte der Kunst des Altertums* (History of Ancient Art), published in 1764, provided not only meticulous descriptions of individual works but also the first comprehensive periodization of Greek and Roman sculpture and a discussion of factors influencing the development of classical sculpture, including social conditions, climate, and craftsmanship. Winckelmann believed

that his successive styles constituted a cycle of cultural development and decline such as the Italian philosopher Giambattista Vico
(1668–1744) had argued characterized all human affairs not associated with the Judaeo-Christian religion. Yet, on the basis of Greek
art, Winckelmann also attempted to define ideal, and in his opinion
eternally valid, standards of artistic beauty and continued to study
material that was of great interest to his aristocratic patrons. Despite
his professed love of the ancient Greeks, he exhibited no interest in investigating their everyday lives. Winckelmann nevertheless
extended a historical knowledge of classical civilization into domains
inadequately dealt with in ancient texts. Not even the most detailed
ancient account of classical art could reveal as much about that art
or its development as did Winckelmann's comparative study of surviving works. His research marked the culmination of an interest in
the material remains of the past begun by Bianchini.

Winckelmann is frequently identified as the founder of classical
archaeology. His demonstration that it was possible to establish a
chronology of styles that could be applied to undated artifacts was
an important step forward in establishing archaeology as a separate
historical discipline. Yet Winckelmann, like most other antiquaries of
the eighteenth century, generally was interested in studying objects
that had been removed from their archaeological context. His primary interest was with genre, not provenience. Hence, in many ways,
the claim that he was the founder of art history may be even more
appropriate than the claim that he was the father of classical archaeology. Winckelmann clearly was responsible for establishing a close
and lasting relation between classical studies and what was to become
the separate discipline of art history.

The eighteenth century also witnessed the development of systematic archaeological excavations, especially at the Roman sites of
Herculaneum and Pompeii, which had been destroyed by an erup-
tion of Mount Vesuvius in AD 79 (Figure 2.1). The earliest digging
was aimed primarily at recovering statues and other works of art for
the king of Naples, often by tunneling. Despite objections by Italian
antiquaries attached to the royal court, who wished art objects to be
recovered as quickly as possible for them to study, the Swiss army
engineer Karl Weber (1712–1764), who supervised later excavations,
his successor Francesco La Vega, and French antiquaries working
for the king of Naples developed a preference for studying public

Figure 2.1 Digging at Herculaneum, 1782 (J.-C. Saint-Non, *Voyage pittoresque et description du royaume de Naples et de Sicile*, Paris 1781–1786)

buildings and large private residences at these sites. In France, since the late seventeenth century there had been a growing interest in examining, recording, and trying to preserve Roman buildings (Schnapp 1997: 247–53). This interest had been stimulated by the great programs of constructing roads and fortifications undertaken during the reign of Louis XIV, which had revealed numerous buried Roman structures. Accurate plans and elevations were recorded, often under very difficult circumstances, of major buildings found at Herculaneum and Pompeii, and axonometric projections of these structures were sometimes prepared. Locations where outstanding artifacts were found were noted on these plans.

Before this time, architects had studied ancient buildings, but they had rarely cleared them in any systematic fashion. In their plans, these architects had restored missing parts and added details in a fanciful manner and generally employed ancient treatises on architecture to interpret ruins. The excavations at Naples were among the first to use carefully excavated ruins to try to understand better such texts. Although few stratigraphic observations were made, these developments were no less important than the work of Winckelmann for helping to transform antiquarian studies into classical archaeology. The systematic excavation and conservation of the ruins of ancient temples and other public buildings carried out by the French between 1809 and 1814, during Napoleon Bonaparte's occupation of Rome, even though the primary goal of these excavations was to uncover works of fine art, suggests that new standards of excavation had been established at Herculaneum and Pompeii during the eighteenth century (Ridley 1992). Antiquaries had been interested in the urban geography of Rome since the early Renaissance, but it was only in the eighteenth century that they began to study systematically the architecture of specific sites as well as collections of fine art.

Although Cyriacus of Ancona had recorded classical antiquities in the eastern Mediterranean in the early Renaissance and classical art from that region was reaching England by the seventeenth century (Parry 1995: 125), the main focus of classical studies long remained in Italy. In 1734, a group of English gentlemen who had toured Italy established the Society of Dilettanti, which funded detailed surveys of ancient monuments in Greece beginning in 1751. Similar work was carried out by the French investigator David Le Roy starting in 1758. Publications of this research provided models for Greek revival architecture and more generally stimulated a growing interest in the art and architecture of ancient Greece as well as that of Italy. Serious archaeological work did not begin in Greece, however, until after that country's independence from Turkey in the early nineteenth century.

The Development of Classical Archaeology

In the late eighteenth century, classical archaeology had begun to develop in an academic context. Following its military defeat by Napoleon in 1806, the north German kingdom of Prussia set out to reform its educational system. The goal of this reform was to educate civil servants so that they could manage the affairs of state more effectively without exposing them to the revolutionary ideas of the French Enlightenment, which were regarded as highly subversive by the conservative, estate-owning Prussian upper class. German humanists had been inspired by Winckelmann's publications to regard the genius, creativity, love of freedom, and sense of beauty of the ancient Greeks as the highest expression of the human spirit. They also believed that the essence of Greek achievements could be recreated in forms suitable for the modern world (Marchand 1996: 16). One of the other leading concepts of German humanism at this period was the belief that every culture was unique and deserved to be understood on its own terms (Zammito 2002). This encouraged an antipathy toward the comparative study of cultures that has continued to characterize classical studies to the present. This antipathy encouraged many philhellenic humanists to forget the ancient Greeks' own accounts of their cultural relations with Egypt and the Middle East and to view classical Greece as a self-contained culture that expressed the noble spirit of its creators, who in turn were identified as quintessential Europeans or Indo-Europeans (M. Bernal 1987). In the course of the nineteenth century, the connection between ancient Greeks and modern Germans was increasingly racialized. Already during the Napoleonic period, many educated Germans viewed modern France as the counterpart of imperial Rome, and modern Germany, which was culturally highly developed but politically disunited and threatened by France, as equivalent to ancient Greece.

Wilhelm von Humboldt (1767–1835), who was in charge of educational reform in Prussia, decided that a high school curriculum based on the study of classical languages, literatures, history, philosophy, and art was the best way to educate future bureaucrats without exposing them to revolutionary ideas. He assumed that Greek philosophy was sufficiently developed to provide German students with all the ideas they required to function in the modern world. Although Winckelmann had attributed the great cultural achievements of the ancient Greeks to their love of freedom, von Humboldt decreed that the study of their culture should remain apolitical. When many educated Germans actively supported the Greek revolt against Turkey in the 1820s, Prussia, Austria, and other conservative German states prohibited the formation of associations for this purpose and in some cases suppressed any public expression of support for the Greeks (Marchand 1996: 32–5).

The implementation of von Humboldt's curriculum reform encouraged an expansion of classical studies or *Altertumskunde* (the science of ancient times) at Prussian and other German universities. Classical studies, as it had been instituted by C. G. Heyne (1729–1812) at the University of Göttingen and formulated more clearly by his student Friedrich Wolf (1759–1824) at the University of Halle, privileged philology as the key to understanding ancient Greek and Roman culture, although it also embraced the study of classical art and architecture, which had been objects of antiquarian research since the Renaissance. Even after Barthold Niebuhr (1776–1831) demonstrated the unreliability of many written "historical" sources, classical scholars chose to rely on the literary source criticism that he advocated rather than on archaeology to check the veracity of ancient texts. Archaeology was regarded mainly as a way to recover data for epigraphers and art historians to study. Whether classical art and architecture were studied in departments of classics or art history, classical archaeology trailed in the wake of the larger discipline into which it was incorporated. Yet, because classical studies enjoyed the support of most educated Germans, including most members of the civil service, unprecedented funding for classical archaeological research gradually became available. In this way, archaeologists benefited from their connections with classics and art history.

In the second half of the nineteenth century, classical archaeologists began to search for ways to recover information that would corroborate and expand what was known from written records. Tracing architectural changes over relatively short periods in urban centers required detailed stratigraphic studies. One of the pioneers of this sort of analysis was Giuseppe Fiorelli (1823–1896) who, with the support of the government of the newly unified Italy, took charge of the excavations at Pompeii in 1860. He proclaimed the recovery of works of art and monumental architecture, which had hitherto dominated work at the site, to be secondary to the detailed excavation of all kinds of buildings in order to learn how they had been constructed and for what purposes different parts of them had been used. This required careful excavation to recover information about the ruined upper stories of houses. He also emphasized classifying artifacts according to function. Fiorelli established a school at Pompeii where students could learn his techniques.

Major advances in excavation techniques were achieved by Alexander Conze (1831–1914) from the University of Vienna on the island of Samothrace in 1873 and 1875 and the German archaeologist Ernst Curtius (1814–1896) at the Greek cult center of Olympia between 1875 and 1881. In their efforts to work out the history of major structures at these sites, both archaeologists endeavored to record the plans and stratigraphy of their excavations of major public buildings, including ones that had been rebuilt several times, in sufficient detail that their reports could serve as substitutes for the evidence that their excavations had destroyed. The report on Samothrace was the first to contain plans prepared by professional architects, as well as photographic documentation of the progress of the work. These excavations constituted prototypes for major excavations at other classical sites.

During the nineteenth century, classical studies, strongly influenced by the German model, became the quintessential expression of humanism and the preferred basis of a liberal arts education across Europe and America (Morris 1994b: 31). At least in countries where Protestantism prevailed, everyone who could read was supposed to be familiar with the stories contained in the Bible. Better-educated people were expected also to be familiar with ancient Greek and Roman history, legends, and mythology. Allusions to these stories were woven into everyday conversation, as well as literature and art. Thus, knowledge of classical times became a token of superior taste, education, and social status and supporting the cultivation of such knowledge constituted evidence of social solidarity (Lowenthal 1985). The upper-middle classes thus financed efforts to produce and disseminate such knowledge. Public funds and private philanthropy supported the creation of museums in major European and North American cities and of national schools to promote classical research in Italy, Greece, and neighboring regions.

Although the Italian government prevented foreign archaeologists from excavating in Italy, foreign archaeologists based in Greece carried out important excavations at classical sites around the northeastern Mediterranean. The Germans dug at Pergamon in modern Turkey from 1878 until 1915 and the Americans at Corinth from 1896 to 1916 and at the Athenian agora beginning in 1931, whereas the French carried out long-term research at Delos and Delphi and the British worked at Sparta and in Crete. Russian classical archaeology was pursued within the borders of the Russian empire, where valuable Greek jewelry was found in Scythian burials and Greek colonies had been established along the north shore of the Black Sea. Classical excavations began in the Crimea early in the nineteenth century, and by 1826 so many finds had been assembled in the city of Krech that an archaeological museum was established there. The study of classical antiquities was vigorously pursued by the Imperial Odessa Society of History and Antiquity, founded in 1839 (M. Miller 1956: 22, 27; Sklenář 1983: 94). Russian classical archaeology continued along traditional lines with a preference for the analysis of ancient art, as Russian medieval archaeology also did.

In general, classical excavators sought to recover information relating to epigraphy, fine arts, architecture, and urban design. The organization of research at major sites was characterized by increasing specialization of tasks and the development of more elaborate hierarchical structures. Directors, who controlled research funds, determined the goals of such research and evaluated the performance of students and junior colleagues. Much of the professional training of classical archaeologists occurred at these digs and within the national schools that often were associated with them. Professional standards and a desire to do work that was precise and could withstand international peer evaluation gradually replaced the romanticism of earlier times. Only major countries possessed the resources required to finance large-scale excavations and they found in archaeology yet another way to compete for international prestige. Accompanying this growing professionalism was an increasingly insistent denial that knowledge of ancient Greece was relevant for the present.

The professed goal of professional archaeologists came to be to know what had really existed in the past, at least in terms of what was of interest to classical studies.

As a result of being employed in university or museum departments of classical studies or art history, most classical archaeologists remained isolated from prehistoric archaeologists and anthropologists; a rare exception being Roman provincial archaeology in countries such as Britain. Although many foreign archaeologists working in Greece were aware of the work being done by prehistoric archaeologists studying the Bronze Age cultures of the Aegean area, they long denied that these cultures were of much significance for understanding the classical period and hence did not pay as much attention to this work as they might have done. One result of this was a remarkable continuity in the practice of classical archaeology. Michael Shanks (1996: 97–9) has proposed that for almost 200 years, into the 1960s, classical archaeologists continued to ask essentially the same questions and to collect the same sorts of data. They searched for ancient texts and works of fine art in the contexts of sanctuaries, other public buildings, and elaborate houses, and sought to recover urban plans with a primary focus on civic centers, but they generally ignored evidence relating to subsistence, overall settlement patterns, rural life, technological processes, or trade. In a remarkable display of conservatism, classical archaeology remained true to its original Renaissance preoccupations.

Within this pattern, changes did occur. During the nineteenth century, as part of the professionalization of classical archaeology, a preoccupation with the analysis of style replaced an earlier interest in beauty. In the 1850s, Eduard Gerhard (1795–1867) argued that archaeology had to be based on the systematic description and comparison of artifacts. Like palaeographers, numismatists, and art historians, classical archaeologists used stylistic analysis to order various kinds of artifacts chronologically, determine where they were made, and even try to ascertain who had made them. Adolf Furtwängler (1853–1907) perfected techniques for stylistically categorizing finds that were widely imitated. His catalogues of Greek vases culminated in John Beazley's (1885–1970) celebrated efforts to assign the manufacture of unsigned as well as what were believed to be signed Attic painted ceramic vessels to individual painters or their schools (Marchand 1996: 104–15; Shanks 1996: 60–3). Yet, Mary Beard

(2001) has observed that no more can be said about Beazley's artists than can be said about the pots he assigned to them.

Classical archaeologists showed little interest in ascertaining the uses made of ancient objects, with the conspicuous exception of the American archaeologist Harriet Ann Boyd Hawes (1871–1945), who employed functional considerations as a basis for classifying many of her Cretan finds. In the late nineteenth and early twentieth centuries, the British classicists Charles Newton, Jane Harrison, and William Ridgeway became interested in studying ancient Greek religious beliefs, everyday life, and other anthropological concerns, but their ideas had no lasting impact on classical archaeology (Morris 1994b: 28–9). For classicists, the main question was not what functions an artifact had served in the civilization that had created it, but the far more subjective issue of what such an artifact might be able to communicate about the general mindset of its creators. Explanations of change were treated as the responsibility of classical epigraphers and historians rather than of archaeologists. Archaeological publications increasingly took the form of site reports and catalogues. Thus, the main objectives of classical archaeologists retreated to the formal study of a limited range of material culture in isolation from its original social or cultural context. Whether working within classical studies or art history, classical archaeologists appeared increasingly unlikely to produce any broad vision of the past.

Stephen Dyson (1989, 1998) and Ian Morris (1994b: 14) suggest that the main reason for the conservatism of classical archaeology was the need for graduate students to go abroad to carry out research, usually within the hierarchical structures created for large, long-term excavation projects. There they found themselves dependent on the goodwill of senior academics who dictated what topics students might study and how they would do their research. By the time even an innovative researcher was in a position to chart his own course, he had become thoroughly enculturated into established ways of doing things. The great importance accorded to teamwork also may have promoted conformity. Yet perhaps an equally important factor maintaining the status quo was the role assigned to archaeologists as providers of data to be studied by epigraphers, historians, and art historians. The best escape for intellectually ambitious archaeologists was to seek to establish themselves in these more prestigious roles.

Since the 1960s, classical studies have been in decline (Morris 1994b: 12). Ancient Greece and Rome do not enjoy the prestige they once did in modern multiethnic societies where classical humanism has been replaced by ethnographic humanism (Marchand 1996: 372–3), or in a world in which human history now extends back four million years. New electronic technologies make classical societies seem more irrelevant to understanding modern life than ever before, and many find Western society's justification in its own success, even if they are not convinced that this success will be long-lived. Diminishing funding for classical studies and increasing questioning of the relevance of the discipline have caused many classical archaeologists to explore new adaptations. These developments will be examined in Chapter 9.

Egyptology and Assyriology

Classical studies provided a model for the development of both Egyptology and Assyriology. In the late eighteenth century, almost nothing was known about the ancient civilizations of Egypt and the Middle East except what had been recorded about them by the ancient Hebrews, Greeks, and Romans. Their scripts could not be read and their writings and works of art were unstudied and largely remained buried in the ground.

Ancient Egypt had long been a subject of speculation and fantasy and, despite the development of Egyptology, remains so in amateur circles. To the Greeks and Romans of antiquity, Egypt was already an ancient civilization and a repository of primeval wisdom, arcane cults, and bizarre customs. It must have impressed visitors from the northern shores of the Mediterranean in much the same way that India did European visitors in the eighteenth century AD. In the Bible, Egypt was portrayed as a land of exotic splendor and a place of refuge but also as a land of oppression, idolatry, and dangerous women. The rediscovery in the fifteenth century of classical writings about Egypt led Renaissance scholars to speculate that, long before Moses, Egyptians had received a pristine revelation of divine wisdom that may have been more complete and less corrupted than was that recorded in the Hebrew scriptures. In 1600, the mystic Giordano Bruno was burned at the stake in Rome for claiming, among other things, that ancient Egyptian religious beliefs were older and more authentic than Christian ones (Yates 1964). By contrast, in the following century the Jesuit priest Athanasius Kircher (1602–1680) supported the idea of ancient Egyptian wisdom as a means of combatting mechanistic philosophy and modern science, both of which he regarded as a serious threat to Christianity. Ideas of this sort eventually became a perennial part of the European intellectual underground through Rosicrucianism and Freemasonry (Stevenson 1988).

Beginning in the medieval period, European visitors to Egypt produced accounts of their travels that included brief descriptions of ancient monuments. The systematic study of ancient Egypt began with observations by the French academics who accompanied Napoleon Bonaparte's invasion of Egypt in 1798–1799 and produced the multivolume *Description de l'Egypte* beginning in 1809. Another result of this military campaign was the accidental discovery of the Rosetta Stone, a bilingual inscription that played a major role in Jean-François Champollion's (1790–1832) decipherment of the ancient Egyptian scripts, which began to produce substantial results by 1822. Most Egyptian texts turned out not to be repositories of esoteric knowledge but to deal with historical, administrative, and secular matters as well as routine aspects of religious cults. Champollion and Ippolito Rosellini (1800–1843), in 1828–1829, and the German Egyptologist Karl Lepsius (1810–1884), between 1849 and 1859, led expeditions to Egypt that recorded temples, tombs, and, most important, the monumental inscriptions that were associated with them; the American Egyptologist James Breasted (1865–1935) extended this work throughout Nubia between 1905 and 1907. Using these texts, it was possible to produce a chronology and skeletal history of ancient Egypt, in relation to which Egyptologists could begin to study the development of Egyptian art and architecture. Champollion was, however, forced to restrict his chronology so that it did not conflict with that of the Bible, in order not to offend the religious sentiments of the conservative officials who controlled France after the defeat of Napoleon (M. Bernal 1987: 252–3). At the same time, adventurers, including the Italian circus performer and strong man Giovanni Belzoni (1778–1823) and agents of the French Consul-General Bernardino Drovetti, were locked in fierce competition to acquire major collections of Egyptian art works for public display in Britain and France (Fagan 1975). Their plundering of ancient Egyptian tombs and temples was halted only after the French Egyptologist Auguste Mariette (1821–1881), who was appointed Conservator of Egyptian Monuments in 1858, took steps to stop all unauthorized work. Even his clearances of ancient temples and tombs were intended to forestall robbers and to acquire material for a national collection rather than to record the circumstances in which finds were made.

W. M. F. Petrie (1853–1942), who began working in Egypt in 1880, set new standards by recording the plans of his excavations and noting where major finds had been made, but only rarely did he record stratigraphic sections. He regarded sections as being of minor importance, as most of the sites he dug had been occupied for relatively short periods (Drower 1985). George Reisner (1867–1942), an American archaeologist who excavated in Egypt and the Sudan beginning in 1899, introduced the routine recording of sections as well as profiles as early as his work at Deir el-Ballas in 1900 (Lacovara 1981: 120). He excavated by natural levels and also recorded in minute detail the precise locations of many precious but often badly decayed objects that he found buried together in the tomb of Queen Hetepheres at Giza. His work brought Egyptian archaeology close to its modern technical standard (J. Wilson 1964: 144–50).

Egyptologists tended to excavate mainly temples and tombs in their search for texts, art treasures, and architectural data. Only a few residential sites were excavated, primarily with the intention of finding papyri and other inscriptions. Unlike in classical studies, archaeology was the sole source of written material produced by the people being studied. John Gardiner Wilkinson (1837) and Adolf Erman ([1886], English translation 1894) used tomb paintings to produce studies of daily life in ancient Egypt (J. Thompson 1992). Later, W. M. F. Petrie sought to trace changes from one period to another in items of the material culture used in everyday life (Drower 1985). Nevertheless, daily life did not become a major focus of scholarly study in Egyptology. Instead, Egyptologists, modeling their work on classical studies, concentrated overwhelmingly on philology, literary studies, political history, and the study of elite art and architecture. One distinctive and enduring feature of Egyptian archaeology was a substantial interest in ancient Egyptian technology (Lucas 1926). Because it was a less populous field than classical studies, Egyptology also was less specialized, the principal division being between archaeologists and epigraphers. The two most distinguished interpretive works produced by Egyptological archaeologists before the 1960s were Breasted's *Development of Religion and Thought in Ancient Egypt* (1912) and Henri Frankfort's *Kingship and the Gods* (1948), a contrastive study of how rulership was conceptualized in ancient Egypt and Mesopotamia.

Beginning in the twelfth century, when Rabbi Benjamin of Tudela in northern Spain encountered the ruins of Nineveh, European travelers to the Middle East noted the remains of ancient cities in Iraq and Persia and occasionally brought back to Europe unreadable inscriptions and other artifacts. In 1616 Pietro della Valle identified and investigated the ruins of Babylon and also visited the site of Ur. In 1786, abbé Joseph de Beauchamp (1752–1801) carried out the first known excavations at Babylon. All three of these cities had been mentioned in the Hebrew Bible. In 1754, Jean-Jacques Barthélemy (1716–95) used his knowledge of Hebrew to decipher the closely-related Phoenician alphabet, thereby initiating the epigraphic study of "lost" Middle Eastern civilizations. The first successful attempt to translate copies of Old Persian cuneiform texts from Persepolis was made by Georg Grotefend (1775–1833) in 1802. Early in the nineteenth century, Claudius Rich, the East India Company agent in Baghdad, inspected the ruins of ancient Mesopotamian sites, including those of Nineveh and Babylon, and collected artifacts that were purchased by the British Museum in 1825. Sporadic digging gave way in the 1840s to Paul-Emile Botta's (1802–1870) more extensive excavations at Nineveh and Khorsabad and Austen Layard's (1817–1891) at Nimrud and Kuyunjik in northern Iraq. The elaborate neo-Assyrian palaces at these sites yielded vast amounts of ancient sculpture and textual material (Figure 2.2). By 1857, beginning with a trilingual historical text that the Persian king Darius I (r. 522–486 BC) had ordered carved on a cliff face at Bisitun in Iran, Henry Rawlinson (1810–1895) and others had succeeded in translating cuneiform texts composed in the ancient Babylonian language, a breakthrough that made it possible to begin reconstructing the history of ancient Assyria and Babylon. This work of decipherment aroused great public interest, as some of these texts confirmed historical events mentioned in the Hebrew Bible.

Figure 2.2 Layard's reconstruction of an Assyrian palace, from *Monuments of Nineveh*, 1853

Major excavations began in southern Iraq only after a hiatus caused by Britain's and France's participation in the Crimean War (1853–1856). Ernest de Sarzec's (1832–1901) work at Tello (ancient Girsu) between 1877 and 1901 provided the first substantial evidence of the Sumerian culture which had flourished in southern Iraq in the third millennium BC. American archaeologists began excavating at Nippur in 1887 (B. Kuklick 1996) and a German team at Uruk in 1912. These and other sites yielded enormous numbers of cuneiform texts. Between 1899 and 1913, the German archaeologist Robert Koldewey (1855–1925) excavated large areas of ancient Babylon, revealing a vast amount of information about the layout of this city during the late Babylonian period. His horizontal clearances did not, however, recover significant information about the earlier periods of this city's history. In contrast, between 1897 and 1908, the French archaeologist Jacques de Morgan dug a deep trench into the citadel mound at Susa, in western Iran. It produced a stratified sequence extending from late historic back into prehistoric times; however, de Morgan's poor stratigraphic controls lessened the value of his work. Between 1922 and 1934, Leonard Woolley (1880–1960) (1950) revealed much about the city of Ur at various phases of its history.

Reconstructing the history of Mesopotamia using written texts made it possible for Assyriologists to study changes in art and architecture over long periods of time. The only sporadic occurrence of first-rate art meant, however, that the study of art history remained less developed in Assyriology than in Egyptology or classical studies. Conversely, because of the extraordinary preservation of written texts epigraphers have devoted unparalleled attention to using them to study the political history, literary genres, religious beliefs, and social and political organization of ancient Mesopotamia. As a result, both epigraphers and archaeologists have exhibited much more concern for understanding changing patterns of everyday life in Mesopotamia than was common until recent decades in Egyptology or classical studies. Yet the diversity of the corpuses of epigraphic data, both linguistically and topically, has caused Mesopotamian epigraphers to be divided into a large number of temporal and topical specializations. This diversity and a more general division between text-based and archaeologically oriented Assyriologists have been major barriers to synthetic interpretations of Mesopotamian data.

The development of Egyptology and Assyriology added 3,000 years of written history to two areas of the world that had hitherto been known only at second hand through the accounts of the ancient Hebrews, Greeks, and Romans. Both disciplines modeled themselves on classical studies. They relied on written sources to supply chronologies, historical records, and information about the beliefs and values of these two civilizations, but they also were concerned with the development of art and monumental architecture as documented by archaeological finds. Both disciplines depended more heavily on archaeology than classical studies did, as almost all the texts they studied had to be dug out of the earth. Although the development of both disciplines was initially supported largely because they were believed to be relevant for biblical studies, as they grew more professionalized, Assyriologists and Egyptologists sought to break free of the limitations that this interest imposed. As knowledge of Egyptian and Middle Eastern history increased, it became increasingly attractive to dismiss Hebrew culture as a late and parochial expression of that of the Middle East (Marchand 1996: 220–7). Although this position was sometimes linked to anti-Jewish sentiments, it was more often associated with increasing secularism.

Another pervasive bias built into Egyptology and Assyriology was the refusal of these disciplines to study the Islamic period in Egypt and Iraq. It was generally assumed that the cultures of these ancient civilizations were superior to Islamic ones. Even most hellenophiles recognized in ancient Egypt and Mesopotamia some of the early roots of classical civilization, whereas Islamic civilization was believed to be different from, and inferior to, what had preceded it. Few provisions were made for modern Egyptians and Iraqis to become professional Egyptologists and Assyriologists (D. Reid 2002). Archaeology thus both mirrored and supported European projects of colonization in North Africa and the Middle East that grew more explicit and interventionist through the nineteenth century. Therefore, as they escaped from the confines of biblical authority, these new disciplines became mired in colonialism, orientalism, and increasingly racism (Said 1978). It is a mistake, however, to conceptualize any of these categories in a unitary fashion. Each discipline and different archaeologists utilized them in different ways and for their own specific purposes.

Other First Archaeologies

In China, a long-standing interest in studying ancient elite artifacts intensified during the Song Dynasty (AD 960–1279) as part of a revival of Confucianism among the literati (G. Barnes 1993: 28). This interest also was stimulated by the accidental unearthing of bronze vessels of the Shang Dynasty, following a displacement in the course of the Yellow River. These vessels formed the nucleus of an Imperial collection of antiquities still preserved in Beijing (Elisseeff 1986: 37–9). Song scholars began to publish detailed descriptions and studies of ancient bronze and jade objects, especially ones bearing inscriptions. The earliest surviving work of this sort, *Kaogutu* by Lu Dalin, describes in words and line drawings 210 bronze and thirteen jade artifacts dating from the Shang to the Han Dynasties, which were kept in the Imperial collection and in thirty private ones. The inscriptions on these objects were studied as sources of information about ancient epigraphy and historical matters and the artifacts themselves were minutely scrutinized in an effort to acquire information about early forms of rituals and other aspects of culture that was not supplied by surviving ancient texts (Figure 2.3). Inscriptions, decorative motifs, and the general shapes of objects also were used as criteria for dating them and assuring their authenticity and in due course scholars were able to assign dates to vessels on the basis of formal criteria only. The inscriptions on these vessels also were employed to evaluate the reliability of surviving texts. In the preface to his book on antiquities, the Song scholar Zhao Mingcheng noted that, when matters such as dates, geography, official titles, and genealogy in surviving classical writings were checked against texts recovered on ancient vessels, the two were in conflict 30 to 40 percent of the time, and on this basis he concluded that in these instances the preserved classical writings were in error (Rudolph 1962–1963: 169–70).

Although antiquarian studies experienced a severe decline after the Song Dynasty, they revived early in the Qing Dynasty (AD 1644–1911). Scholars such as Gu Yenwu (1613–1682) and Yen Rozhü (1636–1704) paid much attention to textual criticism. One of their major concerns was to establish the authenticity of ancient writings. Ancient inscriptions on bronze and stone were used to verify and correct the meanings of characters that were given in early dictionaries. Scholars who belonged to this school also made the earliest

Figure 2.3 Shang cast bronze ritual vessel, illustrated with rubbing of inscriptions and their transcription into conventional characters, from twelfth-century AD catalogue *Bogutu* (Percival David Foundation of Chinese Art, London)

studies of inscriptions on Shang oracle bones that were unearthed at Anyang beginning in 1898 (Li Chi 1977: 3–13; Chang 1981). Yet, although these scholars have been interpreted as providing an indigenous basis for the development of archaeology in modern China, they made no effort to recover data. Their studies also remained a branch of general historiography rather than developing, because of their additional concern with material culture, into a discipline in its own right, as classical studies, Egyptology, and Assyriology did in the West. Li Chi (1977: 32–3) maintains that Chinese scholars viewed their office desks as their proper work domains and physical labor as being unworthy of their learning. Although Chinese scholars eagerly studied antiquities, they also had a deeply rooted antipathy against carrying out excavations. The knowing violation of graves was punishable by death in China into the twentieth century, and all forms of excavation were believed to be potentially capable of disturbing benevolent supernatural influences flowing through the soil (Creel 1937: 27–9).

In Japan, during the prosperous Tokugawa period (AD 1603–1868), gentlemen-scholars of the samurai (warrior) and merchant classes collected and described ancient artifacts. Neo-Confucians adopted a rationalistic approach to antiquities. For example, Hakuseki Arai (1656–1725) maintained that stone arrowheads were not of supernatural origin but had been manufactured by human beings in ancient times. Followers of the Kokugaku, or national learning, movement, sought to eliminate foreign influences from Japanese culture and to restore the primacy of Shinto religion and the power of the emperor. They promoted the study of texts such as the *Kojiki* (Register of Ancient Things) and *Nihon Shoki* (Chronicles of Japan), both composed in the eighth century AD. On the basis of vague evidence, or mere guesses, they claimed that many large artificial mounds (*kofun*) were the burial places of specific early emperors and sought to conserve and repair them. In this way, they turned the landscape into a statement supporting the priority of Shinto temples over Buddhist ones and of centralized government over Tokugawa feudalism. Michael Hoffman (1974) has suggested that these antiquarian activities were the result of European influence but, even though Hakuseki is known to have conversed with Italian missionaries, this is by no means certain. Antiquarianism seems to belong to the same tradition as does the study of Japanese history and folklore. It is therefore likely that in Japan, as in China and Italy, an interest in the material remains of the past developed under propitious circumstances as an extension of historical studies beyond the use of written sources (Hoffman 1974; Ikawa-Smith 1982, 2001; Bleed 1986; Barnes, G. 1990b).

By contrast, systematic antiquarianism did not develop in India before the colonial period. Despite impressive intellectual achievements in other fields, Indian scholarship did not devote much attention to political history (Chakrabarti 1982), perhaps because the Hindu religion and the division of socioregulatory powers between high-caste priests and warriors directed efforts to understanding the meaning of life and of historical events more toward cosmology (Pande 1985; J. Hall 1986: 58–83). Antiquarianism also failed to develop in the Middle East, even where Islamic peoples lived amid impressive monuments of antiquity. Moreover, Islamic culture encouraged a strong interest in history and efforts were made to explain what had happened in the past in naturalistic terms, especially by the historian and statesman Abu Zayd Abd ar-Rahman ibn Khaldun (AD 1332–1406), that modern historians judge to have been far in advance of historical research being done anywhere else in the world (Masry 1981). The failure of antiquarianism to develop in the Arab world may be attributed to Islam's view of pagan pre-Islamic civilizations and their works as an Age of Ignorance, to a tendency to view many features of Islamic history as cyclical, and to a religiously based disdain for and fear of works of art that involved the portrayal of human forms. Too great an interest in pre-Islamic times also could easily have been mistaken for dabbling in satanic arts. In the medieval period, some Arab writers celebrated ancient Egypt's monuments as wonders worthy of respect but mainly because of their association with revered Moslems. By contrast, popular practices that attributed supernatural powers to ancient Egyptian structures were seen by scholars as something that had to be suppressed (Wood 1998). India and the Arab world indicate the highly particularistic factors that must be taken into account in explaining the origins of archaeological research, or its failure to develop, in any specific culture.

Conclusions

The first archaeologies to be developed in a systematic fashion were historical ones. Although an interest in material culture surviving from the past is ubiquitous, disciplines devoted to studying the past by means of such material have developed in only a few societies.

Practices generally anticipating those of modern archaeology developed for religious reasons in Egypt and Mesopotamia, but they were not coherently organized and did not survive into later times. In ancient Greece and Rome and in medieval Europe, the study of the material remains of the past was at best vestigial and disorganized. Comparisons between Renaissance Europe, Song China, and, to a lesser degree, Japan suggest that in some cases where traditions of historiography are well established, studies of written documents may come to be supplemented by systematic research on palaeography and ancient elite culture. In China and Europe, such studies first used texts to date ancient finds and then employed stylistic traits to track changes in art and architecture over time.

The more extensive and systematic development of such research in Europe may be attributed to the vast social and political transformation that occurred there beginning in the late medieval period. The study of classical antiquity began in the context of the rejection of feudalism that started in northern Italy and was closely related to the desire of rising elites to abandon their ties to the immediate past and associate themselves with what they gradually came to recognize as an older and superior cultural tradition. Antiquarianism evolved as a practice that was capable of providing the information that wealthy patrons valued (Parry 1995: 95). Classical archaeology later came to play a major role in defining European culture from the viewpoint of the upper classes. This situation, which contrasted with the greater continuity in Chinese and Japanese society before the twentieth century, may have stimulated the development of archaeology as a major source of information about the literate civilizations of ancient times. The rediscovery of classical antiquity provided detailed information about the glorious pasts of Italy and Greece, which had received little coverage in biblical accounts, whereas the study of Egypt and Mesopotamia was initially motivated by curiosity concerning civilizations that had featured prominently in the Hebrew scriptures. A growing sense of the discontinuity and diversity of the sources of European civilization encouraged research that relied ever more heavily on archaeology as a source of textual data as well as artifacts.

Once classical studies, Egyptology, and Assyriology were formed, these disciplines proved remarkably resistant to fundamental change into the 1960s. Each continued to focus on the high culture of one or more ancient civilizations, supplementing the study of ancient texts with the investigation of fine art and monumental architecture. The primary role of archaeology in these disciplines was to recover material to be interpreted by experts in other subfields. This cast archaeology in an inferior role compared to the study of epigraphy, ancient literature, history, or art history. Yet classical archaeologists, such as D. G. Hogarth (1899: vi), the Director of the British School at Athens, had no doubts that archaeology illuminated by written texts was greatly superior to archaeology that was not. Thus, it seems unlikely that most archaeologists regarded their subordinate position within these larger disciplines as anything but natural.

CHAPTER 3

Antiquarianism without Texts

———

Knowing the past is as astonishing a
performance as knowing the stars.
GEORGE KUBLER, *The Shape of Time* (1962), p. 19

The first archaeologists were only interested in historical times. They sought to use major works of art and architecture from the past to extend their knowledge of ancient civilizations that were already familiar to them from written records. Although they progressively enhanced their ability to elicit information about human behavior from material remains, they did not at first seek to study peoples about whom there was no written documentation. In the German academic tradition, the term archaeology (*Archäologie*) remains generally restricted to this sort of archaeology, whereas prehistoric archaeology is called *Urgeschichte* (history of beginnings) or *Frühgeschichte* (early history). Elsewhere the term archaeology was extended to the study of prehistory as the latter activity became more professionalized (Gran-Aymerich 1998: 128–30). Both classical and prehistoric archaeology grew out of a less professional and at first largely undifferentiated antiquarianism.

As a result of the work of prehistoric archaeologists, today we know that historical archaeologists ignored at least 95 percent of human history extending from the earliest known hominids who existed some four million years ago to the nonliterate peoples who lived in many parts of the world until recent times. In this chapter, we will examine how archaeology began to develop in northern and central Europe, where historical records usually do not antedate the Roman period and in some areas began only after AD 1000. We also will trace how archaeology spread to other parts of the world where there were no written records before the arrival of the Europeans.

Antiquarianism in Northern Europe

In medieval Europe, what we now recognize as prehistoric tumuli and megalithic monuments were objects of local interest and priests occasionally recorded in their chronicles the folk tales that were associated with them. Few of these monuments escaped violation by lords or peasants who believed them to contain treasure (Klindt-Jensen 1975: 9). Abandoned buildings of later times were likewise plundered for construction materials and in search of holy relics and treasure (Kendrick 1950: 18; Sklenář 1983: 16–18). As long as people believed that the world had been created between 4000 and 5000 BC and that the Bible provided a reliable account of events in the Middle East covering the whole of human history, relatively little appeared to lie beyond the purview of written records. There was no agreement whether human beings had reached Europe before Noah's flood, which was calculated to have occurred about 2500 BC, but, if any had, they were believed to have certainly been destroyed by that cataclysm. It would have taken a long time for the few people that the Bible recorded as having survived in the Middle East to have increased in numbers and once again spread north and west. Thus, only a few hundred to a few thousand years of human history in Europe appeared to be unaccounted for. This meant that in much of central and northern Europe and in most other parts of the world little time was available for prehistory as we now understand it.

During the Middle Ages, chroniclers, who were usually priests, constructed colorful histories that traced royal and noble families back to prestigious individuals who were mentioned either in the Bible or in classical writings. These accounts were justified with references to historical records, oral traditions, legends, myths, folk-etymologies, and outright inventions. They had the Goths descended from Gog, one of Noah's grandsons (Klindt-Jensen 1975: 10), and Brutus, a Trojan prince, becoming the first king of Britain after he had defeated a race of giants who had previously lived there. Pagan deities were often reinterpreted as deified mortals whose pedigrees could be traced back to minor biblical figures (Kendrick 1950: 82). In an age that was uncritical of historical scholarship, written records frequently were forged to support these tales (Sklenář 1983: 14). English scholars proudly claimed that King Arthur, and before him Brutus, had conquered much of the world (Kendrick 1950: 36–7).

Individual chroniclers supported particular ruling groups. Geoffrey of Monmouth, who wrote in the twelfth century, stressed England's earlier British, rather than its more recent Anglo-Saxon past, in order not to displease his Norman masters by lauding the achievements of the ruling group they had conquered (Ibid.: 4). As a result of conflicting loyalties, contradictory claims were made in different chronicles.

Other historical studies attempted to establish religious ties with the Middle East. In the late twelfth century, the monks of Glastonbury Abbey, in southwestern England, claimed that Joseph of Arimathea, a minor biblical figure, had in AD 63 brought to England the chalice that Jesus had used at his last supper (Kendrick 1950: 15). Prehistoric monuments were sometimes mentioned in these accounts. Geoffrey of Monmouth associated Stonehenge with the magician Merlin and hence with Arthurian legend (Figure 3.1), whereas German writers often ascribed megalithic graves and tumuli to the Huns, who had invaded Europe in the fifth century AD (Sklenář 1983: 16). The ancient Greeks would have labeled such history *archaiologia*.

The stirrings of patriotism in northern Europe that led to the Protestant Reformation stimulated a new and more secular interest in the histories of the countries of that region that was already evident by the sixteenth century. This patriotism was especially strong among the middle class, whose growing prosperity was linked to the decline of feudalism and the development of nation states, each ruled by an increasingly powerful monarch served by civil servants, lawyers, rural gentry, and clergy. In Protestant countries, the clergy was usually wholly dependent on the government and strongly supported it. Yet the entire middle class, such as it was then constituted, benefited from, and supported, increasingly powerful kings.

In England, the newly installed and still insecure Tudor dynasty (AD 1480–1603) was glorified by renewed historical treatments of Arthurian legends, which reflected the family's Welsh, as opposed to English, origins. Later, there was a marked increase of interest in the history of England before the Norman Conquest as scholars combed early records in an attempt to prove that Protestantism, rather than engaging in heretical innovation, was restoring elements of true Christianity that had been destroyed or distorted by Roman Catholicism (Kendrick 1950: 115).

Figure 3.1 Merlin erecting Stonehenge, from a fourteenth-century British
manuscript (British Library MS Egerton 3028, f.30r.)

T. D. Kendrick (1950) has interpreted the growth of historical scholarship in England during the sixteenth century as a slow triumph of Renaissance over medieval thought. Across northern Europe, newly powerful rulers adopted Renaissance art, architecture, and learning as symbols of their overcoming of feudalism. The Italian historian Polydore Vergil (ca. 1470–1555), who was invited by Henry VII to write a history of England, rejected the uncritical approach of medieval chroniclers and sought to base his work on reliable documentary sources. This led him to reject the historicity of many treasured national legends, such as those concerning King Arthur's conquests on the European continent, because he found no confirmation of them in the historical records of any other country (Ibid.: 38). Critical studies of this sort demolished medieval chronicles and created a significant void in the early history of northern Europe.

In general, until the late 1600s, British antiquaries sought to fill this gap with information derived from written archival sources dating from the medieval and still earlier Anglo-Saxon periods. They began researching the origins of laws, religious practices, and the royal prerogative, as well as genealogy and heraldry. In 1572, a group of antiquaries established the London Society of Antiquaries to promote the preservation of such records and the study of the history of institutions. This society disbanded early in the seventeenth century because King James I feared that the work of its members might undermine his royal powers (Piggott 1989: 22; Parry 1995: 43–4).

From the beginning, however, some antiquaries exhibited an interest in the physical remains of the past. In England, as early as the fifteenth century, John Rous (1411–1491) and William of Worcester (1415–1482) were aware that the past had been materially different from the present. William was working on an account of Britain that involved measuring and describing old buildings (Kendrick 1950: 18–33). This concern with the material remains of the past was strengthened as a result of the destruction of the monasteries in the reign of Henry VIII (1509–1547). The dismantling of these familiar landmarks and the dispersal of their libraries spurred scholars to record what was being destroyed as well as monuments of the more remote past. In this way, the study of physical remains began to supplement that of written records and oral traditions. These leisured, although usually not rich, antiquaries were drawn from the professional and administrative middle class, which was expanding and prospering under the more centralized rule of the Tudors (Casson 1939: 143). For these patriotic Englishmen, local antiquities were an acceptable substitute for the classical art from Italy and Greece that would soon be imported by the king and members of the nobility. They visited monuments dating from the medieval, Roman, and prehistoric periods and described them in the context of county topographies and histories. They also recorded the local legends and traditions relating to these sites. In addition, some antiquaries made collections of local (as well as exotic) curiosities. John Twyne, who died in 1581, collected Romano-British coins, pottery, and glass, as well as studying earthworks and megaliths (Kendrick 1950: 105). A more varied and extensive, but less archaeological, collection of curiosities by the royal gardener John Tradescant was to become the nucleus of the Ashmolean Museum, established at Oxford in 1675. Hitherto, collections containing antiquities had consisted either of church relics or the family heirlooms of the nobility.

At first, no clear distinction was drawn between curiosities that were of natural and those that were of human origin. Scholars, as well as uneducated people, believed prehistoric stone tools to be thunderstones (a view endorsed by the Roman naturalist Pliny [Slotkin 1965: x]) or elf-bolts and in Poland and central Europe it was widely thought that pottery vessels grew spontaneously in the earth (Abramowicz 1981; Sklenář 1983: 16; Coye 1997; Schnapp 1997: 145–8). In a world unaware of biological evolution, it was not self-evident that a prehistoric celt was man-made whereas a fossil ammonite was a natural formation. Most of these curios were found accidentally by farmers and manual laborers and there was as yet no tradition of excavating for prehistoric remains.

John Leland (1503–1552) was appointed King's Antiquary in 1533; evidence of growing royal interest in promoting the secular study of the past. He played an important role in rescuing books following the dispersal of monastic libraries. He also toured England and Wales recording place-names and genealogies as well as objects of antiquarian interest, including the visible remains of prehistoric sites. Only vaguely aware even of major changes in architectural styles in medieval times, his great innovation within the English context was his desire to travel to see things rather than simply to read about them (Kendrick 1950: 45–64).

William Camden's (1551–1623) *Britannia*, first published in 1586, was originally intended as a survey of what was known about England in Roman times based on literary sources and topographic surveys. In adopting this approach, Camden was following the example of Italian topographical antiquaries to whose work he had been introduced by the cartographer Abraham Ortelius in 1577 (Piggott 1989: 18). Camden's studies also extended to pre-Roman Britain and later Saxon England. It is indicative of the limited understanding of prehistory at this time that in his survey of the county of Wiltshire, nothing, not even Stonehenge or Silbury Hill, was recognized as being pre-Roman. *Britannia* was revised and updated in many editions both during Camden's lifetime and posthumously.

Camden's style of research was continued by a succession of historians and topographers, most of whom worked at the county level. They did little digging and had no sense of chronology apart from what could be ascertained from written records. Like classical antiquaries, they sought to explain ancient monuments by associating them with people mentioned in historical accounts. Their lack of an established method for doing this meant that what are now recognized as prehistoric remains were generally ascribed quite arbitrarily either to the ancient Britons, whom the Romans had encountered when they first invaded England, or to the Saxons and Danes, who invaded Britain after the fall of the Roman Empire.

Systematic antiquarian research developed somewhat later in Scandinavia than in England, as part of the keen political and military rivalry that followed the political separation of Sweden and Denmark in 1523. Renaissance historians soon became as fascinated with their respective national heritages as were those in England. They were encouraged by Kings Christian IV of Denmark (r. 1588–1648) and Gustavus II Adolphus of Sweden (r. 1611–1632) to draw from historical records and folklore a picture of primordial greatness and valor flattering to their respective kingdoms. This interest quickly extended to the study of ancient monuments. Royal patronage enabled leading antiquaries to record these monuments in a thorough and systematic fashion. Johan Bure (1568–1652), a Swedish civil servant, and Ole Worm (1588–1654), a Danish medical doctor, documented large numbers of rune stones. The inscriptions on these stones, which date from the late Iron Age, permitted a historical archaeological approach to late prehistoric and early historical times (Figure 3.2).

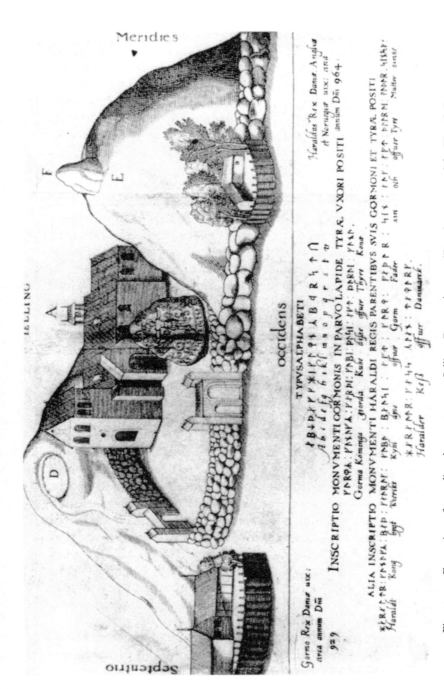

Figure 3.2 Engraving of tumuli and rune stones at Jelling, Denmark, 1591 (Drawing executed for Henrik Ratzau and published in 1591)

These antiquaries also collected information about what we now know were much older megalithic tombs and rock drawings. Yet Worm was of the opinion that Danish barrow graves and stone circles were unlikely to date prior to the beginning of the Christian era (Parry 1995: 284). His publications of Danish antiquities led some British antiquaries wrongly to identify megalithic remains in their own country as the work of Danes, who they knew from historical sources had begun invading and settling in England in the eighth century AD (Piggott 1989: 104).

Bure and Worm learned from each other despite the tense political rivalries between their respective countries and their opposed patriotic loyalties (Klindt-Jensen 1975: 14–21). Some of their work was carried out by means of questionnaires that were distributed nationwide. Museums also were established in which collections of humanly fabricated objects and natural curiosities were assembled. In Denmark one of the first of these was Worm's own museum, which became the basis for the Kunstkammer, or Royal Collection, that was opened to the public in the 1680s. In Sweden, an Antiquaries College was established at Uppsala in 1666 in order to pursue antiquarian research and national laws were passed to protect ancient monuments. These required the surrender of valuable finds to the king in return for a reward. Olof Rudbeck (1630–1702), who taught at the University of Uppsala, trenched and drew vertical sections of Viking-age tumuli at Old Uppsala, and in this way determined the relative age of burials within individual mounds. He wrongly believed that the thickness of sod accumulated above a grave could be used to indicate to the nearest century how much time had elapsed since a burial had been placed in it (Klindt-Jensen 1975: 29–31). Unfortunately, antiquarian research tended to languish in Sweden and Denmark as the political ambitions of these states and their economies faltered toward the end of the seventeenth century.

In late medieval France, historians focused on the Franks, a German-speaking people who had settled in their country after the fall of the Roman Empire. Prehistoric, Roman, and post-Roman structures were ascribed to Germanic heroes, such as Charlemagne and Roland, or to local saints. With the spread of Renaissance learning, Roman antiquities were identified for what they were and Francis I (r. 1515–1547) and Henri IV (r. 1589–1610) built up substantial collections of local and imported classical marble statues and bronzes.

Much local scholarship was concentrated on Roman inscriptions, whereas for a long time pre-Roman antiquities were little valued. The French collector of books and exotic artifacts Nicolas Fabri de Peiresc (1580–1637) played an important role in disseminating an understanding of what Italian antiquaries were doing throughout northern and central Europe.

Beginning with the publication in Lyon in 1485 of Paolo Emilio's (died 1529) *De Antiquitate Galliarum* (Gallic Antiquities), French scholars became more aware of the Gauls, who had lived in France before the arrival of the Romans and the Franks. Yet, because for over a century French humanists avoided any kind of fieldwork, only in the eighteenth century did a substantial antiquarian interest develop in the way of life and origins of these early, Celtic-speaking inhabitants of France. This led to the excavation of some prehistoric monuments. In the 1750s, antiquaries were still debating whether prehistoric megaliths in Britanny dated from the Roman period or that of the Germanic migrations that followed. In the latter part of the eighteenth century, a growing desire to document the cultural achievements of the Celts, who were now recognized as ancestors of the French, encouraged the study of pre-Roman times to develop independently of classical archaeology. This movement, which continued into the nineteenth century, was linked to growing nationalism. Like early English studies of pre-Roman remains, it encouraged more fanciful speculation than sober investigations and ultimately contributed little to the development of archaeology (Laming-Emperaire 1964). Yet the quality of reporting archaeological finds improved over time. In 1653 the tomb of the Merovingian king Childeric I, who had died in AD 481, was accidentally discovered at Tournai. Jean-Jacob Chifflet's description of the magnificent objects recovered from this tomb has been referred to as the first methodical excavation report ever published (Parry 1995: 256), although the find was not systematically excavated (Schnapp 1997: 204). In the 1770s, Pierre-Clément Grignon published a detailed account of his excavations of a Gallo-Roman settlement at Châtelet in Champagne, which resembles the reporting by Weber of his work at Pompeii (Schnapp 1997: 253–7).

In Germany, the rediscovery in 1451 of the Roman historian Cornelius Tacitus's (ca. AD 56–120) *Germania*, with its detailed and laudatory descriptions of the customs of the ancient Germans, encouraged scholars to use classical sources rather than medieval legends to study their early history. This trend laid the basis for the first general historical study of ancient Germany, Philip Klüver's *Germaniae Antiquae* (Ancient Germany), published in 1616 (Sklenář 1983: 24–5). As happened elsewhere, this historical orientation encouraged a growing interest in the material remains of the past. German antiquaries were precocious in resorting to excavation to try to study historical problems. Nicolaus Marschalk (ca. 1460–1527), a Thuringian humanist, investigated the differences between megalithic alignments and tumuli in an attempt to relate them to different, historically recorded ethnic groups. In the late sixteenth century, numerous excavators sought to recover decorated Lusatian urns and to determine whether these vessels were humanly manufactured or grew naturally in the soil (Schnapp 1997: 148).

In 1691, the philosopher Gottfried Leibniz (1646–1716) called on antiquaries to use their skills to reconstruct the ancient history of Germany. Antiquaries, such as Johann Major (1634–1693), J. H. Nünningh (1675–1753), Christian Rhode (1653–1717), and his son Andreas Rhode (1682–1724), excavated to learn more about the customs of their presumed ancestors. In order to accomplish this task, megaliths and funerary vessels were classified according to shape and presumed use. In an essay on the origins of the Germans published in 1750, Johann von Eckart suggested that graves without metal artifacts, graves containing bronze and stone but not iron artifacts, and graves containing artifacts made from all three materials represented three successive phases in human development, an idea that had already been suggested to Montfaucon by the Swiss antiquary Jacques Christophe Iselin. Instructions how to excavate sites were being published by German antiquaries as early as 1688 (Sklenář 1983: 24–5; Malina and Vašíček 1990: 28; Schnapp 1997: 142–8, 205–12).

Antiquarian studies clearly evolved somewhat differently in Britain, Scandinavia, France, and Germany. Developments in Hungary and the western Slavic countries seem to have most resembled those in Germany. Yet everywhere in northern and central Europe early antiquarianism shared important features in common. Political leaders and scholars incorporated archaeological finds into their collections of curiosities. In some princes' collections local discoveries considered to have artistic merit were displayed alongside statues and painted vessels imported from Italy and Greece. Some digging was carried out to recover artifacts and occasionally laws were passed to protect antiquities and secure new finds for royal or national collections (Sklenář 1983: 32–3). Although archaeological discoveries were often fancifully associated with historically known peoples, no effective system was devised for dating prehistoric artifacts anywhere in Europe. In the absence of written inscriptions, it was not even clear which finds dated before earliest written records in any particular area and which did not.

According to Leo Klejn (2001b: 1128), until Russia was "Europeanized" by Peter the Great (r. 1682–1725), no antiquarian tradition existed there as it did in the rest of Europe. The first substantial interest in what we regard as the remains of prehistoric times was directed to the kurgans, or tumuli, many thousands of which had been constructed over a period of 5,000 years in the steppe lands that stretch from the Ukraine eastward into Siberia. For centuries, if not millennia, these tombs had been plundered for treasure. As Russian colonization spread eastward into Siberia in the seventeenth century, the plundering of kurgans in that region was carried out on a massive scale, sometimes under government license. By the 1760s, not enough Siberian tumuli remained unplundered for these commercial operations to remain profitable (M. Miller 1956: 15).

In 1718, Peter the Great ordered officials to collect and forward to his new capital of St. Petersburg old and rare objects as these were discovered. This order embraced geological and palaeontological as well as archaeological finds and Peter's scientific interests were expressed in his request that sketches be made of the circumstances in which the most interesting objects were found. In 1721, a German naturalist named Messerschmidt was sent to Siberia to collect various categories of material, including archaeological artifacts. Five years later, a government office turned over more than 250 objects of gold and silver weighing more than 33 kilograms to the Imperial Art Collection. In 1739, Gerhard Müller (1705–1783), a professor of German attached to the Russian Academy of Sciences, who had been sent to study the peoples and resources of Siberia, supervised the excavation of kurgans in the vicinity of Krasnoiarsk. He recovered numerous bronze weapons and ornaments that he prepared for publication (Black 1986: 71). After the Russians annexed and began to settle the steppes along the north coast of the Black Sea in the second half of the eighteenth century, interests in ancient treasures shifted to that region. Landowners and peasants began to dig into mounds in hopes of recovering precious metals and antiquities. As early as 1763, the governor of the region, Aleksy Mel'gunov, excavated a Scythian royal kurgan, recovering valuable material now in the Hermitage Museum.

Recognition of Stone Tools

The sixteenth and seventeenth centuries marked the beginning of worldwide western European exploration and colonization. Mariners started encountering large numbers of hunter-gatherers and tribal agriculturalists in the Americas, Africa, and the Pacific. Descriptions of these peoples and their customs circulated in Europe and collections of their tools and clothing were brought back as curiosities. At first the discovery of groups who did not know how to work metal and whose cultures abounded with practices and beliefs that were contrary to Christian teaching seemed to confirm the traditional medieval view that those who had wandered farthest from the Middle East and thus lost contact with God's continuing revelation had degenerated both morally and technologically. Gradually, however, a growing awareness of these people and their tools gave rise to an alternative view, which drew a parallel between modern "primitive" peoples and prehistoric Europeans. Yet it took a long time for this comparison to be generally accepted and even longer for all of its implications to be worked out. It did not lead quickly or directly to the adoption of an evolutionary interpretation of human history.

The first step in this process, and one of the most important advances in the development of prehistoric archaeology, was the realization by scholars that the stone tools being found in Europe had been manufactured by human beings and were not of natural or supernatural origin. Until the late seventeenth century crystals, petrified plants and animals, stone tools, and other distinctively shaped stone objects were all classified as fossils. In 1669, Nicolaus Steno (1638–1686) compared fossil and modern mollusc shells and concluded that they resembled each other more closely than either did inorganic crystals. On this basis, he argued that fossil shells were the remains of once living animals instead of objects that had grown as a result of the same creative forces acting on stone that produced living organisms when they acted on animate matter. Ethnographic analogies played a similar role in establishing the human origin of stone tools (Grayson 1983: 5). The possibility that people had once lived in Europe who did not know the use of metal tools was implicitly raised early in the sixteenth century by Pietro Martire d'Anghiera when he compared the indigenous peoples of the West Indies with classical accounts of a primordial Golden Age (Hodgen 1964: 371). In the late sixteenth century, John Twyne used ancient Greek ethnographic accounts to suggest that in the first millennium BC, the northern Europeans had followed a primitive lifestyle that resembled those of the stone-tool using North American Indians of his own time. In the following century, John Aubrey proposed that life in prehistoric England might have resembled that of the indigenous inhabitants of Virginia.

Already in the sixteenth century, the Italian geologist Georgius Agricola (1490–1555) had expressed the opinion that stone tools were probably of human origin (Heizer 1962a: 62) and Michel Mercati (1541–1593), who was Superintendent of the Vatican Botanical Gardens and physician to Pope Clement VII, had suggested in his *Metallotheca* that, before the use of iron, chipped stone tools might have been "beaten out of the hardest flints, to be used for the madness of war" ([1717] Heizer 1962a: 65). He cited biblical and classical attestations of the use of stone tools and was familiar with ethnographic specimens from the New World that had been sent as presents to the Vatican. Ulisse Aldrovandi (1522–1605) also argued that stone tools were human fabrications in his *Museum Metallicum*, published in 1648. In 1655, the heterodox Frenchman Isaac de La Peyrère, one of the first writers to challenge the biblical account of the creation of humanity, identified thunderstones with his "pre-Adamite" race, which he claimed had existed before the creation of the first Hebrews, described at the beginning of the Book of Genesis.

In Britain, by the seventeenth century increasing knowledge of the indigenous peoples of the New World was resulting in a growing realization that stone tools had been made by human beings. In 1656, the antiquary William Dugdale (1605–1686) attributed such tools to the ancient Britons, asserting that they had used them before they learned how to work brass or iron. Robert Plot (1640–1696), Dugdale's son-in-law and the Keeper of the Ashmolean Museum, shared this opinion to the extent that in 1686 he wrote that the ancient Britons had used mostly stone rather than iron tools and that one might learn how prehistoric stone tools had been hafted by comparing them with North American Indian ones that could be observed in their wooden mounts. In 1699, his assistant Edward Lhwyd drew specific comparisons between elf-arrows and chipped flint arrowheads made by the Indians of New England. Similar views were entertained by the Scottish antiquary Robert Sibbald as early as 1684. Around 1766, Bishop Charles Lyttelton speculated that stone tools must have been made in Britain before any metal ones were available and therefore that they dated from some time before the Roman conquest (Slotkin 1965: 223). A decade later the writer Samuel Johnson ([1775] 1970: 56) compared British stone arrowheads with tools made by the modern inhabitants of the Pacific Islands and concluded that the former had been manufactured by a nation that did not know how to manufacture iron. By the eighteenth century such observations had encouraged a growing realization in Britain that antiquities could be a source of information about the past as well as curiosities worthy of being recorded in county topographies. Yet as late as 1655, as distinguished a European antiquary as Ole Worm continued to believe it likely that polished stone axes were of celestial origin even though he had ethnographic examples of stone tools from the New World in his collection (Klindt-Jensen 1975: 23). The repeated realization that stone tools had been manufactured by human beings and the slowness with which this idea was generally accepted indicate how weak were the networks linking European antiquaries interested in such questions during the sixteenth to the eighteenth centuries. The slowness also demonstrates that the artifactual nature of such objects was not self-evident.

Early in the eighteenth century Bernard de Montfaucon, on the basis of his examination of a megalithic tomb containing polished stone axes that had been excavated in Cocherel, Normandy, in 1685, ascribed this class of tomb to a nation that had no knowledge of iron. In reaching this conclusion, he was influenced by knowledge of archaeological research in England and Scandinavia (Laming-Emperaire 1964: 94). Soon after, the French scholar Antoine de Jussieu (1686–1758) drew some detailed comparisons between European stone tools and ethnographic specimens brought from New France and the Caribbean. He stated that "the people of France, Germany, and other Northern countries who, but for the discovery of iron, would have much resemblance to the savages of today, had no less need than they – before using iron – to cut wood, to remove bark, to split branches, to kill wild animals, to hunt for their food and to defend themselves against their enemies" ([1723] Heizer 1962a: 69). In 1738, Kilian Stobeus, Professor of Natural History at the University of Lund, argued that flint implements antedated metal ones in Scandinavia and compared them with ethnographic specimens from Louisiana, an opinion echoed in 1763 by the Danish scholar Erik Pontoppidan (Klindt-Jensen 1975: 35–9). By the eighteenth century, not only the human fabrication of stone tools but also the possibility of their considerable antiquity in Europe were widely accepted as plausible.

Yet a growing realization that stone tools had probably been used before metal ones in Europe and elsewhere did not necessitate the adoption of an evolutionary perspective. Stone tools could be observed being used both instead of metal ones and alongside metal ones in the contemporary world. Noting that, according to the Bible, iron working had been practiced at the latest no more than a few generations after the creation of human beings, Mercati argued that knowledge of metallurgy must have been lost by nations who migrated into areas where iron ore was not found ([1717] Heizer 1962a: 66). Similar degenerationist views were held for a long time. It was frequently suggested that knowledge of metallurgy was lost by many human groups as they spread across the face of the earth after Noah's flood, while at the same time this knowledge persisted in the Middle East. Stone tools were believed to have been invented as a substitute for metal ones. Some thought that at a later date knowledge of bronze and iron working diffused from the Middle East to places like Europe. Others speculated that bronze and iron working might have been independently reinvented in Europe. Only the latter theory postulated an evolutionary sequence, although it, like the others, remained embedded in the larger context of medieval degenerationism (Figure 3.3).

In 1695, John Woodward (1665–1728) hypothesized that humanity as a whole might have been barbarized after the flood (Rossi 1985: 217–22), an even more ambitious evolutionary scheme embedded within a degenerationist context. Although the radical English philosopher Thomas Hobbes (1588–1679) adopted a purely evolutionary view of human origins in his *Leviathan* (1651), it clearly remained dangerous to question the biblical claim that the earliest humans had been familiar with agriculture and metallurgy. Still other

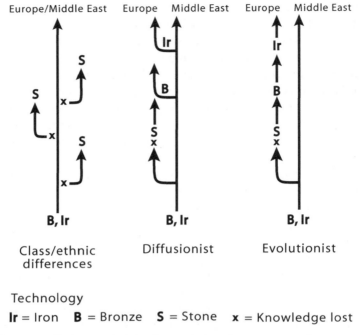

Europe/Middle East   Europe   Middle East   Europe   Middle East

B, Ir   B, Ir   B, Ir

Class/ethnic   Diffusionist   Evolutionist
differences

Technology
Ir = Iron   **B** = Bronze   **S** = Stone   **x** = Knowledge lost

Figure 3.3 Early speculations about relations between stone, bronze, and
iron implements in Europe and the Middle East

antiquaries rejected the proposal that a knowledge of metallurgy
had ever been lost in Europe. They argued instead that throughout
human history stone tools had been used alongside metal ones by
social classes or communities that were too poor to afford metal tools
or by a few isolated nations that, unlike their neighbors, had forgotten how to work metal. Because chronological controls did not exist
for the archaeological record anywhere before the earliest written
records, it was impossible to determine how different materials had
been used to make tools over time in different places.

As late as 1857, it was argued in opposition to the theory that
stone tools antedated metal ones that many stone tools appeared
to be imitations of metal originals (O'Laverty 1857; "Trevelyan"
1857). Without adequate chronological controls and any archaeological data from most parts of the world, it remained possible that
knowledge and lack of knowledge of iron working had existed side
by side throughout most of human history. Before the nineteenth

century there was no factual evidence to make an evolutionary view of human history more plausible than a degenerationist one.

The Enlightenment

The development of an evolutionary view of the past was encouraged far less by a growing body of archaeological evidence than by a gradual transformation in thought that began during the seventeenth century in northwestern Europe, the region that was rapidly emerging as the economic hub of a new world economy (Wallerstein 1974; Delâge 1985). This view was based on growing confidence in the ability of individual human beings to excel and of human societies to develop both economically and culturally. Early in the seventeenth century the English philosopher and statesman Francis Bacon (1561–1626) protested against the idea that the culture of classical antiquity was superior to that of modern times. He urged scholars to ignore the teachings of ancient writers and instead to seek knowledge through observation, classification, and experiment. Although Bacon did not rule out the use of hypotheses to guide research, he maintained that both their formulation and testing had to be grounded in observations. For Bacon, an inductive scientific method was the only way for humanity to overcome the tyranny of customary beliefs.

Bacon's position was echoed in France in the late-seventeenth-century Quarrel between the Ancients and the Moderns, in which the "moderns" argued that human talents were not declining and hence present day Europeans could hope to produce works that equaled or surpassed those of the ancient Greeks or Romans (Laming-Emperaire 1964: 64–6). Although Walter Raleigh and many other Elizabethan writers had continued to believe, in the medieval fashion, that the world was hastening toward its end, by the second half of the seventeenth century a growing number of western Europeans were confident about the future (Toulmin and Goodfield 1966: 108–10).

This optimism was encouraged by the acceleration of economic growth as a result of the application of technological innovations, especially in agriculture and shipbuilding, in Holland and England; by the scientific revolutions brought about by Galileo Galilei (1564–1642) and Isaac Newton (1643–1727), which vastly altered the understanding of the universe inherited from classical antiquity; and by widespread delight in the literary creativity of writers in Elizabethan England and seventeenth-century France. Especially among the middle classes, these developments encouraged a growing faith in progress and a new belief that to a large degree human beings were masters of their own destiny. They also gradually inclined western Europeans to regard the ways of life of the technologically less advanced peoples they were encountering in various parts of the world as survivals of a primordial human condition rather than as products of degeneration.

In the course of the seventeenth century, a growing belief in progress was complemented by an increasing emphasis on rationalism. The French philosopher René Descartes (1596–1650) attempted to account for all natural phenomena, apart from the human mind itself, in terms of a single system of mechanical principles. He expounded the idea that the laws governing nature were universal and eternal in their application. God was viewed as existing apart from the material realm, which he had created as a sort of machine that was capable of functioning without further intervention. These views, which denied God's personal involvement in the everyday affairs of the world, simultaneously promoted Deism and discouraged a belief in miracles. They therefore encouraged a more rationalistic approach to understanding nature as well as the belief that human creative powers were fixed rather than in decline (Toulmin and Goodfield 1966: 80–4).

Neither the Renaissance discovery that the past had been different from the present nor the realization that technological development was occurring in western Europe led directly to the conclusion that progress was a general characteristic of human history. In the seventeenth century, successive historical periods were viewed as a series of kaleidoscopic variations on themes that were grounded in a fixed human nature, rather than as constituting a developmental sequence worthy of study in its own right (Toulmin and Goodfield 1966: 113–14). The Italian philosopher Giambattista Vico (1668–1744) saw history as having cyclical characteristics and argued that human societies evolve through similar stages of development and decay (theocracy, monarchy, democracy, and ultimately barbarism or chaos) that reflect the uniform actions of providence. He prudently stressed, however, that this view of human history as governed by strict laws did not apply to the Hebrews, whose progress was divinely guided. Although he was not an evolutionist, his views helped to encourage the belief that human history could be understood in terms of regularities analogous to those being proposed for the natural sciences (Ibid.: 125–9).

While ideas about cultural evolution were being expounded in France by Loys Leroy and Jean Bodin already in the late sixteenth century (Patterson 1997: 32–3), an evolutionary view of human history that was sufficiently comprehensive to challenge the medieval one not only on specific points but also in its entirety was not formulated until the eighteenth century. Enlightenment philosophy, the most ambitious and influential systematization of a century characterized by system building, began in France, where it was associated with leading philosophers such as Charles-Louis, baron de Montesquieu, François-Marie Arouet Voltaire, Marie-Jean de Caritat, marquis de Condorcet, and the economist Marie-Robert-Jacques Turgot, baron de l'Aulne. It also flourished in Scotland in the school of "primitivist" thinkers, so called because of their interest in the origins of institutions. These included Francis Hutcheson, Henry Home (Lord Kames), William Robertson, David Hume, Adam Smith, John Millar, Adam Ferguson, Dugald Stewart, Thomas Reid, and James Burnett (Lord Monboddo), best known for his insistence that human beings and orangutans belonged to the same species (Bryson 1945; Schneider 1967; Herman 2001).

The philosophers of the Enlightenment combined a more naturalistic understanding of social processes with a firm belief in progress to produce an integrated set of concepts that purported to explain social change. They also created a methodology that they believed enabled them to study the general course of human development from earliest times. In England and the Netherlands, where political power was already in the hands of the merchant middle class, intellectual activity was directed toward analyzing the practical political and economic significance of this change. The continuing political weakness of the French middle class in the face of Bourbon autocracy stimulated French intellectuals to use the idea of progress to reify change as a basis for challenging the legitimacy of an absolute monarch, who claimed to rule by divine will and protected the feudal economic privileges enjoyed by a politically moribund nobility. By proclaiming change to be both desirable and inevitable, Enlightenment philosophers called into question the legitimacy of the existing political and religious order.

Beginning as an intellectual expression of discontent, the French Enlightenment gradually developed into a movement with revolutionary potential. By arguing that social progress was inevitably in the general interest of humanity, middle-class proponents of the Enlightenment sought to recruit support amongst the French lower classes as well as the middle class. Like adherents of most revolutionary movements seeking power, they sought to identify their own class's interests with everyone's general good. Their program also took account of the growth of capitalism and of a world economy dominated by western Europe and sought to create in France a political system that more closely resembled those already established in Britain and the Netherlands, which were more in accord with these developments.

The Scottish interest in Enlightenment philosophy reflected the close cultural ties between Scotland and France but also was stimulated by the unprecedented power and prosperity acquired by the Scottish urban middle class as a result of Scotland's union with England in 1707. Southern Scotland was experiencing rapid development but the highland areas to the north remained politically, economically, and culturally undeveloped. This contrast aroused the interest of Scottish intellectuals in questions relating to the origin, development, and modernization of institutions. By contrast, in England at this period questions of origins generally were regarded as speculative and were avoided. Although Scottish intellectuals made very important contributions to the development of Enlightenment thought and the understanding of the modern world, it was the more revolutionary version of Enlightenment philosophy that developed in France in the second half of the eighteenth century that would become popular among the middle classes seeking more political power for themselves in Europe and North America.

The following are the main tenets of the Enlightenment that were to be important for the development of archaeology and the other social sciences:

1. Psychic unity. All human groups were believed to possess essentially the same kind and level of intelligence and the same basic emotions, although individuals within groups might differ from one another in their talents and natural dispositions. Because of this there was no biological barrier to the degree to which any race or nationality could benefit from new knowledge or contribute to

its advancement. All groups were equally perfectable and hence all human beings were capable of benefiting from European civilization. Psychic unity also implied that an advanced technological civilization was not destined to remain the exclusive possession of Europeans. Closer to home, the doctrine of psychic unity implicitly denied that there was any natural justification for the feudal division of French society into three unequal social orders: nobles, clergy, and commoners. By contrast, few adherents of Enlightenment thought supported the political and social equality of men and women. Most would have read the "Declaration of the Rights of Man and the Citizen," passed by the revolutionary National Assembly in 1789 and regarded as the legal embodiment of the political ideals of the Enlightenment, as referring exclusively to males.

2. Cultural progress is the dominant feature of human history. Change was believed to occur continuously rather than episodically and was ascribed to natural rather than supernatural causes. The main motivation for progress was thought to be the desire of human beings to improve their condition, principally by gaining greater control over nature (Slotkin 1965: 441). Many Enlightenment philosophers regarded progress as inevitable, or even as a law of nature, whereas others thought of it instead as something to be hoped for (Ibid.: 357–91; Harris 1968a: 37–9).

3. Progress characterizes not only technological development but all aspects of human life, including social organization, politics, morality, and religious beliefs. Changes in all these spheres were viewed as occurring concomitantly and as generally following a similar sequence of development. Human beings at the same level of development were believed to devise uniform solutions to their problems; hence their ways of life evolved along parallel lines (Slotkin 1965: 445). Cultural change was frequently conceptualized in terms of a universal series of stages. These stages were usually defined in economic terms. Almost simultaneously Turgot and Home spoke of successive periods of savage hunters, barbarian pastoralists, and civilized farmers. A fourth period of commerce embraced more recent developments in Europe (Herman 2001; Pluciennik 2002). Europeans were believed to have evolved through all these stages, whereas less developed societies had passed through only some of the simpler ones.

Qualitative cultural differences were generally ascribed to climatic and other environmental influences (Slotkin 1965: 423).

4. Progress perfects human nature, not by changing it but by progressively eliminating ignorance and superstition and curbing destructive passions (Toulmin and Goodfield 1966: 115–23). The new evolutionary view of cultural change did not negate either the traditional Christian or Cartesian notion of a fixed and immutable human nature. It was, however, now believed that human nature was essentially good and hence that human beings had the innate capacity to manage their affairs to both their personal and their collective advantage. These ideas had much in common with the traditional Confucian beliefs of China, which were known to at least some Enlightenment philosophers from accounts by Christian missionaries. Human nature as it was now conceived was far removed from the medieval preoccupation with sinfulness and individual dependence on divine grace as the only means of achieving salvation.

5. Progress results from the exercise of rational thought to improve the human condition. In this fashion, human beings gradually acquire greater ability to control their environment, which in turn generates the wealth and leisure needed to support the creation of more complex societies and the development of a more profound and objective understanding of the nature of humanity and the universe. The exercise of reason had long been regarded by Europeans as the crucial feature distinguishing human beings from animals. Most Enlightenment philosophers also viewed cultural progress teleologically, as humanity's realization of the plans of a benevolent, if remote, deity. A faith that benevolent laws guided human development was long to outlive a belief in God among those who studied human societies.

The Scottish philosopher Dugald Stewart labeled the methodology that Enlightenment philosophers devised to trace the development of human institutions "theoretic" or "conjectural" history (Slotkin 1965: 460). This involved the comparative study of living peoples whose cultures were judged to be at different levels of complexity and arranging these cultures to form a logical, usually unilinear, sequence from simple to complex. These studies were based largely on ethnographic data derived from accounts by explorers and missionaries working in different parts of the world. There were disagreements about details, such as whether agricultural or pastoral economies had evolved first. In the New World, evidence of independent pastoral economies was totally lacking. Nevertheless, the evidence suggested similar developmental trends, even if the range of intermediate societies differed in the two hemispheres. It was believed that the resulting pattern could be regarded as an approximation of actual historical sequences, and in turn be used to examine the development of all kinds of social institutions. In the writings of the historian William Robertson and others, the generally similar range of cultures found in the Eastern Hemisphere and the Americas was interpreted as validating the principle of psychic unity and the belief that humans at the same stage of development generally respond to similar problems in similar ways (Harris 1968a: 34–5).

Turgot suggested that the modern world contains examples of all the past stages of human development. The systematic comparison and ordering of existing societies therefore would illustrate the entire history of human progress. This belief has led ethnologists from the eighteenth century to the present to claim that they possess the means required to study the total range of variability in human behavior and to document the general development of human societies without having to depend on archaeological data. This untested assumption has encouraged the formation of the view held by many social anthropologists that archaeology is of minor theoretical importance, if as a discipline it is needed at all. More productively, the theoretic history of Enlightenment philosophers questioned the Renaissance belief that the study of the past could be based solely on written records and ancient art and architecture. Instead, Enlightenment philosophers addressed changes in everyday life – in subsistence patterns, social and political organization, and folk beliefs – as well as in philosophy and the arts.

Enlightenment philosophers were convinced that their beliefs represented the cutting edge of human creativity and were destined to spread around the world and transform human life everywhere. Enlightenment philosophy was both ethnocentric and Eurocentric (Vyverberg 1989). Yet it should not be presumed that Enlightenment philosophers were inevitably preoccupied with the uniqueness of Europe. When Napoleon later considered charges that his efforts to modernize Egypt posed the danger that some time in the future the Egyptians might conquer France, he replied that it was as natural for the world to be ruled from Alexandria as from Paris (Herold 1962: 15–16). The progress and enlightenment of humanity as a whole were of primary importance.

It is generally acknowledged that a cultural-evolutionary perspective was widely accepted for explaining human history long before the publication of Darwin's *On the Origin of Species* in 1859. Yet Glyn Daniel (1976: 41) doubted the importance of Enlightenment philosophy for the development of archaeology because Enlightenment scholars, with few exceptions (see Harris 1968a: 34), ignored archaeological data in their own writings. That they did so is scarcely surprising because, in the absence of any established means for dating prehistoric material, archaeology had little to contribute to their discussions of long-term cultural change. This does not mean, however, that the writings of the Enlightenment did not influence the thinking of antiquaries. On the contrary, at the very least their evolutionary view of human development from the most primitive beginnings to the present suggested that there was much change before the earliest written records for archaeologists to study.

More specifically, the Enlightenment encouraged a renewed antiquarian interest in the materialist and evolutionary views of cultural development that had been expounded by the Roman Epicurean philosopher Titus Lucretius Carus (98–55 BC) in his poem *De Rerum Natura* (On the Nature of Things). He had argued that the earliest implements were hands, nails, and teeth, then stones and pieces of wood. Only later were tools made of bronze and later still of iron. Although Lucretius's scheme was supported by references in earlier classical texts to a period when bronze tools and weapons had not yet been replaced by iron ones, it was based largely on evolutionary speculations, which postulated that the universe and all living species had developed as a result of irreducible and eternal particles of matter, called atoms, combining in ever more complex ways. Neither Lucretius nor any other Roman scholar sought to prove this theory and it remained only one of many speculative schemes known to the Romans. A popular alternative postulated the moral degeneration of humanity through successive ages of gold, silver, bronze, and iron.

Early in the eighteenth century, French scholars were familiar both with the ideas of Lucretius and with the growing evidence that stone tools had once been used throughout Europe. They also were familiar with classical and biblical texts, which suggested that bronze tools had been used before iron ones. In 1734 Nicolas Mahudel read a paper to the Académie des Inscriptions in Paris, in which he cited Mercati and set out the idea of three successive ages of stone, bronze, and iron as a plausible account of human development. Mahudel, like Mercati, differed from Lucretius in assuming that stones had been worked as well as used, a change that must have been inspired by archaeological discoveries (Leroi-Gourhan 1993: 409). In 1758 Antoine-Yves Goguet (1716–1758) supported the Three-Age theory in a book that was translated into English three years later with the title *The Origin of Laws, Arts, and Sciences, and their Progress among the Most Ancient Nations.* He believed that modern "savages set before us a striking picture of the ignorance of the ancient world, and the practices of primitive times" ([1761] Heizer 1962a: 14). Yet to square this evolutionary view with the biblical assertion that iron working had been invented before the flood, he claimed, like Mercati and some other contemporary "evolutionists," that this process had to be reinvented after "that dreadful calamity deprived the greatest part of humanity of this, as well as of other arts."

Glyn Daniel (1976: 40) correctly warned against exaggerating the influence that the Three-Age theory exerted on antiquarian thought during the eighteenth century. Yet, as an interest in cultural progress grew more pervasive, the Three-Age theory gained in popular esteem. In Denmark, this idea was presented by the historian P. F. Suhm in his *History of Norway, Denmark, and Holstein* (1776) and by the anti-quary Skuli Thorlacius (1802), as well as by L. S. Vedel Simonsen in his textbook of Danish history published in 1813. Nevertheless, despite a growing number of supporters, the Three-Age theory remained as speculative and unproved as it had been in the days of Lucretius. Moreover, during the eighteenth century, the Three-Age scheme of technological evolution was not combined with the Enlightenment evolutionary trajectory of economic development from hunting and gathering to commerce. By comparison, the observation that sometime in the remote past at least some Europeans had made and used stone tools was widely accepted.

Scientific Antiquarianism

The study of prehistoric antiquities in the seventeenth and eighteenth centuries was influenced by the same elaboration of scientific methodology that had played a role in the development of the Enlightenment. The ideas of Bacon and Descartes were reflected in the importance that the Royal Society of London, founded by King Charles II in 1660, placed on observation, classification, and experimentation. The membership of that society rejected the authority that medieval scholars had assigned to learned works of antiquity as the ultimate sources of scientific knowledge and devoted themselves to studying things rather than what had been written about them, even if some of them still continued to be pleased when they thought they had found their most recent discoveries anticipated in the great scientific writings of ancient times. Antiquaries were elected fellows of the Royal Society and their work was encouraged and published by the society, except while Isaac Newton was its president between 1703 and 1727. Although Newton was a great physical scientist, his interests in human history were mystical and numerological in character.

The most innovative and celebrated of the seventeenth-century antiquaries who became members of the Royal Society was John Aubrey (1626–1697), who worked mainly in the county of Wiltshire, in south-central England. He had become familiar with Baconian methodology at Oxford University in the 1650s and had begun studying the monumental complex of prehistoric stone ruins at Avebury in 1649 (Figure 3.4). In 1663 Charles II personally encouraged him to prepare detailed descriptions of Stonehenge and Avebury for a projected publication that Aubrey titled *Monumenta Britannica*. In this work, he argued that these great monuments had probably been druidical temples. Aubrey also compared other stone circles, demonstrating that they constituted a distinctive category of monument and maintaining that their distribution over the whole of Britain indicated that they must have predated the Roman occupation of England and southern Scotland only. Aubrey was aware of the originality of what he was doing and called his method "comparative antiquities." He defined its goal as being "to make the stones give evidence for themselves" (Parry 1999: 19). Although it was not published until the twentieth century, the manuscript of *Monumenta Britannica* was available for consultation

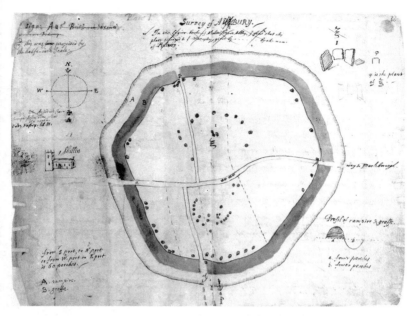

Figure 3.4 Aubrey's plan of Avebury, from his *Monumenta Britannica*, ca. 1675 (Bodleian MS Top. Gen. C. 24, f.39v-40.)

and marks the beginning of the formal study of prehistoric remains in England. Aubrey also used historically dated material to chart the evolution of styles in medieval architecture, dress, and handwriting (Parry 1995: 297).

Over the years, other members of the Royal Society provided accurate and detailed descriptions of archaeological finds. They identified animal bones from archaeological sites and sought to determine by experiment how tools had been made and used. They also tried to work out how large stones might have been moved and monuments constructed in ancient times. The kinds of research that the Royal Society encouraged are exemplified by the fieldwork of William Stukeley (1687–1765) (Figure 3.5). Like Camden, he realized that the geometrical crop marks that farmers had noted in various parts of England since the medieval period (and which they believed were of supernatural origin) resulted from the differential effect that the buried foundations of some demolished structures had on the growth of crops (Piggott 1985: 52). Like Aubrey, Stukeley grouped together as types monuments of similar form, such as linear earthworks or different kinds of burial mounds, in hopes of interpreting them in the light of the meager historical evidence that was available. Stukeley also was one of the first British antiquaries to recognize the possibility of a lengthy pre-Roman occupation, during which distinctive types of prehistoric monuments might have been constructed at different times and different peoples might have successively occupied southern England (Piggott 1985: 67). Such multiple occupations were historically attested by Julius Caesar's reference to a Belgic invasion of southeastern England shortly before the Roman conquest.

At the same time, Stukeley and other antiquaries took the first steps toward trying to ascertain relative dates for archaeological finds for which there were no historical records. Stukeley observed construction layers in barrows and argued that Silbury Hill, the largest artificial mound in Europe, had been built before the construction of a Roman road, which curved abruptly to avoid it (Daniel 1967: 122–3). He also noted that Roman roads cut through Bronze Age disc ("Druid") barrows in several places (Piggott 1985: 67) and used the presence of bluestone chips in some burial mounds near Stonehenge to infer that those burials were contemporary with the building of that structure (Marsden 1974: 5). In 1758, his daughter Anna

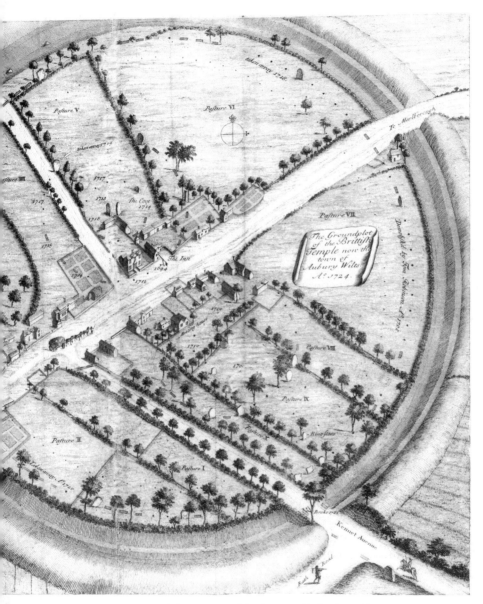

Figure 3.5 Stukeley's view of Avebury published in *Abury*, 1743

dated the White Horse cut in the chalk at Uffington, which had been thought to be a Saxon memorial, to the pre-Roman period because of its stylistic similarity to horses portrayed on pre-Roman British coins (Piggott 1985: 142). In 1720, the astronomer Edmund Halley had estimated that Stonehenge might be 2,000 or 3,000 years old on the basis of the depth of weathering he observed on its stones; whereas a later comparison of relative weathering convinced Stukeley that Avebury was much older than Stonehenge (Lynch and Lynch 1968: 52). These were creditable conclusions.

Similar observations were made by antiquaries in other countries. In Denmark, Erik Pontoppidan carefully excavated in 1744 a megalithic tomb on the grounds of a royal palace in northwest Sjaelland, the main Danish island. He reported on its structure and the finds it contained in the first volume of the *Proceedings of the Danish Royal Society*, concluding that cremation burials found near the top of the mound dated from a more recent era than the stone chamber below them and the mound itself (Klindt-Jensen 1975: 35–6). When three megalithic tombs opened in 1776 were found to contain stone and bronze artifacts but no iron ones, O. Hoegh-Guldberg, the excavator, assumed that they were very ancient (Ibid.: 42–3). Likewise, by 1799, in France Pierre Legrand d'Aussy (1737–1800) proposed a six-period classification of burial practices from earliest times to the Middle Ages (Laming-Emperaire 1964: 100–1).

Studies of these sort helped to advance the investigation of prehistoric times by encouraging more accurate observations and descriptions of ancient artifacts and monuments, more disciplined thought about them, and efforts to date a few in either relative or calendrical terms. Although this research was too fragmentary and the results too disconnected to constitute a discipline of prehistoric archaeology, it helped to lay the groundwork for the eventual development of such a discipline. Under the influence of rationalism, antiquaries were making substantial progress in conceptualizing the problems confronting the study of prehistoric times and taking steps to resolve these problems.

Antiquarianism and Romanticism

Yet the growing influence of cultural-evolutionary thought during the eighteenth century spawned a conservative reaction that at that time had far greater influence on antiquarian research than did evolutionism. In 1724, the French Jesuit missionary Joseph-François Lafitau (1685–1740), who had worked among the Indians of Canada, published his *Moeurs des sauvages amériquains comparées aux moeurs des premiers temps*. Although this book has often been described as an early contribution to evolutionary anthropology, Lafitau argued that the religions and customs of the Amerindians and the ancient Greeks and Romans resembled each other because both were corrupt and distorted versions of the true religion and morality that God had revealed to Adam and his descendants in the Middle East. In his opposition to modernity, Lafitau was upholding essentially the same view of human history as his fellow Jesuit Athanasius Kircher had done in the previous century. Lafitau's arguments, which revived the doctrine of degeneration, also were similar to those of Stukeley, who was obsessed by his belief that the religion of the ancient druids was a relatively pure survival of the primordial monotheism that God had revealed early in human history to the Hebrew patriarchs and hence closely related to Christianity. He maintained that the druids had come as priests to Britain from the city of Tyre in the Middle East with a party of Phoenician colonists (Balfour 1979; Parry 1995: 329). Stukeley associated all the major prehistoric monuments in Britain with the druids and based his extravagant interpretations of them on this premise. His writings on this subject were directed mainly against the Deists, who believed that reasonable people could apprehend God without the help of divine revelation, a view that was in accord with Enlightenment philosophy.

Stukeley's thinking also reflected a growing trend toward romanticism. This literary and philosophical movement, which developed in the late eighteenth century, was anticipated by the back-to-nature philosophy of Jean-Jacques Rousseau (1712–1778). Although Rousseau, as an Enlightenment philosopher, believed in the importance of reason, he also emphasized emotion and sensibility as important components of human behavior. In addition, he attributed greed, envy, and other antisocial forms of behavior to the corrupting influences of civilization. In Germany and England romanticism was embraced as part of a popular revolt against French cultural domination and the literary and artistic restrictions of French neoclassicism.

In addition to emphasizing the importance of powerful emotional reactions, romanticism favored the local and culturally specific over the general. Romantics were deeply interested in the past, but the past of individual peoples or countries, not of humanity as a whole. The poems attributed to the ancient Celtic bard Ossian, allegedly discovered (but actually authored) by the Scottish poet James Macpherson and published by him in the 1760s, were welcomed across Europe as evidence that a primitive people could produce great art and therefore as a concrete refutation of Enlightenment cultural evolutionism. These poems inspired Walter Scott's (1771–1832) historical novels, which established a literary trend throughout Europe. Romanticism championed "primitive" or "natural" societies and the "spirit" of European nations as reflected in their monuments and folklore, especially of the medieval period, as ideal sources of inspiration for modern arts and letters (K. Clark 1962: 66). It found its highest philosophical expression in the relativism of the German scholar Johann Herder (1744–1803), who regarded every people as culturally unique and celebrated their diversity as evidence of the creativity of the human spirit (Barnard 1965, 2003; Zammito 2002).

In this fashion, romanticism became closely linked to nationalism. Following the outbreak of the French Revolution, the middle classes in England feared a rebellion by the English working class, whereas in Germany, Italy, and elsewhere kings and nobles anticipated, not without reason, that the oppressed middle classes in their own countries might welcome French armies as liberators. Conservative elements throughout Europe embraced romanticism as an antidote to republicanism and popular liberty, which they believed were dangerous and inevitable products of Enlightenment philosophy. In the conservative restoration that followed the final defeat of Napoleon Bonaparte in 1815, a concerted effort was made to suppress Enlightenment ideas throughout Europe.

By encouraging an interest in the histories of specific peoples, romanticism also stimulated antiquarianism. The "Gothic" literary movement was preoccupied with ruined castles and abbeys, graves, and other symbols of death and decay, such as human skeletons grinning "a ghastly smile" (Marsden 1974: 18). The late eighteenth century has in the past been portrayed as a time of intellectual decline in antiquarian studies in Britain (Piggott 1985; cf. Ucko et al. 1991). Although the rationalism promoted by the Royal Society had stimulated interesting interpretations of archaeological data before 1750, in the second half of the eighteenth century romanticism appears to

have encouraged an unprecedented increase in archaeological excavation, especially of graves, that also contributed to the development
of antiquarianism. Nor is there evidence of a decline in standards of
interpretation. Between 1757 and 1773, the Reverend Bryan Fausset
(1720–1776) excavated more than 750 Anglo-Saxon burial mounds
in southeastern England. James Douglas (1753–1819), in his *Nenia
Britannica, or Sepulchral History of Great Britain*, which was published in parts between 1786 and 1793 and based on a massive compilation of information derived from barrow excavations throughout
Britain, assumed that graves containing only stone artifacts were earlier than those that also contained metal ones (Lynch and Lynch
1968: 48).

Some of the best work done during this period was by William
Cunnington (1754–1810) and his wealthy patron Sir Richard Colt
Hoare. They surveyed a large area in Wiltshire, locating ancient
village sites and earthworks and excavating 379 barrows. Cunnington and Colt Hoare recorded their observations carefully, divided
barrows into five types, and employed stratigraphy to distinguish
between primary and secondary interments. They used finds of coins
to date some barrows from the historical period and, like Douglas
and still earlier antiquaries, thought it possible that graves containing
only stone artifacts might be earlier than prehistoric burials accompanied by metal ones. Yet, despite these tentative advances, they were
unable to demonstrate to "which of the successive inhabitants" of
Britain various classes of monuments were to be ascribed or even that
specific types were the work of only one people. Moreover, Cunnington could not discover enough regularity in the sorts of grave goods
associated with particular barrow styles to implement the antiquary
Thomas Leman's suggestion that stone, bronze, and iron weapons
could be used to distinguish three successive ages (Chippindale 1983:
123). Thus, as Glyn Daniel (1950: 31) put it, they "failed to find any
way of breaking down the apparent contemporaneity of pre-Roman
remains." There were always antiquaries prepared to argue that graves
containing only stone tools were not necessarily older than the rest
but merely belonged to ruder tribes or poorer social groups. As yet,
there was no satisfactory rebuttal for this claim. Moreover, as Enlightenment ideas fell into disrepute in England, as a consequence of their
association with the French Revolution, the interest of antiquaries in
cultural evolution declined with them.

Because of their lack of adequate chronological controls over pre-historic archaeological data, in the eighteenth century antiquaries often employed other sources of information about the past. Comparative ethnography, comparative philology, physical anthropology, folklore, and oral traditions all were evaluated as sources of information about the prehistory of specific peoples. Monogenists, who believed that all modern societies were derived from a single source (often thought to be the biblical Adam and Eve), hoped they could use these various categories of data to trace the entire history of humanity. It had long been assumed that, if a single ancestral group descended from Adam and Eve had spread around the world and in the course of doing so had split into many descendant peoples, the differentiation of linguistic, racial, and cultural data would have occurred together, making it relatively easy to trace the history of specific human groups into the most remote past. If that were the case, conclusions based on different sorts of data would harmonize (J. Lalemant 1641 in Thwaites 1896–1901, vol. 21: 193–5).

The most important early accomplishment of this sort of research was the identification of the Indo-European language family initiated by the British orientalist William Jones (1746–1794) in 1786 (G. Cannon 1990). This discovery marked the beginning of comparative philology. It proved surprisingly difficult, however, to correlate linguistic findings with archaeological data. Differences over time in human skull morphology were interpreted as evidence of ethnic change, but harmonizing biological and cultural changes was likewise not always possible. In the absence of complementary sets of data relating to changes in languages, human skeletal morphology, and material culture, the most abundant category of data in any particular region tended to be used as a surrogate for the rest. Each of these methods for studying the past would have to undergo its own scientific elaboration and how they can be used together remains to this day controversial.

The New World

The study of the past in colonial settings has always been a highly ideological activity that most often seeks to justify the seizure of land and the exploitation of indigenous peoples. And so it was beginning immediately after Columbus's "discovery" of the New World in 1492.

The first historical questions that Europeans asked themselves about the indigenous inhabitants of North and South America were who were they and from where had they come. Between the sixteenth and eighteenth centuries, scholars speculated that Indians might be descended from Iberians, Carthaginians, Israelites, Canaanites, or Tartars. Still more imaginative writers derived them from the vanished continent of Atlantis. Most of these identifications reflected the pretensions or cultural biases of particular groups of European settlers.

Some early Spanish colonists denied that the Indians had souls, which would have meant they were not human beings. Had that argument been accepted, colonists would have been free to exploit the Indians as they did animals. Supporters of this view strove to document the lack of intelligence and moral sense among indigenous peoples, whereas opponents such as Bartolomé de Las Casas (1474–1566) sought to establish the opposite. The Spanish Crown wanted the Roman Catholic Church to recognize that the Indians had souls, since that would allow the Spanish government to assert its right to govern them and curb the independence of the colonists. When the Church proclaimed indigenous peoples to be human beings, Christians were required to recognize that the Indians were descended from Adam and Eve and hence had originated, like other peoples, in the Middle East (Hanke 1959; Pagden 1982).

In the seventeenth century, the leaders of the Puritan Massachusetts Bay Colony liked to represent their group as constituting a New Israel that God had delivered from spiritual enslavement in England and led to freedom in a new promised land in America. They compared the local Indians to the Canaanites, God having delivered their territories into the Puritan settlers' hands just as the Bible stated he had reassigned Palestine to the ancient Hebrews. This was interpreted as granting the Puritan settlers the right to seize land and enslave the Indians. As late as 1783, Ezra Stiles, the President of Yale University, was expounding the idea that the Indians of New England were literally descended from Canaanites who had fled from Palestine to America when Joshua and his Hebrew followers had conquered their homeland late in the second millennium BC (Haven 1856: 27–8).

Over time, however, there was growing support for the theory, first expounded in 1589 by the Jesuit priest José de Acosta (1539–1600) in his *Historia natural y moral de las Indias*, that the Indians had reached North America by way of Siberia (Pagden 1982: 193–7). This idea was partly based on the early recognition by Europeans of physical similarities between the peoples of East Asia and the New World. Until the middle of the nineteenth century, however, other scholars maintained that the Indians had reached the New World across the Atlantic or Pacific Ocean. Acosta believed that the Indians had lost all knowledge of sedentary life and much of their knowledge of true religion in the course of their migration from the Middle East. Once they arrived in the New World some of them had reinvented agriculture, metallurgy, and civilized life, although knowledge of true religion, being dependent on divine revelation, was lost forever.

Later evolutionists and proto-evolutionists saw in North America evidence of what the childhood of all humanity had been like. This is what John Locke (1632–1704) ([1690] 1952: 29) meant when he stated that "in the beginning all the world was America." By contrast, old-fashioned degenerationists interpreted indigenous cultures as corrupt remnants of the divinely revealed patriarchal way of life described in the Book of Genesis or saw in them evidence of the half-remembered teachings of early and forgotten Christian missionaries who had managed to reach the New World. In the seventeenth century, the technological inferiority and alleged moral degeneracy of indigenous North American peoples by comparison with Europeans were interpreted in theological terms as evidence of divine displeasure with these groups (Vaughan 1982). During the next century, some leading European scholars proposed in a seemingly naturalistic vein that a supposed climatic inferiority of the New World to Europe and Asia accounted for the inferiority of its indigenous peoples as well as of its plant and animal life. Climatic explanations of differences in customs and achievements among human groups had been commonplace since classical times (Haven 1856: 94).

In Mexico and Peru, during the sixteenth and seventeenth centuries, Spanish political and religious authorities sought to ensure that archaeological monuments were routinely destroyed, effaced, or hidden away, as far as this was possible, in order to eliminate the memories that indigenous peoples had of their pre-Christian past and religion (I. Bernal 1980: 37–9; Diehl 1983: 169). A particularly thorough effort was made to destroy symbols of Aztec sovereignty and national identity (Keen 1971). During the struggles preceding

Mexican independence in 1821, Spanish officials continued to discourage the study of the pre-Hispanic period but Creoles turned to it as a source of inspiration and national identity. Only a small number of European visitors discussed the great pre-Hispanic monuments of Mexico, Peru, and other Latin American countries before the nineteenth century, when these monuments were sometimes studied and publicized to provide symbols of identity to newly independent nation states (Chinchilla Mazariegos 1998). Through the nineteenth century, the conservatives among the Mexican ruling elite scorned the study of prehistoric times as a worthless preoccupation with barbarism, whereas liberals supported it as the investigation of a significant period of Mexico's national history (Lorenzo 1981).

Before the late eighteenth century, almost no notice was taken of the less spectacular prehistoric remains in North America, apart from occasional references to rock carvings and rock paintings, which were usually thought to be the work of more or less contemporary Native peoples. Few collections of artifacts recovered from the ground were assembled in North America and the excavation of sites was rarely attempted. Among the exceptions is a splendid collection of polished stone tools from the late Archaic period found during the course of construction work near Trois-Rivières, in Quebec, in 1700 and preserved in a convent there until modern times (Ribes 1966). Equally exceptional was Thomas Jefferson's systematic and carefully reported excavation of an Indian burial mound in Virginia in 1784 (Heizer 1959: 218–21) and the alleged but questionable exploration of another mound in Kansas a decade earlier (Blakeslee 1987; Yelton 1989).

By portraying the Indians as First Americans, Jefferson sought romantically to transform victims of colonialism into national symbols of the new republic (McGuire 1992b). Yet, throughout this period extremely pervasive ethnocentrism caused most Euro-Americans to doubt that anything significant could be learned from archaeological remains about the histories of peoples whom they viewed as savages fit only to be swept aside, or in exceptional cases assimilated, by the advance of European civilization. A notable exception was the naturalist and explorer William Bartram, who in 1789 used contemporary ceremonial structures constructed by the Creek Indians of the southeastern United States as analogues for interpreting prehistoric mound sites. This is one of the earliest known examples of the employment of the direct historical approach to interpret archaeological remains in North America (I. Brown 1993).

The Impasse of Antiquarianism

In North America as well as in Europe, antiquaries who were interested in what are now recognized to be prehistoric remains looked to written records and oral traditions to provide a historical context for their finds no less than did classical archaeologists. Yet in the case of prehistoric remains there were no adequate written records. In his book on the antiquities of the island of Anglesey, published in 1723, the Reverend Henry Rowlands (1655–1723) noted that "in these inextricable recesses of antiquity we must borrow other lights to guide us through, or content ourselves to be without any" (Daniel 1967: 43). He went on to declare that "analogy of ancient names and words, a rational coherence and congruity of things, and plain natural inferences and deductions grounded thereon, are the best authorities we can rely upon in this subject, when more warrantable relations and records are altogether silent in the matter." Generally the explanation of a monument consisted in trying to identify what people or individual mentioned in ancient records had constructed it and for what purpose. This approach left Camden to speculate whether Silbury Hill had been erected by the Saxons or the Romans and whether it had served to commemorate soldiers slain in a battle or was erected as a boundary survey marker. Although Stukeley demonstrated stratigraphically that this mound was older than the nearby Roman road, his conclusion that it was the tomb of the British king Chyndonax, the founder of Avebury, was a mere flight of fantasy (Joan Evans 1956: 121). Stonehenge was alternately attributed to the Danes, Saxons, Romans, and ancient Britons. There was also great confusion as to whether particular stone, bronze, or iron artifacts dated from the pre-Roman, Roman, or Saxon periods.

As a result of their continuing dependence on written records, throughout the eighteenth and into the early nineteenth centuries antiquaries generally despaired of ever learning much about the period before such records became available. In 1742 Richard Wise commented "where history is silent and the monuments do not speak for themselves, demonstration cannot be expected; but the utmost is conjecture supported by probability" (Lynch and Lynch 1968: 57).

Colt Hoare concluded "we have evidence of the very high antiquity of our Wiltshire barrows, but none respecting the tribes to whom they appertained, that can rest on solid foundations." Later in his *Tour in Ireland* he added: "Alike will the histories of those stupendous temples at Avebury and Stonehenge . . . remain involved in obscurity and oblivion" (Daniel 1963a: 35–6). In 1802, the Danish antiquary Rasmus Nyerup expressed similar despair: "everything which has come down to us from heathendom is wrapped in a thick fog; it belongs to a space of time we cannot measure. We know that it is older than Christendom but whether by a couple of years or a couple of centuries, or even by more than a millennium, we can do no more than guess" (Ibid.: 36). The English essayist and lexicographer Samuel Johnson (1709–1784), who had little patience with antiquaries, pressed the case against a future for their research even more trenchantly: "All that is really known of the ancient state of Britain is contained in a few pages. We can know no more than what old writers have told us" (Ibid.: 35). Even J. Dobrovsky, "the father of Czech prehistory," who is said to have argued in 1786 that archaeological finds were "speaking documents" that by themselves might illuminate as yet unknown periods of national history (Sklenář 1983: 52), was unable to demonstrate how this could be done.

Antiquaries continued to believe that the world had been created about 5000 BC. They also thought that reliable written records were available as far back as the time of creation for the most crucial region of human history. If humanity had spread from the Middle East to the rest of the world, in most regions there was likely to have been only a brief period between the earliest human occupation and the dawn of recorded history. Yet scholars remained uncertain whether the general course of human history had been one of development, degeneration, or cyclical change.

Nevertheless, the study of prehistoric times was not as stagnant at this period as it is often represented. Between the fifteenth and eighteenth centuries, European antiquaries had learned that stone tools were artifacts, as well as how to excavate and record finds, how to describe and classify monuments and artifacts, and how to use various dating methods, including stratigraphy, to estimate the relative and even the approximate calendrical age of some prehistoric finds. The varied nature of finds made in particular areas suggested to some antiquaries that more than one people had either coexisted or existed sequentially there. Some antiquaries had concluded on the basis of archaeological evidence that in the past certain of these communities or peoples had used stone artifacts but not metal ones. Others further speculated that an age when only stone and bone tools had been used might have preceded ages of bronze and iron tools, but little archaeological evidence could be marshaled to sustain such a claim. Although these accomplishments seem very limited in retrospect, they had already carried the study of prehistory a long way forward.

Religious constraints continued to hinder the development and explicit advocacy of an evolutionary interpretation of the archaeological record that might have challenged the biblical account of human history even after Enlightenment philosophers had argued that cultural evolution characterized that history. Enlightenment philosophers remained remote from antiquarianism because they focused on "theoretical history" rather than on the material remains of the past and used subsistence patterns rather than tool technologies as their principal index of cultural development. Yet perhaps the most serious stumbling block to establishing a relative chronology of prehistoric times and hence to acquiring more systematic knowledge concerning early human development was the deeply ingrained assumption that artifacts and monuments merely illustrated the accomplishments of peoples who had lived in the past. This view was based on the conviction shared with classical archaeologists that historical knowledge could only be acquired from written records or reliable oral traditions, without which no systematic understanding of the past was possible. The evidence from the late eighteenth century suggests that such an understanding was unlikely to have emerged inductively in the near future. Despite the progress that had been made, the creation of prehistoric archaeology required that antiquaries liberate themselves from assumptions that continued to restrict their vision.

CHAPTER 4

The Beginnings of Prehistoric Archaeology

Within no very distant period the study of antiquities has passed, in popular esteem, from contempt to comparative honour.

E. OLDFIELD, Introductory Address, *Archaeological Journal* (1852), p. 1

The development of a self-contained, systematic study of prehistory, as distinguished from the antiquarianism of earlier times, occurred as two distinct movements, the first of which began in the early nineteenth century and the second in the 1850s. The first originated in Scandinavia with the invention of a technique for distinguishing and dating archaeological finds that made possible the comprehensive study of prehistory. This development marked the beginning of prehistoric archaeology, which soon was able to take its place alongside classical and other text-based archaeologies as a significant component in the study of human development using material culture. The second wave, which began in France and England, pioneered the study of the Palaeolithic period and added vast, hitherto unimagined, time depth to human history. Palaeolithic archaeology addressed questions of human origins that became of major concern to the entire scientific community and to the general public as a result of the debates between evolutionists and creationists that followed the publication of Charles Darwin's *On the Origin of Species* in 1859.

Relative Dating

The creation of a controlled chronology that did not rely on written records was the work of the Danish scholar Christian Jürgensen Thomsen (1788–1865). The principal motivation for Thomsen's work, like that of many earlier antiquaries, was patriotism and the romanticism associated with it, but the antiquarian research of the eighteenth century and the evolutionary concepts of the Enlightenment were indispensable preconditions for his success. Yet all these factors would have mattered little had Thomsen not developed a powerful new technique for dating archaeological finds without recourse to written records. Unfortunately, because Thomsen never published a detailed account of his work, its importance has been underrated, first by poorly informed detractors and later by English, French, and American historians of archaeology. It is therefore necessary to clarify what he actually accomplished.

Thomsen was born in Copenhagen in 1788, the son of a wealthy merchant. As a young man he spent some time in Paris, where he may have been exposed to Enlightenment ideas about cultural evolution. After he returned home, he undertook to order a substantial collection of Roman and Scandinavian coins. Collecting coins and medals had become a widespread gentleman's hobby during the eighteenth century (McKay 1976). From the inscriptions and dates they bore, it was possible to arrange coins in a series according to the country and reigns in which they had been minted. It also was often possible to assign coins on which dates and inscriptions were illegible to such series using stylistic criteria alone. Working with this coin collection may have made Thomsen at least intuitively aware of stylistic changes and their value for the relative dating of artifacts.

The early nineteenth century was a time of heightened patriotism in Denmark, which was reinforced when the British, who were fighting Napoleon and his reluctant continental allies, including Denmark, destroyed most of the Danish navy in Copenhagen harbor in 1801 and bombarded the city again in 1807. The Danish archaeologist Jens J. A. Worsaae (1821–1885) later argued that these calamities encouraged Danes to study their past as a source of consolation and reassurance to face the future. He also noted that the French Revolution, by promoting greater respect for the political rights of the middle classes everywhere, had awakened in Denmark an evolutionary interest. Denmark, with its absolute monarchy, was politically and economically less evolved than some other countries of western Europe. Hence, the ideals of the Enlightenment, which in popular thinking were closely associated with the French Revolution (Hampson 1982: 251–83), appealed to many middle-class Danes. Denmark had a strong antiquarian tradition, although such studies had not been as flourishing in recent decades as they were in England. Yet most English antiquaries were conservatives who had rejected the ideals of the Enlightenment and taken refuge in romantic nationalism. By contrast, although Scandinavian antiquaries were inspired to study the past for patriotic reasons, these interests did not preclude an evolutionary approach. For them, history and evolution were complementary rather than antithetical concepts.

In 1806 Rasmus Nyerup, the librarian at the University of Copenhagen, published a book protesting against the unchecked destruction of ancient monuments and advocating the founding of a National Museum of Antiquity modeled on the Museum of French Monuments established in Paris after the Revolution. The purpose of this national collection would be to remind Danes of their past greatness. In 1807, a Danish Royal Commission for the Preservation and Collection of Antiquities was established, with Nyerup as its secretary. It began to amass a collection of antiquities from all over Denmark, which soon became one of the largest and most representative in Europe. In 1816, the Commission invited Thomsen to catalogue and prepare this collection for exhibition. His chief qualifications for this post, which was not a salaried one, were his knowledge of numismatics and his independent means. For the rest of his life, Thomsen was to divide his time between managing his family business and archaeological research.

The main problem that Thomsen faced was how the diverse assortment of prehistoric material in the collection could be exhibited most effectively. He decided to proceed chronologically by subdividing the prehistoric, or heathen, period into successive ages of stone, bronze, and iron. Presumably he knew of Lucretius's Three-Age scheme through the work of Vedel Simonsen, if not the writings of French antiquaries such as Montfaucon and Mahudel. He also appears to have been aware of archaeological evidence suggesting an era when stone but not metal tools had been used and of the classical and biblical texts, which suggested that bronze had been used before iron. The notion of successive ages of stone, bronze, and iron was not mere speculation but a hypothesis for which there was already some evidence.

In attempting to sort the prehistoric material in the collection into three successive technological stages or eras, Thomsen faced a daunting task. He recognized that even for the stone and metal objects a mechanical sorting would not work. Bronze and stone artifacts had continued to be made in the Iron Age, just as stone tools had been used in the Bronze Age. The challenge was therefore to distinguish bronze artifacts made during the Iron Age from those made during the Bronze Age and to differentiate which stone tools had been made in each era. There also was the problem of assigning objects made of gold, silver, glass, and other substances to each period. Individual artifacts were no help in beginning this work. Yet the Danish national collection contained sets of artifacts that had been found in the same grave, hoard, or other contexts and that could safely be assumed to have been buried at the same time. Thomsen called these "closed finds" and believed that, by comparing the various items from each such discovery and noting which types of artifacts occurred together and which never did, it would be possible for him to determine the sorts of artifacts that were characteristic of different periods (Gräslund 1974: 97–118, 1981, 1987).

Thomsen sorted and classified his artifacts into various use categories, such as knives, adzes, cooking vessels, safety pins, and necklaces. He further refined each category by distinguishing the artifacts according to the material from which they were made and their various shapes. Having in this way established a set of informal artifact types, he began to examine closed finds in order to determine which types did and did not occur together. He also examined the decorations on artifacts and found that these, too, varied systematically from one closed find to another. On the basis of shape and decoration, it became possible for Thomsen to distinguish types of bronze artifacts that never occurred together with iron artifacts from ones that did occur with them. He also was able to demonstrate that large flint knives and spearpoints that had similar shapes to bronze ones had been made at the same time as bronze artifacts. Eventually, he succeeded in dividing the prehistoric artifacts in the collection into five distinct groups. Once these groups were established, he could assign single artifacts to each group on the basis of formal similarities. Thomsen also studied the contexts in which artifacts had been found and discovered that these varied systematically from one group to another.

Thomsen then proceeded to order his groups into a historical sequence. He identified the simplest assemblages, which contained only chipped stone artifacts, as the remains of an early Stone Age. This material came invariably from small, simple sites. Next was a later Stone Age, which he described as the period when polished as well as chipped stone tools were manufactured and the first use was made of metal. At this time, the dead were buried, uncremated, in megalithic tombs, accompanied by crude pottery vessels with incised decoration. In the full Bronze Age, both weapons and cutting tools were made of bronze, the dead were cremated and buried in urns under small tumuli, and artifacts were decorated with ring patterns. In the proposed Iron Age, tools and weapons were made of tempered iron, whereas bronze continued to be used to manufacture ornaments and luxury goods. Thomsen divided the Iron Age into two stages, the earlier characterized by curvilinear serpent motifs and the later by more elaborate dragons and other fantastic animals (Figure 4.1). The latter forms of ornamentation were associated with runic inscriptions and persisted into the historical period ([1837] Heizer 1962a: 21–6).

In the past, a few antiquaries had attempted to divide prehistoric materials into various temporal segments. These schemes were based largely on intuition and failed to convince many people. It had been repeatedly claimed that such divisions might instead represent different cultures or social classes that had lived alongside one another. Yet, especially in a small country such as Denmark, had two or more groups coexisted, some artifacts characteristic of one group ought to have turned up in the sites of another as a result of exchange, theft, or warfare. Because of cultural borrowing, archaeologists also might have expected occasionally to find iron tools decorated with patterns otherwise associated with assemblages containing only bronze metal objects. Discrepancies of this sort would have completely undermined Thomsen's assertion that his groups represented temporal units. Instead, all the characteristics of individual objects and of the objects found together in closed finds displayed coherent patterns with respect to material, style, decoration, and contexts of discovery. This consistency permitted each of them to be assigned to one, and only one, of Thomsen's five groups. Thomsen's crude but effective technique of occurrence sorting produced classificatory units that appeared unlikely to have coexisted and, therefore, most probably represented a chronological sequence.

Thomsen's observations of formal similarities among some of the artifacts that he assigned to the early and later phases of the Iron Age and between his later Iron Age and the historical period constituted the earliest, probably unselfconscious, use of a crude form of seriation to produce a prehistoric cultural chronology. Lack of obvious stylistic cross-ties did not permit a similar chronological ordering of

Bølgezirater:

Ringzirater:

Spiralzirater:

Dobbeltspiralzirater:

Slangezirater:

Dragezirater:

Figure 4.1 Successive styles of ornamentation, from Thomsen's *Guidebook* (older forms at top) (C. J. Thomsen *Ledetraad til Nordisk Oldkyndighed*, part 2, Copenhagen 1836)

Thomsen's earlier periods. Yet, once it was accepted that his groupings most likely reflected chronological differences, it was reasonable to assume that evidence of increasing use of copper and bronze documented the chronological order of the earlier groups. Thomsen also observed that concurrent technological trends supported his sequence: gold and different types of pottery occurred in all the groups he dated subsequent to the early Stone Age, whereas silver did not appear before his Iron Age. Likewise, the fact that in his putative Bronze Age tools as well as ornaments had been made of bronze, whereas in the Iron Age bronze, which was less easily obtained, was reserved for making ornaments and cheaper and more abundant iron was used to make tools, corresponded with his conclusion that the age of bronze had preceded that of iron. Thomsen also sought to demonstrate the historicity of his sequence stratigraphically. As early as 1837, he published a report on a burial mound containing Bronze Age cremations that was constructed on top of a Stone Age burial mound. Stratigraphy offered a more convincing demonstration of cultural change over time than did seriation, although Thomsen's five clearly separated groups enhanced the general importance of his few stratigraphic observations.

Thomsen's work constituted the chronological breakthrough that set the study of prehistory on a scientific basis. His work was as fundamental for the development of prehistoric archaeology as were the major theoretical discoveries in historical geography and biology during the nineteenth century. Although some antiquaries mocked Thomsen for not adding ages of glass, wood, and gold to his sequence and others continued to ascribe his stone, bronze, and iron objects to different economies that had existed alongside one another, these critics failed to recognize that his phases did not result from a mechanical sorting of artifacts but instead were based on the concurrent analysis of style, decoration, and context, which reinforced each other to produce a rudimentary but effective chronology.

Thomsen's Museum of Northern Antiquities, with its prehistoric collection already divided into Stone, Bronze, and Iron Age components, was opened to the public in 1819 (Figure 4.2), but the first written account of his research appeared only in 1836 in the *Ledetraad til Nordisk Oldkyndighed* (Guidebook to Scandinavian Antiquity). Bo Gräslund (1987: 18) believes that Thomsen continued to refine his sequence as more closed finds became available and that it may not have reached its final form before 1824–1825. Thomsen's publication was available in a German translation by 1837, but not in English until 1848. Long before 1836, however, detailed information about Thomsen's system was available to antiquaries who visited his museum. At least some of the appeal of Thomsen's findings was that they offered independent support for an evolutionary view of human development, which was slowly becoming more

Figure 4.2 Thomsen showing visitors around the Museum
of Northern Antiquities

popular, especially in England. As fear of the French Revolution and
of Napoleon receded, the new industrial middle class were increasingly inclined to view progress as universal and themselves as representing its cutting edge in the modern world.

Neither Thomsen nor his successors regarded the Three Ages as
constituting an evolutionary sequence within Scandinavia. Instead,

they argued that knowledge of bronze and iron working was introduced to the region either by successive waves of immigrants from the south or as a result of "intercourse with other nations" (Daniel 1967: 103). Migration and diffusion were traditional explanations of change. The Scandinavian prehistoric archaeologists did, however, assume that somewhere in Europe or the Middle East evolutionary development had taken place. Nineteenth-century evolutionary archaeology did not view diffusion and migration as processes that were antithetical to evolution but as helping to promote evolutionary change (Harris 1968a: 174). They also appear to have regarded the Stone Age as a primal condition and not as the repeated product of cultural degeneration.

The Development and Spread of Scandinavian Archaeology

Even in his earliest work, Thomsen was interested not merely in artifacts and their development over time but also in the contexts in which they had been found and what those contexts might reveal about changing burial customs and other aspects of prehistoric life. He studied incomplete and damaged artifacts in order to learn about how such artifacts had been made and used. Yet it does not appear that Thomsen had any firm views about what sort of subsistence economy was associated with his earlier cultures. During the first half of the nineteenth century, archaeology continued to develop in Scandinavia as a discipline concerned with the evolution of ways of life throughout prehistoric times.

This development was powerfully promoted by Sven Nilsson (1787–1883), who for many years was Professor of Zoology at the University of Lund and whose thinking was deeply influenced by the writings of the leading French palaeontologist Georges Cuvier. Nilsson strongly believed in cultural evolution but, unlike Thomsen, he was more interested in the development of subsistence economies than in the evolution of technology. From eighteenth-century Enlightenment philosophers, he had adopted the idea that increasing population had been the principal factor compelling Scandinavian hunter-gatherers to become first pastoralist herdsmen and then agriculturalists. In 1822, he published one of the world's earliest reports on animal bones recovered from an archaeological excavation. His most important methodological contribution to the study of prehistory was his systematic effort to determine the uses made of stone and bone artifacts by means of detailed comparisons with ethnographic specimens collected from around the world. Because many Scandinavian stone artifacts had been parts of compound tools now decayed, inferring the sorts of implements to which they had belonged was often far from easy. As an exponent of unilinear evolution, Nilsson believed that ethnographic specimens from North America, the Arctic, and the Pacific Islands could shed light on prehistoric Scandinavian cultures that were at the same level of development. He advocated, however, that ethnographic parallels should be verified through replicative experiments and the study of wear patterns on prehistoric artifacts, which could help confirm what they had been used for. He is recognized as the first archaeologist to use flint-knapping experience to explain prehistoric artifacts (L. Johnson 1978). In these ways, Nilsson sought to infer prehistoric subsistence patterns from archaeological data. His most important study of the Stone Age was published in four parts between 1838 and 1843, and a later edition was very freely and misleadingly translated into English as *The Primitive Inhabitants of Scandinavia* in 1868.

Nilsson concluded that Thomsen's Stone Age people had been hunters and fishers and that farming had been introduced to Scandinavia in the Bronze Age. In this manner, he combined for the first time an interest in the evolution of technology, derived from Lucretius, and of subsistence patterns, coming from the Enlightenment. This permitted the development of subsistence to be studied in relation to technological change and the two to be considered as coevolving aspects of human behavior. Previously, these two evolutionary schemes had existed independently of each other. Nilsson believed the Stone Age inhabitants of Sweden to have been Lapps, the Bronze Age people Celts, and the Gothic ancestors of the modern Swedes to have arrived in the Iron Age. Nilsson was also the first person anywhere to coin a word that is translatable as "prehistory" – the Swedish *förhistorie* (Clermont and Smith 1990; Welinder 1991).

Johannes Japetus Steenstrup (1813–1907), a young Danish geologist who was interested in studying environmental changes, discovered stratigraphic evidence of a prehistoric human presence in Scandinavia in the course of the excavations that he carried out in the peat bogs of Denmark. These excavations revealed a pattern of forest change, beginning with what are now known to have been

Figure 4.3 Worsaae boring into one of the large tumuli at Jelling; he explains the procedure to King Frederik VII of Denmark (Drawing by J. Korncrup, 1861)

postglacial aspen forests that were replaced in succession by pine, oak, and finally beech and elm. By the early 1840s, Steenstrup was convinced that stone and bronze artifacts were associated with his oak period, linking the evolution of culture to environmental history. Eventually, he associated pine forests with Stone Age occupation, oak forests with the Bronze Age, and beech and elm forests with the Iron Age, thereby correlating Thomsen's artifact sequence with major environmental changes (Morlot 1861: 309–10). Because Steenstrup estimated that each of these forest successions must have occurred over about 2000 years, he was the first to assign a considerable time depth to the Scandinavian Stone Age.

Jens Worsaae became the first professional prehistoric archaeologist and was the first person to be trained in the discipline, albeit informally as a volunteer working with Thomsen. He was appointed Denmark's Inspector for the Conservation of Ancient Monuments in 1847 and the first Professor of Archaeology at the University of Copenhagen in 1855. Unlike Thomsen, who remained principally a museum researcher, Worsaae became a prolific field worker (Figure 4.3). His excavations helped to confirm Thomsen's chronology by providing more closed finds. One of Worsaae's major contributions to prehistoric archaeology was his refusal to use local oral traditions to explain specific archaeological finds.

In his first book *Danmarks Oldtid* (The Primeval Antiquities of Denmark), published in 1843 (English translation 1849), Worsaae popularized Thomsen's findings and integrated them with those of

Nilsson and Steenstrup to produce a general account of Denmark's prehistory. In 1859, Worsaae formalized Thomsen's division of the Scandinavian Stone Age into an earlier and later period and soon after he observed that both of these periods were later than the Palaeolithic cultures that were being identified in France. He also divided the Bronze Age into two periods on the basis of different burial customs and the Iron Age into three periods. However, his definitions of these periods remained impressionistic. Both in *Danmarks Oldtid* and in many of his later writings, Worsaae sought to use archaeology to validate Denmark's national existence, especially in the context of the wars of 1848–1850 and 1864, in the course of which Denmark lost much territory to an expanding Prussia.

In 1846–1847, with financial support from the Danish king, Worsaae visited Britain and Ireland, mainly to study Viking remains there. His observations of prehistoric finds in these countries convinced him that Thomsen's Three-Age scheme was applicable to large parts of Europe, and maybe to all of it. He also became increasingly aware, however, of significant stylistic (cultural) differences between artifacts from the same stage of development in the British Isles and Scandinavia.

By 1843, it had become known for the first time that Scandinavia's earliest inhabitants had used stone tools, subsisted by hunting and gathering, and inhabited an environment different from that of the present. This understanding was deepened and strengthened by interdisciplinary work that began late in the 1840s. As early as 1837 on Sjaelland, mounds of oyster and cockle shells containing numerous prehistoric artifacts had been observed a short distance inland from the present coastline. As the result of a desire to learn more about geological changes, in 1848 the Royal Danish Academy of Sciences established an interdisciplinary commission to study these shell middens. The commission was headed by Worsaae, Steenstrup, and an older academic, Johan Georg Forchhammer, the father of Danish geology. In the early 1850s, these scholars published six volumes of reports on their studies of these "kitchen middens." They demonstrated that the middens were of human origin and traced the pattern of their accumulation. They also determined that, when the middens had formed, the palaeo-environmental setting had consisted of fir and pine forests and some oak, that the only animals likely to have been domesticated were dogs, and from the bones of animals that had been eaten that the middens had been occupied during the autumn, winter, and spring but not during the summer. The distributions of hearths and artifacts within the middens also were studied to learn more about human activities at these sites. Experiments, which involved feeding chicken carcasses to dogs, were carried out in order to explain the numerical preponderance of the middle part of the long bones of birds over other parts of their skeletons (Morlot 1861: 300–1). The one issue Worsaae and Steenstrup did not agree about was the dating of the middens. Steenstrup maintained that they were Neolithic, and hence contemporary with the megalithic tombs, but, because they contained no ground or polished stone implements, Worsaae correctly concluded that they were earlier (Klindt-Jensen 1975: 71–3).

The archaeology that was developing in Scandinavia provided a model for work elsewhere. Contacts with Worsaae inspired the Scottish antiquary Daniel Wilson (1816–1892) to employ Thomsen's Three-Age system to reorganize a large collection of artifacts belonging to the Society of Antiquaries of Scotland in Edinburgh. This work provided the basis for his book *The Archaeology and Prehistoric Annals of Scotland* published in 1851. In this first scientific synthesis of prehistoric times in the English language, Wilson assigned archaeological data to the Stone (Primeval), Bronze (Archaic), Iron, and Christian eras. Wilson was motivated by the same mixture of evolutionary thinking and romantic nationalism that had inspired the work of Scandinavian archaeologists. It is not clear, however, that he fully understood Thomsen's "closed find" method, as opposed to simply applying the chronological findings of Danish archaeologists to Scottish data. Unlike the Scandinavian archaeologists, Wilson also tended to view the Stone Age, as many Enlightenment philosophers had done, as a base line to which humanity had often descended.

Yet, in this work, Wilson coined the term prehistory, which he used to designate the study of the history of a region before the earliest appearance of written records relating to it. He also made a significant contribution to establishing the goals and potential of prehistoric archaeology. Wilson stressed that the sort of understanding of the past that could be derived from artifacts alone was very different from the kind of understanding derived from written records. In the nineteenth century, historians were preoccupied with the actions and ideas of "great men," which were, and still remain, archaeologically inaccessible. Yet Wilson expressed the hope that in due course archaeologists would be able to learn much about the economy, social life, and religious beliefs of prehistoric times. He also briefly introduced gender studies to archaeology by suggesting that the relative amounts of goods buried with men and women might reveal something about their respective social status. Among English antiquaries, there was much more resistance to accepting the Scandinavian approach and Wilson's call to reorganize the collections of the British Museum in accordance with the Three-Age system fell on deaf ears. Unfortunately for British archaeology, Wilson, although he was awarded an honorary doctorate by the University of St. Andrews for his accomplishments, failed to find satisfactory employment in Scotland. In 1853, he left to teach English, history, and anthropology at University College in Toronto, Canada (Trigger 1992; Hulse 1999).

Scandinavian archaeology also provided a model for significant archaeological research in Switzerland, a country where the political triumph of liberalism in 1847 popularized both Enlightenment and romantic ideas. As the result of a drought in the winter of 1853–1854, lake levels in western Switzerland fell unprecedentedly low, revealing the remains of ancient settlements preserved in waterlogged environments. The first of these sites, a Bronze Age village at Obermeilen, was studied the following summer by Ferdinand Keller (1800–1881), a Professor of English and President of the Zurich Antiquarian Society. His report led to the eventual identification of several hundred such sites, including the Neolithic village at Robenhausen, which was excavated by Jakob Messikommer beginning in 1858. These so-called Lake Dwellings were interpreted as settlements built on piles driven into lake bottoms, based on descriptions of villages of this sort encountered in lowland New Guinea by the traveler C. Dumont d'Urville (Gallay 1986: 167). The Swiss ones are now believed to have been constructed on swampy ground around the edges of lakes.

These excavations yielded the remains of wooden piles and house platforms, stone and bone tools still mounted in their wooden handles, matting, basketry, and a vast array of foodstuffs. Villages dating from both the Neolithic and Bronze Ages provided Swiss archaeologists with the opportunity to study changes in the natural environment, economies, and ways of life of these peoples. The Swiss finds not only revealed many sorts of perishable artifacts not usually found in Scandinavia and Scotland but also verified the reconstructions of stone and bone tools by Nilsson and others. Switzerland was already an important center of tourism and the continuing study of these prehistoric remains attracted wide interest. This confirmation played a major role in convincing western Europeans of the reality of cultural evolution and that ancient times could be studied using archaeological evidence alone (Morlot 1861: 321–36; Bibby 1956: 201–19; Kaeser 2001, 2004a, 2004b).

Prehistoric archaeology thus had developed as a well-defined discipline in Scandinavia, Scotland, and Switzerland before 1859. Artifacts were no longer valued primarily as objects, but as sources of information about human behavior in the past. The essential basis for this new discipline was the ability to construct relative chronologies from archaeological data alone using closed finds, simple forms of seriation, and stratigraphic contexts. For the first time, relative chronologies could be produced into which all the known archaeological data for a region or country could be fitted. This made it possible for artifacts from reasonably well-documented archaeological contexts to be used as a basis for understanding human history and cultural development.

The development of prehistoric archaeology has long been ascribed to influences derived from the study of geological and biological evolution. It has been assumed that the stratigraphically derived chronologies of geological time constructed by geologists and palaeontologists provided a model for the development of archaeological chronologies of prehistory. Yet, in Thomsen's work, we see a chronology of human prehistory inspired by an understanding of the chronological significance of closed finds and implicit knowledge of stylistic change probably derived from the study of numismatics. The roots of prehistoric archaeology clearly lie in European antiquarianism. Prehistoric archaeology did not begin as the result of borrowing one or more dating devices from other disciplines. Instead, it started with the development of a new technique for relative dating that was appropriate to archaeological material.

The kind of history produced by Scandinavian archaeologists made sense only in terms of the cultural-evolutionary perspective of the Enlightenment. Historians had traditionally been concerned with recounting the thoughts and deeds of famous individuals. Yet Worsaae pointed out that in many cases prehistoric archaeologists could not even determine what people had made the implements they were studying. He and Wilson also protested against the idea that the earliest people to be mentioned in the recorded history of a region were necessarily its original inhabitants. In the early nineteenth century, the attraction of Enlightenment views about cultural evolution was the hope they offered the Scandinavian middle classes of political reforms that would better serve their interests. Although Danish archaeology continued to be strongly nationalistic and to enjoy the patronage of successive generations of the royal family, its innovators and increasingly its audience were members of a growing commercial middle class (Kristiansen 1981), for whom nationalism, political reform, and evolutionism were all attractive concepts. By contrast, in the politically reactionary environment of post-Napoleonic Germany, archaeologists, although inspired by nationalism, tended to reject the Scandinavian approach at least partly because its evolutionism was too closely aligned with the Enlightenment philosophy that they opposed (Böhner 1981; Sklenář 1983: 87–91).

An evolutionary approach made possible an archaeology that was not based on chronologies derived from written records and dedicated primarily to the recovery and study of texts and works of art. Scandinavian prehistoric archaeologists and those who were inspired by them did not, however, limit their efforts to demonstrating the reality of cultural evolution. They also sought to learn something about the specific technologies and subsistence economies associated with the various peoples who had inhabited their countries in prehistoric times, as well as about the environments in which these peoples had lived, their social life, and religious beliefs. Studying social life mainly involved examining their houses, when these could be identified, and studying religion was based on investigations of their tombs. The goal of archaeologists was to learn as much as the archaeological evidence would permit not only about patterns of life and death at any one period but also about how those patterns had changed and developed over time. In order to understand the behavioral significance of archaeological finds, archaeologists were prepared to make systematic comparisons of archaeological and ethnographic data, to study unfinished and broken tools, to carry out replicative experiments to determine how artifacts had been manufactured and used, and to perform experiments to explain the attrition patterns on bones found in archaeological sites. They also learned how to cooperate with geologists and biologists to reconstruct palaeoenvironments and determine prehistoric diets. This approach reflected a romantic nationalist desire to know who had inhabited specific countries in prehistoric times and how they had lived.

Thus, in early Scandinavian prehistoric archaeology we discover the origins of the evolutionary, culture-historical, and functional-processual approaches that have characterized prehistoric archaeology ever since. In the early nineteenth century, Scandinavian archaeologists evolved a prehistoric archaeology that exhibited in an embryonic form all the main features of modern prehistoric archaeology. Although the database and the analytical resources of prehistoric archaeology have expanded enormously in the interval, the founders of prehistoric archaeology would experience little difficulty in discussing their goals and aspirations with modern archaeologists. Romantic and evolutionary interests had combined to produce a complex and multifaceted interest in prehistoric times.

What these first prehistoric archaeologists did not do was to question the traditional biblical chronology, which allowed no more than a few thousand years for the whole of human history. Beginning during the Renaissance, various scholars had challenged the shortness of the biblical chronology. They observed that in classical times there had been no fixed view concerning how long human beings had inhabited the earth. The Egyptians and Mesopotamians seemed to have believed that humans had done so for 100,000 years or longer. Christian missionaries also reported that the Chinese and other Asian peoples had records extending far into the past. Such information was used by dissident scholars who wished to subvert Christian authority by arguing that these other cultures were repositories of older and hence greater wisdom than were the Hebrews. This led to a vigorous defense of the traditional biblical chronology and the repression of unorthodox views by means of legal and social sanctions (Rossi 1985). For Thomsen, Worsaae, and even Steenstrup, several thousand years appeared long enough to encompass the past that was being revealed by the archaeological record. Worsaae dated the first arrival of human beings in Denmark around 3000 BC, the beginning of the Bronze Age between 1400 and 1000 BC, and the start of the Iron Age as late as the early Christian era. By an ironic coincidence, Scandinavia, Scotland, and Switzerland had all been covered by glaciers during the Würm glaciation and to this day have produced little evidence of human habitation prior to the Holocene era. Hence, the absolute chronology imagined by the Scandinavian, Scottish, and Swiss archaeologists for their finds was not significantly out of line with reality as we currently understand it. Like the Enlightenment philosophers of the eighteenth century, Scandinavian archaeologists neither challenged the traditional biblical chronology nor embraced an evolutionary view of human biological origins.

The Antiquity of Humanity

The prehistoric archaeology pioneered by the Scandinavians was largely ignored in France and England, where antiquaries seem to have been reluctant to follow the example set by colleagues in peripheral and seemingly backward countries. During the first half of the nineteenth century, archaeology in England and France remained antiquarian in orientation. Although in the 1840s and 1850s there was increasing emphasis on the use of physical anthropological, folkloric, and linguistic data, alone or in combination, to study prehistory, the examination of archaeological remains remained focused on historical peoples such as the Celts, Romans, Anglo-Saxons, and Merovingians and on the medieval period (Van Riper 1993; M. Morse 1999; T. Murray 2001b: 204–10). Only rarely did these antiquaries seriously consider Thomsen's Three-Age system. This conservative attitude ensured that the scientific study of prehistoric archaeology did not begin in these countries before the late 1850s.

Unlike Scandinavia, early scientific archaeology in England and France was concerned primarily with the Palaeolithic period and ascertaining the antiquity of humanity. This archaeology was mostly created not by antiquaries but by people interested in geology and palaeontology and it eventually replaced, rather than transformed, antiquarianism as a method for studying the material remains of all prehistoric periods. The presence in France and southern England of caves and glacial deposits containing traces of human activities going as far back as Lower Palaeolithic times provided archaeologists in these countries with opportunities for studying early phases of human existence that were lacking in Scandinavia, Scotland, and Switzerland.

The development of Palaeolithic archaeology depended on the emergence of an evolutionary perspective in geology and also of some knowledge of palaeontology. Progress in these fields was necessary for a scientific study of human origins to replace reliance on the traditional biblical accounts. Although the major archaeological breakthroughs in studying the antiquity of humanity slightly preceded the first major statement of Darwinian evolutionism, Palaeolithic archaeology was quickly drawn into the controversies that surrounded Darwin's work and was strongly influenced by concepts derived from biological evolution.

When a flint handaxe was discovered near the tooth of a mammoth beneath a street in London in 1690, the antiquary John Bagford interpreted the find as that of a Roman war elephant brought to Britain by the emperor Claudius in AD 43 and slain by an ancient Briton armed with a stone-tipped spear. This explanation was accepted as reasonable, even though it was known from historical records that the ancient Britons fought with iron swords (Burkitt 1921: 10; Grayson 1983: 7–8). Such an interpretation was squarely in the tradition of text-based archaeology, which often used historical records very selectively. By contrast, in 1797 John Frere described a collection of Acheulean handaxes that were found together with the bones of unknown animals at a depth of four meters at Hoxne, in eastern England (Figure 4.4). He argued that the carefully documented overlying strata, which included a presumed incursion of the sea and the formation of half a meter of vegetable earth, could only have been built up over a long period and concluded that "the situation in which these weapons were found may tempt us to refer them to a very remote period indeed; even beyond that of the present world" ([1800] Heizer 1962a: 71). By this he meant that they were probably more than 6,000 years old. The Society of Antiquaries judged his paper to be worthy of publication but it aroused no contemporary discussion. Although the intellectual climate was clearly opposed to assigning a great antiquity to humanity, Donald Grayson (1983: 58) has pointed out that Frere's failure to identify either the animal bones or the shells in his stratigraphy did not demand agreement with his claims.

In the course of the eighteenth century, scientists such as Georges Buffon (1707–1788) began to propose naturalistic origins for the world and to speculate that it might be tens of thousands or even millions of years old. This in turn suggested the need for a symbolic rather than a literal interpretation of the biblical account of the seven days of creation. As early as 1669, Nicolaus Steno (1636–1686)

Figure 4.4 Acheulean handaxe found by Frere at Hoxne, published in
Archaeologia, 1800

had recognized that in any geological formation lower strata can be
assumed to have formed before the layers that cover them. In the
course of the eighteenth and nineteenth centuries, more was learned
about geological stratification because of the increased mining, quar-
rying, and construction of canals that resulted from the industrial
revolution.

The French geologist Georges Cuvier (1769–1832), who established palaeontology as a scientific discipline and whose work inspired

Nilsson's studies of prehistoric artifacts, viewed the bones of each animal as parts of a system and used his knowledge of comparative anatomy to reconstruct hitherto unknown fossil animals on the basis of what he knew about what he determined were similar living species. In this fashion, he assembled evidence that numerous species of animals had become extinct. He also observed that older geological strata contained animal remains that were increasingly dissimilar to those of modern times. Because he assumed a relatively brief amount of time had passed since the creation of the world, he concluded that a series of regional natural catastrophes had destroyed local species of animals and altered the geological configuration of limited areas. He believed that these devastated areas were repopulated by migrations of animals from areas that had been spared, resulting in the number of species worldwide declining over time. This theory can be called regional catastrophism.

As the palaeontological record became better known, it was observed that many more complex life forms had appeared over time and that the biota as a whole grew to be more like that of the present. As a result, geologists, such as William Buckland (1784–1856), an Anglican priest and Professor of Mineralogy at Oxford University, came to view geological catastrophes as universal ones that had wiped out almost all species. This required God to create new species to replace them. The increasing complexity of plant and animal life observed in successive geological strata was therefore not viewed as a developmental sequence but, rather, as a series of ever more complex supernatural creations. Buckland conceived of evolution as occurring in God's mind rather than in the natural world. This un-Cartesian view can be labeled general catastrophism.

Beginning with finds reported by Johann Esper (1732–1781) in 1774, naturalists and antiquaries encountered human physical remains and stone tools associated with the bones of extinct animals in stratified deposits in cave sites in many parts of western Europe. The most important finds were those made in the early nineteenth century by Paul Tournal (1805–1872) near Narbonne and Jules de Christol (1802–1861) northeast of Montpellier, both in France, Philippe-Charles Schmerling (1791–1836) near Liège in Belgium, and the Reverend John MacEnery (1796–1841) at Kent's Cavern in England. Each of these men believed that his discoveries might constitute evidence of the contemporaneity of human beings and extinct animal species. Yet their techniques of excavation were not sufficiently developed to rule out the possibility that the human material was intrusive into older deposits. MacEnery's finds were sealed beneath a layer of hard travertine that would have taken a long time to form. Buckland maintained that ancient Britons had dug earth ovens through the travertine and that their stone tools had found their way through these pits into much older levels containing the bones of fossil animals. Although MacEnery denied the existence of such pits, he accepted that the tools, even though old, need not have been contemporaneous with the bones of extinct animals. It was argued that deposits elsewhere contained animal bones and artifacts from diverse periods that had been mixed together when they were washed into caves by flooding that had occurred in fairly recent times (Grayson 1983: 107). It became obvious that it was not easy for evidence from caves to be conclusive. James Sackett (2000: 47) has suggested that before 1859 Edouard Lartet had accepted the high antiquity of humans on the basis of cut marks he observed on the bones of extinct animals. If so, his failure to publish his evidence until more convincing arguments were forthcoming suggests that he did not believe that his observations were likely to win widespread acceptance.

A much-debated question was whether it was reasonable to expect that traces of human beings and their works might be found in contexts that revealed them to be coeval with extinct mammals. The bones of mammoth and wooly rhinoceros were encountered frequently in the glacial deposits that covered parts of France and southern England. At the beginning of the nineteenth century these deposits were generally believed to have resulted from Noah's flood, the last great catastrophe to convulse the earth's surface. Because the Bible recorded the existence of human beings before that time, it seemed possible that human remains might be found in these diluvial deposits. Nevertheless, fundamentalist Christians believed that the Bible implied that as a result of divine intervention all existing animal species had survived the flood; hence, the presence of extinct species in these levels was interpreted as indicating that they dated before the creation of humanity rather than simply before the last flood. Even those palaeontologists who were inclined to interpret the Bible less literally tended to believe that a beneficent God would have brought the earth to its modern state prior to creating the human species. By the 1830s, it was generally accepted that all the diluvium had not been deposited at the same time. It also was widely believed to antedate the most recent creation and, therefore, that it should not contain human remains (Grayson 1983: 69).

The intellectual problems of this period are clearly exemplified by the work of Jacques Boucher de Crèvecoeur de Perthes (1788–1868), who was the director of customs at Abbeville, in the Somme Valley of northwestern France. In the 1830s, Casimir Picard, a local doctor, reported discoveries of stone and antler tools in the region. Boucher de Perthes began studying these finds in 1837. Soon after, in the canal and railway excavations of the period, he started to find what are now known to be Lower Palaeolithic handaxes associated with the bones of extinct mammoth and wooly rhinoceros, deeply buried in the stratified gravel deposits of river terraces that predated the local peat formations (Figure 4.5).

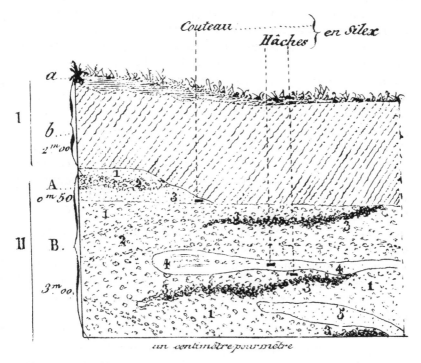

Figure 4.5 Profile showing location of Palaeolithic material, from Boucher de Perthes's *Antiquités celtiques et antédiluviennes*, 1847

Boucher de Perthes's sound stratigraphic observations convinced him that the stone tools and extinct animals were equally old. Yet, as a catastrophist, he decided that these tools belonged to an antediluvian tool-making race that had been completely annihilated by a massive flood that had occurred "prior to the biblical deluge." After a lengthy period of time God had created a new human race – that of Adam and Eve and their descendants (Grayson 1983: 126–30). It is scarcely surprising that when these fanciful ideas were published in the first volume of his *Antiquités celtiques et antédiluviennes* in 1847, they were dismissed by French and English scholars alike. Yet, even when his field observations were duplicated by the physician Marcel-Jérôme Rigollot (1786–1854) at St. Acheul and another site near Amiens, 40 kilometers upstream from Abbeville, and these deposits were confirmed to be of "diluvial age" by geologists, including Edmond Hébert from the Sorbonne, geologists and antiquaries continued to express concern that the artifacts might be intrusive and, hence, of later date. Grayson (1983: 207) has concluded that the rejection of Rigollot's sound evidence "stemmed from the sheer belief that such things could not be" and from Rigollot's status as an outsider with respect to the scientific elite of his day.

The resolution of controversies concerning the antiquity of humanity required an improved understanding of the geological record. In 1785, the Edinburgh physician James Hutton (1726–1797) proposed a uniformitarian view of geological history in which the slow erosion of rocks and soil was balanced by the uplifting of land surfaces. He believed that all geological strata could be accounted for in terms of the geological forces currently at work operating over very long periods of time. In the years that followed, William (Strata) Smith (1769–1839) in England and Georges Cuvier and Alexandre Brongniart (1770–1847) in France recognized that strata of different ages each possessed its own characteristic assemblage of organic fossils and concluded that such assemblages could be used to identify coeval formations over large areas. Smith, unlike Cuvier, accepted the principle of the orderly deposition of rock formations over long periods of time.

Between 1830 and 1833, the English geologist Charles Lyell (1797–1875) published his *Principles of Geology*, in which he assembled an overwhelming amount of data, much of it based on his observations around Mount Etna in Sicily, to support the uniformitarian assumption that geological changes had occurred in the past as a result of the same natural agencies acting over long periods and at approximately the same rate as they do at present. Lyell quickly won support for the principle of uniformitarianism in geology. Contrary to catastrophism, it indicated the past to have been a long and geologically uninterrupted period, during which other events could have happened. This provided a setting for scholars to consider the possibility of biological evolution, a concept that Lyell rejected, although Jean-Baptiste Lamarck (1744–1829) had already argued in favor of it, and Robert Chambers (1844) (anonymously) and others were soon to do so.

This new view of geological history also left the question of the antiquity of humanity requiring an empirical answer. The favorable reception given to Lyell's geology reflected the increasing willingness of English intellectuals and the general public to embrace evolutionary ideas. In the early nineteenth century, the concepts of biological and cultural evolution had still been associated with radical politics in England and therefore were anathema to the respectable middle classes (Desmond 1989). By the middle of the nineteenth century, Britain had become the "workshop of the world" and the growth of industrialism had greatly strengthened the political power and self-confidence of the middle classes, who, especially after the period of economic contraction and social turmoil that lasted from 1826 to 1848 had ended (Wolf 1982: 291), came to view themselves as a major force shaping the history of the world for the benefit of all humanity.

This new confidence was reflected in the writings of the philosopher Herbert Spencer (1820–1903), who in the 1850s began to champion a general evolutionary approach to scientific and political problems. He argued that the development of everything in the universe moved from simple, uniform homogeneity to increasingly complex and differentiated entities. Atoms combined to form molecules and these in turn to create cells, organisms, primitive societies, and ultimately European civilization. By claiming that individual initiative and free enterprise were the driving forces behind cultural evolution and that the self-interested behavior of middle-class entrepreneurs in the course of the industrial revolution was a continuation and intensification of those processes that had brought about progress throughout human history, Spencer cleansed the concept of sociocultural evolution of its former politically subversive associations and helped to make it the ideology of a substantial portion of the British middle classes whose faith in progress had already been expressed by the Great Exhibition celebrating industrial creativity held in London in 1851 (Harris 1968a: 108–41). In this way, Spencer encouraged the middle class to sympathize with arguments favoring biological evolution and the great antiquity of humanity. This shift in sentiment led to a growing interest in what the archaeological record might reveal about human origins.

In 1858, William Pengelly (1812–94), who was a schoolteacher by profession, excavated in Brixham Cave near Torquay in southwestern England. This was a newly discovered site known to contain fossilized bones. His work was sponsored by the Royal and the Geological Societies of London and was carefully supervised by a committee of prestigious scientists, including Charles Lyell. In the course of excavations, stone tools and fossil animal bones were found beneath an unbroken layer of stalagmitic deposits 7.5 centimeters thick, which suggested considerable antiquity (Gruber 1965; Warren and Rose 1994). As a result of growing interest in the antiquity of humanity, in the spring and summer of 1859, first the geologist Joseph Prestwich (1812–1896) and the accomplished amateur archaeologist John Evans (1823–1908) and then a number of other British scientists, including Charles Lyell, visited the sites in the Somme Valley. All these scientists were convinced of the validity of the finds Boucher de Perthes and Rigollot had made there and the geologists also recognized that the strata in which these finds occurred must have been deposited long before 4000 BC. In their reports to leading British scientific associations, including the British Association for the Advancement of Science, the Royal Society of London, and the Geological Society of London, they agreed that there was now solid evidence that human beings had coexisted with extinct mammals at a time that was far removed from the present in terms of calendar years (Chorley et al. 1964: 447–9; Grayson 1983: 179–90). This new view of the antiquity of human beings received what amounted to official approval in Lyell's *The Geological Evidences of the Antiquity of Man* (1863).

Charles Darwin's *On the Origin of Species* was published in November 1859. This book, which summarized the results of almost thirty years of research that had been inspired by uniformitarian geology, accomplished for evolutionary biology what Lyell's *Principles* had done for geology. Darwin's concept of natural selection was accepted by many scientists and members of the general public as providing a mechanism that made it possible to believe that a process of biological evolution accounted for the origins and distributions of modern species and explained the changes observed in the palaeontological record. Natural selection was widely viewed as the biological equivalent of capitalist competition, which was believed to be the driving force behind economic and cultural advancement. Spencer encouraged this conflation by renaming natural selection the "survival of the fittest." Yet the enduring preoccupation of prehistoric archaeologists and anthropologists with unilinear cultural evolution accorded with the views of Spencer and the eighteenth-century Enlightenment philosophers rather than with Darwin's. Darwin conceived of biological evolution as occurring in a dendritic, or branching, rather than a unilinear manner and he believed that natural selection was determined by fortuitous circumstances and not by foresight and conscious decisions, as sociocultural evolution was assumed to be.

The obvious implication of Darwin's theory, that humanity had evolved from some apelike primate, not only made the antiquity of the human species a burning issue that had to be empirically studied but also identified this investigation as being a vital part of the broader controversy that was raging concerning Darwin's theory of biological evolution. Palaeolithic archaeology therefore quickly acquired a high-profile role alongside geology and palaeontology in debates relating to questions of escalating public interest.

Palaeolithic Archaeology

The subject matter of Palaeolithic archaeology was first identified in 1865 when, in his book *Pre-historic Times*, the English banker and naturalist John Lubbock (1834–1913) divided the Stone Age into an earlier Palaeolithic or Archaeolithic (Old Stone) and a more recent Neolithic (New Stone) period. The Palaeolithic Age was defined as an early period of human development when only chipped stone tools had been manufactured and numerous animal species that are now extinct had still been alive. The Neolithic was a later period when many special purpose stone tools, such as axes and gouges, were ground and polished and only modern species of animals were alive. Although Lubbock's observation that chipped stone tools had been manufactured before polished ones was derived from Worsaae ([1859] Fischer and Kristiansen 2002: 45–56), Lubbock failed to note that Thomsen and Worsaae had already defined an intermediary period, which is now labeled the Mesolithic. In the Mesolithic, only chipped stone tools had been manufactured, but the array of animal species already resembled the present. The failure of early Palaeolithic archaeologists to recognize this period suggests the lack of a detailed understanding of the work of Scandinavian archaeologists by their counterparts in France and England. Even the term Mesolithic, as first used by Hodder Westropp in 1872, included what we now designate as the Middle and Upper Palaeolithic periods rather than referring specifically to the cultures of postglacial hunters. It was not employed in its modern sense before the twentieth century (Gräslund 1987: 38; Rowley-Conwy 1996).

After 1860, the main advances in Palaeolithic archaeology took place in France, where the river terraces of the north and the rock shelters of the south provided better evidence than was available in England. The principal goals of these studies were to determine how long human beings had been in the area and whether evolutionary trends could be detected within the Palaeolithic period. Evolutionary theory predicted that over time human beings should have become both morphologically and culturally more complex. The first goal of Palaeolithic archaeologists was therefore to arrange their sites in chronological order and see if this pattern had occurred.

The leading figure in early Palaeolithic research was Edouard Lartet (1801–1871), a French magistrate who had turned to the study of palaeontology and had publicly acknowledged the importance of Boucher de Perthes's discoveries in 1860. Financially supported by the English banker and amateur anthropologist Henry Christy, he began to explore cave sites in the Dordogne in 1863. He quickly realized that the Palaeolithic was not a single phase of human development but a series of phases that could be distinguished according to artifacts and associated prehistoric animals. He preferred a classification based on palaeontological criteria and identified four ages or periods, which from most recent to oldest were: (1) Aurochs or Bison Age; (2) Reindeer Age, of which the cave sites at Laugerie Basse and La Madeleine were typical; (3) Mammoth and Wooly Rhinoceros Age; and (4) Cave Bear Age, although he gradually recognized that the last two periods could not be temporally separated. The Le Moustier site was designated as typical of a new Cave Bear and Mammoth period. To Lartet's periods, Félix Garrigou added a still earlier Hippopotamus Age, when human beings had inhabited mainly open sites and that was not represented in the caves of southern France.

Lartet's work was continued by Gabriel de Mortillet (1821–1898), a geologist and palaeontologist who turned to the study of archaeology. He was assistant curator at the Museum of National Antiquities at Saint-Germain-en-Laye for eight years before becoming Professor of Prehistoric Anthropology at the School of Anthropology in Paris in 1876. Mortillet was a radical socialist and a materialist, who believed that promoting an evolutionary understanding of the origins of human beings and their cultures in opposition to the creationist views of French monarchists and conservatives was a way to encourage the development of socialism in France (Dennell 1990). Although he admired Lartet's work, he maintained that an archaeological subdivision of the Palaeolithic had to be based on cultural rather than palaeontological criteria, in part to minimize the risk of ecological differences being mistaken for temporal ones. In this respect, he chose to follow the example of Lubbock and Worsaae (Mortillet 1883, 1897).

In spite of this, Mortillet's approach to archaeology was greatly influenced by his knowledge of geology and palaeontology. He sought to distinguish each period by specifying a limited number of artifact types that were characteristic of that period alone. These diagnostic artifacts were archaeological equivalents of the index fossils that geologists and palaeontologists used to identify the strata belonging to a particular geological epoch. Mortillet also followed geological practice in naming each of his subdivisions of the Palaeolithic after the type site that he had used to define it. Like palaeontologists, he relied on stratigraphy to establish a chronological sequence. In the Palaeolithic research of the nineteenth century, seriation played only a minor role as a means for establishing chronology. This was partly because technological and stylistic sequences were harder to recognize in Palaeolithic stone tools than in later artifacts, as so little was known about how stone tools had been manufactured, and also because the issues being discussed were so controversial and socially consequential that only the clearest stratigraphic evidence was universally agreed to be able to provide convincing temporal sequences.

The Hippopotamus Age became the Chellean Epoch (later to be divided into the Chellean and Acheulean Epochs), named after a site north of Paris, and most of Lartet's Cave Bear and Mammoth Age became the Mousterian, although Mortillet assigned finds from Aurignac that Lartet had placed late in his Cave Bear and Mammoth Age to a separate and later Aurignacian Epoch. Lartet's Reindeer Age was divided into an earlier Solutrean Epoch and a later Magdalenian one. Mortillet was uncertain about the date of the Aurignacian. He later placed it after the Solutrean and finally dropped it from his classification of 1872 (Figure 4.6). Although the criteria were not evident in advance, because so little was understood about flint-knapping, Mortillet's sequence displayed increasing technological virtuosity and greater economy in the use of raw material over time. Bifacial Chellean and Acheulean handaxes gave way to Mousterian tools prepared from Levallois cores and these in turn to Upper Palaeolithic blade tools. Mortillet added still more epochs to incorporate the Neolithic, Bronze, and Iron Ages into his system, although it is doubtful that he was ever serious about the universality of these highly distinctive western European epochs, as opposed to the technological ages of which they were subdivisions (Childe 1956a: 27).

Mortillet also proposed a Thenaisian and a more recent Puycournian Epoch to cover pre-Chellean finds. Between 1863 and 1940 archaeologists discovered eoliths, or presumed artifacts of exceptionally crude manufacture, in early Pleistocene as well as still earlier Pliocene and Miocene deposits in France, England, Portugal, and Belgium. Evolutionary theory implied that the earliest tools would be so crude that they could not be distinguished from naturally broken rocks; hence, in the absence of human bones or other convincing proofs of human presence the authenticity of these finds was challenged. In the late 1870s, Mortillet and others who supported the artifactual status of eoliths began to develop a set of criteria that might be used to distinguish intentional stone working from natural breakage. Challenges to these criteria alternated with efforts to elaborate new and more convincing tests. Comparative studies were made of eoliths and rocks coming from formations hundreds of millions of years old, and that therefore could not be artifactual. Experimental work also was carried out, including S. H. Warren's (1905) observations of striations on flints broken by mechanical pressure,

TEMPS	AGES	PÉRIODES	ÉPOQUES
Quaternaires actuels.	Historiques.	Mérovingienne.	Wabenienne. (*Waben, Pas-de-Calais.*)
		Romaine.	Champdolienne. (*Champdolent, Seine-et-Oise.*)
			Lugdunienne. (*Lyon, Rhône.*)
	du Fer.	Galatienne.	Beuvraysienne. (*Mont-Beuvray, Nièvre.*)
	Protohistoriques.		Marnienne. (*Département de la Marne.*)
			Hallstattienne. (*Hallstatt, haute Autriche.*)
	du Bronze.	Tsiganienne.	Larnaudienne. (*Larnaud, Jura.*)
			Morgienne. (*Morges, canton de Vaud, Suisse.*)
		Néolithique.	Robenhausienne. (*Robenhausen, Zurich.*)
			Campignyenne. (*Campigny, Seine-Inférieure.*)
			Tardenoisienne (*Fère-en-Tardenois, Aisne.*)
Quaternaires anciens.	Préhistoriques.	Paléolithique.	Tourassienne. (*La Tourasse, Haute-Garonne.*) Ancien Hiatus.
			Magdalénienne. (*La Madeleine, Dordogne.*)
			Solutréenne. (*Solutré, Saône-et-Loire.*)
	de la Pierre.		Moustérienne. (*Le Moustier, Dordogne.*)
			Acheuléenne. (*Saint-Acheul, Somme.*)
			Chelléenne. (*Chelles, Seine-et-Marne.*)
Tertiaires.		Éolithique.	Puycournienne. (*Puy-Courny, Cantal.*)
			Thenaysienne. (*Thenay, Loir-et-Cher.*)

Figure 4.6 Mortillet's epochs of prehistory, from *Formation de la nation française*, 1897

Marcelin Boule's (1905) study of flints that had been churned about in a cement mixer, and A. S. Barnes's (1939) quantitative comparison of edge angles fabricated by human hands and by natural processes. In the course of these studies, much was learned about stone working and many sites were disqualified as evidence of human antiquity (Grayson 1986). Either as a result of direct influence or by coincidence, this research replicated the traditions of archaeological experimentation established by Scandinavian investigators in the 1840s.

Mortillet's training in the natural sciences was reflected in more than his classificatory approach. He and most other Palaeolithic archaeologists were primarily concerned with establishing the antiquity of humanity. Within their evolutionary framework, this meant trying to trace evidence of human presence back as far as possible in the archaeological record and demonstrating that older cultures were more primitive than later ones. The sequence that Lartet and Mortillet established carried out this task admirably. Comparing later with earlier stages of the Palaeolithic, there was evidence of a greater variety of stone tools, a more complicated manufacturing sequence and greater precision in the preparation of stone tools, and an increasing number of bone tools. This demonstrated that the technological progress that Thomsen and Worsaae had documented from the Stone to the Iron Ages had already been occurring through the Palaeolithic period.

Although Palaeolithic archaeologists discussed what Palaeolithic populations had eaten at different stages and debated whether certain art work might indicate that horses had been domesticated in the Magdalenian period (Bahn 1978), they were far less interested in studying how people had lived in prehistoric times than Scandinavian archaeologists were. In this respect, Palaeolithic archaeologists resembled palaeontologists, who at that time were more interested in establishing well-documented evolutionary sequences than they were in studying ecological relations among the plant and animal species preserved in rock formations from individual periods. The main units of archaeological excavation were accumulations of microstrata containing similar artifact types. Sites were frequently excavated with minimal supervision, which meant that detailed cultural stratigraphy and the features within major deposits, which would have been noted in Scandinavia, went unrecorded. Especially in rock shelters where living floors had been preserved, this resulted in a severe loss of information about how people had lived. Evidence of hearths and tent rings often went unnoticed, as did the spatial relations of artifacts and faunal remains to such features. The artifacts that were kept for study in museums often were only those recognized as being of diagnostic value (*fossiles directeurs*) for confirming the age and cultural affinities of sites. Debitage and artifacts that were not believed to have diagnostic significance because they did not change significantly over long periods of time were frequently discarded. This encouraged a narrow view of artifacts as dating devices and evidence of progress, which was very different from the Scandinavian approach to studying archaeological data.

Finally, Palaeolithic epochs were viewed as a unilinear series of stages with little attention being paid to synchronic diversity that might have developed as a result of ecological or ethnic differences. Unilinear evolutionism encouraged the belief that archaeologists could use modern ethnographic cultures to illustrate the ways of life that had been associated with particular epochs. The Chelleans often were compared to the aboriginal Tasmanians, alleged to be the most primitive people alive in the nineteenth century, the Mousterians with the somewhat more advanced Australian Aborigines, and the Solutreans with the Inuit. Such dependence on holistic ethnographic analogies for the behavioral interpretation of archaeological data inhibited the development of techniques for inferring specific aspects of human behavior from particular types of archaeological data and subordinated prehistoric archaeology to ethnology in the sphere of functional-processual interpretation. Even Boyd Dawkins (1874), who criticized Mortillet for his preoccupation with evolutionary development and his failure to allow that some differences among Palaeolithic assemblages might reflect ethnic variation or varying access to different types of stone, did not produce any satisfactory historical analyses.

Mortillet, like the geologists and palaeontologists of the mid-nineteenth century, was caught up in the evolutionary enthusiasm that characterized scientific research at that time. He viewed his Palaeolithic sequence as a bridge between the geological and palaeontological evidence of biological evolution prior to the Pleistocene era and the already established documentation of cultural progress in Europe in post-Palaeolithic times. As Glyn Daniel (1950: 244) has noted, one of the keynotes of evolutionary archaeology was the idea that the development of different groups of human beings could be represented in a single sequence and read in a cave section, just as the geological sequence could be read in stratified rocks.

Mortillet also was influenced by a strong ethnological interest in cultural evolution during the second half of the nineteenth century. In 1851, the German ethnologist Adolf Bastian (1826–1905) began a series of scientific voyages around the world in the course of which he built up the collections of the Royal Museum of Ethnology in Berlin. Impressed by the cultural similarities that he encountered in widely separated places, he emphasized the Enlightenment doctrine of psychic unity by arguing that, as a result of universally shared "elementary ideas" (*Elementargedanken*), peoples at the same level of development who are facing similar problems will, within the constraints imposed by their environments, tend to develop similar solutions to such problems (Koepping 1983; Zimmerman 2001).

After 1860, there was a great revival of theoretic history, as ethnologists sought, by comparing modern societies assumed to be at different levels of development, to work out the successive stages through which European societies had evolved in prehistoric times. These researches ranged from studies of specific issues, such as Johann Bachofen's (1861) theory that all societies had evolved from matrilineal beginnings and John McLennan's (1865) arguments that the oldest human societies had been polyandrous, to general delineations of development from savagery through barbarism to civilization by E. B. Tylor (1865) and Lewis H. Morgan (1877). Unlike the "theoretic" histories of the eighteenth century, these ethnological formulations generally were presented as scientific theories rather than as philosophical speculations. Although reflecting the vogue for evolutionary studies in the mid-nineteenth century and usually addressing questions that archaeological data were ill-equipped to handle, these works derived much of their self-confidence from growing archaeological evidence that technological advances had been a significant feature of human history. Reciprocally, these ethnographic formulations encouraged archaeologists to interpret their data from a unilinear perspective. Although Mortillet did not claim that every detail of the development of material culture in France during the Palaeolithic period had been duplicated elsewhere, he did believe that, because this sequence represented a logical process of technological elaboration, all but its most specific features would have characterized the sequences that early human development would have followed in all other parts of the world.

In his guide to the archaeological displays at the Paris Exposition of 1867, Mortillet proclaimed that prehistoric studies had revealed human progress to be a law of nature, that all human groups passed through similar stages of development (although clearly at different speeds), and that humanity was of great antiquity (Daniel 1967: 144). The first two concepts had their roots in the philosophy of the Enlightenment and the third had been recognized as a result of archaeological research carried out before the publication of *On the Origin of Species*. Yet, although Palaeolithic archaeology had vindicated an evolutionary origin for humanity, Mortillet's first two laws were far from validated. Not enough work had been done outside of western Europe to determine whether or not human groups everywhere had developed – insofar as they had developed at all – through the same Palaeolithic sequence. Although many scholars were prepared to accept the multiple invention of simple artifacts, such as spears or calabash containers, some of them suspected that more complex inventions, such as boomerangs or bows and arrows, must each have had a single origin and diffused from its place of origin to other parts of the world (Huxley [1865] 1896: 213). Likewise, overly rigid applications of notions about what constituted progress led many archaeologists to reject the authenticity of cave paintings because they seemed stylistically too advanced to have been produced at an early stage of human development. In 1889 Mortillet claimed in a letter that the cave paintings at Altamira were a plot by the Spanish priesthood to discredit prehistory as a science. This view was only overcome as fresh discoveries of cave paintings were made in contexts that clearly dated this art to the Upper Palaeolithic period. Even when European cave art was validated, however, it was interpreted largely by analogy with the totemism associated with the Australian aborigines (Reinach 1903; Ucko and Rosenfeld 1967: 123–8; Moro Abadía and González Morales 2003, 2004).

Palaeolithic archaeology was scientifically important and aroused great public interest because it revealed the hitherto unexpected antiquity of humanity and the evolution of European civilization from very primitive beginnings (Moro Abadía 2002). Palaeolithic archaeology also enjoyed great prestige because of its close ties with geology and palaeontology, which were both sciences in the forefront of creating a new vision of the history of the world. All three disciplines were valued because they were viewed as demonstrating the reality of progress before the dawn of history. Palaeolithic archaeology also attracted more attention than Scandinavian prehistoric archaeology had done because it evolved in France and England, which were the main centers of political, economic, and cultural development in the world at that time. Yet Palaeolithic archaeology's view of artifacts mainly as dating devices and evidence of cultural evolution was a very narrow one by comparison with Scandinavian prehistoric archaeology, which was concerned with studying cultural evolution but also sought to learn as much as possible about specific human groups that had lived in the past and how human beings had adapted to individual prehistoric environments. The reciprocal interdisciplinary cooperation of Scandinavian archaeologists with geologists and biologists in their pursuit of these objectives contrasts with the wholesale modeling of archaeological research on often inappropriate natural science methods by Palaeolithic archaeologists. As a result, the prehistoric archaeology that developed in France and England was limited in the range of its interests just as it was enhanced in its time depth by comparison with Scandinavian archaeology.

Reaction against Evolution

Individual archaeologists served on both sides in the struggle between the supporters of revealed religion and evolutionism during the late nineteenth and early twentieth centuries. Those who objected to evolutionary explanations of human origins or the denial of biblical accounts of human history fought evolutionists in various ways. During the 1860s, creationists who accepted current interpretations of the archaeological record could admit that human beings had been created much earlier than had previously been thought and continue to hope that early hominid skeletons, when discovered, would resemble those of modern human beings rather than the "pithecoid forms" predicted by the Darwinians (Casson 1939: 207–8; Grayson 1983: 211). Other creationists rejected an evolutionary interpretation of the archaeological record. As early as 1832, Richard Whately, the Anglican Archbishop of Dublin (1787–1863), had sought to breathe new life into the doctrine of degenerationism. He argued that there was no evidence that savages, unaided, had ever developed a less barbarous way of life. It followed that humanity originally must have existed in a state "far superior" to that of modern savages, a view that he felt was in accord with the Book of Genesis (Grayson 1983: 217–20). This position became increasingly popular among conservatives in the 1860s, although not all degenerationists denied the great antiquity of humanity or attributed its earliest cultural achievements to divine revelation.

One of the most eminent degenerationists was the Canadian geologist and amateur archaeologist John William Dawson, who was Principal of McGill University in Montreal from 1855 to 1893. Dawson accepted the association between human remains and extinct mammals but argued that these associations only confirmed the recency of the Pleistocene gravels in which they were found. On a trip to Europe in 1865, he inspected the geological deposits of the Somme Valley and described his former mentor Charles Lyell as taking very "good-naturedly" his opinion that evidence was lacking "of the excessive antiquity at that time attributed to [these formations] by some writers" (Dawson 1901: 145). In this case, Dawson was simply ignoring the unwelcome findings of uniformitarian geologists. Elsewhere, he noted that North American ethnographic evidence revealed that the indigenous peoples who had produced the best-made stone implements also had produced the rudest ones (this was probably a reference to cores and debitage). More generally, he suggested that the developmental sequence found in Europe might represent an idiosyncratic local trend or the accidental interdigitation of neighboring, contemporary groups with different cultures. From this, he concluded that there was no evidence that cultures at different levels of complexity had not coexisted throughout human history (Dawson 1888: 166–7, 214; Trigger 1966). Although, in retrospect, Dawson can be seen as defending a lost cause, in the nineteenth century it was easier for his opponents to ignore his criticisms of the limitations of important aspects of their research than to refute them. In particular, not enough was yet known about prehistoric sequences outside Europe to establish evolution as a general trend in human history.

Still more affinities existed between Middle Eastern archaeologists and those who sought to prove the literal truth of the Bible. Intense public interest in Mesopotamian archaeology revived in the 1870s after George Smith published a clay tablet from Nineveh containing a Babylonian account similar to the biblical one of Noah's flood. *The Daily Telegraph* newspaper offered 1,000 pounds sterling to send an expedition to Iraq in search of the missing portions of this tablet, which were duly found (Daniel 1950: 132–3). Much of the early work of the Egypt Exploration Society was directed to sites in the Nile Delta, such as Tell el-Muskhuta, that might have been associated with biblical accounts of the Hebrew sojourn in Egypt. In 1896, W. M. F. Petrie was quick to identify the ethnic name *I. si. ri. ar* (the ancient Egyptian script did not distinguish r and l), which appeared on a newly discovered stela of the Pharaoh Merneptah (r. 1236–1223 BC), as the first known mention of Israel in Egyptian texts (Drower 1985: 221). As late as 1929, Leonard Woolley excited great interest by claiming that the thick silt deposits that he had found in his excavations of prehistoric levels at Ur attested a great flood in Mesopotamia that might have given rise to the biblical account of the deluge (Woolley 1950: 20–3; Moorey 1991: 79–80). Until the 1890s, historical archaeologists, fearing to question the biblical chronology, maintained that there were no prehistoric sites in the Middle East. They argued that all sites yielding stone artifacts dated from historical times (Gran-Aymerich 1998: 285–6, 292, 443). Although Egypt and Mesopotamia produced spectacular archaeological discoveries that excited the public because of their intrinsic beauty and interest, those that related to the Bible and appeared to confirm scriptural accounts ensured widespread financial support for archaeological research carried out in those countries and in Palestine.

Archaeology in North America

Although European visitors and to a limited degree local scholars studied isolated facets of Latin American prehistory (I. Bernal 1980: 35–102), the United States was the only country outside Europe to develop a substantial tradition of prehistoric archaeological research before the late nineteenth century. By the time European settlers began to press west of the Appalachian Mountains, starting in the

1780s, the spread of Enlightenment rationalism among more educated Euro-Americans was creating the need for nonreligious explanations of Indian inferiority. As a consequence, racial myths eclipsed religious ones as a justification for seizing Indian lands and violating Indian treaty rights. It was widely maintained that the Indians were brutal and warlike by nature and biologically incapable of significant cultural development. They also were alleged, despite substantial evidence to the contrary, to be unable to adjust to a European style of life and therefore destined to die out as "civilization" spread westward (Vaughan 1982). Even Thomas Jefferson, who regarded the Indians as having been a noble and vibrant race before European discovery, did not believe they possessed the power to resist the corrupting influences of civilization (R. McGuire 1992b; Wallace 1999). These ideas were not the invention of a single individual but spontaneous expressions of widely held prejudices. Many Americans viewed the assumed natural inferiority of the Indians as a manifestation of divine providence, which indicates that the new biological explanations of the supposed inferiority of indigenous peoples did not necessarily exclude older religious ones.

When Europeans began to settle west of the Appalachians, they discovered elaborate earthworks and large earth mounds in the Ohio and Mississippi watersheds. The earthworks are now known to have been associated with the Adena and Hopewell cultures that were centered in the Ohio Valley between 800 BC and AD 500 and many of the mounds with the Mississippian culture that flourished across the southeastern United States from AD 500 to 1550. These constructions, which often contained elaborate artifacts made of pottery, shell, mica, and native copper, challenged the belief that indigenous American cultures were invariably primitive. They also quickly became the focus of the most varied speculations. Some Americans, such as the naturalist William Bartram, the Reverend James Madison, and, most important, the Baltimore physician James McCulloh, concluded that they had been constructed by Indians, but most rejected this identification. The traveler Benjamin Barton attributed these structures to Danes, who had gone on to become the Toltecs of Mexico, whereas De Witt Clinton, the Mayor of New York, said they were the work of Vikings, and the lawyer and soldier Amos Stoddard identified them as being of Welsh origin. The sagacious ethnologist Albert Gallatin linked them with Mexico, although he was uncertain whether Mexicans had moved north or the builders of these mounds had relocated south (Silverberg 1968; Willey and Sabloff 1980: 19–25; Blakeslee 1987).

Although the American public often denigrated the accomplishments of their country's indigenous peoples, they were anxious that North America should have its own history to rival that of Europe and, hence, were intrigued by these finds, just as they were to be intrigued by John L. Stephens's discovery of lost Maya cities in the jungles of Central America in the 1840s. Yet, apart from those who interpreted the prehistoric mounds and earthworks as evidence of degeneration (Bieder 1986: 33–4), most scholars and the general public attributed them to a race of Moundbuilders who were imagined to have been destroyed or driven out of North America by savage hordes of Indians. The various Moundbuilder speculations thus offered a chronicle of American prehistory but, by attributing the major accomplishments of the past to a vanished non-North American Indian people, continued to emphasize the static and hence potentially uncivilizable nature of the Indians. The archaeological record was widely interpreted as further evidence of the menace posed by the Indians, who were thereby revealed as destroyers of civilization when given the opportunity. Indians whose lands and other resources were being seized and who were being confined on reservations or forced to relocate farther west were portrayed by their oppressors as bloodthirsty monsters and new reasons were provided to justify American citizens waging war on them and seizing their lands. Books, such as Josiah Priest's *American Antiquities and Discoveries in the West* (1833), expounding the idea that the Moundbuilders were a lost race of civilized people, quickly became best-sellers. So great was the attraction of these narratives that, even after the American physician and anatomist Samuel Morton (1799–1851) had failed to discover any significant differences between the skulls of Moundbuilders and those of recently deceased Indians, he divided his American race into Toltec and Barbarous families on purely cultural grounds (Silverberg 1968).

More positively, the discovery of mounds and earthworks west of the Appalachians created for the first time a widespread interest in the United States in describing prehistoric monuments and collecting artifacts from them. These finds were viewed as far more sophisticated, both technologically and artistically, than anything produced by Indians. Between 1780 and 1860, archaeology in the eastern and central United States passed through an antiquarian phase, which recapitulated the development of archaeology in England and Scandinavia between 1500 and 1800. In the late eighteenth century, army officers stationed in the Ohio Valley began to draw plans of the earthworks and the Reverend Manasseh Cutler counted the number of rings of trees that had grown on top of the earthworks at Marietta as these were cleared for town building. In 1813, H. H. Brackenridge distinguished between burial and temple mounds and as we now know correctly suggested that the burial ones were earlier (Willey and Sabloff 1980: 23).

Research and the publication of research gradually became more systematic. The American Philosophical Society took an active interest in the Moundbuilder debate. In 1799, as one of its numerous scientific projects, its President, Thomas Jefferson, distributed a circular soliciting information about prehistoric fortifications, tumuli, and Indian artifacts. In 1812, the publisher Isaiah Thomas founded the American Antiquarian Society, which provided a focal point for the still diffuse but growing interest in archaeological questions. The first volume of the society's *Transactions*, which appeared in 1820, contained Caleb Atwater's "Description of the antiquities discovered in the State of Ohio and other western states." This study incorporated valuable plans and descriptions of earthworks, many of which have since been leveled (Figure 4.7). Atwater divided the earthworks into three classes: modern European, modern Indian, and Moundbuilder. He speculated, on the basis of a single three-headed ceramic vessel, that the ancient mounds had been constructed by Hindus, who had come to North America from Asia and later moved south into Mexico.

The next major contribution to American archaeology was *Ancient Monuments of the Mississippi Valley* (1848) by Ephraim G. Squier (1821–1888) and Edwin H. Davis (1811–1888). Squier, a newspaper editor, and Davis, a physician, both lived in Ohio. They carefully surveyed a large number of mounds and earthworks, excavated some, and systematically compiled the findings of other researchers. They recorded a vast amount of data about prehistoric earthworks over the eastern United States, many of which relate to sites that have since been destroyed. Their classification, which was based

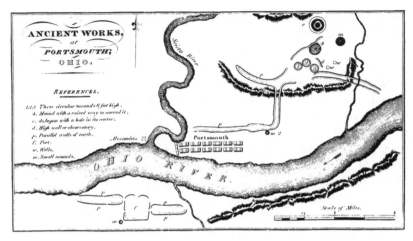

Figure 4.7 Plan of prehistoric earthworks at Portsmouth, Ohio, from
Atwater's "Description of the antiquities discovered in the State of Ohio"
(*Transactions of the American Antiquarian Society*, 1820)

on formal criteria, distinguished between the effigy mounds of the
upper Mississippi Valley, the symmetrical enclosures of Ohio, and
the truncated mounds to the south. Speculation was generally limited to posing questions about the possible uses of such structures
(Figure 4.8).

Although Squier and Davis both strongly supported the Moundbuilder hypothesis, the general tone of their volume was set by Joseph
Henry, a renowned physicist and the first secretary of the Smithsonian Institution, which had been established in Washington, DC,
in 1846. Their volume was the Smithsonian's first publication and
began its *Contributions to Knowledge* series. Henry was determined
to purge American archaeology of its speculative tendencies and to
encourage scientific research in the Baconian tradition. To achieve
that end, he insisted on excising all of what he judged to be Squier
and Davis's unsubstantiated speculations about the Moundbuilders
so that their "positive addition to the sum of human knowledge
should stand in bold relief" (Washburn 1967: 153; Tax 1975; Willey
and Sabloff 1980: 36). Henry also commissioned Samuel Haven, the
librarian of the American Antiquarian Society, to prepare a historical
review of the *Archaeology of the United States*, which was published
in 1856. In it, numerous speculations about American prehistory

Figure 4.8 Grave Creek Mound, West Virginia, from Squier and Davis
Ancient Monuments of the Mississippi Valley, 1848

were systematically examined in the light of available information
and shown to be untenable. The Moundbuilder theory was one of
the principal objects of Haven's attacks.

In order to encourage a more professional outlook, Henry also
published reports on developments in European archaeology in the
Annual Report of the Smithsonian Institution, which was widely distributed in North America. The most successful of these reports was
"General Views on Archaeology," a translation of a paper originally
published in French by the Swiss geologist and amateur archaeologist
Adolf Morlot (1861). Morlot carefully summarized recent advances
in European archaeology, especially in Denmark and Switzerland.
His account of the excavation of Danish "kitchen middens" stimulated the excavation of shell mounds along the east coast of North
America from Nova Scotia to Florida beginning in the early 1860s
(Trigger 1986a). Although Henry's efforts to counteract speculations did not significantly diminish fanciful interpretations of the past
among amateur archaeologists and the general public, his official
encouragement of archaeology and promotion of more systematic

research helped to prepare Americans who were interested in doing archaeology for the more professional era that was to dawn after 1860.

Conclusions

In Europe, prehistoric archaeology developed in the early and middle nineteenth century as a rationalist study of cultural evolution and a romantic investigation of how Europeans had lived before the earliest historical records. It revealed not only that the most complex modern technologies had developed from Stone Age beginnings but also that the Stone Age itself bore witness to the gradual elaboration of the ability of human beings to create technology. Prehistoric archaeology originated in two waves. The first, which began in Denmark in 1816, mainly studied cultural development in Neolithic, Bronze Age, and Iron Age times, while the second, which started fifty years later in England and France, developed around the study of the Palaeolithic period. Although Palaeolithic archaeology did not begin completely independently of the prehistoric archaeology practiced in Scandinavia, the two approaches were distinctive in terms of goals and methods. Palaeolithic archaeology tended to model itself on the natural sciences, whereas Scandinavian archaeology was more interested in learning from archaeological data how specific peoples had lived in the past. Although Palaeolithic archaeology tended to remain evolutionary in orientation, Scandinavian prehistoric archaeologists pioneered the beginnings not only of the evolutionary but also of the culture-historical and functional-processual approaches of later times. They did not view these as alternative approaches but as complementary perspectives on the past.

Both branches of prehistoric archaeology reveal themselves to have been intellectual products of the Enlightenment. They shared the belief that the evolution of material culture betokens social and moral improvement as well. Large numbers of middle-class people, whose economic and political power was increasing as a result of the Industrial Revolution, were pleased to view themselves as participating in a wave of progress that was inherent in human nature and perhaps more generally in the very constitution of the universe. Euro-Americans were happy to share this optimistic view, but they were not prepared to extend it to embrace the indigenous peoples whose lands they were seizing. For them, indigenous people were an exception, who as a result of their biological inferiority were unable to participate in the progress that destiny had made the prerogative of Europeans, wherever they lived in the world. Far from being discordant, these differing views about Europeans and non-Europeans were soon to be combined in a powerful international synthesis.

CHAPTER 5

Evolutionary Archaeology

———

Few of us can observe such indications of the habits and physical
condition of the earliest inhabitants of this island [Britain] as are
afforded by the remains of their rude dwellings, and by the rude
implements occasionally found, without a sense of thankfulness that
our lot has been mercifully cast in times of improved knowledge, of
advanced civilization, and more refined habits.

EARL OF DEVON, "Inaugural Address" at Exeter Congress, 1873,
Archaeological Journal 30 (1873), p. 206

A shared commitment to an evolutionary approach promoted a close
alignment between prehistoric archaeology and ethnology in western Europe and the United States beginning in the 1860s. In Europe,
the foundation for this alignment was the belief in unilinear cultural
evolution forged a century earlier by Enlightenment philosophers.
It was accepted that arranging modern cultures in a series from simplest to most complex illustrated the earlier stages through which the
most advanced cultures had developed in prehistoric times. French
and British Palaeolithic archaeologists did not try harder to eluci-
date the past using archaeological data because their commitment to
unilinear evolutionism led them to believe that ethnology revealed
almost everything they wished to know about prehistoric times.

In the United States, where it was assumed that relatively little
cultural evolution had occurred in prehistoric times, archaeology,
ethnology, physical anthropology, and linguistics had begun by the
1840s to be regarded as different branches of anthropology, which
was identified as the study of American indigenous peoples. The
principal goal of American anthropology was romantically defined by
the ethnologist Henry Schoolcraft (1793–1864) as being to preserve
some records of a dying race for future ages (Hinsley 1981: 20).

One of the main problems that had confronted evolutionism from
the beginning was to explain why some societies had developed

rapidly while others had remained static for thousands of years. In the eighteenth century, such disparities commonly had been attributed to environmental factors. A century later, it was still maintained that a temperate climate encouraged cultural development to a far greater degree than did a less demanding tropical or an extremely harsh arctic one and that the physical conditions in the Old World were naturally more conducive to cultural progress than they were in the Americas – a position still supported by Jared Diamond (1997). Yet specific environmental explanations often were far from convincing. A renewed interest in cultural evolution inevitably focused attention on this problem.

The Rise of Racism

At the same time that a close relationship between prehistoric archaeology and ethnology was developing in western Europe and America, some of the principal ideas on which the Enlightenment had been based were undergoing significant modifications and were even being abandoned. In particular, the nineteenth century witnessed the slow erosion in western Europe of a belief in psychic unity. Especially after Napoleon had stabilized the reforms of the French Revolution in a manner that specifically benefited the middle classes, his conquests tended to be welcomed by these classes in Italy, Germany, and other countries where disadvantaging semifeudal political structures had persisted. His conquests simultaneously provoked nationalist reactions, which continued to be promoted by the conservative regimes that were restored to power in France, Germany, and Italy after his defeat. In place of the rationalism of the Enlightenment, this new conservatism encouraged a romantic celebration of national and ethnic differences in the hope of diverting the middle classes from continuing to demand political and social reform. Although Johann Herder (1744–1803), the German philosopher who was very influential in promoting these ideas, was not a racist or even opposed to reform, this sort of thinking encouraged many intellectuals to view alleged national characteristics as being rooted in biological disparities between human groups that were impervious to change. This belief began to challenge the eighteenth-century Enlightenment assumption of the intellectual and emotional similarity of different ethnic groups (Grayson 1983: 142–9).

Racist ideas found expression in the writings of Joseph-Arthur, comte de Gobineau (1816–1882), especially his four volume *Essai sur l'inégalité des races humaines* (*Essay on the Inequality of the Human Races*) (1853–1855). A member of an aristocratic French family, Gobineau believed that the fate of civilizations was determined by their racial composition and that the more a successful civilization's racial character was "diluted," the more likely it was to sink into stagnation and corruption. Gobineau subscribed to the prerevolutionary belief that the French aristocracy was descended from German-speaking Franks, whereas French commoners were descended from Gauls and Romans. He celebrated the supposed superiority of the Aryans or northern Europeans, including the Germans, and interpreted the execution and exiling of aristocrats during the French Revolution as having deprived France of its most capable leaders. As a result, he believed, France was doomed to lose its national preeminence in Europe. Gobineau also warned that Germans could dominate others only so long as they avoided "miscegenation" with "inferior" peoples, such as Jews, Celts, and Slavs. Gobineau's writings were to influence European racists, including the composer Richard Wagner and the Nazi leader Adolf Hitler, and his ideas were popularized in America by works such as Madison Grant's *The Passing of the Great Race* (1916), which argued against allowing large numbers of immigrants from southern and eastern Europe to enter the United States. Gobineau was not the only source of racist ideas. Already in the 1840s, the German ethnologist Gustav Klemm (1802–1867) was distinguishing between culturally creative and culturally uncreative peoples (Klemm 1843–1852, 1854–1855). It was not long before novelists as well as scholars were routinely invoking alleged racial factors instead of environmental ones to explain the varying degrees to which the cultures of different human groups had evolved.

Some of these theories were founded on the doctrine of polygenesis, or multiple origins of human beings, which can be traced as far back as the twelfth century (Slotkin 1965: 5–6), but was first raised as a major issue in modern times by the French Calvinist librarian Isaac de La Peyrère (1594–1676) in 1655. He argued that the biblical Adam was the ancestor of the Jews alone, whereas God had created the ancestors of other human groups earlier and on different continents, thereby implying in modern terminology that these groups were not simply separate races but separate species.

Although church authorities compelled La Peyrère to retract his thesis, his ideas continued to be debated. Beginning in the late seventeenth century, scholars such as François Bernier (1620–1688), Carolus Linnaeus (1707–1778), and Johann Blumenbach (1752–1840) assigned the peoples of the world to major racial divisions to which they attributed significant differences in behavior as well as physical appearance. Little distinction was drawn between what would now be considered as innate and learned behavior in these classifications. Polygenists identified these groups as separately created species. In 1774, Edward Long (1734–1813), who had worked in the West Indies, argued that Europeans and Africans were separate species and in 1799 Charles White (1728–1813) proclaimed that Europeans, Asians, American Indians, black Africans, and Hottentots constituted a graded sequence of increasingly primitive human groups.

In the United States, the Philadelphia physician Samuel Morton (1799–1851) suggested in his *Crania Americana* (1839) that the American Indian constituted a homogeneous type that providence had created in the New World. In his *Crania Aegyptiaca*, published five years later, he argued that Egyptian skulls and depictions of ethnic groups on Egyptian monuments revealed that human types had not changed in that part of the world for forty-five hundred years; almost as far back as the biblically recorded creation of the earth (Morton 1844). Although Morton initially believed that God had differentiated the races after he had created a common humanity, by 1849 he was advocating divine polygenesis, a position that was endorsed by the influential Swiss-American naturalist Louis Agassiz (1807–1873) and popularized by the Alabama physician Josiah C. Nott (1804–1873) and the amateur Egyptologist George R. Gliddon (1809–1857) in their book *Types of Mankind* (1854). Yet, in the United States, polygenism was generally repudiated by pious Christians, who were offended by its rejection of orthodox interpretations of the Bible. Even among devout slave owners in the southeastern United States, Nott and Gliddon were not popular, despite their alleged proof that negroes were inferior to whites (Stanton 1960: 161–73).

Nevertheless, racist ideas spread. Even the leading British monogenist James Cowles Prichard (1786–1848), who argued that all human beings had differentiated from a single ancestral stock as the result of a process of self-domestication, maintained in the first edition of his *Researches into the Physical History of Man* (1813) that the more civilized peoples became the more they physically resembled Europeans. Although the most primitive groups had black skins, more civilized ones had become progressively lighter (pp. 174–242; Bowler 1992).

Belief in the inequality of races gained in scientific stature as a result of Darwinian evolutionism. In their desire to make credible the evolutionary origins of the human species, Darwin and many of his supporters argued that human groups varied in their biological evolutionary status from highly evolved to ones that were only slightly superior to the most evolved apes. Darwin believed that less civilized peoples were less developed intellectually and emotionally than were Europeans; hence, his estimation of human biological development corresponded with the conventional scale of cultural evolution. In 1863, Thomas Huxley noted similarities between two Neanderthal skulls and those of modern Australian Aborigines, which consisted mainly of both having large brow ridges, and argued on this basis that they must have been culturally similar (Huxley [1863] 1896). Culturally advanced societies were viewed as ones in which the operation of natural selection had produced individuals who possessed superior intelligence and greater self-control.

Alfred Wallace (1823–1913), the codiscoverer of natural selection, had as a naturalist lived for long periods of time among tribal groups in South America and Southeast Asia. On the basis of his personal knowledge of these groups, he denied that these peoples differed significantly from Europeans in their intelligence or other innate abilities and maintained that humanity's higher mental capacities, which so greatly exceeded those of any other animal, could not have been produced by natural selection. Darwin deplored these observations as lack of support for their joint theory of evolution (Eiseley 1958). To those who were predisposed to believe in racial inequality, Darwin's concept of natural selection offered a far more convincing explanation of how biological inequalities had developed among human groups than polygenism had done. Although Darwin vehemently opposed the mistreatment and exploitation of non-Western peoples, his theorizing about human evolution gave an unprecedented measure of scientific respectability to racial interpretations of human behavior. These interpretations provided a biological counterpart to romantic nationalism in challenging and ultimately superseding a belief in psychic unity.

Lubbock's Synthesis

A Darwinian view of human nature was incorporated into prehistoric archaeology by the versatile John Lubbock (1834–1913), who later became Lord Avebury, with his book *Pre-historic Times, as Illustrated by Ancient Remains, and the Manners and Customs of Modern Savages*. Between 1865 and 1913, this book went through seven editions both in England and the United States, and it long served as a textbook of archaeology. It was the most influential work dealing with archaeology published during the nineteenth century. A second book, *The Origin of Civilisation and the Primitive Condition of Man* (1870), also went through several editions. It expounded Lubbock's ideas in a more extreme fashion and with less emphasis on archaeological data. Lubbock grew up as a neighbor of Charles Darwin, whose property bordered on the Lubbock family's estate in Kent. At the age of twenty-two, he became a partner in his father's bank and later in life, as a member of Parliament, he secured passage of an act to provide protection for some ancient monuments (1882) (T. Murray 1989). His research as a naturalist established him as a leading authority on animal behavior. It was as an early supporter of Darwin's theory of evolution that he began to study prehistoric archaeology (Figure 5.1).

At first glance, *Prehistoric Times* (to adopt the spelling of later editions) appears to be a curious compilation of disparate material. A first section, comprising more than half the book, presents a series of chapters dealing in roughly chronological order with archaeological topics: the use of bronze in ancient times, the Bronze Age, the use of stone, megaliths and tumuli, lake-dwellings, kitchen middens, North American archaeology, Quaternary mammals, "primeval man," Pleistocene deposits, and the antiquity of human beings. Lubbock then argued that just as modern elephants provide information about the anatomy of extinct mammoths, so modern primitive societies shed light on the behavior of prehistoric human beings. This observation is followed by a series of sketches of the ways of life of modern tribal societies: Hottentots, Veddahs, Andaman Islanders, Australian Aborigines, Tasmanians,

Figure 5.1 John Lubbock (Lord Avebury) (1834–1913)
(Radio Times Hulton Picture Library)

Fijians, Maoris, Tahitians, Tongans, Eskimos, North American Indians, Paraguayans, Patagonians, and Fuegans. The ordering of these
chapters is clearly geographical rather than evolutionary and no
attempt was made to indicate what particular modern groups provided evidence about specific stages of prehistoric development. The
only common features studied by both archaeologists and ethnologists, and hence the sole basis for justifying broad comparisons of
this sort, would have been similarities in material culture. Among the
few specific parallels of this sort that Lubbock noted was the long-
standing Scandinavian claim that Inuit stone tools were very similar
to those of the European Upper Palaeolithic. He also drew a parallel
between the Fuegans and the people who had produced the Danish
kitchen middens, although he observed that the prehistoric Danes
excelled the Fuegans because they manufactured pottery.

Although nineteenth-century ethnologists often left material culture poorly described, collections of objects from around the world
were available for study in many European museums. Lubbock's failure to present a detailed comparison of stone tools from Fuegan and

Danish kitchen-midden sites or to identify modern cultures manufacturing Chellean handaxes or Levallois cores before using ethnographic comparisons to reconstruct Chellean and Mousterian ways
of life suggests that he was at least to some extent aware that parallels
of this sort in material culture were exceedingly rare. His observation that there was no clear evidence that humanity had invented
specific types of tools in precisely the same order everywhere and
his affirmation that environmental factors clearly had produced differences in "kind" as well as "degree" among human groups were
ways to explain the lack of specific correlations between ethnographic
evidence and the western European archaeological sequence. Yet
Lubbock remained deeply committed to the idea of unilinear cultural evolution. The parallel that he drew between, on the one
hand, Cuvier's reconstruction of extinct species of animals using
living species as analogues and, on the other, his own analogies
between "primitive" peoples and "prehistoric" ones was an attempt
to enhance the scientific respectability of his cultural comparisons.
Neither this comparison nor his caveats concerning the limitations
of a unilinear approach were new.

What was new was Lubbock's Darwinian insistence that, as a result
of natural selection, human groups had become different from each
other not only culturally but also in their biological capacities to
utilize culture. Lubbock viewed modern Europeans as products of
intensive cultural and biological evolution. He believed that technologically less advanced peoples were not only culturally but also
intellectually and emotionally more primitive from a biological point
of view than were civilized ones. He also maintained that, as a result of
the differential operation of natural selection within European societies, the criminally inclined and the lower classes were biologically
inferior to the more successful middle and upper classes. He further
contended that, because women had been protected and cared for
by men throughout history, they had remained biologically inferior
to men in terms of intellectual capacity and emotional self-control.
Thus, his male, middle-class readers did not have to journey to distant lands to observe less evolved types of human beings. Examples
of such people were present in their own communities and even in
their own families. At a time when the genetic mechanisms of biological inheritance remained unknown, the Darwinian concept of natural selection could inspire the creation of a single explanation that

sought to account for and justify the nineteenth-century European class system, gender discrimination, and colonialism.

The widespread support for such ideas among the middle classes suggests that, having achieved political power, middle-class European males had become anxious to regard their exalted status not as a passing phase in human history but as a reflection of their own biological superiority. The Industrial Revolution had terminated the domination of society by the physically strong and martially inclined, as in the feudal period, and provided an opportunity for intelligent and prudent males to rise to the top of society. The new elite wanted to believe that no one was biologically able to challenge their dominance.

Like other late-nineteenth-century evolutionists, Lubbock opposed the idea that cultural degeneration had played a significant role in human history. He consistently described degenerationism as an old-fashioned and discredited doctrine. He also sought to counter the romantic followers of Jean-Jacques Rousseau, who maintained that the development of civilization had resulted in a decrease of human happiness. In order to reinforce an evolutionary perspective, Lubbock consistently sought to portray "primitive" peoples as few in number, wretched, and morally depraved by comparison with civilized ones. He described modern tribal peoples as being unable to control the natural world and having intellects resembling those of European children. Their languages were alleged to lack abstract words and they were claimed to be incapable of understanding abstract concepts. They also were said to be slaves to their passions, being unable to control anger or to follow a predetermined course of action for more than a short time. He maintained that they were more deficient in moral sense than was generally believed and took pains to document how specific primitive groups regularly mistreated children, murdered aged parents, practiced human sacrifice, and ate human flesh. To draw attention to their lack of the most basic middle-class virtues, he also consistently emphasized their alleged dirtiness. He further argued that cultural development inevitably resulted in an increasing population; whereas, left to their own devices, primitive peoples remained static or declined in numbers. Cultural evolution also expanded human consciousness and led to growing material prosperity and spiritual progress.

Lubbock maintained that cultural evolution would continue indefinitely, creating a future marked by ever greater technological and moral improvement and by increasing human happiness and comfort. *Pre-historic Times* ended with a rousing expression of this evolutionary credo:

> Even in our own time, we may hope to see some improvement; but the unselfish mind will find its highest gratification in the belief that, whatever may be the case with ourselves, our descendants will understand many things which are hidden from us now, will better appreciate the beautiful world in which we live, avoid much of that suffering to which we are subject, enjoy many blessings of which we are not yet worthy, and escape many of those temptations which we deplore, but cannot wholly resist.   (Lubbock 1869: 591)

The growth of a capitalist industrial economy, in conjunction with the operation of natural selection on human beings, was clearly seen as leading to an earthly paradise. By offering evidence that such progress was the continuation of what had been occurring ever more rapidly throughout human history, prehistoric archaeology bolstered the self-confidence of the middle classes and confirmed the crucial role they were playing in world history.

Yet not all human groups were believed to be destined to share in this happiness. The most primitive peoples were doomed to vanish as a result of the spread of civilization, as no amount of education could compensate for the thousands of years during which natural selection had failed to adapt them biologically to a more complex and orderly way of life. Nor was their replacement by more evolved peoples to be seriously regretted, as this process was believed to result in an overall improvement of the human race. By applying Darwinian principles, Lubbock came to the same conclusion about the unbridgeable biological differences between Europeans and indigenous peoples that American amateur anthropologists and historians had evolved in the late eighteenth and early nineteenth centuries. His views of such peoples justified British colonization and the establishment of political and economic control abroad on the grounds that such policies promoted the general progress of the human species. He also absolved British and American settlers of much of the moral responsibility for the rapid decline of indigenous peoples in North America, Australia, and the Pacific. These populations were vanishing not because of what colonists were doing to them but rather because, over thousands of years, natural selection had not equipped them to survive as civilization spread. Lubbock was not thinking of their lack of resistance to many communicable diseases introduced by Europeans, about which there was as yet little scientific awareness, but of what he believed was their biological inability to cope with a more complex and demanding way of life. Thus, the imposition of inferior roles on indigenous groups was made to appear less a political act than a natural consequence of their limited innate abilities. Whether dealing with the working classes in Britain or with indigenous peoples abroad, social Darwinism transferred human inequality from the political to the natural realm by explaining it as a consequence of biological differences that could be altered only very slowly, if at all.

This view marked a major break with the ideals of the Enlightenment. The bourgeoisie of eighteenth-century France, wanting more political power and seeking to rally as much support as possible for their cause, had expressed their hopes for the future in terms of a belief in progress in which all human beings could participate. In contrast, the middle classes that dominated Britain in the mid-nineteenth century were increasingly concerned to defend their political and economic gains and did so by trying to assign natural limits to who could reasonably hope to benefit from progress. Beginning in the 1860s, Darwinian evolutionism performed this function admirably. Through Lubbock's version of cultural evolution, prehistory was linked to a doctrine of European biological as well as cultural preeminence.

Although Lubbock's synthesis was clearly a product of Victorian England, there was nothing narrowly chauvinistic about it. Arguments about superiority were formulated in terms of a contrast between European civilization and technologically less developed societies. These arguments sought to explain the expanding world system that was dominated by western Europe. At that time, Britain's political and economic hegemony was so great, compared to the power of any other European nation, that it did not require ideological reinforcement. Hence Lubbock took his own country's leadership for granted. Because of that, the ideas he promoted had appeal far beyond Britain and influenced the interpretation of archaeological data in many parts of the world.

Colonial Archaeology in the United States

Lubbock's writings played a significant role in reinforcing and shaping the development of American evolutionary archaeology in the late nineteenth century, even though not all American archaeologists accepted the relevance of Darwinian concepts for understanding human affairs (Meltzer 1983: 13). Euro-American anthropologists had no difficulty, however, in applying an evolutionary perspective to their own society. The Enlightenment concepts of reason and progress that had played an important role in the American Revolution, and the economic and territorial expansion of the United States throughout the nineteenth century, sustained a belief that progress was inherent in the human condition. In works such as Lewis Henry Morgan's (1818–1881) *Ancient Society* (1877) and Otis Mason's (1838–1908) *The Origins of Invention* (1895), anthropologists traced the overall development of culture from a perspective that placed Euro-American society at the forefront of human advancement. Lubbock provided Americans with a Darwinian explanation for the biological inferiority that they had attributed to American Indians since the late eighteenth century. Many found his explanation more persuasive than any previous one, no doubt partly as a result of the great prestige that many leading biologists accorded to Darwin's work. The declining numbers of indigenous people and their lessening ability to withstand Euro-American expansion also encouraged a growing belief that they were doomed to extinction, which accorded with Lubbock's views. As a result of their belief in the incapacity of indigenous societies to change, most North American archaeologists continued to stress the changeless quality of the archaeological record and tried hard to attribute changes to processes other than creativity in indigenous cultures.

What was known about the archaeology of Mexico, Central America, and Peru constituted a challenge to this view. Some writers, including those who identified the indigenous peoples of Mexico with the Moundbuilders, regarded them as racially superior to the North American Indians. J. L. Stephens's discovery of the ruins of Maya cities in Mexico and Central America was welcomed as proof that the New World had developed its own civilizations by American scholars who were anxious to refute the claims advanced by eighteenth-century European naturalists and historians, including Georges-Louis Leclerc, comte de Buffon, Guillaume-Thomas Raynal, and William Robertson, that the climate of the New World was conducive to the degeneration of plant, animal, and human life (Haven 1856: 94). William H. Prescott's celebrated *History of the Conquest of Mexico* (1843) and his later *History of the Conquest of Peru* (1847) portrayed the Aztecs and Inkas as civilized peoples, although he maintained that, as a result of their superstitions and aggressiveness, by the sixteenth century the Aztecs were destroying the accomplishments of their more civilized predecessors. The ethnologist Albert Gallatin (1761–1849) defended Enlightenment views concerning cultural evolution and strongly opposed polygenesis, but by the 1840s his arguments appeared old-fashioned and unconvincing (Bieder 1975). Nevertheless, E. G. Squier continued to defend both unilinear evolutionism and psychic unity (Bieder 1986: 104–45).

In 1862 Daniel Wilson, who was now teaching at University College in Toronto, published the first edition of *Prehistoric Man: Researches into the Origin of Civilisation in the Old and the New World*. This book was a remarkable synthesis of all that was known about the anthropology of the Americas. Wilson, as a product of the Edinburgh Enlightenment, continued, like Gallatin, to resist racial interpretations of human behavior. He concluded, based on his demonstration of their cranial diversity, that aboriginal peoples had reached the Americas from many directions, but he argued that in the course of settling there they had lost all the advanced knowledge they possessed and reverted to a Stone Age level of existence. The agricultural societies and prehistoric civilizations of the New World had thus evolved locally. Wilson believed that, given enough time, North American Indian tribes living in the temperate zone, such as the Iroquois and the Micmacs, could have created cultures as advanced as those of western Europeans. In 1862 Wilson was still a creationist and accepted the traditional biblical chronology. Only in a later edition of *Prehistoric Man* (1876) did he embrace biological evolution, while continuing to reject ideas of racial inequality.

In the United States, any position that ascribed creativity to indigenous people encountered much resistance. The war between the United States and Mexico that ended in 1848 incited a flood of anti-Mexican feeling. The Mexicans were generally agreed to be inferior to Euro-Americans because Spanish settlers had interbred extensively with the indigenous population (Horsman 1975). Lewis Henry Morgan, doggedly ignoring archaeological evidence, maintained that, in the sixteenth century, Spanish writers had exaggerated the sophistication of the Aztecs and Inkas in order to magnify their own accomplishments in conquering them. He argued that the ways of life of these supposedly civilized peoples had differed little from that of the Iroquois of New York State in the seventeenth century and that no indigenous group anywhere in the New World had ever evolved beyond the level of a tribal society. Although Morgan (1881) published a comparative study of the indigenous architecture of the New World, he continued to equate Mesoamerican stone buildings with Iroquois longhouses. He did not rule out the possibility that on their own indigenous Americans eventually might have evolved more complex cultures, but he believed that cultural advancement depended on an increase in brain size that could occur only very slowly (Bieder 1986: 194–246). This position was long embraced by many Euro-Americans, who saw little to admire among the indigenous peoples of the United States. There was widespread support by the 1860s for the view that the surviving indigenous peoples of the entire hemisphere were biologically primitive and that their cultures had remained static throughout prehistoric times.

It has been suggested that the lack of concern with chronology in North American archaeology before the twentieth century resulted from three causes: the failure of any indigenous group to advance beyond the Stone Age, a dearth of stratified sites, and lack of familiarity with techniques for deriving chronology in the absence of major technological changes (Willey and Sabloff 1993: 39–64). These factors do not, however, agree with the evidence. The low frequency of stratified post-Palaeolithic sites among those known in northern and western Europe during the nineteenth century did not inhibit the use of simple forms of seriation to construct detailed chronologies in those regions (Childe 1932: 207). All the chronological methods used in Europe were known in America and had been successfully applied by archaeologists in situations in which they sought to emulate European research. Beginning at least by the 1860s, shell mounds were studied both seriationally and stratigraphically, and in this way local cultural chronologies were constructed that were characterized by changing pottery styles or adaptive patterns. Such observations were made by Jeffries Wyman (1875), S. T. Walker (1883), and Clarence B. Moore (1892) in the southeastern United States; William Dall (1877) in Alaska; and the visiting German archaeologist Max Uhle (1907) in California. Stratigraphic methods also were employed in mound studies by Squier and Davis in the 1840s and by Cyrus Thomas in the 1880s, as well as by W. H. Holmes and F. W. Putnam in their "Palaeolithic" research in the 1880s (Meltzer 1983: 39). R. L. Lyman, M. J. O'Brien, and R. Dunnell (1997a: 23–8) have demonstrated that stratigraphic techniques were being employed at archaeological sites across the United States in the late nineteenth century, even if not all these sites were being excavated layer by layer (Browman and Givens 1996).

The evidence of local cultural change that these early archaeologists adduced was rejected or dismissed as being of trivial significance by most contemporary archaeologists, including sometimes by those who employed these methods (C. Thomas 1898: 29–34). Discussing Max Uhle's demonstration of evidence for "the gradual elaboration and refinement of technical processes" within the Emeryville shell mound in California, A. L. Kroeber (1909: 16) observed that the indigenous cultures found in that region in historical times had been so primitive as to rule out any possibility that there could have been significant cultural development among them in the past. Similar doubts that evidence of any significant change was being found in the archaeological record continued to be expressed by other ethnologists (Dixon 1913; Wissler 1914). Mainly because of the scarcity and mobility of research personnel, local archaeological studies also did not necessarily display continuous cumulative development at this time. The most insightful and productive research in any one region was not necessarily the most recent (Trigger 1986a).

In accordance with the belief that change had been minimal in prehistoric times, the systematic study of cultural variation in the archaeological record was oriented primarily toward defining geographical rather than chronological patterns. This paralleled the tendency of American ethnologists late in the nineteenth century to organize the study of cultural similarities and differences in terms of cultural areas. In 1887 the German-born and -educated ethnologist Franz Boas (1858–1942) had argued that the ethnological material from across the United States that was accumulating in major museums should be exhibited according to geographical areas and tribes rather than in terms of a hypothetical evolutionary sequence or typological categories applicable to the entire continent. In advocating this display technique, Boas was following the standard German museological practice of that period (Zimmerman 2001). Otis Mason published the first detailed ethnographical treatment of the cultural areas of North America in 1896 and was followed in this approach by Clark Wissler (1914).

Archaeologists had long been aware of geographical variations in the distributions of certain classes of archaeological data, such as the different types of mounds attributed to the Moundbuilders. Cyrus Thomas (1825–1910), an entomologist who worked as an archaeologist for the Bureau of American Ethnology, subdivided these mounds into eight geographical units, which he suggested represented more than one nation or group of tribes, some of which had survived into historical times (1894). Later, in his *Introduction to the Study of North American Archaeology* (1898), he divided all of North America into three major cultural zones: Arctic, Atlantic, and Pacific, with the latter subdivided into several districts. J. D. McGuire (1842–1916) examined the distribution of different types of Indian pipes in terms of fifteen geographical divisions (1899) and W. H. Holmes (1846–1933), who had been trained as an artist, used stylistic analyses as well as technological criteria to define a series of pottery regions for the eastern United States (1903). In 1914, he divided the whole of North America into twenty-six general "cultural characterization areas" on the basis of archaeological data, in a manner that paralleled the procedures being followed by ethnologists (Figure 5.2). Little effort was made to assign relative chronological significance to different units or to trace chronological changes within them.

Cultural areas frequently tended to correspond with major natural ecological zones. Today, many of the features shared by cultures located in the same ecological zone would be interpreted as skillful adaptations by indigenous peoples to the environments in which they lived. In the nineteenth century, they were instead regarded as evidence of the domination of indigenous peoples by natural forces. It was generally believed that soon after Indians first arrived in various regions of the New World their cultures had been reshaped by environmental demands and, once they were adjusted to these forces, they tended to remain the same. Such a passive adaptation of Native Americans to their environmental settings was contrasted with the ability of prehistoric Europeans to create new tool technologies

Figure 5.2 "Cultural characterization areas" of North America, based on
archaeological criteria, by Holmes (*American Anthropologist*, 1914)

that allowed them to impose their will on the environment and
transform it.

Thus, evidence of later change in the archaeological record was
generally interpreted as resulting from movements of people rather
than from alterations within individual cultures. For example, the
change from what would now be called Archaic to Middle Woodland
cultures in upper New York State was attributed to the northward
movement of an original Inuit-like population that was replaced by

Algonquian-speakers. These in turn were pushed farther north and east by Iroquoian-speaking peoples carrying yet another distinctive cultural pattern northward from the Mississippi Valley. That pattern included incised pottery and an agricultural subsistence economy that in general was thought to resemble more closely the ways of life found in the southeastern United States than it did earlier cultures in its historical homeland (Beauchamp 1900; Parker 1916, 1920). The elaborate prehistoric Pueblo sites found in the southwestern United States were similarly assumed to have been built by Mesoamericans who had migrated north and because of that some of them were assigned fanciful names, such as Aztec Ruins and Montezuma Castle. The ethnologist R. B. Dixon (1913) interpreted the complexity of the archaeological record, which by that time was becoming evident to archaeologists in eastern North America, as a "palimpsest" resulting from repeated shifts of population in prehistoric times. These shifts were viewed as largely random movements that characterized aboriginal life on a large and thinly populated continent.

It also was agreed, however, that, where there had been no major shifts in population, ethnographic data concerning tribes that had lived in a region in historical times could be used relatively straightforwardly to explain prehistoric archaeological data. Cyrus Thomas (1898: 23) argued that once America had been settled by indigenous peoples they had tended to remain in the same place; hence, the archaeological record had mainly been produced by the same people who had lived in particular regions in historical times. He even suggested that such stability might be assumed unless there was clear evidence to the contrary. Archaeologists such as Frank Cushing (1857–1900) and J. W. Fewkes (1850–1930), in their studies of the Pueblo Indians, paid much attention to determining by means of careful ethnographic parallels for what purposes prehistoric artifacts had been used and how they had been made (Cushing 1886; Fewkes 1896). It was generally assumed that there were no significant differences between life in prehistoric pueblos and in modern ones. Hence, efforts to learn about the past brought archaeologists into close contact with ethnologists and often with indigenous people. In regions where indigenous people were no longer living in a traditional manner, archaeologists tried to learn how prehistoric artifacts had been made and used by consulting early European historical records about local Indian cultures as well as by replicative experiments and studying only partly finished artifacts. The studies based on local ethnographic or historical data demonstrate increasing use of the direct historical approach to interpret archaeological data (I. Brown 1993; Lyman and O'Brien 2001). Although W. H. Holmes and other archaeologists working with him have been credited with first systematically applying this approach (Meltzer 1999: 183), its earlier employment by William Bartram and by many European archaeologists suggests that it was a method that was invented many times. Only Edgar Lee Hewett (1865–1946) expressed significant reservations about its relevance (1906: 12).

The anthropologists employed by the Bureau of Ethnology (renamed the Bureau of American Ethnology in 1894) favored this "flat" view of aboriginal history because it organically united the study of ethnology and prehistoric archaeology as closely related branches of anthropology. Founded as an arm of the Smithsonian Institution in 1879, the Bureau grew under the leadership of its director, the renowned geologist and explorer John Wesley Powell (1834–1902), into the leading center of anthropological research in North America. Established to study ethnographic and linguistic problems in order to promote the more effective administration of Indian affairs, it also laid "the empirical foundations of archaeology in the United States...on a broad geographical scale" (Hallowell 1960: 84). Although the "flat" past was advocated as a self-evident means for understanding archaeological data, the application of this approach required the assumption that life in prehistoric times was not qualitatively distinct from that recorded soon after European contact. Long before the founding of the Bureau of American Ethnology, Samuel Haven (1864: 37) had observed that "The flint utensils of the Age of Stone lie upon the surface of the ground.... The people that made and used them have not yet entirely disappeared." This denial of cultural change, to no less a degree than the extreme unilinear evolutionism of European archaeologists, subordinated archaeological to ethnological research by implying that nothing could be learned from archaeological data that could not be ascertained more easily ethnographically. Although unifying anthropology, the "flat" view subordinated archaeology as a discipline to ethnology and reinforced negative stereotypes about indigenous peoples. As Meltzer (1983: 40) observed, this view was "a predictable consequence of the government approach to archaeological research [which was] grounded in a subliminal and denigrating stereotype of the Native American."

In order to validate their program, the anthropologists at the Bureau of American Ethnology sought to discredit those aspects of prehistory that could not be studied by means of the direct historical approach (Meltzer 1983). The most influential of these anomalies was the idea of the lost Moundbuilder race. Because of great public interest, the United States Congress had insisted that the Bureau should spend the then large sum of $5,000 each year on mound studies. In 1882 Powell selected Cyrus Thomas to direct this research. Thomas began an extensive program of survey and excavation which led him to conclude that many mounds had been constructed after earliest European contact and, largely on the basis of the direct historical approach (O'Brien and Lyman 1999b), that all of them had been built by the ancestors of modern Native Americans (Thomas 1894). He also sought to demonstrate that the cultures of the Indians who had built the mounds were not more advanced than those of Indian groups who had lived in the eastern United States in the seventeenth and eighteenth centuries.

Thus, the refutation of the Moundbuilder myth involved not only the rejection of inflated claims that had been made about their way of life (such as that they had worked iron) but also undervaluing many of the genuine accomplishments of the various Indian groups that had built the mounds. It appears that at this time archaeologists had either to credit the Moundbuilders with possessing an advanced culture and deny that they were Indians or to accept them as Indians and deny that their culture had been more advanced than those of any Indian groups living north of Mexico in historical times. No archaeologist in the late nineteenth century seems to have been prepared to believe that in prehistoric times indigenous North Americans might have evolved cultures that were more complex than those observed in the seventeenth century, when most Indian groups had already been severely reduced by epidemics of European diseases and many also had been shattered and dislocated by European aggression and by intertribal warfare arising as a result of European settlement. Under these circumstances, it is scarcely surprising that the demolition of the Moundbuilder myth "did nothing to change the prevailing popular attitudes against the Native American" (Willey and Sabloff 1993: 48).

The archaeologists at the Bureau of American Ethnology also adopted a very sceptical attitude toward claims that there existed in North America evidence of human antiquity to rival the Palaeolithic assemblages of Europe. The most significant of these assertions was based on excavations that Charles C. Abbott (1843–1919), a physician by training, carried out in gravel deposits on his ancestral farm near Trenton, New Jersey. By 1877, he was convinced that these finds had been produced not by the recently arrived ancestors of modern indigenous Americans but by inhabitants of the region during the glacial period who were probably not related to the American Indians. Abbott thought it possible that there might have been a long period between the Palaeolithic settlers and the arrival of the first Indians, during which North America was again uninhabited by human beings, although he later suggested that this earlier "race" might have been ancestral to the Inuit (Abbott 1881). For a time, his research enjoyed the limited support and patronage of Frederic W. Putnam (1839–1915), who had been trained as an ichthyologist but since 1874 had been the curator of the Peabody Museum of American Archaeology and Ethnology at Harvard University. Meanwhile, scientists in other parts of the United States began to discover similar "Palaeolithic" tools, sometimes in geological contexts suggesting great antiquity. Holmes and Thomas led the attack on these claims on behalf of the Smithsonian Institution. Their careful research demonstrated that the so-called Palaeolithic tools closely resembled quarry refuse marking the early stages in the manufacture of implements by more recent American Indians. Doubt also was cast on the geological contexts in which so-called Palaeolithic finds were being made.

Later, Aleš Hrdlička (1869–1943), a Czech physical anthropologist who was brought to the United States National Museum in 1903, investigated what was known about all the skeletal material that had been claimed as evidence of "Early Man" and demonstrated that there was no clear evidence that any of it dated prior to the post-glacial period. Although these onslaughts led archaeologists and geologists to abandon the idea of a strictly Palaeolithic age in North America, they did not exclude the possibility that human beings had lived in the New World for many thousands of years. They did, however, indicate the need for more rigorous evidence to prove this had actually happened. It is clear that in this case scientists employed by the federal government were using their power and prestige not only to put archaeology on "a really scientific basis" but also to promote an understanding of the past that accorded with their personal view of how archaeology and ethnology fitted together as branches of anthropology (Meltzer 1983).

Archaeologists were prepared to acknowledge that a limited amount of innovation had occurred in prehistoric times. Warren K. Moorehead (1866–1939) even believed that some progress was likely because "the Indian brain is finer than the Australian or African brain" (1910, vol. 1: 331). There was, however, a tendency, when clear chronological indications to the contrary were lacking, to interpret high-quality artifacts, such as stone effigy pipes or elaborately decorated stone and metal ornaments, as reflecting European influence, in the form of iron carving tools and artistic inspiration. J. D. McGuire (1899) argued that all but the simplest Iroquoian pipes were based on European models, although archaeologists working in the lower Great Lakes region were able to demonstrate that many of the elaborate pipes dated before European contact (Boyle 1904: 27–9). The implication of McGuire's interpretation was that indigenous cultures had been even simpler, and hence more primitive, than the archaeological remains of the past, if viewed uncritically, might suggest.

The period between 1860 and 1910 witnessed the growing professionalization of archaeology in the United States. Full-time positions became available for prehistoric archaeologists in major museums in the larger cities and later teaching positions were established in universities, beginning with Putnam's appointment as Peabody Professor of American Archaeology and Ethnology at Harvard in 1887. The first doctorate in prehistoric archaeology in the United States was granted at Harvard in 1894 (Hinsley 1985: 72, 1999; Conn 1998). Euro-Americans expressed their sense of their own ethnic superiority by locating collections of indigenous American archaeological and ethnological material in museums of natural history rather than together with European and Middle Eastern antiquities in museums of fine art and by teaching prehistory in departments of anthropology rather than of history. Despite the pleas of anthropologists such as John W. Powell and Lewis H. Morgan that "humble Indian antiquities" should not be allowed to perish, it was generally more difficult to secure the support of wealthy patrons for research on North

Figure 5.3 Drawing of the Great Serpent Mound of Ohio, from a popular
article by Putnam (*Century Illustrated Magazine*, 1890)

American Indian prehistory than for collecting classical antiquities
from Europe, which it was argued would "increase the standard of
our civilization and culture" (Hinsley 1985: 55).

Despite these problems, much new information was collected,
new standards of research were established, and the first steps were
taken to preserve major prehistoric monuments, such as the Great
Serpent Mound in Ohio (Figure 5.3) and Casa Grande in Arizona.
The Smithsonian Institution and the Bureau of American Ethnology played a major role in providing leadership to archaeology. This
sometimes involved directing their prestige and resources against
amateurs, who bitterly resented interference in their activities by professional scientists employed by the federal government (McKusick
1970, 1991). Although Putnam, who was employed by a university, encouraged valuable archaeological research in the Ohio Valley
and the use of systematic excavation techniques, his work did little
to promote a clearer understanding of North American prehistory
(Browman 2002). It is possible that the interest he had in chronology was discouraged by the widespread rejection of the evidence for
an American Palaeolithic period, which he had supported.

Despite the progress that was made, there was no change in the
view of Indians that had prevailed in archaeology, and American
society generally, since the late eighteenth century. On the contrary,
the belief that Indian societies were fossilized entities, incapable of
progress and therefore doomed to extinction was reinforced as a

result of being rationalized in terms of Darwinian evolution and seen to accord with the universal perspective on human evolution that had been popularized by John Lubbock. The view of American Indians as inherently primitive and static was now shared not only by vast numbers of Euro-Americans at all social levels but also by an international scientific community that was increasingly receptive to racist explanations of human behavior. Without making any significant changes, the traditional view that Euro-American archaeologists had held of American prehistory could be identified as congruent with that part of Lubbock's evolutionary archaeology that applied to colonial situations.

Australian Prehistory

Developments in American archaeology foreshadowed what was to occur later in other colonial settings. In Australia, studies of Aboriginal customs began with the first European explorers and settlers. By 1850, most of southern Australia was occupied by Europeans and the Aborigines had been driven from their lands or were dead as a result of disease, neglect, and murder (Figure 5.4). As in North America, racial prejudice helped to lessen any sense of guilt that European settlers might have felt about the way they were treating indigenous people.

Beginning in the second half of the nineteenth century, ethnologists in Europe and America encouraged the study of Aborigines as examples of the "most primitive tribes" known to anthropological science. By 1900, major works, such as Baldwin Spencer and F. J. Gillen's *The Native Tribes of Central Australia* (1899), had placed Aboriginal ethnography on an internationally respected basis. Spencer, like his English mentors, was to describe the Aborigines as "a relic of the early childhood of mankind left stranded ... in a low condition of savagery" (Spencer 1901: 12).

Early investigations of Aboriginal prehistory failed to uncover any clear evidence of an association between human beings and prehistoric animals, such as had been found in Europe. Nor did the artifacts discovered in archaeological sites appear to differ significantly from those in recent use. By 1910, naturalists had abandoned the search for evidence of the early presence of aboriginal people in Australia. The assumptions that they had arrived recently and that their cultures

Figure 5.4 "Native police dispersing the blacks," Western Queensland,
ca. 1882 (C. Lumholtz *Among Cannibals*, 1890)

had not changed significantly since that time agreed with the ethnologists' claims that these cultures were extremely primitive and essentially static. From 1910 until the 1950s, most amateur archaeologists collected artifacts "secure in the knowledge that Aborigines were an unchanging people, with an unchanging technology" (Murray and White 1981: 256). Spencer, alleging that Aboriginal culture was characterized by technological opportunism and a lack of concern with formal tool types, attributed variations in the form and function of artifacts to differences in raw material, thereby ignoring the alternative possibilities of change over time, cultural preferences, and functional adaptation (Mulvaney 1981: 63). John Mulvaney (1981: 63–4) has argued that the concept of the "unchanging savage," which was in accord with the popular denigration of Aboriginal culture, inhibited the development of prehistoric archaeology in Australia throughout this period. Significantly, the first archaeology department that was established in Australia, at the University of Sydney in 1948, initially studied only the archaeology of Europe and the Middle East.

Norman Tindale's (1900–1993) excavations, beginning in 1929, at the Devon Downs rock shelter in South Australia of a stratified series of different tool types suggested a longer occupation and called into question the image of a static prehistory. Fred D. McCarthy (1905–1997) made similar discoveries in 1935 at the Lapstone Creek rock shelter in the Blue Mountains of New South Wales. Cultural change was attributed initially, however, to shifting groups replacing one another, some of them recent invaders. In 1938, Norman Tindale linked his sequence to the American physical anthropologist, J. B. Birdsell's, triracial hybrid theory of Australian origins. Tindale also suggested that environmental changes might have occurred during the period of Aboriginal occupation. A systematic concern with cultural change and regional variation did not characterize Australian archaeology until a number of young professional archaeologists began to study Australian prehistory following John Mulvaney's (b. 1925) appointment in the history department at the University of Melbourne in 1953. Most of these archaeologists had been trained at Cambridge University, where Grahame Clark had encouraged them to study prehistory from an ecological perspective. Their research soon made it clear that humans had lived in Australia for at least 40,000 years. Since the 1950s, professional archaeologists have documented numerous changes in environment, adaptation, and nontechnological aspects of Aboriginal culture. Their cultural chronologies also have dispelled the belief that all cultural changes in prehistoric times occurred as a result of external stimuli.

The changing interpretation of archaeological data also reflected a growing concern for a distinctive national identity among white Australians. White artists have drawn inspiration from indigenous art forms and Aboriginal art has been viewed as part of Australia's national heritage to a far greater degree than is the case with indigenous art in North America. Within the context of this growing nationalism, Australian archaeologists were no longer content to treat their country's prehistory as a mirror of the Palaeolithic stage of human development. Instead they began to emphasize the singularities of Australian prehistory, including the considerable degree to which Australian Aborigines managed and altered significant aspects of their environment. The current image of prehistoric Aborigines as "firestick farmers" is far removed from the traditional view of them as Upper Palaeolithic hunter-gatherers (Murray and White 1981; Mulvaney 1981; McBryde 1986; Byrne 1993: 144–5; Griffiths 1996).

It took longer for Australian archaeologists to consider the possibility that their country's prehistory might be more than nineteenth-century ethnology extending back unchanged for fifty millennia and to overcome the accompanying predilection to project the direct historical approach ever further back in time (Murray and White 1981: 258; Mulvaney and White 1987). By the 1980s, however, it was being discussed whether it was legitimate to regard the whole of Australian prehistory as that of the ancestors of the modern Aborigines (White and O'Connell 1982; Flood 1983; T. Murray 1992).

Archaeologists also have been compelled to reassess their goals as a result of the increasing political activities of Aborigines. The federal Labour Party that was elected in 1972 passed legislation granting Aborigines significant membership on decision-making bodies considering matters of concern to them, including the protection of archaeological sites. As a result, archaeologists have come under growing pressure to consider the relevance of their research for indigenous people (Ucko 1983; McBryde 1986; Moser 1995b). The general orientation of modern Australian archaeologists toward a historical rather than an evolutionary view of prehistory, which results from their British training, has made the resolution of these problems in some respects easier than it has been for anthropologically trained North American archaeologists.

Archaeology in New Zealand

In New Zealand, the small and dispersed British settlements that began to be established in the 1840s, in the wake of earlier activities by European missionaries and whalers, were for a long time unable to subdue the indigenous Maori, a Polynesian-speaking people who, especially on the North Island, were numerous and warlike. Armed conflict between the natives and settlers lasted until 1847 and broke out again in the 1860s. Although the Maori were weakened by European diseases, their continuing resistance won them a measure of grudging respect from the European settlers. The Maori remain a dynamic and integral part of New Zealand's cultural mosaic.

No full-time archaeologist was appointed to a university position in New Zealand prior to 1954. Yet, as early as 1843, European settlers had noted stone tools associated with the bones of the giant moa and other extinct species of birds. In the 1870s, Julius von Haast (1822–1887), who was influenced by the writings of Lyell and Lubbock concerning the antiquity of human beings in Europe, argued that the Moa-hunters were a vanished Palaeolithic people, who had subsisted mainly on fish and shellfish and were distinct from the much later Neolithic Maori. He was soon compelled, however, to admit that in terms of their material culture the Moa-hunters were not very different from the Maori (von Haast 1871, 1874).

Hereafter, the main historical research concerned the origins of the Maori. In the course of the nineteenth century, a strong interest developed in their customs, mythology, folklore, and physical anthropology. Much of this research was stimulated by a decline in Maori population and by rapid cultural change, which suggested that soon little of their traditional culture might be available for study. Between 1898 and 1915 S. Percy Smith (1913, 1915) sought to reconcile various tribal accounts of Maori migrations that had been collected in the 1850s, in order to produce an integrated history of their settlement in New Zealand. He concluded that they were Polynesian seafarers who had ultimately originated in India. New Zealand had first been settled by the Maruiwi, an allegedly inferior Melanesian people who were later conquered by the Maori. In 1916, Elsdon Best

(1856–1931) identified the Maruiwi with the South Island Moa-hunters. Some Maori tribes were claimed on the basis of oral traditions to have reached New Zealand around AD 950 and 1150 and these were followed in AD 1350 by a Great Fleet, which carried the groups from which the major tribes are descended. It was generally accepted that the basic pattern of Maori culture had remained the same since that time (Sorrenson 1977).

This scheme of origins was widely accepted by New Zealanders of British and Maori origin, including the Maori anthropologist Peter Buck (Te Rangihiroa, 1877–1951). Peter Gathercole (1981: 163) has drawn attention to the parallels that this account, based on Maori traditional scholarship, drew between the coming of the Maori and the arrival of the Europeans in New Zealand. The Maori were portrayed as being recent colonists in New Zealand, who had seized it from an earlier, culturally less developed people. This suggested that they had little more historical claim to New Zealand than the European settlers had. It also was assumed that ethnology and oral traditions revealed all that needed to be known about Maori prehistory.

In the 1920s, Henry D. Skinner, who had studied anthropology at Cambridge University, began to examine Moa-hunter sites on the South Island. Combining archaeological, ethnographic, physical anthropological, and linguistic data with oral traditions, he sought to demonstrate that the Moa-hunters were Maori, and hence Polynesian, in origin. By debunking the Maruiwi myth, he established the role of the Maori as the "first people of the land" and put archaeology in the forefront of the movement for reenfranchising them (Sutton 1985). Skinner also was sensitive to regional variations in Maori culture, which he interpreted as partly adaptive in nature. In addition, he acknowledged that significant cultural changes had occurred after their arrival in New Zealand.

Yet Skinner's archaeological work lacked any systematic treatment of temporal sequences or cultural change apart from his consideration of the economic impact of the extinction of the moa (Skinner 1921). Like colonialist archaeologists elsewhere, he continued to view archaeology mainly as a way to recover material culture that would complement ethnological collections rather than be an independent source of historical information. He did, however, support the expansion of archaeological research, including the appointment of David

Teviotdale (1932) at the Otago Museum. Teviotdale thus became the first professional archaeologist in New Zealand. Into the 1950s, archaeological research continued to concentrate on the study of the Moa-hunters (Duff 1950), whereas later periods remained understudied (Gathercole 1981). Although oral traditions recounted numerous historical events, New Zealand archaeologists had not yet developed an interest in searching for changes in material culture and styles of life that would have stimulated a comprehensive study of alterations in the archaeological record.

In recent decades, New Zealand archaeology has become increasingly professionalized and developed a more critical and self-conscious relation with Maori ethnology, which has encouraged the study of later prehistory. Much recent work has been done on the North Island, which archaeologists had hitherto ignored, but where most of the Maori population lived and the greatest elaboration of their culture had occurred. This work, which is increasingly involving the Maori themselves, has discovered evidence of dramatic changes in the prehistoric material culture and the economic and social organization of the Maori, which partly reflects climatic changes and regional diversification as Polynesian settlers adapted to living in New Zealand. The Moa-hunters are now interpreted as an episode, possibly a very short one, in the settlement of the South Island. There is increasing archaeological investigation of contacts between New Zealand and neighboring regions of the Pacific, including when and under what conditions people first arrived in New Zealand (H. Allen 2001). New Zealand archaeology provides an example of a colonial situation in which a grudging measure of respect was shown for the indigenous inhabitants. Yet amateur archaeologists there, as elsewhere, viewed indigenous cultures as static and long attributed alterations in the archaeological record to ethnic changes rather than to internal developments. In the course of the twentieth century, a more professional archaeology has played a significant role in dispelling such beliefs.

Racist Archaeology in Africa

Archaeological research was carried out sporadically in sub-Saharan Africa by European visitors beginning in the eighteenth century. According to Brian Fagan, the earliest recorded excavation was by the Swedish naturalist Andrew Sparrman in 1776. He dug into one of a number of stone mounds near the Great Fish River in South Africa. Although he discovered nothing, he concluded that these mounds offered irrefutable proof that a more powerful and numerous population had lived in the area before being "degraded to the present race of Cafres, Hottentots, Boshiesmen, and savages" (Fagan 1981: 42).

In South Africa, the first stone tools were collected by Thomas Bowker in 1858 near the mouth of the Great Fish River. This inspired much local collecting, and by 1905 G. W. Stow had published a speculative but archaeologically informed migrationist prehistory of southern Africa. Systematic archaeological research did not begin in the rest of sub-Saharan Africa before the 1890s, by which time political control of most of the continent had been divided among various European colonial powers. Archaeologists and colonizers both regarded the indigenous cultures of sub-Saharan Africa as a living museum of the human past. There was, however, much more diversity among these cultures than among those of North America, which all could be formally assigned to the Stone Age. In Africa technologies were based on iron as well as stone tools and societies ranged in complexity from tiny hunting bands to large kingdoms. Yet most European scholars agreed that the technological, cultural, and political achievements of African people were less significant than they appeared to be. Many would have concurred with the English traveler Mary Kingsley's (1897: 670) opinion that "the African has never made an even fourteenth-rate piece of cloth or pottery." Yet archaeological discoveries were made that seemed too sophisticated to be the work of people who were as primitive or indolent as Africans were imagined to be (Nederveen Pieterse 1992).

The most spectacular and best studied example of the colonialist mentality at work in African archaeology is provided by the controversies surrounding the stone ruins found in what is now Zimbabwe. Fagan (1981: 43–4) has observed that these controversies constituted an African counterpart to the Moundbuilder debate in North America. Early European investigators of these monuments saw them as proof of prehistoric white colonization in southern Africa.

In the sixteenth century, Portuguese colonists in Mozambique heard reports of stone buildings in the interior. These accounts encouraged European speculation that those buildings had been constructed by King Solomon or the Queen of Sheba in the course of gold-mining activities that were recorded in the Hebrew Bible. The identification of the rumored stone constructions of Zimbabwe with the land of Ophir, mentioned in the Bible, continued to excite the imagination of those who studied the geography of Africa in succeeding centuries. In the late nineteenth century, these speculations greatly appealed to the Afrikaaners, who were newly settled in the Transvaal and whose Calvinist faith led them to welcome the thought that their new homeland bordered on a region that had biblical associations. Information collected in the Transvaal about ruins to the north inspired H. M. Walmsley's *The Ruined Cities of Zululand*, a novel published in 1869. Already in 1868 the German missionary A. Merensky had persuaded the young German geologist Carl Mauch to look for these ruins. In 1871, Mauch became the first European known to have visited the ruins of Great Zimbabwe, which, on the basis of what Merensky had told him, he concluded was the lost palace of the Queen of Sheba.

Speculations of this sort were actively promoted by the businessman Cecil Rhodes after a private army assembled by his British South Africa Company occupied Mashonaland in 1890 and neighboring Matabeleland three years later in order to seize control of those regions' gold resources. Great Zimbabwe soon became a symbol of the justice of European colonization, which was portrayed as the white race returning to a land that it had formerly controlled. The first serious study of Great Zimbabwe was sponsored by the British South Africa Company with the help of the Royal Geographical Society and the British Association for the Advancement of Science. The man chosen for this task was J. Theodore Bent (1852–1897), a Middle Eastern explorer with antiquarian interests. Although his excavations revealed evidence of Bantu occupation containing foreign trade goods no more than a few centuries old, he concluded on the basis of a few architectural and stylistic features that the ruins had been built by "a northern race" that had come to southern Africa from Arabia in biblical times. Supposed astronomical orientations were used to date the stone ruins between 1000 and 2000 BC (Bent 1892) (Figure 5.5).

In 1895, a company called Rhodesia Ancient Ruins Limited was licensed to hunt for gold artifacts in all the archaeological sites with stone buildings in Matabeleland except Great Zimbabwe. This

Figure 5.5 "Approach to the acropolis," from J. T. Bent's *The Ruined Cities of Mashonaland*, 1892

operation, which largely involved robbing graves, was stopped in 1901; after which, in an effort to give his plundering some respectability, one of the prospectors, W. G. Neal, collaborated with Richard Hall (1853–1914), a local journalist, to produce *The Ancient Ruins of Rhodesia* (Hall and Neal 1902). This book presented the first general survey of the ruins of the region. On the strength of this book, the British South Africa Company appointed Hall as Curator of Great Zimbabwe, where he proceeded to remove still more stratified archaeological deposits on the grounds that he was clearing the site of "the filth and decadence of the Kaffir occupation." Later he defined three architectural styles, which he claimed revealed progressive degeneration from the early, finely dressed walls of the elliptical enclosure, and interpreted early Great Zimbabwe as the metropolis of an ancient Phoenician colony (R. Hall 1909). In recent years, careful architectural studies have revealed that the regularly coursed and dressed walls at Zimbabwe are later than short, wavy ones but were followed by walls with uncoursed stones (Garlake 1973: 21–3).

Criticism of Hall's work by professional archaeologists led to his dismissal in 1904, following which the British Association for the Advancement of Science, using funds provided by the Rhodes Trustees, invited David Randall-MacIver (1873–1945), a professional archaeologist who had worked with the distinguished Egyptological archaeologist M. W. F. Petrie, to investigate Great Zimbabwe and other ruins in Rhodesia (1906). More extensive and stratigraphically sophisticated work was carried out under the same auspices by the celebrated British archaeologist Gertrude Caton Thompson (1893–1985) in 1929 (Caton Thompson 1931). These two archaeologists demonstrated conclusively that the ruins were entirely of Bantu origin and dated from the Christian era. Yet, in accordance with the generally low opinion of African cultures, both Randall-MacIver and Caton Thompson offered, as proof of the relatively recent construction of Great Zimbabwe, that it was shoddily constructed, so poorly that in Caton Thompson's opinion it could not have remained standing for several thousand years (H. Kuklick 1991b: 152–3).

Although the conclusions of Randall-MacIver and Caton Thompson were accepted by the world archaeological community, they were unwelcome among the European settlers in Rhodesia and South Africa, where amateur archaeologists kept alive the claim that the ruins of Zimbabwe were the work of invaders, merchants, or metalworkers said to have come from such varied places as the Middle East, India, or Indonesia (Posnansky 1982: 347). In 1909 Hall, supported by subscriptions from a broad cross-section of leading white South Africans, published *Prehistoric Rhodesia*, a massive, polemical work in which he attempted to refute Randall-MacIver's findings. He maintained that the "decadence" of the African, which he attributed to a "sudden arrest of intelligence" that "befalls every member of the Bantu at the time of puberty" (p. 13), is a "process which has been in operation for very many centuries [and] is admitted by all authorities." Thus, as Peter Garlake (1973: 79) has noted, Hall made explicit for the first time the racial biases that had been implicit in excluding Africans from the consideration of Zimbabwe's past. Notions of exotic origin were kept alive after that time by A. J. Bruwer (1965), R. Gayre (1972), Wilfrid Mallows (1985), and Thomas Huffman in an official guidebook to Great Zimbabwe written under the illegal white-settler regime headed by Ian Smith. For the European settlers, who constituted less than 10 percent of the population of Southern Rhodesia, such claims served to disparage African talents and past accomplishments and to justify their own domination of the country. These claims became particularly insistent after those settlers proclaimed Rhodesia to be independent in 1965. In 1971, Peter Garlake, who had been Inspector of Monuments since 1964, resigned in protest over a secret order issued by the settler regime that no official publication should agree that Great Zimbabwe had been built by blacks. By this time, the government was increasingly concerned that the ruins were becoming a powerful symbol of their cultural heritage to local Africans struggling for majority rule. Since the independence of Zimbabwe in 1980, some nationalists have claimed that only Black Africans have the moral right or cultural understanding necessary to interpret the ancient ruins of Zimbabwe and attempts have been made to promote new, and in this case Black African, speculations (Mufuka 1983; Garlake 1973, 1983, 1984).

The comparison of the controversies surrounding the Moundbuilders in North America during the nineteenth century and Zimbabwe beginning in the 1890s reveals striking similarities as well as significant differences. In both cases, amateur archaeologists and public opinion rejected an association of these remains with indigenous peoples in order to avoid having to acknowledge the latter's accomplishments. Similarly, the scientific establishment of the day expressed some reservations about the more fanciful interpretations that were being offered of these monuments. There is also a striking similarity between Caton Thompson's disparaging of the quality of the architecture at Great Zimbabwe after she had proved that it was constructed by Africans and Cyrus Thomas' belittling of the accomplishments of moundbuilding cultures in North America after he had established that these cultures were the creations of North American Indians. What is significantly different, however, is that soon after 1905 the international archaeological community rejected claims that Zimbabwe had not been constructed by Bantus, leaving the maintenance of the Zimbabwe myth to local amateur archaeologists and the general public. By contrast, the Moundbuilder myth had survived for over a century. This suggests that, although the same social pressures to distort the past existed on both continents, by 1905 advances in archaeological techniques for resolving historical questions had reached the point at which these pressures no longer gave free rein to the interpretations of most professional archaeologists. Research carried out in Zimbabwe since the 1950s by locally based professional archaeologists, such as Keith Robinson, R. Summers, and Peter Garlake, has made a distinguished contribution to understanding the history of Zimbabwe during the late Iron Age.

Belief in the biological inferiority of Africans, despite archaeological and ethnographic evidence of major cultural achievements everywhere south of the Sahara, was sustained by ascribing these accomplishments to influences coming from the north. Explorers and missionaries who first encountered sub-Saharan Africa's many complex societies concluded that agriculture, metallurgy, urban life, and various art forms had been introduced from circum-Mediterranean or Middle Eastern civilizations (Fagan 1981: 43; Schrire et al. 1986). The German ethnologist Leo Frobenius interpreted the naturalistic bronze and terracotta heads that he found at Ife, Nigeria, in 1910 as evidence of an early Greek colony along the Atlantic coast of Africa (Willett 1967: 13–14). Miles Burkitt (1890–1971), a lecturer at Cambridge University, saw northern, and frequently specifically European Lower Palaeolithic, Mousterian, and Upper Palaeolithic influences in South African stone-tool assemblages and rock art (Burkitt 1928). His view of southern Africa as a cul-de-sac where older forms of cultures managed to survive was shared by many

Palaeolithic archaeologists during the early twentieth century (Gamble 1992).

In 1880, the German Egyptologist Karl Lepsius suggested that the indigenous peoples of Africa were composed of two major stocks: a lighter-skinned Hamitic population in the north and a Negro population to the south. A large number of ethnologists, including Charles Seligman (1930), identified the Hamites as the "great civilizing force" of sub-Saharan Africa. They sought to account for the more advanced features of sub-Saharan cultures by claiming that culturally more creative Hamitic pastoralists had conquered and imposed the rudiments of a more advanced technology and culture, that were ultimately of Middle Eastern origin, on the culturally "inert" Negro population of Africa until their own creativity was undermined as a result of "miscegenation." This dichotomy between Negroids and Caucasoids, and the accompanying disparagement of African creativity, lingered on in studies of prehistory and ethnology into the 1960s. The role assigned to the prehistoric Hamitic conquerors bore a striking resemblance to the civilizing missions that European colonists had been claiming for themselves since the late nineteenth century (MacGaffey 1966). Such ideas also played an important role in racializing the perception of ethnic differences among indigenous peoples, such as those of Rwanda and Burundi (A. Reid 2003: 73). These historical interpretations were based almost entirely on ethnographic and linguistic, rather than archaeological, data. Until after World War II, no cultural chronologies existed outside of South Africa that might have been used to test the validity of such interpretations of African prehistory. On the contrary, these speculations provided the context for interpreting isolated archaeological finds.

These and similar ideas affected Egyptology, which was significantly influenced by racist beliefs as late as the 1960s. It was commonly maintained that ancient Egyptian civilization was created around 3000 BC, when conquerors from the Middle East, a so-called Dynastic Race, imposed their superior culture on a primitive African population (W. Emery 1961). Likewise, civilization was thought to have been introduced several times to the Sudan by Egyptians or Libyans and then to have decayed as northern contacts became attenuated (Arkell 1961). The cultural status of the Nile Valley south of Egypt at any given period was often correlated directly with the amount of "white" as opposed to "black" blood quotient (genetic material) believed to be present in the population (Reisner 1910, I: 348; Randall-MacIver and Woolley 1909: 2). In these interpretations, Africa was equated with barbarism and civilization with a northern presence. George Reisner (1923a, 1923b) wrongly construed his seriation of the royal cemetery at Kerma as running from complex to simple, rather than from simple to complex, because he believed that Kerma had been established by Egyptian officials and then decayed as these rulers lost contact with their homeland (O'Connor 1993). Although more archaeological research had been done on the development of complex societies in the Sudan than anywhere else in sub-Saharan Africa, that evidence was still being interpreted in accordance with the belief that the ancient Egyptians had been imperial precursors to Europeans (Trigger 1994b; O'Connor and Reid 2003; S. T. Smith 2003).

The Senegalese physicist Cheikh Anta Diop's (1974) writings were a justified protest against such denials of African creativity (M. Bernal 1987). Unfortunately, he had no more archaeological data on which to base his understanding of African prehistory than did those whom he opposed. His identification of the ancient Egyptians as a black African people and the source of African, as well as world, civilization, would later be shown to have grossly underestimated the cultural creativity of peoples living in all parts of Africa.

Another feature of African colonial archaeology was the great attention paid to Palaeolithic studies. In the 1890s, the geologist J. P. Johnson studied the geological contexts of Palaeolithic tools in the Orange Free State and Transvaal. In 1911, Louis Péringuey, the Director of the South African Museum in Cape Town, divided South African prehistory into a Palaeolithic phase, characterized by implements from river gravels, and a later Bushman phase, represented in shell middens and rock shelters (Fagan 1981: 42–3). In the 1920s, A. J. H. Goodwin and Clarence Van Riet Lowe (1929) subdivided the South African Stone Age into Early, Middle, and Late stages that were characterized by Acheulean, Levalloisian, and microlithic tools respectively. At the same time, the Afrikaaner palaeontologist Egbert Van Hoepen (1884–1966) divided the South African Stone Age into a series of cultures that were eventually incorporated (with their names anglicized) into the Goodwin–Van Riet Lowe system (Schlanger 2003). Between 1913 and 1924, remains of fossil hominids were discovered in South Africa tracing human development from

Upper Palaeolithic *Homo sapiens* back to the first identified skull of an Australopithecine.

Stone tools were identified in Kenya as early as 1893, but systematic work did not begin there until 1926, when the Kenyan-born Louis Leakey (1903–1972) organized the first East African Archaeological Expedition from Cambridge University. In *The Stone Age Cultures of Kenya Colony* (1931), Leakey outlined a culture-historical framework for East Africa that continued to be used into the 1950s. Stone-tool assemblages were labeled, as before, with terms used in European Palaeolithic studies, such as Chellean, Acheulean, Mousterian, and Aurignacian. Leakey also worked out a succession of pluvial and inter-pluvial periods that were generally believed to correlate with glacial and interglacial periods in Europe. In due course, it was realized that many finds did not conform to European categories and after the 1920s Goodwin–Van Riet's nomenclature was adopted for cultural assemblages that were recognized to be specific to Africa. The two systems continued to be used alongside one another until the 1960s, when the European one was discarded, except as a source of designations for tool-manufacturing techniques (Posnansky 1982: 348).

Between 1936 and 1962, a large number of Australopithecine discoveries were made at Sterkfontein, Kromdraai, Makapansgat, and Swartkrans in South Africa. These finds encouraged growing interest in earlier phases of cultural development than had been studied anywhere else in the world. In the late 1950s, new geological chronologies were established for the Pleistocene and Pliocene epochs in Africa and potassium–argon dating stretched the period that was covered by evidence of cultural remains back from an estimated 600,000 to 2 million years. Palaeolithic artifacts found in river gravels were shown to be of limited interpretative value and interest shifted to the excavation of presumed "living floors," which favored the preservation of fossil pollens and other palaeoenvironmental data.

In 1959, Louis and Mary Leakey, who had pioneered Palaeolithic living-floor archaeology at Olorgesaillie in the 1940s, made the first of many spectacular early hominid finds in the primitive Oldowan tool levels at Oldovai Gorge (M. Leakey 1984). These finds aroused worldwide interest in Lower Palaeolithic archaeology. International funding for such research increased vastly and large numbers of archaeologists from America and Europe began to work in East

Africa. Their discoveries were seen as confirming Darwin's prediction that Africa was likely to have been the cradle of humanity. Although these finds were proclaimed to be of great scientific importance, much of their interest resulted from their being celebrated in the mass media as marking the origins not only of humanity as a whole but more specifically of Europeans and Euro-Americans. Although the earliest segments of European and Euro-American prehistory were clearly not going to be found in Europe, it was now believed that they could be discovered in Africa. Just as many archaeologists had once regarded the study of ancient Egypt and Mesopotamia as being of interest mainly for what it might reveal about the origins of European civilization, so the African Palaeolithic seemed to be primarily of interest for what it would reveal about the origins of Europeans (Dennell 1990).

Before the late 1950s, Europeans generally regarded recent phases of African prehistory as a time of cultural stagnation. To archaeologists in other parts of the world, these late periods were of little interest compared to the early Palaeolithic ones and many foreign archaeologists living and working in Africa were preoccupied with Palaeolithic archaeology. Fagan (1981: 49) has observed that similarly almost no historians were concerned with precolonial Africa. As late as 1966, the eminent British historian H. R. Trevor-Roper was to state that nothing significant had happened in Africa prior to the arrival of Europeans (p. 9). Such opinions reinforced the belief that there was little for archaeologists to discover about recent millennia. In Grahame Clark's *World Prehistory* (1961), sub-Saharan Africa received far less attention than any comparable region of the world. There were, however, some significant exceptions. Kenneth Murray, an art teacher who had long sought to conserve Nigeria's indigenous traditions and to convince scholars that these traditions were worth studying, was appointed first Director of the Nigerian Antiquities Service in 1943. He persuaded Bernard Fagg, a Cambridge-trained archaeologist, to join his staff and founded a number of regional museums throughout the colony. This work brought traditional art and culture closer to the currents of emerging African nationalism. John Schofield's *Primitive Pottery* (1948) presented the first typology of Iron Age ceramics from sites in Rhodesia and the Transvaal, although major uncertainties about the chronology of the Iron Age were not resolved until the 1950s (Fagan 1981: 48–9).

After 1945, there was a marked expansion of museums, antiquities services, and university departments employing archaeologists, especially in the British and French colonies. Expatriate archaeologists, such as Charles Thurston Shaw (b. 1914) and J. Desmond Clark (1916–2002) used the most recent technical and conceptual advances of European archaeology to build on the pioneer efforts of local amateur archaeologists, most of whom were European colonists or their descendants. As the prospects for independence brightened, there was in some colonies a growing, more broadly based interest in learning more "about the actual peoples who were now to govern Africa rather than about their remote Stone Age ancestors" (Posnansky 1982: 349). There was, in addition, a growing demand that African and not merely European and colonial history be taught in African schools, as had been done in the past; hence, African historians insisted that more attention should be paid to the prehistoric Iron Age. Archaeologists began to investigate important late precolonial sites such as Benin, Gedi, and Kilwa, and to study the development of early African states. The 1960s witnessed the introduction of the first regular courses in archaeology at universities in Uganda and Ghana (Posnansky 1976).

Iron Age archaeologists learned to draw on historical and ethnographic sources to help them to interpret their findings. At the same time, they ceased to attribute changes in prehistoric times almost exclusively to external stimuli and began to try to understand the internal dynamics of prehistoric African development. Many of these archaeologists had been influenced by Grahame Clark's ecological approach at Cambridge University; others sought to explain changes economically or politically. This reorientation was made possible by rapidly accumulating evidence that in precolonial times Africans had played a major role in the development of agriculture and metallurgy and that without major external stimuli they had created numerous civilizations. The same reorientation further encouraged the recovery of such data.

The history of colonial African archaeology reveals that changing social conditions have influenced the periods of prehistory that were studied at different times, the sorts of questions that were asked, and the degree to which internal or external factors were invoked to explain change. It is also clear that a growing corpus of archaeological data, produced by an increasing number of professional archaeologists, and the application of new, internationally accepted techniques for studying the past restricted the freedom of archaeologists to support the views of prehistory that were congenial to colonial ideologies. At the same time, changing fashions in archaeological interpretations in the European countries where most archaeologists who worked in Africa were trained also influenced the interpretation of African prehistory. These fashions were not directly related to the changing colonial milieu. Nevertheless, there was a significant but complex relationship between archaeology and the colonial settings in which it was practiced in Africa.

The Legacy of Evolutionary Archaeology

In the 1860s and 1870s, archaeologists continued to be preoccupied with the evolutionary origins of European societies. Especially in Britain, cultural evolution remained popular with the middle classes because it justified their economic and political ascendancy. Yet, by then, sociocultural evolution was no longer regarded as a project that benefited everyone equally. The privileged position of the middle classes was attributed to the superior intelligence and managerial abilities of middle-class males and the working class was regarded as biologically unfit to share in the governing of society. Thus, the existing social order came to be thought of as biologically grounded and immutable.

Racial explanations also were offered for the failure of other societies to evolve to the same extent as European ones had done. The Darwinian explanation of these differences that was popularized by Lubbock reinforced the racism that had long influenced the interpretation of the prehistoric archaeological evidence in the United States and played a major role in shaping archaeological interpretation in other parts of the world that experienced substantial European settlement and exploitation. These archaeologies differed from one another in many ways but nevertheless shared some key features. Indigenous societies were assumed to be static and, when evidence of change was noted in the archaeological record, it was generally attributed to prehistoric migrations rather than to internal dynamism. Cultural evolutionists had never denied the importance of migration and diffusion as processes bringing about sociocultural change. Yet change brought about in these ways indicated less inherent creativity than characterized societies that appeared to be autonomous centers of innovation, such as those of Europe.

Colonialist archaeology served to denigrate the indigenous societies that European colonists were seeking to dominate or replace by offering evidence that in prehistoric times they had lacked the initiative to develop on their own. Such archaeology was closely aligned with ethnology, which documented the primitive condition of traditional native cultures and their general inability to change. This primitiveness was widely believed to justify Europeans seizing control of the territories of such peoples. In its early stages colonial archaeology tended to reflect, and reinforce, the prejudices of the colonizing group. Although these archaeological interpretations did not long survive the systematic collection of archaeological evidence, which invariably indicated that internal changes had occurred in indigenous cultures, they often impeded the search for such evidence. They also significantly delayed the development of prehistoric archaeology in countries such as Australia, where it was assumed that archaeology had little to reveal about the past. Finally, although it was recognized that migration and diffusion could speed up the rate of change and complicate the archaeological record, it was not believed that these processes could alter the basic pattern of cultural development, which insofar as it occurred at all was believed invariably to exhibit the same general sequence of changes.

Unilinear evolutionism, whether of Lubbock's racist variety or the older, universalistic sort championed by Mortillet, shared certain major weaknesses as a model for collecting and interpreting archaeological data. By arguing that modern cultures, arranged from simplest to most complex, recapitulated the sequence through which European societies had slowly evolved, unilinear evolutionists denied that anything novel might be learned from the archaeological record. The main value of archaeology was its proof that evolution had in fact occurred, to varying degrees and hence at varying rates, in different parts of the world. Lubbock and other archaeologists argued that ethnographic evidence provided an easy way to achieve a rounded understanding of how people had lived in prehistoric times. They believed that, so long as archaeological data, in the form of diagnostic artifacts, could reveal the level of development that a particular culture had reached, ethnographic data concerning modern societies at the same stage of development were capable of supplying all the information that was needed to know what sorts of human behavior had been associated with that culture. Only the earliest archaeological finds were likely to lack corresponding ethnographic evidence. As late as 1911, it was believed that life in Lower and Middle Palaeolithic times must have been generally similar to that of the modern Tasmanians and Australian Aborigines (Sollas 1911).

Little effort was made to try to infer behavior from specific sorts of archaeological data, as had already been done, in the context of culture-historical and functional-processual approaches, by Scandinavian-style prehistoric archaeologists. In these approaches, behavioral analogues were based on similar forms of material culture encountered in archaeological and ethnographic contexts rather than on the comparison of whole cultures. Holistic analogues invited a revival of antiquarianism, in as much as they returned archaeology to a situation in which artifacts once again merely illustrated the past, rather than constituting a basis for investigating prehistoric human behavior. Evolutionary archaeologists had failed to address the task of inferring such behavior from archaeological data.

They also had failed to devise a methodology for implementing holistic comparisons. No systematic effort was made to correlate specific tool types with particular stages of cultural development so that these tool types could be used to draw detailed and controlled comparisons between ethnographic and archaeological assemblages. It went unnoted that Tasmanians did not manufacture Chellean handaxes or Australian Aborigines Levallois cores, although Mortillet argued that these types constituted a logical sequence of technological evolution. Efforts to take account of such differences might have revealed some of the limitations of cultural evolutionism. Archaeologists also were aware of the difficulties posed by geographical and environmental variations, but they never confronted this issue systematically. As a result, comparisons between archaeological assemblages and ethnographic cultures remained impressionistic.

The failure to deal adequately with these problems produced a growing sense of impasse and sterility in evolutionary archaeology after the European Palaeolithic sequence had been delineated. The problem with unilinear evolutionary archaeology was that it had become too integral a part of anthropology and too dependent on ethnology. Far more creativity had survived in Scandinavian-style post-Palaeolithic archaeology, although it had been temporarily eclipsed by the momentous discoveries concerning still earlier phases of human development. Because of their growing realization of the inadequacies of the unilinear evolutionary approach, a new generation of professional archaeologists was to view its decline as a liberation rather than a loss.

CHAPTER 6

Culture-Historical Archaeology

—

*We Danes... have a fatherland in which ancient monuments lie
spread out in fields and moors... this feeling of having a history
and a fatherland actually means that we are a nation.*

JOHAN SKJOLDBORG, quoted by K. Kristiansen (1993), p. 21

*Generally speaking, nationalist ideology suffers from pervasive
false consciousness. Its myths invert reality: it... claims to protect
an old folk society while in fact helping to build up an anonymous
mass society.*

E. GELLNER, *Nations and Nationalism* (1983), p. 124

The culture-historical archaeology of the late nineteenth century
was a response to growing awareness of geographical variability in
the archaeological record at a time when cultural evolutionism was
being challenged in western and central Europe by declining faith
in the benefits of technological progress. These developments were
accompanied by growing nationalism and racism, which made ethnicity appear to be the most important factor shaping human history.
Nationalist fervor increased as spreading industrialization heightened
competition for markets and resources. Toward the end of the century, it was encouraged by intellectuals who sought to promote solidarity within their own countries in the face of growing social unrest
by blaming economic and social problems on neighboring states.

Early Interests in Ethnicity

National consciousness has a long history. Already in the sixteenth
and seventeenth centuries it had played a significant role in the development of antiquarianism in northern and western Europe. Political
scientists frequently distinguish this early patriotism, which tended
to be expressed by loyalty to a king or hereditary prince, from the

nationalism that developed in Europe along with industrialization and has since spread around the world. Nationalism is defined as an all-embracing sense of group identity and loyalty to a common homeland that is promoted by mass media, widespread literacy, and a comprehensive educational system. This new concept was a product of the French Revolution but in France national identity was at first not explicitly linked to ethnicity. As a result of their allegiance to the new French Republic, minority groups such as Celtic-speaking Bretons, German-speaking Alsatians, and Italian-speaking Corsicans became as much French citizens as anyone else. Even so, French authorities sought to ensure national unity by using the educational system to promote the French language and culture at the expense of ethnic diversity. Hence, even in France, national identity gradually became equated with cultural unity (Gellner 1983; Anderson 1991; Dumont 1994).

Most European nation states came to be viewed as political expressions of ethnic identity that was grounded in linguistic, cultural, and racial unity as well as in a shared history. Citizens often were encouraged to regard themselves as constituting an immutable and indivisible biological entity. Efforts were made to strengthen existing states by identifying them with single ethnic groups, by ethnic groups to achieve the status of nation states, and by some countries to expand their borders on the pretext that they were justified in doing so because they were politically uniting a single people. Nationalism also tended to identify racial divisions, which before the nineteenth century had often been thought to correspond with class divisions within countries, with national or ethnic boundaries. Gobineau was a transitional figure in this process. Under these circumstances, prehistoric archaeologists were encouraged to study the origins and early histories of specific ethnic groups.

Throughout the nineteenth century in England and France, nationalism was powerfully expressed in historical writing, which emphasized the internal solidarity of national groups. Yet its influence on archaeology was quite muted, in part as a result of the continuing importance of Lubbock's and Mortillet's evolutionary interests. During the French Revolution, the suppression of the aristocracy was represented as the expulsion of foreign conquerors and the restoration of sovereignty to the descendants of France's indigenous Celtic inhabitants. Henceforth, the origin of the French people was traced back to the Celtic-speaking Gauls. In 1803, Napoleon Bonaparte established the *Académie Celtique* whose members employed archaeological, historical, folkloric, and linguistic data to cultivate a sense of direct continuity between the Gauls and the modern French, despite the replacement of their Celtic language by that of their Roman conquerors.

In the 1860s, Napoleon III (r.1852–1870), who had proclaimed himself Emperor of the French after being elected President of the French Republic, supported major excavations at three Celtic *oppida*, or fortified towns, that had been identified as ones that were associated with major events that had occurred during Julius Caesar's conquest of Gaul in the first century BC. These excavations revealed a close resemblance to the late Iron Age culture found at the La Tène site in Switzerland in 1856. It is suggested that Napoleon III supported these excavations because of his desire to use belief in a common ethnic heritage to craft a uniform national culture that would help to unite modern France (Dietler 1994, 1998; Weber 1976). Yet Napoleon III claimed to sponsor these excavations as part of a massive program of historical and archaeological research that he was carrying out for a biography of Julius Caesar he was writing (Gran-Aymerich 1998: 142). His admiration for Caesar was probably inspired by a tendency for French monarchs, beginning during the Renaissance, to regard themselves as the true spiritual heirs of the Roman imperial tradition (M. Heffernan 1994: 30–1). Napoleon III's uncle, Napoleon Bonaparte, had shared this fascination with ancient Rome.

In Britain, fantasizing about possible Druidical associations of Neolithic and Bronze Age sites, which had been the main form of patriotism antiquaries had indulged in during the eighteenth century, was banished to the realms of popular history and folklore (Owen 1962: 239). The British were as proud of their supposed Nordic or Aryan racial affinities as were the Germans. Yet, unlike the Germans, who could trace themselves back into prehistoric times as the sole occupants of most of their modern homeland, the British were keenly aware from historical records that England had been conquered and settled in turn by Romans, Saxons, Danes, and Normans. Beginning in the late nineteenth century, British archaeologists regularly assumed that similar invasions had occurred in prehistoric times (T. Holmes 1907). Although some English specified that the prehistoric Celtic peoples were only their predecessors and not their ancestors, most historians argued that what was biologically and culturally most desirable in successive indigenous populations had combined with what was most advanced in invading groups to produce a people whose hybrid vigor, composed of various European stocks, made them the best in the world (Rouse 1972: 71–2). This historical chain of increasing biological and cultural superiority corresponded with the modern regional and ethnic hierarchy within Britain. The dominant upper and upper-middle classes viewed themselves as the spiritual, if not the biological, heirs of the Normans, whereas the English as a whole were identified with the earlier Saxons, and the more remote Celtic fringe with the still earlier and more primitive British. It was also argued that, as a result of natural selection, each ethnic group in Britain was best adapted to the locality and condition in which they were living. Each of these interpretations was related to Boyd Dawkins's (1874) proposal that over time in Europe culturally more advanced peoples had pushed aside less developed ones. Already by the middle of the nineteenth century, British archaeologists were interpreting the distributions of distinctive types of pottery as evidence of migrations (Latham and Franks 1856) and by 1913 E. T. Leeds was using similar artifacts found in graves on the European continent and in England to trace the English migrations into Britain following the collapse of the Roman Empire.

In northern and central Europe, the study of prehistory remained closely associated with nationalism throughout the nineteenth century. Although Scandinavian archaeologists continued to be interested in learning about how peoples had lived in the past and in cultural evolution (Fischer and Kristiansen 2002), they were mainly concerned with working out cultural chronologies that elucidated the prehistories of their respective countries and provided them with a source of pride and deeply rooted cultural identity. The revival of German literature in the eighteenth century had been characterized by a glorification of Germany's medieval and ancient past. At the end of that century, the philosopher Johann Herder had defined history as the account of the development of a people as exemplified by their language, traditions, and institutions (Hampson 1982: 241, 248–9; Zammito 2002). By encouraging a sense of pan-German ethnic identity, antiquaries and archaeologists played a significant role in promoting the unification of Germany, which was achieved in 1871.

Yet the study of German prehistory remained largely an amateur activity. It was not encouraged by the conservative Prussian leaders, who exploited German national feeling but, especially after the popular uprisings of 1849, feared to promote it. In eastern Europe, archaeologists, by helping to encourage a sense of national identity amongst Poles, Czechs, Hungarians, Lithuanians, and other ethnic groups living under Austrian, Russian, and Prussian domination, played a role in weakening those multinational empires and promoting the eventual emergence of a series of nation states. For this reason, archaeology was supported by nationalist elements such as the Czech middle class and the Polish landed aristocracy.

During the nineteenth century, growing amounts of archaeological material were collected throughout Europe as a result of more intensive agriculture and land reclamation projects; the construction of roads, railways, canals, and factories; the founding of increasing numbers of museums and research institutes; and the establishment of teaching positions for archaeologists in universities. Nonprofessional recovery peaked in the early nineteenth century, whereas recovery by professional archaeologists gradually increased thereafter (Schnapp and Kristiansen 1999: 29). As more evidence was collected, the attention of archaeologists turned increasingly to the study of artifacts and with that came a growing awareness of variations in their geographical distributions. In the 1870s and 1880s, archaeological research in central and eastern Europe was influenced by the evolutionary archaeology of France and England and by work being done by Scandinavian archaeologists, which encouraged the more detailed classification and comparison of archaeological finds. The development of local chronologies was retarded in some areas, however, by a longstanding reluctance to adopt the Scandinavian Three-Age system, which was opposed, because of personal rivalries and for nationalistic reasons, by a number of prominent German archaeologists (Böhner 1981; Sklenář 1983: 87–91). A concern with historical and ethnic issues nevertheless led archaeologists to pay increasing attention to the geographical distribution of distinctive types of artifacts and artifact assemblages in an effort to relate them to historical peoples. In addition, a nationalist orientation encouraged archaeologists to concentrate on the study of the Neolithic and more recent periods rather than on Palaeolithic times.

The culture-historical approach also drew prehistoric and classical archaeologists closer together than they had been previously in terms of goals, methods, and common interests. The ancient Greeks and Romans had interacted with peoples who had lived to the north of them, which made the findings of classical archaeologists and European culture-historical archaeologists of mutual interest. Among Italians and Greeks, the study of classical archaeology was accompanied by an interest in the prehistoric and postclassical periods of their respective countries that promoted communication between different types of archaeology, even though classical archaeology maintained its distinctive art-historical approach. In Germany, France, Britain, the United States, and elsewhere, classical archaeology remained a separate discipline, but its focus had always been culture-historical in a generic sense, inasmuch as classical archaeologists were devoted to the study of only two ethnic groups and two national cultures. In France and England, the study of local classical sites frequently led prehistoric and classical archaeologists to work together. In southern and western Germany, studies of the Roman frontier played a vital role in the development of prehistoric archaeology, as indicated by the establishment of the Roman-Germanic Central Museum at Mainz in 1852. The creation in 1892 of a special commission to investigate the Roman frontiers of central Europe is credited with making the resources of the well-funded German Archaeological Institute, hitherto reserved for classical archaeology, available for the study of late central European prehistory (Veit 2001: 580–1). Like classical studies, Egyptology and Assyriology were generically culture-historical from the beginning.

Finally, although prehistoric archaeologists frequently were interested in the pre- and protohistory of specific peoples or countries, this did not rule out a concern with the archaeology of Europe as a whole or even of Europe and the Middle East. Ian Morris (1994b: 11) calls this "continentalist," as distinguished from "national," archaeology. Very often, this sort of archaeology sought to define the distinctive features of European civilization and to account for the development of what was believed to be its superiority over all others. Many European archaeologists viewed the national and continental approaches as entirely complementary to one another.

Diffusionism

Although evolutionary archaeologists attributed cultural change to diffusion and migration as well as independent invention, the rejection of evolutionism led to diffusion and migration becoming privileged explanations and independent development being almost totally abandoned. By the 1880s, growing social and economic difficulties in western Europe were encouraging a new emphasis on the conservatism and rigidity of human nature in the heartland of evolutionary anthropology. The problems of the Industrial Revolution had been becoming increasingly evident for some time, especially in Britain where it had been going on the longest, in the form of slums, economic crises, and growing foreign competition. The political supremacy of the middle classes also was being challenged by the first labor movements, which sought either to share power by electoral means or to seize it through revolution. As a result of these developments, the younger generation of intellectuals turned against the idea of progress. Industrialism, which had formerly been a source of pride, was now seen as a cause of social chaos and ugliness (Trevelyan 1952: 119). The influential writer and art critic John Ruskin (1819–1900) had long argued that the preindustrial past had been superior to the present and sought to revive artisanal skills. His views promoted romanticism and devalued rationalism and Enlightenment values.

The efforts that were made at this time to externalize the economic and social conflicts that were going on within nation-states also encouraged a growing emphasis on racism. It was argued that French, Germans, and English were biologically different from one another and that their behavior was determined, not by economic and political factors, but by essentially immutable racial differences. Middle-class intellectuals sought to assure their readers that workers of different nationalities were so different in temperament that they could never unite to pursue a common goal. In contrast, these intellectuals sought to promote national unity by arguing that within each nation everyone, regardless of social class, was united by a common biological heritage, which constituted the strongest of human bonds. Therefore, instead of seeking political power for themselves, the working classes should trust that middle-class politicians would do their best to help ordinary people.

Disillusionment with progress, together with the belief that human behavior was biologically determined, encouraged growing scepticism about human creativity. Writers and social analysts maintained that human beings were not inherently inventive and that change was therefore contrary to human nature and potentially harmful to people. It was argued that an unchanging society was most congenial to human beings, who were naturally predisposed to resist alterations in their styles of life. This led to declining credence in independent development, to a belief that particular inventions were unlikely to be made more than once in human history, and hence to a growing reliance on diffusion and migration to explain cultural change. It also encouraged an increasing interest in the idiosyncratic features associated with particular ethnic groups rather than with the general characteristics of successive stages of cultural development. If the insecurity of the middle classes of western Europe in the 1860s had led Lubbock and other Darwinians to abandon the doctrine of psychic unity and view indigenous peoples as biologically inferior to Europeans, the still greater insecurity of the 1880s led intellectuals to jettison the doctrine of progress and regard human beings as far more resistant to change than they had been viewed since before the Enlightenment.

Increasing reliance on diffusion and migration, as well as the concept of cultures as ways of life related to specific ethnic groups, were soon evident in the work of German ethnologists such as Friedrich Ratzel (1844–1904) and Franz Boas (1858–1942). Ratzel, a geographer and ethnologist, rejected the German ethnologist Adolf Bastian's concept of psychic unity. In works such as *Anthropogeographie* (1882–1891) and *The History of Mankind* ([1885–1888] 1896–1898), he argued that, because the world was small, ethnologists must beware of thinking that even the simplest inventions were likely to have been made more than once, let alone repeatedly. Both invention and diffusion were described as capricious processes; hence, it was impossible to predict whether a particular group would borrow even a useful invention from its nearest neighbors. Ratzel maintained arbitrarily that because of this it was necessary to rule out the possibility of diffusion in order to prove that the same type of artifact had been invented more than once. He asserted that items such as the blowpipe and the bow and arrow, wherever they occurred in the world, could be traced back to a common source. This argument was directed against Bastian's claim that, in the absence of evidence to the contrary, all similarities should be attributed to the operation of psychic unity (Zimmerman 2001: 204). Both positions were equally unscientific, as most archaeologists appear to have intuitively realized, but there was as yet no detailed archaeological record against which each claim might be evaluated. Ratzel also argued that, despite its capriciousness, the prolonged diffusion of traits created culture areas or blocks of similar cultures located adjacent to each other (H. Kuklick 1991a: 121–30; Zimmerman 2001: 203–6).

Ratzel's ideas influenced the younger Boas, who introduced them to North America. Boas opposed the doctrine of cultural evolution and argued that each culture was a unique entity that had to be understood on its own terms. Doing this required accepting two concepts: cultural relativism, which denied the existence of any universal standard that could be used to compare the degree of development or worth of different cultures, and historical particularism, which viewed each culture as the product of a unique sequence of development in which the largely chance operation of diffusion played the major role in bringing about change. Boas believed that, if the development of cultures displayed any overall regularities, these were so complex as to defy understanding. The only way to explain the past was to determine the successive idiosyncratic diffusionary episodes that had shaped the development of each culture (M. Harris 1968a: 250–89). About the same time, the Viennese school of anthropology, developed by the Roman Catholic priests Fritz Graebner (1877–1934) and Wilhelm Schmidt (1868–1954), argued that a single series of cultures had developed in central Asia, from where these cultures had been carried to various parts of the world. The complex cultural variations observed on every continent resulted from the mingling of cultures at different levels of development (M. Harris 1968a: 382–92; Andriolo 1979). This approach was applied to European archaeology and then carried to Argentina after World War II by the Austrian archaeologist Oswald Menghin (1888–1973) (Kohl and Pérez Gollán 2002). Menghin's religious conservatism and his hostility to socialism led him to embrace a variant of culture-historical anthropology that not only rejected cultural evolution and psychic unity but also embraced primitive monotheism and degenerationism.

Diffusion displaced an evolutionary approach in English ethnology as a result of the work of the Cambridge scholar W. H. R.

Rivers (1864–1922) (1914). Unable to detect an evolutionary pattern in his detailed study of the distribution of cultural traits in Oceanic societies, he rejected evolutionism and adopted a diffusionist approach (Slobodin 1978). Diffusionism was carried further in British anthropology by Grafton Elliot Smith (1871–1937). Born in Australia, Smith studied medicine and became interested in mummification while he taught anatomy at the University of Cairo, before moving to the University of London. Noting that embalming was practiced in various forms elsewhere, he decided that it had been invented in Egypt, where it had reached its most highly developed form, and that it had degenerated as it spread to other parts of the world. He went on to theorize that all early cultural development had occurred in Egypt. Before 4000 BC, there had been no agriculture, architecture, religion, or government anywhere in the world. Then the accidental harvesting of wild barley and millet in the Nile Valley led to the discovery of agriculture, which was followed by the invention of pottery, clothing, monumental architecture, and divine kingship, producing what hyperdiffusionists called the "Archaic Civilization." Smith maintained that these events had occurred in a unique environment and were unlikely ever to have happened elsewhere. Egyptian innovations were carried to all parts of the world by merchants who were searching for raw materials that had the power to prolong human life. Although these influences acted as an "exotic leaven" encouraging the development of agriculture and civilization in other parts of the world, many secondary civilizations, such as that of the Maya, declined when cut off from direct contact with Egypt (Smith 1911, 1915, 1928, 1933).

Smith's hyperdiffusionist ideas were elaborated using ethnographic data by W. J. Perry, who taught cultural anthropology at the University of London. His two major works, *The Children of the Sun* (1923) and *The Growth of Civilization* (1924), still make fascinating reading, although the real explanation of the worldwide parallels that he noted in political organization and religious beliefs remains illusive. Lord Raglan (1939) also advocated hyperdiffusionism but believed Mesopotamia rather than Egypt to have been its source. The ideas on which these three men agreed were that most human beings are naturally primitive and will always revert to a state of savagery if not stopped from doing so by the ruling classes; that savages never invent anything; that the development of civilization, and by extrapolation the Industrial Revolution, were accidents that produced results contrary to human nature; and that religion was a prime factor promoting the development and spread of civilization. Yet, in denying that progress was natural or that there was any plan to human history, the hyperdiffusionists were only carrying to an extreme ideas that had come to be shared by a growing number of anthropologists since the 1880s.

Some European archaeologists were influenced by Smith to the extent that they argued that megalithic tombs might be a degenerate form of pyramid, the idea of which had been carried from Egypt to western Europe by Egyptian agents seeking for life-giving natural substances (Childe 1939: 301–2, 1954: 69). Yet, by the 1920s, the archaeological record was sufficiently well known that hyperdiffusionism had little appeal to archaeologists as an explanation of world prehistory. Insofar as archaeologists thought about the problem, cultures in the Old and New Worlds were recognized to be distinct stylistically and in many other ways and hence were assumed to have developed largely independently of one another from hunting and gathering to civilization. Yet, within the diffusionist intellectual milieu that had begun to evolve in the 1880s, the human capacity for innovation was considered to be sufficiently limited and quixotic that basic discoveries, such as pottery and bronze working, seemed unlikely to have been invented twice in human history and hence they were believed to have spread from one part of the world to another. The chronologies that had been elaborated before radiocarbon dating, especially on an intercontinental scale, were not sufficiently cross-dated to rule out such interpretations. Almost all cultural change in the archaeological record was attributed to the diffusion of ideas from one group to another or to migrations that had led to the replacement of one people and their culture by another.

Because they accepted the capacity of one group to learn from another, archaeologists who emphasized diffusion tended to be more optimistic about the capacity of human societies to change than were those who attributed almost all change to migration. The latter fashion is exemplified by the work of W. M. F. Petrie (1939), who, in discussing the prehistoric development of Egypt, attributed all cultural changes either to mass migrations or to the arrival of smaller groups who brought about cultural change by mingling culturally and biologically with the existing population. According to Petrie, the early

Neolithic Fayum culture represented a "Solutrean migration from
the Caucasus," which also was the homeland of the Badarian people.
Amratian white-lined pottery was introduced by "Libyan invasions,"
whereas the Gerzean culture was brought to Egypt by an "Eastern Desert Folk" who invaded and dominated the country. Finally,
Egypt was unified by the "Falcon Tribe" or "Dynastic Race" that
"certainly had originated in Elam" (Iran) and came to Egypt by way
of Ethiopia and the Red Sea. In each case, Petrie's arguments were
based on tenuous resemblances between a few traits in Egyptian culture and those in some culture or cultures outside Egypt, while the
general patterns were ignored. Petrie saw no possibility of significant cultural change without accompanying biological change. Still
earlier, he had written in a Vicoesque style about millennium-long
cycles of growth and decay in which he believed racial struggle to be
of paramount importance (Petrie 1911).

Archaeological interpretation everywhere in Europe was influenced by growing pessimism about human creativity. Changes in
the archaeological record were attributed mainly to migration and
diffusion. Multiple inventions of the same items were now believed to
be highly improbable. There also was no sense of pattern to human
history. The archaeological record made it hard for archaeologists
to deny that cultural development had taken place, but few now
regarded this development as universal, inevitable, or even desirable.

The transition between evolutionary and migrationist-diffusionist
modes of thought was gradual and "diffusionist" explanations often
shared many of the features of evolutionary ones. W. J. Sollas, in
his *Ancient Hunters and their Modern Representatives* (1911), based
on a series of lectures delivered in 1906, appears to be following
an evolutionary model when he compares successive ages of Palaeolithic development with different modern hunter-gatherer groups.
Thus, the Mousterians are "represented" by the Tasmanians, the
Aurignacians in part by the Bushmen, and the Magdalenians by the
Inuit and the American Indians. Yet Sollas maintains that most of
these modern counterparts are appropriate analogues because they
are the literal descendants of these Palaeolithic groups, who, as more
"intelligent" races emerged, were "expelled and driven to the uttermost parts of the earth" where they remained in an arrested state of
development (1924: 599). Under the impact of diffusionism, holistic
analogies based on the assumption that historically unrelated groups

at the same level of development would be culturally similar gradually were replaced by the assumption that because cultures are inherently static only the comparison of historically related ones could facilitate the interpretation of archaeological data (Wylie 1985a: 66–7; Bowler 1992).

The Montelian Synthesis of European Prehistory

The growing interest in cultural variation and diffusion in the social sciences provided a theoretical framework that allowed archaeologists to account for the evidence of spatial as well as temporal variation that was becoming obvious as archaeological data accumulated across Europe. As early as 1847, Worsaae had noted major stylistic differences between Bronze and Iron Age artifacts in Scandinavia and Ireland. In the course of the nineteenth century, archaeologists in Britain, France, Switzerland, Germany, and central Europe traced the geographical and temporal distributions of coins (J. Evans 1864), megaliths, and other Stone (J. Evans 1872), Bronze (J. Evans 1881), and Iron Age remains. As La Tène finds were more firmly identified with late prehistoric Celtic groups, their status as a culture rather than a stage of development or a period became clearer; a process that was accelerated in 1870 when Mortillet interpreted La Tène artifacts found in northern Italy as archaeological evidence of a historically recorded Celtic invasion of that country. In 1890, Arthur Evans identified a late Celtic urnfield in southeastern England with the Belgae, who the Romans reported had invaded England in the first century BC. John Abercromby (1841–1924) (1902, 1912) associated Early Bronze Age beaker pottery, probably wrongly (Harrison 1980), with a putative "Beaker folk" who he believed had migrated over much of western Europe. In 1898, the Danish archaeologist Sophus Müller (1846–1934) argued that, although the Single Graves and Megalithic Burials of the Danish Neolithic were at least partly contemporary, the weapons, pottery, and ornaments associated with them were different and hence they must represent two distinct peoples (Childe 1953: 9). As early as 1874, Boyd Dawkins (p. 353) had suggested the possibility of regional variations in the Palaeolithic.

This growing emphasis on the geographical distribution as well as the chronology of archaeological finds led to important creative work being done by archaeologists who were interested primarily

Figure 6.1 Oscar Montelius (1843–1921)

in the European Neolithic, Bronze, and Iron Ages rather than the Palaeolithic period. Their work would replace the evolutionary preoccupation that western European prehistoric archaeologists had with a succession of cultural stages with a historical orientation focused on cultures, but this change occurred slowly. The major figure in initiating this transition was the Swedish archaeologist Gustaf Oscar Montelius (1843–1921) (Figure 6.1). He was trained in the natural sciences but became interested in archaeology and was employed full time at the Museum of National Antiquities in Stockholm beginning in 1868. He shared Thomsen's and Worsaae's interest in elaborating a prehistoric chronology. Between 1876 and 1879, he also traveled throughout Europe in order to study collections, thus becoming the first archaeologist to investigate prehistory on a continental scale. The enlarged scope of his research was made possible by the increasing tempo of archaeological activity throughout Europe and by the development of a network of railways, which made travel easier.

During the mid-nineteenth century, Scandinavian archaeologists had subdivided the Bronze and Iron Ages into an increasing number of periods, often using limited criteria, such as grave types or dated trade goods, and without taking account of whole assemblages. The typological method, as Montelius developed it, was a refinement of Thomsen's chronological approach. The creation of systematic typologies or classifications of prehistoric artifacts began with the Swedish archaeologist Hans Hildebrand (1842–1913). He derived the idea of a clearly defined type from numismatic work by his father, Bror Emil Hildebrand (1806–1884), who in 1846 formally identified different types of Anglo-Saxon coins (Gräslund 1987: 96–101). Hans Hildebrand was, however, little interested in chronology. Montelius, by contrast, carefully defined artifact types on the basis of variations in form and decoration for numerous classes of artifacts throughout Europe and on this basis sought to work out and correlate a series of regional chronologies. He did this by examining, as Thomsen had done, material from closed finds, such as graves, hoards, and single rooms, to determine what types of artifacts occurred and never occurred together. Experience taught him that, after comparing two hundred to three hundred finds of this sort, clusters of association would form that represented, not large units of time such as the Bronze Age, but subdivisions of these ages that he believed must each have lasted for only a few hundred years. Because of the vastly greater amount of data available and Montelius' more detailed artifact classifications, it was possible for him not only to identify shorter periods but, by identifying artifact types that were common to more than one period, to order these periods chronologically. For such a sequence to be persuasive, materials, techniques of manufacture, shape, and decoration had to covary in a coherent pattern. Montelius established seriation as a self-contained and convincing technique for constructing archaeological sequences.

After Montelius had established chronological sequences on the basis of formal criteria and closed finds, he drew attention to evolutionary trends in these sequences. Bronze celts, for example, began as flat axes that were later flanged to strengthen them. Next they were provided with a crossbar and cylindrical shaft and finally with a heavy cast socket to facilitate mounting and use (Figure 6.2). Montelius viewed such a developmental sequence as a natural and logical one and drew parallels between the evolution of material culture and of biological organisms. Yet, as Gräslund (1974) has shown, despite Montelius's training in the natural sciences, his thinking about human behavior owed little to Darwinism. On the contrary, it continued the traditions of Scandinavian archaeology. Montelius believed, as had the philosophers of the Enlightenment, that technology developed because human beings used their powers of reason to

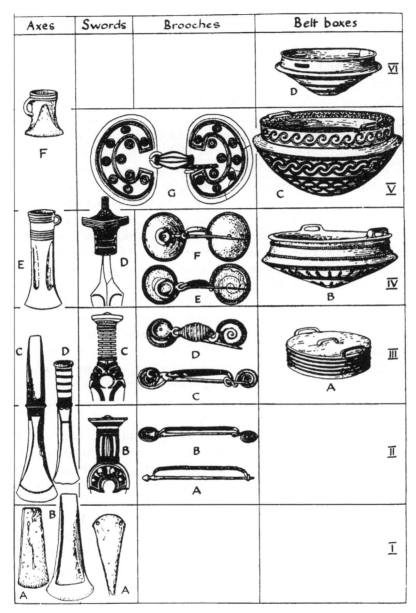

Figure 6.2 Bronze Age artifacts arranged according to Montelius's system, 1881

226

devise more effective ways of coping with nature and thereby making their lives easier and more secure. His references to biological evolution seem to have been intended mainly as analogies designed to enhance the status of archaeology in an era dominated by Darwinian evolution. It is also significant that not all Montelius's evolutionary patterns were unilinear. He demonstrated, for example, that during the Bronze Age fibulae (safety pins), which were used to fasten clothing, had been manufactured in Italy as one piece with a coiled spring and in Scandinavia as two pieces with a hinge (Bibby 1956: 180–1). In due course, the best features of both types were merged to form a new pan-European variety. Hence, Montelius took account of how idiosyncratic historical factors as well as logical ones influenced the evolution of material culture.

By the 1880s, Montelius (1885) had worked out a detailed chronology of the Scandinavian Bronze Age. By 1903, he had divided the European Neolithic into four periods, the Bronze Age into six periods, and the Iron Age into ten periods. Although he regarded such periods as applicable in general terms to the whole of Europe, he had noted considerable regional variation within each period and had come to doubt the assumption that all parts of Europe had reached the same stage of development at the same time. Instead, he sought to use artifacts that he assumed had been exchanged from one region to another, or been copied from more advanced areas, as geographical cross-ties to temporally correlate various periods in different parts of Europe. As a result of the discovery of Mycenaean Greek pottery in historically dated Egyptian sites and Egyptian goods in Greece, it was possible for archaeologists to date the Mycenaean period in Greece to the fifteenth century BC. Cylindrical faience beads found across Europe that were presumed to have come from Egypt through the Mycenaean civilization provided a benchmark calendrical dating for a number of Bronze Age cultures. In general, these beads turned up in typologically less evolved Bronze Age contexts in central, western, and northern Europe than in the southeast, suggesting that the farther a region was from the Middle East, the later most technological innovations had been adopted there. This correlation gave rise to what was later called the "short chronology" of European prehistory (Bibby 1956: 181–2). Other periods were aligned using goods that on the basis of stylistic criteria appeared to have been traded from one part of Europe to another. It was assumed that all these goods were exchanged soon after they had been manufactured.

Montelius believed that his cultural chronology of European prehistory was derived objectively from the archaeological evidence. Today, archaeologists are not so certain that presuppositions did not play a significant role in determining his selection of the cross-ties that he used to correlate the chronologies of different parts of Europe. Montelius thought that his chronology indicated that in prehistoric times cultural development had occurred in the Middle East and achievements had been carried from there to Europe by waves of diffusion and migration making their way through the Balkans and Italy. Because of that, the level of cultural development in southeastern Europe in prehistoric times was always ahead of that to the north and west and Europe as a whole "was for long but the pale reflection of Eastern civilization." Montelius became the most distinguished exponent of a diffusionist explanation of European cultural development, the so-called *ex oriente lux* ("light from the east") school (Renfrew 1973a: 36–7).

Montelius's (1899, 1903) interpretation of the development of European civilization required a belief not only in diffusion but also that over long periods innovation tended to occur in particular areas and to diffuse outward from those areas to peripheries. A similar concept of cultural cores and peripheries played a significant role in Boasian anthropology, together with the age/area assumption, which maintained that more widely distributed traits tended to be older than ones spread over a smaller territory. In general, American anthropologists tended to view broad natural zones, such as the Great Plains or boreal forests of North America, as constituting the most active spheres of diffusion. The concepts of cultural cores and age/area were later subjected to a withering critique by the anthropologist R. B. Dixon (1928). In Europe, however, these theoretical assumptions were neither articulated nor criticized so clearly.

Many archaeologists supported Montelius's interpretation of European prehistory. Moreover, the most vocal objections were directed not against his idea of diffusion from a center of innovation but, rather, against his claim that this center was located in the Middle East. Some archaeologists objected to an interpretation that ran counter to European convictions of their own superior creativity by deriving civilization from beyond Europe. Carl Schuchhardt

(1859–1943), Adolf Furtwängler (1853–1907), and other German archaeologists maintained that the Mycenaean civilization of Greece was the creation of "Aryan" (Indo-European-speaking) invaders from the north. Montelius's thesis was opposed on more general principles by the Austrian archaeologist Matthäus Much (1832–1909) (1907) and by the French prehistorian Salomon Reinach (1858–1932) in *Le Mirage oriental* (*The Eastern Mirage*) (1893). Overthrowing Montelius's scheme required, however, either ignoring or refuting his chronology, which most impartial prehistorians were convinced was based on sound evidence.

There were, however, subjective reasons as well as scientific ones for the support given to Montelius. His diffusionist views clearly accorded with the conservative opinions denying human creativity that were fashionable at the end of the nineteenth century. Tracing the origins of European civilization to the Middle East also appealed to many Christians because it appeared to offer support for the biblical view of world history. In the late nineteenth century, growing social and economic problems led many members of the middle class in western Europe to turn once more to religion. Montelius's scheme also accorded with a biblically based interpretation of history dating from the medieval period that saw successive empires – Babylonian, Persian, Hellenistic Greek, and Roman – gradually transferring the center of power and creativity westward from the Middle East to Europe. Finally, throughout the nineteenth century, European powers, especially England and France, had been intervening to an ever greater degree in the political and economic affairs of North Africa and the Middle East (Silberman 1982; Gran-Aymerich 1998). A scheme of prehistory that treated the western European nations rather than the modern Arab peoples as the true heirs of the ancient civilizations of the Middle East helped to justify European colonial interventions in that region, just as myths about the nonindigenous origin of Great Zimbabwe were used to support the European colonization of sub-Saharan Africa. Montelius's demonstration that early technological innovations in the Middle East had constituted the origins of European civilization may help to explain why his arguments were of greater interest in France and England than in Germany, where political interventions in the Middle East began only toward the end of the nineteenth century.

Montelius did not subscribe to racial interpretations of human history. Moreover, although he believed that diffusionary processes accounted for the spread of civilization to Europe in prehistoric times, he saw evolutionary ones explaining its origins in the Middle East. As the citizen of a geographically peripheral European nation whose cultural and academic life was being transformed during the nineteenth century by influences coming principally from Germany, he must have regarded diffusion as a powerful stimulus for beneficial change. His views about the origins of European technology were generically similar to those of Thomsen and Worsaae. Furthermore, despite his pioneering contributions to the study of pan-European prehistory, the primary focus of his research remained Scandinavia. Although he was the first great archaeological innovator to be strongly influenced by a specifically diffusionist view of cultural change, his position in the debate about human inventiveness was a moderate one and much of his thinking continued in an evolutionist mode.

Montelius's influence was not limited to central and western Europe. In the late nineteenth century, Russian archaeology, inspired by patriotism and romanticism, shifted rapidly from being an antiquarian to being a scientific pursuit. The models Russian archaeologists followed were the Scandinavian and German archaeologists who were in the process of creating culture-historical archaeology. The Russian government's forbidding as early as 1826 of the publication of any studies dealing with human evolution had effectively discouraged the consideration of evolutionary archaeology during the mid-nineteenth century (Klejn 2001b: 1130–1).

In the second half of the nineteenth century, Russia experienced rapid development in industry, transport, trade, and educational opportunities. The middle classes expanded and the educated segment of the population became interested in natural science, philosophy, history, and political economy. Archaeological research, publications, museums, associations, and congresses proliferated. All the archaeologists at this period were landowners, teachers, civil servants, or military officers who were self-instructed in the discipline. Yet they carried out research comparable to that being done elsewhere in Europe (M. Miller 1956: 28). The rapid development of archaeology in Russia, and a growing number of remarkable finds, led the government to establish the Imperial Russian Archaeological Commission in St. Petersburg in 1859. It was intended to safeguard archaeological remains. Already in 1851 a Russian Archaeology Society had been founded in St. Petersburg and in 1864 Count Aleksey Uvarov, who had excavated over 7000 burial mounds, organized the Moscow Archaeological Society, which he, and later his widow, Countess Praskovia Uvarova, directed until 1917. Each of these bodies established major publications series, which continued until the Bolshevik revolution of that year. In the late 1870s and 1880s, regional archaeological societies were established in Tbilisi, Kazan, Pskov, and other provincial cities. Although the Russians, like the Americans and other European colonizing powers, were seizing control of regions occupied by tribal peoples, the Russians did not invoke archaeological evidence to justify their actions racially. Having been conquered and ruled for centuries by the Mongols, they were less inclined to despise racially different peoples than were the Americans.

Beginning in the 1870s and continuing into the early twentieth century, archaeological interests diversified. Kurgans and classical sites continued to be excavated, but there was a growing emphasis on settlements and cemeteries from all periods of Russian history. The Palaeolithic sites at Kostenki, in the Ukraine, began to be studied in 1879 and Neolithic sites, including those of the Tripolje culture, as well as Bronze and Iron Age ones were excavated across western Russia. There also was much interest in Slavic and medieval Russian archaeology, especially among the members of the Russian Archaeology Society, where a special section was established for such research. This interest reflected the pan-Slavism that played a significant role in Russian foreign policy in the late nineteenth century and supported the government's efforts to strengthen Russian influence throughout eastern Europe. By this time archaeology was being taught, although not yet in separate departments, at the universities in St. Petersburg and Moscow.

Many archaeologists working in Moscow and St. Petersburg were influenced by recent developments in prehistoric archaeology in northern and central Europe. The most prominent of these was Vasily Gorodtsov (1860–1945), who began to excavate in the 1880s but remained employed as a military officer until 1906. In the early 1900s, he became senior curator at the Moscow Historical Museum and also a lecturer at the Moscow Archaeological Institute, where he trained a large number of professional archaeologists. Gorodtsov was the outstanding exponent of what later was labeled the formalist school of Russian archaeology, which was inspired by the work of Montelius and other Scandinavian typologists. His systematic classification of Neolithic ceramics according to material, then shape, and finally decoration enabled him to trace the distribution and establish the boundaries of clusters of similar sites and to note material evidence of contacts between such clusters. He accepted that diffusion and migration were important processes bringing about cultural change. He also produced the first periodization of pre-Scythian burial mounds along lines similar to those employed by Sophus Müller in Denmark. In 1899, Aleksander Spitsyn (1858–1931), who was the leading member of the St. Petersburg school, combined archaeological data about temple ring types and historical information to trace the distribution of some early Russian tribes in a manner resembling that being developed by the German archaeologist Gustaf Kossinna.

The Concept of Culture

In the late nineteenth century, a growing interest in ethnicity encouraged increasing use of the concept of the archaeological culture. Archaeologists in Scandinavia and in central and eastern Europe began to draw an explicit parallel between the numerous geographically restricted remains of a distinctive character they were finding and ethnographic cultures. The term "culture" seems first to have been used in Italian and Spanish, where it originally referred to the cultivation of the human mind. By the seventeenth century, it was employed to designate the distinctive way of life of a people and in the late eighteenth century, Herder was maintaining that each people (*Volk*) had their own culture (*Kultur*). The equivalent term in French was *civilisation* (Díaz-Andreu 1996a: 51–7). In Germany, *Kultur* came to be used more narrowly to designate the slowly changing ways of life ascribed to tribal or peasant groups, or modern rural dwellers, as distinguished from the cosmopolitan, rapidly changing "Zivilisation" of urban centers.

After 1780, works on *Kulturgeschichte* (culture history) began to proliferate and, beginning in 1843, the German ethnologist Gustav Klemm published books titled *Allgemeine Cultur-Geschichte der Menschheit* (*General Culture History of Humanity*) (1843–1852) and *Allgemeine Kulturwissenschaft* (*General Ethnology*) (1854–1855).

Friedrich Ratzel based his antievolutionary theories on the use of the concept of culture to denote distinctive ways of life transmitted by specific peoples from one generation to another as well as on the concept of diffusion. The English ethnologist Edward B. Tylor (1832–1917) was aware as early as 1865 of Klemm's use of the term culture, but it was only in *Primitive Culture* (1871) that he adopted the word and provided it with its now classic English definition as "that complex whole which includes knowledge, belief, art, morals, law, custom, and other capabilities and habits acquired by man as a member of society" (p. 1). In general, nineteenth-century evolutionary archaeologists tended to use the term culture only in the singular. It referred to all the knowledge and beliefs of humanity that were transmitted by teaching and imitation and that were believed to grow more complex and refined over time. This holistic usage contrasted with the German use of the word (often in the plural) to designate the distinctive ways of life of various peoples (Stocking 1987: 18–19).

The labeling of geographically and temporally restricted assemblages of formally similar prehistoric archaeological material as cultures or civilizations and identifying them as the remains of ethnic groups seem to have occurred independently to a number of archaeologists. In V. G. Childe's (1935b: 3) view, the concept of the archaeological culture was "forced" on Scandinavian and central European archaeologists by the wealth of material that their excavations had produced for the Neolithic and later periods. The early Scandinavian archaeologists were aware of the German ethnographic use of the concept of culture, and the oldest known use of the term culture to designate an archaeological unit is found in Thomsen's contribution to the *Ledetraad* (1836). In his discussion of the Bronze Age, Thomsen refers to the diffusion in prehistoric times of technological knowledge from one culture to another. In *Danmarks Oldtid* (1843), Worsaae made even more use of the term culture to designate archaeological entities, referring to "higher cultures," "later cultures," and "Roman culture" among others. No need was felt to explain this usage, which seems to have been regarded as self-evident. Nor, because of the general homogeneity of prehistoric cultures at any one time in Denmark, was a need perceived to assign specific geographic boundaries to archaeological cultures. Yet both Thomsen and Worsaae were aware that different cultures had coexisted in different parts of Europe and even different parts of Scandinavia in prehistoric times.

In 1866, the Norwegian archaeologist Olof Rygh interpreted distinctive spear points and arrowheads found in his country as the products of a particular Stone Age "culture and people" and by 1871 he had noted the existence of two "Stone Age cultures" and "Stone Age peoples" in Norway (Meinander 1981: 106). In his multivolume *Geschichte des Alterthums* (*History of Ancient Times*), which began to appear in 1884, the historian Eduard Meyer (1855–1930) wrote casually of the Egyptian, Greek, Trojan, and Mycenaean cultures, while in the works of Heinrich Schliemann and others the terms Aegean, Mycenaean, Helladic, and Cycladic were used to distinguish various Bronze Age "civilizations" of the eastern Mediterranean region (Daniel 1950: 243; Meinander 1981).

By 1891, A. Götze was referring to the Bandkeramik and other Neolithic cultures; V. V. Hvojko wrote about the Tripolje culture in 1901; and Spitsyn about the Fatyanovo culture in 1905 (Meinander 1981). In 1908 Raphael Pumpelly (1837–1923), an American geologist turned archaeologist, who was excavating at the stratified site of Anau in central Asia, used the term culture to distinguish successive levels of occupation at that site, explaining that "culture" was employed as a synonym for "civilization" (p. xxxv). In some cases, it is possible to trace the process by which specific cultures were recognized. Following the excavations at a Bronze Age cemetery at Únětice in Czechoslovakia, archaeologists began to identify Únětice-like finds in nearby regions and finally organized these to establish a Únětice culture. In a similar manner, the Burgwall-type pottery that had been defined in central Europe in 1870 was broadened into the concept of a Burgwall culture (Sklenář 1983: 110). These developments generally occurred first in northern and central Europe, where there had been a longstanding interest in tracing ethnic identities in the archaeological record. Yet, despite the enormous influence that the concept of the archaeological culture was to exert on the development of archaeology, it would be erroneous to regard the development of a culture-historical approach at this time as inherent in the nature of archaeology. Had archaeologists in northern and central Europe been more interested in studying ecological adaptation than in nationalism, race, and ethnicity, it is possible that their concern with geographical variation in the archaeological record might instead have led to the early development of an ecological approach.

The Birth of Culture-Historical Archaeology

A growing interest in the concept of the archaeological culture did not lead immediately to the development of culture-historical archaeology, which occurred in Germany. There anthropology had evolved as a positivist, human-science alternative to the text-based humanism of German universities. Most of its practitioners were employed in museums. Led initially by Adolf Bastian, they advocated the study of all cultures, not simply ones that had produced "great" art and literature. The professionalization of prehistoric archaeology began in Germany with the establishment of the German Society for Anthropology, Ethnology, and Prehistoric Archaeology (*Urgeschichte*) in 1869, three years after the first meeting of the *Congrès international d'anthropologie et d'archéologie préhistorique* was held in Neuchâtel, Switzerland. The leading figure in this new German society was the eminent pathologist and left-wing politician Rudolf Virchow (1821–1902), who had become actively involved in archaeological research in Germany. He advocated the incorporation of prehistoric archaeology, along with physical anthropology and ethnology, into a comprehensive prehistoric anthropology. Together with his followers, he sought to identify prehistoric cultures, to trace their origin and movements, and if possible to associate them with known peoples, often largely on the basis of pottery types, although grave types, settlements, and historical data were also considered. The excavations of prehistoric sites carried out by archaeologists such as Carl Schuchhardt were modeled on the best work being done by classical archaeologists (Ottaway 1973; Fetten 2000). Yet, although their work offered insights into European prehistory, it did not provide an understanding of the past that was comprehensive enough to challenge Mortillet's evolutionary approach. This was to be produced by a professional librarian who had little interest in doing fieldwork and who regarded prehistoric archaeology not as a branch of anthropology but as an independent discipline dedicated to the study of German prehistory.

Gustaf Kossinna (1858–1931) first presented his views in 1895 in a lecture that traced the German tribes historically recorded as living between the Rhine and Vistula Rivers about 100 BC back to the Neolithic period. His approach was expounded in greater detail in *Die Herkunft der Germanen* (*The Origin of the Germans*) (1911) and his two-volume *Ursprung und Verbreitung der Germanen* (*Origin and Expansion of the Germans*) (1926–1927). A fanatical German patriot, Kossinna declared archaeology to be the most national of sciences and the ancient Germans the most noble subject for archaeological research. He criticized German archaeologists for their interest in classical and Egyptian archaeology, which he viewed as indicating a lack of patriotism. Before 1918, however, some caution was required, as the German emperor, Wilhelm II, was both a zealous nationalist and an enthusiastic supporter of classical and Middle Eastern archaeology. Although Kossinna had been trained in philology, he turned from linguistics to archaeology in an effort to discover the original homeland of the Indo-European speaking peoples and hence of the Germans. He was appointed Professor of Archaeology at the University of Berlin and in 1909 founded the German Society for Prehistory (*Vorgeschichte*), which was soon renamed the Society for German Prehistory to publicize more clearly its nationalist commitments.

Die Herkunft der Germanen, the first systematic exposition of Kossinna's approach to archaeology, was a mixture of important theoretical innovations and a fanciful glorification of German prehistory. His work helped to reinforce German nationalism and won the favor of high-ranking conservatives, such as Field Marshall Paul von Hindenburg, who was to be elected President of Germany in 1925. Because of Kossinna's misuse of archaeological data for political purposes, careful attention is required to separate his positive contributions from the pernicious aspects of his work. It also should be remembered that, in interpreting archaeological evidence in a way that encouraged Germans to regard Slavs and other neighboring European peoples as inferior to themselves and which justified German aggression against these peoples, Kossinna was not acting differently from the amateur and semiprofessional archaeologists of other countries who at the same time were portraying the indigenous peoples of North America, Africa, Asia, and Australia as inferior to Europeans. In different ways archaeology in all these countries was reflecting racist attitudes that in the course of the late nineteenth century had become widespread not only in Germany but throughout

Western civilization (Césaire 1955). The Polish archaeologist Józef Kostrzewski (1885–1969), who had studied with Kossinna, sought to use his methods to emphasize the great achievements of Poland's prehistoric Slavic inhabitants.

Kossinna proposed that from Mesolithic times onward the archaeological record of central Europe could be organized as a mosaic of cultures (*Kulturen, Kultur-Gruppen*), the location and content of which had altered over time. On the basis of his belief that cultures are invariably a reflection of ethnicity, he argued that similarities and differences in material culture correlate with similarities and differences in ethnicity. Hence, clearly defined cultural provinces always correlate with major ethnic groups or peoples, such as the Germans, Celts, and Slavs, whereas individual cultures correspond with tribes, such as the Germanic-speaking Saxons, Vandals, Lombards, and Burgundians. Like many other archaeologists, Kossinna believed that cultural continuity indicated ethnic continuity. Hence, he argued that, by mapping the distributions of types of artifacts that were characteristic of specific tribal groups, whose homelands could be pinpointed for the early historical period by using written sources, it would be possible to identify the material culture associated with each of these groups and use that information to determine archaeologically where they had lived at earlier periods of prehistory. He called this procedure *Siedlungsarchäologie* (settlement archaeology), which did not signify the study of habitation sites but, rather, determining where particular ethnic groups had lived in earlier times. At some point in the past, it would not be possible to distinguish individual German tribes, as they would not yet have differentiated from each other, but archaeologists could still differentiate among Germans, Slavs, Celts, and other major groups of Indo-Europeans. For still more remote periods, it might only be possible to differentiate Indo-Europeans from non-Indo-Europeans.

In all of his later writings, Kossinna specifically identified cultural and ethnic variations with racial differences. In particular, he accepted the commonly held belief that the original Indo-European speaking peoples and hence the direct ancestors of the Germans were members of the blond, longheaded Nordic (or Aryan) racial group. He also believed that racial characteristics were the fundamental determinants of human behavior. Kossinna also accepted Klemm's distinction between *Kulturvölker*, or culturally creative peoples, and

Naturvölker, or culturally passive peoples. For him, this was a distinction between Indo-Europeans, and above all Germans, and all other peoples. He believed that the Indo-Europeans could be traced back to the Mesolithic Maglemosian culture found in northern Germany. In particular, he traced their origins to the vicinity of Schleswig and Holstein, which Germany had recently annexed from Denmark. By claiming maximum antiquity for the cultural chronology of Germany, he sought to demonstrate that this region had been the center of cultural development for Europe and the Middle East. Late Neolithic flint daggers were interpreted as evidence of a noble German pride in weapons and as prototypes for later bronze ones and Bronze Age trumpets were construed as evidence of the superior musical ability of the Germans in prehistoric times. In another flight of fantasy, Kossinna proposed that even the alphabet had a Stone Age European origin rather than a Phoenician one.

Because more advanced cultures were believed to manifest the biological superiority of their creators, it was assumed that they could spread from one region to another only as a result of migrations of people, not by diffusion. Kossinna acknowledged that diffusion occurred but assigned it a minor role in bringing about cultural change. Although most of his studies were limited to northern and central Europe, Kossinna stated that race was the key to understanding world history. He proclaimed an original Indo-European mentality to be common to the Greeks, Babylonians, and Sumerians (Schwerin von Krosigk 1982: 53, 69). These ideas conjured up visions of waves of Indo-Europeans migrating south and east, conquering indigenous populations and using them to build civilizations in the Middle East, Greece, and Italy. Each of these waves in turn, however, interbred with local populations and as a result impaired their creative abilities. Hence, even the Indo-European speaking peoples of ancient Greece and Italy eventually became incapable of sustained cultural creativity. Kossinna argued that, because the Germans had stayed in their original homeland, they remained the racially purest and therefore the most talented and creative of all the Indo-European peoples. They alone were still capable of carrying out the historical responsibility of creating civilization and imposing it on inferior peoples. Hence, the Germans became the first-born (*Erstgeborenen*) of the Indo-Europeans. These fantasies resembled the "Hamitic" hypothesis and other speculations that attributed ancient civilizations to conquering peoples coming from the north. Kossinna also viewed archaeology as establishing a historical right to territory. Wherever allegedly German artifacts were found was declared ancient German territory, which modern Germany either held by right or was entitled to win back. The same argument did not, of course, apply to non-German groups, such as the Slavs, who in medieval times had settled as far west as the recent border between East and West Germany (Klejn 1974).

Finally, Kossinna stressed the need to learn as much as possible about how human groups, or at least Germans, had lived in prehistoric times. Cultures were not to be defined simply as artifact assemblages but archaeologists were urged to try to determine the nature of prehistoric lifestyles. Yet, in his own work, Kossinna paid little attention to archaeological evidence of house types, burial customs, and rituals but based his interpretations on artifacts in museum collections. His speculations about prehistoric German life often were fanciful in the tradition of Stukeley and his latter-day druidical followers. Nevertheless, in its intention, Kossinna's desire to understand individual archaeological cultures as evidence of how people had lived in prehistoric times had more in common with the Scandinavian approach to archaeology than it had with a "scientific" archaeology modeled on French and English Palaeolithic studies.

There was much about Kossinna's work that was not new and much that remained controversial. The idea that the Indo-Europeans had originated in northern Europe had been supported for some time by various linguists and physical anthropologists on the basis of evidence that is no longer persuasive. Much of Kossinna's understanding of northern European prehistory and archaeological method was borrowed with little public acknowledgement from Montelius, including the principle that continuity of material culture in the archaeological record indicates ethnic continuity. Virchow and the Polish archaeologists Erzam Majewski (1858–1922) and Leon Kozłowski (1892–1944) expressed reservations about Kossinna's defining of cultures and his migrationism. More specifically K. H. Jacob-Friesen (1886–1960) (1928), A. M. Tallgren (1885–1945) (1937: 156–7), and Ernst Wahle (1889–1981) (1941) questioned his uncritical interpretation of archaeological cultures as being the same as ethnographic ones and argued that data derived from different sources could not be expected always to coincide. It also was observed that, especially in his later work, his culture units tended to be defined on the basis of only one or a few items of material culture that he assumed were correlated with ethnic identity. It is possible that the variations in brooches that he used to equate late Iron Age cultures with specific historical German tribes may in fact correlate with production centers and not with ethnic differences.

Yet Kossinna's work, for all its chauvinistic nonsense and its often amateurish quality, marked the final replacement of an evolutionary approach to prehistory by a culture-historical one. By organizing archaeological data for each period of prehistory into a mosaic of archaeological cultures, he sought not simply to document where different groups of Europeans had lived at different stages of prehistoric development but also to learn how particular peoples, many of whom he believed could be identified as the ancestors of specific modern groups, had lived in the past and what had happened to them over time. To many of his contemporaries his approach, grounded in the familiar concept of ethnicity, offered a plausible means to account for the growing evidence of geographical as well as chronological variations in the archaeological record. Kossinna must therefore be recognized as an innovator whose work was of very great importance for the development of culture-historical archaeology.

Although Kossinna died in 1931, in his final years he was increasingly attracted to the Nazi party (Grünert 2002). Calling themselves National Socialists, the Nazis promoted an ethnic policy that sought to unite all German-speakers within a single state. When the Nazi party came to power in 1933, much of Kossinna's interpretation of German prehistory was incorporated into a new history curriculum for German schools (Frick 1934). A large number of teaching and research positions in German prehistory were established for Kossinna's followers in German universities, whereas archaeologists who were politically or racially anathema to the regime were dismissed from their positions. Most German prehistoric archaeologists had been nationalists already before 1933 and their sort of archaeology benefited sufficiently from Nazi patronage that opposition from within the archaeological community was limited. One of the chief uses that the Nazis made of archaeology was to reinforce or create myths about German behavior in antiquity that were designed to promote their own policies, such as the claim that Germans had always respected and obeyed their leaders (Hassmann 2000). Two rival Nazi organizations recruited archaeologists to carry out research for ideological and propaganda purposes. Curiously Adolf Hitler, the Nazi leader, was enamored of ancient Greek and Roman art and architecture. He is reported to have deplored prehistoric archaeology for revealing how culturally primitive the ancient Germans had been (Speer 1970: 141) and appears to have believed that the alleged biological superiority of the modern Germans resulted from selective pressures exerted during the medieval period. His personal views were never made public.

Childe and The Dawn of European Civilization

Kossinna's interpretations of prehistory had little direct influence on archaeology outside German-speaking countries, except in Poland, no doubt because his chauvinism was so repellant. Because of their positive attitude towards foreign influences, British archaeologists were receptive to Montelius's arguments that prehistoric Europe owed much of its cultural development to the Middle East. Yet they did not hold his views and those of more Eurocentric archaeologists to be mutually exclusive. One of the two main themes of John L. Myres's (1869–1954) *The Dawn of History* (1911) was the spread of technology from Egypt and Mesopotamia to Europe. The second was his belief that all hierarchical societies developed when politically dynamic, pastoral peoples, such as the Semites and the Indo-Europeans, were forced by drought to leave their homelands and to conquer and rule politically less innovative peasant societies. This scenario was, like the Hamitic hypothesis, based on the widespread belief that pastoralists, who were equated with the medieval European aristocracy, were natural rulers, while farmers, like medieval peasants, were by nature submissive and predisposed to be ruled by others. According to Myres the Indo-Europeans, whom he believed to be nomads from the steppes of central Asia, were particularly adept at imposing their language, beliefs, and social customs on conquered peoples, while adopting the latter's material culture. Out of the encounter between cultural influences that had been transmitted to Europe from the Middle East and Indo-European political skills a vital and distinctive European way of life was created. Similar views were held by Arthur Evans (1851–1941) (1896), who was Myres's colleague at Oxford University. Yet, although Myres wrote of "peoples" in *The Dawn of History*, he did not yet refer to archaeological cultures.

In the early 1920s, individual cultures were being mentioned by British archaeologists such as M. C. Burkitt (1921), Stanley Casson (1921), J. L. Myres (1923a, 1923b), Harold Peake (1922), and Cyril Fox (1923). Burkitt idiosyncratically defined industries, cultures, and civilizations as nested cultural units of increasing generality, but he referred indiscriminately to entities such as the Mousterian and Solutrean as both cultures and civilizations. In *Man and his Past*, O. G. S. Crawford (1921: 78–9) discussed geographical methods for delineating the origins, extent, and frontiers of cultures. Yet no effort was made to apply the concept of the archaeological culture in a systematic fashion in Britain before the publication of V. Gordon Childe's (1893–1957) *The Dawn of European Civilization* (1925a). Through this book, which Glyn Daniel (1950: 247) called "a new starting-point for prehistoric archaeology," the archaeological culture became the working tool of all European archaeologists.

Childe was born in Sydney, Australia in 1893, the son of a conservative Church of England minister. He studied Classics at the University of Sydney, where he became committed to socialist politics. At an early stage he also grew interested, like Kossinna, in locating the homeland of the Indo-European-speaking peoples. He went on to Oxford University where he studied with Myres and Evans. In 1916 he returned to Australia and political activities became the focus of his life until 1921. Then, disillusioned with politics, he returned to the study of archaeology. His already extensive command of European languages and an acute visual memory enabled him to visit and assemble a vast amount of data from museums and excavations across the whole of Europe (Figure 6.3). He presented the results of this research in two books: *The Dawn of European Civilization* (1925a), which was a synthesis of European prehistory to the end of the Bronze Age, and *The Danube in Prehistory* (1929), a more narrowly focused and more detailed examination of a hitherto little-known region. In 1927, as part of his research for the latter book, Childe participated in a joint Cambridge University–Hungarian excavation at the site of Tószeg in Hungary (Makkay 1991). The theoretical basis of both books was outlined at the beginning of *The Danube*. At this period, theoretical discussions were not a common feature of archaeological literature.

Figure 6.3   Childe (wearing tie) with a party of workmen at Skara Brae,
Orkney, 1928–1930 (Royal Commission on Ancient Monuments, Scotland)

In *The Dawn of European Civilization*, Childe adopted Kossinna's
basic concept of the archaeological culture and his identification of
such cultures as the remains of prehistoric peoples, while exhibiting
no awareness of the racist connotations that Kossinna had attributed
to both of these concepts. It is possible that Childe had come to
understand Kossinna's concept of the archaeological culture mainly
through his close associations with the Polish archaeologist Leon
Kozłowski (1892–1944) (he visited Poland in 1923), and hence was
not fully aware of the ethnic and racial prejudices that Kossinna
had built into it (Lech 1999: 49–51). Childe combined this concept
with Montelius's chronology and Montelius's belief that in prehistoric times technological skills had diffused to Europe from their
place of origin in the Middle East. This is one of the earliest examples of an archaeologist's combining the different approaches and
results of more than one previous researcher to create a new way of

interpreting archaeological evidence. Childe's doing this constitutes evidence of the existence of a growing body of archaeological theory. His interpretations of European prehistory were also influenced by those of Myres and Evans, inasmuch as he stressed the creativity of prehistoric Europeans to a much greater extent than Montelius had done.

Childe defined an archaeological culture, unfortunately with deceptive brevity, as "certain types of remains – pots, implements, ornaments, burial rites, house forms – constantly recurring together" (1929: v–vi). He stressed that each culture had to be delineated individually in terms of constituent artifacts and that cultures could not be created simply by subdividing the ages or epochs of the evolutionary archaeologists either spatially or temporally. Instead, the duration and geographical limits of each culture had to be established empirically and individual cultures aligned chronologically by employing stratigraphy, seriation, and synchronisms. In this way, he interpreted the prehistory of the whole of Europe as a complex mosaic of cultures. Although this mosaic was represented using small-scale maps and tables in *The Dawn of European Civilization*, a detailed chart showing the chronological and geographical distributions of all the archaeological cultures known in the Danube Valley was published in *The Danube in Prehistory* (Figure 6.4) and a chart by Childe and M. C. Burkitt covering all of Europe appeared in *Antiquity* in 1932. In preparing this chart, the authors were able to utilize cultures that had already been provisionally identified by local archaeologists to a far greater extent for central and eastern than for western Europe. These charts were the prototypes for ones that other archaeologists would use to represent regional cultural chronologies around the world.

Most of Childe's cultures were defined on the basis of a small number of diagnostic artifacts. Yet his selection of these artifacts was based on a functionalist view of material culture. Childe argued that the historical significance of different types of artifacts could only be ascertained by considering what role they had played in prehistoric cultures. He decided, apparently on the basis of common sense, that home-made pottery, ornaments, and burial rites tended to reflect local tastes and were relatively resistant to change; hence, they were useful for identifying specific ethnic groups. By contrast, the marked utilitarian value of tools, weapons, and other items of technology

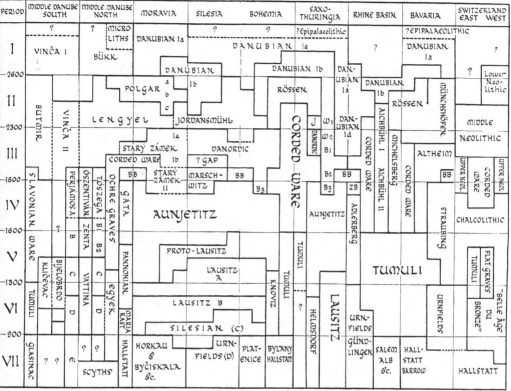

BB = BELL-BEAKER   ZB = ZONED BEAKER   W1 etc. = WALTERMENBURG   B1 etc. = BERNBURG   J = JORDANSMÜHL
TABLE GIVING CORRELATIONS OF THE SEVERAL CULTURES IN TIME AND SPACE

Figure 6.4 Childe's first chart correlating the archaeological cultures of central Europe, from *The Danube in Prehistory*, 1929

caused them to diffuse rapidly from one group to another, as a result of either trade or copying. Hence, he considered these types of artifacts especially valuable for assigning neighboring cultures to the same period and establishing cultural chronologies before the invention of radiocarbon dating (Childe 1929: viii, 248; cf. Binford 1983a: 399–400). Childe concluded that the synchronisms produced by this operation supported the same picture of the diffusion of material culture westward across Europe as had emerged from Montelius's work.

Childe believed that although diagnostic artifacts might serve to define an archaeological culture, they did not suffice to describe it. For that purpose every type of artifact was relevant. Childe was interested in viewing archaeological cultures not simply as collections of traits but also as the means for providing an ethnographic interpretation of how specific groups had lived in prehistoric times. Yet he went about doing this more systematically than Kossinna had done. In the first edition of *The Dawn of European Civilization* he attempted to summarize what could be inferred about the way of life associated with each major culture. In later editions, he surveyed each culture more systematically, covering – insofar as this was possible – economy, social and political organization, and religious beliefs (Childe 1939, 1956a: 129–31). When it came to interpreting cultural change, Childe paid equal attention, as Montelius had done, to diffusion and migration. He interpreted diffusion as the spread of functionally advantageous or stylistically more attractive traits from one culture to another, whereas migration resulted in the replacement of one culture by another or in cultural mixing. Cultural continuity was ascribed to ethnic continuity in the absence of these processes. Childe's approach thus bore a close resemblance to the diffusionist ethnology found in Europe and North America in the 1920s.

Yet, although equating archaeological cultures and peoples, as Kossinna had done, Childe developed grave doubts about the possibility of tracing specific peoples in the archaeological record. Unlike Kossinna, he attributed great importance to diffusion and had come to believe that over time this process could obscure even the most tenacious cultural continuities. Because of this he abandoned his efforts to use archaeological data to identify the homeland of the Indo-Europeans. In *Prehistoric Migrations in Europe* (1950a), he tentatively associated the Indo-Europeans with the Urnfield culture but that identification was refuted within a decade (Childe 1958b: 73). His avoidance in *The Dawn of European Civilization* of the Iron Age, with its connecting links to the historic period, may have been related to his decision to avoid discussing specific ethnic identities. In any case, although not doubting that cultures had been produced by prehistoric peoples, as a diffusionist Childe was far more sceptical than Kossinna, or even Montelius, had been about it being possible to trace specific ethnicities far back in the archaeological record.

The Dawn of European Civilization provided a model that was to be applied to the study of archaeology throughout much of Europe into the 1950s. It was an approach that Childe, despite his own changing interests, followed closely in his later regional syntheses, such as *The Prehistory of Scotland* (1935a) and *Prehistoric Communities of the British Isles* (1940a). The primary aim of archaeologists who adopted this approach was no longer to interpret the archaeological record as evidence of stages of cultural development. Instead, they sought to identify often nameless prehistoric peoples by means of archaeological cultures and to trace their origins, movements, and interactions. The Neolithic period was no longer seen primarily as a stage of cultural development but, rather, as a mosaic composed of sharply delineated cultural groups. The questions being addressed were of a particularist, historical variety. There also was a general interest in learning about how specific peoples had lived in prehistoric times.

Childe was fully aware of the revolution that he had brought about in archaeology. In 1925, he noted with satisfaction that the clarity with which the migrations of nameless prehistoric peoples stood out in the archaeological record when it was studied as a mosaic of cultures was a revelation to fellow archaeologists (Childe 1925b). He thus distinguished between an older evolutionary archaeology and a new culture-historical approach. He also observed, with reference to the British and French rather than the Scandinavian school, that in the nineteenth century evolutionary archaeologists had become more interested in artifacts than in their makers. He claimed that in constructing evolutionary sequences they had treated artifacts as dead fossils rather than as expressions of living societies (1940a: 3). In his opinion, scientific progress had left archaeologists with no alternative but to adopt the concrete methods of history. Yet the concept of the archaeological culture, which he had borrowed from Kossinna, and the diffusionist views of Montelius were both closely related to the widely held interpretations of human behavior that had developed as a reaction against cultural evolutionism in western Europe beginning in the late nineteenth century. The new culture-historical view of prehistory was as deeply rooted in a pessimistic assessment of cultural change and human creativity as the previous evolutionary one had been rooted in an optimistic assessment.

Childe, despite his left-wing political radicalism, did not wholly escape the racism that was part of this new outlook. In *The Aryans* (1926), which may have been based on material he had written before *The Dawn of European Civilization*, he argued that the Indo-Europeans succeeded, not because they possessed a material culture or natural intelligence that was superior to those of other peoples, but because they spoke a superior language and benefited from the more competent mentality it made possible. He pointed out that the Greeks and Romans had only a diluted Nordic physical type but that each had realized the high cultural potential that was inherent in their language. This interpretation contrasted with Kossinna's belief that ethnic and racial mixture in these countries had resulted in cultural decline. Yet, at the end of *The Aryans*, Childe bowed to prevailing racist sentiments by suggesting that the "superiority in physique" of the Nordic peoples made them the appropriate initial bearers of a superior language (Childe 1926: 211). In later years, as he adopted other explanations for cultural variation, he repudiated these early speculations, which he had come to regard as shameful.

European Archaeology and Nationalism

The gradual development of culture-historical archaeology in Scandinavia, Germany, and England took place while prehistoric archaeology was being professionalized across Europe and strongly influenced the sort of archaeology that emerged. Prehistoric archaeology clearly developed differently in every country (Ucko 1995b: 8). Yet that does not rule out identifying some shared features. Hodder (1991b) has observed that European archaeology has been and remains deeply historical. Most archaeologists seek to learn about the history and prehistory of specific parts of Europe or the whole continent. Their original goal was to extend history as it was known from written sources back into the still more remote past. They did this by defining archaeological cultures and trying to explain their origins and changes by means of diffusion and migration. Because nationalism was ubiquitous in Europe, it seems likely that it played a significant role in shaping the practice of archaeology. Yet it is going too far to claim that nationalism was embedded in the very concept of archaeology and was the only cause of its development (Díaz-Andreu and Champion 1996b: 3) or that nationalism cannot do without archaeology (Slapšak and Novaković 1996: 290). Everywhere in Europe, the discipline of document-based history played an early and continuous role in cultivating ethnic identities and encouraging patriotic and later nationalist sentiments. These studies usually focused on the early modern and medieval periods or on any earlier ages for which there were written records. The role played by archaeology was generally subordinate to that of history, while at the same time not all archaeology was national in orientation (Kaeser 2002).

Archaeology's greatest asset was the heightened and immediate sense of connection with the past that material objects can provide. Sites such as Tara in Ireland or Biskupin in Poland at various times have played important roles as foci of national sentiment in their respective countries. Archaeological finds also have provided enduring symbols of national identity. Examples include Neolithic barrows, bronze lurs (trumpets), golden drinking horns, and a ceremonial object, the sun wagon, in Denmark and the Tara brooch and Ardagh chalice in Ireland (Sørensen 1996; Cooney 1996). In recent years, the right to use the star of Vergina, associated with the Greek-speaking kings of ancient Macedonia, has been bitterly contested between the governments of Macedonia and Greece (K. Brown 1994). Yet the sentiments associated with such archaeological finds can also be transitory and they can as easily be local or regional as they are national in scope. Much important archaeological research has been done by archaeologists who were primarily interested in sites or historical problems that were of only local concern.

The significance of archaeology for national projects has varied greatly in duration and intensity. Political unrest, national crises, and rapid economic and social change frequently stimulate interest in a nation's past, which often is romantically represented as having been more stable than the present and therefore as having valuable lessons to teach modern times. Greeks have long derived a sense of ethnic continuity and identity from their combined prehistoric, classical, and Byzantine archaeological heritage, which has helped them to cope with repeated episodes of political instability and multiple foreign threats to their country's survival. The urgent concern of Greek archaeologists to control this past has been sustained by their resistance to the efforts of foreign archaeologists to appropriate the study of ancient Greek civilization for themselves (Kotsakis 1991: 66–7). Throughout much of the nineteenth century, a strong public interest in Danish prehistory was spurred by the military threat posed to Denmark by more powerful European nations (Sørensen 1996). By contrast, Norwegian archaeology played a prominent role in supplying symbols of ancient achievements mainly in the period that immediately followed Norway's political independence in 1905 (Dommasnes 1992: 2), whereas in France Celtic archaeology appears to have been invoked by political leaders to promote unity in the 1860s and again only in 1985 (Dietler 1998).

Political events also can influence how archaeological data are interpreted. After the unification of Italy in 1861 by the northern Italian kingdom of Piedmont, archaeologists working for Luigi Pigorini (1884–1925) attributed the cultural development of prehistoric Italy to the spread southward during the Bronze Age of more advanced northern Italian peoples who superimposed themselves on the Neolithic southerners. Although the implications were not explicitly emphasized by Pigorini, this interpretation made the modern political domination of southern Italy by the north appear to be merely another example of a long established historical process (Guidi 1996: 111–2).

Archaeological research has been suppressed or controlled by governments for political reasons in some European countries. The study of Polish archaeology was interrupted by the repression that followed the Polish November Uprising of 1831 against the Russian occupation of eastern Poland and the Russians banned the study of local archaeology by Lithuanians between 1863 and 1904 after a Lithuanian nationalist uprising was crushed (Puodžiūnas and Girininkas 1996). In Spain, where archaeological research had previously displayed strong regional tendencies, during the dictatorship of Francisco Franco (1939–1975) the study of prehistory from such multiple perspectives was suppressed. Archaeologists were to some extent encouraged to identify the origin of the Spanish people with the prehistoric arrival of the Celts, which was construed as the triumph of Europeans over earlier African elements of the population. Nevertheless, the Franco government's recognition of the period that followed the discovery of America in AD 1492 as Spain's Golden Age resulted in chronic underfunding of prehistoric archaeology (Díaz-Andreu 1993, 1997; Ruiz Zapatero 1996; Ruiz et al. 2002). Culture-historical archaeology also was controlled for political purposes in Italy, where the fascist regime of Benito Mussolini (1922–1943) promoted classical archaeology as a means of identifying itself as the modern reincarnation of the ancient Roman state. Despite lavish financing, much of the archaeological research that was carried out during the fascist period aimed to publicize the grandeur of ancient Rome rather than to understand ancient Rome better (Guidi 1996).

In 1935, when the Soviet Union was threatened by Nazi expansion, the Communist party ordered archaeologists to combat German claims of racial and cultural superiority and strengthen Russian patriotism by bolstering the image of the Slavic peoples in prehistoric times. This involved demonstrating that Slavic culture had evolved independently of German influence, that it was older and more developed than German culture, and that no Germans had ever lived on modern Slavic territory in prehistoric times. This endeavor expressed itself in a growing concern with "ethnogenesis," which involved searching for ways to trace the origins of specific national groups in the archaeological record. Previously, Soviet archaeologists had ridiculed the debates between Polish and German archaeologists as to whether the late Neolithic and early Bronze Age Lusatian culture was Slavic or German, observing that those two linguistic groups had probably not yet differentiated at that time (M. Miller 1956: 83–4). In the late 1930s, Russian archaeologists sought to demonstrate that from ancient times their ancestors, the East Slavs, had occupied the European territory of the Soviet Union, as well as to refute German claims that throughout history the Slavs had been culturally backward peoples. Both before and after World War II research was carried out to trace the origins of the Russian people and the development of their ancient culture and handicrafts (M. Miller 1956: 135–44).

The post-World War II study of medieval Russian towns, especially the excavations at Novgorod, set new standards for urban archaeology for that period (Figure 6.5). The recovery at Novgorod of numerous letters written on birch bark revealed an unexpected degree of literacy that was not restricted, as many scholars had previously believed, to the clergy. These studies demonstrated that the development of towns in ancient Russia started at the same time as, and proceeded simultaneously with, the development of towns in central and western Europe. They also showed that the Russians were

Figure 6.5   Excavations at Novgorod after World War II
(Institute of Archaeology, St. Peterburg)

abreast of other European groups in the development of crafts, trade, and culture (M. Thompson 1967). The long-held view that Russian towns had begun as Scandinavian colonies was vehemently rejected. Yet in studies of ethnogenesis the concept of autochthonous development was frequently ignored and cautious use was made of diffusion and migration to explain changes in the archaeological record. Leo Klejn (1974) has observed that Russian archaeologists adopted a German culture-historical approach but used it, as Polish archaeologists had done, to counter German myths concerning their own racial and cultural superiority. As with much Soviet archaeology, the general nature of the results was ordained by the government before the research was carried out. After 1945, when Eastern Europe was recognized as a Soviet sphere of influence, an International Congress of Slavic Archaeology was founded to encourage closer relations among

Slavic nations. In the Soviet Union, the allocation of substantial resources for researching Slavic ethnogenesis did not result in the significant curtailment of research on other problems.

European archaeologists were not always successful in using the potential national relevance of their research to secure government funding. In Portugal, foreign and local archaeologists had by the 1930s produced what they believed was evidence of continuity between the local Copper Age and the modern nation and also established that still earlier Portugal had been a major center of the development of megalithic culture. Yet the right-wing regime of António Salazar, which controlled Portugal from 1932 to 1974, chose, like the Franco regime in Spain, to ground Portuguese nationalism on historical accounts of the medieval period and the Age of Exploration. The lack of support for archaeological research resulted in Portuguese archaeology falling behind that of all other countries in Europe (Oliveira and Jorge 1995; Lillios 1995; Fabião 1996).

In Ireland, a strong identification with the past developed in the mid-nineteenth century as part of the Celtic revival (Sheehy 1980). Perhaps because of the Irish perception of their struggle for independence from Britain as being as much a religious conflict as it was an ethnic one, their interest in the past did not stimulate a major involvement with prehistoric archaeology, despite the presence of Newgrange and other extraordinary prehistoric monuments in Ireland. Instead, Ireland's Golden Age was identified with the historically documented early Christian period that followed the conversion to Christianity of a supposedly ethnically pure Celtic society. The Keeper of Irish Antiquities of the National Museum of Ireland from 1927 to 1939 was the Austrian archaeologist and Nazi sympathizer Adolph Mahr and the first large-scale scientific excavations in Ireland were carried out by the Harvard Archaeological Expedition beginning in 1932.

The scientific prestige and predominance of evolutionary archaeology in nineteenth-century England and France impeded the development of culture-historical archaeology in those countries. It also tended to identify prehistoric peoples as generic savages rather than heroic national ancestors, although for romantics these two categories were not mutually exclusive. Nor was there much doubt among intellectuals in these countries that for much of human history cultural development in the Middle East had been in advance of that in western Europe. Although these factors limited the political scope of ethnic archaeology, they did not prevent archaeology from serving the cause of nationalism in other ways. By appropriating the archaeological heritage of foreign lands – especially ones that had produced great civilizations in ancient times – it was possible for European nations to affirm their leading role in the modern world. In 1794 the victorious Napoleon Bonaparte systematically carried off many major classical art works from Italian museums to Paris, on the grounds that the cultural supremacy of the French allowed them to be better appreciated there than in Italy. In 1816, the British Museum purchased from Lord Thomas Elgin the marble sculptures that he had removed from the Acropolis in Athens in 1801–1802 and competition between French and English agents to acquire ancient works of art from Egypt and northern Mesopotamia continued throughout the first half of the nineteenth century (R. Chamberlin 1983; M. Larsen 1996; Ridley 1998; Mayes 2003). Only powerful and wealthy nations could afford to carry out such activities on a truly impressive scale. Chief among these were Britain, France, Germany, the United States, and to a lesser extent Italy. Another expression of national preeminence was the ability to carry out archaeological research not only in one's own country but around the world. In such endeavors, the same five nations excelled. Although such activities did not contribute to an understanding of national prehistory, they were a source of national distinction and pride (Jenkins 1992). In that sense, although it collected artifacts from all parts of the world, the British Museum was, despite recent claims to the contrary (Champion 1996: 130–2), truly a national museum (Díaz-Andreu 2004).

It was not until after World War I that a culture-historical approach replaced an evolutionary one in Britain and France. Childe was the leading archaeologist, but not the only one, who brought this about in Britain. In France, Joseph Dechélette (1862–1914) had already worked out a detailed pottery chronology for the Gallo-Roman period and published a manual of prehistoric, protohistoric, and early historical archaeology. Yet his primary focus was artifact types not cultures and his career was cut short when he was killed in action early in World War I (Binétruy 1994). Beginning in the 1920s, Henri Breuil (1877–1961), a Roman Catholic priest and the first Professor of Prehistory at the Collège de France, applied a culture-historical approach to the evolutionary stronghold of French Palaeolithic archaeology.

His interpretation of the European Palaeolithic was based on the belief of the physical anthropologist Marcellin Boule (1861–1942) that modern-type human beings had existed in Europe alongside the Neanderthals and their ancestors and on Hugo Obermaier's (1877–1946) division of the Lower Palaeolithic into contemporary flake and core traditions. All three men were opposed to Gabriel de Mortillet's unilinear evolutionism and his anticlericalism. Breuil argued that archaeological evidence indicated that two hominid groups had coexisted in France from earliest times. One group, making bifacial tools, had produced the Abbevillian, Acheulean, and Micoquian cultures, whereas the other, producing flake tools, accounted for the Clactonian, Languedocian, Levalloisian, Tayacian, and Mousterian sequence. Breuil argued that the Aurignacian culture had been introduced to France by *Homo sapiens* coming from the east and that in France some bearers of this culture had mingled with the Mousterian Neanderthals. He also maintained that the Solutrean culture originated in central Europe and the Magdalenian came from the northeast (C. Cohen 1999). After World War II, François Bordes (1919–1981) defined sixty-three tool types that were recurring features of Middle Palaeolithic assemblages and used these to identify several archaeological cultures that he associated with a number of distinct Neanderthal tribes that he believed had lived in southern France. The replacement of an evolutionary by a culture-historical approach in Palaeolithic archaeology epitomized the success of this approach in French archaeology (Binford 1983b: 79–94; Bisson 2000).

In the late nineteenth and early twentieth centuries, European archaeologists became interested in the prehistory of Egypt and the Middle East. In the 1870s and 1880s, Heinrich Schliemann (1822–1890) excavated late prehistoric sites in Greece and Turkey in an effort to confirm Homeric legends. At the same time, historical archaeologists generally extended their research back into prehistoric times when they inadvertently encountered prehistoric material. Systematic study of the prehistory of the Middle East increased after World War I, when large areas of the former Ottoman Empire were placed under French and British political control. In the 1920s and 1930s work was carried out in the Middle East by archaeologists familiar with European prehistory, such as Dorothy Garrod (1892–1968), or who specialized in studying the prehistory of the Middle East, such as Gertrude Caton Thompson. These archaeologists sought to define prehistoric cultures and trace their origins and the influence they had exerted on each other. To do this, they had to rely far more on stratigraphy and cross-dating cultural sequences than did historical archaeologists working in the region. Gradually, a set of local cultural sequences was produced extending temporally from Palaeolithic times to the historical period and geographically from Europe and North Africa eastward through the Middle East to India. This research reinforced the idea of the Middle East as the cradle of European civilization. It also established the maximum effective range of interest for most European archaeologists before the invention of radiocarbon dating. Although European archaeologists also carried out research in East Asia and the Americas, their inability to correlate findings in these areas with cultural developments in Europe and the Middle East precluded the development of world prehistory. When Henri Berr launched his global history project *L'évolution de l'Humanité*, its volumes dealing with prehistory were restricted to covering Europe and the Middle East (Gran-Aymerich 1998: 268–98, 349–57, 408–16). In general, prehistoric archaeology in the Middle East reflected and confirmed the Montelian view of the priority of cultural development in this region and of its impact on Europe.

In most European countries, the cruder and more obvious uses of archaeology to promote ethnic and nationalist agendas disappeared after 1945, as growing political and economic cooperation and gradually improving standards of living resulted in less blatant political manipulations of nationalist sentiments. One of the strongest continuing engagements of archaeology in national projects was in Poland, the borders of which had been radically altered after World War II and were not universally accepted until the early 1970s. By the 1960s, the culture-historical approach, as it had been defined by Childe in 1925, also was being abandoned as many archaeologists sought for other explanations of cultural change to supplement or replace diffusion and migration. Yet European archaeologists did not become less interested in studying the history of Europe at the local, national, and continental levels. In part, this continuing influence was assured by the institutionalization of prehistoric archaeology as an independent historical discipline or a branch of history in many universities. It also reflected a strong, broadly held conviction among Europeans that archaeology was first and foremost a study of their past. Under these circumstances, it is not surprising that archaeological interpretation continued to be influenced in various ways by national political, ethnic, and cultural concerns that were sometimes serious and sometimes fanciful in nature (Gjessing 1968; Rowlands 1984b).

In Scandinavia, a commitment to peace and social welfare was accompanied by a compensatory, whimsical fascination with the Viking period, which was conceptualized as a violent, wanton, and romantic time in contrast to the dull and peaceful present. In the 1970s, 20 to 25 percent of all archaeological publications were devoted to these 300 years (Moberg 1981: 215). As Britain's role as a world power declined, there was a resurgence of popular interest in that country's rich assemblage of megalithic circles and stone alignments, which were interpreted as evidence that highly skilled engineers and "astronomer priests" had lived there in prehistoric times. On these grounds, some archaeologists maintained that Britain had been a center of scientific excellence since the Neolithic period (Ellegård 1981; Fowler 1987). According to Gabriel Cooney (1995: 273), Irish archaeology remains essentially nationalistic in outlook. Migration is still an important explanatory device, reflecting a continuing interest in ethnicity. On the other hand, suggestions of links with Britain generally tend to be played down (Cooney 1995, 1996; Woodman 1995; Crooke 2000). The evidence produced by the excavations at Wood Quay of Dublin as a Viking center during the Dark Ages, although exciting much local public interest, accorded less well with a Celtocentric nationalist view of Irish history (Sheehy 1980; T. Heffernan 1988).

Other archaeological projects have played a major role in countering centrist narratives and the prejudices associated with them. In England, the discovery that during the Dark Ages the Viking settlement at York was a center of manufacturing and trade has confirmed to northerners that their region was culturally as advanced as southern England, contrary to establishment history, which portrays Saxon Wessex as an outpost of civilization valiantly resisting the incursions of barbarous Scandinavians who eventually settled in the north (Graham Campbell and Kidd 1980). In Spain, following the demise of the Franco regime, regional archaeologies reemerged in various parts of the country, including for the first time in the south, where archaeologists began seriously to study that region's Islamic period (Díaz-Andreu 1996b). Yet archaeological findings were used much less for polemical purposes than they had been in the past.

Across Europe, nations seemed more interested in achieving and affirming modernity than in recalling past hostilities and injustices.

Culture-historical archaeology survived more completely than anywhere else in West Germany and in neighboring German-speaking Austria and Switzerland. Despite the devastation of World War II and the denazification program that followed, a large number of professional archaeologists who had been working before and during the war continued to do so after 1945. The experiences these archaeologists had with adjusting to new political programs during and immediately after the Nazi period led to a heightened mistrust of all theories and generalizations and an even greater emphasis than in the past on empirical and inductive approaches. In 1987, the distinguished prehistorian Ulrich Fischer declared that, with a few minor exceptions, all the basic theoretical knowledge that prehistoric archaeologists required had been invented before the end of the nineteenth century. All that was needed was to discover better ways of applying such knowledge. Racial interpretations were abandoned immediately after the war and a growing emphasis was placed on the technical excellence of excavation, typological analysis, the production of artifact catalogues, and using seriation to create more refined chronologies. These all were aspects of archaeology in which German archaeologists had taken pride before World War II.

Although the concept of the archaeological culture continued to be regarded as a valuable classificatory device, Kossinna's belief that this entity necessarily coincided with a specific people or language group was widely abandoned (Eggers 1950; Veit 1989). Ethnic interpretations of archaeological cultures were replaced by ones referring to economic spheres, trading zones, political or social structures, and cult activities. A heavy emphasis was placed by Herbert Jahnkuhn (1905–1990) (1977), B. Sielmann (1971), Georg Kossack, and others on the study of prehistoric settlements in their ecological and economic settings. This type of analysis was favored because the examination of zoological and botanical finds, soils, and sources of raw materials added the prestige of "value-free" scientific research to such studies. It was generally accepted that the best way to interpret archaeological data was by employing the direct historical approach, although comparisons of this sort often were made in an impressionistic and uncontrolled fashion (Härke 1991, 1995; Kossack 1992; Arnold and Hassmann 1995; Wiwjorra 1996; Wolfram 2000).

Despite the emphasis on empiricism, some highly innovative theoretical work was accomplished. In 1950, Hans-Jürgen Eggers (1906–1975) published a study of how knowledge concerning the deposition, survival, and recovery of archaeological material influenced an understanding of the past that anticipated modern taphonomic studies in Britain and the United States by several decades. In keeping with the historical orientation of German archaeology, Eggers thought of these procedures as the archaeological equivalents of historical source criticism. In 1964, Günter Smolla analyzed the role of uniformitarian assumptions for evaluating analogies in a way that anticipated some aspects of middle-range theory. He received support from Karl Narr, one of Germany's few senior archaeologists who had an understanding of anthropology. Although Eggers's practical suggestions were incorporated into German archaeological practice, neither his publications nor Smolla's gave rise to significant archaeological discussion (Wolfram 2000: 189–92). While efforts have been made since the late 1980s, mainly by younger archaeologists, to encourage theoretical debates, German archaeology appears to have persisted as a culture-historical approach from which the concept of ethnicity has been largely eliminated. There has been little serious examination of the reasons for cultural change. In a world in which archaeological interpretations have been changing rapidly, German archaeology remains characterized by craft, continuity, consensus, and an abiding faith in the efficacy of accumulating data (Härke 1995: 47–51). The empirical approach has been strongly championed by the students and followers of Otto von Merhart (1866–1959), who beginning in 1928 held the first German chair in prehistoric archaeology, which was established at Marburg University.

Although nationalism continues to influence European archaeology to varying degrees in different countries, the concern with Europe as a whole and with the status of Western Civilization in world perspective that was evident in the work of Montelius and Childe still seems to be as strong as it was in the past, or even more so. Colin Renfrew (1973a), by using calibrated radiocarbon dates to argue that metallurgy may have developed independently in Europe as early as it did in the Middle East and to demonstrate that megalithic structures were being erected in Malta and western Europe before any known monumental constructions in the Middle East, except perhaps at Jericho, played a major role in challenging the Montelius–Childe diffusionary model of European prehistory and emphasizing the technological superiority of Europe in prehistoric times. His more recent proposal to link the arrival of the Indo-Europeans in Europe with that of agriculture also assigns most modern European peoples a longer in situ history there than was previously envisaged (Renfrew 1988). The neoconservatism of the 1980s was accompanied by a resurgent emphasis on economic dynamism, equality before the law, and the sharing of political power within a society as special features of Western Civilization (Wells 1984; Lamberg-Karlovsky 1985; Willey 1985). Ian Hodder in *The Domestication of Europe* (1990) has attempted to use archaeological evidence to trace assumed distinctive patterns of European thought back to the Neolithic or even the Upper Palaeolithic period. With the growing importance of the European Union, efforts were made to adopt the widespread Celtic culture of the Iron Age as a symbol for European unity. This endeavor has been criticized by various archaeologists (Collis 1996; Díaz-Andreu 1996a: 56–7; Fitzpatrick, A. P 1996) and does not appear to have generated much public enthusiasm.

A concern with heritage management began in Europe in the late nineteenth century, but for a long time it was mainly concerned with preserving a small number of buildings and archaeological sites deemed to be of special importance. It thus reflected, often in an extreme manner, the historical values of specific times and places. In the late twentieth century, governments increasingly competed in ensuring the conservation and rational management of cultural resources. Where this management process has resulted in archaeological surveys and investigations being extended to cover all periods of a nation's history and all parts of its territory, it has helped to counter the biases introduced into archaeology by political partisanship. In France, this approach is said to have resulted in the development of a "national," rather than a "nationalist," archaeology (Fleury-Ilett 1996). Such an approach also has increased the ability of regional and local concerns to influence archaeological research and in some cases has produced "community archaeology," which seeks to involve local groups in the planning and carrying out of research projects that are of direct interest to them (S. Moser 1995b; Marshall 2002). Similar engagements of dispersed ethnic minorities, occupational groups, social classes, and alternative life styles further increase the multivocality of inputs into archaeological research. The ongoing acrimonious debates concerning the use, management, and interpretation of Stonehenge indicate how difficult it can be to accommodate conflicting demands (Bender 1998). Although contributions of this sort help to counteract narrow, elite biases and to generate valuable research problems, Kristian Kristiansen (1996: 143) has appropriately stressed the need for archaeologists to be critical of all efforts to manipulate archaeological findings for political and ideological purposes. Doing this requires archaeologists to exercise their professional judgment about what is archaeologically possible and to strive as much as possible to be objective in their designing and execution of research projects.

Other National Archaeologies

The European culture-historical approach, with its emphasis on studying the prehistory of specific peoples, provided a model for national archaeologies around the world. It remains the dominant approach to archaeology in many countries. Like nationalist history, to which it is usually closely linked, the culture-historical approach can be used to bolster the pride and morale of nations or ethnic groups. It is most often used for this purpose among peoples who feel thwarted, threatened, or deprived of their collective rights by more powerful nations or in countries where appeals for national unity are being made to counteract serious internal divisions. It is also used to strengthen insecure political regimes, and to justify aggression against neighboring peoples and the oppression of ethnic minorities. As in Europe, the culture-historical approach often promotes its agenda by stressing specific periods of history and assigning particular ethnic identities to archaeological finds. It celebrates the achievements of indigenous early civilizations and usually pays more attention to the recent past than it does to the Palaeolithic period. History and late prehistory tend to be treated as a continuum. This section will examine a few examples of the culture-historical approach from Asia, Africa, and Latin America.

Western-style field archaeology was introduced into Japan by American and European natural scientists and physicians who were hired to teach there after the Meiji revolution of 1868, when the new government determined to catch up with advances in Western science, technology, and medicine. The most important of these visiting scholars was the American zoologist Edward Morse (1838–1925), who had participated in shell-mound research in the eastern United States. He identified and excavated a shell mound at Omori in 1877 and recorded a great interest in archaeology among the Japanese he encountered (Morse 1879). Those who became Japan's leading archaeologists in the late nineteenth and early twentieth centuries were often educated in other disciplines and many of them had studied in Europe. Hence, their backgrounds were similar to those of self-trained or informally trained professional archaeologists in the West during the nineteenth century.

Although Morse was an evolutionist, the Japanese archaeologists who followed him had more in common with the European culture-historical archaeologists of the late nineteenth century. The first generation of Japanese professional archaeologists was led by Tsuboi Shogoro (1863–1913). In 1884, he and several other science students established the Anthropological Society of Tokyo and nine years later he was appointed Professor of Anthropology at the University of Tokyo. Tsuboi conceived of anthropology, in the continental European fashion, as a branch of zoology interested in human physical remains and regarded archaeological evidence as providing clues for identifying racial groups. He specialized in the study of the Mesolithic Jomon culture, which he attributed to a pre-Ainu population. Already by 1919 Matsumoto Hikoshichiro had demonstrated stratigraphically that some variations in Jomon ceramics were the result of chronological rather than tribal differences.

In 1895, historians working at the Imperial Museum (today the Tokyo National Museum) founded the Archaeological Society. It had closer links with pre-Meiji antiquarian scholarship than did the Anthropological Society of Tokyo. Its aims were to study the "archaeology of our country, with the view to throwing light on customs, institutions, culture and technologies in the successive periods of our national history" (Ikawa-Smith 1982: 301). These scholars concentrated on the late prehistoric Yayoi and the protohistoric Kofun periods and had a special interest in fine art, as exemplified by bronze mirrors and elite weapons. The main tradition of Japanese archaeology was established by Hamada Kosaku (1881–1938), an art historian by background who was appointed Professor of Archaeology at Kyoto University after he returned from Europe in 1916, where he had studied archaeology with W. M. F. Petrie. Hamada encouraged the development in Japan of systematic excavation techniques, which he combined with a rigorous typological approach within the general framework of culture-historical archaeology. His reports on sites he excavated in Japan, Korea, and China provided models for many Japanese researchers. His ablest student and successor at Kyoto University, Umehara Suezi (1893–1983), excavated more than 200 sites. Umehara's primary interest was the detailed study of artifacts, including Chinese and early Japanese metal objects.

Before World War II, Japanese archaeologists of all schools continued to pursue a culture-historically oriented archaeology, which did not preclude an interest in understanding "the outline of human development and regularities of social transformations" (Ikawa-Smith 1982: 302). Political pressures, particularly those associated with efforts to promote national unity by stressing the veneration of the emperor as the direct descendant of the gods and the divinely appointed head of the Japanese national family, impeded archaeological development at certain periods. Government regulations issued in 1874 and 1880 made it difficult to excavate large burial mounds that were identified as tombs of the royal family. Some excavations of tombs of this sort were carried out in the politically relaxed atmosphere of the 1920s. At that time, historians also published Marxist interpretations of Japanese history in which archaeological data were used. From the nineteenth century onward, however, most archaeologists were careful not to contradict officially sponsored accounts of ancient Japanese history based on the *Kojiki, Nihon Shoki,* and other chronicles recorded in the eighth century AD. The Jomon culture, which was dated before 1500 BC and therefore antedated the events described in these accounts, was ascribed to the Ainu by the anatomist Koganei Yoshikiyo (1859–1944) and to a pre-Ainu people by Morse and Tsuboi, but was not associated with a people regarded as ancestral to the modern Japanese. Either interpretation justified the late-nineteenth-century colonization of the island of Hokkaido, where the Ainu lived, by representing it as the continuation of a historical expansion of the Japanese people northward through the Japanese archipelago (Fawcett 1986). In the ultranationalist atmosphere of the 1930s, it became extremely dangerous to engage in any research that even inadvertently might cast doubt on Shinto myths concerning the divine origin of the royal family. Those involved in such activities risked removal from their posts and imprisonment.

As a result of these pressures physical anthropologists and linguists avoided discussions of ethnicity, while archaeologists concentrated on elaborating artifact typologies and did not engage in discussions of cultural change that could have any bearing on the official version of history.

After 1945, archaeologists helped to provide a view of the development of the Japanese people that filled the ideological vacuum left following military defeat in World War II. Immediately after the war, Wajima Seiichi (1909–1971) used Marxist theories and information about pre- and protohistoric settlement systems to infer social transformations that had produced the early Japanese state and class system. Kobayashi Yukio (1911–1988) studied similar developments from a technological perspective. As Japan was steered politically away from left-wing radicalism and toward a more centrist position, the culture-historical approach that was entrenched before the war prevailed. Japanese archaeology provided tangible contact with the past and helped to reinforce a sense of stability through successive phases of postwar economic and cultural change and uncertainty. It was looked to as an important source of information about what was distinctively and inalienably Japanese.

In keeping with new ideas about the sovereignty of the people, popular accounts of archaeological discoveries were characterized by a fascination with the origin of the Japanese people and their culture. There has been a growing tendency to trace the Japanese as an ethnic group as far back as the Jomon or even the Palaeolithic period (Fawcett 1986). The following Yayoi period is celebrated as a prehistoric analogue of modern times that was characterized by the selective adoption of items of culture from abroad and their integration into Japanese life. The leading role assigned to the upper classes as mediators in this process resembles interpretations of British history offered by nationalist historians and prehistorians in England in the late nineteenth and early twentieth centuries (Mizoguchi 2002). By tracing current features of Japanese life deeply into the past, change and foreign ideas are made to appear less threatening to the nation's core values.

Archaeological activities have expanded enormously in Japan since the 1940s. Japanese archaeologists are proud of the technical excellence of their work and most of them seek to understand their findings from the perspective of Japan's national history. Public interest in archaeology is high, surveys and rescue work are mandatory, and archaeological finds are exhibited to the public in many places (Tanaka 1984). The high quality of excavation and artifact analysis has produced detailed intrasite chronologies that permit questions about changes in social organization to be addressed in ways that are equalled in few other countries (Mizoguchi 2002).

The political problems and revolutionary changes that overtook China beginning in the nineteenth century produced a renewed interest in historiography and the development of a more critical attitude toward ancient texts as sources of information about the past. In particular, it was suggested that accounts of the two earliest royal dynasties were largely mythical creations of later times (G. Wang 1985: 184–8). The study of art objects and calligraphy was a long-established part of the Chinese tradition of historiography. Field archaeology developed, however, for the first time within the context of the reformist May 4th Movement, which, beginning in 1919, sought to replace literary scholarship with scientific knowledge from the West. There was a receptive audience for geology, palaeontology, and other sciences capable of collecting empirical data from the earth.

The first major archaeological fieldwork was carried out by Western scientists attached to the Geological Survey of China, which had been established in Peking (Beijing) in 1916. The Swedish geologist J. G. Andersson (1874–1960) (1934: 163–87) identified the Neolithic Yangshao culture in 1921 and major work at the lower levels of the Palaeolithic site of Zhoukoudian began under the direction of the Canadian anatomist Davidson Black (1884–1934) in 1926 (Hood 1964). The first indigenous Chinese scholar to direct the excavation of a major archaeological site was Li Ji (Li Chi) (1895–1979), who had earned a doctorate in anthropology at Harvard University in 1923. From 1928 to 1937, as first head of the Department of Archaeology in the National Research Institute of History and Philology of Academia Sinica, he dug at the late Shang site of Yinxu, near Anyang. These excavations, carried out at a site that yielded many inscriptions and works of art, played a major role in training a generation of Chinese archaeologists and also in turning the new science of archaeology into an instrument for studying Chinese history. Ironically, the written materials excavated at Anyang confirmed traditional historical sources concerning the late Shang Dynasty, contrary to the expectations of the science-oriented Doubters of Antiquity (*yigupai*), who had grown out of the reformist May 4th Movement and had promoted Western-style archaeology. The work done at Anyang fueled a resurgence of pride in China's ancient past.

Foreign scholars, such as Andersson, sought to trace the origins of Chinese culture, or at least of major aspects of it, such as the Neolithic painted pottery, back to the Middle East, thereby implying that Chinese civilization was derived from the West. Chinese archaeologists sought the origin of Chinese civilization in the Neolithic Longshan culture, where what was assumed to be Western influence seemed less evident. Later they argued that Yangshao and Longshan represented an indigenous continuum of development that culminated in Shang civilization (W. Watson 1981: 65–6). Archaeological research was curtailed by the Japanese invasion in 1937 and, following the Communist victory in 1949, many archaeologists, including Li, retreated to Taiwan taking valuable collections with them.

Marxism had begun to influence the study of ancient China as early as 1930 in the works of Guo Moruo (1892–1978). A writer and revolutionary, Guo had been forced to flee to a still relatively liberal Japan in 1927 to escape the death squads of Chiang Kai-Shek, the current military dictator of China. During the ten years Guo lived in Japan, he produced a series of studies on ancient inscriptions and the stylistic evolution of bronze artifacts. Unlike Li and his associates, who were primarily interested in art, religion, and ideology, Guo stressed production as the basis of society and interpreted the Shang and Zhou Dynasties as examples of a slave society. More than any other Chinese scholar, Guo sought to place his country in a comparative framework of world history (G. Wang 1985: 188). After the Communist revolution, he became a major figure in Chinese intellectual life. From 1950 until his death in 1978, he was President of the Chinese Academy of Sciences.

Following the Communist victory of 1949, archaeology became a state-directed activity. Except briefly, when the value of any study of the past was challenged by extremists near the beginning of the Cultural Revolution (1966–1977), archaeology has been supported as an important instrument of political education. This was done in accordance with Mao Zedong's dictum that "the past should serve the present." A National Bureau of Cultural Relics administered thousands of provincial and local museums either directly or through provincial and district Bureaus of Culture. Vast amounts of archaeological data were unearthed throughout China in the course of unprecedented industrial and agricultural development (Chang 1981: 168). Within the research divisions of Academia Sinica, Palaeolithic archaeology was separated from the study of the Neolithic and historical periods and attached to the Institute of Vertebrate Palaeontology and Palaeoanthropology. This arrangement may have reflected a lack of close identification of the earliest periods of human development with a specifically national history, although pride was officially expressed about the great antiquity of China's Palaeolithic record. On a practical level, this division reflected the close working relations among Palaeolithic archaeologists, geologists, and palaeontologists in China.

In keeping with nationally sanctioned Marxist tenets, the Chinese past was conceptualized in terms of a unilinear sequence of stages: primitive society, slave society, and feudal society. No questioning of this model was tolerated. Yet very little archaeological research was directed towards actually utilizing Marxist theories of social evolution, which would have involved the detailed investigation of social and political organization, subsistence systems, settlement patterns, and trade. This may partly have resulted from the scarcity of well-trained personnel, but unpredictable shifts in Chinese government policy also may have discouraged archaeologists from addressing problems that politically were potentially dangerous. Instead, archaeological finds were interpreted as required by the government to promote a variety of specific political goals. They were used to remind people of the cruelty and exploitation that had characterized life for the Chinese masses under successive royal dynasties. The great tombs, temples, and other monuments of the past also were interpreted as testimonials to the skills and energy of the workers and artisans who had created them. Archaeological finds were used to promote national dignity and pride and respect abroad by documenting China's accomplishments over the ages. Despite a Marxist veneer, these functions encouraged the continuation of an archaeology that remained culture-historical in practice and nationalistic in its goals (Falkenhausen 1993).

Chinese archaeology also played a significant role in promoting national unity, as historiography in general had done before 1949. The interpretation of the archaeological record continued to accord with long-standing northern-centered Chinese traditions. Chinese material culture and institutions were interpreted as first having evolved in the Yellow River Valley and spreading out from there to produce the pan-Chinese culture of the Iron Age. The cultural creativity of other parts of China was thereby minimized, even though under the Communists China was officially recognized to be a multi-ethnic nation and the past chauvinism of its Han majority was officially repudiated.

During the 1980s, as a result of the decentralization brought about by the government of Deng Xiaoping, decision-making powers increasingly became the responsibility of provincial archaeological institutions. Archaeologists began to develop culture-historical sequences for individual provinces and to identify these sequences with ancient nations and ethnic groups that had been incorporated into the Chinese state, usually in the first millennium BC. By drawing attention to the special roles individual provinces had played within China, archaeologists were accommodating to new sources of financial support. At the national level, beginning in the early 1980s, Su Bingqi (1909–1997) evolved a model in which, in accordance with Marxist "laws of social evolution," distinctive cultures were seen as having developed alongside one another in the different regions of China. This model accounted far better than did the older northern core-periphery one for the growing evidence of regional cultural diversity and increasing social and cultural complexity throughout China in prehistoric and early historical times. Su's multiregional model of cultural origins also validated the current regionalist tendencies of Chinese archaeology within a broader national context (Falkenhausen 1995, 1999). These early regional divisions had been noted earlier by Western archaeologists (Meacham 1977) and by Chinese archaeologists working abroad (Chang 1986: 234–94) but their interpretations had been publicly rejected by archaeologists in China (W. Watson 1981: 68–9). National unity remains a crucial issue in China. Su's formulation struck an even balance between Marxist and culture-historical interpretative trends and between central and provincial interests in contemporary China.

Archaeological research in India began in a colonial setting and for a long time remained remote from traditional Indian scholarship. European travelers noted ancient monuments as early as the sixteenth century and systematic scholarly interest in these monuments began about 1750. This interest was further stimulated beginning in 1786 by the realization that the modern languages of northern India were related to the Indo-European ones of Europe (G. Cannon 1990). In the nineteenth century, amateur British archaeologists began to examine and report on megaliths, Buddhist stupas, and other monumental sites with some regularity. Often, they treated these monuments as evidence of a Golden Age in India's remote past and implied that these finds indicated that the duty of British colonial rulers was to rescue India from the decline that had followed (Harding 2003). The Archaeological Survey of India, first established in 1861, published an immense amount of research under directors such as Alexander Cunningham (in charge from 1861 to 1865) (U. Singh 2004), John Marshall (1902–1929), who discovered the Indus Valley civilization, and Mortimer Wheeler (1944–1948). Wheeler trained many Indian students in modern field methods and encouraged several Indian universities to begin offering instruction in archaeology. Lallanji Gopal (1985: i) has observed that the "glorious cultural heritage, which was unearthed by archaeologists ... aroused the self-confidence of the Indian people [and] was one of the major factors contributing to the Indian renaissance, which ultimately ushered in independence."

In general, the British justification of colonialism was based on historical and linguistic data rather than archaeology. Colonial historians argued that cultural progress had been brought about by the migration into India of successive waves of racially superior northern peoples who introduced important innovations but then interbred with the general population. The primary message was that India was unable to change without external influences. In this scheme, the British presented themselves as the latest and most advanced standard bearers of progress in India, while acknowledging a distant ethnic affinity to the allegedly racially purer Indo-European elements in the population of northern India. In this way, the Indian caste system was racialized and the higher castes portrayed as a separate ethnic group. Dilip Chakrabarti (2001: 1192) notes that British-educated colonial collaborators and freedom fighters alike were pleased to believe that they stood racially aloof from the non-Aryan autochthonous peoples at the lower end of the caste hierarchy. This use of "Aryanism" to coopt the Indian elite into a high status position in the racial and class hierarchy of colonial India may explain why most Indian historians did not seriously challenge a migrationary view of their country's past (Chakrabarti 1997). Because direct historical sources for early Indian history are few, historians had to rely on ancient religious and literary texts and on archaeological evidence and tended to interpret both in conformity with the migrationary model. It is largely within the framework of this model that India's archaeological heritage was understood by those who brought India to independence in 1947.

In the years following independence, archaeological activities continued to receive moderate levels of government financial support and there was little interference by governments or public opinion with what archaeologists did. Indian archaeology became well established in universities and much research was carried out (Thapar 1984). Many archaeologists kept abreast of world trends in archaeology and adopted the most recent scientific methods for analyzing their finds. More so than in China and Japan, researchers were aware of new theoretical trends, such as processual archaeology, and some participated in international discussions relating to these developments (Jacobson 1979; Paddayya 1980, 1982, 1983, 1986; Lal 1984). Yet archaeology remained closely attached to the study of ancient history and most archaeologists remained content to work out cultural sequences and attach ethnic and linguistic labels to cultures rather than trying to explain cultural processes. As late as the 1980s, it appeared to outsiders that Indian archaeologists continued to adhere to what they had learned during the late colonial period.

With the growing influence of Hindu nationalism in Indian politics, marked changes have occurred in archaeology. Archaeologists who support Hindu nationalism have challenged traditional explanations that derive changes from outside India. There now is a tendency to search for innovations inside India, including ones that relate to the domestication of plants and animals, iron-working, and the development of Indian scripts. Some Indian archaeologists assign the "Aryans" a local origin along the now dried-up Sarasvati River in northwestern India. In southern India, Dravidian-speaking archaeologists analogously emphasize the primordial status of Dravidians as India's first people. Reacting against such tendencies, Dilip Chakrabarti (2003) rejects ethnicity as a legitimate focus of archaeological enquiry and stresses the importance of an approach that traces the gradual development of Indian culture in relation to India's landscape as a way of uniting India's ethnically diverse peoples. Although the Hindu and Dravidian nationalist approaches remain resolutely culture-historical, Chakrabarti's might better be described as processual-historical. The internalist viewpoint that is shared by his approach and the nationalist ones has the great advantage of encouraging archaeologists to examine India's prehistory and early history on their own terms rather than treating them as reflections of what was happening elsewhere.

Most Arab and other Moslem countries in the Middle East have extensive bureaucratic organizations to protect and administer cultural heritage. The duty of these organizations is to guard and develop archaeological sites, control museums, regulate foreign archaeologists working in the country, and perform rescue excavations. Yet in these countries there is relatively little public interest in the archaeological remains of pre-Islamic times. Archaeology, as we have seen, was introduced by Europeans who developed and long monopolized research under *de facto*, if not official, colonial regimes. In the early part of the twentieth century, the Egyptian middle class developed considerable interest in ancient Egyptian civilization within the context of a secular and modernizing nationalism. Ancient Egypt provided symbols and a shared past around which both Moslem and Christian Egyptians could rally to resist continuing British domination of their country. During this period, monuments displaying Pharaonic motifs were constructed to commemorate heroes of the struggle for national independence. Yet, beginning as early as the late 1920s, Moslem intellectuals were claiming that Egypt could not exist in isolation but had to take part in, or lead, a broader pan-Arab or pan-Islamic world. To do this, the revival of paganism implied by an interest in Egypt's Pharaonic past had to be swept away. They reminded Egyptians that in the Quran pharaohs were portrayed as archetypal villains. Since the 1940s, the growing influence of pan-Arabism and more recently of Islamic movements has resulted in a political discourse that is increasingly hostile to the glorification of ancient Egypt. The Pharaonic heritage has largely been reduced to being a source of tourist revenue (J. Wilson 1964: 159–77; D. Reid 1997; Hassan 1998; Wood 1998).

In Iraq, during the 1970s and 1980s, the secularist Baath Party stressed the country's distinctive Mesopotamian heritage as a focus of national loyalty that might symbolically help to counter modern Iraq's powerful religious and ethnic divisions, especially as relations with neighboring Arab and Moslem states became more troubled. Iraq's dictator, Saddam Hussein, liked to be portrayed as an ancient Babylonian king. However, as his regime's difficulties increased, this interest in pre-Islamic times was played down in an effort to stress his regime's Islamic religious credentials (Bahrani 1998; Bernhardsson 2005).

In Iran, Persian ethnicity long has played an important political role. Before the Islamic Revolution of 1979, much of the archaeological research in Iran was carried out by foreign expeditions. The work done by Iranian archaeologists also tended to be focused on the more recent Parthian, Sassanian, and Islamic periods. The last Shah of Iran, Mohammad Reza Pahlavi, sought to emphasize the glories of pre-Islamic Persian civilization and to identify his secularist and modernizing regime with the ancient Persian Achaemenian dynasty (539–330 BC) rather than with a more recent Islamic past. This included a magnificent celebration in 1971 of the supposed 2,500th anniversary of the founding of that monarchy held in the ruins of its greatest palace at Persepolis. Archaeological fieldwork came to an almost total standstill in the decade following the Islamic Revolution and now seems to be heavily focused on the Islamic period (Abdi 2001; S. Brown 2001). Although Iranian concerns with their national identity have traditionally encouraged more interest in the study of pre-Islamic periods than has been common in Arab countries, in recent decades there has been an increasing emphasis on Islamic archaeology in most Arab and Islamic countries (Masry 1981).

In few areas of the world has the development of culture-historical archaeology been more complex, or its history more studied, than in Palestine and Israel. In the nineteenth century, European and American archaeologists conducted surveys in an effort to locate places mentioned in the Old and New Testaments. Beginning in the late nineteenth century, excavations were carried out at important sites that were thought to be associated with biblical accounts. Biblical archaeologists, such as the American William F. Albright (1891–1971), were mainly believing Christians, who sought to confirm the historical truth of biblical accounts. As a consequence, little research was done on prehistoric sites, the most important work being that carried out by Kathleen Kenyon (1906–1978) in the lower levels at

Jericho in the 1950s. The primary motive for doing archaeology in Palestine was religious (Dever 2001a).

Israeli archaeology, as it developed in the 1950s and 1960s, served the very different purpose of affirming links between an immigrant population and the homeland that they believed God had given to their ancestors (Benvinisti 2000). Israeli archaeology was not primarily religious in orientation but was promoted by the Zionist movement to heighten national consciousness and strengthen Israeli ties to the land they were settling. By encouraging Israelis to view the Bible as a source of national history, archaeologists also were promoting a secular view of modern Israel. Although Israeli archaeology was closely related to biblical archaeology in terms of many of the problems both groups of archaeologists studied, and there was close cooperation between biblical and Israeli archaeologists in the early stages of the development of Israeli archaeology, archaeology in Israel from the beginning was primarily a nationalist not a religious enterprise.

Like many other nationalists, Zionists viewed archaeology as a source of potent symbols. After it was excavated with great publicity by Yigail Yadin (1917–1984) between 1963 and 1965, Masada, the site of the last Jewish resistance to the Romans in AD 72–73, became a monument possessing great emotional and ceremonial value as a symbol of the will to survive of the new Israeli state (Paine 1994). This site and the heroic narrative associated with it also were used to promote a more proactive sense of Jewish personal identity to replace that of the diaspora (Ben-Yehuda 1995, 2002). The identification of ancient Hebrew sites throughout Israel reinforced a sense of unity between present and past at the local level that aided the formation of a national identity. Archaeological projects, by altering the landscape, in some instances erased evidence of Arab settlement and materially enhanced a sense of continuity between ancient and modern Jewish settlement (Abu El-Haj 2001: 167), a process also promoted by the imposition of Hebrew place names (Benvinisti 2000). Zionists interested in archaeology further encouraged an interest in the past to ensure the protection of biblical sites at a time of rapid Jewish settlement and economic expansion (Abu El-Haj 2000: 49).

Like most national archaeologies, Israeli archaeology was selective. It was primarily interested in studying the history of Jewish settlement and culture in the region and relatively little attention was paid to the archaeology of the Christian and Islamic periods (Bar Yosef and Mazar 1982; Dever 2001b). Most Israeli archaeologists were trained in historical and biblical research and devoted much time to studying history, philology, and art history. Palaeolithic archaeology was of relatively little interest and the influence of anthropological archaeology was generally limited to encouraging the use of new technical aids to analyse data (Hanbury-Tenison 1986: 108).

In the 1970s, archaeology was becoming less important for Israeli nation-building. Nevertheless, political and religious groups used the archaeological discovery of numerous early Iron Age settlements on the West Bank, following the annexation of the region in 1967, to help promote Jewish settlement in the "heartland of ancient Israel" (Hallote and Joffee 2002). Reacting to this partisan political exploitation of archaeological data, some Israeli archaeologists sought to upgrade the professional status of Israeli archaeology by advocating a more critical attitude toward historical data when they were being used to interpret archaeological finds. This development also was related to a broader trend among biblical scholars to question the historicity of biblical narratives dealing with the period before the eighth century BC (Finkelstein and Silberman 2001; Dever 2003: 137–42). Efforts also were made to expand the temporal range of Israeli archaeology to make it national in scope rather than simply ethnic or nationalist, a development that some commentators associate with a new, "post-Zionist" appropriation of all the history associated with the national territory claimed by Israel. Processual archaeology also encouraged a growing concern with economic and ecological interpretations of the past. Today, Israeli archaeology is interpretationally far less unified than it was in the 1960s and 1970s. It is challenged from within by critical scholars and by the commitments of Israeli archaeologists to various political agendas and research priorities. It is also challenged by ultraorthodox Jewish religious groups who oppose it on the grounds that excavation violates ancient Hebrew burials (Paine 1983).

William Dever, an American archaeologist, sought to replace biblical archaeology with a local variant of processual archaeology that he called "Syro-Palestinian" archaeology (2001a). His approach involved ignoring texts and emphasizing ecology. Yet even he has found it difficult to avoid questions of ethnicity (Dever 2003). Recent decades have also witnessed the emergence of Palestinian archaeology. Specifically, Palestinian archaeology seeks to fill the gaps caused by the failure of most Israeli and Christian archaeologists to study the material remains of recent phases of Palestinian history (Ziadeh 1995); but, more generally, it claims the right to study the material remains of all the people who have ever lived in Palestine, and hence are referred to as Palestinians, as a continuity extending from earliest times to the present (E. Fox 2001); thus completely overlapping with Israeli "national" archaeology.

The decolonization of sub-Saharan Africa in the 1960s accelerated the changes in the archaeology of that region that had begun in the late colonial period. This was a time of great hope for the continued development of archaeology at least within some of Africa's most prosperous nation states. Archaeologists of African descent were not necessarily interested in the same problems as were foreign scholars. Like nationalist archaeologists elsewhere, they were more concerned with recent prehistory and issues related to national history than with Palaeolithic archaeology. Topics of interest included the origin of specific states, the development of regional trade, the evolution of historically attested social and economic institutions, and the history of relations among ethnic groups living within the borders of modern African states (Tardits 1981; Posnansky 1982: 355; Andah 1985). Later Bassy Andah (1995), Nigeria's leading archaeologist, maintained that African archaeologists had to study the past in terms of local, culturally specific meanings, as daily life was guided by such concepts. This required archaeologists to become familiar with local ethnography and to use such information rather than Western anthropological generalizations to explain archaeological data. Thus, he advocated a cognitively oriented form of the direct historical approach.

There also was much interest in the study and preservation of major sites that related to precolonial African history. Although archaeology was seen as a means of increasing awareness of, and pride in, Africa's past, there also was political concern about how the presentation of archaeological findings might help to enhance national unity or promote regional and local self-awareness (Nzewunwa 1984). While African archaeologists, who were often tied to administrative positions, generally welcomed research by anthropologically trained colleagues from abroad, anthropology as a discipline was not well regarded. Across Africa, archaeology was becoming increasingly aligned with history in the 1960s, just as ethnological studies were being redefined as sociology (Ki-Zerbo 1981). As a result of this realignment, as well as a growing involvement with the study of oral traditions and historical linguistics, it was believed that Africans would be equipped to investigate periods of their history for which no written records were available and that archaeology would become African rather than colonial in its orientation (McCall 1964; Ehret and Posnansky 1982). Yet these dreams have not been realized. As a result of economic downturns, wars, political instability, lack of concern by governments, and other misfortunes, African archaeology has generally been unable to live up to the hopes of the 1960s. Where it did not die out completely, archaeologists were either starved of resources or compelled to collaborate with foreign institutions or partners, often on the latter's terms (McIntosh 2001: 28–34). Over most of Africa, colonial archaeology seems to have been followed, not by national, but by neocolonial archaeology.

Throughout Latin America, individual archaeologists, such as Julio C. Tello (1880–1947) and Rafael Larco Hoyle (1901–1966) in Peru, have made distinguished contributions to understanding pre-Columbian culture-history. Yet, lack of funds, political instability, government interference, and the massive intervention of large numbers of foreign archaeologists and archaeological projects have impeded the development of coherent national traditions of doing archaeology in many Latin American countries (Politis and Alberti 1999; Funari 2001; Politis 2003; Politis and Pérez Gollán 2004). The most successful development of a national archaeology has been in Mexico. It began with Leopoldo Batres's massive restoration projects at Teotihuacán that were carried out to celebrate the 1910 centenary of Mexico's independence from Spain.

Porfirio Díaz's lengthy dictatorship was brought to an end by the Mexican Revolution of 1910–1917, which was successful largely as a result of armed support by peasants, who were mainly Indians and constituted a majority of the population. The revolution resulted in major changes in government policy towards these people. The injustices of the colonial period were acknowledged and far-reaching economic and social reforms promised. The government undertook to integrate Indians into national life and increase their sense of self-respect by encouraging the study of Mexico's rich pre-Hispanic heritage and making its findings an integral part of Mexican history. In this way the government also hoped to assert Mexico's cultural distinctiveness to its own citizens and the rest of the world (Gamio 1916). Large sums of money were allocated for archaeological instruction and research. A Department of Anthropology was established in 1937 at the National Polytechnical School, which had as one of its duties to train archaeologists. It later became part of the National Institute of Anthropology and History, which was granted an absolute monopoly to license archaeological excavations throughout Mexico.

Since the revolution, Mexican archaeology has exhibited a strong historicist orientation. Already in 1913, Manuel Gamio (1883–1960) conducted a series of stratigraphic excavations at San Miguel Amantla that provided the first prehistoric cultural sequence for the Valley of Mexico. Since then, Mexican and foreign archaeologists have produced cultural chronologies for all the diverse regions of the country. Mexican archaeologists accepted that it was their duty to provide Mexicans with a past of their own that would promote national unity by formulating a historical understanding that could be shared by all sections of the population. This required the humanization and popularization of prehistory. An important feature of this policy was the creation of public museums and the development of major archaeological sites or zones for the entertainment and instruction of Mexicans and foreign visitors alike (Lorenzo 1981, 1984). Early projects included Gamio's excavations at the Ciudadela complex at Teotihuacán and Alfonso Caso's work at Monte Albán. Today, over 100 major archaeological zones have been at least partially restored and are open to the public. Archaeology continues to document a continuity in Mexican history from earliest pre-Hispanic times to the present. It also seeks symbolically to unite all the people of Mexico and to affirm Mexico's uniqueness by documenting the country's vast cultural achievements prior to the Spanish conquest. This approach reinforces the culture-historical orientation of Mexican archaeology, even though Mexican archaeologists are familiar with and make use of alternative approaches (I. Bernal 1983). Yet, in recent decades, the continuing political uses of archaeology have been accompanied by chronic underfunding of scientifically oriented research. Many of the most important longterm research projects in Mexico continue to be carried out by foreign expeditions. Archaeology done by Mexicans looks increasingly like tourist archaeology and a token way to honor indigenous peoples while ignoring the current daily needs of large numbers of them (Vázquez León 2003).

The national archaeologies we have examined all have much in common with the culture-historical archaeology that developed in Europe. All have as their primary objective to trace the histories of specific nations or ethnic groups in the archaeological record. They also tend to focus on those periods and cultures that are of greatest interest to the people whose past they are studying. Only a strong commitment to cultural resource management results in equal attention being paid to all periods and all cultures. Even where ideas derived from processual and postprocessual archaeology have deflected attention from migration and diffusion as explanations of cultural change, a nationalist orientation tends to preserve a historical perspective.

Culture-historical archaeologists also wish their findings to be popular. Although they validate their scientific credentials by employing internationally recognized archaeological methods, the historical narratives they construct tend to be highly intuitive and subject to change as political conditions alter. Their interpretations also diversify in situations in which political debate encourages alternative views of the past. Public interest in the findings of archaeologists fluctuates according to changing social, political, and economic circumstances. There is also considerable variation in the extent to which national and foreign archaeologists work together. In China and Japan, most research is carried out by local archaeologists; Indian and Mexican archaeologists work together with, or compete with, foreign archaeologists; whereas in many smaller and poorer countries foreign archaeologists tend to dominate archaeological practice.

Culture-Historical Archaeology in the United States

In the United States, a culture-historical approach was adopted soon after 1910 as a response to growing familiarity with the archaeological record. Archaeology also was increasingly influenced by Boasian cultural anthropology, which during the first half of the twentieth century enjoyed great prestige as a result of many of the nation's key social problems relating to the assimilation of various ethnic groups being defined in cultural terms. The spread of central European cultural theory to North America as a result of the activities of Boas and his followers encouraged similar developments in archaeological interpretation on both continents.

Continuing archaeological research revealed temporal changes that could not be explained by the simple replacement of one group of people by another. As a result of the first confirmed Palaeo-Indian finds, made in a late Pleistocene context at Folsom, New Mexico, in 1927, it also became evident that indigenous people had lived in North America for longer than most archaeologists had hitherto believed and that their cultures must have changed considerably over time (Willey and Sabloff 1993: 141–3). Boasian anthropology had already popularized the ethnographic culture as a basic unit of study and diffusion as the major cause of cultural change. In addition, Boas's persuasive advocacy of cultural relativism and his strong opposition to racism encouraged the view that Indians were capable of change. Yet, although Boas had some interest in archaeology, which he actively promoted in Mexico, there is no evidence that he introduced the European concept of the archaeological culture to the United States. On the contrary, the distinctive way in which this concept developed in North America and the fact that the term as applied archaeologically was used in North America before it received any formal definition in Europe suggest an independent origin. By contrast, the American concept of the ethnographic culture had its roots in the teachings of Friedrich Ratzel, which were expounded in America in an explicit, albeit modified, form by Franz Boas.

We have already noted that, during the nineteenth century, American archaeologists became increasingly aware of geographically circumscribed cultural manifestations in the archaeological record, especially in the central United States, where a concern with the Moundbuilders had led to much archaeological activity. In 1890, G. P. Thruston defined a prehistoric Stone Grave "race" in Tennessee, which he believed was the remains of a single tribe or a group of related tribes (pp. 5, 28). The term *culture* was first applied to groups of sites containing distinctive artifact assemblages in the Ohio Valley. By 1902, William C. Mills had distinguished the Fort Ancient and Hopewell cultures. In 1909, W. K. Moorehead identified the Glacial Kame culture and soon after H. C. Shetrone (1920) was noting more such units in that area. These archaeological "cultures" differed from European or later American ones inasmuch as they remained primarily cultural-geographical, not culture-historical, entities; their temporal relations to one another not yet being established. Not until 1936 was the Hopewell culture securely dated as being earlier than the Fort Ancient one.

In 1913, the American ethnologist Berthold Laufer (1913: 577) diagnosed the most serious shortcoming of American archaeology as being its lack of chronological control. This was a problem that American archaeologists had already recognized and begun to remedy. Stratigraphic excavations had been undertaken with increasing frequency since the 1860s and for a long time important conclusions had been flowing from such excavations, such as Richard Wetherill's demonstration that the Basketmaker culture had preceded the more sedentary Pueblo one in the American Southwest (Kidder 1924: 161). Wetherill may have learned the value of observing stratigraphy from the Swedish explorer and scientist Gustaf Nordenskiold when Nordenskiold collected archaeological material in the southwestern United States in 1891 (McNitt 1990: 38–43). On somewhat speculative typological grounds, Adolf Bandelier in the 1880s and Edgar Lee Hewett in 1904 had attempted to work out a rough chronology of prehistoric Pueblo sites (Schwartz 1981). In many parts of the United States, archaeological evidence was being collected which showed that local cultures had varied markedly over time.

The systematic study of North American culture history developed in the southwestern United States, beginning with the work of Nels C. Nelson (1875–1964) and Alfred Kidder (1885–1963). In 1914, Nelson carried out important stratigraphic excavations at the San Cristóbal Pueblo site in New Mexico (Nelson 1916). His earlier excavations at the Ellis Landing shell midden near San Francisco already seem to have been influenced by Max Uhle's stratigraphic work at nearby Emeryville. In 1913, Nelson toured Hugo Obermaier's and Henri Breuil's stratigraphic excavations at Palaeolithic sites in Spain and dug at the Castillo Cave. His excavations in New Mexico were done using arbitrary levels. Kidder had studied archaeological field methods at Harvard University with the celebrated Egyptologist George Reisner, who was one of the most meticulous excavators of the early twentieth century (Givens 1992a: 25; Wauchope 1965: 151). Beginning in 1915, Kidder excavated in the thick refuse deposits at Pecos Pueblo, New Mexico, collecting artifacts from

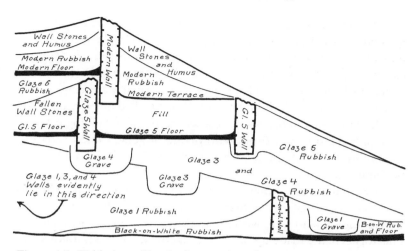

Figure 6.6 Kidder's profile of refuse stratigraphy and construction levels at
Pecos Ruin, New Mexico, from *An Introduction to the Study
of Southwestern Archaeology*, 1924

distinct depositional units (Figure 6.6). Both archaeologists discovered that in these middens the frequencies of various pottery types
varied in an orderly fashion from top to bottom. They interpreted
these variations as evidence of gradual changes in preferred pottery
styles. Such alterations provided evidence of simultaneous cultural
continuity and cultural change (Browman and Givens 1996; Lyman
et al. 1997a: 34–55). These excavations and the innovative observations that Nelson and Kidder made while carrying them out laid the
basis for the development of culture-historical archaeology in the
United States. By 1917, Clark Wissler was describing the revolution
that the preoccupation with cultural chronology was bringing about
as a "new archaeology."

Kidder believed that studying the spatial distributions of combinations of artifact types was as important as studying their chronological
transformations. In his *An Introduction to the Study of Southwestern
Archaeology* (1924), he attempted the first culture-historical synthesis
of the archaeology of any part of the United States. This study was
published one year before Childe's *The Dawn of European Civilization*. In it, Kidder discussed the archaeological material from nine
river drainages in terms of four successive periods, or stages, of cultural development: Basket Maker, Post-Basket Maker, Pre-Pueblo,

and Pueblo. He sometimes called each period a culture but also designated regional variants of each period that were associated with individual river drainages as the Chihuahua Basin culture, Mimbres culture, and Lower Gila culture. Kidder's imprecise utilization of the concept of "culture" closely paralleled the way it was being used in Britain before 1925. Although the term *culture* had not yet acquired a standard meaning in the Southwest, as a result of chronological studies supplementing an existing knowledge of geographical variation, something approaching the concept of an archaeological culture was beginning to evolve.

Yet what interested other archaeologists most about Kidder's work was his chronology. At the first Pecos Conference, held in 1927, the archaeologists who were working in the area adopted a general classificatory scheme made up of three Basketmaker periods followed by five Pueblo ones. H. S. Gladwin (1883–1983) complained, however, that among its other shortcomings the Pecos classification was better suited to the northern Pueblo area of the Southwest than to more southerly regions, where quite different cultures were found. In a paper entitled "A method for designation of cultures and their variations" (1934), he and his wife Winifred Gladwin (born McCurdy) proposed a hierarchical classification of cultural units for the region, the most general of which were three roots called Basketmaker (later Anasazi), Hohokam, and Caddoan (later Mogollon). Each of these roots, which respectively were found in the northern, southern, and intervening mountainous areas of the Southwest, was subdivided into stems, that were named after regions, and these in turn into branches and phases that were given more specific geographical names. Phases could follow one another in the same locality and each was defined as a set of sites with a high degree of similarity in artifact types. Although the Gladwin classificatory hierarchy was based on relative degrees of trait similarities, its dendritic pattern involved geographical considerations and it was implicitly chronological; roots formed before stems and stems before branches. The Gladwins followed much earlier archaeologists in believing that Indians, after they had arrived in North America, adapted to increasingly specific areas, but they differed from their predecessors in assuming that once a specific group was established in a particular location, its material culture might continue to change. Willey and Sabloff (1993: 123) observed that the Gladwins's belief that the prehistoric cultures of the southwestern

United States had become increasingly differentiated "while a possibility, was by no means demonstrated."

A different and even more influential classificatory scheme was proposed in 1932 by a group of archaeologists, including Thorne Deuel, Carl Guthe, and James B. Griffin, all of whom worked in the midwestern United States. The leader and chief spokesman for this group was William C. McKern (1892–1988) (1939). This scheme, called the Midwestern Taxonomic Method, was soon used throughout the central and eastern United States to classify material being recovered in a region where few stratified sites displaying occupations over long periods of time were yet known. The goal of the Midwestern Taxonomic Method was to classify finds on the basis of formal criteria alone. Artifact assemblages representing a single period of occupation at a site were designated a "component" and they in turn were grouped to form five nested taxa. Components sharing an almost identical set of artifact traits were assigned to the same focus; foci with a "preponderating majority of traits" to the same aspect; aspects sharing only more general characteristics to the same phase; and phases sharing a few broad traits to the same pattern. The traits used to define a pattern were said to be "a cultural reflection of the primary adjustments of peoples to environment, as defined by tradition." The patterns that were identified were Mississippian, with sedentary sites, incised pottery, and small triangular points; Woodland, characterized by semisedentary sites, cordmarked pottery, and stemmed or sidenotched projectile points; and Archaic, which lacked pottery but was marked by ground slate artifacts.

Foci and aspects were defined by drawing up lists of various sorts of cultural traits (types, attributes, and burial patterns) for each component and determining how many of these traits different components had in common. This approach corresponded with the historical particularist conception championed by Boas during the early part of his career, which viewed cultures not as integrated systems but as collections of traits that had come together as a result of random patterns of diffusion. No inferences about human behavior were included in defining traits, nor was any attention paid, unlike Childe, to the functional significance of different types of artifacts or the ecological significance of what was being found. The prevalence of different traits also was rejected in favor of simply noting their presence or absence in each unit being compared. Contrary to what was being done in the Southwest, changing frequencies of traits were not viewed as having chronological or functional significance. The problem was noted, but not resolved, that artifacts that were stylistically highly variable, such as pottery, were a potential source of many more traits than were stone or bone tools. It also was recognized that cemeteries and habitation sites belonging to the same culture might contain a different selection of artifact types. Because of this, some archaeologists proposed to base foci on a range of different types of sites or on a balanced selection of traits from various functional categories of finds representing the complete cultural manifestations of a people, rather than simply on components (McKern 1939: 310–11). McKern recommended rather obscurely "the selecting, from the traits comprising a complex subject, of those trait details which have sufficient cultural significance to qualify them as cultural determinants" (p. 306). He also argued that these considerations, as well as the incompleteness of archaeological data, precluded the statistical method from being used to establish degrees of relations among components, although he accepted that quantitative similarity was important for determining the classificatory status of archaeological manifestations. John C. McGregor (1941) proposed that components should have more than 85 percent of traits in common, foci 65 to 84 percent, aspects 40 to 64 percent, phases 20 to 39 percent, and patterns fewer than 20 percent. These recommendations were ignored.

Both the Gladwin system and the Midwestern Taxonomic Method eschewed the term *culture*, which McKern (1939: 303) believed archaeologists used to designate too broad a range of phenomena. Nevertheless, these two systems initiated the systematic use of cultural traits for classifying archaeological data as cultural units in the United States, in the guise of the Gladwins' phases and McKern's foci and aspects. These units were widely regarded as the archaeological expression of a tribe or group of closely related tribes. The Gladwin scheme assumed that cultures, like biological species, differentiated along irreversible paths, thereby ignoring the convergence brought about by diffusion. McKern and most others who formulated the Midwestern Taxonomic Method appear to have regarded foci and phases as culturally and historically significant taxa. They acted on the assumption that formal differences among such units in a single locality usually indicated temporal differences, whereas similar cultures distributed over large areas dated from the same period. By contrast, they generally understood the higher taxa of the Midwestern Taxonomic Method as pragmatic groupings that were useful for classifying foci and aspects on the basis of formal similarities until they could be understood historically. Yet many archaeologists who used this system in its early days assumed that shared traits at all levels signified common origins, history, and ethnicity. They also believed that traits that were more generally shared were older than more culturally specific ones, a fallacy that even in the 1930s would have made the Coca-Cola bottle older than the Acheulean hand-axe. This view had some retrograde effects on the interpretation of archaeological data. For example, in New York State McKern's Woodland pattern embraced prehistoric cultures that archaeologists traditionally had associated with Algonquian-speakers, whereas his Mississippian pattern embraced the historical cultures of linguistically unrelated Iroquoians. The assumption that cultures could not evolve from one pattern to another, any more than an Algonquian language could change into an Iroquoian one, hindered the realization that the historical Iroquoian cultures had developed from local Middle Woodland antecedents (Ritchie 1944; MacNeish 1952). As a result of this misunderstanding, the Midwestern Taxonomic Method, although struggling for classificatory objectivity and quantitative precision, inadvertently helped to perpetuate the pessimistic views about the Indians' capacity to change that had characterized American archaeology during the nineteenth century.

Yet in practice this misunderstanding was of short duration. Phases in the Southwest and foci in the East were soon being aligned to form local chronologies by means of stratigraphy and seriation, as was being done with cultures in Europe. As this happened, the higher levels of both the Gladwin scheme and the Midwestern Taxonomic Method were abandoned and archaeological cultures were viewed as forming mosaics, in which each culture had to be assigned its own empirically determined spatial and temporal boundaries. Cultures, as well as artifact types, were viewed as persisting in particular areas, possibly with slow modifications, to form traditions, or spreading geographically to create cultural horizons, which were used to align traditions chronologically. As regional cultural chronologies were constructed and archaeologists became increasingly aware of the complex patterning of material culture both within and among archaeological cultures, they began increasingly to credit diffusion with playing an important role in bringing about cultural change. Yet diffusion was employed mechanically. Most archaeologists continued to pay little attention to understanding the internal dynamics of cultural change or trying to determine why a particular innovation did or did not diffuse from one group to another. By 1941, enough data had been collected for James A. Ford and G. R. Willey to present a synthesis of the culture history of eastern North America in which the known cultures were grouped to form five stages of development: Archaic, Burial Mound I (Early Woodland), Burial Mound II (Middle Woodland), Temple Mound I (Early Mississippian) and Temple Mound II (Late Mississippian) (Figure 6.7). In this arrangement, the three patterns of the Midwestern Taxonomic Method were transformed into three stages of cultural development. Each new stage was viewed as coming from the south, and ultimately from Mesoamerica, and then spreading north through the Mississippi Valley. Thus an interpretation of eastern North American prehistory was created that closely resembled what had been presented sixteen years earlier for prehistoric Europe in *The Dawn of European Civilization*.

Although diffusion implied recognition of the capacity for indigenous cultures to change, diffusionist explanations were employed very conservatively. Innovations, such as pottery, burial mounds, metal working, and agriculture were almost always assigned an East Asian or Mesoamerican origin (Spinden 1928; McKern 1937; Spaulding 1946), thus implying that indigenous North Americans were imitative rather than creative. Moreover, archaeologists still tended to attribute major changes in the archaeological record to migrations. For example, into the 1950s the transitions from the Archaic to the Woodland pattern and from Woodland to Mississippian in the northeastern United States were usually explained as resulting from the entry of new populations into that region. As had happened in Europe, theories of cultural change and chronologies became linked to form a closed system of interpretation. A very short chronology was adopted in which late Archaic cultures, that are now radiocarbon dated around 2500 BC, were placed no earlier than AD 300 (Ritchie 1944). This short chronology reflected the belief that major changes had been brought about quickly by migrations. Yet, so long as that chronology was accepted, it discouraged archaeologists

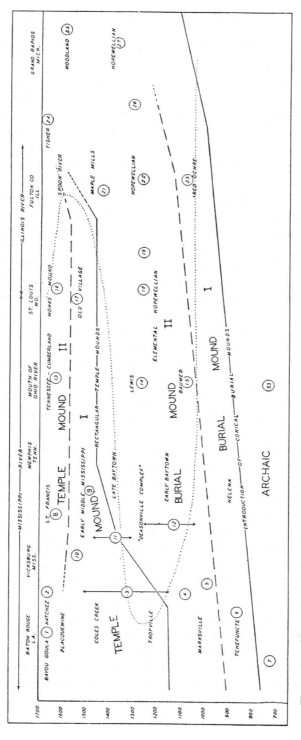

Figure 6.7 Chronological chart from Ford and Willey's synthesis of eastern North American prehistory (*American Anthropologist*, 1941)

from considering internal developments as an alternative explanation of cultural change in that area.

With the notable exception of Ford and Willey (1941), interpretations of archaeological data during the culture-historical period were characterized by a lack of will to discover, or even to search for, any overall pattern to North American prehistory. Only a tiny portion of P. S. Martin, G. I. Quimby, and Donald Collier's *Indians Before Columbus* (1947) was devoted to interpreting rather than describing the archaeological record. The authors concluded that from the arrival of the first Asian immigrants "there existed a continuous process of adaptation to local environments, of specialization, and of independent invention" that "led to the development of a series of regional Indian cultures" (p. 520). Yet they believed that the innovations they had selected as representing basic trends of cultural development, such as pottery making, were of external origin. Although their book documented change as a basic feature of North American prehistory, it made little effort to explain that change. Kidder was a rare exception to the prevailing diffusionist perspective when he maintained in 1924 that the prehistoric southwestern United States owed little more than the "germ" of its culture to the outside and that its development had been a local and almost wholly independent one that was cut short by the "devastating blight of the white man's arrival" (1962: 344). In this, as in much else, Kidder was intelligently far-sighted.

American culture-historical archaeology did not remain a passive victim of the stereotypes of Indians as being incapable of change that had dominated archaeology throughout the nineteenth century. Yet, although in the decades after 1914 cultural change and development were perceived for the first time as being a conspicuous feature of the archaeological record for North America, the main product of this period was a series of regional chronologies. Although overtly racist views concerning indigenous peoples were abandoned, the stereotypes of the American Indian that had been formulated before 1914 remained largely unchallenged. Major changes documented in the archaeological record continued to be attributed whenever possible to migration and diffusion was only grudgingly admitted to indicate creativity on the part of North American Indians. Because there was less concern than previously with reconstructing prehistoric patterns of life, the links between archaeology and ethnology, as well as between archaeologists and indigenous people, were weakened. No alternative links were forged and to a large degree American archaeologists came to be preoccupied with creating typologies of artifacts and cultures and working out cultural chronologies.

The most influential programmatic statement of culture-historical archaeology was G. R. Willey and Philip Phillips's *Method and Theory in American Archaeology* (1958), based on two earlier and much discussed papers (Phillips and Willey 1953; Willey and Phillips 1955; see also Phillips 1955). Their primary concern was the methodology of "culture-historical integration." The principal formal units that they used for this purpose were components and phases, the Gladwins' term for culture being preferred to McKern's focus because they had assigned it a stronger temporal implication. Phases were characterized as arbitrary divisions of space-time-cultural continua. Willey and Phillips also defined three spatial units of different scales: localities, regions, and areas, the first two of which might correspond to a community or local group and a tribe or society respectively. Temporal series consisted of local (intrasite) and regional (multisite or phase) sequences. The integrative units that were used to link cultures were traditions and horizons, which were interpreted as evidence of any kind of historical relations, not just phylogeny. In addition, Willey and Phillips assigned all archaeological cultures to one of five developmental, but in their view not evolutionary, stages based on economic and political criteria: Lithic, Archaic, Formative, Classic, and Postclassic. The result was a programmatic statement that unintentionally drew the attention of readers to the limitations of American culture-historical archaeology. Willey (1966, 1971) went on to produce an attractive two-volume culture-historical synthesis of what was known about the prehistory of the New World. In 1972, Irving B. Rouse published what he had intended as the theoretical introduction to a major culture-historical synthesis of world prehistory. By the time it appeared, however, this introduction was no longer framed entirely in relation to culture-history. These works represented the final, synthesizing output of American culture-historical archaeology.

American archaeologists did not simply adopt a ready made culture-historical approach from Europe but reinvented much of it, as increasing knowledge of chronological variations in the archaeological record supplemented an older awareness of geographical variations. The culture-historical approach had developed differently in Europe, where a growing sense of geographical variation in the archaeological record complemented a long-standing evolutionary preoccupation with chronological variation (Trigger 1978a: 75–95). Moreover, nationalist rivalries played no role in the evolution of the concept of the archaeological culture in North American prehistoric archaeology as they had done in Europe. Yet American archaeology did not, as a result of this enhanced perception of change in prehistoric times, totally overcome the negative views about indigenous peoples that had characterized the "colonial" phase of its development. The minimal acceptance of change in prehistoric times was primarily an adjustment of cherished beliefs to fit new archaeological facts. American archaeology remained colonial in spirit at the same time that it adopted a culture-historical methodology. The same problems were later to characterize archaeology in other white-settler countries, such as Australia, Canada, New Zealand, and South Africa.

Technical Developments

The adoption of a culture-historical approach by prehistoric archaeologists encouraged a considerable elaboration of archaeological methods. This was especially evident in terms of stratigraphy, seriation, and classification. As prehistoric archaeologists became increasingly interested in historical rather than evolutionary problems, they perceived the need for tighter controls over chronological as well as cultural variations. Temporal changes within sites over relatively short periods of time became crucial for answering many questions of a historical nature.

Classical archaeologists with their strong historical orientation were the first to perceive the need for more controlled excavations of sites. In the second half of the nineteenth century, Fiorelli, Conze, and Curtius devised new methods for the more detailed excavation and recording of plans and sections in major classical sites. In southern Europe and the Middle East, where text-based and prehistoric archaeology were pursued in close proximity and stratified sites often contained both historic and prehistoric components, these methods diffused rapidly. Wilhelm Dörpfeld (1853–1940), who had excavated under Curtius's direction at Olympia, worked for Heinrich

Schliemann from 1882 to 1890. Schliemann, who had begun digging at Hisarlik in Turkey in 1871, had pioneered the stratigraphic excavation of a multilayered "tell" site in an effort to discover the remains of Homer's Troy. He identified seven superimposed settlements at the site, most of them unaccompanied by any texts. Using more refined excavation methods, in combination with a pottery sherd chronology, Dörpfeld identified nine major levels and revised Schliemann's chronology. In 1890, Petrie recorded idealized profiles at Tell el-Hesy, a stratified site in southern Palestine that he dug by arbitrary levels, using Egyptian objects to date his finds (Figure 6.8). In 1897, Jacques de Morgan began his stratigraphic excavations at Susa, in western Iran, at the bottom of which he encountered prehistoric levels. Like Dörpfeld, he used different sherd types to establish a chronology. These stratigraphic excavations and the opening up of large areas of sites by archaeologists such as Petrie and Koldewey gradually spread improved methods for excavating and recording archaeological data through the Middle East, where they influenced both historical and prehistoric archaeology. Eve Gran-Aymerich (1998: 473) has described these developments as representing the transformation of archaeology from being a science of objects to being a science of buildings and sites.

Although prehistoric monuments in Europe occasionally were excavated with considerable attention to detail beginning in the seventeenth century (Klindt-Jensen 1975: 30), detailed recording techniques developed more slowly in this field than in classical archaeology. Until the 1870s, as a result of evolutionary preoccupations, across much of Europe interest was focused on the recording, frequently in an idealized fashion, of cross-sections of excavations, the main exception being richly furnished graves, such as those found in the early Iron Age cemetery at Hallstatt in Austria in the 1850s, which often were recorded in considerable detail (Sklenář 1983: 71–2, 77) (Figure 6.9). General Augustus Lane Fox (1827–1900), who took the name Pitt Rivers in 1880, altered this situation with his detailed excavations of sites on the extensive estates he had inherited in southern England. In the 1850s, he had become interested in anthropology as the result of a detailed study he made of the history of firearms in order to help select a new rifle for use by the British Army. Through the 1860s, he built up a large ethnographic collection and wrote about primitive warfare, navigation, and principles

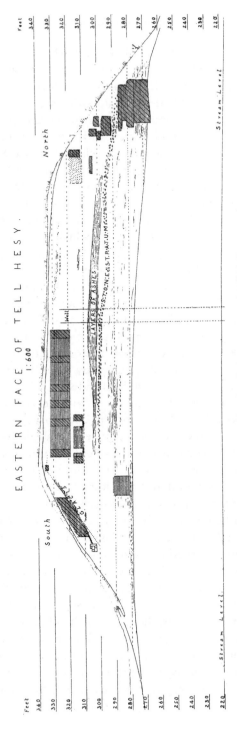

Figure 6.8 Petrie's profile of Tell el-Hesy, 1890 (*Tell el Hesy*, 1891)

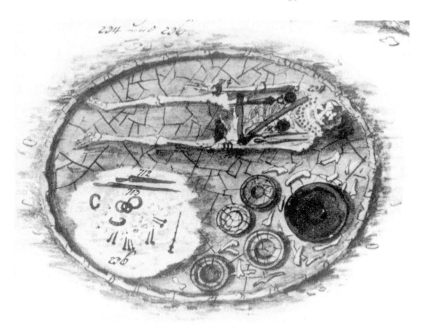

Figure 6.9   Grave from Hallstatt cemetery, Austria, recorded by the painter
Isidor Engel in the mid-nineteenth century

of classification (Pitt-Rivers 1906). To control the temporal dimension of change better, Pitt Rivers wanted to extend his studies to
include prehistoric archaeological data. He soon realized, however,
that many sites in England contained material from more than one
prehistoric time period and that these sites would have to be excavated carefully to distinguish different periods if his findings were
to be of any value for investigating evolutionary processes. Hence,
the principal goal of the evolutionist Pitt Rivers as an archaeologist
came to be to understand the history of individual archaeological
sites. He did this by trenching ditches at right angles, leaving baulks
to record stratigraphy, and carefully relating individual finds to their
stratigraphic contexts. After he inherited the estates of his cousin,
Horace Pitt, at Cranborne Chase in 1880, he had the resources to
excavate, in an exemplary manner, numerous sites located on or near
them. In his lavish excavation reports, he stressed the need for archaeologists to publish a complete record of their work, rather than only
what was of immediate interest to them (M. Thompson 1977). Much

of the fieldwork and analysis was done by a small group of assistants whom he specially trained.

After Pitt Rivers died, several of these assistants continued to do archaeological work. Harold St. George Gray remained a prolific fieldworker to the end of his life. He and Arthur H. Bulleid, whose work had been mentored by Pitt Rivers before Gray joined him, recorded their excavations at the Late Iron Age settlement at Glastonbury between 1892 and 1911 in sufficient detail that their findings concerning houses and building levels could be reanalyzed in the 1970s (Bulleid and Gray 1911, 1917; Clarke 1972b; Coles et al. 1992). The general ebb in the quality of archaeological fieldwork and excavation in Britain in the early decades of the twentieth century had less to do with a lack of skilled excavators than with the lack of adequate funding for such work (M. Thompson 1977; Bowden 1991).

With the development of publicly funded excavations in Britain, Mortimer Wheeler (1890–1976), one of the few young British archaeologists to survive World War I, sought to emulate and surpass Pitt Rivers's excavating and recording techniques. He perfected his system in a series of excavations between 1921 and 1937. Excavation was carried out using plotted grid squares separated by baulks of soil which provided numerous sections for study. Sections were drawn only after they were interpreted, and the context of each find was carefully recorded. Wheeler's system emphasized the vertical sequence of a site rather than its horizontal features and hence was admirably suited for the study of site histories. He taught his method to British and foreign students from around the world and to Indian archaeologists during his brief appointment as Director General of the Archaeological Survey of India. His book *Archaeology from the Earth* (1954) expounded the philosophy of this style of excavation. By the 1930s, similar excavation techniques were being followed in North America (Willey and Sabloff 1993: 143–6).

Techniques of seriation also were refined in response to growing historical interests. In the 1890s, Petrie, who normally dated Egyptian sites by means of inscriptions, excavated a number of large cemeteries in southern Egypt that contained material that was unfamiliar to him and lacked any inscriptions. Eventually, it was established that these cemeteries dated from the late prehistoric and very early historical periods. There was considerable stylistic variation in the artifacts found in different graves, suggesting that the cemeteries had been used for a long time, but no stratigraphy or obvious general patterns of expansion that could be used to arrange the graves even roughly in a chronological sequence. In order to devise a chronology, Petrie (1901) divided the pottery from the cemeteries at Diospolis Parva into nine major groups or classes and these in turn into several hundred types. He then recorded what types occurred in each of about 900 graves that contained more than five different types of pottery and tried to seriate the graves to produce a maximum concentration of each type (Heizer 1959: 376–83). This task, which proved to be a formidable one even when duplicated using modern computers (Kendall 1969, 1971), was facilitated by Petrie's having inferred, based on his knowledge of early historical Egyptian pottery, certain trends in major wares, in particular the tendency of Wavy-handled vessels to become smaller, cylindrical rather than globular, and their handles more vestigial as the historical period was approached. He was finally able to order his graves into fifty divisions that were arranged to form a series of "sequence dates" (Figure 6.10). The resulting chronological sequence was then tested against trends in nonceramic artifacts from the graves and overlaps resulting from later graves being cut into earlier ones. Petrie's chronology for Predynastic Egypt, which in general terms has stood the test of time (Kaiser 1957), differed from Montelius's seriation by defining intervals that in some cases may have lasted less than a decade rather than periods of several hundred years. Curiously, although Petrie presented his many pottery types as each increasing and then decreasing in relative popularity over time, he attributed their introductions to incursions of new peoples. While his seriation was an astonishing achievement by an intuitive mathematical genius, its cumbersomeness ensured that it was an approach that few archaeologists were ever likely to emulate.

In 1915, A. L. Kroeber, who was doing ethnographic fieldwork among the Zuñi Indians of western New Mexico, observed a number of archaeological sites and noted that the pot sherds visible on the surface differed in color combinations from one site to another. Almost certainly aware that Nelson had very recently demonstrated variations in the frequency of pottery types from one level to another at San Cristóbal Pueblo, Kroeber collected pot sherds from eighteen of these sites, divided them into three general types, and by comparing changes in the frequency of each type worked out a

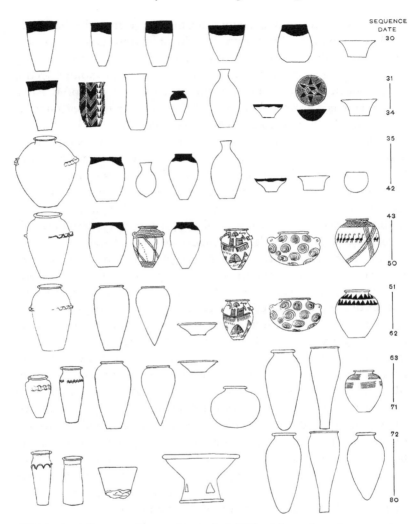

Figure 6.10 Pottery of successive periods in Petrie's predynastic sequence, from *Diospolis Parva*, 1901

historical sequence of these sites (Kroeber 1916; Heizer 1959: 383–93). This approach was adopted by Leslie Spier (1917), who applied it to a larger number of Zuñi sites and then conducted stratigraphic excavations that corroborated his findings (Lyman et al. 1997a: 55–62). Beginning in the 1930s, James Ford (1936) used this sort of frequency seriation of pottery types to supplement stratigraphic sequences as a basis for working out the prehistoric cultural chronology of the Mississippi Valley (Ford 1938; O'Brien and Lyman 1998). Petrie's "occurrence seriation" depended on the individual occurrence or nonoccurrence in specific closed finds of a large number of different types, whereas Kroeber's "frequency seriation" depended on the changing frequencies of a much smaller number of types (Dunnell 1970). The greater ease with which frequency seriation could be implemented ensured its rapid spread and development. It has become the basis of all modern seriation. In both cases, seriation was being used to establish a detailed historical sequence of villages or graves rather than a succession of periods, as evolutionary archaeologists from Thomsen to Montelius had done. Petrie and Kroeber both chose to work with pottery because its stylistic attributes provided more sensitive indices of change than did the stone and metal tools that had been studied by the Scandinavian archaeologists.

Growing interest in defining cultures and working out more detailed seriations encouraged more systematic and elaborate classifications of artifacts in both Europe and North America. In Europe, these classifications tended to build on ones originally established by evolutionary archaeologists, usually by splitting or otherwise refining existing types. Types tended to be viewed pragmatically as a means for achieving chronological objectives or for understanding life in prehistoric times. Perhaps for these reasons, the discussion of the nature and significance of types generally remained low-keyed in Europe. Gorodtsov, however, continued to develop his typological approach, in which categories were divided into groups and groups into types on the basis of function, material, and form respectively. His final description of this system was translated into English and published in the *American Anthropologist* (Gorodzov 1933). After World War II, François Bordes (1919–1981) and Maurice Bourgon developed a new and more systematic approach to classifying Middle and Lower Palaeolithic assemblages to replace a reliance on diagnostic types. Bordes distinguished the description of artifact assemblages from that of the artifacts they contained and the description of artifact forms from the identification of the techniques that were used to produce them (Bordes 1953). Still later, G. Laplace (1964) produced an elaborate alternative classification of Palaeolithic stone tools, and finally David Clarke (1968) provided a systematic treatment of archaeological classifications at all levels that sought to improve the procedures inherent in culture-historical archaeology as it was practiced in Britain (Shennan 2002: 72).

In the United States, artifact classification has been discussed from a theoretical point of view since the 1920s. In 1930, Winifred and Harry Gladwin argued that, because of processes such as trade, artifact classification had to be done independently from cultural classification. Although they viewed pottery styles as sensitive indicators of spatial and temporal variations in culture, they also believed that it was necessary to define pottery types in terms that were free from temporal implications, if subjectivity was to be avoided. They therefore proposed a binomial nomenclature in which the first term indicated a geographical location where the type was found and the second its color or surface treatment: for example, Tularosa black-on-white. Type descriptions were published in a set format involving name, vessel shape, design, type site, geographical distribution, and inferred chronological range. In 1932, Harold S. Colton proposed an elaborate, Linnaean-style system for classifying pottery (which was seen as equivalent to a Linnaean Class) on the basis of paste and temper (Order), surface color (Family or Ware), surface treatment (Genus or Series), and more specific features (types). In a systematic classification of southwestern pottery, based on the examination of several million sherds, published by Harold Colton and Lyndon Hargrave (1937), only wares, series, and types continued to be used. William Adams (2001: 347) has noted that, although this hierarchical approach did not find general acceptance, the individual wares that Colton and Hargrave defined have nearly all withstood the test of time.

James Ford (1938), by contrast, stressed that types should be recognized only if they could be demonstrated to be useful for interpreting culture-history and that there should be no formal splitting of types unless the results clearly correlated with spatial or temporal differences. Ford in particular regarded types as heuristic constructs to be used for historical analysis and therefore he sought empirically to isolate traits that had chronological significance. Later discussions centered on the reality of types to the people who had made and used artifacts, on the relations between types and the attributes or modes that are used to define them, and on the nature of attributes and their usefulness for artifact seriation. Rouse (1939) proposed that an emic type could be recognized by the statistical clustering of attributes around the high points of statistical curves, which represent the norms or ideal mental templates shared by a group of artisans. In the 1950s, it was maintained that types could be discovered as regular clusterings of attributes and that these "natural" types would reveal much more about human behavior and cultural change than would Ford's arbitrary creations (Spaulding 1953). This prolonged discussion of artifact classification was the first substantial manifestation of the concern of American archaeologists to articulate and make explicit the analytical basis of their discipline.

Although the concept of the archaeological culture had been developed separately and from different baselines in Europe and North America, it came to be viewed on both sides of the Atlantic as a recurrent set of components characterized by similar material culture, normally occupying a small geographical area and lasting for a relatively brief interval of time. The spatial and temporal boundaries of each culture had to be determined empirically. When the cultures being compared represented successive stages of a single cultural tradition, the boundaries separating them were recognized as being arbitrary. Nevertheless, differences existed in how archaeological cultures were perceived in Europe and America. In America, especially under the influence of the Midwestern Taxonomic Method, cultures (foci) were established on the basis of the number of different kinds of traits components had in common, not the frequency of individual traits, even though frequency was recognized as being vital for seriation and neglecting it enhanced the classificatory importance of rare items that were traded or otherwise intrusive into single sites. Archaeologists also rejected their former interest in the functional roles that artifacts or traits had played. This new, formalistic approach was believed to be more objective and scientific than earlier, more "impressionistic" concerns with the functions of artifacts.

In Europe, archaeologists adopted a more functional view of material culture. It was widely recognized that cemeteries might contain a narrower, or even a different, set of artifacts from those found in habitation sites, and this difference was welcomed as providing a deeper insight into prehistoric cultures. Childe argued that cultures were best defined pragmatically on the basis of ethnically sensitive traits that were resistant to change rather than by using utilitarian ones that diffused quickly over broad areas. He also emphasized that the boundaries of cultures were not the same as those of their constituent artifact types, thus in effect adopting what David Clarke (1968) would later call a polythetic concept of archaeological cultures. Childe also acknowledged that all types of artifacts were significant for understanding how people had lived in the past. He stressed, however, that their importance was not equivalent to their number: a single bronze axe might provide as much information as did 500 potsherds. This orientation probably reflected the greater interest in the "people behind the artifact" among European than among American prehistoric archaeologists in the early twentieth century. Childe did not suggest, however, that the relative frequencies of different types of artifacts might be important for understanding cultures.

A growing interest in how particular groups of Europeans had lived in prehistoric times, that was encouraged by nationalism but had its roots in the Scandinavian archaeology of the early nineteenth century, led archaeologists to pay attention to classes of archaeological data that previously had been ignored. A long-standing interest in cemeteries was supplemented by increasing study of the remains of settlements. This encouraged the development of large-scale, open-plan, horizontal excavations at the expense of vertical stratigraphic ones, as well as the recording of many new types of data. The first post molds sealed below ground were noted by Pitt Rivers before 1872 (Bowden 1991: 77). In the 1890s, the Roman-German Boundary Commission, studying sites along the northern frontier of the Roman empire in central Europe, developed techniques for recognizing post molds in all kinds of soils (Childe 1953: 13). German archaeologists, such as Carl Schuchhardt and Gerhard Bersu (1889–1964), were soon using postmold patterns to reconstruct decayed wooden structures. Archaeologists also began to record more systematically where in sites artifacts were found, so that these could be plotted in relation to features such as hearths and house walls. Gradually, lithic debitage and floral and faunal remains that hitherto had generally been dismissed as unimportant were saved and studied. This style of excavation was applied in the Netherlands by Albert Egges van Giffen (1884–1973) and was transmitted from Germany to England in the late 1930s, when Bersu arrived there as a refugee from Nazi persecution (C. Evans 1989).

These developments encouraged a new precision in excavation techniques. The principal goal of such research was not to reconstruct details of social organization or what people had thought in the past but rather to reconstruct a visual impression of life in the past. That involved determining what houses looked like, what kind of clothing people wore, what utensils they used, and in what activities they had engaged. These impressions could be reconstructed in drawings (Figure 6.11) or three-dimensionally in the form of open-air museums. One site that did not require much reconstruction was Skara Brae, a Neolithic settlement in the Orkneys that was excavated by Gordon Childe (1931). In this site not only houses but also furniture, such as beds and cupboards, were preserved as a result of being constructed from stone slabs. The most impressive developments in this sort of archaeology occurred in continental Europe between 1920 and 1940. Houses and their surroundings were completely excavated and post molds, hearths, pits, and artifact distributions interpreted as evidence of patterns of daily life (De Laet 1957: 101–3; Sieveking 1976: xvi).

In the United States, the development of a culture-historical approach initially encouraged archaeologists to excavate sites to recover artifact samples that could be used to elaborate trait lists, define cultures, and work out cultural chronologies. It was assumed that the sorts of artifacts found in any one part of a site were typical of the whole and therefore excavations were frequently directed toward middens, where artifacts were most abundant and could be recovered most cheaply. In addition to artifacts, archaeologists sometimes sought to obtain floral and faunal data as evidence of subsistence patterns and skeletal remains that could identify the physical types of the people who had occupied sites. During the economic depression of the 1930s, U.S. federal government relief agencies, working through park services, museums, and universities, made large sums of money available for archaeological research. Archaeological excavation was supported because it could be learned easily by unemployed manual laborers and did not produce anything that competed with private industry. Much of the work was rescue archaeology. Large sites were completely excavated in areas that were to be flooded by the construction of hydroelectric dams (Fagette 1996; Lyon 1996). The massive horizontal excavations carried out during the depression years resulted not only in the recovery of vast amounts of data

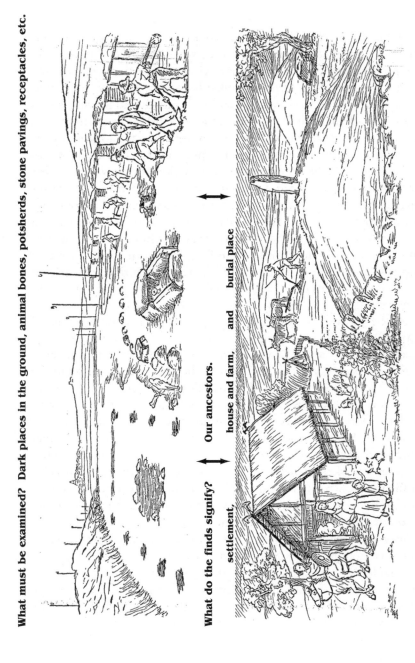

What must be examined? Dark places in the ground, animal bones, potsherds, stone pavings, receptacles, etc.

What do the finds signify?

Our ancestors.

settlement,   house and farm,   and   burial place

Figure 6.11 Illustration of horizontal excavation and reconstruction of a prehistoric German site, from a pamphlet issued by Halle Museum, republished in *Antiquity*, June 1938 (captions translated)

relating to the culture-history of the eastern United States but also in growing attention being paid to features such as hearths, house patterns, and community plans, in relation to which distributions of artifacts took on additional significance. These excavations expanded knowledge about the construction of houses and ritual structures and the plans of entire settlements (Willey and Sabloff 1993: 143–4). Yet these findings were initially envisaged as a means to expand trait lists and only slowly stimulated a renewed interest in how people had lived in prehistoric times. Government-supported archaeological rescue projects resumed in the 1950s, when the American government built additional dams along the Missouri and Colorado Rivers.

Convergences in European and American culture-historical research programs did not produce equivalent convergences in attitudes toward the past. Although Europeans were deeply involved emotionally in what they regarded as the study of their own prehistory, Euro-Americans continued to view the prehistoric archaeological record as the product of an alien people. Yet, on both sides of the Atlantic Ocean, the development of a culture-historical approach to archaeology carried classification, chronology, and cultural reconstruction far beyond the point they had reached previously. The switch from "scientific" to "historical" objectives stimulated rather than inhibited the development of archaeological methodology.

Theory

In recent decades archaeological theorists have looked to philosophy to provide guidance in matters relating to epistemology, or theories of knowledge. It is widely supposed, however, that culture-historical archaeologists did not make significant use of philosophical concepts (Spaulding 1968; M. Salmon 1982; Gibbon 1989; W. Salmon 1992). Even Gordon Childe had largely abandoned the culture-historical approach before he began in the 1940s and 1950s to employ philosophy to help him understand what archaeologists were doing. In fact, a profound encounter between culture-historical archaeology and philosophy took place in Romano-British archaeology, a field that traditionally has spanned the divide between classical and prehistoric archaeology. This encounter occurred in the person of the Oxford academic Robin Collingwood (1889–1943), who was simultaneously a leading classical archaeologist and one of the most distinguished British philosophers of his time. Collingwood was perhaps the first philosopher who viewed efforts to understand the past as a testing ground for investigating the nature of thought in general and hence as a basis for philosophical enquiry. Beginning in 1911, he concentrated on archaeological studies that made him the leading authority on Roman Britain. This work culminated in his definitive study of this subject, *The Archaeology of Roman Britain* (1930). After that time, he produced his most important philosophical work, *The Idea of History*, which was published posthumously in 1946. A briefer and more accessible exposition of his philosophical ideas is available in *An Autobiography*, which appeared in 1939, at a time when, because of illness, he feared he might not live long enough to complete his major work.

Collingwood was an advocate of idealist philosophy in the Kantian tradition. He believed that even the simplest perceptions make sense only as the result of concepts, or categories, that already exist in the human mind. Individuals cannot perceive or make sense of the world independently of their existing understanding of the nature of things. Many of these concepts are learned, but others, such as basic notions of time, space, and causality, appear to be innate. Whatever the origin of such concepts, without them the observations that constitute the basis of a positivist epistemology would remain meaningless. As an idealist, Collingwood had much in common with the Italian philosopher Benedetto Croce (1866–1952), whose belief in history as the history of ideas and hence as a branch of philosophy greatly influenced the development of Italian archaeology (d'Agostino 1991: 53–4).

For Collingwood, the past that the archaeologist studies is not a dead past, but one that exists entirely in the present. He maintained that all we know about the past comes from texts and artifacts that exist in the modern world, together with knowledge that we believe is relevant for understanding the past when applied to this material (Collingwood 1939: 97–9). Collingwood's idealism also led him to deny that facts and theories are distinct from one another. Archaeologists, he argued, only perceive what they are conditioned to look for and nothing acquires meaning except in relation to clearly formulated questions that the archaeologist poses (pp. 24–5). As an idealist, Collingwood maintained that, because what is real to people is only what exists in their minds, archaeologists must seek to understand the past by determining the intentions, goals, and knowledge that motivated the behavior of the people being studied. They therefore must attempt to replicate the intentions, purposes, and ideas that caused people to make and do things in particular ways in the past. Archaeological interpretation consists of the ideas that modern archaeologists have about the ideas that people once had, and is an activity in which a scholar strives to relive the past in her or his own mind. Only by seeking to reconstruct the mental activities that shaped events, and by rethinking the past in terms of their own experiences, can archaeologists hope to discern the significant patterns and dynamics of ancient cultures. Collingwood also stressed the importance of the convergence of multiple lines of independent evidence for establishing a persuasive understanding (Collingwood 1946: 276).

To study the past adequately, however, archaeologists also must try to expand their own consciousness by seeking to learn as much as possible about variations in human behavior and about specific ancient cultures from literary sources. There is no evidence that Collingwood viewed social anthropology as a useful source of information about variations in human behavior, although this would have been a productive way for him to expand his awareness of diversity. Instead, his classical bias led him to use the written records of ancient Greece and Rome to become more aware of the thoughts and practices of those civilizations that were distinct from modern ones and would help to place the past on a different plane from the present by contradicting the archaeologist's conventional beliefs (Collingwood 1939: 120–46, 1946: 302–15). Collingwood did not believe that such understanding would provide the basis for a definitive knowledge of the past. For him, the most that was possible was an imagining of the past that the archaeologist might hope approximated the understanding held by the people who had lived in the past. Working within the confines of the classical tradition, Collingwood seems to have been unaware of the dangers of ethnocentrism involved in this process.

Many British archaeologists of the 1940s and 1950s read Collingwood, or at least became generally familiar with his ideas. Yet most of them knew little about philosophy and were culturally predisposed toward some form of naive positivism or empiricism. That led archaeologists such as Glyn Daniel (1975), Stuart Piggott (1950,

1959), and Christopher Hawkes (1954) to interpret Collingwood's ideas along lines that in some respects were very different from what Collingwood had intended. Like Collingwood, they accorded ideas a major role in shaping human behavior, but, unlike him, they drew a clear distinction between facts and interpretations. They believed that archaeological data constituted the real and cumulative core of the discipline. Interpretations, by contrast, were matters of opinion that had little lasting importance. They argued that all archaeological interpretations are shaped by intellectual fashions and are invariably undermined by new data and new understandings. This position, which had much in common with the views of contemporary historians who followed the influential nineteenth-century German empirical historian Leopold von Ranke (1795–1886), combined extreme scepticism regarding the objectivity or lasting value of interpretations with unquestioning faith in the objectivity of archaeological facts (Carr 1967: 5–6; Iggers and Powell 1990). These archaeologists argued that, as the past no longer exists, there was no possibility of comparing inferences about the past with the actual events to establish if the inferences were correct. Because of the complexity of human phenomena, varying interpretations were possible and these were influenced to a considerable degree by the various standpoints or beliefs of individual archaeologists.

The idealist epistemology of these archaeologists influenced how they evaluated archaeology's potential and how they believed it should be organized. In 1954, Christopher Hawkes (1905–1992) maintained that, when totally unaided by written texts or oral traditions, it was easier for prehistoric archaeologists to learn something about ancient technologies than about economies, considerably more difficult to reconstruct sociopolitical institutions, and hardest of all to address religious and spiritual beliefs. The logic underlying this scale of increasing difficulty, which has come to be called "Hawkes's hierarchy" or "Hawkes's ladder," is that universal physical laws play a major role in shaping technology, whereas idiosyncratic and highly variable cultural factors influence human beliefs and behavior. Similar ideas had already structured the first edition of Grahame Clark's *Archaeology and Society* (1939), but as a materialist Clark believed that even working under these limitations archaeologists could learn much that was important about human behavior in prehistoric times. Hawkes, as an idealist, deplored the idea that archaeology was limited to studying what was "generically animal" about human behavior rather than what was "specifically human," by which he meant human cognitive behavior (C. Evans 1999). Hawkes's argument evidently struck a responsive chord and was endorsed by M. A. Smith (1955), Childe (1956a: 129–31), Piggott (1959: 9–12), and André Leroi-Gourhan (1964), and more recently by J. Friedman and M. J. Rowlands (1978b: 203–4).

During the 1950s, British culture-historical archaeologists also tended to dichotomize the collection and interpretation of prehistoric archaeological data. The collection and primary analysis of data were widely viewed as the tasks of "dirt archaeologists," but the synthesis of their findings was the domain of prehistorians. Ironically, although data were believed to be the stable basis of archaeology and interpretations were regarded as little more than opinions, prehistorians were assigned much higher status than were archaeologists. This assignment of tasks was based on the assumption that there was no significant feedback between the synthesis and the collection of data. British empiricism suggested that fieldwork was best done in a theoretical vacuum, which was the opposite of Collingwood's belief that it should be undertaken to answer questions. Although this division of labor was noted by some American archaeologists (Rouse 1972: 6–11), it was not widely accepted in the United States. Yet Philip Phillips (1955: 249–50) agreed that the "integration" and "interpretation" of archaeological data were separate "operations."

Most prehistoric archaeologists, like palaeontologists, believed that analogical reasoning provided a means for interpreting their data. Within this general category, palaeontologists distinguished between analogies in the strict sense and homologies. Analogies are similar features that different species share as a result of natural selection having separately adapted them to a similar environment. An example is the streamlining acquired by fish and whales as a result of convergent evolution having adapted them to live in the water. Homologies are features species share as the result of a genetic relationship, such as the similarities between elephants and mammoths. Evolutionary archaeologists had believed that, as a result of psychic unity, different groups of people at the same level of development responded in similar ways to similar challenges and such resemblances were explained from a rational, adaptive point of view. Yet they did not rule out the possibility that two or more cultures shared features because they were descended from a common ancestral culture or as the result of diffusion (something that could not happen between reproductively isolated species). Hence, they tended to explain similarities among distant cultures analogically and among neighboring cultures historically. Culture-historical archaeologists generally distrusted evolutionary explanations and relied almost exclusively on homologies to explain archaeological findings, very often by means of the direct historical approach. This choice reflected both their strong commitment to cultural particularism and their pessimism about human creativity, which resulted in diffusion and migration being almost the only mechanisms invoked to explain cultural change.

Culture-historical archaeologists long assumed that an archaeological culture was produced by a group of people who shared a common language and way of life and hence that ethnicity could be inferred from archaeological data (Kossinna 1911; Childe 1925a). By the 1950s, Eóin MacWhite (1956), Willey and Phillips (1958: 48–9), and other archaeologists had concluded that no single type of social unit corresponded with an archaeological culture. The distribution of the Chellean and Acheulean "cultures" over large parts of Africa, western Asia, and Europe and the great length of time they had endured made nonsense of the idea they could be equated with a single people. For this reason, these taxa often were called "industries" rather than cultures. The late prehistoric Thule culture, which spread over much of the Canadian Arctic, may have been associated with a single ethnic group, but it too clearly did not correspond with a single society. It was suggested that the archaeological remains of the ways of life of the Maya peasantry and elite might be classified as two linked "subcultures" or ethnic groups, although both groups almost certainly regarded themselves as members of a single social and economic system (Rouse 1965: 9–10). It was also observed that the geographical extent of the archaeological cultures of the European Neolithic was much larger than that of analogous ethnographic entities, an observation recently confirmed by H. P. Wotzka (1997). With the development of modern settlement pattern studies, new means for inferring prehistoric social and political units became available. It was gradually accepted that social organization had to be inferred from archaeological data on a case by case basis and that patterns of material culture were only one source of information. As a result, archaeologists in English as well as German-speaking countries became increasingly aware that the social interpretation of archaeological cultures was more problematic than had generally been believed.

The ethnic significance of the archaeological culture also was being questioned on other grounds. Although Childe (1935a, 1940a) continued to produce detailed culture-historical syntheses, by the late 1920s he had begun to doubt that much could be learned about ethnicity from archaeological data alone or that ethnicity was a concept that could be central to the study of prehistory (Childe 1930: 240–7). The ethnographer Donald Thomson (1939) revealed that different seasonal manifestations of hunter-gatherer cultures might be associated with radically different material remains. It also became apparent that not all archaeological "cultures" had clearly defined boundaries. When variation in material culture occurred along clines or gradients, the delineations of archaeological cultures could be highly arbitrary and subjective and therefore be manipulated in accordance with interpretative agendas (Renfrew 1978b). This further called into question the relation between archaeological cultures and ethnic groups. As culture-historical archaeology declined in importance, the critiques of ethnic interpretations of the archaeological culture grew sharper. Processual archaeologists were inclined to construe variation in material culture as an expression of ecological adaptation rather than ethnicity.

Archaeologists now recognize that variations in material culture have numerous causes. Some of them reflect temporal differences, others differences in environmental settings, the availability of resources, local traditions of craft production and ornamentation, trading patterns, status emulation, gender identities, intergroup marriage patterns, and religious beliefs, as well as ethnic differences. It also has been shown that some peoples derive more powerful and enduring affiliations from clans or religious associations than they do from membership in tribes and communities. In these cases, material culture associated with clans and religious cults rather than with archaeological cultures is proving to be ideally suited for tracing the movement of groups of people in prehistoric times (T. Ferguson 2003: 141–2). Frederick Barth's (1969) demonstration that ethnicity is a subjective sense of identity that is manipulated by individuals and groups within many different contexts, that often have little to do with the material culture archaeologists study, makes ethnicity unlikely to be the sole, or even the primary explanation either of cultural variation in the archaeological record or of cultural change (S. Jones 1997; Gosden 1999: 190–7; Shennan 2002: 84–5; Snow 2002; Chrisomalis and Trigger 2004).

Today, many archaeologists ignore or reject the concept of the archaeological culture (Shennan 1989b). Yet, where sharp breaks in material culture occur between adjacent groups of archaeological sites, the archaeological culture remains a useful concept for analyzing archaeological data. Archaeological cultures are increasingly being viewed as summary descriptions of patterns of spatial and temporal variation in material culture that were produced by many different factors. Hence, they are not explanations but phenomena that it is the duty of archaeologists to explain in specific instances. The search for ethnicity, which shaped the development of culture-historical archaeology for over a century, can now be understood as based on a misunderstanding of to what degree various factors shaped the archaeological record that persisted because of archaeologists' prolonged and largely uncritical preoccupation with producing ethnic or national prehistory. Although Kossinna and other German archaeologists pioneered this sort of archaeology, other German archaeologists were the first to discuss its shortcomings.

By the 1950s, culture-historical archaeology was running out of new ideas. In Britain, this era was characterized by the publication of numerous books dealing with how to dig sites and analyze finds using techniques derived from the physical and biological sciences. This approach culminated in Don Brothwell and Eric S. Higgs's *Science in Archaeology* (1963). Nowhere were there sustained discussions of how the interpretation of archaeological data might be grounded in archaeological and social science theory. The closest to such a body of theory was Eóin MacWhite's (1956) scheme of levels of archaeological interpretation, but this approach was not developed any further.

Although some culture-historical archaeologists traced the prehistoric development of technology (Piggott 1983) and art styles (Megaw and Megaw 1989), most continued to try to identify ethnic groups in the archaeological record and attributed changes in material culture to diffusion and migration. Archaeological findings were interpreted behaviorally or symbolically only when written texts or the direct historical approach provided additional sources of information. The resulting narratives displayed little systematic grounding in archaeological data, with the result that they were increasingly criticized for being merely expressions of their authors' opinions (Clarke 1968: 30–1). The most striking shortcoming of culture-historical archaeologists was that change continued to be attributed to external processes, lumped under the rubrics of diffusion and migration, but little effort was made to discover why cultures accepted or rejected new traits or how innovations transformed societies. What was missing, despite a growing interest in what archaeological sites had looked like and what activities had gone on in them, was the will to learn how individual cultures had functioned and changed as systems. Without such an understanding, diffusion and migration were doomed to remain nonexplanations. These problems had been recognized for a long time, but ultimately the solutions would come from outside the culture-historical approach not from within it.

Conclusions

An approach centered on defining archaeological cultures and trying to account for their origins in terms of diffusion and migration developed as European archaeologists became more aware of the complexity of the archaeological record and ceased to view cultural evolution as a natural or desirable process. European archaeology became closely aligned with history and was seen as offering insights into what had happened to particular peoples in prehistoric times. Its findings became incorporated into struggles for national self-determination, the assertion and defense of national identity, and promoting national unity in opposition to class conflict. Archaeology of this sort also had great appeal elsewhere in the world. Ethnic and national groups continue to seek to learn about their early history as a means of enhancing group pride and solidarity and helping to promote economic and social development. Although the findings of culture-historical archaeology are now frequently enriched by the use of techniques for reconstructing prehistoric cultures and explaining cultural change that developed in other branches of archaeology, an approach that seeks to trace the histories of specific peoples continues to serve the needs of nation building in a postcolonial era. For this reason, culture-historical archaeology remains socially attractive in many countries. In the United States, efforts to explain increasing evidence of complex patterning in the archaeological record slowly resulted in the grudging and limited acceptance of a formerly denied capacity of indigenous Americans to change.

Over the years, research by supporters and opponents of culture-historical archaeology has revealed the limitations of the archaeological culture as a source of information about ethnicity. Ethnicity is only one of many factors that shape the patterning of material culture; hence, archaeological cultures are not a privileged source of information about ethnicity but phenomena to be explained in many different ways. There is also considerable ongoing disagreement concerning to what extent archaeological cultures exist as bounded entities or are subjectively extracted from continua of variability.

Nevertheless, a more limited and formalist version of the culture-historical approach remains important. In places where little archaeological research has been done, it is necessary to construct culture-historical frameworks as a prerequisite for addressing other problems. In Canada, early in the twentieth century, cultural anthropologists asserted that ethnographic and linguistic data about indigenous peoples should be recorded before their old ways disappeared, whereas archaeological data could safely be left in the ground (Jenness 1932: 71). As a result, there was little government funding for archaeological research before the 1960s. Since then, Canadian archaeologists have been constructing cultural chronologies over half a continent. In this research, archaeological cultures have had to compete with social units, such as villages and site clusters, and with clinal variation for describing spatial and temporal variations in material culture. At the same time, processual archaeology has stimulated a strong focus on understanding how Canada's indigenous hunter-gatherer peoples adapted to diverse environments over many millennia. The resulting combination of culture-historical and processual archaeology continues to dominate Canadian archaeology. Even in countries where detailed chronologies already exist, functional and cognitive understandings of the past almost invariably require a more detailed understanding of the temporal and geographical variations of material culture in the archaeological record. Although Lewis Binford has made important contributions to understanding human behavior in Palaeolithic times, Palaeolithic archaeologists such as Olga Soffer and Clive Gamble continue to pursue a more detailed culture-historical understanding of that era (Gamble 1999: 828–9).

The enduring value of a culture-historical approach is not its emphasis on ethnicity or on diffusionist and migrationist explanations of culture change but its ability to trace real lineages of the development of material culture in the archaeological record. Culture-historical, not evolutionary, archaeology is the equivalent of palaeontological research in biology. Like palaeontology, culture-historical archaeology's chief asset is its ability to trace historical relations through time and space. Such historical findings are the necessary prerequisites for evolutionary generalizations about the processes of change. Long ago A. L. Kroeber (1952: 63–103) observed that this relationship holds true in all historical sciences, whether they deal with natural, biological, or human phenomena.

CHAPTER 7

Early Functional-Processual Archaeology

———

Forms and types, that is, products, have been regarded as more real and alive than the society which created them and whose needs determined these manifestations of life.

A. M. TALLGREN, "The method of prehistoric archaeology" (1937), p. 155

As the inadequacies of culture-historical archaeology for understanding how prehistoric cultures operated and changed became obvious to a growing number of archaeologists, they adopted new approaches to the study of prehistory that were based on systematic anthropological and sociological investigations of human behavior. These approaches are generally designated as being functional and processual in nature. Culture-historical studies traditionally explained changes from the outside by attributing them to diffusion and migration. Functional and processual studies try to understand social and cultural systems from the inside by determining how different parts of these systems are interrelated and how these parts interact with one another. Functionalism is a synchronous approach that attempts to understand how systems operate routinely without accounting for major changes. Processual approaches seek to understand how and why such systems change irreversibly. Yet, many self-styled functionalist anthropologists also were interested in how systems changed (Malinowski 1945; Evans-Pritchard 1949, 1962). Although functionalist approaches are often presumed to have preceded processual ones in anthropology, both have been employed at least incipiently in prehistoric archaeology since the mid-nineteenth century and they were often used together. The two sorts of explanation are not only closely related but also are complementary, in the sense that it is impossible fully to understand either stasis or irreversible change without understanding the other.

Environmental Functional-Processualism

Already by the 1830s, Steenstrup was attempting to relate archaeological finds to the succession of forest types he was discovering in Danish bog sites. Beginning in 1848, Worsaae, Steenstrup, and Forchhammer, as members of what has come to be called the First Kitchen-Midden Commission, pioneered the field study of archaeological finds in relation to their palaeoenvironmental settings and combined their archaeological, biological, and geological skills to investigate how people had lived in prehistoric Denmark. Around the same time, Nilsson argued that pastoralism had given way to farming in Sweden as population densities had increased, perhaps the earliest example of a processual approach being used to explain prehistoric change. These projects were the first manifestations of an interest in ecological research that has persisted to the present in Scandinavian archaeology. Although Scandinavian archaeologists were mainly preoccupied with culture-historical questions in the late nineteenth century and the Second Kitchen-Midden Commission (1885–1900) largely addressed such issues, Georg Sarauw (1862–1928) studied the plants and seeds that were recovered by that project. Gradually, Scandinavian geologists learned more about how the retreat of the glaciers and the combined results of changing sea levels and isostatic rebound of land that accompanied this process had altered distributions of land surfaces, lakes, and oceans in Scandinavia. Other scientists investigated changes in climate, flora, and fauna. These findings provided archaeologists with information that allowed them better to understand human land use in prehistoric times.

Beginning in 1905, the geologist Gerard de Geer (1858–1943) used successions of overlapping varve deposits, which formed annually in lakes in front of glaciers, to date the retreating ice front in Scandinavia over the past 12,000 years. This varve sequence was tied in with 30 meters of annual silt deposits on the bed of former Lake Raganda, which had been drained in 1796. As a result, this study provided the first calendrically calibrated natural chronology anywhere in the world in relation to which adjacent prehistoric finds could be dated. This permitted cultural change to be considered in relation not only to sequence but to the actual amount of time involved.

Another Swede, E. J. Lennart von Post (1884–1951), utilized Gustav Lagerheim's observation that pollen grains could be preserved in soil for thousands of years to elaborate Steenstrup's pioneering studies of postglacial floral changes. By 1916, he had produced graphs that purported to show the percentages of various species of trees at successive periods of Scandinavian prehistory. The old sequence of birch, pine, oak, and beech-elm forest was vindicated but, because pollen is preserved not only in bogs, it was now possible to examine prehistoric variation in plant communities over larger areas and to provide evidence of tree cutting and the introduction of domestic plants. It also became possible to trace fluctuations in different plant species over much smaller intervals of time than had been done previously. Forest contour lines were worked out showing the northern limits of various trees at different periods and these were correlated with De Geer's geochronology of glacial margins to achieve a high degree of calendrical precision (Bibby 1956: 183–94). Between 1940 and 1960, the ecological approach dominated Scandinavian Stone Age research (Kristiansen 2002). Pollen analysis was introduced into England in the early 1930s and applied to archaeological problems by the biologist Harry Godwin (1901–1985) (1933).

In 1898, the geologist Robert Gradmann (1865–1950) noted a close correlation between wind-deposited loess soils and early Neolithic settlement in central Europe and erroneously concluded that, because early farmers were incapable of clearing forests, the first agricultural settlements had been in areas that were naturally either devoid of trees or lightly forested (Gradmann 1906). It is now believed that early farmers preferred loess soils because they were light and therefore easy to work with wooden tools. The relations between loess soils and Neolithic settlement continued to be examined by Alfred Schliz (1906), Ernst Wahle (1915), and Max Hellmich (1923). Attempts to reconstruct central European natural palaeoenvironments and early cultural landscapes led to more intensive archaeological studies concerning why certain terrains were or were not settled at various times in prehistory. Wahle (1889–1981) (1921) continued to play a major role in this research. Both before and after World War II, German archaeologists paid much attention to studying the reciprocal relations between settlement systems and their ecological contexts (Kossack 1992: 91–2, 101–2). In Russia, during the late nineteenth century, Dimitri Anuchin, a geographer and ethnologist who was also interested in archaeology and had embraced the culture-historical approach, urged the need to create archaeological maps of Russia and interpret archaeological finds in relation to geographical factors (Klejn 2001b: 1139).

In the account of his excavations at the stratified site of Anau in Russian Turkestan (now Turkmenistan) in 1904, the American geologist and archaeologist Raphael Pumpelly (1837–1923) proposed the desiccation or oasis theory of the origins of food-production (1908, I: 65–6). He argued that, as the Middle East became much drier following the last Ice Age, hunter-gatherers were compelled to gather around surviving sources of water and to "conquer new means of support" by domesticating wild animals and grasses. This theory, which was to become extremely popular among Old World archaeologists in succeeding decades, is another early example of a processual explanation (G. Wright 1971: 451–6).

In *Origines Celticae* (1883), the Oxford University historian Edwin Guest (1800–1880) urged that the history of England had to be understood against the background of British geography. Shortly after, the Oxford geographer H. J. Mackinder (1861–1947) argued that the geographical location of nations in relation to one another played a major role in shaping their political and economic history. In 1912, F. J. Haverfield (1860–1919) demonstrated a correlation between the extent of Roman settlement in Britain and particular types of geographical terrain and John Myres was inspired by Guest and Mackinder to expound the value of a geographical approach to archaeology. Also beginning in 1912, O. G. S. Crawford (1886–1957), who had studied at Oxford and was to work for many years for the British Ordnance Survey, concentrated on studying prehistory in relation to the geographical environment. This involved detailed mapping of the distribution of artifacts and sites associated with specific periods. It was not until later, however, that archaeologists, such as Grahame Clark, would use palaeoenvironmental data, such as fossil pollen, to reconstruct original patterns of vegetation. Among Crawford's many contributions, he encouraged the employment of aerial photography to detect ancient ditches, banks, and crop marks that were not visible from the ground. The importance of aerial reconnaissance for archaeological research had first been recognized during military operations in the course of World War I (Crawford 1923; Crawford and Keiller 1928).

W. G. Clark, J. P. Williams-Freeman, Herbert Fleure, W. E. White-house, and Cyril Fox undertook studies of the relations between prehistoric settlement and ecology in various parts of Britain. As early as 1916, Fleure and Whitehouse noted, on the basis of their research in Wales, that the introduction of bronze, and more especially of iron, tools had resulted in a major shift of settlement from lighter, more easily worked, but poorer highland soils to heavier, harder to work, but more productive lowland ones. These important observations were published in a paper that was mainly concerned with accounting for modern "racial" distributions. Fox's (1882–1967) *The Archaeology of the Cambridge Region* (1923) confirmed that in the pre-Roman Iron Age, and even more so in Anglo-Saxon times, agricultural set-tlement had shifted to heavier soils, that were harder to work but more drought resistant and productive. Still later, in *The Personality of Britain*, Fox (1932) combined the ecological-distributional approach of Gradmann and Crawford with the positional geography of Mackinder to produce some broad generalizations about the relations between British landscapes and culture-history. He observed that, because of differences in soil types and more effective agricultural technology, the southern part of England, with its light soils, had been the major center of population in the Bronze Age, whereas the greatest concentration had shifted to central England, with its heavier clay soils, during the Iron Age. His most widely cited contribution was his distinction between the lowlands of southeastern England, which he saw as always exposed to migrations and diffusion of culture from continental Europe, and the highland areas of western and northern Britain, which were more sheltered from such disruptions and, hence, whose inhabitants were more selective in adopting new items of culture. The approach Fox used in this book was later applied to other parts of the world (Daniel 1963b; Trigger 1969).

As early as 1915, Grafton Elliot Smith had championed the idea that the invention of agriculture, which he believed had occurred as a result of fortuitous circumstances in Egypt, rather than the production of polished stone tools, was the primary criterion of the Neolithic and marked one of the crucial turning-points in human history. Both this idea and Pumpelly's oasis hypothesis were popularized by Harold Peake (1867–1946) and H. J. Fleure (1877–1969) in the third volume of their *The Corridors of Time* (1927), a widely read, multivolume series dealing with prehistory. About the same time, W. J. Perry (1924: 29–32) popularized the claim of the agronomist T. Cherry that agriculture had been invented in Egypt when people began to increase the amount of millet and barley that grew spontaneously on the flood plain by irrigating dry land adjacent to wild stands and scattering barley seeds in the wet mud left behind at the end of the annual flood. These contributions raised the discussion of the origins of agriculture to a new level of theoretical importance.

Although not constituting analyses of whole cultures, growing interest in the relations between human societies and their environmental settings encouraged a functional-processual view of one major aspect of human behavior. This approach stimulated the study of palaeoenvironments and of the ecological adaptation of prehistoric cultures to them. Such an approach to analyzing these relations accorded with the human geography of the period, which was dominated by the possibilist approach advocated by the French geographer Paul Vidal de La Blache (1845–1918). Geographical possibilism assumed that the natural environment set limits to the sorts of adaptations that were possible rather than determining the specific nature of the response, which was significantly influenced by cultural traditions and personal choices (Vidal de La Blache 1952). Possibilism, like diffusionism, emphasized indeterminacy and unpredictability as the dominant features of cultural change.

Social Anthropology

In the 1920s, a sea-change occured in British anthropology. Ethnologists reacted against the sterile diffusionism of Grafton Elliot Smith and his followers by adopting the structuralist-functionalist approach of Bronislaw Malinowski (1884–1942) and E. R. Radcliffe-Brown (1881–1955), whose first major works, Malinowski's *Argonauts of the Western Pacific* and Radcliffe-Brown's *The Andaman Islanders* both were published in 1922. Both of these anthropologists argued that human behavior could be understood best in relation to social systems that were conceived as made up of functionally interdependent elements. Malinowski stressed that the institutions that composed social systems were grounded in biological needs, a view not shared by Radcliffe-Brown, who sought only to define the social role played by institutions. The common features of their approaches came to be called social anthropology to distinguish them from ethnology, which was associated with unilinear evolutionism and diffusionism.

Both Malinowksi and Radcliffe-Brown rejected historical accounts and missionary records as sources of data on the grounds that they were anecdotal and unreliable. They stressed the importance of doing lengthy fieldwork and the need for the detailed analysis of personal observations by professional anthropologists. Fieldwork ideally required individual anthropologists to live in a community for a year or longer. The focus of Malinowski and Radcliffe-Brown on observation privileged the study of behavior rather than of people's ideas. The latter approach was associated with now outmoded ethnographic efforts to investigate cultures by collecting norms of socially sanctioned behavior from indigenous informants. This emphasis on observing behavior was in keeping with the growing popularity of behaviorism in psychology (J. Watson 1925). Social anthropology also privileged synchronic analysis.

British social anthropology was grounded on the work of the French sociologist Emile Durkheim (1858–1917). Like Karl Marx, Durkheim viewed societies as systems made up of interdependent parts. Coming from a family of modest means whose status was threatened by the rapid social and economic changes taking place in late-nineteenth-century France, Durkheim interpreted these changes as threatening the equilibrium of society and the well-being of the lower-middle class. Although Marx had elaborated theories of internal conflict to explain social change, Durkheim directed his attention toward factors that promoted social stability. Like Henri de Saint-Simon (1760–1825) and Auguste Comte (1798–1857), he advocated sociology as a practical means to counteract what he saw as social disintegration in a capitalist society. At the same time, he avoided a critique of the economic basis of such societies by viewing social relations as causal in their own right and therefore as capable of being regulated without significant reference to the economy (Wolf 1982: 9). His interpretations were elaborated in a series of major publications: *De la division du travail social* (1893), *Les Règles de la méthode sociologique* (1895), *Le Suicide* (1897), and *Les Formes élémentaires de la vie religieuse* (1912).

Durkheim argued that the objective of social science studies was to understand social relations and that the explanation of all social processes should be sought in the internal constitution of human groups.

He maintained that simpler societies exhibited in embryo many of the basic features of more complex ones and therefore provided an opportunity to study the basic facets of behavior in a setting uncluttered by the complexities of more evolved societies (Gosden 1999: 75). Individual aspects of culture, whether they were invented internally or externally, were said to acquire their significance in terms of their functional relations to specific social systems. Durkheim rejected the culture-historical view that social systems and the cultural norms that were associated with them could be understood as a mechanical collection of traits that diffusion had brought together largely as a result of chance. Instead he argued that societies constituted integrated systems, whose institutions were interrelated like the parts of a living organism. The science of society was thus conceptualized as a comparative study of social morphologies, similar in its objectives to comparative anatomy.

Durkheim also maintained that no change could occur in one part of a social system without bringing about varying degrees of change in other parts. Yet he believed that the normal state of society was one of social solidarity and that rapid changes led to feelings of anomie or alienation. Thus, he agreed with the diffusionists that change was contrary to human nature and aligned himself with the conservative antievolutionists of the late nineteenth century. Nevertheless, he was interested to some degree in problems of social evolution, which he studied using ethnographic data. He argued that as societies became more complex they ceased to be held together by mechanical solidarity, or shared beliefs, and were increasingly united by organic solidarity, resulting from growing economic interdependence. This new form of cohesion freed individuals from the tyranny of custom and tradition (Durkheim 1893).

Malinowski and, to a still greater extent, Radcliffe-Brown rejected all evolutionary and historical interpretations of ethnographic data as speculative and argued that the comparative study of the structure and functioning of societies currently available for detailed examination was sufficient to produce generalizations that eventually would explain the morphological variation among all societies. For Radcliffe-Brown in particular, the study of change had no significance apart from the investigation of this variation.

Although such rejection of an interest in historical processes might seem to have provided an unpromising basis for a relation between social anthropology and archaeology, social anthropology and Durkheimian sociology encouraged an interest among archaeologists in how prehistoric cultures had functioned as systems. That interest increased as archaeologists became disillusioned with the limitations of a diffusionist or culture-historical approach. With its conservative views of human behavior, social anthropology provided a respectable alternative to Marxism for those archaeologists who were primarily interested in how societies had worked rather than how change came about. Yet a functional view of archaeological data had begun in archaeology long before the development of social anthropology, in the form of a concern with relations between prehistoric cultures and their environments.

Economic Approaches

As Childe in the late 1920s turned away from the culture-historical approach, which he later stated he had come to view as merely an archaeological version of old-fashioned political history in which cultures replaced statesmen and migrations replaced battles (Childe 1958b: 70), he did not deny the importance of diffusion as a process bringing about cultural change. He did, however, realize that diffusion was of no more value for explaining such changes than unilinear evolutionary concepts had been, unless archaeologists could determine what factors within prehistoric cultures favored the adoption of new technologies and practices and influenced the roles that these innovations came to play. Childe sought to emulate the work of economic historians by searching for broad economic trends in prehistory, in terms of which specific instances of diffusion might be explained. He presented the results of this research in three books: *The Most Ancient East* (1928), *The Bronze Age* (1930), and *New Light on the Most Ancient East* (1934). Economic interpretations of prehistoric data also played a significant role in *The Danube in Prehistory* (1929), which was written before *The Most Ancient East*.

Although Childe's concern with economic factors has been interpreted as an early reflection of his commitment to Marxism, he did not publicly claim to be a Marxist at this time and nothing that is specifically Marxist is evident in his archaeological work of this period. British archaeologists such as Peake and Fleure had already been offering economic interpretations of the archaeological record and Childe used many of their ideas to construct a more comprehensive model of economic development. It is also evident that his thinking evolved only slowly from a primary interest in subsistence patterns to a view that emphasized aspects of the economy that were not primarily related to subsistence. The importance that he ascribed to viewing prehistoric cultures as patterns of social relations reflects a knowledge of Durkheimian sociology that he acquired primarily as a result of translating into English *From Tribe to Empire* by Alexandre Moret and Georges Davy (1926). Davy was a student of Durkheim who had collaborated with Moret, an Egyptologist, to produce a Durkheimian interpretation of the development of ancient Egyptian civilization.

The Most Ancient East was written as a textbook and a companion volume to *The Dawn of European Civilization*. It sought to trace the origins of the technological innovations that had later spread to Europe. Childe followed Smith and Fleure in stressing the development of agriculture as a crucial turning-point in human history. He also agreed with Pumpelly that desiccation in the Middle East at the end of the last Ice Age had caused people to domesticate plants and animals in order to feed the growing densities of population that clustered around surviving sources of water. In keeping with the environmental possibilism that was fashionable at that time, he stressed that individual hunter-gatherer bands could have perished or moved north or south into areas where big game survived rather than developing agriculture.

According to Childe, only three regions in the vicinity of the Middle East had enough fertile soil to support the development of a major early civilization: the Nile, Tigris-Euphrates, and Indus Valleys. In each of these areas surplus wealth increased even faster than population, resulting in the concentration of political power, the rise of city life, and the progress of the industrial arts. Yet, although these civilizations evolved from a common Neolithic base and maintained contact with each other, Mesopotamia developed as a series of city-states, whereas Egypt quickly was united as a divine monarchy. Technological knowledge spread from these early civilizations to outlying regions, such as Europe, as a result of the civilizations' trading surplus food and manufactured goods for raw materials, especially copper and tin. Although Childe based this model on relations between modern industrial and third-world countries, he argued that it was necessary to give "trade" a precise definition whenever the term was used by specifying the particular sociological, economic, and environmental conditions that shaped such activities in a specific area and at a given point in time (Childe 1928: 221; G. Wright 1971).

In *The Bronze Age*, Childe studied the origins and spread of metallurgy, as documented in the archaeological record. He considered the possibility that metallurgy might have been invented independently in Egypt, the Middle East, Hungary, and Spain, but, like most diffusionists, concluded that it was such a complex process that it probably had been invented only once in human history. He also interpreted specific similarities in the processes used to work bronze and in the shapes of the earliest metal artifacts in Europe and the Middle East as proofs of a single origin. Childe was convinced, almost certainly wrongly, on the basis of Homeric texts, that metal casting required full-time, although initially itinerant, specialists, who, along with prospectors and miners, became the first human beings to function independently of tribal affiliations. The adoption of a metal tool technology therefore was thought to have produced a double loss of Neolithic self-sufficiency, as it required communities to become dependent on craftsmen who were often unrelated to them as well as on the maintenance of extensive trade routes that were not closed by periodic outbreaks of tribal warfare and could ensure the regular delivery of supplies of copper and tin. Although he viewed bronze working as an important prerequisite for the development of civilizations in the Middle East, he argued that in Europe it was mainly used to supply weapons to tribal societies, as an increasing population and spreading forests (resulting from climatic changes) resulted in greater competition for agricultural land.

In *New Light on the Most Ancient East*, which was written after a visit to major archaeological excavations in Iraq and the Indus Valley, Childe synthesized and elaborated the arguments advanced in his two previous books. He maintained that two revolutions had occurred in prehistoric times in the Middle East that were equivalent in their importance to the Industrial Revolution. These were the transition from food-collecting to food-producing and from self-sufficient food-producing villages to urban societies. He believed that each of these revolutions had resulted in a more productive technology and a massive increase in population. The population increase was, however, assumed by Childe rather than demonstrated by him using archaeological evidence. He also overestimated the extent to which the inhabitants of ancient Middle Eastern cities engaged in industry, trade, and commerce rather than agricultural activities. He believed that migrations of surplus population, the exchange of manufactured goods for raw materials, and surplus craftsmen seeking employment abroad had spread the technologies produced by these revolutions to Europe. The result was the development in Europe of a large number of small and fiercely competitive Neolithic and Bronze Age societies that were structurally very different from those that had evolved in the Middle East. In due course, conspicuous consumption by the upper classes and the military conflicts of the Middle Eastern civilizations began to waste more goods than they produced, while the growth of secondary civilizations reduced the amount of raw material that was reaching the Middle East. Childe believed that, as a result of both processes, economic progress eventually ground to a halt in that region. At the same time, European societies continued to progress until they were able to outstrip and dominate those of the Middle East. With this economic explanation, Childe was able to exorcize the ethnic stereotypes and semiracist theories that he had invoked to explain the ultimate dominance of European cultures in *The Aryans.*

Childe's interest in economic development in prehistoric times drew its inspiration from trends that were active in the European, and more specifically the British, archaeology of the early twentieth century. Yet he advanced beyond the interpretations of G. E. Smith, Peake, and Fleure in the consistency with which he applied an economic approach to the study of prehistory and in the scope of his formulations. Also, instead of interpreting cultural change as the result of technological innovation, he saw broader economic and political contexts influencing the uses that were made of innovations. This allowed him to explain how the same technological innovations could produce very different types of societies in Europe and the Middle East.

A multilinear evolutionary perspective was inherent in such an economic approach. Yet Childe was not primarily concerned with cultural evolution at this time. He stated categorically that "archaeology's revelations . . . disclose not abstract evolution but the interaction of multiple concrete groups and the blending of contributions from far-sundered regions" (Childe 1928: 11). Like other European archaeologists, he accepted that increasingly complex technologies had developed in the Middle East and later in Europe. Yet he regarded human beings as inherently uninventive and relied heavily on diffusion and migration to explain cultural change. Readers were told at the end of *New Light on the Most Ancient East* that the principal aim of the book was to justify "the general doctrine of cultural diffusion" (Childe 1934: 301). Nor was his materialist perspective complete at this time. Although he interpreted some economic change as a response to environmental challenges, much innovation that actually occurred was attributed in a Montelian fashion to the spontaneous exercise of human intelligence to achieve greater control over nature and make human life easier and more secure. Childe also was lax in using archaeological data to test his theories. Most of his explanations purported to account for general rather than specific observations concerning the archaeological record. As a result, they did not provide clear direction for further archaeological research. The same was true of most archaeological explanations of this period. Nevertheless, by considering how economic activities might have brought about changes within cultures, Childe had helped to narrow the gap between static reconstructions of prehistoric cultures and the appeal to external factors to explain change that had characterized his earlier culture-historical studies.

Soviet Archaeology

It has been claimed that "no previous government in history was so openly and energetically in favor of science" as was the Soviet regime that came to power in the autumn of 1917 (L. Graham 1967: 32–3). The revolutionary leaders of the new state looked to scientific knowledge to modernize the Russian economy and to eliminate Russia's age-old religious mysticism, which was viewed as a hindrance to social and economic progress. The social sciences, including archaeology, had a crucial role to play in the ensuing ideological struggle. A decree of the Council of People's Commissars dated 18 April 1919 and signed by V. I. Lenin established the Russian Academy for the History of Material Culture (RAIMK) in Petrograd (St. Petersburg). It embraced all branches of archaeology. Following the creation of the Soviet Union, the RAIMK became the State Academy for the History of Material Culture (GAIMK) and was assigned ultimate jurisdiction over archaeological institutions not only in the Russian Republic but throughout the Union (M. Miller 1956: 47). In 1922, separate archaeology units were organized at the Universities of Petrograd and Moscow. Talented students who completed their undergraduate studies at these and other universities were admitted to the Institute of Postgraduate Studies of the GAIMK. The best of these students could hope to become research associates of the Academy or to find employment in large museums across the Soviet Union. Thus, a pattern of separating archaeological research and undergraduate teaching was established (R. Davis 1983: 409). The encouragement by the Communist Party of the popularization of scientific knowledge and research also led to the establishment across the Soviet Union of a network of museums and regional studies organizations that were responsible for the investigation and protection of archaeological sites. By 1928, there were five times as many museums as there had been before World War I. Archaeology was a popular subject in the regional studies societies, where professional archaeologists, students, and interested amateurs united to carry out and publish research.

In 1921, in an effort to promote economic recovery and broaden the basis of support for the revolution, Lenin inaugurated the New Economic Policy, which until 1928 restored a limited market economy to the Soviet Union. As part of this policy, the Soviet government adopted an accommodating policy toward the intelligentsia, most of whom had not supported the Bolshevik Revolution. To the disgust of hardline revolutionaries, established intellectuals were entrusted with positions of power and influence, given well-paid jobs, and allowed considerable scholarly freedom, so long as they did not actively oppose the regime.

During the period of the New Economic Policy, a large amount of archaeological research was carried out and the culture-historical approach that had begun to develop before 1917 was further elaborated. In Moscow and Petrograd, the followers of D. N. Anuchin and F. K. Volkov pursued their own variants of the palaeoethnological approach. They treated archaeology as a branch of ethnology and maintained that, because of unpredictable idiosyncracies from one cultural tradition to another, the direct historical approach was essential to interpret archaeological data. Palaeoethnological archaeologists advocated the combined archaeological and ethnographic study of individual regions. They also maintained that generalizations about change had to be arrived at empirically and without preconceptions. The leader of the Moscow group was B. S. Zhukov, whereas P. P. Efimenko, A. A. Miller, and S. I. Rudenko were prominent members of the Petrograd (later Leningrad) group. In Moscow, Gorodtsov and his followers continued to view archaeology as an independent discipline with its own objectives and methods. Gorodtsov also continued to promote a diffusionist approach resembling that of Montelius, although his analytical techniques were modelled specifically on Sophus Müller's, not Montelius's, works. Gorodtsov's emphasis on the primary importance of tools and his interest in formulating regularities that would explain changes in the archaeological record were indulgently construed by old Marxists as "progressive," if not Marxist. Under the influence of the Marxist sociologist V. M. Friche, some of Gorodtsov's students, most notably A. V. Artsikhovsky (1902–1978), developed a "Marxist" approach to the interpretation of archaeological data. This approach was based on the belief that technology directly determined the nature of society and belief systems. None of the approaches being used at this time was Marxist, in the sense that it treated socioeconomic factors as the main driving force behind change, while palaeoethnological archaeology, with its preference for ties with anthropology and for inductivism, left itself vulnerable to charges of being anti-Marxist (Klejn 2001b; Platonova, personal communication).

Political struggles within the leadership of the Communist Party following the death of Lenin in 1924 played a role in deciding cultural policy at this juncture. Joseph Stalin's program of intensive industrialization and the collectivization of agriculture, which began with the first Five Year Plan in 1928–1929, reversed the basic economic principles of the New Economic Policy. As part of his campaign to consolidate power, Stalin allied himself with cultural radicals who demanded that intellectuals should be subjected to strict party discipline (S. Fitzpatrick 1974; T. O'Connor 1983: 54, 89). The cultural revolution, which was initiated by the arrest of engineers and technicians on charges of sabotage and treason, lasted from 1928 to 1932. It involved a massive campaign to bring Soviet intellectual life into line with the tenets of Marxist philosophy as they were understood by the Soviet Communist Party. Many non-Marxist intellectuals and institutions were purged as the Stalinist bureaucracy sought to suppress

Figure 7.1 V. I. Ravdonikas (1894–1976) (Institute of Archaeology, St. Petersburg)

all opposition to its control. Among the early victims of this campaign were the regional studies societies. From 1930 on, contacts between Soviet and foreign scholars were forbidden and for a time current issues of foreign archaeological publications could be found only in the GAIMK library (M. Miller 1956: 73, 93–4).

In the late 1920s, a communist cell had been established in the GAIMK. It was composed mainly of postgraduate students and research associates. At the beginning of the cultural revolution, this group began to criticize archaeologists of the old schools and challenge them to reveal their attitude toward Marxism. In 1929, Vladislav I. Ravdonikas (1894–1976), a young archaeologist, on orders from the GAIMK party organization, read a report in the Academy titled "For a Soviet history of material culture" (Figure 7.1). This paper was published the following year and widely read by archaeologists throughout the Soviet Union. It criticized the theoretical positions of prominent archaeologists and called for a "Marxist history of material culture" to replace the old archaeology. The very concept of archaeology was rejected as that of a bourgeois science hostile to Marxism. At the Pan-Russian Conference for Archaeology and Ethnography held at the GAIMK the following May, the party organization of the academy mounted an exhibition of Soviet archaeological literature in which books and papers written since 1917 were denounced for their alleged adherence to formalism, bourgeois nationalism, and other anticommunist tendencies. The Montelian typological method was criticized for its idealism, for making fetishes of artifacts (artifactology), and for improperly interpreting human history in biological terms (M. Miller 1956: 71–8). This criticism was followed by the dismissal, and in some cases the exiling, imprisonment, or execution of archaeologists who were unable or unwilling to alter their views or who were regarded as politically dangerous by the Communist Party. Adherents of the palaeoethnological schools were suppressed with particular rigor. This suppression was documented and condemned by the Finnish archaeologist A. M. Tallgren (1885–1945) (1936) after he was allowed to visit Leningrad in 1935. In retaliation, he was deprived of his honorary membership in the GAIMK and denied further entry to the Soviet Union.

The younger generation of archaeologists, who under Ravdonikas's leadership came to occupy leading positions, had to elaborate a Marxist approach to archaeology. These scholars included Yevgeni Krichevsky (1910–1942), who studied Neolithic cultures, A. P. Kruglov (1904–1942) and G. P. Podgayetsky (1908–1941), who studied the Bronze Age in southern Russia, and P. N. Tret'yakov (1909–1976), who studied the Old Russian and Slavic cultures. Most of them were enthusiastic, but not very experienced in Marxism or in archaeology (Bulkin et al. 1982: 274). The leading theoretician in these formative years was Ravdonikas, whom even his enemies credited with exceptional ability. The Communist Party, while supporting the creation of a Marxist approach to archaeology and reserving the right to pass judgment on its theory and practice, does not appear to have provided archaeologists with explicit guidelines. Communist officials generally knew little about archaeology and hence, while mandating the creation of a Marxist archaeology, had no idea what it should look like. Yet they reserved the right, within the terms of their own dogmatic understanding of Marxism, to pass judgment on the theories and methods that archaeologists proposed and to hold archaeologists accountable for the ideological purity of their proposals.

Nor could any specific guidelines be found in the writings of Marx and Engels. The most relevant statement that Marx had made about archaeology was that:

> Relics of by-gone instruments of labor possess the same importance for the investigation of extinct economic forms of society, as do fossil bones for the determination of extinct species of animals. It is not the articles made, but how they are made, and by what instruments, that enables us to distinguish different economic epochs. Instruments of labor not only supply a standard of the degree of development to which human labor has attained, but they are also indicators of the social conditions under which labor is carried on. (Marx 1906: 200)

Marx had devoted most of his career to studying capitalist societies and how they had developed from feudal ones. He had begun to investigate preclass and early class societies late in life and to do so had to depend on the highly defective and polemical anthropological literature that was available in the late nineteenth century (Bloch 1985: 21–94). Thus, he and Engels left many questions about the sorts of societies that archaeologists study unanswered, including how these societies had evolved. This meant that archaeologists had to rely, not on the well-developed Marxist concepts that were available to most other social scientists, but on the basic principles of Marxism, as these were formulated in Marx's and Engels's own writings and in later exegeses.

Marx summarized the basic principles on which he based his analyzes of society in the preface to his *Contribution to the Critique of Political Economy* (1859):

> In the social production that human beings carry on, they enter into definite relations that are indispensable and independent of their will, relations of production which correspond to a definite stage of development of their material forces of production.... The mode of production in material life determines the general character of the social, political, and intellectual processes of life. It is not the consciousness of humans that determines their existence; it is on the contrary their social existence that determines their consciousness. (Marx and Engels 1962, I: 362–3)

Nineteenth-century Marxism was characterized by an unswerving devotion to a materialist analysis of the human condition. The crucial factor that Marx identified as shaping social systems was the economic base, which consists of the forces and relations of production.

Although Marxists disagree concerning the precise definitions of these terms, the forces of production are widely interpreted as embracing not only all forms of technology but also all utilized resources, human and nonhuman, and all scientific knowledge (L. Graham 1967: 34–5). The relations of production signify the ways in which individual human beings relate with one another to utilize the forces of production to produce and distribute goods. They therefore embrace not only what Western anthropologists would identify as economic behavior but also various facets of social behavior. The economic base is seen as playing a powerful role in shaping other aspects of society, such as concepts of property, family life, political organization, law, religious beliefs, aesthetics, and philosophical and organizational aspects of scientific activities. All of these are collectively referred to as society's superstructure. Marx did not believe that technological change came about as a result of human beings' using their intellect to develop more effective ways to control their environment, as Victorian evolutionists and Enlightenment philosophers did. Instead, he argued that technological change must be understood in a social context. Although new technologies bring about social and political changes, they themselves are the products of specific social contexts that influence what innovations are likely or unlikely to occur. This is what Engels meant when he wrote that "the determining element in the historical process in the final analysis is production, and the reproduction of human life.... If somebody distorts this principle into the belief that the economic element is the only determining element, then [that person] has transformed [the materialist understanding of history] into an empty, abstract phrase" (Marx and Engels 1962, 2: 488).

Marx and Engels stressed internal contradictions of interest and conflicts between different classes as being prominent features of complex human societies and the most important sources of social change. They analyzed every society of this sort as containing within itself tendencies that both promote and oppose change. They believed that each such society contains the seeds of the destruction of its present state and at the same time the embryo of a future condition. The antagonism between these two tendencies generates the energy that brings about change. Marx did not deny that superstructural factors, such as entrenched political hierarchies or powerful religious beliefs, can be of great historical importance but he maintained that this is so only insofar as they are capable of preventing change. More positively he emphasized that all "human beings make their own history . . . not under circumstances chosen by themselves . . . but directly encountered, given, and transmitted from the past" (Marx 1852 in Marx and Engels 1962, I: 247). Although Marx attributed great importance to beliefs, values, and patterns of behavior inherited from the past, he also believed in the considerable power of individuals to evaluate their material self-interest rationally and to unite in collective action to modify existing conditions in their own interests and those of their class. He did not rule out the possibility that cultural traditions might be so strong or the ability of ruling groups to manipulate beliefs to serve their own purposes so great as to stifle opposition and prevent socioeconomic change. Yet he maintained that changes that benefit an ever larger number of human beings can occur only if progressive economic transformations are not overwhelmed by such reactionary forces. For Marx, freedom was not just freedom from toil and political constraint but the ability of individuals to participate in the creation of new social options for themselves (Miller et al. 1989b: 4).

In his own research, Marx endeavored both to explain concrete historical events and to generalize about evolutionary trends in human history. In *The XVIIIth Brumaire of Louis Bonaparte* and *The Class Struggle in France, 1848–1850*, he sought to account for historical events not as collective responses to economic conditions but in terms of the conflicting interests of various social and economic groups that were seeking to preserve or enhance their power. These studies stress intentionality and the social reproduction of reality rather than treating human behavior as the passive consequence of social forces. He also observed that every society was the product of its own separate history and therefore responded to economic changes in its own distinctive fashion. Because of this, it was impossible to formulate general laws that would explain all of the concrete reality of cultural change in a predictive fashion. In some of his writings, there is a suggestion that he believed in multilinear evolution, at least in the short and middle range (Hobsbawm 1964). Yet he also believed in an ideal course for human development that would run from primitive egalitarian societies, through class societies, to the technologically advanced, egalitarian societies of the future. Over the years, Marxists have varied in the degree to which they have emphasized the historical complexity or evolutionary regularity of human history. Soviet scholarship, rooted in the writings of G. V. Plekhanov (1856–1918) and reinforced by Stalin's dogmatic views, tended to stress a strongly evolutionary and deterministic view of social change (Bloch 1985: 95–123).

Marx also maintained that, because of entrenched beliefs and class loyalties, it was impossible to create a socially and politically neutral social science in a class society, since such studies inevitably are influenced by the class prejudices of the scholars who undertake them. Yet Marx did not view the ancient Sumerian and modern capitalist world views relativistically. Instead, he interpreted them as positions that are qualitatively distinct in terms of their potential for human action. He also claimed for Marxism a privileged position compared to all other philosophical or scientific approaches to understanding human behavior. Insofar as it discouraged self-criticism among Marxists, the belief that in a future classless society knowledge would be free of all class bias and therefore objective, and that Marxism was an anticipation of such knowledge, constituted a dangerous flaw in Marxist thinking.

Ravdonikas and his colleagues attempted to render archaeological data valuable to society by making them useful for the Marxist study of history. They were committed to using their data to illustrate the laws and regularities of historical processes and by doing so to demonstrate the accuracy and utility of Marxist concepts. The specific task they set themselves was to explain in Marxist terms the changes that had occurred in prehistoric times. The primary context in which such changes were held to be comprehensible was no longer technology but social organization. The concept of successive ages of stone, bronze, and iron was abandoned on the ground that it had its source in an understanding not of society but too narrowly of the raw materials prevailing in the development of technology. Archaeologists were called on not only to describe their finds but also to reconstruct the societies that had produced them. This involved defining the modes of production of these societies and determining as much as possible about their technology, social organization, and ideological concepts (M. Miller 1956: 79).

This approach had many valuable consequences. By directing the attention of archaeologists to how ordinary people had lived, it encouraged them to undertake large-scale horizontal excavations of

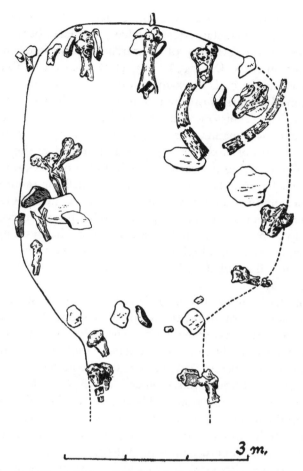

Figure 7.2 Plan of Palaeolithic hut found at Buryet, reproduced in
Antiquity by Childe, 1950

settlements, camp sites, and workshops (R. Davis 1983: 410). Greater
attention also was paid to evidence of dwellings and the relations of
different types of artifacts to these structures. This resulted in the
first identification of Palaeolithic dwellings anywhere in the world
(Childe 1950b) (Figure 7.2) and some of the first total excavations
of Neolithic villages. When cemeteries were excavated, it was mainly
to investigate religious beliefs and to ascertain the social structures
of the societies that had produced them.

Some interpretations were unsound, such as P. I. Boriskovsky's suggestion that female statuettes and what appeared to be the remains of longhouses were evidence of matriarchal clan societies in Upper Palaeolithic times (R. Davis 1983: 413–4). By contrast, in 1934 P. N. Tret'yakov, on the basis of examination by forensic experts, determined from fingerprints on the interiors of vessels that the pottery associated with prehistoric hunter-fisher cultures of northern and central Russia was manufactured by women. He went on to argue that the uniformity of pottery styles within individual sites and the considerable variation between sites indicated a matrilocal marriage pattern, which resulted in the potters of each small community handing on their traditions from one generation to the next undisturbed by external influences (Childe 1943: 6). Similar interpretations were not attempted by American archaeologists before the 1960s and these studies were less archaeological in that the identification of the sex of the potters depended entirely on the direct historical approach (Binford 1972: 61).

This emphasis on how people had lived led to one of Soviet archaeology's major contributions to world archaeology. S. A. Semenov (1898–1978) had considerable success in determining the uses that had been made of prehistoric stone and bone tools by experimentally reproducing the processes that had caused the patterns of use-wear found on them. Although this approach, which is closely aligned to a Marxist interest in production, had been pioneered by Nilsson in the first half of the nineteenth century, it was almost completely ignored by Western archaeologists until an English translation of Semenov's *Prehistoric Technology* (1964) was published.

Archaeologists also were encouraged to explain changes in the archaeological record as the results of internal social developments. For example, in their *Clan Societies of the Steppes of Eastern Europe*, Kruglov and Podgayetsky (1935) related changes in Copper Age burial customs in southern Russia to developing concepts of property. They suggested that collective tombs correlated with the communal ownership of the means of production and individual barrows with patriarchal pastoral societies. They also suggested that, as property became more important in evolving societies, the greed of heirs gradually curtailed the burial of large amounts of valuable possessions with the dead (Childe 1942d: 133, 1945a). Because of their concern with social change, Soviet archaeologists revived an interest in cultural evolution as well as associated concepts of development and progress, at a time when diffusionism was in the ascendant in North America and the rest of Europe.

Yet Marxist studies of archaeological data labored under severe intellectual restrictions at this time. Social evolution was conceptualized in terms of a unilinear scheme of socioeconomic formations loosely derived from Engels's *The Origin of the Family, Private Property, and the State*, which in turn had been based largely on Marx's study of Morgan's *Ancient Society*. Preclass societies were divided into successive preclan, matriarchal clan, patriarchal clan, and terminal clan stages followed by three forms of class society: slave, feudal, and capitalist; and two more forms of advanced classless society: socialist and communist. The latter form, characterized by economic as well as social and political equality, was regarded as the final stage of human development and not subject to further change (M. Miller 1956: 78–9; Yu. Semenov 1980). This formulation was accorded canonical status during the Stalin period and scientific criticism of it was not allowed. Archaeologists had to interpret their findings in accordance with this scheme and also in agreement with the classics of Marxism-Leninism. The only leeway permitted was the recognition that many archaeological cultures might be in a transitional rather than a pure state with respect to their stage of development. There also was debate concerning the archaeological criteria that might reveal to which stage of development an archaeological culture belonged. The dogmatism with which Soviet social scientists adhered to this scheme contrasts sharply with the views expressed by Marx and Engels, who were prepared to consider multilinear models of social evolution, especially with regard to earlier and less well understood periods of human development.

Still worse, within the GAIMK, Soviet archaeological research was now subjected to the intellectual as well as the administrative control of Nikolay Marr (1865–1934), a linguist with archaeological interests. Marr rejected the universally held belief that new languages evolve from ancestral forms as the result of a gradual process of phonological, grammatical, and lexical differentiation. Instead, he believed that linguistic change occurred as a response to alterations in the socioeconomic organization of the societies with which languages are associated. As a result, similarities among languages indicate the stage of evolution that various societies have reached rather than their historical affinities. In Marr's view of human history, there was no place for proto-languages, linguistic homelands, or language families. On the basis of a superficial resemblance between this theory and the Marxist scheme of unilinear sociopolitical evolution, Marr's theory of linguistic change enjoyed political favor. It enabled archaeologists to ignore even the most blatant evidence of ethnic movements in the archaeological record and to interpret the archaeological sequence for each region from earliest times to the present as stages in the history of a single people.

Ravdonikas argued that in the Crimea an autochthonous population had in turn manifested itself as Iranian-speaking Scythians, German-speaking Goths (whose language was proclaimed to be historically unrelated to German languages farther west), and, finally, Slavs. Mikhail Artamonov maintained that the Khazars had not come from farther east to the Don Valley and the northern Caucasus but had evolved locally and hence were not Turks and M. Khudyakov asserted that the Volga Tatars were likewise not Turks but had developed as a result of the amalgamation of local tribes (M. Miller 1956: 81–2). This view also tended to inhibit an interest in physical anthropology, insofar as the latter was directed toward distinguishing ethnic groups in the archaeological record (Trigger 1980a: 104). Skeletal differences often were interpreted as physical changes that had accompanied sociocultural evolution.

Although Soviet archaeologists professed to be interested in the prehistory of various ethnic groups, their unilinear evolutionary approach discouraged the investigation of sorts of cultural variation that might have had ethnic significance. Diffusion also was rejected on the grounds that it denigrated human creativity. The only historical process that was acknowledged was the gradual merging over time of various small human groups to form larger and more complex ones, each of which evolved its own distinctive ethnicity and culture. Because each larger group could be the mixture of a heterogeneous assortment of older ethnic groups, it was impossible to identify any early prehistoric archaeological culture with any recent language and no modern ethnic group could be regarded as having a deep history. Some archaeologists abandoned the concept of the archaeological culture as having any analytical utility. What emerged was a powerful emphasis on all human groups evolving independently through a uniform series of stages, which in turn was construed as evidence of the ability of all humans to participate in human progress.

V. A. Shnirelman (1995, 1996) correlates this formulation with Stalin's emphasis on uniform administrative structures and his repression of "local nationalism," which replaced an earlier Leninist policy of granting more autonomy to various ethnic groups. Yet, in the 1930s, Marr's concept of the autonomous development of peoples was represented as a rejection of what Soviet authorities viewed as the antievolutionary and often racist theories of cultural development prevailing in western Europe. After Marr died in 1934, his doctrines continued to enjoy official patronage and dominated archaeological interpretations until 1950. At that time, Stalin, in his essay "Concerning Marxism in linguistics," denounced Marr's teachings as absurd, pointing out that contrary to Marr's prediction the same Russian language continued to be spoken in the Soviet Union as had been spoken in tsarist Russia.

The heavy emphasis that was placed on the sociological interpretation of archaeological data and the rejection of the Montelian approach inhibited an interest in the systematic classification of artifacts, which was labeled *goloye veshchevedeniye* (naked artifactology). The attention paid to classification in the past was condemned as part of a bourgeois tendency to ignore the social and political significance of archaeological data. Hence classification, like diffusion and migration, acquired negative political connotations. The neglect of classification had long-term adverse effects on Soviet archaeology, which continued, in terms of typology, cultural chronology, and the defining of cultural units to lag far behind research being done in central and western Europe (Bulkin et al. 1982: 288–90).

The cultural revolution was followed by an officially mandated period of consolidation. Although the government accepted Soviet archaeology as being adequately developed in a political sense, greater technical expertise was now required to improve the general practice of the discipline. In 1934 there was a call, in all branches of Soviet historical scholarship, for greater professionalization, better techniques, and higher quality research. The polemical and programmatic literature that had dominated the previous period was abandoned in favor of more conventional empirical studies. The term archaeology had been revived, early in 1931, as the name of a discipline, although to distinguish it from "bourgeois archaeology" the form practiced in the Soviet Union was henceforth to be called "Soviet archaeology" (M. Miller 1956: 108–9). All branches of archaeology continued to be studied in history departments and higher degrees in archaeology were always in history. It was argued that this unity of history and archaeology and their shared commitment to a Marxist historical approach helped archaeologists to understand their findings from a holistic perspective that united an interest in specific culture-historical processes with a more general concern with the evolution of society and culture. It also was once again possible to refer to the traditional technological stages of development, although technology alone was no longer accorded explanatory significance.

During the 1930s, chairs and archaeology units were established in a large number of universities, new monographs and monograph series were published, and *Sovetskaya Arkheologiya*, which was to become the leading Soviet archaeological journal, was begun. Archaeological salvage work expanded rapidly in conjunction with the massive industrial projects that started in 1928. Special archaeological expeditions were attached to each major construction project. These investigated the affected terrain before and during construction, carried out excavations, and studied the findings. In the 1930s, nearly 300 expeditions were at work annually (Bulkin et al. 1982: 276). Tours of excavations, exhibitions, and popular publications served as means of public instruction. Archaeologists also applied themselves to practical work, such as studying ancient irrigation systems as guides to modern development and locating ancient mining sites that might still be of commercial value. This practice was especially common between 1935 and 1941 (M. Miller 1956: 112).

The development of Slavic archaeology and its use to promote Slavic patriotism beginning in the late 1930s, which already has been discussed in Chapter 6, were accompanied by efforts to cultivate the loyalty of other ethnic groups to the Soviet Union. Archaeologists began to trace the ethnic particularities of such groups into antiquity, to define their ethnic territories, and to glorify their ancestral cultures. There was a dramatic increase in knowledge of the prehistoric archaeology of the Caucasus, Central Asia, and Siberia. Various rich finds were made in these areas, such as remains of the ancient states of Urartu and Parthia and the tumuli at Trialeti and Pazyryk (Frumkin 1962). Researchers were now taking account of culturally specific characteristics of the archaeological record and of types of prehistoric human behavior that they had previously ignored. The archaeological record was becoming more diverse and colorful as it was seen to be filled with ethnic groups whose cultural differences were now acknowledged to be of considerable interest.

The cultural diversity that was becoming increasingly evident in the archaeological record in turn raised questions about how such data were to be analyzed and related to the prevailing unilinear evolutionary scheme. Leo Klejn (2001b: 1140) has observed that many archaeologists who began to research and theorize about "ethnogenesis" in the late 1930s, such as M. Artamonov, P. N. Tret'yakov, and S. P. Tolstov, had been students of palaeoethnologists, such as Alexander Miller, Petr Efimenko, and B. S. Zhukov, in the 1920s. These archaeologists sought to discover "ethnic indictors" and use them to identify various ethnic groups in prehistory. Yet ethnographic research weakened this approach by demonstrating the complexity of the relations between material culture, language, and group identity as revealed by a self-bestowed name (Dragadze 1980). It also was discussed whether systematic variations in Mousterian assemblages in the Caucasus region reflected ethnic groups or functional variations in site use, producing a debate that had much in common with that between Bordes and Binford concerning the Mousterian of western Europe (R. Davis 1983). By the 1940s, the discussion of diffusion and migration was no longer prohibited, although the evidence had to be very convincing and usually was confined to the territory of the Soviet Union (Trigger 1980a: 104). These tendencies were reinforced after Marr's theories were officially repudiated in 1950 and with them the main underpinning for the concept of autochthonous development. By the 1950s, some migrations of ethnic groups were seen as covering great distances.

Nevertheless, the evolutionary approach persisted, most notably in the form of V. M. Masson's "sociological archaeology." This approach was notably associated with research being done in the Caucasus and Central Asia, where the earliest agricultural economies and the first urban civilizations had evolved within the territory of the Soviet Union. Sociological archaeology sought to reconstruct the economic, social, and ideological structures of ancient societies in order to establish the laws as well as the particular phenomena and processes that brought about change (Bulkin et al. 1982: 281).

Systematic studies begun in 1937 by S. P. Tolstov in Turkmenia documented the development of ancient irrigation systems. Later research in southern Turkmenia investigated the sequential development of a food-producing economy and of Bronze Age class societies in that region (Kohl 1981a). Although major efforts were made to reconstruct tool use, the operation of irrigation systems, and the economy and social composition of urban centers, at least one American commentator noted the absence of detailed discussions of the relative importance of population pressure, irrigation agriculture, settlement patterns, warfare, economic exchanges, and religious integration as factors bringing about change (Lamberg-Karlovsky 1981: 388). Sociological archaeology reflected a continuing belief that Marxist stadial theory provided a detailed explanation of cultural change rather than a desire to use archaeological data to refine and elaborate an understanding that would take account of the distinctive features of the archaeological record.

Many of the more traditional Soviet archaeologists believed that historical information could be extracted from archaeological data using only common sense and the theoretical apparatus of conventional historical analysis. These inferences could then be combined with the findings from written historical sources, ethnography, historical linguistics, art history, folklore, and any other information that was deemed relevant for studying the past. Although not denying that they employed distinctive methods to recover and analyze their data, these archaeologists did not believe that it was necessary to elaborate any specifically archaeological concepts that would distinguish archaeological interpretation from the general stream of historical analysis.

The period following Stalin's death in 1953 witnessed less political interference in Soviet scholarship and in Soviet life generally. Although this era has been described as one of "problems" (Gening 1982) or even "crisis" (Soffer 1985: 11–13), it also was a time when Soviet archaeologists attempted discretely to repair the damage inflicted on their discipline during the cultural revolution. No archaeologist publicly questioned archaeology's status as a historical discipline or the appropriateness of interpreting human behavior in Marxist terms. Some archaeologists did suggest, however, that the progress of archaeology was hampered by failure to pay adequate attention to the specific characteristics of archaeological data. This trend was assisted as Western books and periodicals became more available and more personal contacts were established between Soviet and Western archaeologists. To give them political legitimacy, these new ideas were implied to constitute a shift from the evolutionary and polemical to the historical and more scientific poles of Marxist explanations (Bulkin et al. 1982).

Many Soviet archaeologists urged the necessity for strict indicators and standardized procedures for the analysis of archaeological data. Although central European archaeologists could refer to specific types of fibulae, such as Almgren 67 or 236, which have carefully defined formal characteristics and temporal associations, Soviet archaeologists used general descriptive phrases, such as "fibula with a high catch-guard" (Bulkin et al. 1982: 288; Klejn 1982). Some work was done using attribute analyses and complex mathematical-statistical procedures. These procedures made it possible to recognize artifacts as multivariate phenomena rather than simply as products of cultural norms. Opponents of this trend in archaeology accused it of overestimating the potential of a typological approach to reveal historical information (Bulkin et al. 1982: 282).

In the Soviet Union, archaeological cultures had generally been larger-scale taxonomic units than they were in central and western Europe, perhaps partly as a result of the vast areas that had to be studied. Beginning in the early 1970s, efforts were made to formulate a uniform definition of the archaeological culture for use throughout the Soviet Union. In 1972, V. M. Masson suggested a hierarchy of units – local variant, archaeological culture, and culture group – which was explicitly modeled on the scheme that David Clarke had presented in his *Analytical Archaeology* (1968). Masson also proposed that the levels of this hierarchy could be defined in terms of the extent of the coincidence of artifact types. An even more elaborate scheme was proposed by Klejn (1982). Yet it was no easier in the Soviet Union than in the West for archaeologists to agree about how archaeological cultures were to be defined or their precise sociological meaning. Nor could it be agreed how they fitted into a Marxist analysis of social change.

Beginning in 1928, to avoid committing the sin of "artifactology," Soviet archaeologists not only had shunned creating artifact typologies and defining cultures but also had avoided the systematic construction of relative chronologies using archaeological data.

In 1957, Childe expressed to Glyn Daniel his opinion that the prehistoric chronology of the Soviet Union was a series of hopelessly vague guesses that did not attract, still less convince, him (Daniel 1958: 66–7). After the 1950s, neglect of this activity was reinforced by a growing reliance on radiocarbon dates to date sites. Because of their failure to construct a detailed prehistoric cultural-chronology, Soviet archaeologists were unable to correlate changes in material cultures in adjacent regions with desirable precision. Such an approach had been alien to Soviet archaeology in its early stages as a result of its preoccupation with unilinear evolution and its advocacy of the autochthonous development of cultures. Only gradually was the need for detailed cultural chronologies articulated and efforts made to begin to rectify the damage inflicted on Soviet archaeology as a whole by decades of politically enforced neglect of this subject.

Archaeological activity continued to expand in the Soviet Union from 1956 to 1991. In 1985, about 700 expeditions were active, and toward the end of that decade 4000 archaeological books and papers were being published annually. Yet Klejn (2001b: 1135) views the continuing combination of relative scholarly independence in technical matters and overall political supervision as leading to intellectual stagnation. Despite the suffocating political environment in which it developed and continued to function, Soviet archaeology is notable as the first form of functional-processual archaeology to try to account for changes in the archaeological record not simply in terms of environmental, ecological, or narrowly defined economic relations but also in terms of social factors, in particular the relations of production. Soviet archaeology's greatest shortcoming was its failure to operationalize its theory by connecting it more systematically to its data. Given the political circumstances, this was impossible even to attempt.

Childe as a Marxist Archaeologist

In 1935, Childe visited the Soviet Union for the first time. When he was there, he met Russian archaeologists, toured museums, and gathered information about recent archaeological discoveries relating to the prehistory of eastern Europe (S. Green 1981: 76–7). He was impressed by the lavish government support for archaeology, the vast scale on which archaeological research was being conducted, and the use being made of archaeological finds for public education. Above all, he was fascinated by the efforts of Soviet archaeologists to explain history in terms of processes internal to societies and on explicitly materialist principles. Their work revealed the narrowness of his own economic interpretations, which he henceforth contrasted unfavorably with the Marxist view that the forces and relations of production played a major role in determining the general character of societies.

On the basis of his own experience, Childe did not accept the entire program of Soviet archaeology. He rejected its detailed scheme of socioeconomic formations and any other unilinear formulation of social evolution. Later, he criticized the Soviet government for compelling archaeologists to assume in advance that this scheme was correct rather than encouraging them to use archaeological evidence to test and refine it (Childe 1951: 28–9). Moreover, he did not see how archaeologists might infer many of the specific details of social organization that were required to relate this stadial scheme to their work. He also refused to stop regarding diffusion as a major factor promoting cultural development (Childe 1933a, 1933b, 1946a: 24) and to abandon the major emphasis he had placed on typology, which he saw as essential for constructing regional chronologies and tracing cultural influences between one region and another. His experience as a prehistoric archaeologist led him to incorporate what he believed were the important innovations of Soviet archaeology into his own work and to reject what he saw as its shortcomings. In the post-Stalin era, Soviet archaeologists confirmed the wisdom of his choices by working to modify precisely those features of early Soviet archaeology that Childe had found objectionable.

Following his visit to the Soviet Union, Childe sought to replace his earlier emphasis on economic factors as the principal cause of social change with analyses that were more in accord with Marxist principles. He also paid attention for the first time to cultural evolution, which was a topic of theoretical interest that had remained important in Marxist scholarship but had not been significant in his own writings or in cutting-edge western European archaeology since the 1880s. In the course of a decade he published three books dealing with cultural evolution: *Man Makes Himself* (1936), *What Happened in History* (1942a), and *Progress and Archaeology* (1944a), as well as a case study *Scotland Before the Scots* (1946a). The first two were written for the general public as well as for professional archaeologists and were widely read.

In *Man Makes Himself*, Childe interpreted the archaeological record as evidence of a general directional process whereby the scientific knowledge accumulated by human beings gave progressive societies ever greater control over nature and led to the formation of new and more complex sociopolitical systems. He later regarded these views as not being significantly different from the idealist Montelian conception of cultural change (Childe 1958b: 72). In *What Happened in History*, he attempted in a more explicitly Marxist fashion to formulate explanations of cultural change that were focused not on technological knowledge as a prime mover but on social, political, and economic institutions and the role they played in bringing about change.

Childe did not embrace unilinear evolutionism in these studies any more than he had done previously or was to do later, although he was erroneously accused of doing so by Julian Steward (1953, 1955: 12), who influenced many American archaeologists to regard Childe as a typical nineteenth-century evolutionist. In *Man Makes Himself* and *What Happened in History*, in which he concentrated on the development of cultures in the Middle East, Childe presents a more unilinear view of cultural change than he does in his works in which developments in Europe and the Middle East are examined alongside one another (Childe 1930, 1951). Nevertheless, even in these two books he continued to attribute the differences between the city-states that developed in Mesopotamia and the divine monarchy that united Old Kingdom Egypt to divergent social and political techniques for controlling agricultural surpluses that had been created in the course of the transformation of different tribal societies into class ones. Writing under the shadow of expanding Nazi power and World War II, Childe also rejected the naive faith in the inevitability of progress that characterized many vulgarized versions of Marxism no less than it did the unilinear cultural evolutionism of the nineteenth century. Childe's pessimism led him to make a significant contribution to Marxist studies of change by providing a detailed analysis of the social conditions that impede progress.

Childe argued that at any level of social development, but especially in the early civilizations, entrenched political hierarchies and inflexible systems of religious beliefs could slow or even halt social and economic change. He distinguished between progressive societies, in which relations of production favor an expansion of productive forces and there are harmonious relations among the means of production, social institutions, and the dominant system of beliefs, and conservative societies, in which social and political factors block change. The ruling classes in early civilizations, according to Childe, sought to prevent technological changes that might threaten their control of society. They did this not only by the use of force but also by monopolizing surplus wealth, exercising bureaucratic control over craftsmen, inhibiting the pursuit of technical knowledge, and patronizing magic and superstition on a lavish scale. They only succeeded, however, at the cost of making it more difficult for their own societies to compete with more progressive ones. He offered this explanation for what he saw as the eventual backwardness of Middle Eastern civilizations by comparison with European ones as a replacement for the older, more narrowly economic explanation he had provided in *New Light on the Most Ancient East*. Childe now ascribed important roles in shaping history to both the economic base and the superstructure of societies. Yet he was careful to specify that, where a dogmatic ideology was dominant, its influence could only be negative.

This position provides a definitive answer to those British Marxists, such as George Thomson (1949), who accused him of ignoring class conflict in the early civilizations. Childe argued that social evolution occurred slowly, if at all, in those early civilizations because such struggles were blunted by highly effective political and religious techniques of social control. He did not ignore the concept of class struggle in the early civilizations or reject it because he thought it inapplicable for studies based on archaeological data; rather, he did not find it useful for explaining ancient Middle Eastern civilizations, which he believed remained static for long periods. In his analyses of later classical civilizations, and in particular of the Roman Empire, he placed greater emphasis on struggles among groups within societies to control wealth and power and on shifting patterns of political control.

Despite Childe's growing interest in evolutionary processes, he remained as sceptical as were most culture-historical archaeologists about the value of ethnographic analogies, except where historical continuities were apparent. He regarded modern hunter-gatherer societies, such as those of Australia, as ones that had failed to develop technologically, and suspected that instead they had elaborated complex forms of social organization and "painful" and "incoherent" rituals that had blocked further technological development. Hence, he believed that in crucial respects modern hunter-gatherer societies were unlike the Palaeolithic ones from which more complex societies had evolved. He also believed that the same dichotomy held at the level of tribal cultivators. Childe thus proposed two general lines of cultural evolution: a progressive one, characterized by continuous technological development combined with a flexible social organization and ideology, and a conservative one, characterized by a static technology and the elaboration of convoluted social structures and ideologies (1936: 46). Although based on Marxist ideas, this model bore little relation to generally held Marxist evolutionary concepts. His interpretation of cultural development, like his changing efforts to explain what he saw as the eventual superiority of European culture, looks curiously like an attempt to reformulate Lubbock's view of human evolution in nonracist terms.

In *Scotland Before the Scots*, Childe attempted to apply a Soviet-style approach to the interpretation of a specific corpus of Western archaeological data. He sought to use archaeological information concerning subsistence patterns, houses, handicrafts, trade, and burial customs to infer changing modes of production and the accompanying development of larger and more hierarchical groups and new ideologies. Inspired by Kruglov and Podgayetsky's explanation of the evolution of Bronze Age society in southern Russia, he saw Scotland gradually developing from a network of egalitarian tribal societies based on communal property into a state society. The key factor bringing about change was the emergence of private property, which he believed was mirrored archaeologically in the replacement of communal tombs by various types of individual burials expressing status differences. Childe concluded that this approach produced "a picture of Scotland's development which was far more realistic and far more historical" than he had achieved by means of migrationist hypotheses in his early studies of Scottish prehistory (1958b: 73). Yet he refused categorically to subscribe to the dogmatic scheme of social evolution used by Soviet archaeologists or to rule out diffusion and migration as significant factors bringing about social and cultural change.

During and after World War II, Childe continued to cultivate a Marxist understanding of social change. Yet, as a result of his growing disillusionment with the low quality of archaeological research being done in the Soviet Union, he turned away from Soviet archaeology as a major source of creative inspiration and began to investigate the philosophical basis of Marxism itself. He worked hard to acquire a more profound and less dogmatic understanding of Marxism as an analytical tool and to apply it to the interpretation of archaeological data. He also read widely in philosophy and studied British social anthropology and American cultural anthropology (Childe 1946b).

Childe's reading of Marx led him to pay increasing attention to the cognitive aspects of human behavior. From Marx's observation that, although human beings shape their own history, their point of departure is inevitably the social organization and traditions of the societies into which they are born, Childe (1949: 6–8) concluded that all human behavior was cognitively mediated. Like later post-processual archaeologists, he maintained that humans do not adapt to the world as it really is but to the world as people imagine it to be. The landscape of central Australia as perceived by Aborigine hunter-gatherers was not the same as that perceived by European mineral prospectors. Yet, as a materialist, Childe, like later processual archaeologists, maintained that, although humans can only know the world through their minds and brains, minds and brains exist in organisms that must survive in the natural world. Hence, every socially shared view of the world must accord to a significant degree with the world as it really is in order to endure (1956b: 58–60). He argued that both the beliefs of hunter-gatherers and those of modern industrial nations must be judged effective according to how well they achieved the goal of survival in a particular ecological setting. Thus, Childe, as a Marxist, simultaneously subscribed to, and reconciled, two of the key tenets that later were to distinguish processual and postprocessual archaeology. Like Marx, he took cultural traditions seriously, although he believed that under favorable circumstances these traditions could be transcended fairly easily in the pursuit of economic interests that were cross-culturally meaningful.

In Childe's view, a Marxist analysis, although assigning a privileged role to the relations of production, ruled out any form of narrow determinism. Functional constraints account for many similar features of social organization and ideology possessed by historically unrelated cultures that share a common mode of production. Yet he believed that the specific content of cultures and of individual sequences of change is determined to so great a degree by preexisting cultural patterns, fortuitous contacts with other cultures, and interactions among neighboring societies that it cannot be predicted in detail. Childe already had observed that the precise form of the British constitution in the nineteenth century could never be deduced from the capitalist mode of production alone. Although the domination of political life by middle-class industrialists reflected changing economic forces, the monarch, the House of Lords, and the House of Commons were institutions surviving from the feudal period minimally adapted to serve the political requirements of the present (Childe 1936: 98). This analysis implied that there was no easy way to predict the precise nature of one aspect of a society on the basis of knowledge of some other aspect. Insofar as each feature of a prehistoric culture was to be reconstructed, this would have to be done inductively, using archaeological data.

In *Social Evolution* (1951), Childe reaffirmed his belief in multilinear evolution, but he argued in accordance with Marxist principles that over time cultures sharing the same mode of production tend to evolve increasingly similar social, political, and cultural institutions, which are in ever greater harmony with the economic base. Yet these institutions develop in varied ways and in different sequences even in adjacent cultures because of environmental differences, historical accidents, and the societies involved being initially dissimilar. Thus, there are many more ways to move from one level of social organization to another than there are forms in which the superstructure is in close accord with the base. Because of this and the rapid rate at which traits diffuse from one culture to another, social reality rarely corresponds with an ideal type. This view of cultures as less than perfectly integrated systems was shared by a number of non-Marxist American anthropologists, most notably G. P. Murdock (1949).

Childe defined knowledge in Marxist terms as shared mental approximations of the real world that permitted human beings to act upon that world and insisted that archaeologists must treat artifacts as concrete expressions of human thoughts and ideas. He also argued that innovations and their applications to social needs require new forms of thought that have ramifications extending through entire societies. Advances in technology thus reflect not simply an increase in scientific information but also the evolution of the total knowledge at the disposal of a society, including its understanding of how human beings perceive themselves and their relations to nature. He maintained that notions of causality had remained anthropomorphic until the growing use of inanimate power to work machines had engendered the idea of mechanical causality embodied in the thinking of Isaac Newton. Childe had no qualms about pronouncing modern civilization to be superior to all preceding ones, insofar as it was able to provide a reliable guide to a far greater number of actions (Childe 1949). Yet Childe was pessimistic about the extent to which archaeology could make use of such Marxist ideas.

In *Society and Knowledge* (1956b), Childe elaborated his concept of knowledge in terms of the Marxist dichotomy between "true" and "false" consciousness. True consciousness is characterized by the operational correspondence between views of reality and external reality itself. In the form of basic technological knowledge, it exists to varying degrees in all societies. False consciousness occurs in situations where there is no operational correspondence between what is believed and external reality. It embraces the myths that all societies create to mask and compensate for their technological ineffectualness and that class societies use to disguise exploitation as altruism. Childe observed that false consciousness, in the form of religious beliefs, magic, and superstition, leaves its mark on the archaeological record no less conspicuously than does technological knowledge. Yet, because the possible variations in the details of magical and religious beliefs are infinite, the archaeologist has no hope of being able to infer the specific content of these beliefs in the absence of written records or oral traditions. By contrast, the number of practical solutions to any technological problem is limited by material constraints that can be inferred with a high degree of accuracy, using the laws of physics and chemistry. Childe therefore concluded that the archaeological study of knowledge must be restricted largely to technological matters and framed in terms of practical results rather than the subjective goals of those who possessed it.

Childe also believed that the evolution and functioning of technology could only be understood if archaeologists were able to reconstruct the social context in which it had operated. Doing this was the problem that he turned to in his last book, *The Prehistory of European Society* (1958a). He identified social relations, which from a Marxist perspective he viewed as including the relations of production, as the principal aspect of human behavior that was capable of orderly cross-cultural explanation. He observed that variation in the essential features of economic, social, and political organization was far more limited than variation in most cultural traits and argued, as did social anthropologists, that cultural traits acquired their functional significance in terms of their relation to the social system. The main practical problem that he confronted was how archaeological evidence could be used more effectively to infer prehistoric sociopolitical systems (Childe 1958a: 12–14).

Yet, in this his last major work, Childe seemed more constrained than ever before by the typological method that had been the basis of his early culture-historical research, and less able to make effective use of settlement-pattern or funerary data. Although he had done much archaeological fieldwork in Scotland, most of it bore little relation to his theorizing. His most innovative results had come from his early use of ethnographic descriptions of rustic dwellings in eighteenth-century highland Scotland to interpret the use of house-space at the Neolithic village of Skara Brae (Childe 1931) and his later use of a survey of megalithic tombs to estimate the size and distribution of the population on the island of Rousay in the Neolithic period (Childe 1942f). It is perhaps indicative of failing creativity in the last years of his life that his earlier pioneering of settlement-pattern research did not suggest to him effective techniques for studying prehistoric social and political organization.

Although Childe devoted much of his career to trying to understand the nature of sociocultural change from a critically viewed Marxist perspective, he paid little attention to devising ways by which fieldwork could be used to test and refine his theories. He also did not train students to carry on his work and, because his contemporaries found his later theoretical writings difficult to understand, these works were soon forgotten. Perhaps the archaeologist who in the years following Childe's death did the most to develop and operationalize some of Childe's most innovative ideas was Robert McC. Adams (b. 1926). A student of Linda and Robert Braidwood, who were much influenced by Childe, Adams (1966) used archaeological data to study the technology, demography, social organization, and social evolution of early civilizations. He viewed ancient states as seldom being fully integrated or stable polities. Elites sought to be despotic, self-serving, and manipulative and, whenever possible, ignored the interests of rural populations and the urban poor. Yet, especially in the early stages of the development of civilizations, they had only limited success in overcoming the resistance of these groups to their efforts at centralization (Yoffee 1999). Adams's grounding of his interpretations of his archaeological findings not simply in ecological relations but also in economic and political contexts and his analyses of technological innovations in their social settings have much in common with Childe's theorizing. In recent years, Childe's later writings have been rediscovered and are inspiring the work of a growing number of archaeologists.

Grahame Clark

An alternative and in many ways complementary functionalist approach was pioneered by Grahame (J. G. D.) Clark. Through his training of numerous graduate students at Cambridge University, this approach exerted a strong influence on the development of archaeology in many parts of the world (Murray and White 1981; Clark 1989a). Although Clark, too, was committed to a material-ist perspective, he consistently criticized Childe's attempts to apply Marxist concepts to archaeology (Clark 1936, 1976). Clark's views were closer to those of Cyril Fox and other early British ecological archaeologists than they were to Childe's economic and sociopoliti-cal ones. Unlike Childe, he also attempted to develop new methods of fieldwork to complement his theoretical innovations.

Clark studied at Cambridge University, where he became a lecturer in 1935. His doctoral thesis was a conventional typological study of Mesolithic material from Britain and a comparison of this material with Mesolithic finds from continental Europe (Clark 1932). Yet, during his early years at Cambridge, three different influences ori-ented him toward a functionalist view of prehistoric cultures. The first was his growing awareness of the manner in which Scandina-vian archaeologists studied prehistoric cultures in their environmen-tal settings. This awareness was encouraged by the close similarities between Mesolithic finds in England and the Maglemosian culture of Denmark and the eventual realization that the latter culture had exploited marshlands extending across the present bed of the North Sea before their being flooded by rising sea levels. He also worked closely with Harry Godwin, the biologist who had introduced pollen analysis from Scandinavia into Britain. Second, he was exposed to the functionalist views of social anthropologists such as Malinowski and Radcliffe-Brown. Finally, in his own words, he "responded eagerly" to the call by the Finnish archaeologist A. M. Tallgren that archaeologists should stop regarding artifacts as more real and alive than the societies that had created them and the people whose needs had brought them into being (Tallgren 1937; Clark 1974). Ironically, Tallgren's views had been shaped in large part through his close contacts with Soviet archaeologists.

In 1939, Clark published the first edition of *Archaeology and Society*, a theoretical study of archaeology that remains a milestone in the history of the discipline. He maintained that archaeology should be "the study of how [human beings] lived in the past" (p. 1) and that to achieve that goal archaeological finds, which Clark believed had meaning only in relation to society, had to be examined from a functionalist point of view. He further argued that the primary function of a culture, or way of life, was to ensure the survival of a society; which implied that all aspects of cultures were influenced at least to some degree by ecological constraints. He maintained that archaeologists should aim to determine how human beings had lived in prehistoric times by reconstructing as far as possible their economies, their social and political organizations, and their systems of beliefs and values and trying to understand how these different aspects of culture related to one another as parts of functioning systems. This formulation reflected Clark's conviction that, by influencing individual human behavior, culturally transmitted patterns facilitated the social interaction on which the survival of individuals and groups depended. In *Archaeology and Society*, Clark published a flow chart linking various aspects of culture to food supply (Figure 7.3). To a more complex version of that chart that he produced a few years later, he added *habitat* and *biome* as twin foundations below subsistence (Clark 1953) (Figure 7.4). Rowley-Conwy (1999: 511) believes that this chart, which Clark henceforth regarded as being central to his work, was probably the first ever published that linked cultural and environmental factors as parts of a single system. Clark also maintained that someone with no excavation experience was not equipped to interpret archaeological data, thereby implicitly denying the distinction that some British culture-historical archaeologists were drawing between archaeologists and prehistorians.

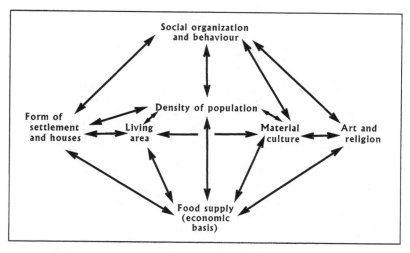

Figure 7.3 Grahame Clark's original systems diagram from
Archaeology and Society, 1939

Clark systematically assessed the strengths and limitations of archaeological data for studying prehistoric social life. He noted that some aspects of material culture are better preserved in the archaeological record than are others: bronze survives better than iron or silver and bone better than soft plant parts. By contrast, because of its high value, gold is less likely to make its way into the archaeological record than is a less expensive metal or to escape plundering once it is there. He also observed that material culture generally survives better in desert or arctic environments than in tropical forests. Because people living in tropical forests tend to use perishable materials and because of the greater difficulties of preservation and recovery, it is likely that archaeologists will always know less about prehistoric cultural development in tropical forests than in deserts or the high arctic. In temperate zones, wet sites, such as bogs, preserve a wider range of evidence than do well-drained sites. Clark stressed that it was essential to study settlements as well as burials in order to understand how people had lived in the past. In a lengthy discussion of the interpretation of archaeological data, he made it clear that, when working only with archaeological data, archaeologists are likely to learn more about the economies of prehistoric societies than about their social organization and religious beliefs.

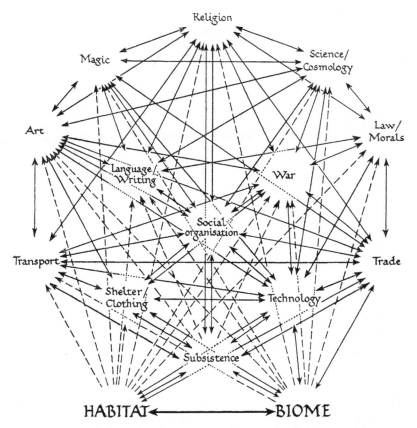

Figure 7.4 Clark's refined ecosystems diagram with habitat and biome
added, first used in his Reckitt Lecture, 1953

In *Archaeology and Society*, Clark asserted that the ultimate goal
of archaeologists should be to interpret their data in terms of social
history. They could do that, however, only after they had defined a
succession of cultures in the archaeological record and had a clear idea
of how the prehistoric communities associated with these cultures
had functioned. He regarded an archaeologist studying a prehistoric
habitation site as the equivalent of an ethnologist studying a living
community. He did not, however, critically examine the appropriateness of this analogy or of the social anthropologists' assumption that
a single community was necessarily representative of some larger cultural unit, a belief that is now generally repudiated. He also accepted

that ethnographic analogies had to be used to interpret archaeological data. Yet his adoption of an ecological perspective and his belief in the relatively loose articulation between the different parts of a cultural system led him to reject the unilinear evolutionary view that cultures at the same stage of development would be similar to one another in any detailed fashion.

Clark specified, as Nilsson had done, that ethnographic analogies had to be drawn between individual types of artifacts rather than between whole cultures, in the unilinear evolutionary fashion, and that such analogies had to be treated as suggestive rather than definitive. In general, he preferred to use analogies derived homologically from folklore rather than from comparative ethnology for the interpretation of European prehistory, because he believed that historical continuity guaranteed the greater relevance of the former. He argued that when archaeologists were seeking to interpret data about prehistoric times "it was helpful to know how people occupying the same territory managed to provide for themselves before the rise of modern economies" (Clark 1974: 41). In this respect, his position was similar to that of Childe and in line with earlier diffusionist doctrines.

During the next decade, Clark sought to develop his ecological approach by elaborating techniques for using archaeological evidence to document social life and particularly the ways in which natural resources had been utilized. In *Prehistoric England* (1940), his chapters were organized not chronologically but functionally to provide a review of what was known about subsistence patterns, dwellings, handicrafts, mining, trade, communications, defense, burial, and sacred sites in England from Palaeolithic times to the end of the Iron Age. This was followed by a series of papers on the utilization of various resources in European prehistory and on basic subsistence activities such as seal hunting, whaling, fowling, fishing, forest clearance, farming, and stock raising. In a paper on "Bees in Antiquity," he outlined an ecological perspective that linked an increase in the number of wild bees in Europe to the introduction of farming and demonstrated how the resulting increase in the supply of beeswax facilitated bronze casting (Clark 1942). Although these papers all addressed biological issues, Clark sought, by identifying the functions of artifacts and the seasons when specific subsistence activities took place, to use the archaeological record to document economic and social life. The need to study seasonality was stressed by Donald Thomson (1939), who demonstrated ethnographically that a single group of Australian Aborigines produced totally different material culture assemblages at different times of the year, as they exploited the resources of different areas. These remains could easily be mistaken for separate cultures within a traditional culture-historical framework.

Between 1949 and 1951, Clark excavated a waterlogged Mesolithic site at Star Carr in East Yorkshire. The primary objectives of this excavation were to recover organic materials as well as stone tools, to date the site in relation to postglacial vegetation patterns, to recover food remains that would reveal the subsistence pattern, and to determine what sort of social group had used the site. With the help of palaeobotanists and zoologists, he was able to conclude that a small group of hunters had visited Star Carr over a number of winters to hunt deer (Figure 7.5). Although Clark's recording of what was found was inferior to Knud Andersen's excavations of the Mesolithic lakeside sites of Ulkestrup I and II, in Denmark, between 1947 and 1950, and the area Clark dug is now interpreted as a waterlogged dump for a much larger summer encampment, Clark's innovative emphasis on ecological and economic issues went far beyond the artifact orientation of the Danish excavations. Star Carr set a new standard for the archaeological investigation of hunter-gatherer sites and called into question the value of all previously excavated Mesolithic sites for the economic study of prehistory in Britain (Clark 1954, 1972; Andresen et al. 1981; Rowley-Conwy 1999: 515–16).

At the same time Clark was excavating at Star Carr, he wrote *Prehistoric Europe: The Economic Basis* (1952). In this book, which was based on a series of lectures he delivered in 1949, he sought to "mine and quarry" existing archaeological literature and museum collections to see what could be learned from them about the economic development of Europe from late glacial times to the historical period. The main topics that he addressed were subsistence patterns, shelter, technology, trade, travel, and transportation. He did not examine data in terms of specific societies or archaeological cultures but sought to trace economic changes as they related to three major climatic and vegetation zones in Europe: Circumpolar, Temperate, and Mediterranean. The relations between culture and environment were viewed as reciprocal and the economy defined as "an adjustment to specific physical and biological conditions of certain needs, capacities, aspirations and values" (p. 7). A similar ecological approach

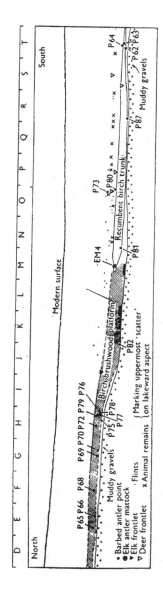
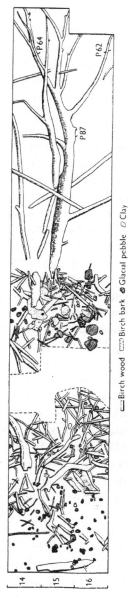

Figure 7.5 Plan and section of Cutting II, Star Carr (*Excavations at Star Carr*, 1954)

359

had been applied by the social anthropologist E. E. Evans-Pritchard (1940) in his ethnographic study of the ecology of the Nuer people of the southern Sudan.

Prehistoric Europe was distinguished, however, by being the first systematic application to archaeology of the botanist A. G. Tansley's (1871–1955) concept of the ecosystem, with its notion of a self-correcting mechanism, or homeostat, which keeps the whole system in balance (Tansley 1935; Odum 1953). Clark viewed cultural change as a response to "temporary disequilibrium" brought about by environmental changes, fluctuations in population, labor-saving innovations, and cultural contact. He thus ascribed change to all the major factors that evolutionary and diffusionist archaeologists had invoked over the previous century, without reviewing the status of these concepts. Nor did he attempt to interrelate them, apart from his commonplace observation that the natural environment imposed certain restrictions on economic exploitation at particular stages of technological development. If Clark excelled Childe in the detailed reconstruction of subsistence activities from archaeological data, his work fell short of Childe's as an attempt to explain cultural change. Clark never developed an explicit model of cultural change to complement his behavioral interpretations of archaeological data. Nevertheless, *Prehistoric Europe* exemplifies what European archaeology might have been like if archaeologists in the 1880s had chosen to interpret spatial variations in the archaeological record in terms of ecological factors rather than ethnicity. Clark (1957: 169–70), however, continued to recognize the usefulness of the archaeological culture as a classificatory device.

Later, Clark's interests turned to the social and symbolic significance of artifacts. He paid increasing attention to how the integrity and cohesion of social groups was reinforced by distinctive symbols and patterns of behavior in the same way, as he put it, that individuals signal their identity by conforming to or violating social norms. Clark combined this interest with a growing concern with the use of the landscape by hunter-gatherer peoples. In *The Earlier Stone Age Settlement of Scandinavia* (1975), he examined archaeological evidence relating to social territories, home bases, social hierarchies, and redistribution networks to address questions of hunter-gatherer seasonality, social organization, and mobility. He argued that so long as form and style were studied in order to define the territories of social groups rather than as ends in themselves, they had a significant role to play in scientific archaeology (Clark 1974: 53–4, 1975).

Clark also continued to play a major role in moving British archaeologists away from a preoccupation with typology and encouraging efforts to understand prehistoric economies and related forms of social organization. Under Clark's guidance, the laboratory study of animal bones and plant remains recovered from archaeological sites, and their interpretation in ecological and economic terms, became major interdisciplinary specializations covered by labels such as zooarchaeology, palaeobotany, and bioarchaeology. Under the leadership of Clark's student Eric Higgs (1908–1976) and the British Academy's Major Research Project in the Early History of Agriculture, a school of palaeoeconomy developed that attempted to understand such findings by comparing them with the results of site catchment analysis, which sought to determine all the resources that would have been available at specific times in the past within an exploitable radius around an archaeological site (Vita-Finzi and Higgs 1970; Higgs 1972, 1975; Sieveking 1976: xxii; Jarman et al. 1982). Both Higgs and Jarman regarded "ecofacts" as more productive sources of information about past human behavior than were "artifacts." They also viewed economic factors as being the only ones that were of long-term explanatory importance or significantly detectable in the archaeological record. Higgs objected to the idea that social, cultural, or cognitive variables could be studied without reference to the powerful selective forces of the economy, which he viewed as constraining free will. He also proclaimed that archaeological research must begin with the search for natural laws governing human behavior (Bailey 1999: 552–7). Much of David Clarke's (1968) focus on artifacts was a reaction against what he regarded as the narrowness, determinism, and ecofactology of the Higgsian approach (Sherratt 1979: 199–200). Clark appears to have regarded both archaeologists as carrying on his work.

Early Functionalism in the United States

In the United States, a functionalist approach to archaeological analysis began in the nineteenth century. It took the form of an interest in how artifacts were manufactured and what use had been made of them. This approach was developed and systematized in Harlan Smith's (1872–1940) *The Prehistoric Ethnology of a Kentucky Site* (1910), which was based on the analysis of artifacts that he had recovered from the Fox Farm site in 1895. Smith sought to reconstruct the lifeways of the inhabitants of that site, which was later assigned to the prehistoric Fort Ancient aspect of the Midwestern Taxonomic Method. Artifacts were described and analyzed in terms of a series of functional categories: Resources in Animal and Plant Materials; Securing Food; Preparation of Food; Habitations; Tools used by Men; Tools used by Women; Processes of Manufacture; History of Manufactured Objects (stages in the manufacture of tools as illustrated by unfinished artifacts); Games; Religious Objects; Pipes and Amusements; Warfare; Dress and Ornament; Art; Injuries and Diseases; and Methods of Burial. Individual artifacts were discussed from different points of view under multiple headings. Although ethnographic analogies were employed to determine the functions of specific artifacts and artifacts that were incomplete or damaged in use were studied to learn how they had been made and used, guesswork played a major role in assigning artifacts to specific classes.

There was widespread interest in this sort of functional interpretation in the early twentieth century. The Canadian archaeologist William Wintemberg (1876–1941), whose professional career developed under Smith's supervision closely followed Smith's approach in his analysis of material from the Iroquoian sites that he excavated in southern Ontario (Trigger 1978c). A former craftsman, he conducted many experiments to determine how artifacts were made and used. He also acquired an extensive knowledge of traditional Indian material culture and ways of life (Swayze 1960: 178). A. C. Parker's (1881–1955) report on the Iroquoian Ripley site, in northwestern New York State (1907), has been described as "an early attempt to delineate the entire culture of a group from archaeological remains interpreted in the light of ethnography" (Brose 1973: 92). M. R. Harrington, who worked for the American Museum of Natural History when Harlan Smith was employed there, consulted local Indians in order to understand better the material he had excavated at the Shinnecock site on Long Island in 1902 (Harrington 1924). Beginning with *Ancient Life in Kentucky* (Webb and Funkhouser 1928), William S. Webb (1882–1964) studied how prehistoric Indians had made and used artifacts and how these artifacts reflected less tangible ancient customs. He was trained as a physicist and is said to have approached archaeology with an amateur's "interest in local antiquities and the ancient life of the local Indians" (W. Taylor 1948: 75). Working in Kentucky, he had special reason to be influenced by Smith's report on the Fox Farm site. Similarly William Ritchie's early publications on the "pre-Iroquoian" sites of New York State manifested a widely ranging, if unsystematic, interest in using artifacts to reconstruct prehistoric human behavior. After they were influenced by the Midwestern Taxonomic Method, both Webb and Ritchie concentrated on the elaboration of trait lists and ceased (in Ritchie's case only until the 1950s) to study the behavior of prehistoric peoples (W. Taylor 1948: 70–80).

The large, labor-intensive, horizontal excavations carried out during the depression years of the 1930s helped to revive the interest of American archaeologists in viewing archaeological data from a functionalist perspective (Figure 7.6). In *Rediscovering Illinois* (1937), a report on archaeological excavations carried out in and around Fulton County, Illinois, Fay-Cooper Cole (1881–1961) and Thorne Deuel listed all the artifact types from a single occupation level within a site under a number of broad functional headings, which they labeled complexes. These complexes included Architecture and House Life, Costume and Dress, Ceremonial, Military and Hunting, Economic and Artistic, Agricultural and Food-Getting, and Pottery. A similar approach was adopted by Charles Fairbanks (1942) when he listed artifact types from the Stallings Island midden in Georgia according to whether they appeared to relate primarily to subsistence, community plan, burial, or technological and artistic activities. In Martin, Quimby, and Collier's *Indians Before Columbus* (1947), the major archaeological cultures so far defined for North America, organized by regions and successive periods, were summarized under the headings of location, people (physical type), village, livelihood, pottery, tools, utensils, weapons, pipes, costumes, ornaments, and burials.

In each of these cases, despite a growing variety of data, the emphasis was largely on listing traits in an ethnographic or pseudo-ethnographic format rather than on trying to interpret material culture as evidence of human behavior. Although functional interpretations before the 1930s have been rightly castigated for remaining

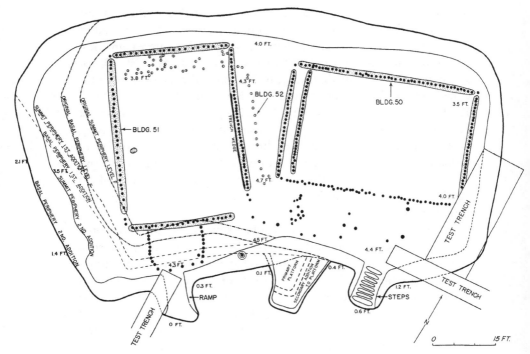

Figure 7.6 Structures on mound platform, from *Hiwasee Island*, by T. Lewis and M. Kneberg, 1946

"on a relatively superficial level" consisting "mainly of the obvious inferences to be drawn from artifacts...by visualizing how they might have been used" (Rouse 1972: 147), for the most part they constituted a more serious effort to infer human behavior from archaeological remains than did the ethnographic trait lists of the 1930s and 1940s. This indicates that the classificatory approach of the Midwestern Taxonomic Method, and of chronological studies generally, stifled a professional interest in the behavioral interpretation of archaeological data in North America for longer than Taylor (1948: 91) or Willey and Sabloff (1980: 134) believed.

Nevertheless, a growing minority of American archaeologists began to call for the functional interpretation of archaeological data within the framework of more holistic views of culture than had been adopted hitherto in American archaeology. They may have been responding to the more functionalist views of human behavior that were being popularized in American anthropology by Radcliffe-Brown, who taught at the University of Chicago between 1931 and 1937, and by Malinowski, who taught at Yale University from 1938 until his death in 1942. Exposure to social anthropology also seems to have encouraged the development of a different sort of functionalist trend in Boasian cultural anthropology. Originally, Boasian anthropologists had viewed each culture as a random collection of traits brought together by diffusion and migration. They believed that, provided the basic functional requirements that were needed to sustain individuals and groups were supplied in some minimally adequate fashion, other cultural traits could be of any sort (Aberle et al. 1950).

In the 1930s, Boasian anthropologists began to argue that cultures displayed patterns or configurations that made them psychologically meaningful and reassuring to people. One culture might emphasize social harmony, another violent competition among individuals. By providing guidance for human conduct, such configurations, however psychologically demanding they might be on individuals, reduced the still greater psychological stress that would have arisen in their absence as a result of people not knowing how they should behave. The most widely read expression of this view was Ruth Benedict's *Patterns of Culture* (1934), which contrasted the self-effacing cooperativeness of the Hopi way of life with the ruthless competitiveness of the Kwakiutl. These ideas led to the development within Boasian anthropology of what was called the "culture and personality" school and later "psychological anthropology," an approach that persisted into the early 1960s. As a result of the development of psychological anthropology, functionalism became as important within idealist Boasian cultural anthropology as it already was for behaviorist social anthropology.

American archaeologists also were increasingly aware of the interpretations of archaeological data offered by Childe, Clark, and other European archaeologists. These archaeologists provided theoretical as well as practical evidence that leading American ethnologists, such as Robert Lowie and Frank Speck, erred when they claimed that, because archaeologists could study only material culture, they were unable to say anything significant about nonmaterial aspects of human behavior. To provide behavioral interpretations, however,

American archaeologists had to view artifacts as parts of total cultural systems and as having been integrated within social, political, and economic frameworks, rather than simply as material objects that had only typological significance.

The desire to understand archaeological remains from a functional point of view led some American archaeologists to renew their ties with ethnology. These ties had become attenuated during the early culture-historical period, when the main goal of archaeologists had been to construct cultural chronologies. Many of these functionally oriented archaeologists were directly or indirectly connected with the Smithsonian Institution. In 1936, William D. Strong (1899–1962) stressed the interdependence of archaeology, history, and ethnography and argued that archaeologists should look to ethnologists for theoretical leads as well as factual information. He had already applied this principle in his direct-historical approach to Nebraskan prehistory, which had revealed a far more complex and varied past than had hitherto been envisaged (Strong 1935). In 1951, he divided New World prehistory into seven epochs or stages with parallel sequences in each of nine regions. Rather than depending on distinctive ceramic styles, he defined each epoch by economic features, the artistic level achieved, and the political organization "in so far as it can be envisaged." In his study of native subsistence economies on the Great Plains, Waldo R. Wedel (1908–1996) (1941) stressed the importance of relations between culture and environment and argued that factors other than historical accidents shaped archaeological cultures. Paul Martin (1899–1974) attempted to use the ethnologist Robert Redfield's concept of "folk culture" to explain variations in the size and contents of Pueblo ruins (Martin et al. 1938; Martin and Rinaldo 1939). A. J. Waring, Jr. and Preston Holder (1945) interpreted elaborately decorated copper and shell artifacts in widely dispersed Mississippian sites as evidence of a widespread religious cult.

Similar functional explanations were used to account for stylistic distributions in Peru, such as the Chavin and Tiahuanaco horizons, which had hitherto been considered purely in diffusionist terms. In these studies, efforts were made to identify sociopolitical or religious characteristics of the material by considering their intrasite provenience or other features that typological studies had ignored (W. Bennett 1945; Willey 1948). In a study of the contentious issue of

Mesoamerican influences on the cultures of the southeastern United States, John W. Bennett (1916–2005) (1944) stressed the need to consider the functional implications of traits, the social context from which they were derived, and, above all, the context into which they would have been introduced. He hypothesized that some Mesoamerican traits would readily have been accepted by the less complex cultures of the United States, whereas others would have been rejected, however many times they were transmitted. Hence, he maintained that diffusionist explanations required a detailed functional understanding of the recipient cultures. Still other archaeologists sought to interpret the interaction between neighboring cultures using the concept of acculturation, which was popular at that time among ethnologists (Keur 1941; Lewis and Kneberg 1941). Although these and other studies were highly disparate and provisional, enough of them had appeared by 1943 to be recognized as constituting a trend in American archaeology, which J. W. Bennett (1943) labeled a "functional" or "sociological" approach to archaeological interpretation.

The Conjunctive Approach

These studies and the ethnologist Clyde Kluckhohn's (1940) advocacy of a "scientific" approach, which he defined as making a search for generalizations about human behavior and cultural change the ultimate goal of archaeology and ethnology, prepared the way for Walter Taylor's (1913–1997) *A Study of Archeology* (1948), a polemical work that was written in the early 1940s as Taylor's PhD thesis, although its publication was delayed by World War II. Although Taylor's criticism of the work of some senior American archaeologists outraged many established members of the profession, he failed to recruit support from archaeologists of his own generation. Taylor later saw his work as anticipating processual archaeology and was embittered because he felt he did not receive due recognition for his contributions to this movement (Reyman 1999).

Taylor observed in *A Study of Archeology* that the majority of American archaeologists claimed that their goal was to reconstruct prehistory, although some of them, like Kidder, went further and expressed the hope that eventually archaeological data would provide a basis for generalizing about human behavior and cultural change. Yet, Taylor claimed, few culture-historical archaeologists had displayed any interest in systematically reconstructing prehistoric ways of life or explaining what had occurred in prehistoric times. Instead, they occupied themselves with "mere chronicle," which he defined as working out the geographical and temporal distributions of different sorts of archaeological evidence and explaining them in terms of diffusion and migration.

Taylor proceeded to demonstrate that the limited goals of American culture-historical archaeologists had encouraged slackness in archaeological fieldwork and analysis. Many classes of artifacts, especially those that were not regarded as important for defining cultures or for working out cultural chronologies, were neither examined nor described in more than a cursory manner. Pottery and lithic material were studied much more carefully than was surviving evidence of basketry. Floral and faunal remains often were inadequately recovered and identified; hence, archaeologists did not know what foods were eaten and why particular sites were used or at what season. Archaeologists also failed to record, and more often to report, the intrasite provenience of artifacts in sufficient detail. Because of this, it was impossible to identify activity areas within sites or to determine how frequencies of artifacts might have varied from one part of a site to another. Finally, although archaeologists sought to elaborate lists of all the traits or types of artifacts associated with particular sites and compared these lists to determine their cultural affinity, they were normally content to consider merely the presence or absence of traits. As a result, quantified data, that might have been very important for understanding the functional roles played by particular kinds of artifacts, were lacking. Taylor devoted much of his study to providing a detailed critique of the shortcomings of the work of leading American archaeologists in order to demonstrate how their cultural-chronological objectives had limited their investigations of the archaeological record.

To remedy these defects, Taylor offered the conjunctive approach. He proposed to add to the traditional investigation of chronological problems and intersite relations intrasite studies in which careful attention would be paid to all artifacts and features and how they were interrelated. Special note would be taken of the quantitative aspects and spatial distributions of archaeological finds, as well as of their formal properties and evidence of how they were made and used. In this way, archaeologists might hope to learn as much as possible about the nature of life in prehistoric times and about the functional relations within a prehistoric culture. A distinctive aspect of the conjunctive approach was the importance that Taylor, like Clark, attached to sites as primary units of analysis. Taylor, however, was an adherent of Boasian anthropology; hence his approach, unlike Clark's, was primarily cultural and configurational rather than social.

Taylor sought to avoid the problems inherent for archaeologists in the concept of material culture by following Kroeber and other Boasian anthropologists in defining culture as mental constructs and viewing material remains as products of culture rather than culture itself (Osgood 1951). He believed that mental constructs, which were partly a heritage from the past and could be either idiosyncratic or shared by varying numbers of people, provided beliefs and values that guided social activities as well as the technical knowledge required to produce material culture. He concluded that, although culture was ideational and hence did not survive in the archaeological record, many aspects of culture other than the knowledge that went into manufacturing artifacts were reflected archaeologically.

Taylor maintained that archaeologists should strive to recover as much information as possible from archaeological sites, including seemingly trivial evidence. They also must collect information concerning the palaeoenvironmental context of sites as well as any related historical and ethnographic data. The first analytical task relating to a site as a whole was to work out its internal chronology and thus determine what evidence was synchronous or successive. Archaeologists should next turn to the major task of synthesizing the material from the site, or from each period that it was occupied. Two sorts of synthesis had to be done. The ethnographic synthesis consisted of determining everything possible about how people had lived at the site. The archaeologist, like an ethnographer, should try to fill out the *Outline of Cultural Materials* (Murdock et al. 1938), a checklist documenting all conceivable patterns of cultural behavior. The ethnographic synthesis was to be followed by a historiographic one that traced how ways of life at a site had changed during the course of its occupation and tried to account for how these changes had come about. Taylor did not provide any detailed instructions how to interpret archaeological data. Like most culture-historical archaeologists, he recommended drawing analogies (homologies) among historically related cultures and, hence, the application of the direct historical approach. He appears to have viewed interpretation as a commonsense operation, as American archaeologists had done for a long time. His main point was that this should be done more systematically.

Having synthesized the cultural significance of individual sites, Taylor saw archaeologists ready to undertake what he called comparative studies. He believed that such studies should involve the comparison of whole cultural contexts as manifested at individual sites rather than of individual items of culture, and that the immediate aim of such a study should be to understand how a site related to the broader pattern of life in a surrounding territory. In this way, seasonally occupied hunter-gatherer sites could be linked to form year-round patterns, or peasant hamlets associated with elite centers to provide information about the hierarchical structures of ancient civilizations. Thus, a functional understanding could be gained that was equivalent to the ethnologists' insights into the nature of living cultures. Archaeologists could then proceed to work alongside ethnologists to achieve the principal goal of anthropology: a general understanding of the nature and working of culture.

Under the influence of contemporary Boasian anthropologists, including Kluckhohn, Taylor appears to have been trying to understand archaeological data in terms of functionally integrated cultural patterns. Like all Boasian anthropologists, his goal was to recover the ideas that he believed accounted for human behavior. His concept of integration was derived from the ideas of configuration and psychological consistency advocated by Boasian anthropologists such as Ruth Benedict rather than from the concepts of structural and functional integration being promoted by social anthropologists. In one of his more explicit demonstrations of the sort of work he was proposing, he contrasted the lack of symmetry in basketry designs recovered from Coyote Cave and site CM 79 in Coahuila, Mexico, with the highly symmetrical patterns that dominated San Juan baskets in the southwestern United States. He interpreted these variations, which could not be attributed to differences in material or weaving techniques, as reflecting a fundamental difference between two ethnic groups concerning how things should be ordered. This, he believed, was quite possibly a difference that would have expressed itself in many other ways of doing things that were not necessarily reflected in the archaeological record. In 1950, the psychological anthropologist Anthony Wallace published an analysis of the personality structure of prehispanic Maya upper-class males based on a culture-and-personality study of artwork from their codices that he compared with early Spanish descriptions of Maya behavior and Rorschach studies of the personalities of modern Maya. Although much hope was expressed at the time that techniques of this sort might provide deep insights into the nature of prehistoric cultures, such configurational studies were generally ignored by archaeologists. By the 1960s, psychological anthropology in general was being abandoned, and Boasian anthropology along with it, as it became increasingly clear that such approaches had no way of demonstrating their far-reaching claims.

There has been considerable discussion concerning to what extent Taylor's approach represented a break with the past or marked the beginning of the New Archaeology of the 1960s (W. Taylor 1972; Binford 1972: 8–9, 1983a: 229–33). Yet little attention has been paid to connections between Taylor's work and what was going on in archaeology in the late 1930s. In *A Study of Archeology*, Taylor ignored much of the innovative fieldwork of that time and the accompanying movement toward a functionalist interpretation of archaeological data. Instead of trying to position himself as the spokesperson for younger and more innovative archaeologists, he alienated them by ignoring their works. This failure, combined with his harsh criticism of the work of senior American archaeologists, was a recipe for academic disaster. He also failed to cite the recent works of innovative British archaeologists, such as Childe and Clark. Yet Taylor's emphasis on the first task of archaeologists being to use archaeological evidence to reconstruct how people had lived at individual prehistoric sites closely paralleled the approach that Clark had advocated in 1939. So, too, did Taylor's insistence on palaeoethnography as a vital goal of archaeology and his view of cultures as functioning entities embracing social, political, and ideological as well as economic components that the archaeologist must try to study holistically from the inside.

Yet Taylor did not follow Clark or anticipate the New Archaeology in viewing cultures as ecologically adaptive systems. Instead, he adopted an idealist view of culture as a pattern of psychologically integrated concepts, a position that closely resembled the configurational Boasian anthropology of that period. Like the Boasians, he did not presuppose that any one part of a culture plays a more important role than any other in bringing about cultural change. Instead, he regarded defining the relations between parts and explaining change as problems that must be approached inductively. Taylor contributed almost nothing to explaining how or why cultural change occurred. Like the Boasians, he was amenable to the idea that different aspects of culture might play a leading role in bringing about change in different societies and continued to believe that much change occurs as a result of fortuitous contacts between human groups. His idealist and inductive approach prevented him from using a functionalist view of prehistoric cultures to achieve a new understanding of cultural change. His contribution was mainly important as a critique of current standards of archaeological research and a call for archaeologists to recover and analyze archaeological data more intensively than they had done in the past. He did not challenge the basic tenets of Boasian historical particularism or introduce any major innovations into archaeological interpretation. In all these ways, his ideas were very different from those of the New Archaeology, and Binford was justified in regarding him as being a Boasian archaeologist. Yet a significant challenge to culture-historical archaeology in North America did not have to await the New Archaeology.

Ecological and Settlement Archaeology

Julian Steward (1902–1972), who was one of the first American ethnologists to adopt an explicitly materialist view of human behavior, greatly enhanced an awareness of the role played by ecological factors in shaping prehistoric sociocultural systems. In 1938, he and the archaeologist F. M. Setzler published a landmark paper in which they argued that archaeologists as well as ethnologists should seek to understand the nature of cultural change and that both disciplines could contribute to an ecological analysis of human behavior. To play a significant role, however, archaeologists would have to stop focusing on the stylistic analysis of artifacts and begin to use their data to study changes in subsistence economies, population size, and settlement patterns. Steward was convinced that, because archaeologists could study changes in these three variables over time, they could contribute significantly to understanding human behavior and cultural change. Steward himself had carried out archaeological research on the *Ancient Caves of the Great Salt Lake Region* (1937a) and written a paper in which he had drawn together archaeological and ethnographic settlement-pattern data in a study of interaction between culture and environment in the southwestern United States (1937b). Of all the American ethnologists of this period, he had the greatest respect for archaeological data and the greatest awareness of their potential value for studying problems of human behavior over long periods.

After World War II, increasing awareness of the importance of the ecological approach, resulting from the writings of Steward and Clark, stimulated major American research programs involving interdisciplinary teams. One of the most important of these was the Iraq Jarmo Project, directed by Robert Braidwood (1907–2003), which between 1948 and 1955 examined a series of late Palaeolithic to early Neolithic sites in the Kirkuk region of Iraq (Braidwood 1974). Another was the Tehuacan Archaeological-Botanical Project, led by Richard S. MacNeish (1918–2001), which between 1960 and 1968 revealed an unbroken cultural sequence in highland Mexico running for 12,000 years from PalaeoIndian times to the Spanish conquest (MacNeish 1974, 1978, 1992) (Figure 7.7). These projects, which were funded in part by the United States National Science Foundation, brought together archaeologists, botanists, zoologists, geologists, and other specialists to carry out research relating to the origin of food production in the Middle East and Mesoamerica. They succeeded in delineating changes in the subsistence economies of their respective regions and MacNeish, whose team located 456 sites, also was able to infer changes over time in group composition and land utilization. Using radiocarbon dates, they demonstrated that in both the Old and the New Worlds food production had begun earlier and increased in economic importance far more slowly than archaeologists, including Childe, had previously believed. In the politically charged atmosphere of the Cold War prevailing in the United States, these findings were welcomed as proof of the normalcy of gradual evolutionary changes and a major setback for Childe's much criticized and apparently Marxist-inspired theory of a Neolithic "revolution" (Redfield 1953: 24; Patterson 2003: 53–4). Braidwood's findings also ruled out the likelihood that desiccation had played a significant role in initiating the development of food-producing economies in the Middle East. These two studies pioneered the use

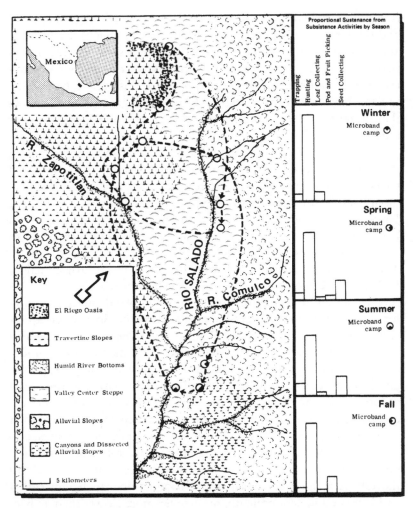

Figure 7.7 MacNeish's interpretation of subsistence-settlement pattern of
Ajuereado Phase (11,000–7,000 BC) in Tehuacan Valley, Mexico
(*The Science of Archaeology?* 1978)

of archaeological data to study in detail one of the major economic
and social transformations of human history. Like Clark's excavation at Star Carr, they also demonstrated the importance of a multidisciplinary approach in which archaeologists and natural science specialists worked together to analyze archaeological data.

In *Trend and Tradition in the Prehistory of the Eastern United States,* Joseph Caldwell (1916–1973) adopted a more rounded ecological approach to understanding cultural change (1958). He argued that ecological adjustments to the disappearance of big game at the end of the last Ice Age had resulted in more complex and intensive patterns of food collection that increased the carrying capacity of most areas and promoted denser populations and sedentarization throughout eastern North America. Reduced mobility had encouraged the acquisition of heavier and more varied types of equipment than had been useful or usable previously, including soapstone, and later ceramic, cooking vessels. Caldwell stressed not only the capacity for internally initiated change among the indigenous cultures of the Eastern Woodlands but also the need for archaeologists to understand artifacts such as pottery vessels with reference to the roles they had played within adaptive systems. Such interpretations had been foreshadowed in Ralph Linton's (1944) study of developmental trends in the shapes of eastern North American ceramic vessels.

Steward also inspired the development of settlement archaeology, which was initiated by Gordon Willey's *Prehistoric Settlement Patterns in the Virú Valley, Peru* (1953), the report of a study that was carried out in 1946 as part of the combined archaeological and anthropological investigation of a small coastal valley in Peru by American and Peruvian anthropologists. Before World War II, regional archaeological surveys had been conducted mainly to select sites for excavation (W. Sumner 1990: 87–8), although some archaeologists had used archaeological survey data to infer prehistoric distributions of population. In 1904, Sophus Müller had employed some 60,000 barrows and several thousand megaliths to determine the general distribution of settlement in Neolithic and Bronze Age Denmark (Schnapp and Kristiansen 1999: 40). Later, Crawford (1921) used artifact densities to plot population distributions in the United Kingdom. The site surveys by William Albright (1891–1971) and Nelson Glueck (1901–1971) in Palestine and Jordan between the early 1920s and 1949 also have been recognized as forerunners of settlement-pattern archaeology (Moorey 1991: 68–77). In 1940, the classical archaeologist Carl Blegen (1887–1971) stressed the need for surveys to locate all sites in Greece in order to trace the distribution and movements of population from one historical period to another. This appeal is credited with inspiring the Messenia Project of the 1960s (W. McDonald 1966: 414–15). And, in 1942, Childe (1942f) used the distribution of tombs on Rousay to estimate the size and distribution of population on this Scottish island during the Neolithic period. None of these studies, nor the study of settlements by German archaeologists, gave rise to settlement archaeology as a standard archaeological practice.

It was Steward who persuaded Willey to conduct a settlement-pattern survey as part of the Virú Valley project (Willey 1974b: 153). Aerial photographs and ground surveys were used to locate several hundred prehistoric settlements as well as traces of prehistoric irrigation systems. Pottery was surface collected from each site to determine during which periods it had been inhabited. The traces of buildings that were visible on the surface of sites were also recorded in order to determine what roles different sites might have played. Then maps were produced showing which sites had been occupied at successive phases in the history of the Virú Valley.

Yet Willey's interpretation of the data he collected marked a significant departure from Steward's ecological approach. Steward had regarded archaeological settlement patterns as evidence of relations between human groups and the natural environment. Willey, who had been trained in culture-historical archaeology but was familiar with more recent funtional-processual trends, chose instead to view settlement patterns as a "strategic starting point for the functional interpretation of archaeological cultures." He went on to assert that settlement patterns "reflect the natural environment, the level of technology on which the builders operated, and various institutions of social interaction and control which the culture maintained" (p. 1). He did not deny that ecological factors played a significant role in shaping settlement patterns but observed that many other factors of a social and cultural nature also were reflected in the archaeological record and was unprepared to view these factors as merely a reflection of the general patterns of ecological adaptation. Instead, he treated settlement patterns as a source of information about many aspects of human behavior. The major advantage of settlement patterns over artifacts was that, whereas artifacts frequently are found not where they were used but where they had been disposed of, the remains of structures, where they survive, do so *in situ*, and hence provide direct evidence concerning the settings in which human activities were carried out. Willey recognized the full potential of settlement-pattern data for the systematic study of the economic, social, and political organization of ancient societies.

Willey employed the concept of the archaeological culture mainly to distinguish successive phases in the history of the Virú Valley and to identify sites that had existed at approximately the same time. Cemeteries, habitation sites, palaces, temples, forts, and irrigation networks that appeared to be contemporary were used to try to reconstruct the changing patterns of life in the Virú Valley over several millennia (Figure 7.8). These studies revealed that population growth had been associated with the development of more intensive forms of food production, changing distributions of population, and ever more complex forms of social and political organization. Instead of viewing social and political phenomena as attributes of culture, Willey interpreted them as an evolving system of social relations that provided a behavioral context integrating other aspects of culture. Thus, in addition to identifying social and political organization as a legitimate object of archaeological study, Willey provided an analytical device for studying such organization in prehistoric contexts. Recognizing long-term continuities in the occupation of the Virú Valley also led Willey to try to explain changes in the archaeological record in terms of internal transformations rather than attributing them to diffusion and migration as had commonly been done in the past. His study was therefore an important pioneering effort in using archaeological data to interpret long-term social and political change.

Within the context of settlement archaeology, individual sites ceased to be studied as ends in themselves or to be regarded as representative of a particular culture or region. Instead, they were seen as forming networks within which single sites often played very different and complementary roles. Site surveys no longer sought merely to locate the largest or most representative sites for excavation but to recover information that was important in its own right for archaeological analysis.

Although ecological studies of settlement patterns continued and are recognized as often, if not always, being a necessary preliminary for social and political interpretations, a growing number of American archaeologists came to view settlement patterns as an important source of information concerning demographic trends and the social,

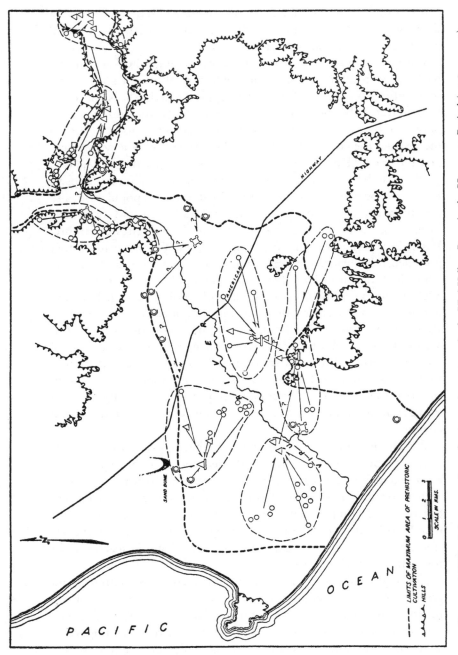

Figure 7.8 Willey's interpretation of community patterns in the Virú Valley, Peru, in the Huancaco Period (AD 800–1000) (*Prehistoric Settlement Patterns in the Virú Valley, Peru*, 1953)

political, and religious institutions of prehistoric societies. They also came to think of settlement patterns in terms of a hierarchy of levels: activity areas within structures, structures, associated activity areas around structures, communities, and the distribution of communities across landscapes. Each of these levels was recognized as having been shaped by factors that differ in kind or degree from those that influence other levels. Individual houses reflect family organization, settlements community structure, and spatial distributions the impact of trade, administration, and regional defense. Because of this the combined study of two or more levels is likely to shed more light on prehistoric societies than is the study of only one level (Trigger 1968b; Flannery 1976; Clarke 1977b; Kent 1984). Of all the functionalist approaches, settlement archaeology, with its focus on inferring patterns of social behavior and its rejection of ecological determinism, is the one that most closely relates to the interests of Durkheimian social anthropology.

For archaeologists interested in studying social and political organization, Willey's research in the Virú Valley constituted the most important methodological breakthrough in the history of archaeology. Even from a broader archaeological perspective, it was perhaps the most important innovation since Thomsen had succeeded in periodizing prehistory. Willey's findings inspired intensive regional surveys of the origin and development of complex societies in various parts of the world. These surveys addressed a variety of functional and processual issues, some of them of considerable importance to anthropologists as well as archaeologists. As the result of a detailed study in southern Iraq, Robert McC. Adams was able to demonstrate convincingly that in that region irrigation systems had expanded and collapsed as a consequence of political change rather than being a major cause of it (Adams 1965, 1981; Adams and Nissen 1972). K. C. Chang (1963) used settlement data to demonstrate continuity in the development of social and political systems in northern China from the early Neolithic period through the Xia, Shang, and Zhou dynasties and Makkhan Lal (1984) examined relations between technology and environment in northern India during the period of development of Gangetic civilization. Karl Butzer (1976) demonstrated that overall population pressure could not have played a major role in the rise of ancient Egyptian civilization, which developed most rapidly in the far south, where the exploitation of the smaller, natural agricultural basins required less effort than did that of the larger and more productive basins farther north. Trigger (1965) used mainly cemetery data to compare the relative importance of changes in technology, the natural environment, trade, and warfare in determining shifts in the size and distribution of population in Lower Nubia during the four millennia that followed the introduction of agriculture. Richard E. Blanton (1978) correlated changing settlement patterns in the Oaxaca area of Mexico with altering configurations of political organization, while William T. Sanders's detailed study of the Valley of Mexico demonstrated that idiosyncratic factors played a major role in shaping the size and distribution of settlements (Sanders et al. 1979) (Figure 7.9).

Archaeologists also recognized the value of settlement patterns for studying social change within smaller-scale societies. Early work at this level resulted in a unilinear scheme of types of community patterning devised at a seminar on the functional and evolutionary implications of such patterning held under the chairmanship of Richard Beardsley in 1955 (Beardsley et al. 1956). As a result of this seminar, terms such as "free wandering," "restricted wandering," "central based wandering," and "semipermanent sedentary" came to be used to describe the settlement and subsistence systems of aboriginal American peoples. It was not long, however, before settlement pattern studies utilizing Willey's approach were revealing much about the social and political organization of small-scale societies as well as about their adaptive patterns (Willey 1956; Ritchie and Funk 1973; B. Smith 1978).

Systematic studies of the settlement patterns of particular regions have increased awareness of regional diversity and the complexity of adaptations. They also have revealed the rapidity with which these adaptations sometimes changed, thereby demonstrating the erroneousness of the claim that cultural changes invariably occur in a slow, gradual fashion. Finally they have challenged simplistic beliefs that population increase or the development of irrigation agriculture played a preponderant role in shaping the evolution of complex societies. Settlement archaeology, like ecological approaches, encouraged archaeologists to study human behavior rather than culture and ethnicity, which had been associated with culture-historical archaeology. These changes in American archaeology, which corresponded with a growing interest in behaviorist approaches in all the

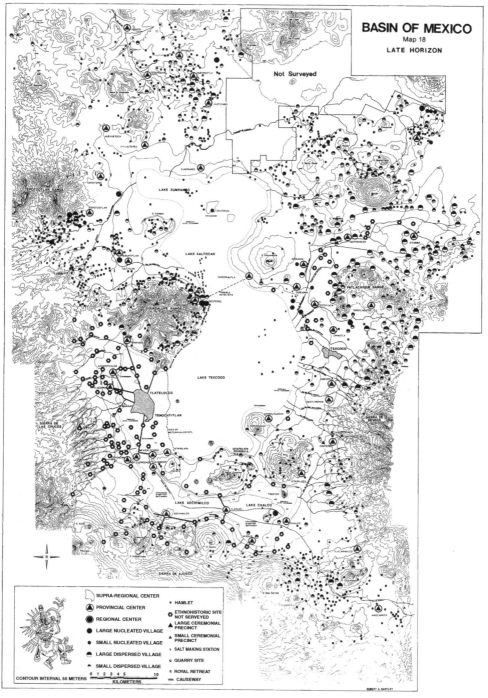

Figure 7.9 The settlement pattern of the Basin of Mexico for the Late Horizon
(Sanders et al. *The Basin of Mexico*, 1979)

social sciences and with growing familiarity with the work of Childe and Clark, constituted a major break with culture-historical archaeology.

World Archaeology

In the early 1950s, archaeology began to be transformed by a major scientific innovation: radiocarbon dating (Marlowe 1999). This method of dating was developed by Willard F. Libby (1908–1980) in the late 1940s and almost immediately tested by using it to date archaeological material of known age (Libby 1955). Ancient Egyptian artifacts and the chronology already worked out by Egyptologists played a major role in demonstrating that the original assumption that the rate of carbon-14 formation was a constant was incorrect and in the initial calibration of radiocarbon dates. Radiocarbon dating reduced, although it did not eliminate, the need for archaeologists to rely on seriation and cross-dating to construct cultural chronologies.

It also became possible for the first time to date prehistoric sites around the world in relation to one another and assign calendrical dates rather than only relative ones to them. Archaeologists were thus able to study rates as well as sequences of change. It had been possible for several decades to date geological or archaeological phenomena calendrically by means of varves and tree-rings, but these methods were applicable in only a few areas (Nash 1999, 2000a; Truncer 2003). Hitherto archaeologists had been able to create complex, relatively dated prehistoric cultural sequences covering geographically contiguous areas, but they could not correlate sequences in the Old and New Worlds or even in East and West Asia. Because they were unable to date most prehistoric sites calendrically, they also had no certain idea of whether cultural changes had occurred quickly or slowly.

The first archaeologist to exploit systematically the potential of radiocarbon dating for creating a global perspective in archaeology was Grahame Clark in his book *World Prehistory* (1961), which appeared in significantly revised editions in 1969 and 1977 as increasing arrays of radiocarbon dates and archaeological discoveries became available from around the world. In the second edition, lists of relevant radiocarbon dates appeared at the end of each chapter. Already in

1943, at a conference on the future of archaeology, Clark had urged the need to create a common history and prehistory of humanity as an antidote to nationalism (Clark 1945; C. Evans 1995: 313–15). After World War II, Dorothy Garrod introduced a course on world prehistory at Cambridge University that sought to present archaeology as a subject that spans the entire globe (Clark 1999: 407). In the late 1950s, Clark used available radiocarbon dates to construct a worldwide chronology covering the last 50,000 years and then attempted to delineate the successive patterns of ecological adaptation in each region and to determine when each pattern appeared in different places. In keeping with his functionalist interests, Clark's goal was not to explain change but to ascertain the degree of similarity of developmental sequences on a worldwide basis. By the 1960s, a growing number of Clark's former students were working in many parts of the world, which Clark visited to collect material for successive editions of his book. Although 57 percent of the first edition dealt with Europe and western Asia, by the third edition this coverage had dropped to 33 percent and more attention was being paid to East Asia, Africa, the Americas, and Australia (Rowley-Conwy 1999: 517–18); although, like many British academics of that period, Clark tended to undervalue the achievements of sub-Saharan Africa (Trevor-Roper 1966: 9). Clark was not the only archaeologist to view prehistory from a global perspective, but he took advantage of radiocarbon dating to produce the first modern-style textbook of global prehistory. His comparison of sequences of adaptive patterns around the world encouraged the development of comparative ecology and helped to renew an interest in evolutionary processes.

Radiocarbon dating had an important impact on understanding rates of cultural change. Preferring diffusionist and migratory explanations, culture-historical archaeologists had believed that cultures could change quickly, which encouraged the creation of short chronologies. Nineteenth-century evolutionists had preferred longer chronologies, which provided more time for internal changes to occur, but even they greatly overestimated the rate of change for the Palaeolithic period. As early as 1966, Clark was questioning migratory explanations of changes in the archaeological record of prehistoric Britain. Colin Renfrew's (1973a, 1979) reinterpretation of European prehistory was based almost entirely on calibrated radiocarbon dates that indicated that Neolithic and Bronze Age sites north and west of the Aegean area were considerably older than Montelius and Childe had estimated using Aegean sites that had been cross-dated with historically dated Bronze Age sites in Egypt and the Middle East. This revision suggested that in terms of technology and architecture early central and western Europe had been more innovative than previously had been believed.

Radiocarbon dating had a similar effect on the study of North American prehistory. There, everywhere except in the Southwest, where calendrical dates for sites back to the beginning of the Christian era had been derived dendrochronologically since the 1920s, radiocarbon chronologies revealed that cultural sequences had developed over longer periods and far more slowly than had previously been believed (cf. Ritchie 1944, 1965). By greatly slowing the rate of cultural change in the eastern United States and western Europe, radiocarbon dating made it far easier for archaeologists to credit the possibility that major changes had come about as a result of internal processes rather than because of diffusion and migration. This in turn made evolutionary explanations of change in the archaeological record seem more plausible. The chronology of the Palaeolithic period, especially that of the Lower Palaeolithic period, was greatly lengthened in the 1960s as a result of the application of potassium-argon dating to new archaeological discoveries that were being made in east Africa. That, too, created new facts that were in need of explanation.

Conclusions

Functional and processual interpretations of archaeological data had long been associated with studies of the relations between cultures and their environments and how artifacts were made and used. Beginning in the late 1920s, Soviet archaeologists sought to pioneer ways to infer social, economic, and political behavior from the archaeological record. What was completely new was their determination to understand how social and cultural systems changed in terms of their own internal dynamics. This marked a sharp break with earlier efforts by archaeologists to explain cultural change in terms of external influences or human inventiveness considered without reference to social and economic conditions. The new approach also was characterized by an explicit rejection of the racism and pessimism about human creativity that characterized archaeology in central and western Europe in the 1920s. Yet the development of Soviet archaeology was blighted by extreme ideological regimentation, which restricted the range of analytical techniques that could be employed to construct cultural chronologies and explain change in the archaeological record.

In the West, the proliferation and increasing sophistication of functionalist views that represented a significant trend in British and American anthropology, beginning in the 1920s, encouraged archaeologists to view prehistoric cultures as internally differentiated and to some degree integrated ways of life. That development in turn promoted a consideration of the internal as well as the external causes of change. At first the examination of internal causes was directed mainly toward ecological and economic factors. Yet, although Taylor and Clark did much to encourage the use of archaeological data for reconstructing prehistoric patterns of life, they made few contributions toward explaining changes in the archaeological record. In contrast, Childe, although developing some very interesting models of social change, failed to address how these models could be applied in any detail to the study of the archaeological evidence. Ecological and settlement archaeology, by contrast, encouraged the study both of prehistoric cultures at specific points in time and of how these cultures changed. The development of functional and processual approaches to archaeological data resulted in the gradual replacement of the increasingly sterile preoccupation of culture-historical archaeology with ethnicity by a vital new interest in how prehistoric cultures operated and changed. A declining interest in the study of culture and a growing interest in behavior not only accorded with trends in other social sciences but also foreshadowed continuing changes in prehistoric archaeology.

CHAPTER 8

Processualism and Postprocessualism

———

I am unwilling to admit that the abundant literature published in the last fifteen years in praise of "archaeology as anthropology"... marks a turning point in the intellectual history of our discipline.

JEAN-CLAUDE GARDIN, *Archaeological Constructs* (1980), p. 29

The proper analogy for human behaviour is not natural law – of a physical kind – but a game of chess.

EDMUND LEACH, "Concluding Address" (1973), p. 764

In Europe and North America, culture-historical and functional-processual archaeology might have continued to develop alongside one another in a complementary fashion as they had done in the 1950s. Instead, in the early 1960s, a group of American processual archaeologists launched an all-out attack on culture-historical archaeology, which they proposed to replace with an approach that was evolutionist, behaviorist, ecological, and positivist in orientation. In the late 1980s, archaeologists, mainly in Britain, offered an equally dogmatic, culturally oriented postprocessual archaeology as a solution for what they proclaimed were processual archaeology's shortcomings. Neither option has lived up to its promise to solve all of archaeology's problems, although together they offer productive ways to consider many, but not all, of the questions archaeologists must address. In retrospect, these two antagonistic positions can be seen to reflect successive theoretical fashions in anthropology.

Neoevolutionism

The two decades following World War II were an era of unrivaled prosperity and unchallenged political power for the United States. Despite the threat of nuclear war, this also was a time of great optimism and self-confidence for middle-class Americans. As had happened in Britain and western Europe in the middle of the nineteenth century, this self-confidence encouraged a relatively materialistic outlook and a greater readiness than in the past to believe that there was a pattern to human history and that technological progress was the key to human betterment. In American anthropology, these trends were manifested in the revival of an interest in cultural evolution. Although evolutionism never became the predominant trend in American anthropology, it increased greatly in popularity in the 1950s and 1960s and exerted a significant influence throughout the discipline.

The resurgence of cultural evolutionism in American anthropology also was encouraged by a growing consensus that Boasian anthropology could not adequately explain cultural changes. Boasian anthropology, with its emphasis on cultural relativism, had generally been hostile to the study of cultural evolution as opposed to cultural history. Hence, it is not surprising that opposition to Boasian anthropology took the form of a renewed interest in cultural evolution. In addition, Boasian idealist epistemology did not accord with the growing interest in positivism and behaviorism that spread through the social sciences in the 1940s and 1950s, ironically at a time when behaviorism was starting to fall out of favor in psychology, where it had first been applied in the 1910s (J. Watson 1925).

The two principal exponents of neoevolutionism in anthropology in the 1950s were the ethnologists Leslie White (1900–1975) and Julian Steward (1902–1972) (White 1949, 1959; Steward 1955). White regarded himself as the intellectual heir of L. H. Morgan and the nineteenth-century evolutionary tradition of American anthropology. He rejected the historical particularism, psychological reductionism, and belief in free will inherent in Boasian anthropology. In their place he offered the concept of "General Evolution," which treated progress as a characteristic of culture in general, although not necessarily of every individual culture. White deliberately ignored the influence of environments on culture and of one culture on another and concentrated on explaining what he regarded as the main line of cultural development, which was marked by the most advanced culture of each successive period regardless of the historical relations between these leading cultures. He argued that this approach was justified because, in the long run, cultures that failed to keep ahead were superseded and absorbed by more progressive ones. Hence, from an evolutionary point of view, they were irrelevant.

White defined cultures as elaborate thermodynamic systems. In his early writings, he argued that they functioned to make human life more secure and enduring, although later he rejected that view as anthropocentric and claimed that cultures evolved to serve their own needs (White 1975: 8–13). His perception of cultural change was materialistic and narrowly deterministic. He maintained that cultural systems were composed of technoeconomic, social, and ideological subsystems and that "social systems are . . . determined by technological systems, and philosophies and the arts express experience as it is defined by technology and refracted by social systems" (White 1949: 390–1). He formulated his concept of technological determinism in terms of a "basic law of evolution," which stated that, all things being equal, culture evolves as the amount of energy harnessed per capita increases or the efficiency of putting energy to work is increased. This law was summarized by the formula:

$$\text{Culture} = \text{Energy} \times \text{Technology} \; (C = E \times T).$$

Despite the sweeping claims that White sometimes made for his theory, he emphasized that, although it accounted for the general outlines of cultural development, it could not be used to infer the specific features of individual cultures (White 1945: 346).

Because White was a radical socialist, his technological determinism is often assumed to be of Marxist origin. Yet conceptually it had in common with Marxism only a general materialist orientation. It more closely reflected one of the principal themes of mid-twentieth-century American social science scholarship, which privileged the relation between technology and society at the expense of other kinds of relations, such as that between self and society (Noble 1977; Kroker 1984: 12). In the 1950s and 1960s, most Americans viewed technological progress as the main cause of economic, political, and intellectual progress and the main cure for all social problems. Either White deliberately disguised the Marxist basis of his ideas to protect his academic appointment at the University of Michigan (Peace 1993) or he disagreed with Marxists on this matter. Marxists were not technological determinists.

Julian Steward championed an alternative multilinear, ecological, and more empirical approach to the study of cultural evolution. He assumed that there were significant regularities in cultural development and that ecological adaptation was crucial for determining the limits of variation in cultural systems. He sought by means of comparative studies to determine the different ways in which cultures had developed in various types of natural environments, believing that they would tend to acquire the same forms and follow similar developmental trajectories in similar natural settings. These cross-cultural similarities constituted a "cultural core," which was constituted by those features of a culture that were functionally most closely related to subsistence activities. The core embraced economic, political, and religious patterns that could be empirically determined to have major adaptive significance. Steward argued that the aim of evolutionary anthropology should be to explain the shared features of cultures at similar levels of development rather than "unique, exotic, and non-recurrent particulars," which can be attributed to historical accidents (Steward 1955: 209).

M. D. Sahlins and E. R. Service (1960) tried to reconcile White's and Steward's approaches by differentiating between general and specific evolution. These were defined as being concerned with progress and adaptation respectively. Although the concept of evolution was thereby dissociated from automatically implying progress, in later studies Sahlins (1968) and Service (1962, 1975) used ethnographic data to construct speculative, highly generalized sequences of unilinear development, employing evolutionary concepts such as band, tribe, chiefdom, and state. Implicit in their approaches, and in the alternative scheme of political evolution developed by Morton Fried (1967), was the assumption that the greater selective fitness of technologically advanced societies ensured that progress had characterized cultural change throughout human history.

The most theoretically sophisticated approach of this sort was Marvin Harris's (1979) cultural materialism. He assigned a privileged role in shaping cultural systems to an array of material conditions, including technology, demography, and economic relations, and sought to explain all sociocultural phenomena in terms of the relative costs and benefits of alternative strategies, as measured in terms of those criteria. Much of his work was directed toward trying to explain the origin of food taboos, religious beliefs, and other cultural esoterica in terms of the functional relations these customs had to basic economic considerations (Harris 1974, 1977, 1981). Although overtly less concerned with delineating evolutionary sequences than were Sahlins, Service, and Fried, Harris was no less an evolutionist than they were.

What distinguished the various materialist approaches that developed in American anthropology in the 1960s from the evolutionary schemes of the nineteenth century was their view of causality. White adopted a very narrow form of technological determinism that reflected his belief in technology as a source of social progress, whereas Steward embraced a less restrictive ecological and Harris a still broader economic determinism. Yet neoevolutionists continued to argue, as diffusionists and social anthropologists had done, that humans sought to preserve a familiar style of life unless they were compelled to change by forces that were beyond their control. This position was very different from the deliberate search by individuals for better ways to control nature and improve the quality of human life that Spencer and most nineteenth-century evolutionists had used to explain cultural change.

Already by the middle of the nineteenth century some North American archaeologists were constructing sequences to describe the development of indigenous cultures in the New World. Like Acosta, Daniel Wilson (1862) believed that indigenous peoples had originally come from the Old World but, because of hardships they had encountered in the course of doing so, they had all declined to a hunter-gatherer level of culture and had to reinvent more complex forms of society in the Americas without further stimulus from the Eastern Hemisphere. Evolutionary approaches, which located the main centers of New World development in Mesoamerica and Peru, did not disappear following the adoption of a culture-historical approach. In *Ancient Civilizations of Mexico and Central America*, H. J. Spinden (1879–1967) (1928) distinguished three levels of development: Nomadic (hunting and gathering), Archaic (agriculture), and Civilization; while in *Method and Theory in American Archaeology*, Willey and Phillips (1958) assigned all cultures to five levels of increasing complexity: Lithic, Archaic, Formative, Classic, and Postclassic. Yet, despite their evolutionary appearance, these formulations sought to describe, rather than to account for, cultural change in developmental terms. They relied heavily on diffusionist explanations, as did other culture-historical works. By the late 1940s and 1950s, however, archaeologists living in Mexico, such as Pedro Armillas, and anthropologists from the United States, such as René Millon and Eric Wolf, were using their own understandings of Marxism and of Childe's evolutionary writings to explain cultural change in prehistoric Mesoamerica in terms of the development of productive forces and the dialectic of class and state formation (Peace 1988; Patterson 1994, 2003: 61–2).

Although most archaeologists in the United States were hostile or indifferent to Marxist ideas, as a consequence of their growing interest in functionalist and processual explanations of the archaeological record, many of them were predisposed to be receptive to neoevolutionary concepts, which emphasized regularities in culture. They noted that many of the key variables that neoevolutionists posited as causes of cultural change, including changing subsistence and settlement patterns and demography, were relatively accessible for archaeological study, unlike the idealist explanations of Boasian anthropologists. Because of their lack of direct information concerning human behavior and beliefs, archaeologists also were less inclined to be critical of the shortcomings of neoevolutionary theory than were ethnologists. Only a few objected that neoevolutionism failed to take account of the regional variation that was evident in the ethnographic record (Lamberg-Karlovsky 1975: 342–3).

One of the first applications of neoevolutionary theory to archaeology was B. J. Meggers's "The Law of Cultural Evolution as a Practical Research Tool" (1960). She argued that, because of the absence of nonhuman sources of energy in small-scale societies, White's law, as it applied to them, could be rewritten:

$$\text{Culture} = \text{Environment} \times \text{Technology.}$$

This formulation suggested that any archaeologist who was able to reconstruct the technology and environment of a prehistoric culture should be able on the basis of that information to infer what the key features of the rest of the culture had been like. Furthermore, any shortcomings in making such inferences were not the responsibility of archaeologists but resulted from the failure of ethnologists to elaborate adequate theories relating technology and environment to the rest of culture. Meggers believed it to be advantageous that archaeologists were "forced to deal with culture artificially separated from human beings" (Meggers 1955: 129) and that her formulation placed so much emphasis on technoenvironmental determinism that there was no need to use archaeological data to study nonmaterial aspects of cultural systems. In that respect, her attitude toward the employment of ethnographic analogy resembled that of many nineteenth-century evolutionary anthropologists. Her position was, however, too lacking in direct application to attract much support among archaeologists. Finally, Meggers could not offer any independent proof that her specific reconstructions were correct. Even more than what had been done by nineteenth-century Palaeolithic archaeologists, this procedure made archaeological interpretation so dependent on ethnology as to question the need for archaeological research.

Early New Archaeology

In 1959, Joseph Caldwell published an article in *Science* titled "The New American Archaeology." In it, he surveyed major trends that he believed were transforming archaeology. He cited growing interest in ecology and settlement patterns as evidence of a new concern with cultural progress. Archaeological cultures were no longer regarded merely as the sum total of their preserved artifact types or traits, each of which could be treated in a stylistic fashion as independent and equally significant. Instead, cultures had to be analyzed, as Taylor had proposed, as configurations or even as functionally integrated systems. Caldwell also supported the neoevolutionary belief that behind the infinite variety of cultural facts and specific historical situations was a finite number of general historical processes. Finally, he adopted the neoevolutionary position that not all cultural facts are of equal importance in bringing about change. The primary aim of archaeologists must be to explain changes in archaeological cultures in terms of cultural processes. From this perspective, the study of cultural idiosyncracies was stigmatized as old-fashioned and unscientific.

Caldwell's paper reveals that during the decade following the publication of Taylor's *A Study of Archeology* the concept of processual change within cultural systems had achieved a new level of importance in American archaeology. Although this transformation was encouraged by developments within archaeology, in particular the

growing study of ecology and settlement patterns, it also was promoted by the growing popularity of neoevolutionary anthropology,
with its emphasis on cultural regularities. Hence, the essential and
enduring elements of the New Archaeology were the collective creation of a considerable number of American archaeologists during
the 1950s.

The ideas that Caldwell noted were popularized among the
younger generation of American archaeologists by Lewis Binford
(b. 1929), who added some new elements to create what since the
1960s has been recognized around the world as the beginnings of
American New or processual archaeology. Binford engaged in a
series of vigorous polemics in which he sought to demonstrate the
advantages of New Archaeology over traditional approaches, which
he identified primarily with the modified form of the Midwestern Taxonomic Method that had been practiced at the University
of Michigan when he was a graduate student there in the 1950s.
Binford attracted much support among young American archae-
ologists, including J. A. Brown, Geoff Clark, James Deetz, Kent
Flannery, James Hill, Frank Hole, Stephen LeBlanc, Mark Leone,
William Longacre, Fred Plog, William Rathje, Charles Redman, Sally
Schanfield (later Sally Binford), Michael Schiffer, Stuart Struever,
Patty Jo Watson, Fred Wendorf, Robert Whallon, and Howard
Winters. Many of these archaeologists had connections with the
University of Chicago, where Binford taught from 1961 to 1965,
and some had initiated substantial research projects before being
drawn into the New Archaeology movement. At least one senior
archaeologist, Paul Martin (1899–1974) (1971), rallied publicly to
Binford's support. Binford also significantly influenced the young
British archaeologist Colin Renfrew (1979, 1984). New Archaeology
marked its formal debut with a symposium organized by Lewis and
Sally Binford at the American Anthropological Association meeting
held at Denver in 1965 (S. and L. Binford 1968).

Binford and his supporters represented New Archaeology as a
radical break with the past and a new and clearly better way of
doing archaeology. The ensuing polarization made New Archaeology appear to be the antithesis of culture-historical archaeology, while ignoring the extent to which it was grounded in the
functionalist and processual trends that had been developing for a
long time in American and European archaeology. Although there

was considerable passive support for old-fashioned culture-historical archaeology, many who were stigmatized as being "traditional" archaeologists were adherents of functional-processual trends who merely objected to particular facets of Binford's program. The rapid adoption of New Archaeology was in part a result of predisposing tendencies already at work in the 1950s, although Binford's polemics diverted attention from the considerable consensus that already existed concerning the general direction in which American archaeology should evolve. It also was widely accepted that culture-historical archaeologists had substantially accomplished their goal of creating a prehistoric cultural chronology for the United States and it was now time to begin explaining the archaeological record.

Binford outlined the program of New Archaeology in two papers: "Archaeology as Anthropology" (1962) and "Archaeological Systematics and the Study of Culture Process" (1965). He formally identified the goal of archaeology as being the same as that of traditional American anthropology: to explain the full range of similarities and differences in cultural behavior. He proposed to achieve that goal by relating human behavior to functionally integrated cultural systems; a position that accorded with the reductionist equating of culture and behavior prevalent in American anthropology at that time. Binford also maintained that archaeological data were particularly useful for studying changes that occurred over long periods of time. Explanations were seen as taking the form of generalizations about systemic change and cultural evolution. As a student of Leslie White, Binford was predisposed to believe that there were strong regularities in human behavior and that because of this there was little difference between explaining a single instance of social change and a whole class of similar changes. Hence, his main concern was to account for cross-cultural similarities rather than differences. Binford has devoted much of his career to explaining general processes such as those accounting for patterns of variability in hunter-gatherer adaptation, the development of agriculture, and to a much more limited extent the evolution of civilizations (Binford 1968a, 1983b).

Binford viewed culture as humanity's extrasomatic means of adaptation. Changes in all aspects of cultural systems were therefore interpreted as adaptive responses to alterations in the natural environment, changes in population pressure, and competition with adjacent cultural systems. Binford described evolution as "a process operative at the interface of a living system and its field" (1972: 106). He believed that cultural changes came about as a result of human groups' responding rationally to the stresses produced by natural ecological changes. Because all aspects of culture could be understood in terms of their adaptive significance, it was not necessary to ascertain what specific groups of people had actually known or believed in order to understand change. Thus, culturally specific beliefs, cultural traditions, and idiosyncratic behavior need be of no interest to archaeologists. Binford assumed that prehistoric groups had possessed a nearly perfect knowledge of their environment and therefore were able to calculate the most rational ecological response to any problem. That meant that human beings could be analyzed in the same manner as any other part of the ecosystem. All changes were ultimately caused by ecological factors rather than by diffusion and migration, contrary to what culture-historical archaeologists had believed. This ruled out the need for an interest in cultural norms and traditions, which were construed merely as epiphenomenal facilitating devices that were reshaped by adaptational forces but did not themselves play a significant role in influencing change. Within the context of neoevolutionism, there was a growing tendency to believe in the capacity of human rationality to invent and reinvent new forms of technology, social behavior, beliefs, and values as these were required by evolving social systems. Steward (1955: 182) had already argued that every cultural borrowing might be treated as an "independent recurrence of cause and effect" and Marvin Harris (1968a: 377–8) had dismissed diffusion as a "nonprinciple."

The belief that Binford and other New Archaeologists held concerning the power of individual rationality to solve problems meant that they paid little attention to the cultural transmission of knowledge. Although they recognized that knowledge of adaptive innovations was transmitted intergenerationally, they believed that, if such transmissions failed, behavioral patterns could easily be reinvented. The study of interaction between societies also was never ruled out in principle. For example, Binford (1972: 204) strongly approved of Caldwell's (1964) concept of an "interaction sphere," which had been developed to explain how the Hopewellian burial cult, which involved the interment of goods manufactured from exotic materials with individuals of high status, came to be shared by many prehistoric societies in the American Midwest. Yet growing interest in the development of specific sociocultural systems and the neoevolutionary emphasis on independent invention led many followers of settlement archaeology and the New Archaeology to minimize the importance of intersocietal contact and competition. There also was no awareness that adaptive strategies might become better adapted as a result of long-term selective cultural transmission (Boyd and Richerson 1985). Binford likewise showed little interest in traditional archaeological cultures and cultural traditions, which he assumed were either arbitrary creations by culture-historical archaeologists or of no use for understanding adaptive behavior. Any phenomenon that could not be accounted for adaptationally was labeled stylistic and dismissed as inconsequential (Shennan 2002: 72). For Binford, the concept of culture signified primarily the different ways in which groups of human beings adapted to their environmental settings.

Neoevolutionary archaeology thus combined the unilinear perspective of nineteenth-century cultural evolutionists with Julian Steward's hypothesis that cultural change represented a response to altering ecological conditions. This hypothesis represented a major departure from the ideas of nineteenth-century unilinear evolutionary anthropologists. They had assumed, as Enlightenment philosophers had done in the previous century, that cultural change occurred as a result of human efforts to control nature more effectively. That view had already been challenged by Marxist evolutionists, who ascribed sociocultural change to different social classes struggling for control of political power and resources. Loss of faith in evolutionism in the late nineteenth century had been coupled with declining faith by intellectuals in human creativity. Neoevolutionary anthropologists, by believing that cultures changed only when ecological conditions compelled them to do so, continued to support the idea that humans were inherently conservative. That position protected them against charges that neoevolutionary anthropology was a form of Marxism during the period of Senator Joseph McCarthy's anticommunist witchhunts and their aftermath (Price 1993). Neoevolutionary archaeologists propagated the idea that changes in all parts of a cultural system were brought about by ecological, not social, factors. They continued to believe that evolution from hunting-gathering to modern industrial societies was a progressive and liberating process, even if they now thought that it shaped human behavior rather than came about as a result of human agency. The development of capitalism from an early entrepreneurial stage, when individual initiative was highly valued, into a corporate phase, dominated by large, bureaucratically managed companies within which the individual was no longer idealized as responsible for bringing about economic growth, may have made the concept of ecological determinism more acceptable.

Like Caldwell, Binford stressed the internal differentiation and systemic integration of cultures. He objected to the established normative view of archaeologists who regarded cultures as collections of ideas held in common by the members of particular social groups. Like Caldwell, Binford also objected to each item of culture being regarded as equal in significance to all others and to the percentage of similarities and differences in artifact traits being treated as a measurement of the amount of effective communication between groups. He maintained that traditionally archaeologists had interpreted differences between cultures as resulting from geographical barriers or resistant value systems, which prevented ideas being spread from one culture to another by diffusion and migration. Although this description may have represented accurately the views about cultures held by culture-historical archaeologists working in the midwestern United States or even those of Walter Taylor, it did not take account of the views of a growing number of functionally oriented archaeologists in the United States or of Grahame Clark and Gordon Childe in Britain. As early as 1925, Childe had employed a functional view of culture to facilitate his culture-historical analyses when he distinguished between ethnic traits, which did not diffuse readily, and technological ones, which did.

Binford argued that cultures were not internally homogeneous. All were differentiated at least according to age and sex roles, and the degree to which they were internally shared by individuals varied inversely with their overall complexity. Individuals always participated in cultures differentially, making a total cultural system a set of functionally interrelated roles. Because of this, it was wrong for archaeologists to treat artifact types as equal and comparable traits. Instead, they must try to determine the roles that artifacts had played within living cultural systems. This necessitated an effort to achieve a relatively holistic view of these systems.

At this point, Binford could have opted, as Willey (1953), Childe (1958a), and various settlement archaeologists had done, largely to ignore the concept of culture and focus on reconstructing social systems. Such an approach would have concentrated on delineating patterns of human interaction and determining the functional relations of cultural traits to social systems. Instead, Binford followed White in viewing cultures as adaptive systems composed of three interrelated subsystems: technology, social organization, and ideology. Thus, he supported the view that human behavior was determined by forces of which human beings are largely unaware and that frequently are located in the natural realm. Because Binford believed that changes occurred mainly as a result of interactions between cultures and their natural environments, he also focused almost exclusively on what was happening in single communities or sociocultural systems. In that respect, his outlook was similar to that of many American settlement pattern archeologists who did not identify with New Archaeology.

Binford argued that material items do not interact within a single subsystem of culture but reflect all three subsystems. Technomic aspects of artifacts reflect how they were used to cope with the environment; sociotechnic ones had their primary context in the social system; and ideotechnic ones related to the ideological realm. In 1962, he suggested that each type of artifact might be interpreted as relating primarily to one of these subsystems, but by 1965 he noted that individual artifacts frequently encoded information about all three. A knife might be used for cutting, but its gold handle could denote the upper-class social status of its owner and a symbol engraved on the blade might invoke divine protection for him.

Binford went further than either Clark or Taylor had done in arguing that, because artifacts have primary contexts in all subsystems of culture, formal artifact assemblages and their contexts can yield a systematic and understandable picture of total extinct cultures. He maintained that the first task of archaeologists was to determine what roles artifacts had played in cultural systems. The second task was to reconstruct cultures as functionally operational systems. He repudiated the idea that it was inherently more difficult to reconstruct social organization or religious activities than it was to infer economic behavior. The idea that archaeologists could study any problem that ethnologists could, and over much longer periods of time, attracted support from many young archaeologists who were frustrated by the artifact-centered culture-historical approach that continued to pervade American archaeology in the early 1960s. They were anxious to demonstrate that ethnologists were wrong when they smugly proclaimed that archaeology was "doomed always to be the lesser part of anthropology" (Hoebel 1949: 436).

Binford observed that archaeologists had already made significant progress in using knowledge derived from the physical and biological sciences to interpret those aspects of the archaeological record relating to technomic behavior, especially subsistence patterns and technological practices. By contrast, anthropologists did not know enough about correlations between social behavior or beliefs and material culture to infer much sociotechnic or ideotechnic information from archaeological finds. Only after such correlations had been established and archaeologists had acquired a holistic knowledge of the structural and functional characteristics of cultural systems could they begin to investigate problems of evolutionary changes in social systems and ideology.

Binford argued that in order to establish such correlations archaeologists must be trained as ethnologists. Only by studying living situations in which behavior and ideas could be observed in conjunction with material culture was it possible to establish correlations that could be used to infer social behavior and ideology reliably from the archaeological record. Binford saw ethnoarchaeology, or the study by archaeologists of regularities in living cultures, as a promising approach to understanding the past because, as a neoevolutionist, he believed that there was a high degree of regularity in human behavior which comparative ethnographic studies could reveal. These regularities could then be used to infer many behavioral aspects of prehistoric cultures. If human behavior were less regular than he assumed, such correlations would be fewer in number and less useful for reconstructing prehistoric cultures and understanding change.

Among Binford's principal original contributions was his insistence that the correlations used to infer human behavior from archaeological data had to be based on the demonstration of a constant articulation of specific variables in a system. He argued that all analogies were inconclusive, whether they were based on worldwide evidence or were homologies drawn from the same cultural tradition as the archaeological data being interpreted. Instead, all behavioral explanations of archaeological material had to be based on a lawful demonstration that in the living (actual) world there was a constant correlation between a particular form of human behavior and a specific type of material culture. Only if a particular behavioral trait could be shown always to correlate with a specific item of material culture, wherever both could be observed, could such behavior be inferred from the occurrence of that item in the archaeological record. This positivist epistemology in turn necessitated a deductive approach in which relations between variables that are archaeologically observable and ones that are not were formulated and tested in a statistically significant number of ethnographic situations in which both variables could be observed. Only by means of such measurement of concomitant variation could regularities be established that were useful for understanding prehistoric cultural systems. Binford (1972: 33–51) insisted that analogies were not explanations but merely a source of hypotheses to be tested in this manner.

Thus, an implicit test of Binford's most fundamental assumption about the nature of culture was built into New Archaeology. If, as Binford assumed, there was a high degree of regularity in human behavior and this was reflected in material culture, ethnoarchaeology should quickly provide the generalizations needed to infer a broad range of human behavior from archaeological evidence. Under these conditions, further ethnoarchaeological evidence would soon become unnecessary and archaeologists could proceed with the still more challenging and rewarding task of explaining human behavior. If human behavior was less cross-culturally uniform than Binford and other neoevolutionists assumed, ethnoarchaeology would not produce the broad range of generalizations that Binford expected.

Binford championed the already challenged positivist view that explanation and prediction are equivalent and that both rest upon the demonstration of a constant articulation of variables. The rigorous application of a positivist approach was seen as eliminating subjective elements and establishing a basis for the objective, scientific interpretation of archaeological data. To achieve this level of rigor, however, archaeologists had to adhere to deductive canons which utilized well-established correlations, as outlined by the philosopher Carl Hempel (1942, 1962, 1965, 1966; Hempel and Oppenheim 1948) in his covering-law model of explanation. Binford also maintained that a single way of doing science, exemplified in its most rigorous form by the work of physicists, constituted the model for carrying out all archaeological enquiries. From that perspective, the only useful correlations are those that hold true whenever specific conditions are present. The application of the covering-law method to the explanation of cultural change tended to exclude consideration of all but situations of notable regularity.

This epistemology required Binford and his followers to repudiate historical studies, which they equated with an unscientific preoccupation with chronology, description, and accidental occurrences (Binford 1967b: 235, 1968b). This viewpoint had been introduced to American archaeologists by the ethnologist Clyde Kluckhohn (1905–1960) (1940), when he argued that Mesoamerican archaeologists had to abandon an exclusive commitment to historical studies, which sought to recreate unique events in all their idiosyncratic detail; instead, they should embrace scientific research by seeking to identify and explain significant cross-cultural uniformities in cultural change. A dichotomy between history and science, which paralleled the distinction that American anthropologists drew between history and evolution, was reinforced by Walter Taylor (1948: 156–7) and Willey and Phillips (1958: 5–6), who regarded culture-historical integration as an objective that was inferior to formulating general rules of cultural behavior. Binford viewed archaeologists' efforts to explain particular historical events as an inductive practice that would doom archaeology to remain a particularistic, nongeneralizing, and hence unscientific field. He argued that instead archaeologists must seek to formulate laws of cultural dynamics. Although in historical retrospect this position can be seen as reflecting the belief that human history is governed by strong regularities, it deflected archaeological interest from significant aspects of cultural change that do not display such regularities. Today, most philosophers of science do not support such a distinction between history and science (Bunge 2003).

Binford also denied the relevance of psychological factors for understanding prehistory. He identified their use with Boasian epistemological idealism and the culture-historical approach and argued that they had no explanatory value for ecological interpretations of culture and cultural change. On the contrary, within an ecological framework specific psychological factors could be viewed as an epiphenomenal aspect of human behavior that was shaped by ecological adaptation. He also argued that archaeologists were poorly trained to function as palaeopsychologists (Binford 1972: 198). This view corresponded with a more general repudiation of Boasian psychological anthropology in the United States and the growing influence of behaviorism, which rejected beliefs and feelings as objects of scientific enquiry.

New archaeologists also advocated the use of sampling strategies to guide both surveys and excavations and economize on the time and labor needed to carry out research. Underlying this advocacy was their belief that, because strong regularities were inherent in cultural systems, a small part of a system could be representative of the whole. Now, however, it was no longer a single site, but some portion of a site network that was thought to be typical of the entire system. Various forms of sampling also were used to try to recover a more representative selection of the material to be found in large heterogeneous sites. Yet random intrasite sampling came to be seen as an initial excavation strategy that had to be supplemented in the later stages of research by an increasing number of informed decisions about what areas should be excavated (Redman 1986).

Studies of early civilizations based on total regional surveys provided the data to allow examination of the representativeness of various sampling strategies. Sanders, Parsons, and Santley's (1979: 491–532) survey of the Valley of Mexico revealed marked diversity in local patterns of development and therefore the need to study the entire region in order to understand what was happening in its various parts. For example, the massive increase in population and growth of urbanism in the Teotihuacán Valley early in the Christian era could only be understood properly once it was realized that similar population growth was not occurring elsewhere in the Valley of Mexico, but on the contrary the population of those areas was declining at that time. Robert Adams (1981) has shown similar local diversity in his studies of Mesopotamian settlement patterns. These findings have severely challenged the belief that patterns from one area are necessarily representative of a whole region (Fish and Kowalewski 1990). Similar diversity also was demonstrated within communities (Bellhouse and Finlayson 1979). As a result, it was gradually recognized that much larger samples than had hitherto been thought necessary were required before they became representative of a whole and that the study of changes over long periods required something approaching total samples.

The earliest publications of New Archaeology sought to apply Binford's ideas concerning the adaptive nature of culture and to demonstrate the value of a deductive covering-law approach. In 1966,

Lewis and Sally Binford published "A Preliminary Analysis of Functional Variability in the Mousterian of the Levallois Facies." Before that time, Sally Binford had demonstrated that the four assemblages into which Bordes had divided the Mousterian material from France were intermingled over a vast area of Europe and the Middle East and, hence, were unlikely to be cultures as Bordes had suggested. Lewis and Sally Binford divided each assemblage into groups of tool types that they assumed had been used to perform different tasks. They concluded that the varying percentages of these toolkits at different sites and in different layers within sites suggested that Bordes's assemblages were associated with the performance of different tasks rather than with different groups of Neanderthals. Although the ensuing controversy with Bordes (1972) attracted widespread interest and epitomized the confrontation between culture-historical and New Archaeology, critics complained that the Binfords' propositions about toolkits had not been tested by use-wear analysis nor by the examination of accompanying plant and animal residues.

Other important early applications of New Archaeology involved attempts to use ceramics to infer the residence patterns of prehistoric communities. "Ceramic sociologists" assumed that, if women manufactured the pottery used by their families, specific design elements would tend to cluster where knowledge of pottery making was transmitted from mothers to daughters in matrilocal societies but would become randomized in patrilocal societies, in which female potters from different lineages would have lived and worked adjacent to one another and hence copied aspects of each other's work. Evidence of matrilineages would emerge in the form of different design combinations showing up in different parts of sites (Hill 1968, 1970) (Figure 8.1) or, where pottery from the different parts of a site became mixed in the course of disposal, in nonrandom associations of design elements on the pottery from the whole site (Longacre 1968, 1970). J. N. Hill, W. A. Longacre, and James Deetz (1965) had begun their research separately from Binford, the first two grounding their studies on still earlier work by Constance Cronin (1962), while Whallon's (1968) work was inspired by that of Deetz (O'Brien et al. 2005: 67–75). The sex of potters was determined by applying the direct historical approach rather than by means of forensic evidence, such as Tret'yakov had used in the 1930s. The same patterns also could have been produced had men made pottery and the residence pattern been

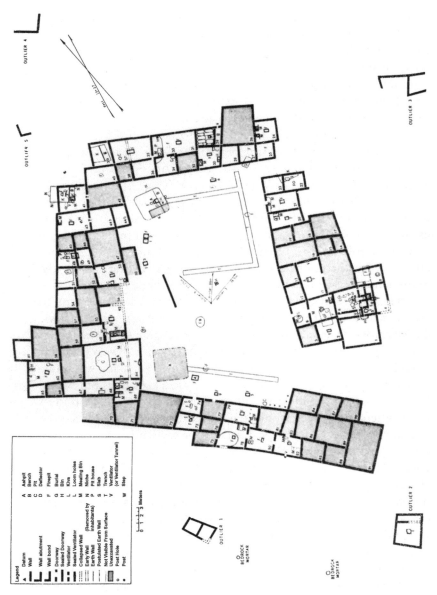

Figure 8.1 Sampling at Broken K Pueblo, J. N. Hill, 1968; shaded rooms were not excavated (J. N. Hill in S. R. and L. R. Binford, *New Perspectives in Archeology*, 1968)

patrilocal. In these early studies of ceramic sociology, the alternative possibilities that pottery was made by a smaller number of professional potters or that it might have been traded over long distances were not examined, nor were the conditions under which broken pottery had been discarded (S. Plog 1980). These pioneering efforts by American archaeologists to infer social organization from archaeological evidence therefore did not reach the high standards Binford had set for such work.

Somewhat later, efforts were made to infer social stratification from variations in the burials associated with different cultures. It was postulated that patterned segregation of bodies or variations in the size of tombs, the quantity and elaborateness of grave goods, and the treatment of dead children might provide information about the nature and extent of status differentiation in prehistoric societies. Underlying these studies was the more general assumption that variations in burials would directly reflect social organization (Saxe 1970; Binford 1971; J. Brown 1971; O'Shea 1984). The analysis of burials gradually became as important a focus of theoretical discourse among archaeologists as the study of kinship had once been for sociocultural anthropologists (Parker Pearson 1999).

New Archaeology encouraged the proliferation of ethnoarchaeological research, which sought to establish correlations between human behavior and material culture by studying living cultures. Important examples of such research were W. A. Longacre's studies of pottery making and use among the Kalinga of the Philippines (Longacre and Skibo 1994) and Patty Jo Watson's (1979) examination of community organization in western Iran. The most celebrated project was Lewis Binford's (1977, 1978) study of settlement and subsistence among the Nunamiut Eskimos of Alaska between 1969 and 1973, which he says he initiated in order to gain deeper insights into the behavioral significance of the Mousterian assemblages of western Europe (Binford 1983b: 100–4). Although the Nunamiut hunted with guns and participated in the international fur trade, they were investigated as an example of a traditional hunter-gatherer culture. Binford recorded how hunting practices and camp life patterned the entry of material remains into the archaeological record (Figure 8.2). He sought to establish what the remains of kill sites and main residential camps looked like, what archaeological evidence household groups left behind, and what sleeping areas looked like.

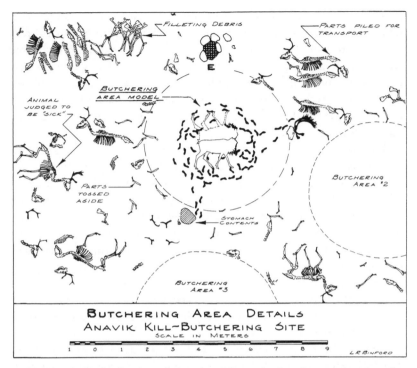

Figure 8.2   Binford's plan of a modern Nunamiut butchery area at Anavik
Springs, Alaska, showing where caribou were dismembered and waste
products were disposed (*In Pursuit of the Past*, 1983)

Binford (1983b) later applied what he had learned about the economy and spatial behavior of the Nunamiut and other modern hunter-
gatherer societies to a series of problems relating to Old World Palaeolithic sites.

In addition to gathering data ethnoarchaeologically, Binford produced a number of cross-cultural studies using ethnographic data
collected from many living societies in an effort to establish universal generalizations about the behavioral implications of hunter-
gatherer site distributions (1980, 2001) and burial practices (1971).
These studies demonstrate that, although ethnoarchaeologists collect data that are useful for generalizing about human behavior, systematic cross-cultural studies are necessary to generalize about the
relations between material culture and human behavior. Contrary

to expectations, when correlations could be established, they more often took the form of trends, tendencies, and tilts than of absolute correspondences.

Some critics argued that New Archaeology represented a revolution in the technical and methodological spheres rather than in archaeological theory (Meltzer 1979). Yet the stand that Binford took against the still influential culture-historical approach in the United States was no less a break with that past in terms of high-level theory than it was methodologically. Historical questions that must be answered are why did his approach appeal so powerfully to a rising generation of American archaeologists and why was Binford able so quickly to popularize views that until then had been spreading only slowly through American archaeology.

The nomothetic or generalizing orientation of New Archaeology strongly appealed to the deeply engrained tendency of Americans to value what was useful. Their contempt for what was not practical manifested itself in the low respect they accorded to historical studies generally (Bronowski 1971: 195), an opinion epitomized by the industrialist Henry Ford's remark that "History is ... bunk" (Lowenthal 1985: 244). The low value accorded to history also reflected the "present-mindedness" of American society, which romantically viewed itself as having prospered by throwing off the shackles of the past, as represented by claims of class, tradition, and hereditary descent, and creating a new society rationally designed to serve the interests of enterprising people (Kroker 1984: 8). The culture-historical approach reduced prehistoric archaeology's prestige and led to its being regarded by the American public and by cultural anthropologists as a dilettantish pursuit.

New Archaeology followed the lead of the generalizing social sciences, such as economics, political science, sociology, and ethnology by claiming to be able to produce objective, ethically neutral generalizations that were useful for the management of modern societies. This desire to conform to a more prestigious model of scholarly behavior was reinforced as the National Science Foundation emerged as a major source of funding for archaeological research and the era of major dam building and government-funded salvage archaeology along the Missouri, Colorado, and other rivers came to an end in the 1950s (Braidwood 1981: 24–5; Kehoe 1998: 126). Such funding had freed archaeologists from dependence on museums and having to discover exhibitable material and allowed them to dig sites in order to learn about how people had behaved in the past. New archaeologists argued that archaeology could provide information about the nature of long-term interactions between human groups and the environment that would be of value for modern economic and social planning (Fritz 1973), a view shared by some archaeologists who rejected the general philosophy and methodology of New Archaeology (Dymond 1974). It was believed that the detailed study of prehistoric irrigation systems in Arizona might reveal unsuspected long-term problems associated with modern irrigation systems in the same area and stratified archaeological sites in California were looked to for information about the frequency of major earthquakes that could help to decide whether or not it was safe to install atomic-energy generators nearby (F. Plog 1982). These suggestions are reminiscent of the practical applications that were used to justify Soviet archaeology in the 1930s and later by Childe (1944b) as a practical reason for public support of archaeological research. On a more ambitious scale, in *The Archaeology of Arizona* Paul Martin and Fred Plog (1973: 364–8) argued that generalizations about human reactions to stress derived from ecological studies of prehistoric Arizona might help to explain the behavior of underprivileged black and hispanic groups living in the ghettos of modern American cities.

An emphasis on the possible practical applications of their research encouraged social scientists to abandon holistic attempts to understand human behavior and instead to seek solutions to problems conceived of in narrow technical terms (Wolf 1982: ix). Such research was endowed with further scientific credentials by positivist claims of ethical neutrality. To produce "relevant" findings that would justify an honored place for archaeology in a society in which "technocratic efficiency is considered as the supreme value" (Kolakowski 1976: 229), many American archaeologists saw themselves having to turn away from seeking a historical understanding of the past to create the generalizations about human behavior that were now the hallmark of successful social scientists. It is within this context that we must understand Binford's (1967b: 235) assertion that historical interpretation was unsuited to play more than a "role in the general education of the public." He was not the first archaeologist to promote the idea that behavioral generalizations were to be regarded as archaeology's supreme achievement. Kidder (1935: 14) had maintained that the ultimate goal of archaeological research should be to establish generalizations about human behavior, while Taylor (1948: 151) and Willey and Phillips (1958: 5–6) also had seen such generalizations as constituting a common anthropological focus for both archaeological and ethnological research.

The antihistorical bias of the New Archaeology can also be viewed as an ideological reflection of the increasing economic and political intervention of the United States on a global scale after World War II. Its preoccupation with nomothetic generalizations implied that the study of any national tradition as an end in itself was of trivial importance. Richard Ford (1973) questioned the legitimacy of "political archaeology" and of any connection between archaeology and nationalism, urging archaeologists instead to embrace a "universal humanism." This was different from Grahame Clark's advocacy of a world prehistory to balance the impact of studying the past from a national point of view. By denying that local or regional studies were worthwhile for their own sakes, New Archaeologists both wittingly and unwittingly cast doubt on the importance of national traditions and anything else that stood in the way of American economic activity and political influence in foreign countries. The corrosive effects of similar arguments in other fields on the national cultures of neighboring Western countries have been well documented for this period (G. Grant 1965; Lord 1974: 198–215; Fuller 1980: 114–15). Although most New Archaeologists may not have been conscious agents in the promotion of the economic and cultural hegemony of the United States, their antihistorical program accorded with that policy.

The most striking impact of this antihistorical viewpoint was exhibited in relation to indigenous North American history. It unintentionally cut in two opposed directions. By making the explanation of internal changes central to its interpretation of archaeological data, New Archaeology stressed the creativity of indigenous North Americans to a much greater extent than diffusionist explanations had done and for the first time placed these people on an equal footing in this respect with Europeans and other ethnic groups. Only amateur or ideologically driven archaeologists who continued to work purely in the culture-historical tradition, such as Barry Fell (1976, 1982), R. A. Jairazbhoy (1974, 1976), and Irvan Van Sertima (1977), continued to belittle indigenous peoples by attributing major elements of their cultural heritage to prehistoric visitors from the Old World.

New Archaeology thus implicitly ended over a century of condescending and often overtly racist interpretations of indigenous prehistory by white archaeologists. Yet, from the beginning processual archaeologists ignored the significance of their own achievements as a result of their insistence that generalizations, not history, were the principal goal of their discipline and their focusing on ecological adaptation at the expense of historically specific aspects of indigenous cultures, such as their artistic traditions and religious beliefs. As Kent Flannery (1967: 120) observed, the processual theorist was not "ultimately concerned with 'the Indian behind the artifact,' but rather with the system behind both the Indian and the artifact."

The theories of change that were first associated with neoevolutionary archaeology were rudimentary and contradictory. Steward and Binford interpreted cultural change as adaptation to ecological change. This approach assumed that human groups were able to devise nearly optimal adjustments to ecological change and that they gained increasing control over nature as technologies and social organization grew more complex. Hence, even if human groups were seen as changing in response to outside factors, the long-term results still were believed to benefit humanity. In the 1970s, neoevolutionary theories of change underwent a major transformation that challenged this optimistic view.

Since the late 1950s, the optimism and security of the middle classes in the United States had been seriously eroded by a succession of deepening economic crises that were exacerbated by repeated failures of foreign policy, especially in Vietnam. These events produced a marked decline of faith in the benefits to be derived from technological development. This uncertainty in turn spawned a proliferation of middle-class protest movements. Although these movements consistently avoided addressing directly the crucial economic and political problems of American society, they profoundly altered social values and influenced the social sciences.

The first of these was the ecology movement, which viewed unrestrained technological development as poisoning and gradually destroying the world's ecosystem. Its beginnings were signaled by the publication of Rachel Carson's *Silent Spring* (1962). This movement went on to promote awareness of an immediate danger to public health from a broad array of technological processes and warned that in the long term even greater catastrophes might result from the continuing pollution of the environment. The second movement, to promote a conserver society, stressed that certain resources essential for industrial processes are available only in finite quantities in nature and hence the world was rapidly reaching a point where further industrial expansion might become impossible. It was predicted that the exhaustion of key resources would result in declining living standards, or even the collapse of civilization. Hitherto, it had generally been assumed that new raw materials or sources of energy would be found before old ones became depleted. Paul Ehrlich's *The Population Bomb* (1968) drew attention to yet another cause for anxiety. He argued that, if unprecedented population growth were not checked, the results would be disastrous in the near future.

As a result of these movements, social scientists and the general public became increasingly sceptical about the benefits of technological progress. As their political and economic insecurity increased, they, like the late-nineteenth-century European middle classes, came to view cultural evolution as a source of danger and perhaps ultimately of disaster. Even rapid cultural change was condemned for producing dysfunctional "future shock" (Toffler 1970). These shifting attitudes laid the groundwork for a conceptual reorientation of archaeology that marked yet another retreat from the optimistic view of change formulated during the Enlightenment. They also intensified neoevolutionists' rejection of the belief that technological innovation was the result of a process of rational self-improvement and the driving force promoting cultural change. Two specific developments, one in economics and the other in social anthropology, served as a catalyst for this shift.

The economist Ester Boserup (1965) had argued that, although increasingly intensive modes of agriculture yielded more food per unit of land, they required more labor for each unit of food produced. Therefore, only the necessity to support slowly but inevitably increasing population densities would have led groups to adopt such systems. Her thesis was construed as evidence that developments which previous generations of archaeologists had interpreted as desirable results of humanity's ability to solve problems and make life easier and more fulfilling were in fact responses to forces beyond human control. Throughout history these forces had compelled most people to work harder, suffer increasing exploitation, and degrade their environments (M. Cohen 1977).

The demonstration by Richard Lee and Irven DeVore (1968) that hunter-gatherer economies could support a low population density with less effort than was required by even the least demanding forms of food production not only was interpreted as support for Boserup's position but also led archaeologists to adopt radically new interpretations of prehistoric big-game hunting societies. Instead of being viewed as living on the brink of starvation, they were portrayed as leisured groups with plenty of spare time to devote to religious and intellectual pursuits. Even relatively conservative archaeologists began to idealize the more egalitarian prehistoric cultures as examples of "conserving societies" that provided models of how we ourselves should behave in relation to the environment (Cunliffe 1974: 27). Some archaeologists questioned the evidence on which these formulations were based and their general applicability (Bronson 1972; Cowgill 1975; M. Harris 1968a: 87–8; Kelly 1995). Yet the rapid and relatively unchallenged way in which these studies came to influence the interpretation of archaeological data, often in the absence of reliable measures of prehistoric population size or even of relative population change, suggests the degree to which they accorded with the spirit of the time.

These new ideas about the nature of cultural change promoted the development of a pessimistic and even tragic version of cultural evolution that interpreted demographic, ecological, and economic factors as constraining change to occur along lines that most human beings did not regard as desirable but that they were unable to control. This eschatological materialism implied that the future was likely to be worse than the present and that humanity was journeying from a primitive Eden filled with happy hunter-gatherers to a hell of ecological collapse or nuclear annihilation. Instead of denying that there was any necessary order to human history, as diffusionists had done in the late nineteenth century, cataclysmic evolutionists stressed a fixed trajectory of change that at best human beings might hope to slow or halt, but which otherwise would result in their certain ruin (Trigger 1981a). Only a few evolutionary archaeologists continued to argue that it was possible to learn from the past how to "adjust and cope" (J. Bradley 1987: 7).

In response to these new ideas, archaeologists also began to express reservations about conventional neoevolutionary theories that analyzed change as if it occurred in slow, gradual trajectories of the sort that Braidwood and MacNeish had documented in their studies of the development of agriculture in the Middle East and Mesoamerica. Robert Adams (1974: 248–9) pointed out that there had been abrupt shifts in the development of early civilizations, sometimes separated by long periods when relatively few changes occurred. Other archaeologists sought to imbue the concept of discontinuous cultural change with additional scientific prestige by drawing parallels between it and the punctuated equilibrium being promoted by some evolutionary biologists (S. Gould 1980; Eldredge 1982). Soon after, Colin Renfrew (1978a; Renfrew and Cooke 1979) attempted to use catastrophe theory, which had been invented by the French mathematician René Thom, to explain changes in the archaeological record. Catastrophe theory demonstrated how, as the result of particular conjunctions of internal states, a set of up to four fluctuating variables could produce discontinuous effects (Saunders 1980). Although both Thom and Renfrew were interested in a "catastrophe theory" that permitted the understanding of the development of more complex as well as simpler societies, the popular view of catastrophe theory as an analysis of social disintegration reflected widespread fears that Western societies might be sliding toward catastrophe in the conventional sense. Archaeologists began to examine specific examples of the collapse of complex societies (Culbert 1973; Yoffee and Cowgill 1988), while Joseph Tainter (1988) in a generalizing study attributed the collapse of such societies to the unchecked growth of increasingly expensive bureaucratic structures.

These views of cultural change made archaeologists more aware of the need to identify varying rates of change as well as gaps produced by sociopolitical collapse in the archaeological record. It became obvious that, despite the large numbers of "vanished societies" that had been identified in the archaeological record, archaeologists had failed to recognize the need to explain their collapse as a general problem. Even the collapse of individual societies had rarely been studied in any detail by nineteenth-century evolutionists or early-twentieth-century culture-historians. Gaps also were recognized in the archaeological record that in the past would have been filled by projecting known cultures backward and forward in time to close them or by hypothesizing the existence of as yet undiscovered intermediary forms. These discoveries challenged archaeologists to acquire tighter control over cultural chronologies. A growing concern with collapse also reinforced the belief that cultural systems are more fragile and cultural change more fraught with danger than archaeologists had hitherto believed.

Cataclysmic evolutionism, whatever its intrinsic merits as a theory of change, encouraged archaeologists to look for evidence of population pressure, environmental degradation, and the collapse of social systems in the archaeological record. This stimulated the study of ecological degradation and ecological catastrophes in the past as well as of societal collapse brought about by political and economic mismanagement. The investigation of such processes resulted in a more rounded understanding of the archaeological record.

As the ethnoarchaeological search for correlations between human behavior and material culture, especially at the social and ideological level, proved less productive than had been anticipated, Binford (1977, 1978) sought to clarify the relations between archaeology and ethnology by reconceptualizing the frames of reference for offering behavioral interpretations of archaeological data. This resulted in the development of middle-range theory, which, unlike Binford's earlier, more narrowly focused searches for correlations between specific types of artifacts and human behavior, involved seeking to establish the spatial, temporal, and formal correlates of specific forms of human behavior and their material expressions in the ethnographic record and to identify similar residues in archaeological contexts (Binford and Sabloff 1982; Binford 1987b; O'Brien et al. 2005: 209–10). To use ethnographic findings for such purposes, Binford believed that it was necessary to establish constant and unique causal relations between processes and their results.

Although multiple case studies are necessary to establish such contexts, this approach lessened the need for broad cross-cultural studies. Formulating middle-range theory utilized not only the results of ethnoarchaeological research and of cross-cultural studies using ethnographic data but also the findings of other forms of actualistic studies, such as use-wear analysis, experimental archaeology, and taphonomy (Tringham 1978). Middle-range theory embraced acts of identification, such as distinguishing different classes of habitations or base camps, as well as diagnosing the economic, social, and ideological functions of artifacts. It also involved identifying patterns of human behavior as these might relate to subsistence activities, family organization, community structure, and political relations.

In addition, middle-range theory also subsumed the investigation of cultural and natural site-formation processes, thereby embracing the study of regularities in physical processes as well as in cultural behavior.

Subsequently, some of Binford's (1984) most important archaeological research involved using a combination of taphonomic evidence and arguments about natural site-formation processes to challenge the hominid origin of many of the patterns observed in the archaeological record for Lower Palaeolithic times. He showed that data that often had been interpreted as evidence of big-game hunting or even scavenging at that time could be merely natural distributions of animal bones coincidentally associated with traces of human activity. Binford also questioned the evidence for cannibalism and possibly the use of fire in the Lower Palaeolithic levels at Zhoukoudian. His research thus cast doubt on some long-standing interpretations of early hominid behavior (Binford 1981, 1984; Binford and Stone 1986). Binford demonstrated that, because of their support for particular theories about hominid behavior, archaeologists frequently failed to consider possible alternatives or to analyze data sufficiently thoroughly.

Growing emphasis on middle-range research as well as better understanding of the contexts of finds encouraged a greater awareness of the differences between the data base of ethnology, which includes direct observation of human behavior as well as of material culture, and of prehistoric archaeology, which is limited to the observation of material culture. Archaeologists also distinguished more clearly between general theory, which seeks to explain human behavior, and middle-range theory, which is concerned with inferring such behavior from archaeological data. Middle-range theory was of interest only to archaeologists, whereas general theory was of concern to all social scientists. A growing awareness of the difference between archaeology and the other social sciences led many archaeologists to question whether the ultimate goal of archaeology really should be to become anthropology and to what extent that goal, even if desirable, was possible. The distinguishing of middle-range and high-level theory had its roots in Irving Rouse's (1972) differentiation of analytical and synthetic interpretations of archaeological data, Carl-Axel Moberg's (1976) distinction between archaeography and archaeology proper, and Leo Klejn's (1977) argument that archaeological data must be understood in their own right before they can be used to address historical problems.

Binford noted that employing present regularities to explain the past involved uniformitarian assumptions and argued that these claims must be warranted by supporting arguments. He suggested, for example, that the behavioral and anatomical characteristics of still extant animal species that ancient human beings exploited are "enduring objects for which uniformitarian assumptions might be securely warranted" (Binford 1981: 28) and expressed the hope that other domains could be elaborated as research progressed. Other archaeologists saw these uniformitarian assumptions as involving a great leap of faith (P. J. Watson 1986: 447–8).

Uniformitarian assumptions have their problems. One of the most insidious and uncontrollable of these is ignorance of what is happening at the present time. Scientists may misunderstand the past because they fail to take account of slow, long-term processes, as was the case with geology before the recognition of plate tectonics and continental drift (Marvin 1973). Social scientists also may consider to be universal, characteristics of human behavior that are specific to a particular stage of cultural development. Marxists, who believe that human nature is substantially altered by social evolutionary change, are less willing to invoke universal features of human behavior than are most archaeologists who assume, along with the philosophers of the Enlightenment, that human nature remains unaltered by social change. Binford does not take account of possible effects of the modern world system on ethnographic analogies. This has suggested to other archaeologists that the degree of similarity between modern hunter-gatherer societies and Palaeolithic ones is a question for archaeologists to investigate, not something for which an answer can be assumed.

Problems also can arise in applying analogies because archaeologists have great difficulty differentiating between what is characteristic of humanity in general (or of societies sharing a particular mode of production) and what is specific only to historically related cultures. Anthropologists remain unable to distinguish on theoretical grounds between analogies and homologies. Instead, they must do so empirically, using historical and archaeological evidence. The sheer variety of forces bringing about social change also complicates the question of what modern societies can provide in the way of useful analogies of prehistoric ones. Although Binford (1980, 2001) established that the settlement patterns of hunter-gatherers in high latitudes shared many features that distinguished them from hunter-gatherer patterns in warmer climates, all these northern societies were engaged in trapping and selling furs to Europeans long before they were studied by anthropologists. We still do not know whether the common features Binford described represent an ecological adaptation extending back thousands of years or had developed in recent centuries as a consequence of new economic relations. In this case, archaeological data about prehistoric settlement patterns are essential to provide insights into the developmental significance of modern hunter-gatherer behavioral patterns and produce convincing warranting arguments. Yet, despite such cautionary tales, the total rejection of uniformitarianism would have far worse consequences for the development of archaeology than its continuing cautious and self-questioning use.

An even more important limitation appears to be that human behavior in general is considerably less uniform than Binford, as a neoevolutionist, continues to believe. Although Binford has been highly critical of assumptions that the behavioral patterns of early hominids resembled those of modern hunter-gatherers, in work dealing with more recent times his neoevolutionary faith in strong regularities governing human behavior leads him to minimize the difficulties involved in interpreting archaeological data. This is evident in his studies of hunter-gatherer use of camp space and hunting territories. Much more empirical ethnographic documentation is needed before archaeologists can agree with his assertion that all hunter-gatherers use their camp space in much the same way, producing easily recognizable features such as bedding areas, drop zones, toss zones, and aggregate dumping areas, and proceed to interpret all upper Palaeolithic archaeological sites in terms of models derived from the San, or Bushmen, and the Nunamiut (Binford 1983b: 144–92) (Figure 8.3). Generally speaking, human behavior is not so regular that convincing generalizations about spatial behavior can be based on only two or three ethnographic case studies, even if these are very detailed ones and plausible causal relations can be established that account for what is observed. Although the use of camp space may eventually be proved to be relatively uniform, there are many aspects of human behavior that cannot be accounted for in terms of universal

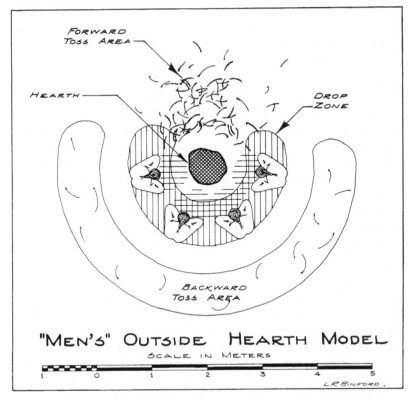

Figure 8.3 Model of drop and toss zones, as developed by L. R. Binford
from his ethnoarchaeological study of the Nunamiut of Alaska
(*In Pursuit of the Past*, 1983b)

generalizations, whether these concern behavior in general or societies at specific levels of development (Watson et al. 1984: 264).

The Diversification of Processual Archaeology

Despite Binford's key role in systematizing New Archaeology, almost from the beginning his followers disagreed about the causes of cultural change and the degree to which human behavior was shaped by these factors. They also disagreed about the key tenets of processual archaeology, as New Archaeology gradually came to be called (Kushner 1970). At first, these differences were regarded as disputes about the way processual archaeology should develop but, as differing opinions multiplied and became more entrenched, competing approaches emerged. Despite early efforts to maintain a common front, processual archaeology was never a frozen creed but a diverse and dynamic movement.

Ecological studies of change continued to be very important, although unicausal theories, such as those that attributed the origins of civilization to the development of complex irrigation systems (Wittfogel 1957), were soon abandoned. So, too, was Stuart Struever's (1968) contention that the means by which a population derived its subsistence from the environment played such an important role in shaping the entire cultural system that the nature of settlement patterns could be predicted and hence explained in terms of technology and the natural environment. Struever viewed settlement patterns as "an essential corollary of subsistence" and interpreted "variations between cultures [as] responses to differing adaptive requirements of specific environments" (pp. 133–5). He therefore believed that the study of archaeological settlement patterns only served to confirm that relation. Out of early ecological research developed a concern with optimal foraging theory that continues to play an important role in processual archaeology (Mithen 1990; Janetski 1997a; Shennan 2002: 142–53). Studies such as Binford's (2001) investigation of relations among hunting-gathering, social organization, and resource availability also continue the ecological research interests of early processual archaeology.

In his programmatic statements concerning New Archaeology, Binford frequently called for cultural change to be studied in terms of systems analysis. Kent Flannery (1965, 1966, 1967, 1968, 1973), the most distinguished advocate of systems theory in prehistoric archaeology, stressed the importance of General Systems Theory as a way to study ecologically driven cultural change from a processual rather than a historical point of view. This concept was popularized by P. J. Watson et al. in *Explanation in Archeology* (1971), the first textbook expounding the ideas of processual archaeology. General Systems Theory was a body of concepts that the biologist Ludwig von Bertalanffy had begun to develop in the 1940s, which sought to establish the underlying rules that govern the behavior of entities as diverse as thermostats, digital computers, glaciers, living organisms, and sociocultural systems. He assumed that all of these could be conceptualized as systems made up of interacting parts and that rules could be formulated that described how significant aspects of any system functioned, regardless of that system's specific nature (Bertalanffy 1969; Laszlo 1972a, 1972b, 1972c). Systems theory allowed archaeologists to transcend the limitations of traditional social anthropological analyses of static structures by studying not only structure-maintaining but also structure-elaborating (or morphogenetic) processes. Many of the most important of these studies were based on cybernetics, which sought to account for how systems functioned by mapping feedback between their various parts. Negative feedback maintains a system in an essentially steady state in the face of fluctuating external inputs, whereas positive feedback brings about irreversible changes in the structure of the system. The concept of feedback appeared to offer archaeologists a more precise, and potentially quantifiable, mechanism for interrelating the various components of a changing cultural system than did the essentially static social anthropological concept of functional integration (Watson et al. 1971: 61–87).

Feedback was measured in various ways, most notably by tracing the transfer of goods, information, or energy or all three combined. Although the transfer of goods and information both require the expenditure of energy, this did not deprive the study of the transfer of goods and information of special explanatory value; nevertheless, the concept of energy flows was regarded as especially appropriate by those who were committed to an ecological approach. If cultures were adaptive systems, the most rigorous way to understand prehistoric ones was empirically to trace energy flows from the natural world into and through the interrelated parts of a cultural system and then back into the natural realm. The remarkable system flow chart that David Thomas (1972) constructed as part of his inductive simulation model of historical Shoshonean subsistence and settlement patterns demonstrated the complex interrelations that were associated with the economic activities of this indigenous American hunter-gatherer people (Figure 8.4).

Flannery's early work was closely aligned with Binford's. In an influential pioneering study, Flannery (1968) argued that favorable genetic changes in maize and beans might have encouraged Mesoamerican hunter-gatherers to reschedule their food procurement patterns in order to increase their dependence on these two

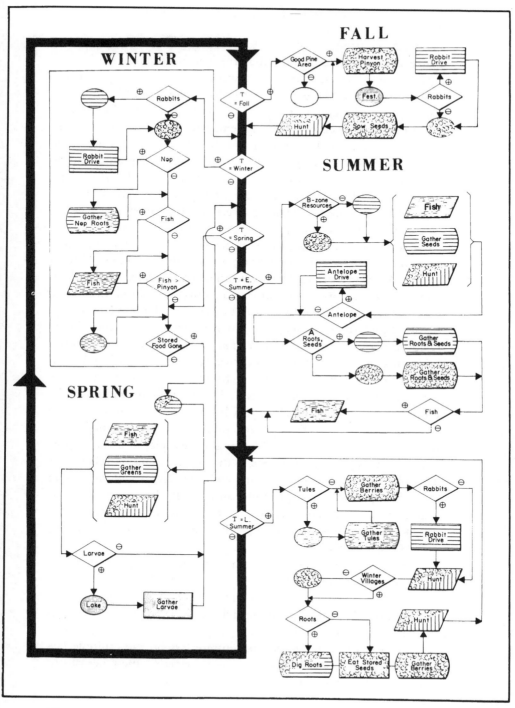

Figure 8.4 System flow chart for Shoshonean Indian subsistence cycle, by D. H. Thomas (D. H. Thomas in D. L. Clarke, ed., *Models in Archaeology*, 1972)

plants, thus setting in motion systemic changes that did not stop until maize and beans had become the principal foci of intensive agriculture. Flannery played a key role, however, in expanding the concept of systems analysis beyond a concern with ecology and adapting it for studying broader issues of social and cultural change. The concept of information processing became central to discussing the development of social hierarchies and complex societies. In these studies, the main emphasis was on administration rather than adaptation and on functional approaches rather than ecological ones. This theorizing drew upon and helped to elaborate a body of propositions derived from General Systems Theory concerning disproportional growth. These propositions attempted to explain the effects of increasing social scale on the development of institutions for collecting information and making decisions (Flannery 1972; Rathje 1975; G. Johnson 1978, 1981) (Figure 8.5). Although archaeologists rarely were able to apply systems theory in a rigorously quantitative fashion, their work gave substance to Binford's call to study cultural change systemically.

Although systems theory produced many explanations of the interrelations between a small number of key variables that were believed to be useful for accounting for change cross-culturally (Watson et al. 1971), they also encouraged archaeologists to investigate whole cultural systems. That perspective stimulated identification of the numerous interlinked variables that brought about cultural change in specific situations. These observations caused archaeologists to recognize that even key variables might have played a less important role in shaping cultural systems than they had hitherto believed. This observation in turn led many archaeologists to adopt a more inductive approach to explaining causality. It also was recognized that, because of the complexity of cultural systems, the same factors might in different circumstances produce different effects or different ones the same effects.

Flannery continued to pursue a systemic approach but recognized an increasing number of general causes for change. In his study of "The Cultural Evolution of Civilizations" (1972), he moved beyond explaining changes in the archaeological record as outcomes of specific adaptive processes, by suggesting that explanations of cultural development should concentrate less on the multiple factors that bring about change than on ascertaining the types of systemic changes that can be observed in the archaeological record.

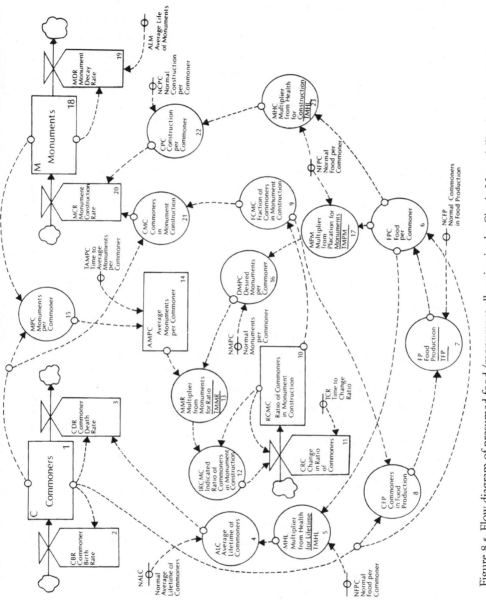

Figure 8.5 Flow diagram of presumed food/monument allocation in the Classic Maya civilization (J. A. Hosler, J. Sabloff, and D. Runge in N. Hammond, ed., *Social Process in Maya Prehistory*, 1977)

423

He offered, as examples of evolutionary mechanisms, "promotion" and "linearization." Promotion involved established institutions rising in a developing hierarchy of control to assume transformed and more far-reaching roles. Linearization occurred when higher-order controls cut past and eliminated traditional lower-order ones after the latter had failed to function in a more complex setting. Such a systemic approach was extremely valuable for producing an understanding of change from a social-structural point of view. It also drew attention to a source of constraint on human behavior that was different from, and seemingly independent of, the ecological constraints that American archaeologists previously had been considering. If social and political systems could assume only a limited number of general forms (a point Childe had already made in *Social Evolution* [1951]), these forms restricted the variation that was possible in human behavior and the routes that cultural change could follow.

Inspired by the work of the ecologist Roy Rappaport (1968), Flannery came to view cultural traditions and belief systems as playing active roles in regulating ecological adaptation. As a result, he paid increasing attention to beliefs and cognition as factors shaping cultural development (Flannery and Marcus 1993). Comparing the cultural development of the adjacent Mixtec and Zapotec peoples of Mexico, Flannery (1983) observed that unilinear evolution was by itself inadequate to realize the general anthropological goal of explaining sociocultural differences as well as similarities. His collaborator in this study, Joyce Marcus (1983a: 360), commented that "the familiar variables of agricultural intensification, population growth, warfare, and interregional trade are by themselves insufficient to explain the diversity of Mesoamerican cultures." Although Flannery and Binford agreed that the ultimate goal of archaeologists was to explain similarities as well as differences in cultures, evidence led Flannery and many other systems analysts to believe that differences were more ubiquitous and, hence, understanding them was more important and demanding than Binford had assumed.

Another disagreement that arose early on was whether the primary object of archaeological research should be to study cultural systems or social behavior. Although Binford, following White, claimed to study cultural systems, like White, he denied ideas more than epiphenomenal status; they facilitated human action but did not play any role in determining it. This suggested that the real system consisted of social relations. These considerations, together with the growing popularity of behaviorism, led some processual archaeologists to embrace the study of prehistoric societies rather than cultures, as Grahame Clark, Gordon Childe, and many settlement archaeologists (Willey 1953; Trigger 1967a, 1968c) had already done. Latterly, Julian Steward (1968: 337) had also displayed a growing tendency to talk about society rather than culture. Among the first processual archaeologists to advocate a social or societal archaeological approach were Colin Renfrew (1973c) and Charles Redman (Redman et al. 1978), although O. G. S. Crawford had coined the term "social archaeology" as early as 1921 (p. 100) and, in the late 1960s, I had suggested that societal and cultural interpretations of archaeological evidence should be pursued independently (Trigger 1968c). One of the factors that encouraged the development of social archaeology was the belief, already cited, propagated by many social anthropologists and accepted by most processual archaeologists, that ideas facilitated human behavior but played no significant role in changing it. There also was considerable, and growing, uncertainty about how integrated cultures were. Many archaeologists were disposed to believe that ideas acquired their significance according to how they were deployed in contexts of social interaction rather than in their own right.

There was also much disagreement about the nature of cultural subsystems. Although Binford followed Leslie White in distinguishing a technoeconomic, social, and ideological subsystem, David Clarke (1968: 102–3) added a psychological and a material culture subsystem and Colin Renfrew (1972: 22–3) divided cultural systems into subsistence, technological, social, projective or symbolic, and trade or communication subsystems. Binford had described material culture as relating to all subsystems rather than constituting a subsystem in its own right and had denied that psychological states were significant factors producing change or that they could be studied using archaeological data alone. Yet, to some other archaeologists, social systems seemed more real than did cultural ones. Social interaction provided the means by which each society sustained its members and biologically reproduced itself as a minimal condition for its survival. "Cultural systems," by contrast, consisted of concepts that might or might not be functionally related to one another.

Another specialization was behavioral archaeology. It grew out of an increasing realization, shared by Binford, that the systemic or living context that produced the archaeological record was radically different from the archaeological record (Schiffer 1972, 1976; Reid et al. 1974). From the beginning, behavioral archaeologists, as David Clarke (1968) had already done, focused on the need to create a science of material culture. This approach included research such as William Rathje's (1974) Garbage Project, which employed techniques of archaeological analysis to study changing patterns in the use and disposal of goods by residents of the modern city of Tucson, Arizona. Behavioral archaeologists maintained that cultural variability in the archaeological record was best explained by determining the interactions involving people and artifacts. In pursuing this course, they were carrying on Binford's search for universally-valid correlations between material culture and human behavior. Michael Schiffer (1995: 24) maintained that this could best be accomplished by creating a science of material culture based on a corpus of regularities that could account for archaeological findings. These regularities included generalizations that explained why people behaved as they did in specific living contexts as well as what happened to artifacts after they entered an archaeological context. Such theories of behavior related to artifact design, manufacture, use, and alteration over time. Not only was the primary emphasis of behavioral archaeology on behavior rather than culture but, as with the systemic approach, ecological adaptation provided only one source of explanation among many. This openness led Binford (1983a: 237) to describe Schiffer's approach as being primarily inductive.

In his book *Behavioral Archeology*, Schiffer (1976), in the tradition of Grahame Clark (1939), described the archaeological record as "a distorted reflection of a past behavioral system" (p. 12). Schiffer believed that the challenge for archaeologists was to eliminate this distortion in order to gain a more accurate understanding of past human behavior. He was optimistic this could be done provided that three sets of factors were controlled. The first were "correlates," which related material objects or spatial relations in archaeological contexts to specific types of human behavior. Correlates provided reliable indicators permitting archaeologists to infer how artifacts were made, distributed, used, and recycled in living societies. If a material cultural system were frozen at a specific moment in time, as to some extent happened to the Roman city of Pompeii as a result of being quickly buried and perfectly preserved under the ash of Mount Vesuvius in AD 79, no distortions of the archaeological record would have to be taken into account in order to study what had been going on at that moment. The interpretation of archaeological sites normally, however, required archaeologists to consider various sorts of site formation processes, the most important of which involved determining how material was transferred from a systemic to an archaeological context and what happened to that material after it was deposited in the archaeological record. The first of these were "cultural formation processes," or C-transforms, which attempted to account for how items were discarded in the normal operation of a cultural system; the second were "non-cultural formation processes," or N-transforms. Through the detailed study of discard rates, discard locations, loss probabilities, and burial practices, C-transforms could predict the materials that would or would not be deposited by a social system in the archaeological record and thus establish a set of relations that would permit the cultural system to be inferred more accurately from what remained for the archaeologist to study. Ethnographic research on problems of this sort suggested that artifacts and artifact debris were more likely to be abandoned in the localities where they had been used in temporary hunter-gatherer sites than in larger and more sedentary ones, where the disposal of waste material was much more highly organized (P. Murray 1980).

The realization that larger numbers of artifacts usually are found in contexts of disposal rather than in those of manufacture or use stimulated much ethnoarchaeological research that aimed to discover regularities in patterns of refuse disposal. It also prompted observations that archaeology might necessarily be doomed to being primarily a science of garbage. J. A. Moore and A. S. Keene (1983: 17) pronounced studies of site formation processes to be "the archaeological agenda for the 1980s." Other studies sought to determine the transformations that artifacts underwent in the course of usage. Stone tools are likely to be curated and reused much more intensively at sites lacking easy access to sources of raw material than in ones located close to such sources (Binford 1983a: 269–86). C-transforms also included postdepositional human activities, such as plowing and looting, that might distort the archaeological record. Some of these distortions can happen in predictable ways, such as the greater likelihood that robbers will remove gold objects rather than less precious ones from graves. Finally, noncultural formation processes, or N-transforms, permitted archaeologists to determine the interactions between cultural materials and the noncultural environment from which they were recovered. Schiffer argued that by accounting for the ways in which archaeological data functioned in systemic contexts, entered the archaeological record, and were transformed by it, archaeologists should be able to eliminate the "distortions" caused by formation processes and infer the original systemic context in which the artifacts had functioned.

Schiffer's approach helped to stimulate much research that has resulted in a more sophisticated understanding of the behavioral significance of archaeological data. Previously, factors such as discard rates had barely been considered by archaeologists, except in assessing the significance of animal bones. It was increasingly recognized, however, that many cultural processes were so complex and varied and the chances of equifinality so great that the neutralization of distorting influences could not produce a complete interpretation of the archaeological record from a behavioral point of view (von Gernet 1985; P. J. Watson 1986: 450). As belief in neoevolutionism waned and the diversity of human behavior increasingly was accepted, this limitation tended to be acknowledged as being inherent in the data rather than a methodological weakness. Hence, although behavioral archaeologists continued to apply Schiffer's approach profitably, few of them, including Schiffer himself, expected his original program to be fully realized.

The early period of processual archaeology in the United States also witnessed the beginning of selectionist ideas that were to become the core of Darwinian or evolutionary archaeology. Selectionism was not an entirely new concept in archaeology. Childe (1942a: 10) had maintained that, if a conservative ideology effectively blocks change, a society might eventually succumb to more aggressive neighbors, whereas Higgs (1968: 617) had argued that human preferences should be regarded "as selective factors determining survival." In 1972, the American archaeologist Mark Leone described cultural systems as self-regulating, exhibiting variation, and adjusting to environmental settings by selecting the most appropriate strategies from among the variants that are available (p. 18). In Leone's view, innovation, although rational, did not occur from nothing but was based on existing knowledge. This position implied that culture was not so much an adaptive system as a reservoir of information from which different ideas could be deployed as needed (Shennan 2002: 80). In *The Archaeology of Arizona*, Paul Martin and Fred Plog (1973) viewed cultures as adaptive systems and argued that those possessing the greatest amount of random variation were the best equipped to survive when confronted by environmental or demographic challenges or competition from neighboring groups. Linda Cordell and Fred Plog (1979) and Robert Dunnell (1980a) also assumed that there was present in every society a broad spectrum of alternative behavioral patterns on which the cultural equivalent of natural selection could operate. This position was far removed from that of many social anthropologists, ecologists, or even Boasian configurationalists, who viewed cultures as being reasonably well integrated systems, although advocates for these approaches did not deny that cultural systems conserved information about alternative ways of dealing with problems, including ones that arose only occasionally (Salzman 2000). The selectionist view of cultures more closely resembled that of early Boasian cultural anthropologists.

Robert Dunnell (1980a), David Braun (1983), and David Rindos (1984, 1989) opted for a systemic approach that used biological ("scientific") evolutionary theory to explain cultural as well as biological variability. Darwinian, or evolutionary, archaeology was further developed by Dunnell and his students (Wenke 1981). They argued that traditional cultural evolutionism had failed to internalize such key tenets of scientific evolutionism as random variation and natural selection. Although generally acknowledging that mechanisms of trait transmission are more varied and that the units on which selection operates are less stable in the cultural than in the biological realm (issues that Kroeber [1952] and other anthropologists had discussed in detail long before), they maintained that an approach based on general principles of scientific evolutionism could offer explanations of human behavior that were superior to those provided by cultural evolutionary theory. Doing so often involved the radical reformulation of traditional questions. For example, David Rindos (1984: 143) defined domestication as a mutualistic relation of varying degrees between different species. He did not view the adaptation of plants and animals to human needs as being inherently different from the adaptation of human beings to the needs of plants and animals.

Thus, Rindos carried to a new extreme the denial that consciousness and intentionality play a significant role in shaping human behavior (Peregrine 2000).

The revolt against culture-historical archaeology occurred more slowly in Britain than in the United States and did not manifest the extreme antihistorical posturing of processual archaeology found in America. David Clarke (1938–1976), who studied and then taught at Cambridge University, developed his key ideas independently of American processual archaeologists and identified himself as a New Archaeologist only in the sense that he was rebelling against the strictures of culture-historical archaeology. Although many American processual archaeologists, who often knew little about his work, chose to regard Clarke as an overseas adherent of their movement, Binford (1972: 248–9, 330–1) was not convinced.

Clarke (1968: 12–14) was scornful of the intuitive manner in which many British culture historians sought to compose historical narratives without first analyzing archaeological data in a rigorous manner in order to extract as much behavioral data from them as possible. He denounced such premature narratives as "an irresponsible art form" (1973: 16). In *Analytical Archaeology* (1968), almost a decade before Schiffer, Clarke had treated archaeology as the potential nucleus of a new science of material culture that he believed would complement social and cognitive anthropology. Clarke modeled his analysis on the systems theory approach of the New Geography that was being expounded in the 1960s at Cambridge University by the physical geographer Richard Chorley and the human geographer Peter Haggett (Chorley and Haggett 1967).

Clarke focused mainly on the study of artifacts, which he sought to interpret from morphological, ecological, geographical, and anthropological perspectives, often employing elaborate statistical analyses. For Clarke, detailed analyses of this sort were indispensable preliminaries for the production of any sort of historical interpretation or narrative, a view that he shared with Eric Higgs, despite their disagreement about whether the best way forward was the study of artifacts or ecofacts (Bailey 1999: 547, 553). Morphologically, Clarke sought to define and interrelate a series of nested concepts: trait, type, culture, and technocomplex. Although he stressed the internal variability of types and cultures, he was more interested in assigning artifacts to classes than in explaining variability (Clarke 1968). Binford

(1972: 248–9) criticized Clarke for adopting an inductive approach to taxonomy that failed to consider adequately the specific goals of any particular classification. In many respects, Clarke's treatment of taxonomy represents a continuation of European culture-historical methodology rather than a break with it. That is precisely why Soviet archaeologists valued it so highly in the 1980s.

In *Analytical Archaeology* (1968), Clarke's chief interest in American anthropology was not processual archaeology but the wealth of detailed information about the cultural and linguistic variation among indigenous North American societies that Boasian ethnologists had recorded. Clarke valued these data, which he regarded as superior to any collected by European ethnologists, as a factual basis for developing a general understanding of material culture from an anthropological (or behavioral) perspective (Herzfeld 1992: 78).

Clarke pursued his efforts to relate archaeological finds to human behavior in a rigorous and systematic fashion that took him into new theoretical domains. As a result of the work of Robert Ascher (1961: 324), archaeologists had become increasingly aware that artifacts were made, used, and frequently discarded in different contexts, not all of which were equally represented in the archaeological record. Recognition that archaeologists possessed only an attenuated sample of what they proposed to study was encapsulated in Clarke's (1973: 17) memorable comment that archaeology was "the discipline with the theory and practice for the recovery of unobservable hominid behaviour patterns from indirect traces in bad samples." Clarke maintained that the scientific interpretation of archaeological data depended on recognizing that, of the full range of hominid activity patterns and social and environmental processes that had occurred in the past, archaeologists had access only to the sample of associated material remains that in turn were deposited in the archaeological record, survived to be recovered, and actually had been recovered.

Inspired by the earlier work of S. G. H. Daniels (1972) and possibly also by B. K. Swartz's (1967) delineation of a logical sequence of archaeological objectives, Clarke (1973) identified five bodies of theory that archaeologists intuitively employed in their interpretive leaps from excavated data to final report. The first of these was predepositional and depositional theory, covering the relations of human activities, social patterns, and environmental factors with each other and with the samples and traces that are deposited in the archaeological record. Postdepositional theory treated the natural and human processes that affected the archaeological record, such as erosion, decay, ground movement, plundering, plowing, and the reuse of land. Retrieval theory dealt with the relations between what survives in the archaeological record and what is recovered. It is largely a theory of sampling, excavation procedures, and flexible response strategies. Analytical theory, which Clarke studied in the greatest detail, dealt with the operational treatment of recovered data, including classification, modeling, testing, and experimental studies. Finally, interpretive theory governed relations between the archaeological patterns established at the analytical level and directly unobservable ancient behavioral and environmental patterns. Thus interpretive theory infers the processes that predepositional theory explains. Clarke believed that a major challenge for archaeologists was to develop a corpus of theory appropriate for each of these stages of analysis. Only a small portion of such theories, mainly relating to the predepositional and interpretive levels, could be derived from the social sciences; the rest had to come from the biological and physical sciences. Clarke believed that the totality of this theory, together with metaphysical, epistemological, and logical theory relating to archaeological operations, was necessary to create a scientific discipline of archaeology.

Yet Clarke's emphasis on analytical procedures did not lessen his regard for the historical analysis of archaeological data or his interest in specific cultures. Nor was his ultimate goal the creation of generalizations about human behavior as contributions to social science theory. From his early analysis of Beaker pottery (Clarke 1970), he was concerned with better understanding European prehistory. His later papers addressed the ecological basis of European cultural development, understanding the social milieus in which economic transactions occurred, and a balanced interest in local development and regional networks of interaction. In "The Economic Context of Trade and Industry in Barbarian Europe till Roman Times" (Clarke 1979: 263–331), which he wrote for *The Cambridge Economic History*, he attempted to summarize the relevant archaeological data guided by Karl Polanyi's theories concerning the social embeddedness of primitive economies. This paper has been described as "a great advance on previous work in its discussion of the social functions of artefact-types and its inference of the circulation-systems of which they are the fossilized remains" (Sherratt 1979: 197). Other studies addressing central issues of European prehistory included a reinterpretation of the social organization and economy of the late Iron Age settlement at Glastonbury (Clarke 1972b) (Figure 8.6) and a survey, utilizing ecological, ethnographic, demographic, and economic, as well as archaeological data to counteract the traditional faunally oriented interpretations of the Mesolithic economies of Europe (Clarke 1979: 206–62).

Unlike Clarke, Colin Renfrew (b. 1937) acquired firsthand experience of New Archaeology when he taught briefly in the United States. Perhaps because of his undergraduate training in the physical sciences, Renfrew regarded the most important defining characteristic of processual archaeology as being its positivist orientation. Yet he remained wary of the search for general laws of human behavior as an end in itself, even though he embraced neoevolutionism and systems theory (Renfrew 1982a; Champion 1991: 132–4). His early research focused on social archaeology (Renfrew 1973d). In a monumental study of the development of complex societies in the Aegean region, he emphasized the role played by positive feedback relations involving the natural environment, population size, subsistence, craft production, exchange, communication, sociopolitical organization, settlement patterns, and religion, arguing that a synergistic "multiplier effect" among these variables resulted in increasing sociocultural complexity (Renfrew 1972). This book strongly reflects the theoretical influence of Kent Flannery. Renfrew also made significant contributions to studying the evolution of social and political organization from a unilinear, neoevolutionary point of view, including his distinction between simpler group-oriented and more complex individualizing chiefdoms (Renfrew 1973c). Like Clarke, Renfrew emphasized the quantitative and geographical analysis of archaeological data, which in some cases he combined with trace-element sourcing of the origin of raw materials in studies of prehistoric trade (Renfrew et al. 1968; Renfrew 1975).

In the 1980s, Renfrew (1982b) became increasingly interested in studying cognitive aspects of human behavior. He sought to employ scientific methods to do this, as a result of which his approach has come to be known as cognitive-processual archaeology. Like Childe (1958c: 5), who saw archaeology as offering a history of effective technological knowledge, Renfrew called for a cognitive approach

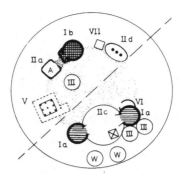

FIG. 21.1. The modular unit – the social and architectural building block of which the settlement is a multiple. The analyses of vertical and horizontal spatial relationships, structural attributes and artefact distributions convergently define a distinct range of structures (I–VII) repeatedly reproduced on the site. Each replication of the unit appears to be a particular transformation of an otherwise standardized set of relationships between each structural category and every other category. The basic division between the pair of major houses (Ia) and their satellites, and the minor house (Ib) and its ancillaries may be tentatively identified with a division between a major familial, multi-role and activity area on one hand and a minor, largely female and domestic area (see Fig. 21.6).

Below: the iconic symbols used to identify the structures in the schematic site models, Figs. 21.2–21.5.

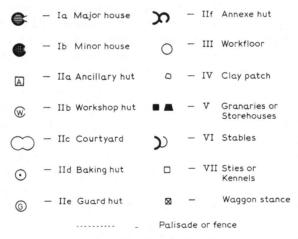

Figure 8.6 Modular housing unit at Glastonbury Iron Age site, as identified by D. L. Clarke (*Models in Archaeology,* 1972a)

434

that addressed the mind behind the artifact in the practical terms of its usage rather than the more abstract terms of its symbolic meaning. This approach functions well when attempting to infer how a prehistoric system of weights and measures worked (Renfrew 1982b: 16–18; J. Bell 1994: 17–19), as the goal is to determine the logic that governed the original system. Yet, without textual sources, it is very difficult to reconstruct culturally specific beliefs from archaeological data (Renfrew and Zubrow 1994). In recent years, Renfrew's cognitive interests have focused more on the study of the evolution of human symbolic and cognitive abilities than on trying to determine specifically what humans thought in the past (Renfrew and Scarre 1998). He does not appear to have evolved a clear theoretical position about how cognitive abilities relate to other forms of human behavior, leaving it uncertain to what extent he is a materialist or an idealist. Cognitive-processual archaeology is important for its insistence on methodological rigor in studying mental processes, but it has made little progress in determining on the basis of archaeological data alone what people actually may have thought.

Like Clarke, but unlike American processual archaeologists, Renfrew has never embraced the idea that historical interpretation and evolutionary generalization are antithetical. Instead, he has remained deeply interested in the study of prehistoric Europe and its peoples (Renfrew 1973a, 1979). In the 1970s, he used radiocarbon dates to emphasize the creativity and originality of early European food-producing cultures (Renfrew 1973a). More recently, he equated the arrival of the Indo-Europeans with the introduction of agricultural economies to Europe (Renfrew 1988). He has since attributed the geographical expansion of other language families to assumed population increases brought about by the invention of agriculture elsewhere in the world (Bellwood and Renfrew 2003). That in turn has led him to seek to correlate linguistic, physical anthropological, and archaeological data in an effort to trace human groups into remote antiquity (Renfrew 1992). Renfrew thus has duplicated, using modern scientific methods, a methodology that incorporates some of the key features of a multidisciplinary approach to studying prehistory that had been elaborated by Boasian anthropologists (Sapir 1916), but many assumptions of which were critiqued and repudiated by Boas (1940) himself. Renfrew provides an interesting example of an archaeologist shifting from processual archaeology to what might be regarded as an upgraded version of culture-historical archaeology.

At the same time that different approaches were developing within processual archaeology, archaeologists as a whole were becoming increasingly concerned about issues that processual archaeology was ignoring rather than solving. During the 1970s, a growing number of American archaeologists became convinced that more diversity was being found in prehistoric cultures than could be accounted for by general evolutionary schemes, such as those of Sahlins and Service, or even by Steward's multilinear evolutionism. There also was a slowly but continuously growing recognition that neoevolutionism had unduly restricted the questions about the past that archaeologists were prepared to consider important.

Critiques made by anthropologists who were not fundamentally hostile to evolutionary studies also undermined the credibility of unilinear evolution. It was pointed out that Sahlins and Service had characterized the tribal stage of development mainly on the basis of New Guinea big-men societies, which have very different social and political structures from indigenous societies at the same level of development in North America, Africa, or Southeast Asia (Whallon 1982: 156). It also was evident that the chiefdom stage of development had been based primarily on the Polynesian societies with which these anthropologists were most familiar. Yet, rather than representing an evolutionary sequence, as Sahlins and Service had assumed, both of these groupings embraced societies of varying degrees of complexity. The ethnographic evidence also suggested that in Polynesia hereditary chiefships might have antedated the development of complexity. Growing awareness of problems such as these led some archaeologists to replace discrete evolutionary categories with quantifiable dimensions of social variability (R. McGuire 1983). Morton Fried's (1975) claim that many of the more complex features associated with tribal societies were products of acculturation resulting from contacts with Western peoples, rather than spontaneous internal developments, also led some archaeologists to view the evolutionary status of such societies with increasing suspicion. It was similarly demonstrated that key features of at least some chiefdoms had developed as a result of their contact with more complex societies (Wolf 1982: 96–100).

Such observations caused archaeologists to become increasingly interested in trying to explain the cultural diversity that used to intrigue historical particularists (Renfrew 1982b). There also was growing willingness to admit that human behavior was shaped by diverse factors. Although most archaeologists continued to interpret their data from a materialistic, and often more specifically an ecological, perspective (P. J. Watson 1986: 441), there was increased questioning of the extent to which ecological and economic factors played a determining role with respect to human behavior. These developments brought about many changes in archaeological analysis. Alison Wylie (1985a: 90) went so far as to observe that "there is a strong case to be made that [idiosyncratic variability at a societal or individual level] is the distinctively human and cultural feature of the archaeological subject; hence, it should be the special interest of an anthropological archaeology." At least some of these trends involved a revival of interest in topics associated with culture-historical archaeology that long had been ignored as a result of the development of processual archaeology. These developments were strengthened by a growing awareness that in evolutionary biology ideas of punctuated equilibrium, indeterminacy, and historical contingency were replacing views that emphasized more gradual, progressive, predictable, and narrowly deterministic change (Gould and Eldredge 1977, 1993).

Another development was a tendency to abandon the view that societies or cultures were closed or tightly bounded units that could be studied independently of one another, and once again to pay more attention to the role played by external stimuli in bringing about cultural change. Wolf (1982: ix) argued that anthropologists, especially under the influence of neoevolutionism, "seem to have forgotten that human populations construct their cultures in interaction with one another and not in isolation." He went on to state that the cultural connections that an older generation of anthropologists studied as diffusion could only be rendered intelligible in systemic terms when they were set into a broader political and economic context. Such views encouraged archaeologists to pay increasing attention to intersocietal relations.

Those working in the Middle East argued the need to view Mesopotamian civilization as part of a much larger zone within which from early times many cultures had influenced one another's development through various forms of political and economic interaction

(Lamberg-Karlovsky 1975; Kohl 1978; Alden 1982). There also was discussion of "peer polity" interaction in prehistoric Europe (Renfrew and Shennan 1982) and elsewhere (Renfrew and Cherry 1986) and of "cluster interaction" in Mesoamerica (B. Price 1977). Blanton and his coauthors (1981) argued that, because of the intensity of economic, political, and ritual interaction among the ruling classes throughout Mesoamerica in prehispanic times, the development of any one region, even a clearly demarcated one such as the Valley of Mexico, could not be understood independently of that of neighboring regions. They therefore proposed to treat the whole of Mesoamerica as a single "macroregional unit" bound together by the interaction of local elites; an approach that placed prodigious demands on the information-gathering capacity of archaeologists. This approach also raised major questions about how the boundaries of macroregions were to be defined. Blanton and his associates argued that what is recognized as Mesoamerica was a network of states and chiefdoms united by intensive reciprocal interaction of a political and ritual nature, that could be recognized in the archaeological record. It had long been surmised that economic and ritual influences of Mesoamerican origin also marked the cultural development of the southwestern United States and eastern North America, although it has rarely been possible to define the social contexts in which those presumed contacts occurred (Griffin 1980).

Other archaeologists were attracted by Immanuel Wallerstein's (1974) world-system theory (Kohl 1978, 1979, 1987; Ekholm and Friedman 1979; Blanton et al. 1981; Renfrew and Shennan 1982: 58). This approach involved the study of large-scale spatial systems, assuming an interregional division of labor in which peripheral areas supplied core areas with raw materials, the core areas were politically and economically dominant, and the economic and social development of all regions was constrained by their changing roles in the system. Philip Kohl suggested that the world systems of antiquity probably only superficially resembled those of modern times. In particular, he argued that the rankings of cores and peripheries may have been less stable than they are now and that political force might have played a more overt role in regulating such rankings. Migrations of individuals and peoples were also once again being discussed (Anthony 1990). What was of greatest importance was the growing realization that societies were not closed systems with respect to neighboring societies any more than in relation to their natural environments and that the development of a society or culture might have been constrained or influenced by the broader social network of which it was a part. There also was increasing recognition that the rules governing these processes were themselves worthy of scientific investigation.

These observations raised additional and even now unresolved questions relating to the nature of sociocultural systems. Social boundaries are defined by reduced levels of interaction. Yet archaeologists began to wonder if a hierarchy of levels could be distinguished, in which individuals were grouped as members of families, families as parts of communities, communities as components of larger societies or polities, and neighboring societies or polities to form larger interaction spheres. Or do individuals simultaneously participate differentially in patterned interactions at many levels and as members of many different kinds of social groupings (R. McGuire 1983)? One must not arbitrarily minimize the importance of brokers and decision makers, such as chiefs, government officials, and kings, who mediate between different levels of society and thereby reflect and make possible varying degrees of social closure between these levels. Yet a detailed analysis of social, political, and economic interaction has called into question the idea that so-called societies or cultures are necessarily more significant units of analysis than are larger and smaller categories (Clarke 1968). More recently, it has been proposed that the concept of society should be replaced by that of social networks (Shanks 1996: 168). The social entity to be studied appears to be something that must be determined in relation to the specific problem being investigated and the evidence available from the archaeological record.

Binford had maintained that cultures were tightly integrated systems in which changes in technology and relations with the environment brought about alterations in social organization and belief systems. Because of this, he and other processual archaeologists, such as Stuart Struever, believed that little variation existed from one culture to another at the same level of development. Systems analysis, by encouraging the detailed study of individual cases, promoted growing awareness of the cross-cultural diversity cultures exhibited. It also became apparent that cultures and societies were not as tightly integrated or as narrowly determined as neoevolutionary archaeologists had imagined. Systems analysts discovered a wide range of ecological, social, and cultural factors bringing about changes in various ways and to different degrees within more loosely integrated entities. Even when subjected to a variety of similar ecological and other functional constraints, societies at the same level of development displayed considerable cross-cultural variation (Trigger 1982a). This gradually led to the abandonment of ecological determinism and of the idea that universal generalizations alone could explain the past.

It was further realized by many archaeologists that, because of the complexity and diversity of human behavior, archaeologists cannot use evolutionary generalizations to explain specific historical situations but must understand specific historical situations as a basis for trying to formulate evolutionary generalizations. George Odell (2001: 681) has asserted that the search for cultural laws has been finished in the United States since the publications of M. Salmon and W. Salmon (1979) and Flannery (1986). Salmon and Salmon argued that, because of the causal complexity of much human behavior, explaining it requires a statistical relevance model, whereby an event is explained when all factors statistically relevant to its occurrence are assembled and the appropriate probability values for its occurrence are determined in the light of these factors (W. Salmon et al. 1971; M. Salmon 1982: 109; W. Salmon 1967, 1984). This approach is similar to the traditional method of historical explanations (Dray 1957). Since then, most archaeologists have realized that correlations relating to human behavior are generally statistical rather than absolute in nature and that most statistical correlations are of a lower rather than a higher degree of magnitude, a problem with which anthropologists engaged in cross-cultural studies have long had to contend (Textor 1967). Under these circumstances, the problem of equifinality, or different causes producing the same effect, becomes increasingly troublesome, as archaeologists engaged in early simulation studies soon realized (Hodder 1978b; Sabloff 1981). Although Binford continued to champion something resembling an ecological determinist view of human history, he became increasingly an exception.

Renewed interest in interaction among cultures also reopened the often-debated question of the significance of ethnographic analogies for archaeological interpretation. Evolutionary anthropologists had assumed that the earliest recorded descriptions of indigenous cultures revealed what these cultures had been like before European contact and that such information could be used without serious question for cross-cultural studies of behavioral variation. The Australian Aborigines and the San of southern Africa were regarded as paradigmatic hunter-gatherer societies. Yet archaeology was revealing that many indigenous cultures had been vastly altered as a result of European contact before the earliest descriptions of them were recorded by Europeans (Ramsden 1977; Cordell and Plog 1979; Wilcox and Masse 1981; J. Bradley 1987). It seemed possible that every hunter-gatherer and tribal society in the world was influenced to some degree by contact with technologically more advanced societies prior to ethnographic study (Brasser 1971; Fried 1975; Wobst 1978; Monks 1981: 228; Trigger 1981b; Alexander and Mohammed 1982).

There was growing archaeological and historical evidence that the San way of life had been modified significantly in recent centuries by contacts with European settlers and over a longer period by interaction with their pastoral Bantu and Hottentot neighbors (Schrire 1980, 1984). The impact that these other groups had on the southern African environment also may have altered San life in many ways. It was further proposed that San groups might have moved out of and back into hunter-gathering many times (Denbow 1984; Wilmsen and Denbow 1990; Gordon 1992). Under such circumstances, it was dangerous for anthropologists to assume that the San, or any other modern hunter-gatherer societies, were necessarily equivalent to Palaeolithic ones. These studies, although revolutionary after a long period dominated by neoevolutionism, resumed a pattern established by Strong (1935) and Wedel (1938), with their archaeological demonstrations that the highly mobile equestrian hunting populations found on the Great Plains of North America in the historical period were a relatively recent phenomenon and that in some areas sedentary agriculturalists had preceded them. In *Stone Age Economics*, Sahlins (1972: 38–9) suggested that social anthropology was nothing but the record of cultures destroyed by colonialism.

The various economic ties that link modern hunter-gatherers to their non-hunter-gatherer neighbors also call into question whether modern and ancient hunter-gatherers (or tribal societies) shared the same mode of production and can therefore be treated as societies at the same stage of development. Binford (1980) used northern indigenous groups that had been engaged for generations in trapping and exchanging furs with Europeans as a basis for offering certain generalizations about the nature of hunter-gatherer adaptations to high-latitude environments. Some anthropologists believe that, because of the flexibility of their adaptation to the boreal forest, the economies of at least some of these groups have not been radically altered by the fur trade (Francis and Morantz 1983: 14–15); others strongly disagree. Only detailed archaeological studies can determine objectively to what extent ethnographic descriptions of hunter-gatherer or tribal agricultural societies provide a representative picture of what these societies were like in prehistoric times (D. Thomas 1974). Until more such investigations are made, the significance of major cross-cultural studies based on ethnographic data must remain doubtful. It has clearly been demonstrated that comparing societies that have been influenced by European colonization can give an exaggerated impression of the degree of variation occurring in cultural phenomena such as kinship terminologies (Eggan 1966: 15–44).

Archaeology therefore came to be viewed as having an important role to play not only in unraveling the complex history of the past but also in providing a historical perspective for understanding the significance of ethnographic data. A growing number of anthropologists began to accept that ethnologists and social anthropologists, whether studying social structure or change, were investigating the results of acculturation because their data were derived from small-scale societies that were being either destroyed or integrated ever more completely into the modern world system. History and archaeology alone could study the evolution of cultures in the past. It was also becoming clear that no society could be properly understood or even classified from a structural point of view without taking account of its relations with other societies (Wolf 1982; Flannery 1983). The persistent Enlightenment belief that ethnologists by themselves could study all facets of cultural development was finally coming to an end.

In the 1960s, Binford had inspired young American archaeologists by arguing that all aspects of sociocultural systems were reflected in the archaeological record. Yet, over the next twenty-five years, processual archaeologists had continued to study mainly the lower echelons of Hawkes's ladder. With the notable exceptions of Flannery, Marcus, and Renfrew, leading processual archaeologists concentrated on subsistence patterns, trade, and to a lesser extent social organization. Of the papers dealing with the interpretation of archaeological evidence in the first eight volumes of Schiffer's *Advances in Archaeological Method and Theory* (1978–1985), 39 percent dealt with data recovery and chronology, 47 percent with ecology, demography, and economic behavior, 8 percent with social behavior, and only 6 percent with ideology, religion, and scientific knowledge. Binford's own research remained focused on technology and settlement-subsistence patterns as they related to ecological adaptation. Processual archaeologists paid little attention to studying the specific religious beliefs, cosmology, iconography, aesthetics, scientific knowledge, or values of prehistoric cultures. Studies of archaeoastronomy (Aveni 1981) and prehistoric iconography (Donnan 1976; Nicholson 1976; Gimbutas 1982) generally were carried out by archaeologists who were not associated with processual archaeology. It also was observed that ecological and evolutionary approaches were not designed to explain motivation and symbolic meaning (Leach 1973: 768–9; Dunnell 1982a: 521). Gradually, however, a growing number of archaeologists began to regard this situation as anomalous because, from at least Upper Palaeolithic times onward, abundant evidence of religious and symbolic behavior occurs in the archaeological record in the form of art, temples, burials, and other remains of ritual behavior (Mithen 1996). By the late 1970s, it appeared as if a Kuhnian paradigm shift might be in the making. Few remembered that Childe (1956b) had argued that the incorporation of cognitive aspects was essential for a persuasive and reasonably complete explanation of human behavior.

Thus, although processual archaeologists generally continued to be materialists and to adhere to positivistic canons of scientific method, they soon diverged from each other in a number of different theoretical directions. In the course of doing so, they embraced numerous conflicting tendencies, often without adequately assessing the scientific credentials of theories or seeking to determine whether they were appropriate for what was being studied. Although processual archaeologists became more familiar with social science, and especially anthropological, theory than archaeologists had ever been before, they remained for the most part consumers of theory. In due course, the questions they refused to discuss began to be interpreted as evidence of theoretical inadequacy rather than of professional sophistication.

At the same time that its adequacy was being called into question, processual archaeology was playing an increasingly important role in shaping archaeological practice as a result of its leading ideas being incorporated into the research-design protocols that government agencies, especially in the United States, used to mandate and evaluate the rapidly expanding roster of archaeological projects that they funded. Because rescue archaeology and cultural resource management soon were providing employment for most professional archaeologists, this was a development that was of great importance for determining how archaeology would be practiced in the United States over the next few decades.

Postprocessual Archaeology

A conscious alternative to processual archaeology began to develop in the 1970s and by 1985 Ian Hodder had labeled this new trend postprocessual archaeology. The beginnings of this movement had been predicted by the social anthropologist Edmund Leach (1973: 763) as early as 1971, when he warned a meeting on "The Explanation of Culture Change," held at the University of Sheffield and largely attended by processual archaeologists, that although the concept of cultural structuralism, currently popular among social anthropologists, had not yet caught up with them, eventually it would. Postprocessual archaeology can be regarded as the inevitable rediscovery of the concept of culture as a source of cross-culturally idiosyncratic variation in human beliefs and behavior (Robb 1998). But this discovery was accompanied by archaeologists being exposed to several interrelated intellectual movements, at least two of which were keen on challenging authority in the political as well as the intellectual arena.

The first influence was the Marxist-inspired social anthropology that had developed in France in the 1960s and already had influenced British social anthropology. This movement had its roots not in orthodox Marxism but in efforts to combine Marxism and structuralism by anthropologists such as Maurice Godelier, Emmanuel Terray, and Pierre-Philippe Rey, as well as by the philosopher Louis Althusser. Although structuralists traditionally practiced an ahistorical form of analysis and Marxism was historical in orientation, the protagonists of French anthropology believed that these two approaches could be made to complement one another. French Marxist anthropologists also were influenced by the idealism of the Frankfurt School, especially as the ideas of that school were represented in the writings of Jürgen Habermas (1971, 1975) and Herbert Marcuse (1964). The Frankfurt School was a rethinking of Marxism dating from the 1920s by Theodore Adorno, Max Horkheimer, Herbert Marcuse, and others who stressed the important role played by beliefs in controlling human behavior. They attributed the failure of the working class to seize power in central and western Europe during World War I to the influence of nationalist propaganda, which had led them to act contrary to their economic and political interests. The economic studies by Claude Meillassoux (1981) constituted yet another influence on French Marxist anthropology.

Despite individual differences, these neo-Marxist anthropologists emphasized the considerable variations among simple modes of production, the important role played by human consciousness in bringing about change, the major significance of clashes of interest between men and women or people of different ages in promoting conflict and hence change in classless societies, and the inescapable impregnation of all human activities, including scientific research, by ideology. They also shared the conviction that Marx and Engels had failed to produce a detailed analysis of preclass societies and that it was their duty to remedy this defect not by returning to the flawed works of the founders of Marxism but by constructing new Marxist theories of precapitalist societies on the basis of current knowledge of such groups (Bloch 1985: 150; R. McGuire 1992a, 1993). They also rejected neoevolutionism, traditional structuralism, cultural materialism, and cultural ecology because these approaches unduly reified stability, treated the causes of cultural change as being external to social relations, and regarded human beings as passive objects that were molded by external factors. Ecology was viewed as constraining rather than directing change and new technologies were interpreted both as responses to social and economic change and as a major force bringing such change about. Social conflicts arising from contradictory interests were identified as vital and pervasive features of all human societies and a major source of change. In preclass societies conflict centered on control of food and labor, gender roles, personal and family status, exotic goods, possession of knowledge, and ritual prerogatives. This view was contrasted with the integrative concerns of functionalism, classical structuralism, and phenomenology, to the disadvantage of these three established positions.

Marxist anthropologists also championed a human-centered view of history. They refused to explain meaning, symbolism, and social phenomena in terms of nonsocial determinants. Instead of treating social behavior as passively shaped by external (ecological) forces, as Binford and many other processual archaeologists did, Marxist anthropologists stressed intentionality and the social production of reality. They also insisted on a holistic approach; in a Marxist and Hegelian fashion, parts of society always had to be studied in relation to the whole and individual social systems in terms of broader networks of intersocietal relations. Marxist anthropologists sought to explain not only cross-cultural regularities but also the particularities, individual differences, and specific contexts that distinguished one concrete instance of social change from another. They clearly identified with the historical orientation that was part, but not all, of Marx's approach. They also insisted on the social basis of knowledge, viewing information and self-consciousness as the products and intellectual capital of specific societies. Finally, the social context of social science research was seen as influencing interpretations of human behavior. This suggested that certainty of the sort envisioned by positivistically oriented researchers could not be achieved (Trigger 1993).

During this period a more broadly based reaction against positivism and behaviorism was developing in the humanities and social sciences. Postmodernism, as archaeologists experienced it, originated in comparative literature, literary criticism, and cultural studies. Following the decline of Boasian anthropology, cultural studies successfully challenged anthropology's claim to be the primary discipline studying culture. Postmodernists emphasized the subjective nature of knowledge and embraced extreme relativism and idealism. Many denied that such a thing as objective knowledge existed. All established approaches, with the possible exception of postmodernism itself, were represented as serving special interests (Lyotard 1984; Jencks 1986; Harvey 1989; Hunt 1989; Laudan 1990; Rose 1991; Rosenau 1992). Postmodernists also violently rejected the hegemonic implications of cultural evolutionary theory and the notion of progress, which they denounced as a morally bankrupt set of concepts that served to rationalize colonialism, the repression of minorities, and the abuse of nature. Postmodernists romantically celebrated random, idiosyncratic cultural variation. They construed the rationalism of the Enlightenment as an effort to impose hegemonic values and political control on the world and believed that by asserting the integrity of local cultures they were defending freedom and helping weaker peoples to oppose their oppressors. In architecture, the austerity and universalism of functionalist modernism was countered by adding local and historical references to it. As idealists, postmodernists also rejected proposals that human behavior was shaped to any significant degree by physical constraints (Goffman 1963; Latour and Woolgar 1979; Knorr-Cetina 1981; L. Shepherd 1993).

Postmodernists agreed that there could never be a single, objective version of human affairs; instead there were multiple versions or truths seen from different standpoints, such as those of poor and rich, winners and losers, females and males, different professions, and various ethnic groups. Postmodernists embraced not only relativism, which emphasizes the varied ways in which different groups of people understand the world and what is happening to it, but also a subjectivist viewpoint, which maintains that every person sees the world differently. Postmodernists emphasized that no two people attending a performance of Shakespeare's play *Hamlet* would perceive that performance in exactly the same way because no two people bring precisely the same experiences and understandings to it. They also maintained that in transmitting information from one person to another every decoding of a message by the recipient is another encoding. This process was identified as a major source of essentially random cultural change.

Radical postmodernists sought to decenter and disempower what they characterized as hegemonic knowledge, which they maintained had been created to serve the interests of the most powerful, conservative, and usually the male members of society. They did this by encouraging weaker members of society to express their own viewpoints and by themselves exposing the self-interest, misrepresentations, and self-deception that permeate the pronouncements of the rich and powerful. Such people, it was maintained, habitually claim that the social arrangements that serve their interests are good for everyone, in order to persuade the weak to acquiesce in being exploited and to resent their bad treatment less.

Although many postmodern ideas were of Marxist origin, post-modernism flourished after the failure of the radical student upheavals in Europe and North America in 1968, at a time when "truth" was no longer seen as necessarily liberating (Hegmon 2003: 232). The extreme subjectivism and opposition to grand narratives of postmodernists made it impossible for them to gain much clear or useful insight into the origins, structure, and transformations of social systems at the very time when worldwide political and economic changes were affecting everyone's life, often for the worse (Sherratt 1993: 125). Such inability to understand and critique what is actually happening in the world may explain why postmodernism has flourished symbiotically as the cultural accompaniment of the emergence of a highly exploitative transnational economy that continues to be driven by a self-assured and very unpostmodern neoconservative ideology (Marchak 1991). This symbiosis also may explain why postmodernists rarely draw attention to the Marxist origins of many of their ideas.

The Polish philosopher Lezek Kolakowski (1978c: 524–5) has observed that, although some Marxist concepts have permeated the historical sciences and humanities in the West, by the late 1970s Marxism as a system had largely ceased to be an intellectual force there and what was left of it seemed to duplicate most of the materialist and idealist viewpoints found in non-Marxist social science. This may help to explain why, when Marxism and Marxist institutions collapsed around the world in the early 1990s and French Marxist anthropology ceased to be regarded as being on the cutting edge of theory production, postmodernism, lacking the historical liability of a Marxist identity, flourished in archaeology.

Finally, the distinction between modernism and postmodernism is far from complete (Hegmon 2003: 232). Critical theory and classical Marxism in general, which have played important roles in shaping postmodern thought, are modernist, not postmodernist, movements. Moreover, postprocessual archaeology, with its interests in other modernist approaches, such as structuralism, cannot be equated with postmodernism. Yet postprocessual archaeologists have given both Marxism and structuralism a postmodern gloss.

The third and politically the most conservative source of inspiration for postprocessual archaeology was the new cultural anthropology that developed in the United States following the collapse of Boasian anthropology. Neoevolutionary anthropology never succeeded in becoming the dominant approach in sociocultural anthropology even during the 1960s, as processualism did in anthropological archaeology. Clifford Geertz (1965: 101) countered an ecological emphasis on functional aspects of behavior by proclaiming cross-cultural regularities to be meaningless intellectual constructions and stressing the need to try to understand every culture on its own terms. He also emphasized the great effort that was needed for anthropologists to acquire even a limited understanding of a single culture other than their own.

New cultural anthropologists denounced studies of cultural evolution as being ethnocentric and intellectually and morally untenable in a multicultural, postcolonial environment (S. Diamond 1974). All cultures were viewed as unique and all sequences of change as historically contingent. This encouraged the revival of a pervasive concern with documenting cultural diversity, idiosyncracy, and uniqueness, while at the same time ignoring cross-cultural regularities (V. Turner 1967, 1975; Geertz 1973; Clifford 1988). The most dramatic event in anthropology was Marshall Sahlins's (1976a) abandonment of neoevolutionism and his embracing of new cultural anthropology. Although this revival of cultural anthropology was formulated largely in a politically neutral idiom, many new cultural anthropologists embraced postmodernism or ideas derived from it. Thus, new cultural anthropology became a force encouraging postprocessual archaeology in the United States and elsewhere.

By the mid-1970s, the discussion of Marxist ideas by social scientists was no longer tabooed in the United States and Marxism began to penetrate prehistoric archaeology in the United States as well as Britain. In 1975 Philip Kohl and Antonio Gilman organized the first symposium on relations between Marxist ideas and archaeology at that year's annual meeting of the American Anthropological Association. Their work and Carole Crumley's tended to be based on classical Marxist theory (Kohl 1975, 1978; Gilman 1976, 1981; Crumley 1976), whereas that of Thomas Patterson (1983), stimulated by his contact with Marxist archaeologists in Latin America, combined elements of both classical Marxism and neo-Marxism. All these archaeologists disagreed with major aspects of processual archaeology. In 1977, Matthew Spriggs (1984a) organized another major conference on Marxist archaeology at Cambridge University. He noted that at that time French Marxist anthropology seemed to offer young archaeologists "a potentially unifying perspective" (Spriggs 1984b: 5).

Postprocessual archaeology, as an explicit movement, began to develop in Britain as a result of the work of Ian Hodder and his students, who attempted to apply insights gained from French Marxist anthropology to the study of material culture. The first public manifestation of this tendency was a conference on "Symbolism and Structuralism in Archaeology" held at Cambridge University in 1980. This conference resulted in *Symbolic and Structural Archaeology*, edited by Hodder (1982c), a postprocessual showcase and counterpart to *New Perspectives in Archeology* (S. and L. Binford 1968). Hodder had been a student of David Clarke and as a processual archaeologist had made significant contributions to the economic analysis of spatial patterns and the early development of simulation studies (Hodder and Hassall 1971; Hodder 1978a, 1978b; Hodder and Orton 1976). Nevertheless, he grew increasingly dissatisfied with the limitations of processual archaeology and interested in the role played by culture in shaping human behavior. The development of processual archaeology in Britain had already stirred an interest in anthropology and Hodder and his students, like Spriggs, found in French Marxist anthropology concepts that seemed relevant for their own work. As was the case with early processual archaeology, the initial contributions to postprocessual archaeology were in the form of papers. These papers reflected an interest in symbolic, structural, and critical approaches to the study of archaeological data. They also revealed a considerable degree of uncertainty and disagreement about what constituted Marxist theory and how it might be applied to archaeology.

A preoccupation with noneconomic phenomena was evident in the unprecedented attention that early postprocessual archaeologists accorded to religion and other beliefs (Miller and Tilley 1984a). Ideology was described by Kristian Kristiansen (1984) as an active factor in social relations and Michael Parker Pearson (1984: 61) asserted, without even referring to their economic functions, that tools were as much the products of ideology as was a crown or a law code. A. B. Knapp (1988) analyzed how elites manipulated ideology to maintain or enhance their power. Some archaeologists discussed ideology within an explicitly materialist context. Thus, Kristiansen described the megalithic religion of western Europe as an extension of production and Miller and Tilley (1984b: 148) stated that ideology was not an autonomous comment but a part of efforts to produce, maintain, and resist social changes that related to the clash of interests between groups. By contrast, Parker Pearson's (1984: 63) suggestion that ideology can direct economic activity, Mary Braithwaite's (1984: 107) claim that understanding the role of material culture in ritual and prestige practices was a necessary first step in reconstructing other aspects of changes and patterns represented in the archaeological record, and Christopher Tilley's (1984: 143) approval of Habermas's efforts to elevate the ideological sphere to "an important explanatory role" must be interpreted as support for an idealist interpretation of human behavior. Susan Kus (1984) and Peter Gathercole (1984) questioned the traditional Marxist distinction between economic base and superstructure; a distinction that Gathercole suggested reflected Western society's cultural preoccupation with economics. John Gledhill (1984) claimed that Western Marxists generally viewed noneconomic factors as dominant in precapitalist societies. Ritual was described as a "discourse" that served to reaffirm existing social relations by making them appear to be part of the natural order and hence enhanced the power of privileged groups or individuals. Tilley (1984: 143), however, following Marx and Engels and the Italian Marxist philosopher Antonio Gramsci (1992) closely on this point, reminded readers that such views underrate the ability of oppressed individuals to analyze their situations and that ideology is never all-embracing in its control.

Postprocessual archaeologists disagreed about how much needed to be known about prehistoric ideologies to establish what role they had played. Some argued that specific symbolic meanings and social processes are "recursively related" and therefore the meanings must be known in some detail if cultural change is to be explained (Hodder 1984a). Braithwaite (1984: 94) suggested that the exact content of belief systems might be irretrievable archaeologically, although their operation was not. Her concept of "operation" seems little different from a functionalist approach to ritual and ideology.

M. Parker Pearson (1984) maintained that in preclass societies "interest groups" consisting of young and old, men and women, and members of different clans or lineages, struggled in much the same manner as classes do in more advanced societies. He also asserted as an essential premise of Marxism that all human beings are motivated by self-interest and seek power to pursue such interests. Tilley (1984) followed Meillassoux and Terray in claiming that exploitative social relations existed in all social formations. Such uniformitarian views of society ran contrary to the traditional Marxist claim that human nature is transformed in substantial ways by social change (Fuller 1980: 230–64; Geras 1983).

Postprocessual archaeologists generally disapproved of positivist approaches to the analysis of archaeological data. Daniel Miller (1984: 38) asserted that positivism, which he defined as accepting only what can be sensed, tested, and predicted as knowable, seeks to produce technical knowledge that will facilitate the exploitation of commoners by oppressive elites, whereas Miller and Tilley (1984: 2) claimed that it encouraged the acceptance of social injustice by persuading people that human societies were irresistibly shaped by external pressures. Hodder (1984b) maintained that archaeologists had no moral right to interpret the prehistory of other peoples and that their main duty should be to provide individuals with the means to construct their own views of the past, although it was not explained how this information could be supplied without introducing inherent biases into it. Gathercole (1984) and others stressed the subjectivity of archaeology by portraying it as primarily an ideological discipline. Miller and Tilley followed scholars of the Frankfurt School in interpreting Marxism as simply another subjective perspective on the human condition. Marx's claim for a special status for his approach was rejected as a vain attempt to give his work a "veneer" of positivist science. M. J. Rowlands (1984a), by contrast, viewed extreme relativism as a danger threatening archaeology. Relativist ideas and opposition to professional elitism as well as to hegemonic pretensions by archaeologists associated with politically, economically, and culturally dominant countries or institutions became further radicalized as a result of the controversy leading to the establishment of the World Archaeological Congress in 1986 (Ucko 1987). This worldwide organization of like-minded archaeologists is opposed to racism, colonialism, and professional elitism.

The importance of postprocessual archaeology was irrevocably established by a series of brief ethnoarchaeological surveys that Ian Hodder and his students carried out in various parts of sub-Saharan Africa (Hodder 1982b). These studies definitively refuted the key assumption by processual archaeologists that archaeological finds must necessarily reflect social organization. Hodder provided overwhelming documentation that material culture was not merely a reflection of sociopolitical organization but also an active element that could be used to disguise, invert, and distort social relations. Overtly competing groups may use material culture to emphasize their dissimilarities, whereas one ethnic group wishing to have easy access to another's resources may attempt to minimize the material manifestations of such differences. High-status groups actively use material culture to legitimize their authority (Hodder 1982b: 119–22), while in some African countries calabash and age-graded spear styles, which cut across ethnic boundaries that are clearly marked by other aspects of material culture, signal the tacit resistance of women and young men to the authority of dominant elders (Ibid.: 58–74) (Figure 8.7). Even tensions within an extended family were found to be expressed and reinforced by variations in pottery decoration (Ibid.: 122–4).

Hodder's demonstration that material culture is used as an active element in social interaction contradicted the carefully developed arguments of processual archaeologists that the relative elaboration of individual graves within a society accurately mirrors the degree of social differentiation. Further research by Hodder and his students has demonstrated that complex ideas relating to religion, hygiene, and status rivalry also have played significant roles in influencing burial customs (M. Parker Pearson 1982). In some societies, simple burials reflect a social ideal of egalitarianism that is not put into practice in everyday life. For example, in Saudi Arabia, kings and commoners are buried in the same simple manner as a material expression of Islamic belief in the equality of all believers before the transcendence of God and in the ideal social equality of all Moslems (Huntington and Metcalf 1979: 122). Aubrey Cannon (1989) demonstrated that during the nineteenth and early twentieth centuries changing strategies of status emulation altered the social significance of burial practices in England. The geographical and social dislocations brought about by industrialization induced newly wealthy families to affirm their social status with elaborate burials and funeral monuments. Then, less wealthy families copied these practices with the result that wealthy ones placed less emphasis on this form of display. Thus, without taking account of its specific historical context, the social and symbolic significance of any particular burial cannot be established.

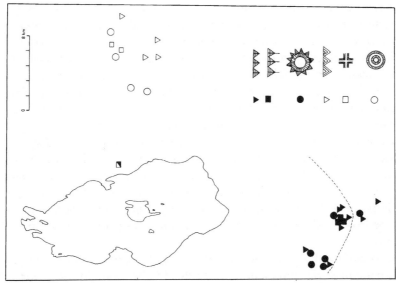

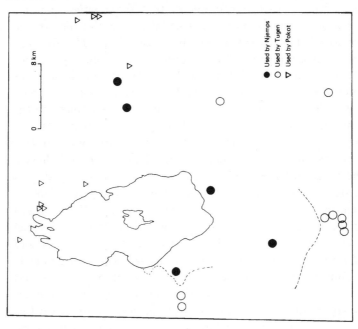

Figure 8.7 Hodder's recording of ethnographic distribution of shield types (above) and calabash motifs (right) among different ethnic groups in the Baringo area of Kenya (*Symbols in Action*, 1982)

454

Ironically, Hodder was able to use ethnoarchaeology – the means by which Binford had hoped to demonstrate detailed regularities in the relations between material culture on the one hand and all forms of social organization on the other – to refute the crucial assumption of processual archaeologists that material culture invariably directly reflects social organization. Hodder's discovery was as significant a contribution to the development of archaeological interpretation as was Willey's demonstration of the importance of settlement pattern studies for investigating prehistoric social and political organization or Thomsen's discovery of occurrence sorting and seriation as effective means for establishing prehistoric chronologies.

Hodder (1987b) went on to apply this discovery to the interpretation of archaeological data by developing what he called contextual archaeology. This approach accords with the general Hegelian-Marxist conviction, transmitted through French anthropology, that social researchers need to examine all possible aspects of a problem in order to understand the significance of any one part of it. Thus, to determine the social significance of burial customs archaeologists have to examine not only cemeteries but other aspects of the archaeological record, such as settlement patterns. It might be assumed that in a situation resembling the Saudi one already mentioned the discrepancy between uniformly simple burials and the vast differences in size and elaboration of dwellings would reveal the ideological character of the burials, once it could be established that burials representing all social classes had been recovered. Even so, without relevant texts or oral traditions, it would be impossible for archaeologists to infer the specific content of the beliefs that had produced this behavior. By drawing attention to properties of material culture that had hitherto been ignored, Hodder revealed the dangers inherent in all interpretations of archaeological evidence analyzed in isolation from its broader cultural context. Even animal bones cannot convincingly be used to reconstruct diet until it has been demonstrated that the animals involved had been slaughtered for eating rather than as sacrifices to the gods or for the use of their hides only. By demonstrating that an archaeological culture cannot be interpreted adequately in a piecemeal fashion, Hodder placed heavy new demands on archaeologists to undertake a comprehensive internal study of archaeological finds that in principle resembled Walter Taylor's conjunctive approach, but in its conceptualization went far beyond it. The contextual approach differed radically from the belief of processual archaeologists that a few selected variables can be studied at a single site to answer a specific archaeological question (Brown and Struever 1973).

Contextual archaeology also rejected the validity of the neoevolutionary distinction between what is culturally specific and what is cross-culturally general that constituted the basis of Steward's dichotomy between science and history (Hodder 1987a). This validated an interest in culturally specific cosmologies, astronomical lore, art styles, religious beliefs, and other topics that had lingered on the fringes of processual archaeology in the 1960s and 1970s. Hodder encouraged archaeologists once again to take account of the complexities of human phenomena and to realize that universal generalizations do not exhaust the regularities that characterize human behavior. He urged them to look for order within individual cultures or historically related cultures both in terms of specific cultural categories, such as the canons governing artistic productions, and in the way different cultural categories related to one another (Bradley 1984). Although contextual archaeology suggested how the detailed study of patterning in the prehistoric archaeological record might distinguish when material culture was being used symbolically to distort or invert rather than to reflect social relations, hard work lay ahead in determining how far and in what ways more specific meanings might be attached to such patterns.

In the United States, postprocessual archaeology developed largely independently and along different lines from what was happening in Britain, with much of the theoretical rationalization for what was being done coming from critical theory. Initiatives involved a more diverse array of archaeologists and there was also less formal organization of what was happening than was the case in Britain. By the early 1980s, as a result of growing doubts about the adequacy of positivism and an increasing awareness of relativism, many American archaeologists recognized for the first time that more than purely objective "scientific" considerations played a role in archaeological interpretation (Gibbon 1984; Leone 1984; Wilk 1985; Patterson 1986a). This in turn promoted a growing interest in the history of archaeology (Trigger 1985a, 1989a, 1994a). Many archaeologists now were prepared to admit that not only the questions they asked but also the answers they were willing to accept as persuasive were influenced by the presuppositions that guided their research (Saitta 1983).

The testing of propositions used to interpret archaeological data was no longer viewed as objective and clearcut, but as a procedure in which significant subjective elements were involved (M. Salmon 1982; Wylie 1982, 1985b). Many now suspected that archaeologists and other scientists accepted lower standards of proof for propositions they held to be reasonable or self-evident than they did for hypotheses of which they disapproved. Even the most strongly supported hypothetico-deductive proposition required faith that what had applied in cases already studied would apply to all similar cases encountered in the future. Many now maintained that archaeologists, both individually and collectively, were influenced in their interpretations, largely unconsciously, by their social milieu (Patterson 1986a). This was not a simple belief that all archaeologists reacted in the same way to a particular set of social conditions (Shanks and Tilley 1987a: 31). Yet it was widely believed that shared class membership or political loyalties encouraged large numbers of archaeologists, but not necessarily all of them, to interpret archaeological data from a similar perspective.

The first major bias to be recognized by American archaeologists was ethnic prejudice. This is scarcely surprising since not only had racial prejudice historically played a major role in American society but it had long influenced the study of American prehistoric archaeology. Robert Silverberg's *Mound Builders of Ancient America* (1968) documented how ideas about the Moundbuilders reflected nineteenth-century Euro-American prejudices against North American Indians and how in a circular fashion interpretations of archaeological finds that had accorded with those beliefs had reinforced such prejudices. In 1980, I argued that assumptions that North American indigenous peoples were primitive and incapable of change had encouraged misreadings of the archaeological record, especially in the nineteenth century when little archaeological work had yet been done (Trigger 1980b). Evidence of cultural change over time was either ignored or attributed to migrations of people rather than to internal transformations. As the archaeological record became better known, archaeologists were slowly, and usually reluctantly, compelled to acknowledge that changes had occurred within cultures, but for a long time these changes were attributed to diffusion from Mesoamerica and Siberia. Only in the second half of the twentieth century did a growing realization of the complexity of the archaeological record compel most archaeologists to consider the possibility that significant internal development had taken place among indigenous groups in prehistoric times.

Archaeologists came to perceive that similar ethnic prejudices had influenced the interpretation of archaeological evidence in other parts of the world, especially in colonial situations and where archaeology was subservient to various nationalist political agendas (Trigger 1984a). Unfortunately, in the United States a growing appreciation of the creativity of indigenous peoples was not accompanied by closer relations between prehistoric archaeologists and the peoples whose pasts they studied. Processual archaeologists, in keeping with their programmatic goals, treated the archaeological record as a basis for generalizing about human behavior and hence their interests had little in common with those of indigenous peoples. Even most post-processual archaeologists looked to the abundant ethnographic data recorded in earlier times rather than to living Indians as sources of the cultural information that was needed to interpret archaeological finds. It was not until Indian activists began to acquire increasing legal control over licensing the study of archaeological material relating to their cultural heritage that, out of political necessity, a dialogue began – a dialogue that continues to be dominated by political issues and is often confrontational (Bray and Killion 1994; Lynott and Wylie 1995; Nicholas and Andrews 1997; Swidler et al. 1997; Dongoske et al. 2000; D. Thomas 2000; Watkins 2000; R. McGuire 2004).

Although feminism and gender studies had become a significant component of Norwegian archaeology already in the 1970s (Dommasnes 1992), it was not until the early 1980s, when Joan Gero (1983) and Margaret Conkey and Janet Spector (1984) published their pioneering studies, that North American archaeologists began to discuss gender bias in both the interpretation of archaeological data and the practice of American archaeology. Historical and sociological studies quickly established that women were seriously underrepresented among the ranks of professional archaeologists and that in the past most of them had worked as technicians and laboratory analysts rather than as directors of field projects, which was regarded as a more prestigious activity. It also was demonstrated that the marginalization of women had resulted in biased and androcentric interpretations of archaeological evidence. The dramatic exposure of the limitations of the "man the hunter" view of cultural evolution was an opening salvo in critiquing the intellectual consequences of the male domination of archaeology (N. Tanner 1981; Fedigan 1986). Accompanying that critique was a demand that more women should be recruited into the discipline and empowered within it in order to enhance archaeology's intellectual credibility as well as to promote social justice (Gero and Conkey 1991; Walde and Willows 1991; Hanen and Kelley 1992; Claassen 1994; Nelson et al. 1994; Conkey and Tringham 1995; R. Wright 1996; S. Nelson 1997).

There was little overt resistance to this movement, no doubt because it began so much later in archaeology than it had in sociocultural anthropology and the other social sciences that male archaeologists despaired of winning such a battle. They quickly conceded that the lack of adequate female representation had resulted in many relevant questions going unasked and in many unduly partial or erroneous interpretations of the past. Because they addressed the organization as well as the practice of archaeology, critiques from the perspective of feminism and gender studies played a major role in revealing the generic nature of bias to many archaeologists. This further undermined the authority of a positivist epistemology and led a growing number of archaeologists to consider seriously the claims that relativists and postprocessual archaeologists were making about other issues.

Alison Wylie (1996, 1997) has described how gender archaeology evolved from critiques of androcentrism to a search for women in the archaeological record and then to a rethinking of issues of difference and relatedness as these concern gender. More recently, third-wave feminism has sought to treat gender issues not as an isolated focus of study but as an aspect of life that inevitably intersects with other aspects, such as age, class, ethnicity, personal appearance, wealth, and occupation (Meskell 1999, 2002). This development bears witness to the success of the feminist critique of archaeology, which has resulted in the acceptance of gender not simply as another standpoint but as a significant consideration in all forms of archaeological interpretation and practice. Excellent gender archaeology has been done in Britain (Gilchrist 1994, 1999), but gender issues have not been discussed as widely there as in the United States. Feminist archaeologists have called on British male postprocessual archaeologists to explain this failure (Engelstad 1991; Preucel and Chesson 1994: 70–1).

Gender archaeologists, like gender specialists in other disciplines, continue to debate to what extent gender is wholly a culturally constructed category or it is also grounded in human biology. Either from conviction or as a default position, most gender archaeologists maintain that archaeologists should never seek to generalize cross-culturally about relations between men and women. Some more radical relativists affirm that even sex, as opposed to gender, consists not of biology but of the changing ideas that specific groups of people have about biological differences (Gosden 1999: 132–51).

It is perhaps symptomatic of the limited interest in the formal study of class in the United States that archaeologists have paid less attention to class biases than to ethnic and gender ones. Most of this work has been done by historical archaeologists, its early advocates including Russell Handsman (1981) and Mark Leone (1981), whose studies, inspired by the pioneering research of Henry Glassie (1975) and James Deetz (1977), challenged Stanley South's (1977a, 1977b) processual approach. Much of Leone's work has sought to counter efforts by those who manage colonial heritage sites to use them to project modern power relations and social values back into earlier times in order to make such relations and values appear natural, changeless, and unproblematical (Figure 8.8). Historical archaeologists also devote much attention to researching the everyday life of slaves and industrial workers, as those groups usually are poorly documented in written records and therefore archaeologists can hope to contribute significantly to knowledge concerning them. Increasing efforts also are being made to involve the descendants of people being studied in helping to formulate the questions that direct such research (Leone and Potter 1988; McGuire and Paynter 1991; M. Johnson 1996; Shackel 1996). These developments have greatly enriched the scope and quality of research in historical archaeology.

Critical theory, which is concerned with deconstructing explanations and revealing the biases that are intentionally and unintentionally built into them according to the different standpoints of their creators (Held 1980), has been used to structure and rationalize discussions of bias in archaeology. The most important impact of the research outlined earlier has been the empirical evidence it has provided of the extent to which biases have permeated archaeological

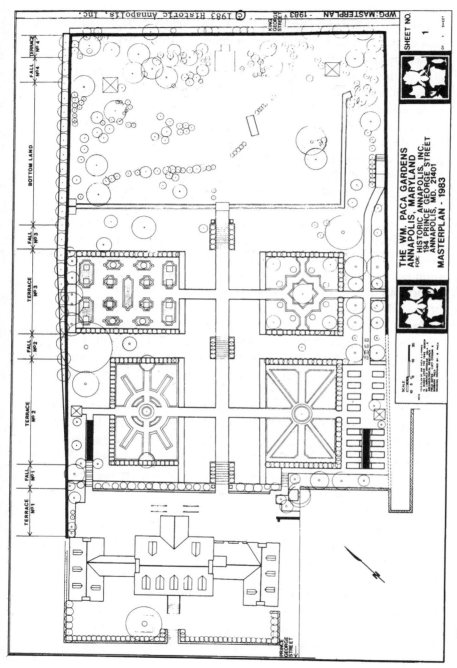

Figure 8.8 Eighteenth-century William Paca Garden, Annapolis, Maryland; the outlines of the garden are archaeologically determined (D. Miller and C. Tilley, eds., *Ideology, Power and Prehistory*, 1984a)

research in the past. This insight has led many archaeologists to believe that similar biases may be influencing their own work. The possibility that this is so has further sensitized American archaeologists to the significance of a relativist epistemology and made them more willing to accept at least some of the claims of postprocessual archaeologists.

Most American prehistoric archaeologists remained convinced of the utility of studying the archaeological record from an ecological point of view, but many of these were prepared to consider cultural explanations for those aspects of the archaeological record to which ecological explanations did not seem to apply. Strictly speaking, this position was not anathema to Binford, although he continued to believe that everything important about human behavior could be explained ecologically. Richard Gould (1978b) argued that archaeologists should explain ecologically all they could and interpret only residual observations symbolically. According to this procedure, preferences for different types of chert should be studied initially in terms of the relative utility of these types for manufacturing specific sorts of tools. Only if the preferred type turned out to perform less well or to be more difficult to work should a cultural explanation be considered. This approach unfortunately made the current limitations of an archaeologist's knowledge or analytical skills the determining factor differentiating between ecological and symbolic explanations. As time went on, a growing number of American archaeologists relied on common sense or current consensus as the basis for deciding what kind of explanation was appropriate. Although American archaeologists were increasingly open to theoretical diversity, most of them lacked the ambition to try to determine in an operational manner under what circumstances specific sorts of theories were and were not applicable.

In Britain, postprocessual archaeology has generally been presented as a self-sufficient alternative to processual archaeology. Partisans assume that one or the other position is correct and that the main goal of postprocessual archaeologists should be to discredit and replace processual archaeology. Beginning in the early 1980s, postprocessual archaeologists sought to explain artifact variation and change in terms of the creation and manipulation of social meanings, especially in the context of asserting, maintaining, or resisting social power.

In the early years, a favorite explanatory device was cultural (as distinguished from social) structuralism. The creator of this approach was the French anthropologist Claude Lévi-Strauss (b. 1908), whose ideas were based on the observation by the distinguished Swiss linguist Ferdinand de Saussure (1857–1913) that all speech is made possible by rules of grammar of which speakers are normally unaware and knowledge of which can be uncovered only by formal linguistic analysis. This observation prompted Lévi-Strauss to conclude analogically that cultural patterns need not be caused by anything outside themselves. He assumed that underlying every culture was a deep structure, or essence, governed by its own laws, that people were unaware of but which ensured regularities in the cultural productions that emanated from it. More specifically, Lévi-Strauss assumed that all human thought was governed by conceptual dichotomies, or bilateral oppositions, such as culture/nature, male/female, day/night, and life/death. He believed that the principle of oppositions was a universal characteristic inherent in the human brain, but that each culture was based on a unique selection of oppositions that could experience significant permutations in their mutual relations, while at the same time the system which they constituted remained unchanged. A careful analysis of written or spoken texts would reveal what oppositions were important in each culture and how they were related to each other (Leach 1970). Although Lévi-Strauss's structuralism has much in common with Boasian configurationalism, the underlying pattern is a cognitive rather than a psychological one. While bilateral oppositions are a widespread feature of human thought, since Lévi-Strauss first presented his theory in the 1950s neuroscience has provided no evidence that the human brain is biologically programmed to think exclusively or even primarily in terms of such oppositions.

The first substantial application of the structuralist approach to prehistoric archaeology was made by the French archaeologist André Leroi-Gourhan (1911–1986), the most anthropologically sophisticated of all European archaeologists. He assumed that a careful structural analysis of material culture might reveal the conceptual oppositions underlying it and how these oppositions were related to each other. Beginning in the 1940s, before becoming a structuralist, Leroi-Gourhan had developed a complex ethnography of artifacts, which embraced a mixture of ideas of a sort that later would be associated with both processual and culture-historical archaeology. He sought to classify artifacts in ways that simultaneously took account of their convergent functional constraints (*tendances*) and their divergent cultural (or ethnic) variations (*faits*). He also developed the concept of the *chaîne opératoire*, or sequence of morphological changes that occur in the production and life history of artifacts. He saw cultural evolution as beginning with the tool, a joint product of mind and body, followed by the diversification of ethnic groups, and finally by the elaboration of technologies that expanded human memory ([1964, 1965] 1993). In this early work, Leroi-Gourhan was inventing an anthropology suited for the needs of archaeologists (Coudart 1999; Audouze and Schlanger 2004). This did not, however, prevent him from adopting a structuralist approach to study the meaning of symbols.

In the 1950s, Leroi-Gourhan (1964) began an analysis of statistical regularities in the distribution of images of animals and human beings and accompanying abstract signs in the Upper Palaeolithic cave art of western Europe. He and Annette Laming-Emperaire (1962) proceeded to interpret in structural terms not individual images but what they believed were planned compositions filling entire caves. They proposed that these compositions referred to myths dealing with relations between male and female principles, which they agreed were symbolized by the numerically dominant paintings of horses and bison. Leroi-Gourhan associated horses with the male principle and bovids with the female principle, whereas Laming-Emperaire supported the opposite association. It proved impossible to persuade other archaeologists that either of these interpretations was correct and by the late 1970s Leroi-Gourhan had completely abandoned this approach (R. White 1993: xiv; Ucko and Rosenfeld 1967).

Ian Hodder became the leading exponent of a structuralist approach in postprocessual archaeology. In 1982, he examined similarities in the layouts of Neolithic tombs and houses in Europe and attempted to infer their symbolic meaning (Hodder 1984a). About the same time, Tilley (1984) examined the orientation of Neolithic tombs in Sweden and the distribution of human bones and pottery in relation to them in an effort to infer prehistoric rituals and their associated meanings. His generalized linking of death and destruction with the promotion of fertility, life, and the social order was not substantially different from the speculative generalizations of the Victorian anthropologist James Frazer (1854–1941).

The most ambitious application of a structuralist approach to interpreting prehistoric archaeological data was Hodder's *The Domestication of Europe* (1990). This book remains the most substantial structuralist work in prehistoric archaeology and hence constitutes the best case study for evaluating the strengths and weaknesses of this approach. Hodder examined changing plans and locations of European houses, settlements, enclosures, and tombs, as well as changes in associated iconographic elements, from Neolithic times to the Iron Age, with still earlier evidence from the Middle East also being considered since it was judged historically relevant for understanding the beginning of this sequence. Hodder sought to relate changes in these patterns to structural adjustments in relations among a set of binary oppositions that he believed included nature and culture, male and female, wild and domestic, outer and inner, front and back, light and dark, and life and death. His most important opposition was between field (*agrios*) and house (*domus*), which often was mediated by the concept of boundary (*foris*). Hodder maintained that the archaeological evidence indicated that from the Neolithic period into the Iron Age the primary symbolic emphasis had shifted from *domus* to *agrios*, as prehistoric European society became more male-centered.

It is not always clear how Hodder went about assigning meanings to the patterns he observed in the archaeological record. Sometimes he appears to have assumed universal meanings, a procedure that runs contrary to his insistence on the mutual incomprehensibility of cultures, but which he employed elsewhere, as for example in his argument that trash disposal is deployed by many small-scale societies as a strategy for marking social boundaries (Hodder 1982a: 60–5, 1982b: 125–84, 1990: 127, 1991d: 4, 6). It seems unlikely, however, that the distinction between nature and culture that is central not only to Hodder's analyses but also to much of the work of Lévi-Strauss meant anything to Europeans or anyone else before about 500 BC. Historical and ethnographic evidence suggests that before that time people would have conceptualized what we view as the natural world as being animated by spiritual powers that possessed minds and wills similar to those of humans. This understanding made no use of the distinctions that Europeans and others later would draw between nature, society, and the supernatural. It was only after the desacralization of nature that took place in Greece, parts of the Middle East, India, and China around the middle of the first millennium BC that a distinction between nature and culture probably existed anywhere in the world (Childe 1949, 1956b; Frankfort 1948; Jaspers 1953; Hallpike 1979; MacCormack and Strathern 1980; Eisenstadt 1986). Similarly, ethnographic evidence suggests that many peoples, especially hunter-gatherers, do not view the wild as being dangerous and the home as being protective, however obvious that dichotomy appears to Westerners and perhaps to most other sedentary peoples. Instead, the wild is perceived as a nurturing sphere controlled by powers on whose friendship and benevolence humans must rely (Bird-David 1990; Ingold 1996).

More generally, Hodder appears to have assumed that because of continuities in the deep structure of European culture, an archaeologist who has grown up in a modern European society would have privileged insights into the thought patterns that had shaped the archaeological record of Europe in prehistoric times (Hodder 1990: 2–3, 282–300). Those insights presumably would not be shared to the same extent by an archaeologist who had grown up in China but had specialized in the study of European prehistory, whereas analogous insights concerning China would be less accessible to European archaeologists trained as Sinologists. This attempt to exploit what structuralists believe to be the long-term persistence in underlying patterns of thought in individual cultural traditions so far has not been demonstrated to have carried the symbolic interpretation of patterning of material culture in the archaeological record beyond the intuitive level.

The structuralist approach encouraged the detailed study of intricate forms of patterning of material culture in the archaeological records of specific cultures that hitherto both culture-historical and processual archaeologists had tended to ignore. Yet neither Leroi-Gourhan nor Hodder discovered how to advance beyond speculation in interpreting the meaning of such regularities in the absence of associated nonarchaeological information. By the 1990s, structuralism itself was in deep trouble. Despite its skillful deployment to analyze many sorts of data, it had exhibited no significant theoretical development since Lévi-Strauss had introduced it, nor had its ontological validity been demonstrated. In recent years, the more general concept of metaphors has come to be viewed as providing more productive insights into the nature of human thought (Lakoff and Johnson 1980; Lakoff 1987), an idea that Tilley (1999) has accepted. The failure of archaeologists to discover ways to use a structural approach to gain insights into the specific meanings of prehistoric data and growing doubts about the ontological validity of Lévi-Strauss's claims have resulted in archaeologists slowly losing interest in structuralism.

A second, poststructural wave of postprocessual archaeology in Britain was primarily concerned with political action, encouraging opposition to authority, and emphasizing the transformative power of human agency. This wave was represented during the 1980s and 1990s in the works of Michael Shanks, Christopher Tilley, and Peter Ucko, a senior culture-historical archaeologist who had become radicalized while serving during the 1970s as director of the Institute of Aboriginal Studies located in Canberra, Australia (Moser 1995b). Shanks and Tilley both explored structuralism but appear to have decided that its ahistorical character did not make it useful for understanding change. After that they focused on ideas derived largely from French Marxist anthropology, as well as from the works of Louis Althusser and Anthony Giddens. They replaced a processual emphasis on behavior with an emphasis on symbolically mediated social and political action that required paying close attention to the specific cultural milieus, beliefs, and goals of the actors involved. They also sought, by undermining archaeology's claims to be an authoritative source of knowledge about the past, to encourage people to question and resist all sorts of authority. In doing this, they were following the Frankfurt School's teaching that authoritative knowledge is an instrument of ideological subjection from which it was necessary for radical intellectuals to try to free ordinary people. It also was assumed that such power was a feature of all societies, not just ones divided by social classes, although the nature of inequality was believed to vary from one society to another (Ucko 1989a: xii). By making domination appear to be an inherent feature of the human condition, this position promoted a belief about the universality of inequality that Marx and Engels had strongly opposed.

Sometimes Shanks and Tilley (1987a: 114–15; 1989; *Lampeter Archaeological Workshop* 1997) acknowledged that archaeological findings had at least some limited power to resist erroneous interpretations being imposed on them. For the most part, however, Shanks, Tilley, and Ucko, like strong relativists in other disciplines, maintained that there was no empirical basis on which archaeologists could demonstrate that one interpretation was right and another wrong.

They argued that scholars were so blinded by their beliefs that archaeological findings could exert little, if any, influence over how they interpreted such evidence. The only way to refute an archaeological theory was to demonstrate that it was illogical (Miller and Tilley 1984b: 151; Shanks and Tilley 1987b: 195; Tilley 1990b: 338–40; Ucko 1989b: xix–xx). The goal of strong relativism was to demystify the knowledge claims of specialists by showing them to be merely expressions of opinion similar in nature to those of nonspecialists or, better still, by exposing them as deliberate lies or myth-making. Such critiques drew heavily on the efforts of the philosopher Paul Feyerabend (1975) and the sociologist of science Barry Barnes (1974, 1977) to demolish the distinction between scientific and nonscientific knowledge. Archaeologists' claims to possess special qualifications to explain their findings were branded as attempts to control the past in the interests of dominant groups. It was asserted, as Hodder had already done, that any individuals or groups had the right to use archaeological data to create the pasts they wanted and for good measure it often was added that there was no factual basis for challenging the validity of any logically coherent interpretation. This position was hailed by its supporters as democratizing archaeology and purging it both of elitist pretensions and of the "grip of all closed systems of thought" (Held 1980: 150; Hodder 1984b; Shanks and Tilley 1987b: 195; Tilley 1990b: 338; Ucko 1989b: xix–xxi).

It also was argued that material objects are symbolically "irreducibly polysemous," which means they signify different things to different people and perhaps even to the same person at different times (Shanks and Tilley 1987b: 115–17; B. Olsen 1990: 195; Shanks 1996: 121). That position denies that there ever was an "original meaning to be textually recreated in an analysis of a set of objects" (Tilley 1990b: 338). Under these conditions, the only meanings that artifacts can have today are ones that archaeologists and others assign to them. There is no way to determine whether these messages are similar to or different from the ones that were assigned to them in the past or, if they could be shown to be different, which meaning is more legitimate. On these grounds, Shanks and Tilley (1987b: 195) asserted that "there is no way of choosing between alternative pasts except on essentially political grounds."

Shanks and Tilley attributed great importance to the concept of agency as a means of countering the deterministic claims of processual archaeologists that there was no possibility of individuals' significantly altering the conditions in which they found themselves. They argued that more attention should be paid to decisions by individuals when trying to account for stability and change in societies. Instead of viewing human actions as controlled by adaptive forces and social systems, they should be viewed as directed by purposeful action.

This approach led postprocessual archaeologists into encounters with a wide variety of disparate and conflicting theories about what was clearly a contentious issue. Some archaeologists attempted to extend and adapt Marx's assumption that class conflict and rational self-interest were the main factors bringing about change so that it also might explain changes in small-scale societies. Sahlins (1976a: 12) argued against this that concepts of utility and self-interest were socially constructed. Others embraced Anthony Giddens's (1984) theory of structuration, which, like Marxism, posited a recursive relation between social structure and agency but viewed self-interest as more deeply embedded in culture than Marx had done and agency as invested in the individual, rather than in classes or in interest groups. Matthew Johnson (1989) and others have complained that, while agency has received much lip service, few archaeologists have attempted seriously to deal with it. More recently, Martin Byers (1999, 2004) has proposed that a cognitive understanding of archaeological data may be advanced by focusing on intentionality, which he views as the causal interface governing interactions between human beings and the world. In keeping with the ideas of the psychologist John Searle (1983), Byers argues that intentionality must be analyzed in terms of four mutually irreducible states of consciousness: beliefs, wants and desires, intentions, and perceptions.

The development of poststructuralism countered an interest in agency with a renewed concern with the structures and forces that might limit and shape human behavior, although the individual was now seen as buffeted by a multiplicity of fragmented structures rather than by a single underlying one (Bapty and Yates 1990). Louis Althusser had long regarded preexisting social conditions as the main factor limiting human freedom. The practice theory of Pierre Bourdieu (1977) likewise analyzed how individuals reshaped their societies by using existing behavioral patterns, beliefs, and institutional resources to achieve their objectives. His concept of *habitus* stressed the extent to which learned, but unconscious, forms of behavior limited the ability of individuals to act as free agents, much as did Michel Foucault's (1970, 1972) concept of *epistemes*. Some postprocessual archaeologists, such as Julian Thomas (2000: 149–50), flatly deny that the agency of individuals is a useful concept, thereby seemingly embracing a cultural determinist position. The role played by individuals has been further called into question by those who maintain that the concept of the individual is present only in some societies, most notably modern capitalist ones (Shennan 2002: 212); others deny that individualism and the individual are related concepts (Meskell 2002). It is also debated to what extent individuals are controlled by dominant ideologies or oppressed groups create counterideologies that facilitate resistance (Gramsci 1992). For the most part, postprocessual archaeologists who are concerned with studying social action have functioned as consumers and advocates for a wide variety of conflicting theories advocated by other social scientists. There is little evidence that they have systematically attempted to use archaeological data to evaluate, improve, and integrate these theories.

The effort by Shanks and Tilley to reduce archaeological interpretations to political practice provoked a strong response from archaeologists who were moderate relativists, mainly in North America. These moderate relativists agreed that major problems of objectivity existed in all archaeological interpretation and that no one can be certain that any interpretation is free of bias. Yet they agreed with the philosopher Alison Wylie that archaeological evidence was produced independently of any archaeologist and therefore such evidence offers resistance to the totally free exercise of archaeologists' imaginations and to erroneous interpretations. Archaeologists' presuppositions and expectations influence what archaeological sites are recognized and chosen for excavation, which artifacts are identified and how they are classified, and how archaeological data are interpreted. Yet, in the long run, erroneous interpretations tend to be challenged and often are falsified as a result of the discovery of contrary new data. This process is aided by disputes among archaeologists who support differing interpretations of the same data and by shifts in interpretative fashions (Trigger 1980b, 1989a: 407–11; Leone 1982; Wylie 1982, 1992, 1996, 2000). It also was observed that there was no guarantee that subjective political interpretations of archaeological data would be used for benevolent and socially responsible purposes. On the contrary, the history of archaeology documents poorly supported interpretations often being employed to support unwholesome political projects (Kohl and Fawcett 1995). Today, most postprocessual archaeologists acknowledge that archaeological evidence can impose constraints on the interpretation of data (M. Johnson 1999). Yet many of these same archaeologists still seek to undermine and relativize the arguments of archaeologists who are not postprocessualists and who pursue research programs that attempt systematically to test the claims they make about beliefs that were held in prehistoric times (S. Jones 1997: 139–44; Gosden 1999; M. Johnson 1999; Hodder 2001b; A. Jones 2002; Hodder and Hutson 2003).

The rejection by postprocessual archaeologists of grand narratives, their advocacy of multivocality and the empowerment of minority interpretations, and their decreasing support for the idea that objectivity is an ideal worth striving for encouraged a new emphasis on producing multiple, small-scale narratives about the past (Joyce 2002). Examples of this genre include Janet Spector's (1993) informed speculation about how a decorated bone-hafted awl came to be lost in a nineteenth-century Wahpeton Dakota village, Ruth Tringham's (1991) imagining of one woman's participation in the deliberate burning of a house at the Neolithic Opovo site in Yugoslavia, and Ian Hodder's (1999: 137–45) arguments about the events surrounding the death of the 5000-year-old Austrian Ice Man. Hodder (1991c) designated this sort of approach "interpretive archaeology" and described it as characterized by a hermeneutic method that was welcoming to multivocality and aimed mainly at satisfying internal criteria of plausibility (Hodder et al. 1995). Even when significant amounts of historical or ethnographic information are available for such an interpretation, it is regarded as desirable to interpolate invented details to enhance the narrative qualities of the story.

The narrative approach closely resembles the story-telling that David Clarke (1968) found so objectionable in the irresponsible form that British prehistorians practiced it in the 1950s and against which he launched his campaign to discover rigorous ways to infer human behavior from archaeological data. Such an approach often ignores the basic rules of historiography that require that, when different interpretations can be derived from the same body of data, historians should seek to determine whether these versions are complementary and can be synthesized into a more comprehensive, persuasive, and theoretically interesting whole, or they are contradictory, in which case new data should be sought and further analyses carried out to discover whether and to what extent each interpretation is correct. Philip Kohl (1993: 15) maintains that when the information needed to answer a specific question is lacking, instead of inventing a tale archaeologists should admit the problem and seek to answer other questions. Even as a means of popularizing archaeological finds, deliberately introducing unsubstantiated and often ideologically driven speculation into narratives raises serious ethical issues. Finally, it is debatable whether fanciful stories are what the public expects from archaeologists. Brit Solli (1996: 225) suggests that instead they desire informed opinions based on professional research.

The third wave of postprocessual interpretation, introduced by Christopher Tilley (1994), has been variously labeled intuitive, constructivist, or humanist archaeology. Humanist archaeology has been defined as an approach that sees biologically grounded humans overlaid by experience, although Julian Thomas rejects its concern with the individual (J. Thomas 2000: 147–8). Among the leaders of this movement are John Barrett (1994), Christopher Gosden (1994), Julian Thomas (1996), and Cornelius Holtorf (2002). The humanist approach has influenced the work of a large number of archaeologists in Britain, the United States, and elsewhere (Tilley 1994; Ashmore and Knapp 1999). Humanist archaeology is based on phenomenology, a branch of philosophy developed by the German academics Edmund Husserl (1859–1938) and Martin Heidegger (1889–1976). Phenomenology is distinguished from most other forms of Western idealist philosophy by its repudiation of the separation between the observer and the observed. Its proponents view human beings not as subjects manipulating objects in the real world but as creatures living in and reciprocally engaged with that world. Both Husserl and Heidegger believed that philosophy alone was sufficient to understand human behavior; hence, they avoided contact with psychology and the social sciences and were poorly informed about developments in these fields. Heidegger also wrote in a style that was very difficult, and some would say impossible, to understand (Bunge 1996: 295). Humanist archaeologists understand phenomenology as indicating that human thought and behavior, whether intuitive or conscious, always relate to things, whether they are part of the natural world or human creations. According to Gosden (1999: 120), this makes objects social agents. Human behavior is learned through socially prescribed comportment which involves engagement with artifacts, buildings, and a natural environment that has been transformed through human use. By understanding how that environment was perceived and used by humans in the past, it should be possible to learn something about the general beliefs, feelings, and attitudes that motivated these people.

Much early humanist archaeology was concerned with studying the meanings that prehistoric landscapes had for the people who inhabited or used them and how these understandings channeled human activity. This approach is often referred to as landscape archaeology and regarded as a postprocessual, culturally oriented counterpart of settlement archaeology (Bender 1993; Bradley 1993, 1998, 2000; Tilley 1994; Sherratt 1996; Ashmore and Knapp 1999; J. Thomas 2001; Ashmore 2002, 2004). Many of the concerns of landscape archaeology seem to have grown out of Hodder's (1984a) study of the symbolism of prehistoric European houses and tombs in relation to their geographical settings. A major weakness of many of these studies is their failure adequately to use the detailed information about ecological and sociopolitical behavior that archaeologists have already inferred for the specific societies being studied. Two major exceptions, as far as sociopolitical behavior is concerned, are Bradley's recent studies of the socially organized relations between people and place and Adam Smith's (2003) non-Heideggerean examinations of the constitution of political authority in space and time through the creation and remodeling of landscapes in early complex societies. In recent years, it has been recognized increasingly that in most locations still older monuments and human modifications to the natural terrain have been part of landscapes for many thousands of years. Memory archaeology has developed as a new branch of archaeology concerned with studying how people have understood the surviving remains of earlier ages throughout human history (Alcock 2002; Bradley 2002; Van Dyke and Alcock 2003; H. Williams 2003).

An archaeological interest in how the human body was understood and manipulated in prehistoric cultures was initially stimulated by Foucault's concern with the cultural disciplining of human actions and behavior (Shanks and Tilley 1982). With the development of landscape archaeology, increasing attention was paid to the role played by architecture and other spatial controls in imposing such discipline. The goal of the archaeology of the body is to ask questions about how in the past humans may have experienced their world both discursively and nondiscursively through their bodies and in relation to specific cultural settings (Kus 1992; Treherne 1995; Meskell 1996, 1999; Rautman 2000; Hamilakis et al. 2002; Fraser 2004; Joyce 2004). Hodder and Hutson (2003: 169) suggest that what archaeologists may hope to learn most about is the "semi-conscious, bodily harmonising" by which humans relate to such settings. Elsewhere they identify this understanding with *habitus* (pp. 94–5).

The most ambitious humanist archaeology study to date is Katsuo Mizoguchi's (2002) examination of how evolving concepts of self-identity related to changing social organization and built environments in Japan from the Jomon into the Kofun periods. Although Mizoguchi specifically seeks to refute essentialist ideas of a monolithic and unchanging Japanese identity beginning in Jomon times, the main source of his insights appears to be the direct historical approach controlled by very detailed studies of short-term changes in material culture at specific sites. Producing data of this sort is a specialty of Japanese culture-historical archaeology.

Heideggerian philosophy has encouraged postprocessual archaeologists to imagine that through an act of contemplation they can sense what landscapes would have meant, symbolically and aesthetically, to the people who inhabited them long ago (Fraser 1998). The idea that a modern, highly educated Western archaeologist can understand the past contemplatively or intuitively reflects the phenomenological belief that underlying cultural diversity are a common human nature and common human bodily needs that make such an operation possible. This idea seems to have been implicit in much German idealist philosophizing for at least two centuries. Anthropologists have empirically demonstrated that cultural differences are sufficiently great as to make it highly unlikely that such a procedure could control for ethnocentrism and produce reliable results. This is especially so given the great amount of cognitive polyvalence that postprocessual archaeologists have demonstrated is inherent in material culture. Many postprocessual archaeologists concur that it is impossible to demonstrate that such interpretations are likely to be valid, but maintain that this impossibility justifies a speculative approach, since it is the best that is possible and without it prehistoric archaeology would be irrelevant to the present (Bender et al. 1997). Other archaeologists view such behavior as irresponsible. Stephen Shennan (2002: 210) also objects that such interpretations tend to ignore ecological realities, and even social relations are left extremely vague, often amounting to no more than an acceptance of highly schematic social evolutionary generalizations, despite a general repudiation of evolutionary approaches by postprocessual archaeologists.

Postprocessual archaeologists have long sought to minimize the differences between the study of purely prehistoric societies and studies where archaeological findings are supplemented by ethnographic or historical data referring to the same period, location, and ethnic group. It was maintained in the 1980s that material culture could be regarded as the equivalent of a text that archaeologists might eventually learn to read (Hodder 1988, 1991d: 126–8; Shanks and Tilley 1987b: 95–117, 1989: 4–5; Tilley 1990b). Yet growing awareness that material culture tends to be conceptually less specific and more polysemous than are written texts eventually revealed the inappropriateness of that expectation (Hodder and Hutson 2003: 167–9). Alain Gallay (1986: 198–200, 281) has argued that there is no purely archaeological way to demonstrate an isometric relation between our inferences about ideas in the past and what was actually believed.

When contemporaneous textual data are not available, unlike the situation with historical archaeology, archaeologists have attempted to use ethnographic data and the direct historical approach to infer symbolic meaning. George Hamell (1983) employed regularities in religious beliefs found in myths recorded since earliest European contact among diverse Iroquoian-, Algonquian-, and Siouan-speaking peoples to explain the inclusion of natural crystals, mica, marine shell, and native copper, as well as artifacts manufactured from these materials, as life-giving objects in indigenous eastern North American burial contexts for over 6,000 years, from the late Archaic into the historical period. In a study of pottery designs from the Mesa Verde area of the southwestern United States, Scott Ortman (2000) provided convincing evidence that, during the Great Pueblo period (AD 1060–1280), pottery designs reproduced weaving patterns associated with cloth and basketry. Similar designs were used to decorate kiva ritual structures that in some modern Pueblo groups are believed to represent a cosmos made up of an earth bowl and a sky basket. Ortman speculated that in prehistoric times the transmission of particular designs from one generation to another may have been reinforced by cultural pressure to behave in conformity with cosmological beliefs that were held sacred by local communities. Alexander von Gernet and Peter Timmins (1987) have demonstrated that the material expression of a belief may fluctuate repeatedly over time in the frequency of its occurrence in the archaeological record.

Although these studies provide evidence that the direct historical approach permits interesting and plausible conclusions to be drawn about symbolic matters for some prehistoric cultures, the results have not been as detailed or as certain as they are with historical archaeology. Contextual analyses of European Palaeolithic art have been attempted, but, as Leroi-Gourhan's work demonstrates, in the absence of compelling homologies or analogies, convincing interpretations of the original meaning of this art have not been forthcoming. As a result of these differences, historical archaeology has emerged as the preeminent testing ground for theories seeking to establish relations between meanings and material culture. Some prehistoric archaeologists regard such historical research as a means to an end, arguing that it is merely a way for cross-cultural regularities to be discovered that will allow specific meanings to be attributed to material culture in prehistoric societies. So far, this approach has not succeeded and evidence of the great pervasiveness of cultural idiosyncrasies suggests that such cross-cultural generalizations will remain limited in number and at a high level of generality. Even J. D. Lewis-Williams and T. A. Dowson's (1988) theories about the influence of drug-induced trances on the production of cave images has little that is convincing to say about the specific meanings that were originally assigned to these representations. Rigorous attributions of meaning to material culture in societies inaccessible to the direct historical approach, if they are to be achieved, will have to depend on the development of cross-cultural generalizations and hence on a cognitive-processual rather than a postprocessual methodology. This suggests that historical archaeology is likely to remain the most productive focus of postprocessual archaeology.

Postprocessual archaeologists, like processual ones, are consumers of anthropological theory. They, however, draw theories from the cultural and idealist side of the anthropological spectrum rather than from the materialist, adaptational, and functional side. Like processual archaeologists, they also have embraced many mutually contradictory theories. Unlike processual archaeologists, however, they tend to be highly conscious of their theoretical diversity and to celebrate it.

Postprocessual archaeologists generally embrace relativism and subjectivism. They reject cultural evolution and grand narratives, positivist scientific methodology, ecological determinism, the idea that culture is primarily an adaptive system, and the value of comparative analysis. They also accept Hodder's demonstration that material culture can distort or invert as well as simply reflect social reality. Yet, although postprocessualists generally deny that human behavior is determined primarily by economic factors, they disagree about the extent to which it is determined by objective self-interest, as conceptualized by classical Marxists, or by cultural considerations. While postprocessual archaeologists are greatly interested in culture as a factor mediating human behavior, they also disagree whether culture is more effectively studied at the level of regions, individual societies, gender, class and occupational divisions, or individual human beings; the individual being the unit where the greatest variety of cultural categories intersect. Although they agree that all artifacts had meanings in the past and that in the symbolic realm the relation between the signifier and the signified is often arbitrary, they disagree about how meaning can be ascribed to archaeological finds. They also disagree about whether archaeologists' interpretations are independent of the meanings artifacts had in the past or bear some unknown relation to those meanings. Finally, they subscribe to many different and competing social anthropological theories about how cultures operate and change.

There is also continuing geographical variation in how processual and postprocessual archaeology are seen as related to one another. In Britain, many archaeologists continue to treat the two approaches as mutually exclusive and to assume that the success of one will eventually result in the disappearance of the other. Most American archaeologists regard them as complementary. They view the processual approach as useful for explaining subsistence patterns and economic behavior and the postprocessual approach as better suited to account for religious beliefs. Yet this eclecticism has remained naive, because little effort has been made to specify the conditions under which one or the other approach applies. Because most American prehistoric archaeologists were trained as anthropologists, they also recognize

that postprocessual archaeology has revived the interest that idealist culture-historical archaeologists once had in culture. This interest
was sidelined by New Archaeology, even if Binford recognized style
as a default explanation for aspects of the archaeological record that
could not be explained ecologically. Now, however, culture is treated
as a cognitive process mediating all human behavior.

Continental European Alternatives

Processual and postprocessual archaeology spread far beyond Britain
and the United States. In Scandinavia and the Netherlands they are
understood as coherent systems and local archaeologists have played
significant roles in the debates concerning their respective merits.
Carl-Axel Moberg's (1915–1987) theoretical position was significantly influenced by the ideas of Lewis Binford and Stig Welinder's
by those of David Clarke (Hegardt 2001: 1234–5). Throughout most
of Europe, processual archaeology has encouraged a greater interest
in the study of ecological adaptation and the scientific analysis of data
among archaeologists who remain broadly committed to a culture-
historical approach. It also temporarily increased interest in Palaeolithic archaeology (Zvelebil 1996: 151). The influence of postprocessual archaeology has been more sporadic. Among some groups
of European archaeologists it has stimulated the study of material
culture from the point of view of its symbolic meaning (Chapman
2003: 15–17). By contrast, Leroi-Gourhan's distinctive theoretical
contributions, although largely ignored by English-speaking archaeologists, have in various ways influenced the development of both
processual and postprocessual archaeology, especially his concept of
the *chaîne opératoire* and his application of a structural approach to
archaeological data.

Across continental Europe, the strong historical orientation of
archaeology encouraged awareness of theoretical developments in
economic, social, and intellectual history, as well as in the philosophy of history and human geography, as these closely related disciplines co-evolved in the course of the twentieth century. This contact has resulted in the application to archaeology of many ideas
used by historians that were derived from various rival schools of
Marxist thought, the Annales School, and the writings of Georg

Hegel, Antonio Gramsci, Ludwig Wittgenstein, Benedetto Croce, Claude Lévi-Strauss, Georges Dumézil, Mircea Eliade, and many others. Although some of these ideas have made their way through European archaeology into mainstream processual and postprocessual archaeology (Bintliff 1991; Knapp 1992), nowhere in Europe have theoretical ideas derived from the humanities and social sciences been cultivated by archaeologists with the same intensity that they have been as a result of the fierce competition between processual and postprocessual archaeologists, especially in the United Kingdom, and the desire of adherents of these rival positions to establish new theoretical niches for themselves. Although the highly innovative theoretical work of the Swedish archaeologist Mats Malmer (b. 1921) influenced how processual archaeology was accepted in Scandinavia, it failed to attract the dedicated followers needed to develop into a school in its own right (Myhre 1991: 166–7; Sørensen 1999).

While European culture-historical archaeology has grown more social-science oriented, subjectivist, and theoretically pluralist, it also has remained particularist, historical, qualitative, and artifact oriented. Its main interests also have continued to focus on producing European and national histories and prehistories (Hodder 1991a). Although archaeologists in German-speaking countries have remained conspicuously loyal to the traditions of culture-historical archaeology, adherents of this approach have independently replicated at least some of the theoretical findings of processual and postprocessual archaeologists (Härke 2000c). These findings have not, however, come to be viewed within the broader theoretical contexts provided by processual or postprocessual archaeology and hence they have had less systemic impact on the practice of German archaeology.

The most coherent and influential theoretical development in continental European archaeology after World War II, apart from the work of Leroi-Gourhan, was Jean-Claude Gardin's *logicism* (Gardin 1980, 2004). Since the 1950s, Gardin's interests have been focused on documentation techniques and the study of archaeological reasoning. Gardin (1980: 5) defines archaeology as the sum of studies bearing on material objects that shed light on the history and ways of life of ancient peoples. Most of his theoretical work has been devoted to determining which analytical operations must be performed to assess the scientific status of the work done at each stage of a chain of logical operations that includes defining objectives, data collection, description of data, ordering of data, interpretation of data, and validation of interpretations. Gardin has argued that, by using expert systems to study the mechanisms of archaeological reasoning at each of these stages, logicism can establish a central position for itself as the means by which the merits and practical advantages of all other archaeological approaches may be appraised.

Logical coherence is clearly an essential characteristic of sound archaeological reasoning, which before Gardin's work had not received as much explicit attention as it deserved. Between the late 1960s and 1980s, his research attracted considerable attention among English-speaking archaeologists (Gardin 1965, 1967, 1980, 1992). Yet, in the long run, logicism failed to secure a central role for itself outside of France. Epistemologically, even before the development of postprocessual archaeology, Gardin had equated his rationalist orientation with positivism. He also embraced the idea of unified science and rejected humanistic and hermeneutic approaches (Gallay 1989). The main reason for logicism's lack of enduring appeal is, however, its lack of ontological content. Although formalizing the procedures of archaeological reasoning is useful, by itself this cannot lead to an understanding of archaeological data. Doing that requires considering what forces have shaped the archaeological record and demonstrating how they have done so. Despite Gardin's aspirations, logicism was destined by its very nature to remain of operational rather than theoretical significance. It also finds its primary reference points within the context of European historical archaeology.

Discussion

At least into the 1990s, both processual and postprocessual archaeologists were doing the same thing: learning more about anthropological theory. Processual archaeology grew out of the neoevolutionary anthropology that was fashionable in the United States in the 1960s; postprocessual archaeology developed several decades later largely as the result of a growing interest in cultural phenomena in anthropology. Processual and postprocessual archaeologists shared a desire to apply their knowledge of anthropological theory to explain how societies or cultures had functioned and changed in the past. Both also were continuations of early functional-processual archaeology. Although processual and postprocessual archaeology claimed to represent the opposite poles of a theoretical spectrum, each came to embrace numerous incompatible theories, while the boundary between them grew less distinct. Within each approach archaeologists continuously adopted new theories, mainly from anthropology, but discarded most of them before fully exploring their potential and limitations (Chippindale 1993).

The most important accomplishment of this process was the effort some archaeologists made to adapt these anthropological theories to the study of material culture, a process that resulted in a slowly growing awareness of what specifically high-level archaeological theories might be like and what they might be used for. This work underlined the importance of Marvin Harris's (1968b: 359–60) early warning that many anthropological concepts were unsuitable for archaeological research. Such discoveries in turn made archaeologists increasingly aware of how different archaeology was as a discipline from sociocultural anthropology.

Schiffer (1976: 193) maintained that archaeologists should seek systematically to assemble theories that they found useful for interpreting archaeological data. Yet, growing awareness by archaeologists of the complexity of the factors that influence human behavior gradually made endeavors of this sort seem less useful than processual archaeologists had originally anticipated. Ironically, the most successful example of a "law" that was useful for archaeologists was Hodder's demonstration that material culture plays an active role in social strategies and hence can invert and distort as well as reflect social reality.

Anthropological theory was adapted for inferring human behavior from archaeological data in many different ways. Binford's (1977, 1978) middle-range theory had very different theoretical underpinnings from Hodder's (1987b) structural and contextual analysis, the direct historical approach (Trigger 1995), the hermeneutical approach (Y. Sherratt 2006), or Wylie's (1989a, 1993) concept of "tacking." Yet no sustained effort was made to determine in what ways these approaches were mutually contradictory or complementary. It also was generally assumed that explaining most forms of belief, behavior, and cultural change did not require special archaeological theories.

Regardless of what they employed them for, most archaeologists tended to accept anthropological theories as givens, even when it was obvious that many of them were mutually contradictory. Archaeologists generally did not attempt to use archaeological data to evaluate these theories. Instead, they stubbornly defended ideas that appealed to them and ignored those that did not. Although many archaeologists recognized that there were numerous issues relating to long-term change that only archaeologists could study and that only archaeology could provide the developmental context within which the findings of all the other social sciences acquired meaning, they remained consumers of anthropological theory. It also has become clear that much of what passed for theoretical debate was focused on rhetoric, political issues, and self-justification. Most of this literature now seems dated and largely irrelevant.

It can appropriately be asked how far by the 1990s archaeologists had advanced in their understanding of anthropological theory beyond Childe's two key propositions: (1) that the world people adapt to is not the world as it really is but the world as people imagine it to be and (2) that every understanding of the world must accord to a significant degree with the world as it really is, if people and their ideas are to survive. It is tempting to conclude that archaeological theory might have developed more quickly and many tedious and unproductive debates between processual and postprocessual archaeologists might have been avoided, had more attention been paid to Childe's later theoretical writings. Yet I do not believe that such fast track development would have been possible. Closely argued, passionate, and dramatic debates seem essential for theoretical development to occur in the social sciences (Trigger 2003d). Moreover, despite the extraordinary lucidity of Childe's later theoretical writings, most facets of his ideas remained undeveloped and this made his basic concepts very difficult for most archaeologists to understand. An oppositional approach encouraged archaeologists to assimilate and learn to use anthropological concepts in a far more detailed and comprehending manner than was likely to have occurred in a less competitive, *laissez-faire* intellectual environment. As a result of this process, archaeologists in the United States and Britain collectively acquired a far more thorough working understanding of anthropological theory than they had possessed at any time in the past. Yet, with the exception of Hodder's one truly outstanding theoretical discovery, they had yet to prove that they could assess anthropological theory critically or create major new theories to serve the needs of their discipline.

CHAPTER 9

Pragmatic Synthesis

Niels Bohr said that the most fundamental truths were so profound that quite the opposite ones were also true!

LEO KLEJN, *Metaarchaeology* (2001a), pp. 55

Papers that end with the depressingly banal conclusion ... that "we should look for a middle ground" should be banned.

MATTHEW JOHNSON, *Archaeological Theory* (1999), p. 187

There is no evidence that in their interpretation of archaeological data archaeologists today are less influenced by the milieu in which they live than they were formerly. Archaeological interpretations consciously and unconsciously (it is often impossible to determine which) echo current concerns. These relate to a vast array of issues, including globalization, American hegemony, international terrorism, pandemics, rising debt loads, environmental pollution, the changing role of government, and the disintegration of the family. Current understandings of ideologies, such as Marxism, neoconservatism, and nationalism, also color interpretations of the past. Like everything else in modern society, these biased understandings are growing more varied, complex, and individualized and are changing more rapidly than ever before. By contrast, the history of archaeology suggests that a growing body of archaeological data offers ever stronger resistance to the misapplication of such ideas and the specific misinterpretation of archaeological evidence. Although there can be no certainty about the "objectivity" of any specific interpretation of archaeological findings, the chances of archaeologists construing such findings in whatever way they wish appear to be lessening.

Since 1990, there also has been a continuing diversification of theoretical viewpoints in both prehistoric and historical archaeology. As a result, archaeological theory resembles more closely than ever

484

before that of sociocultural anthropology and the other social sciences, even if it is being anchored ever more specifically to understanding the past through the medium of material culture. Theoretical debates are often described as being increasingly factional, divisive, and exclusionary and concern is expressed that archaeological theorists are trapping themselves in separate, noncommunicating discourses (Hodder 1999: 12, 2001b: 10–11; R. Chapman 2003: 14).

Complaints also have been leveled against the trivial and self-serving aspects of many theoretical confrontations. Susan Kus (2000: 169) has observed that "Too often the way to attention in our discipline . . . is to wrest agenda setting by producing the next theoretical 'heresy-aspiring-to-dogma.' Given the 'nature of the game,' we have all been pushed into stronger stances of critique and argumentation than we might feel stylistically comfortable with." Robert Kelly (2000: 78) has complained more trenchantly that archaeologists "reward polemic, bombast, and showmanship rather than the serious testing of ideas." Some fear that archaeology as a discipline may be fragmenting, as sociocultural anthropology to some extent is doing (G. A. Clark 2003), although this concern seems exaggerated. There are also contrary signs of enhanced toleration and new efforts at synthesis. What seems increasingly to be dismissed is the idea that particular topics can be rejected as research subjects simply because a particular theory is unable to deal with them.

Competing Approaches

The battle between processual and postprocessual archaeologists continues (A. Smith 2003; Yoffee 2005), with the adherents of these two clusters of theories frequently talking past or ignoring one another rather than engaging in productive discourse. Belief that ecological explanations can account for all or most of the archaeological record has declined sharply in recent years, encouraging the resurgence of ecological possibilism. This development also has resulted in behavioral archaeology becoming an increasingly important expression of processual archaeology. At the same time, a growing number of postprocessual archaeologists are explicitly embracing idealist explanations of change. Jacques Cauvin (2000) in his work on the origins of agriculture, Gregory Possehl (2002) in his study of

the Indus Valley civilization, and Martin Byers (2004) in his reinterpretation of Hopewell ritual structures identify ideas as the primary
forces shaping culture and cultural change. Yet there is understand-
ably widespread reluctance among both processual archaeologists
and postprocessual archaeologists who stress the idea of agency to
embrace cultural determinism. There is also a growing sense among
archaeologists that the debate between processual and postprocessual archaeologists has run its course and interest is turning to other
options (Hegmon 2003; Kristiansen 2004a).

Since the early 1990s, Robert Dunnell and two generations of his
students have been promoting Darwinian, or evolutionary, archaeology as a substitute for processual archaeology on the materialist side
of the theoretical spectrum. This approach views selection, which
synergistically combines the properties of function and adaptation,
as being the main factor producing changes in adaptive aspects of
human behavior. Selectionism clearly transcends a functionalist concern with what works. It seeks to explain the material culture observable in the archaeological record using the concepts of biological
evolutionary theory (Teltser 1995; O'Brien 1996b; Barton and Clark
1997; O'Brien and Lyman 2000; T. Hunt et al. 2001; Hurt and Rakita
2001; Hart and Terrell 2002; G. A. Clark 2003). Darwinian archaeology's main accomplishment so far has been its freeing of evolutionary concepts in archaeology from the Spencerian assumptions of
unilinearity and teleological development that were associated with
neoevolutionism.

Darwinian archaeology, no less than processual and postprocessual
archaeology, has become a cluster of related positions. Purists argue
that selection operates on material culture by determining the reproductive success of individual human beings (Dunnell 1970, 1980a).
Less biologically oriented Darwinian archaeologists view selection
as acting mainly on ideas or artifacts and allow that choices made
by individual human beings play a significant role in this form of
selection (Leonard and Jones 1987: 214; O'Brien and Holland 1990;
Leonard 2001). The latter position also recognizes that innovation
and cultural selection are not wholly separate processes, as muta-
tion and selection are understood to be in biological evolution
(Boone and Smith 1998: S148–S149; Cowgill 2000: 52). In addition,
cultural selection brings about change much faster than does natural
selection (Neff 2000; Roscoe 2002). Supporters of cultural selection

argue that the selection of culturally transmitted traits (*memes*) is no less Darwinian in nature than is that of genes; instead, each form of selection is a specific instance, with its own properties, of information transfer being affected by various processes that lead to the modification of heritable characteristics over time (Shennan 2002: 264).

There is no doubt that human beings have the cognitive ability to make choices based on their beliefs about what is likely to be the outcome of different options. Yet humans are not omniscient and frequently their actions, even when well informed, do not have the expected consequences. Sometimes bad choices result in the deaths of individuals or whole groups. Long ago Gordon Childe (1928: 46) speculated that hunter-gatherer groups who refused to relocate or change their subsistence habits would perish if the region where they lived was transformed into desert. Tragedies also can befall people who, perhaps as a result of poverty or population pressure, are forced to settle in areas that are prone to natural disasters. Millions of Germans who supported Nazism because they were persuaded that its aggressive policies would bring wealth and prosperity to their homeland soon paid for that decision with their lives. It also has been argued that conservative attitudes are increasing in the United States because those who subscribe to these views produce more children than do liberals and a significant number of these children adopt the beliefs and values of their parents. This increase is probably an unintended consequence of religious beliefs relating to morally appropriate sexual behavior. Finally, many people die as a result of smoking tobacco, even though they are aware that doing so involves major health risks.

Although these are all examples of natural selection operating on human behavior, the concept of natural selection has major limitations when one is trying to account for cultural change. Natural selection alone does not determine the number of people who smoke any more than it has determined the large number of Inuit who in recent years have decided to start using snowmobiles. The desire to have large families is not biologically inherent in people who happen to be conservatives nor do young people necessarily adhere to, rather than rebel against, the customs of older generations. Nazi policies also resulted in the deaths of millions of people who opposed their views, suggesting that in that case in its totality selection was random.

Even more important, biological death is not the most common outcome of significant human miscalculations. A more likely possibility is for humans to recognize from experience that what they are doing is not a good idea and alter their behavior. Many dysfunctional behavior patterns are recognized as such and abandoned before they harm many people (Boyd and Richerson 1985). The appropriation of land and resources belonging to small-scale hunter-gatherer societies by powerful neighboring states may terminate the existence of these smaller societies, but it does not invariably impose a similar fate on their individual members. The fact that all human behavior is culturally mediated may explain why selection in the form of conscious choice plays a far more important role in altering such behavior than does biological selection, even though both processes are at work simultaneously. Darwinian archaeology in both its biological and cultural variants is a significant addition to the corpus of theory that accounts for human behavior. Yet, despite the claims that have been made for it, it does not provide a complete explanation for such behavior or the ideas and material culture associated with it; hence it is not the only scientific approach that is required to explain the archaeological record (G. A. Clark 2003: 53; O'Brien 2005).

Nor does it make for clarity to treat the material remains of human behavior as an "external phenotype" as Darwinian archaeologists frequently do. The capacity to create material culture is almost certainly biologically grounded in human beings (Mithen 1996) but, unlike the situation with bees or beavers, the specific repertoire is not. The unparalleled cognitive flexibility of human beings is complemented by their ability to learn not only from experience and observation but also by means of verbal inculcation. In Darwinian terms, this combination of features constitutes an adaptive pattern, but it is a highly unusual and unpredictably open-ended one.

Evolutionary ecology is another approach, with close ties to Darwinian archaeology and processual archaeology, that seeks to use the concepts of evolutionary biologists to assess the role that specific behaviors play in the survival and reproductive success of individual members of social groups. Work of this sort has focused on the evolutionary fitness of the breadth of diet and of various aspects of social behavior such as sharing and status roles. Archaeologists, for example, have sought to establish links between the way artifacts were made and used and the exploitation of specific items contributing to the diet. Cost-benefit analyses assume that, all things being equal, natural selection will lead to an optimal solution for any particular adaptive problem. An explanation is then sought for the differences between what is expected and the actual strategy that was employed. Evolutionary ecology so far has generally been applied to studies of hunter-gatherer or small-scale horticultural societies (Broughton and O'Connell 1999; Bamforth 2002; Shennan 2002).

Culture-historical archaeology, contrary to what might have been expected, has been developing in several independent directions. In the 1990s, a widespread revival of traditional culture-historical archaeology followed the collapse of Soviet control first in Eastern Europe and then in the Soviet Union (Dolukhanov 1995: 337–9). Marxist archaeology seems generally to have vanished with the collapse of communist control, except in East Germany and Poland, where some archaeologists sought to sustain what they regarded as worthwhile Marxist approaches. This initiative by East German archaeologists was suppressed by West German academic authorities following the reunification of Germany (Härke 2000b: 12; Jacobs 2000; Barford 2004). Efforts were made by American archaeologists to interest former Soviet archaeologists in processual archaeology, but this effort was unsuccessful because Soviet archaeologists decided that processual archaeology too closely resembled Soviet archaeology (Kohl 1993: 18). Almost everywhere in the former Soviet sphere of influence culture-historical archaeology reemerged as the preferred approach.

In eastern Europe, culture-historical archaeology had predominated until after World War II, whereas in the Soviet Union it had been practiced commonly prior to 1928. In the late 1930s, significant aspects of culture-historical archaeology were reintroduced to Soviet archaeology in an effort to counter the Nazi use of archaeological data to denigrate Slavic peoples and their cultural achievements (Klejn 1974). Because this approach isolated archaeology from the other social sciences and made practicing it relatively safe politically, after World War II many Soviet archaeologists preferred to continue to focus on culture-historical forms of analysis to which appropriate Marxist glosses referring to matters of current interest to the Soviet authorities were added when politically required. After the collapse of the Soviet Union, Leo Klejn (2001a: 6) announced that, although he had briefly embraced Marxism as a student, he had never been a Marxist archaeologist. Culture-historical archaeology also was an approach that was relatively easy to understand, and its revival was further encouraged beginning in the 1990s by German research funding and by cooperative projects that involved German and East European or Russian archaeologists working together.

Archaeologists became involved with the nationalist ferments that accompanied and helped to bring about the collapse of Soviet power. Following the collapse, some became associated with renewed ethnic and racist speculations of the sort that had been banished from German archaeology after 1945 (Klejn 1991, 1994a; Ligi 1993; Chernykh 1995; Kohl and Tsetskhladze 1995; Shnirelman 1995, 1999; T. Kaiser 1995). Archaeologists who behaved in this manner were either unaware of, or chose to ignore, the critiques concerning the concept of ethnicity that had been published since 1945 by German culture-historical and Western postprocessual archaeologists. The result has been the revival or reinvention of a number of crudely nationalistic and competing archaeologies. This situation has not for the most part characterized archaeology in countries such as Poland and the Czech Republic, where archaeologists had more contacts with the West and were already familiar with alternative ways of doing archaeology. In Russia, the resurgence of culture-historical archaeology has resulted in the achievements of Soviet archaeologists in inferring behavior from archaeological data being largely ignored. The outstanding exception to this retrograde trend is Leo Klejn (2001a), who continues to construct a comprehensive theoretical framework for transforming archaeological evidence into an understanding of human behavior and human history. This was a task that he began, of necessity, under the disguise of being a Marxist.

Darwinian archaeologists have, meanwhile, been reviving and developing selected aspects of culture-historical archaeology in order to explain stylistic as opposed to functional aspects of material culture. Dunnell (1978) argued that style and function could only be distinguished by the patterns of change they display over time, with style changing gradually in the form of unimodal curves. Yet some selectionists now acknowledge that both stylistic and functional change can display this form (O'Brien and Leonard 2001), whereas Stephen Shennan and J. R. Wilkinson (2001) have concluded that the idea of style as being neutral with respect to selection does not account for actual frequency distributions. Yet, despite these problems, analytical concepts of culture-historical archaeology that processual archaeologists rejected in a peremptory manner are now being refurbished by Darwinian archaeologists. There can be no doubt that a more detailed understanding of formal changes in material culture is essential for dealing more effectively with many problems raised by processual and postprocessual archaeologists.

Finally, the widespread rejection of the unilinear evolutionism that was associated with processual archaeology has created a renewed role for culture-historical accounts of the human past at both the regional and the world levels. The techniques of culture-historical archaeology are essential for tracing phylogenetic changes in specific cultures and societies in prehistoric times. Such studies are required to ascertain actual patterns of change and stability and provide the evidence needed to address questions relating to possible evolutionary patterning in the development of human societies (Kehoe 1998; Trigger 1998a). In this new form of culture-historical archaeology, internal explanations of change are regarded as no less important than those involving diffusion and migration.

Another focus of increasing interest to archaeologists is how human biology, including the working of the brain and the endocrine system, influences human behavior. This interest is sometimes referred to as "cognitive archaeology" and it clearly overlaps to some extent with Renfrew's cognitive-processual approach. Yet, because it considers noncognitive factors that influence human behavior, such as moods and drives, in addition to cognitive ones, it is perhaps better to label this field of enquiry biological archaeology. At the cognitive level, it addresses the sorts of cross-cultural uniformities that nineteenth-century evolutionary archaeologists attributed to "psychic unity," a term that they misleadingly treated as if it were an explanation rather than something to be explained. It is curious that the existence of cross-cultural similarities in beliefs and values was not more apparent to neoevolutionary anthropologists and processual archaeologists who could have used them to extend the range of the cross-cultural similarities they studied. This failure can perhaps be attributed to their overwhelming preoccupation with ecological explanations, as well as to the general rejection by anthropologists of biological explanations of human behavior after 1945. Edmund Leach (1973: 763–4) drew to the attention of processual archaeologists the importance of such an approach when he spoke of human consciousness and intentionality creating a "unique human capacity to engage in 'work' (*praxis*)." Leroi-Gourhan (1993) in *Le geste et la parole* explored such capabilities in considerable detail and Merilee Salmon (1982: 132) cited, as a simple example of a causal account of the regularities connecting small population size and egalitarian social structure, the social anthropologist Anthony Forge's (1972) claim that, as societies grew larger, the cognitive inability of individual human beings to handle more than about eighty close personal relations would compel the development of forms of segmentary social organization and more clearly defined patterns of decision making. For a long time, Roland Fletcher (1977, 1995) has argued that the human mind possesses proxemic abilities that result in significant uniformities in the built environment. Structuralism also has been based on complex, but in that case totally inconclusive, speculation about how the human mind works.

Today, a growing number of archaeologists agree that the human capacity to reason, combined with basic human biological needs and culturally transmitted knowledge and beliefs, are not enough to explain human behavior. The universal tendency of human beings to produce or appreciate art and hold religious beliefs (Boyer 1994, 1996; Mithen 1996) suggests that over millions of years hominids have evolved capacities for complex forms of cognition and symbolically mediated analysis, as well as hormonally based drives that, along with organic needs, constitute an internal environment to which individuals must adjust both behaviorally and conceptually. Recent research has revealed that certain specific grammatical capacities, such as the ability to form plurals and alter tenses, are linked to a single gene (Gopnik 1997). This suggests that philosophers such as Immanuel Kant may have been correct in assuming that some concepts, such as space and time, are hardwired into the human brain, probably it now seems to adapt early lemur-like primates to a life that involved jumping from one tree branch to another. Stephen Mithen (1996) has hypothesized that cognitive abilities relating to social skills, technology, and the observation of nature developed independently of one another and at different times during the course of hominid history and only became linked together in modern *Homo sapiens*. This may have given rise among other things to the capacity to anthropomorphize, which may lie at the root of much or all religious thought. Likewise, the hierarchical behavior that is pervasive in all complex societies seems to exceed what is functionally required to process information and for authorities to administer such societies (Trigger 2003a). This behavior may reflect competitive tendencies that, along with sociability, are common to African higher primates (Conroy 1990). Although overtly hierarchical behavior was largely suppressed by gossip, ridicule, and fear of witchcraft in small-scale hunter-gatherer societies, in which generalized reciprocity made ecological sense, these cultural mechanisms for controlling a natural tendency ceased to be effective as societies grew larger and more complex (Lee 1990; Trigger 1990). No substitute has ever been evolved that curbs such behavior equally effectively in larger societies.

There is also evidence that significant cross-cultural regularities underlay the specific idiosyncratic religious beliefs of early civilizations. In many widely separated early civilizations that had no contact with one another, it was believed not only that deities who animated, or were, the universe nourished and sustained humanity but also that, if humans in turn did not nourish these deities with sacrifices, the deities would die and the universe lapse into chaos. Although farmers produced most of the food that fed the deities, the upper classes, and especially kings, claimed a unique role in channeling this nourishment back into the supernatural realm and thus in sustaining the cosmic order. These views of deities differed greatly from those associated with ethnographic examples of less complex societies, where supernatural powers were approached, sometimes by ritual specialists such as shamans and sometimes by anyone, either as hopefully benevolent parents or as powerful ancestors who had to be placated (Bird-David 1990; Ingold 1996). I have suggested that the beliefs that evolved independently multiple times in early civilizations were probably metaphorical projections of tributary relations that existed on the human plane into the cosmic realm. By grounding the survival of the cosmic order on both the productivity of farmers and the administrative and ritual skills of the upper classes, this view also may have enlisted supernatural concepts to help maintain a political balance between rulers and ruled that was necessary for emerging early civilizations, with their still rudimentary mechanisms of political control, to survive (Trigger 2003a: 472–94). Even so, it is remarkable that the same basic metaphor should have been elaborated in so similar a manner in many historically unrelated early civilizations. This evidence of human groups' symbolically interpreting social relations in the same way accords with Marshall Sahlins's (1976a: 211–12) more general proposal that, when societies grew too complex for kinship to supply the metaphors used to understand all social relations, new metaphors were drawn first of all from the religious sphere.

By contrast, I see little direct evidence to support claims by sociobiologists, evolutionary ecologists, and Darwinian archaeologists that human beings are biologically programmed to try to maximize the number of their biological descendants. A large number of cultural factors have been documented as influencing reproductive behavior, and restricting the number of children produced is a feature of many societies (Trigger 2003a: 310–11). This suggests that, if maximizing progeny ever constituted a biological predisposition of our primate ancestors, it may have been eliminated in the course of hominid evolution.

Very little is yet known for certain about the biological basis of almost any aspect of human behavior. Much of what is being published about this subject by ecologists, psychologists, and neuroscientists is speculative and supported only by anecdotal evidence. It is also produced by researchers who know little about anthropology (Donald 1991; Gazzaniga 1992, 1998; Butterworth 1999; Low 2000; Pinker 2002; Dennett 2003). The social sciences, especially economics, are not without their own unsubstantiated speculations about innate aspects of human behavior. Yet in recent decades anthropologists have generally avoided this topic because of their revulsion against the racism that pervaded the social sciences before 1945 and also because of the radical relativism promoted by the new cultural anthropologists since the 1970s (Sahlins 1976b). Extreme postprocessual archaeologists are opposed in principle to recognizing cross-cultural generalizations or anything that encourages the search for cross-cultural generalizations. Anthropologists also have feared rightly that countenancing biological interpretations will be used to essentialize whatever researchers want to believe about human behavior (S. Jones 1997: 65–7). Historically, the biologization of human behavior has been favored by conservatively minded social scientists. Liberals and radicals, by contrast, seek to minimize the importance of biological constraints in the hope that their absence allows social and political change to occur more quickly and easily. Yet, failure to develop closer relations exposes neuroscientists, psychologists, and social scientists alike to being misled by the unsubstantiated claims of sociobiologists and racists. The sooner social scientists, psychologists, biologists, and neuroscientists learn to work together, the sooner archaeologists will be able to apply their findings to understanding the past. The greatest promise of such an approach from an archaeological point of view is that it offers hope of more cross-cultural generalizations that can be used to interpret archaeological findings as evidence of human behavior and beliefs.

Despite the claims of neoracialists such as J. P. Rushton (1995), there is no evidence that, as a result of natural selection, acquired behavior quickly becomes embedded in the genetic constitution of human beings as sociobiologists have assumed (E. Wilson 1975). Human behavioral predispositions generally appear to be shared by the entire species (Carrithers 1992). This suggests that natural selection genetically embeds human behavioral patterns only very slowly. It also indicates that natural selection has provided very little specific biological adaptation for dealing with problems related to managing large-scale social and political entities, long-term planning, and rapid change, all of which have come to characterize human life in recent millennia (Boyd and Richerson 1985).

In recent decades there has been little direct follow-up in the United States and Britain to the social approaches for understanding prehistoric societies that were initiated by Gordon Childe, Robert McC. Adams, Colin Renfrew, Kent Flannery, and Henry Wright in the 1950s and 1960s. Much of what is called "social archaeology" has become a form of cultural archaeology closely identified with postprocessualism (Meskell and Preucel 2004). Obvious exceptions include recent works in Monica L. Smith (2003) and by Norman Yoffee (2003). Yet, the most important efforts to maintain social archaeology are found in the writings of Marxist archaeologists, such as Robert Chapman, Philip Kohl, Randall McGuire, and Thomas Patterson. The important functional role played by social and political organization in shaping economic life and other aspects of human behavior (Trigger 2003a: 264–75) ensures that there is no way that archaeology can in the long run dispense with a societal approach. That in turn suggests that before long social archaeology will again be playing a significant role within the discipline.

The desire to study how human groups interact with material factors to reshape social life has remained an important objective of Marxist Latin American social archaeology, which also seeks to make the practice of archaeology socially relevant and politically active (Lorenzo et al. 1976; Baté 1998: 98–9; R. Chapman 2003). Latin American social archaeologists drew inspiration from the writings of Gordon Childe, the Peruvian archaeologists Emilio Choy (1960) and José Mariátegui (1952), and the Cuban archaeologists Ernesto Tabío and Estrella Rey (1966). They associate the beginnings of this movement with the eminent Peruvian archaeologist Luis Lumbreras (1974), the Venezuelan archaeologists Mario Sanoja and Iraida Vargas (1978), and the Chilean archaeologist Luis Baté (1977, 1978). Yet this approach has not produced a unified body of theory. In general, Marxism is engaged as high-level theory, with little effort being directed toward creating an appropriate methodology for conducting archaeological research. Even the work of Lumbreras has been described as "essentially a sophisticated culture-historical interpretation" (Politis 2003: 251). Marxist archaeology does not predominate in any Latin American country; wherever it is present, it is subordinate to culture-historical, processual, or eclectic approaches (Politis and Alberti 1999; Funari 1999b, 2001; Politis 2003; Politis and Perez Gollán 2004).

In Spain, a Barcelona-based group of archaeologists working from a materialist Marxist perspective has been developing archaeological techniques for studying local (site-based) systems of production and consumption and tracing the development of social inequality and classes in prehistoric times. They argue that this sort of research is necessary to produce a controlled understanding of prehistoric political systems on a geographically larger scale (González Marcén and Risch 1990; Ruiz and Nocete 1990; Vásquez Varela and Risch 1991). They also stress the need to study aspects of prehistoric behavior that leave clear signatures in the archaeological record, such as the presence of producers and non-producers in a society, in order to infer the existence or non-existence of class divisions. Basic information of this sort is regarded as necessary to understand other aspects of the archaeological record, such as fortifications, monumental architecture, and cult centers (R. Chapman 2003: 23–6). Many of these ideas are similar to those of the orthodox Marxist Italian archaeologist Maurizio Tosi (1984), who devoted much time to studying manufacturing processes in the archaeological record.

Theoretical Convergence

Although some archaeologists have opposed the theoretical diversification of archaeology on the grounds that this diversification threatens its credibility as a discipline (P. J. Watson 1986), especially in the United States attempts are being made to promote dialogue between various theoretical approaches in an effort to determine to what extent they are complementary and might serve as the basis for constructing more comprehensive and useful hybrid theories. For over a decade, many American archaeologists have argued that, rather than being rival theories, processual and postprocessual archaeology are complementary approaches, addressing behavior and culture respectively (Duke 1991, 1995; Preucel 1991; Wylie 1993, 2000; VanPool and VanPool 1999, 2003). Behavioral archaeologists are particularly active in seeking to "build bridges" with other approaches (Skibo et al. 1995; Schiffer 1996, 2000b: Skibo and Feinman 1999). In addition, Michelle Hegmon (2003) documents the various positions that are being linked to form what she calls "processual-plus" archaeology and Timothy Pauketat (2003) expounds a theoretical amalgam that he has named "historical-processual archaeology." The chief resistance to such outreach has come from Darwinian archaeologists, many of whom have seemed intent on establishing a hegemonic status for their own position (Lyman and O'Brien 1998; O'Brien, Lyman, and Leonard 1998). Even they, however, have sought to incorporate what they regard as the most valid and enduring concepts of culture-historical archaeology into their own theoretical formulations (Lyman, O'Brien, and Dunnell 1997a; O'Brien and Lyman 2000), and more recently some of them have demonstrated greater willingness to cooperate with and consider the claims made by archaeologists of other persuasions (O'Brien 2005; O'Brien, Lyman, and Schiffer 2005). Sometimes what are alleged to be efforts to reconcile very different approaches appear to be undertaken in the hope that by this means one theoretical position may destabilize and destroy another. Yet many archaeologists clearly are seeking to derive mutual benefits by trying to reconcile existing positions (Preucel 1991; VanPool and VanPool 1999, 2003; Schiffer 2000a; Kristiansen 2004a). Work of this sort helps to advance archaeology beyond the naive eclecticism that characterized it in the recent past. This development, combined with growing interest in the biological aspects of explaining human behavior and the archaeological record, suggests a theoretical sophistication that transcends the sectarianism of earlier decades.

Although parsimony is often stated to be desirable when constructing scientific theories, theoretical economy is self-defeating if it ignores the diversity and complexity of what is being explained. Understanding the material products of human behavior requires considering emergent and systemically related properties of a cultural, social, psychological, and biological nature (Bunge 2003). Recent studies indicate that, while the postprocessual claim that every culture is unique is true, some properties of human behavior and belief tend to be culturally idiosyncratic, whereas others display cross-cultural uniformity. In addition to culture-historical and ecological explanations, which account for both cross-cultural differences and regularities, there is room for biological, functional, and selectionist explanations that account for various sorts of cross-cultural regularities (D. Brown 1988; Trigger 2003a). The ultimate goal of archaeologists must be to account for both similarities and differences in the archaeological record by means of a scientific method that addresses idiographic as well as nomothetic explanations and is rooted in the concepts of materiality, systemicity, lawfulness, and belief in the knowability of the universe (Bunge 2003: 282).

By far the most striking development in archaeology during the late twentieth century was the gradual diminution of the long-standing estrangement between prehistoric archaeology and various forms of historical or text-aided archaeology. Since the eighteenth century, classical and prehistoric archaeology had developed separately from one another, pursuing different goals, employing different methods, and usually being institutionalized in different university departments or faculties. Classical archaeologists remained deeply interested in texts and elite culture, whereas by the 1960s prehistoric archaeologists had become increasingly committed to an ecological approach. Moreover, the traditional role that archaeologists played in humanistic disciplines, such as classics, Egyptology, and Assyriology, was not particularly creative or satisfying. The specialized studies of literary texts and works of fine art were believed to be what brought scholars into intimate contact with the most important ideas of ancient civilizations. Archaeology was viewed as a lesser pursuit devoted to the recovery of texts and works of fine art that would be studied by epigraphers and art historians, as well as incidentally shedding light on mundane and little regarded matters, such as how ordinary people had lived in those societies. In the early twentieth century, new historical archaeologies developed, including medieval, colonial, and industrial archaeology (J. Harrington 1955; Barley 1977; Schuyler 1978, 2001; Gerrard 2003; Orser 1996, 2004: 28–55; Linebaugh 2005). In general, those specializations had closer relations with prehistoric archaeology than did the older historical archaeologies, as a result of which many archaeologists working in these fields strove to create a broader interpretive role for themselves.

In recent decades, it has been recognized that all forms of historical archaeology can address many important aspects of life not adequately documented in written texts (Andrén 1998). Growing use has been made of archaeological data to complement and correct what is known about human behavior and cultural change from historical sources, to set information derived from written records into a broader social context, and even to understand better the role played by literacy in early societies. These developments are helping to broaden the role and enhance the prestige of archaeologists in classical studies, Egyptology, and Assyriology, while reducing the barriers that prehistoric archaeologists and archaeologists working in these disciplines had erected against one another.

Many British culture-historical archaeologists, such as Gordon Childe, Christopher Hawkes, and Stuart Piggott, were interested in both prehistoric and historical archaeology, which they viewed as equally important components of European history. A similar view was shared by archaeologists elsewhere in Europe and around the world who studied the past from national perspectives. Archaeologists such as James Deetz (1968: 121) concluded that historical archaeology was suitable for testing theories about relations between human behavior and material culture, which they hoped eventually would improve the interpretation of prehistoric data. By contrast, processual archaeologists who sought to interpret archaeological data using generalizations based on cross-cultural correlations between material culture and ethnographic data viewed the use of information derived exclusively from historical sources as compromising the scientific status of archaeology.

Recently, many historical archaeologists, especially those studying colonial and industrial archaeology, have reacted against the limited and subordinate role still being assigned to their work by both prehistoric archaeologists and historians. They argue that historical archaeologists should use their findings to study the historical processes that underlie Eurocentrism, capitalism, global colonization, and modernization and that, through the study of material culture, historical archaeologists have much to contribute to understanding processes that lie beyond the purview of ordinary historians (Little 1994; Orser 1996; Funari et al. 1999; Funari 1999b; Majewski 2003; T. Murray 2004a). Recently, Christopher Gosden (2004) has extended the archaeological study of colonialism back to the earliest civilizations (see also Trigger 1976). These works, which involve comparison and address general problems that are avoided by most postprocessual archaeologists, seem once again to be investigating issues that formerly were associated with evolutionary archaeology, although they approach them realistically from a contingent historical perspective rather than a unilinear one.

Although some classical archaeologists attempted to break out of their traditional mold of doing archaeology in the late nineteenth and early twentieth centuries, these efforts had little impact. During the twentieth century, classical archaeology remained a technique for recovering data, whereas prehistoric archaeology, although often institutionally a branch of anthropology, became *de facto* a self-contained discipline. Michael Shanks (1996: 98–9) observed that the 1985 annual meeting of the Archaeological Institute of America addressed essentially the same range of topics that had been addressed at its meeting fifty years earlier. After World War II, a decline in funding for long-term excavations undermined the authoritarian structures that controlled the practice of classical archaeology. At the same time, classical studies lost its traditional cultural importance as the ancient Greek and Roman cultures ceased to be viewed as the supreme early creations of humanity and came to be regarded as only two interesting cultures among many (Renfrew 1980; Gibbon 1985; Dyson 1993; Snodgrass 1985; Wiseman 1980a, 1980b, 1983).

This encouraged some classical archaeologists to consider new ways of doing things and more particularly to compare their work with what prehistoric archaeologists were accomplishing. As a result, there was growing awareness of the narrow cultural focus of classical archaeology and how far behind prehistoric archaeology classical archaeologists were in studying issues relating to everyday life in ancient Greece and Italy. This produced a growing number of settlement pattern surveys, small-scale excavations in rural locations, and greater emphasis on the study of trade and technology, which supplemented classical archaeology's traditional preoccupation with art and architecture. The earliest substantial field surveys were carried out in the late 1950s and early 1960s in Messenia by classical archaeologists from the University of Minnesota led by William McDonald (b. 1913). Although partly inspired by work done by Carl Blegen (1887–1971) (McDonald 1966), the Minnesota surveys and later ones carried out by John Fossey (1988) and other archaeologists elsewhere in Greece were significantly influenced by the prehistoric settlement pattern studies pioneered by Gordon Willey.

These new developments were encouraged and legitimated by Anthony Snodgrass (1987), whose doctoral dissertation on weapons and armor of the preclassical period in Greece had extended the rigorous analysis of fine works of art by classical archaeologists to a more functional category of artifacts (Snodgrass 1964). Inspired by Colin Renfrew (1972), Snodgrass attributed the rise of Greek city-states to demographic increase, which he considered to be a prime mover that resulted in more intensive agriculture and increasing agglomerations of population (Snodgrass 1980). Snodgrass urged classical archaeologists to supplement their existing archaeological investigations of a historical and art-historical nature with ecological and settlement pattern studies that he associated with New Archaeology. He also reminded classical archaeologists that the kind of history they could investigate was not the sort dealing with events and personalities that traditionally had been associated with the study of texts. Shanks (1996: 132–5) described Snodgrass's efforts to combine the traditional strengths of classical archaeology with elements borrowed from prehistoric archaeology as a form of soft processual archaeology, whereas Ian Morris (1994b: 39) labelled it the "new classical archaeology." James Wiseman and Stephen Dyson strongly supported Snodgrass's efforts, Wiseman in part by playing a leading role in the establishment of a flourishing Department of Archaeology at Boston University in which classical and prehistoric archaeologists work together.

Postprocessual archaeology was introduced to classical archaeologists by Ian Morris (b. 1960) (1987), who interpreted classical burials as reflecting a symbolic denial of status differences that was intended to unite aristocrats and enfranchised commoners against a growing number of slaves and other resident noncitizens. Morris (2000) views his work as a form of culture-history that studies the lives of ancient peoples through material culture by treating objects as analogues of the societies that produced them. Morris argued that, because the textual evidence for Greek social and economic history was limited, the study of material culture had to be integrated into the writing of ancient Greek history. Thus, over several decades some classical archaeologists have been narrowing the divide between classical and prehistoric archaeology in the Mediterranean region, as well as the gap between archaeology and history (Sauer 2004). Nevertheless, most classical archaeologists probably continue to ignore these innovations and analyze material as they did in the past.

Perhaps because of their fewer numbers and greater academic isolation, Egyptological archaeologists have been even slower than classical ones to bridge the gap between themselves and prehistoric archaeologists. In the 1960s, they were content to let the geographer Karl Butzer (1976) carry out field studies relevant to understanding the nature of ancient Egyptian hydraulic agriculture, while confining their own research on the subject to epigraphic sources. Over the years, there has been an increasing number of studies of ancient Egyptian settlements, most notably those led by Michael Hoffman and Barbara Adams at Hierakonpolis, David O'Connor at Abydos, Barry Kemp at Amarna, and Manfred Bietak at Tell el Daba'a. Yet, these projects, which partly reflect a long-standing interest by some Egyptologists in how ancient Egyptians lived, have proceeded in a slow and piecemeal fashion and until recently few systematic regional settlement pattern surveys were carried out. Only O'Connor and some of his students have exhibited a sustained interest in what anthropologically trained archaeologists are doing. Hence, the impact of processual archaeology has tended to be indirect and limited (Weeks 1979). Postprocessual archaeology has attracted much more interest among Egyptologists, as Egyptological archaeologists and art historians try to read more cultural meaning into Egyptian art and architecture. In this case, the postprocessual approach has been encouraging Egyptologists to pursue old interests in new and more systematic ways (Lustig 1997). Despite these developments, relations between archaeologists and epigraphers have not altered as much in Egyptology as they have in classical studies.

Although the Maya civilization had created a writing system, before the 1980s the script could not be read to any significant degree and hence Maya culture had to be studied as if it were a prehistoric one. Archaeologists applied a culture-historical and then a processual approach, in the course of which they learned much about Maya art and later about Maya domestic architecture, subsistence, settlement patterns, trade, and social inequality (Sabloff 1990). Following the more complete translation of the Maya script, epigraphers began to claim intellectual primacy, as did epigraphers in classical studies, Egyptology, and Assyriology (Coe 1992). They maintained that knowledge of a relatively small number of surviving texts gave them a privileged insight into the beliefs that had shaped the development of Maya culture. Some suggested that these beliefs had been derived from a still earlier substratum of peasant beliefs that had survived the collapse of Maya civilization and continued to flourish among the Maya populations of present-day Mexico and Guatemala (Wilk 1985; Freidel et al. 1993). Dirt archaeologists countered that the written records of a literate elite, who would have constituted a tiny fraction of the total Maya population, were of little significance compared to the broader picture of Maya society created using other sorts of archaeological evidence that related to the everyday life of ordinary people. Thus, Maya archaeologists became embroiled in an acrimonious dispute about the relative importance of their two approaches. Joyce Marcus (1992) cogently pointed out that royal texts in other early civilizations often deliberately misrepresented events and therefore understanding such texts requires carefully comparing them with each other and with other forms of evidence. As a result of such arguments, confrontation has gradually given way to cooperation (Marcus 2003). Because Maya archaeology had developed within the context of American prehistoric archaeology, these disputes about the priority of different approaches tended to be viewed more as a turf war between processual and postprocessual archaeologists than as a battle between prehistoric and historical archaeologists.

Nowhere else in archaeology has the role of texts been more dominant or problematical than in the study of ancient Israel, about which the Hebrew Bible, despite its numerous glaring internal historical contradictions and cultural anachronisms, was long accepted, and continues to be accepted by many conservative Jews and Christians, as an infallible historical source. For a long time, the primary task of archaeology was assumed to be to confirm and illustrate biblical accounts. This led to enormous problems of interpreting the archaeological record. Only in recent years has a growing number of archaeologists ventured to claim that the archaeological record must on the contrary be used to evaluate the usefulness of the Bible as a historical source and to contextualize its origins. These critiques have increasingly called into question the historicity of the Bible before the ninth century BC, when its accounts begin to be confirmed by written texts from neighboring regions (Finkelstein and Silberman 2001; T. Davis 2004).

One of the chronic problems with historical archaeology has been a tendency to use written records only to supply information that cannot be extracted from archaeological data and archaeological data only to fill gaps in what can be learned from written texts. Still worse, archaeologists often use texts to relieve themselves of having to perform the detailed analyses that are necessary to infer specific sorts of information from the archaeological record. It is assumed on the basis of written documents that a particular society was matrilocal without checking to what extent this claim can be confirmed from the archaeological record. This approach has prevented historical and archaeological data from being studied independently, using methods appropriate to each, before the findings from either source are compared with one another (Graves and Erkelens 1991; Alisson 2001, 2003). There is even considerable disagreement about how and by whom these operations ought to be carried out (Sauer 2004). One archaeologist has complained that more might be known about the prehistoric Wendat, a North American Indian people, had such abundant ethnographic data not been recorded about this group in the early seventeenth century (Ramsden 1996). Although no archaeologist should deliberately ignore any sort of relevant data, Ramsden's exasperation bears witness to the underutilization of archaeological data that has often characterized historical, and all text-aided, archaeology. Ian Morris (1994b: 45) points out that, far from archaeological data becoming less important as texts grow more abundant, they become more crucial, as a basis for making more complex and subtle comparisons that utilize both archaeological and historical data to create a more detailed historical understanding.

In recent years, progress has been made in remedying this problem. Postprocessual archaeologists have recognized that information

in verbal (historical, ethnographic) form can play a vital role in helping to shed significant light on the specific symbolic meanings that
once were attached to material culture, especially when both the
archaeological and textual data relate to the same group. That is
why historical archaeology has been proving so useful for studying
relations between symbolism and beliefs on the one hand and material culture on the other (Leone and Potter 1988; Cannon 1989;
McGuire and Paynter 1991; Gilchrist 1994; Shackel 1996). Archaeologists have had much success in relating the changing layouts
of houses and gardens and the styles of household furnishings in
colonial North America to shifting class and gender values, tastes,
and personal values that are documented in the voluminous written records of that period (Glassie 1975; Deetz 1977; Isaac 1982;
Leone 1984; Yentsch 1991). Matthew Johnson (1996) has likewise
documented how changes in domestic architecture in early modern
England were related recursively to changing ideas about individu-
ality and household life. François Lissarrague (1990) has combined
the study of Greek texts and images on drinking vessels in order to
understand better the meaning of the ancient Greek *symposion*, or
aristocratic drinking party. Stuart T. Smith (2003) has likewise used
both archaeological and textual sources to study ethnic interaction
in Nubia during periods of ancient Egyptian occupation. In all these
cases, archaeological and textual data interact synergistically, with
each data set revealing more about the significance of the other than
could be learned from studying only one type of source. It is anticipated that increasing numbers of studies of this sort will shed light on
general relations between material culture and beliefs. Nevertheless,
historical archaeology still has a long way to go to develop methodologies that are optimally suited to exploit the available data (Graves
and Erkelens 1991; Kirch and Sahlins 1992).

Despite these convergences, there has been continuing disagreement among archaeologists about whether the ultimate objective of
archaeological research should be to understand the material culture
that constitutes its database or to use material culture to investigate
past human behavior and human history. The emergence of archaeology out of antiquarianism involved the development of an interest in
artifacts as sources of information about human behavior rather than
as objects to be studied for their own sake. Yet objects, rather than
people, remained central to culture-historical archaeology, which

focused heavily on classifying artifacts and tracing their distributions in time and space, even though culture-historical archaeologists were interested in identifying ethnic groups and sought to explain cultural change in terms of diffusion and migration (Shennan 2002: 266). Ian Morris (1994b: 45) has argued that classical archaeology, as a variant of culture-historical archaeology, has far too long continued to study material culture as an end in itself. He maintains that creating a truly historical classical archaeology requires that material culture be regarded as a means to an end. Only by doing this is there any hope of archaeologists achieving an actor-based perspective on the past. Ecological archaeologists, whether or not they were processual archaeologists, generally adopted a behavioral approach, while idealists such as R. G. Collingwood and later most postprocessualists maintained that understanding beliefs, ideas, and habits must be the ultimate goal of archaeological research.

By contrast, some processual archaeologists, such as David Clarke (1968) and Michael Schiffer (1976: 4), who were less committed to an ecological approach, maintained that, if the goal of a science was to understand its specific subject matter, that of archaeologists must be to understand material culture. Both Clarke and Schiffer viewed archaeology as constituting the potential core of a new science of material culture that would complement both social and cognitive anthropology. Schiffer and other behavioral archaeologists also viewed the discipline as a methodology that facilitated the study of material culture ethnographically as well as archaeologically (Rathje 1974; Reid et al. 1974). Starting out as ethnoarchaeologists, some of Clarke's students have developed the study of material culture into a flourishing branch of anthropology (D. Miller 1985; Chilton 1999). Lewis Binford (1981: 28) has continued, however, to affirm that the ultimate goal of archaeology cannot be to study relations between human behavior and material culture "since the archaeological record contains no direct information on this subject whatsoever!" Robert Dunnell (1980a) has argued more radically that archaeologists cannot and need not infer human behavior from archaeological data in order to understand how selection works on the "extended phenotype" of material culture. This position, which is accepted by many Darwinian archaeologists, has been viewed as evidence of Dunnell's continuing adherence to many of the core ideas of culture-historical archaeology (Peregrine 2000).

Although these opposed views of the goals of archaeology have implications concerning priorities in archaeological research, they are not in fact mutually exclusive. Contrary to Dunnell's assertions, there is no way in which either the archaeological record or modern material culture can be understood without taking account of human beliefs or behavior. Conversely, if archaeologists are to learn more about human behavior and beliefs and about cultural change in the past, they must seek for ways to infer such behavior from material culture. Archaeological research, whatever its ultimate goal, must embrace a social science component and it is only through the study of human activities that archaeology can be linked theoretically to the social sciences. Finally, to argue, as Gardin (1980: 27) has done, that the need to refer to "laws of behavior" to explain the archaeological record as a product of past ways of life does not make those laws part of archaeology, is to lose sight of the important role that material culture has come to play within the context of the social sciences.

There is general agreement that studying the archaeological remains of subsistence patterns, settlement patterns, and artifacts is the only way that it is possible to learn what has happened to humans over the entire course of human history. It is also the only way to investigate long-term sociocultural processes, many of which are not apparent to living people and become discernable to archaeologists only in retrospect. Hence, archaeology provides the general framework within which the findings of sociocultural anthropology and the other social sciences can be understood and related to one another. Thus, for all its evidential limitations, archaeology, after a long period of underachievement, has begun to realize its capacity to make important contributions to the social sciences. To sustain this momentum, archaeologists must continue to develop their ability to study past human behavior.

Archaeologists around the world and starting from many different theoretical positions have increasingly realized the importance of developing a corpus of theory that will permit them to infer human behavior and ideas in as rigorous and convincing a manner as possible from the material remains that have survived from the past (Malmer 1963; Binford 1977; Klejn 2001a). Although inferring and explaining human behavior may not be as separate as many archaeologists believe, because both operations depend on many of the same theoretical assumptions concerning human behavior, archaeologists have become increasingly aware that only by developing rigorous techniques for inferring human behavior and beliefs from the archaeological record will it be possible for them to address problems of explaining human behavior, history, and cultural change that are of interest to themselves and to other social scientists. Growing awareness of the complexity of factors that influence human behavior has also convinced many archaeologists that developing the knowledge required to infer human behavior will not be the quick and easy operation that in the 1960s processual archaeologists optimistically anticipated it would be. The creation of such theory is now viewed as the primary task of archaeologists and one that will require attention indefinitely.

Middle-Ranging Theory

Today, it is generally understood that past human behavior and beliefs are not "discovered" or "reconstructed" by archaeologists but, rather, "constructed," "inferred," or "conjectured" with varying degrees of probability. Such inferences are clearly recognized as being archaeologists' ideas about the past. From the point of view of nomenclature, it would be convenient to refer to all approaches used to infer behavior or beliefs from archaeological data as middle-range theory. Yet Binford has already employed that term to designate a specific technique of inference. I therefore propose to refer generically to all approaches of this sort as middle-ranging theory. The major types of middle-ranging theory are:

1. *Middle-range theory.* Originally, Binford (1962) proposed that, if a specific type of artifact or attribute could be demonstrated to be correlated with a particular form of behavior or belief in every instance in those ethnographic cultures where its presence was recorded, it could be assumed that such a behavior or belief had been associated with every archaeological culture in which the same sort of artifact or attribute was found. Later, Binford (1978) proposed that, if a distinctive combination of material traits could be demonstrated to correlate with a specific pattern of behavior in living societies, the discovery of the same combination of material traits in the archaeological record would permit similar behavior to be associated with an archaeological culture. Contrary to

Binford's original expectation, this technique works best when relations between material culture and human behavior are mediated by invariant physical and biological laws, as is the case with flint-knapping or bronze casting, or when material constraints in the form of energy or labor consumption play a dominant role, as often happens with ecological or economic behavior. Even Dean Saitta (1992), a self-styled radical archaeologist who believes that social context is fundamental to archaeological interpretations, advocates the use of middle-range theory within such a context.

2. *Behavioral correlations.* These interpretations depend on establishing, on the basis of ethnographic evidence, a cross-cultural correlation between two forms of behavior or between a behavior and a belief. In many cases, this is the same as basing an interpretation on a general law relating to human behavior. For example, if the argument could be sustained that in all early civilizations for which relevant textual evidence is available material goods were sacrificed to deities because it was believed that such a sacrifice would sustain these deities and the cosmic order (Trigger 2003a: 473–94), it would be logical to assume that such sacrifices also were made in other early civilizations for which confirming textual evidence so far has not been discovered. This claim could be at least partially tested by looking for archaeological evidence of religious sacrifices in those civilizations. Because such sacrifices involved different materials, were performed using different rituals, and took place in different settings in each well-documented early civilization, it would not be possible for archaeologists to predict the precise nature or setting of such sacrifices in any one civilization, but it might be possible for them to identify archaeological evidence of sacrifices and even to reconstruct the precise form such sacrifices took in any one society.

Research of this sort can address cross-cultural uniformities arising from psychological or other biological causes. In each case, however, the generalization must be treated as a hypothesis to be tested against specific archaeological evidence. One serious problem with this approach, which applies to the example cited above, is that it encourages the application of inadequately tested generalizations. For example, Mircea Eliade's (1954) ideas about the universality among hunter-gatherers of shamanism and associated cosmological representations as known in Siberia have encouraged the interpretation of fragmentary data in ways that probably exaggerate the extent of cross-cultural uniformity of ideas relating to these two subjects. Hence, considerable rigor is required in both formulating behavioral generalizations and applying them to specific archaeological situations.

3. *Historical interpretation.* In this form of interpretation, archaeological finds are examined in relation to historical, ethnographic, or any other sorts of written records that relate to the same time, place, and social group. Such interpretations deal with ideas, human behavior, or specific events. Ian Morris (1994b: 45–6) maintains that, because of the multivalency and ambiguity of meaning of material culture, written texts and oral traditions are the only means by which archaeologists can directly access all but the simplest and most general ideas from the past. We have already discussed the challenges involved in correlating and interrogating both texts and archaeological data in ways that yield a maximum amount of information about the past. Although limited to a small number of cultures that were literate or well documented by literate visitors, this approach provides the only opportunity for archaeologists to acquire a detailed and accurate understanding of precisely what material culture meant to members of an earlier society and how that meaning influenced their behavior. This sort of understanding also helps archaeologists to investigate how meaning relates to material culture in general. The historical approach is thus of disproportionately great importance for gaining a general understanding of the meaning and behavioral significance of material culture.

4. *Direct historical approach.* The direct historical approach employs historical or ethnographic information about living cultures to interpret archaeological finds relating to earlier, historically undocumented stages of the same, or of historically closely related, cultures. Like historical interpretation, this is a homological method. Major problems in applying this method are created by historical evidence that meaning and form can alter independently of one another. The same symbol or icon can acquire new meanings over time or the same meaning can be expressed in new and unrelated forms (Goodenough 1953–1968). By contrast, there is also historical evidence that in some cultures, such as that of ancient Egypt, meanings persisted for millennia without

significant change. The direct historical approach also can be used to demonstrate how in particular areas there was radical cultural change before the historical period. In these cases, the direct historical approach cannot be used to assign culturally specific meanings to older and different cultures, unless these older cultures in turn can be shown to be historically related to yet some other historically attested culture. Bassy Andah's (1995) argument that the interpretation of African archaeological finds must be grounded in a detailed knowledge of African meanings of artifacts derived from local ethnography failed to specify how archaeologists might ascertain the relevance of such homologies to finds that date from ever earlier periods. When applied over long periods of history, careful culture-historical documentation is required to distinguish homologies from analogies with respect to material culture (von Gernet 1993). Much more research needs to be carried out before it is possible to reach informed opinions about what long-term continuities in material culture can tell us about continuities in beliefs. In general, however, the more complex the material manifestation, the more likely there is continuity at least in general meaning (Hamell 1983).

5. *Empirical approach.* This method involves attempting to work out ancient systems of weight, measurement, or monetary value by searching for orderly differences in weights, the size of buildings or rooms, and currency (Renfrew 1982b: 16–19). This approach, which has long been known, is limited to sets of objects that were standardized according to strict mathematical criteria. It has recently been employed by some cognitive-processual archaeologists, who generally use middle-range theory.

6. *Structuralist approach.* This approach to trying to reconstruct the patterns of thought associated with prehistoric cultures is based on Lévi-Strauss's assumption that binary oppositions that are believed to be part of the "deep structure" underlying culture constitute the foundation of all communication codes. Although this approach has encouraged the search for patterning of material culture in the archaeological record, its underlying assumptions remain unproved and there is no way to link symbolic variations in the archaeological record in a convincing manner to hypothesized bilateral oppositions (Anthony 1995: 84–6). In a more general sense, Christopher Hallpike (1986: 288–371) and John Hall

(1986: 33–110) have suggested that in preindustrial civilizations idiosyncratic and change-resistant core principles, or patternings of behavior, beliefs, and habit that are not directly related to modes of subsistence, supply complex sets of propositions that play an important role in shaping the elaboration of social organization, knowledge, and values in historically related societies, often for thousands of years. Hallpike maintains that these patterns originated as a result of historical accidents analogous to the operation of random variation or founder effects in biological evolution. Finally, some archaeologists have been trying to conjecture the meaning that was ascribed to stylistic parallels in the material culture of individual societies by treating these parallels as manifestations of underlying metaphors (Tilley 1999; Ortman 2000). Although both of these approaches exhibit promise for providing deeper insights into the beliefs that shaped aspects of the material culture of individual societies, verification depends on the direct historical approach.

7. *Intuitive approach.* The intuitive approach is based on the questionable phenomenological assumption that because all humans share similar general cognitive systems and capacities for feelings, it should be possible for archaeologists, on exposure to archaeological remains and their natural settings, to understand the past in at least some general fashion in the same way that prehistoric people experienced it as their present. Alain Gallay (1986: 198–200) has argued, however, that no way can be found to demonstrate an isometric relation between modern ideas about the past and ideas that were actually held in prehistoric times. The only ways that such ideas could be tested would be by means of behavioral correlations or (more likely) by the direct historical approach. Insofar as some behavioral interpretations might take the form of proxemic generalizations about relations between people and spaces, they might be demonstrable by means of middle-range theory.

The first five of these methods constitute a set of techniques for inferring behavior and beliefs from archaeological data, each of which has something to contribute but none of which is sufficient by itself to do all that can be done. Together, they form a powerful battery of techniques, each with a sound ontological grounding. The first two offer analogical interpretations based on physical, biological, and psychological constants. These techniques are suited to deal with ecological and economic factors as well as neurologically embedded, species-specific operations of the human mind. The empirical approach is based on mathematical constants and the historical and direct historical approaches are constructed in accordance with cultural theory. In contrast, structuralism in the strict sense is based on a theory of how the human mind works that is unproved and probably erroneous, while the intuitive approach does not employ any recognized scientific method, including hermeneutics as practiced by philologists.

There is, in addition, the contextual approach, which combines the results of independent studies of multiple data sets relating to a single archaeological site or culture to determine more reliably the behavioral or cultural significance of archaeological data. David Edwards (2003) has demonstrated how the results of the examination of food, cooking methods, serving dishes, and evidence of the use of food and dishes as found and illustrated in tombs can shed light on the use and meaning of food in ancient Nubia. As already discussed, the occurrence of uniformly simple burials in a society characterized by a highly stratified series of housetypes and by other differential wealth criteria suggests that these burials reflect some sort of egalitarian ideal that was not realized in everyday life. Archaeologists have employed the contextual approach in an unselfconscious manner for a long time. The idea that the Maya constructed ceremonial centers that were inhabited by priests and only visited for ritual purposes by a rural farming population gradually was dispelled as growing archaeological information about Maya subsistence, household organization, craft production, and political organization revealed that Maya centers were urban in nature (M. Becker 1979). The ability of some archaeologists who have long studied a particular culture or region to contextualize evidence on the basis of their general knowledge explains how they accurately can grasp the significance of archaeological finds in ways that seem intuitive and unscientific to outsiders.

Complementing the contextual approach is a reviving interest in multidisciplinary studies of the past, which were discouraged for no valid scientific reason by the methodological purism and exclusivity of early processual archaeology. There has been renewed recognition that human skeletal evidence, when analyzed by biological anthropologists, can complement, reinforce, and amplify what may be learned about prehistoric diets by means of floral and faunal analyses (Cohen and Armelagos 1984) and reveal even more about band exogamy than would the study of artifacts. Yet, for a long time, little attention was paid to the value of systematically comparing the results of archaeological studies with those of historical linguistics, biological anthropology, oral traditions, historical ethnography, and historical records, although Jesse Jennings (1979) published a multidisciplinary study of prehistoric Polynesia and Joyce Marcus (1983b) a similar study dealing with the Maya. In recent years, there has once again been growing interest in this method (Shennan 2002: 267–8; T. Ferguson 2003: 142). The findings of each contributing discipline are no more reliable than the data and methodologies on which they are based. If their interpretations correspond, however, that reinforces the likelihood that the separate conclusions of each discipline are correct. If they do not, specialists in each field are challenged to determine who is wrong. When combined, the findings of these various approaches also may offer a more rounded understanding of the past than any one approach could provide. The multidisciplinary approach seeks to avoid past mistakes and misinterpretations by treating race, language, and culture as separate variables and not assuming that changes in one of these categories automatically imply parallel changes in another (F. Boas 1940; Sapir 1921: 121–235; Trigger 1968a: 7–13).

There is also a revival of interest in the method of multiple working hypotheses (Chamberlin 1890), which in the 1960s was ignored because processual archaeologists were promoting a deductive method grounded in a single high-level theory. Following this method, archaeologists propose alternative interpretations that each accord with available data. They then specify the test implications that would confirm or refute each of these alternatives and seek out, or await, further evidence that may support or refute particular interpretations. Although this method is limited, as are all methods, by the capacity for imaginative thinking, factual knowledge, and theoretical sophistication of individual archaeologists, it combines many of the advantages of both deductive and inductive approaches, and of Collingwood's method of asking questions. Over time, new alternatives can be added and, once a problem seems definitively solved, archaeologists can move on to investigate new problems using this method.

Clearly the simplistic deductive schemes for inferring behavior and culture from archaeological data that prevailed in the 1960s have given way to more diverse, overlapping strategies. This permits the "tacking" that Alison Wylie (1989a, 1993) sees as essential for such operations. Tacking involves the use of independent lines of evidence to test theories and of data structured by one theory to test propositions generated by another. This highly flexible approach reflects a more realistic appreciation of the complexity of factors that shape human behavior and cultural change.

A very important technique for promoting a more objective understanding of the past is multivocality. This involves having people with many different understandings about how human societies operate, many different interests in the past, and many different views about how the archaeological record should be studied involved in the planning and carrying out of archaeological research projects. The goal is to ensure that a maximum number of alternative explanations of the archaeological record are considered. When the questions being asked lead to complementary findings, the result is a more richly contextualized view of the past, and when they contradict each other they challenge archaeologists to do more work to resolve these differences. Thus, multivocality is closely linked to the method of multiple working hypotheses. Ian Hodder (1999) has attempted with his recent excavations at Çatalhöyük to combine many independently conceived research projects with a maximum exchange of ideas and information among the researchers (Balter 2005).

Alison Wylie (1992) sees multivocality as a major way of helping to overcome bias, while at the same time relating archaeology to a broader constituency. This approach is exemplified by a growing number of historical archaeology projects that invite the participation of interest groups in their design and execution. Such projects include the 5-Points Project in New York City, the African burial ground in New York City, research on the Ludlow Massacre in Colorado, and the involvement of African American communities in research on Annapolis (McGuire and Reckner 2002, 2003; Ruppel et al. 2003; Walker 2003; Leone 2005). Like the method of multiple working hypotheses, multivocality rejects the idea of processual archaeology that archaeological research should be guided by hypotheses formulated in accordance with a single high-level theory.

By the year 2000, archaeology in the English-speaking world was no longer dichotomized into processual and postprocessual camps that were battling for supremacy. Both materialist and idealist approaches had produced numerous alternative positions, most of which offered useful ideas about inferring human behavior and beliefs from archaeological data. All of these approaches can be grouped under a larger theoretical umbrella that is ontologically materialist and epistemologically realist. For anyone who accepts the evolutionary origin of the human species, no other general perspective is possible. Analogical approaches have proved valuable for inferring many features of technological, ecological, and economic behavior. These approaches can be applied to both historical and prehistoric cultures. Behavioral correlations based on innate biological tendencies of human beings also provide analogies that facilitate inferring some forms of social and ritual behavior and associated general beliefs. Inferring culturally determined beliefs depends on homologies and, hence, is usually restricted to historical cultures and to prehistoric cultures that are closely related both phylogenetically and temporally to historical cultures.

Archaeologists experience considerable difficulty in acknowledging the limited circumstances under which they can infer culturally determined beliefs and behavior from archaeological data. Over the past 150 years, they have slowly become aware of the purely subjective nature of ethnicity and, as they have done so, ethnicity has become an increasingly intractable problem in the absence of relevant historical or ethnographic data (S. Jones 1997). The study of gender, insofar as gender is understood to be likewise a purely cultural construction, has become subject to similar limitations, which have eliminated the uniformitarian, androcentric biases that until recently seriously distorted archaeological interpretations. Although most prehistoric archaeologists continue to study relations between biological sex, as ascertained by physical anthropologists, and material culture, usually in the context of burials, radical relativists are now trying to demonstrate that sex as well as gender is a cultural construction (Gosden 1999: 147–51). If gender behavior could be demonstrated to be biologically grounded in significant respects, it would be easier for prehistoric archaeologists to infer. Yet, given the currently limited state of a biological understanding of human gender behavior, it seems more responsible to study such behavior as if it were determined purely by cultural factors. Likewise, arguments that shamanism is universally involved in the rock images produced by hunter-gatherer cultures (Lewis-Williams 2002) appear to require far more substantiation before they can be applied to the interpretation of all such representations (Price 2001; Whitley and Keyser 2003). Finally, although historical records have been used to demonstrate that some oral traditions have been accurately transmitted for over a century (Treaty 7 Elders et al. 1996), it has been shown that other oral traditions have been altered over equally short periods for social and political reasons (Vansina 1985; R. Mason 2000; Whiteley 2002). Roger Echo-Hawk (2000) and Vine Deloria (1995) have made extravagant demands for the uncritical acceptance of the factual nature of indigenous oral traditions. Such traditions, as cultural creations that are subject to both social and cultural manipulation, require independent confirmation before they can be accepted as reliable sources of historical information.

Although the establishment of additional behavioral generalizations may facilitate the inference of more general beliefs and ritual behavior using archaeological data, Hawkes's hierarchy currently appears to describe correctly the limitations of what can reliably be inferred about prehistoric societies for which no historical or relevant ethnographic data are available. Those limitations suggest that in the future the most important division within archaeology may be between historical and prehistoric archaeology. Historical cultures and to a lesser extent cultures for which some forms of indirect textual information are available can be studied from the point of view of both behavior and culturally specific beliefs, whereas fully prehistoric societies must be examined mainly from a behavioral perspective. Unlike the difference between processual and postprocessual archaeology, that between the study of prehistoric and historical cultures is pragmatic rather than theoretical and hence should not arouse such strong sectarian tensions, although historical archaeology will be the primary arena where the interests traditionally associated with postprocessual archaeology have fullest scope, whereas fully prehistoric archaeology will be the field that corresponds most closely with the current interests of processual archaeologists.

The refusal of many postprocessual archaeologists to consider the evidential limitations of their efforts to study prehistoric material has resulted in attempts to justify inferences regarding habits and beliefs

associated with prehistoric cultures that are based largely on speculation and intuition. Such approaches are justified on the grounds that
they offer hypotheses that may later become testable or, even more
lamely, that nothing more convincing is currently possible. Such
interpretations become conduits through which all sorts of unexamined prejudices and personal biases are introduced into archaeology. They ignore the alternative course of remaining silent regarding
matters that are unknowable. Unsubstantiated speculation currently
threatens to return archaeological interpretation to the highly subjective and irresponsible state of "story-telling" from which Lewis
Binford and David Clarke, each in his own way, sought to rescue it
in the 1960s. I do not deny the importance of formulating hypotheses for advancing a scientific understanding of the past, but maintain
that, if this activity is to be useful, it must be accompanied by serious
efforts to test such propositions. It is appropriate to recall Marvin
Harris's (1968b) advice that archaeologists should focus on questions that their data permit them to examine and hopefully to answer.
Instead of developing theory for its own sake or because of the belief
that archaeologists should be able to do anything that historians or
sociocultural anthropologists can do, archaeologists should seek to
craft theories that are appropriate for their own database and the
analytical methods they can hope to devise for examining them.

In reality, there are many different kinds of archaeology, each with
its own distinctive traditions. Despite all the practices that professional archaeologists have in common, each sort of archaeology is
produced by a different network of archaeologists who study different kinds of data, ask different questions, employ different sets
of analytical techniques, and exhibit different attitudes toward what
they are studying (Shennan 2002: 14; G. A. Clark 2003). Lower and
Middle Palaeolithic archaeology ("deep prehistory") is studied differently from Upper Palaeolithic and more recent hunter-gatherer
archaeology, Neolithic archaeology, or the archaeology of early civilizations. Likewise, the practices of medieval, colonial, and industrial
archaeology differ from one another. Idiosyncratic differences also
can be observed among the work of archaeologists who pursue these
lines of research in different regions. Each early civilization tends
in significant ways to be studied and interpreted differently from
every other. In general, the differences that result from variations in
the sorts of data that are available conform with the more general

differences between historical and prehistoric archaeology that have already been noted, while those differences that reflect the cultures of specific work groups tend to be more idiosyncratic. The latter are also more likely to change in unpredictable ways as personnel and the social contexts in which they work alter.

High-Level Theory

Although Gardin (1980: 27) rejects the idea that high-level theory is a part of archaeology and many archaeologists who adopt a purely inductive approach believe that high-level theory can be dispensed with entirely (Courbin 1988), we have already argued that archaeologists can ignore high-level theory only at the risk of their interpretations of archaeological data being unconsciously shaped by the largely unexamined beliefs of the societies in which they live. The racist prejudices that dominated culture-historical archaeology in the late nineteenth and early twentieth centuries were not the result of too much theoretical sophistication but of too little. Archaeologists who ignore theoretical debates in the social sciences risk being dominated by the prejudices of their own societies or social groups, which can influence the interpretation of archaeological evidence at all levels. Idealists tend to assume that every culture is unique and must be understood on its own terms, whereas those who believe cultures to be shaped to a considerable degree by material constraints or psychic unity strive to discover generalizations that can be applied cross-culturally. My own study of similarities and differences among early civilizations indicates that, although every early civilization was unique in its totality, some aspects were shaped by factors that were culturally specific, whereas others can be understood only in terms of cross-cultural generalizations (Trigger 2003a).

Palaeontologists have long understood that uniqueness does not necessarily indicate a lack of orderly and hence understandable processes. In 1852, Karl Marx made a major contribution to understanding how change occurred in human societies when he observed that human beings make their own history not on their own but within the context of institutions, beliefs, values, and patterns of behavior inherited from the past (Marx and Engels 1962, vol. I: 247). Thus, Marx ascribed historical importance to cultural traditions, although he believed that they could be altered relatively easily by the pursuit of cross-culturally meaningful economic interests. Since then, social scientists have debated how easily changeable or intractable cultural heritages may be. Pierre Bourdieu (1977) has drawn attention to the considerable extent to which nonverbalized and often unconscious forms of learned behavior (*habitus*) inhibit change. There is also much debate about what factors produce social and cultural change. Self-interest has been joined by ecological conditions, functional limitations, selection brought about by competition within and between societies, and the biologically based nature of human beings. There is also debate concerning to what degree change comes about as a result of decisions made by individuals or interest groups or because of factors beyond human control, located both in the ecological system and in society itself. Mario Bunge (1979) has eloquently argued the advantages of a systemic approach over either methodological individualism or holistic ones. Even if archaeologists were able to study the behavior of individual human agents in a wide variety of circumstances, as they cannot do, they would find the interests of these agents defined and controlled to a great extent by a vast array of ecological factors, functional constraints, competing interests, and cultural traditions operating at both the conscious and unconscious levels. The outcome of efforts by individuals to bend or change the rules is rarely predictable, nor is the manner in which circumstances unforeseen by individuals or groups may play a significant role in determining what happens next. That is why in human affairs events can be explained but never predicted with any certainty.

So far, no single generally accepted high-level theory has guided the work of archaeologists or any other social scientists. Instead, they embrace a spectrum of theories with orientations ranging from extreme materialism to extreme idealism. Materialism has spawned various technological, ecological, economic, and selectionist explanations, while idealism has produced varied historical, structural, and cultural options. The popularity of individual high-level theories rises and falls, but none of them has ever succeeded in excluding all rival theories and few of them have completely died out. At present racial explanations of human behavior are seeking to make a comeback after sixty years of deserved obscurity (Rushton 1995). As the social climate and intellectual fashions change, theoretical preferences shift toward either the materialist or idealist end of the theoretical spectrum. Marxism was once a culturally aware materialist theory, but in recent decades it has shifted increasingly toward an idealist position (Godelier 1986; McGuire 1992, 1993; Trigger 1993).

Archaeologists and other social scientists disagree among themselves concerning whether it is possible to transcend this plethora of high-level theories by constructing a general framework that might resolve their differences and integrate them in a harmonious fashion. There is now broad agreement that no unicausal explanation can account for all, or even most, of the similarities and differences observed in human behavior or material culture. Ecological, economic, and technological determinisms appear increasingly to be outmoded, except among popular intellectual gurus (J. Diamond 1997). Testable middle-level theories, such as Karl Wittfogel's (1957) irrigation hypothesis or Ester Boserup's (1965) theory of agricultural intensification, have been demonstrated not to correspond with evidence in numerous instances (Spooner 1972). It is increasingly accepted that, because many different factors influence human behavior, the theoretical structure needed to explain this behavior will be complex. There is also a growing consensus that an adequate general theory must account for both cross-cultural regularities and idiosyncratic cultural variation (van der Leeuw and McGlade 1997). This is different from the tendency of cultural evolutionists to try to explain cross-cultural similarities while ignoring cultural differences or of new cultural anthropologists to account for homologies while ignoring analogies.

The contrary opinion, that it is impossible to create an integrated body of high-level theory, has been supported by postprocessual archaeologists (Hodder 2003b). As it did the new cultural anthropologists and the Boasians before them, cultural relativism leads postprocessual archaeologists to deny the existence of cross-cultural regularities and view each culture as a unique example of human creativity. The nature and importance of variables that determine behavior are believed to vary greatly from one culture to another. In large measure, cultural change comes about as a result of accidents and culturally specific processes. From the beginning, this was a problematical view, as even the early Boasians had to admit that each viable culture had to provide for a set of minimal cultural prerequisites that would keep enough people alive for the culture to survive (Aberle et al. 1950).

The relativist response was that no prerequisite determined how that prerequisite was provided for in any given culture (Sahlins 1976a).

Ian Hodder (2001b) has questioned the wisdom of efforts to create a unified body of archaeological, or social science, theory. He suggests that instead we should view such theory as a collection of discourses that often, like Kuhnian paradigms, are mutually incomprehensible. This perspective accords with a relativist, culturally-oriented approach that seeks to deny that there are other than contingent explanations for human behavior. Yet, such a position ignores major cross-cultural regularities. Some of these are the result of functional constraints that permit only certain types of economic, social, and political institutions to coexist. Others result from convergent cultural selection. Human history also demonstrates greater unilinearity than a relativist position can countenance. This comes about as a result of large, complex societies appropriating the resources of their smaller and weaker neighbors (Trigger 1998a). Evidence of the occurrence of numerous analogies in sociocultural systems distributed around the world supports the likelihood that functional and selective factors play a significant role in shaping human behavior (D. Brown 1988; Trigger 2003a). Rosemary Joyce (2002: 76) argues that our inevitably limited and situated view of what is possible precludes our ability ever to achieve an objective understanding of the forces that shape human behavior and sociocultural systems. This view rejects the role of anthropology as a comparative study of culture. It also repudiates one of the basic working principles of science, which is to assume that the world is knowable until the contrary has been clearly demonstrated. Science does not claim ever to know the truth, but scientists constantly strive to learn the truth. Postprocessualists are like spectators who tell the blind men studying an elephant that the beast is too big for them ever to learn much about it or that they ought to establish whether an elephant is really there before they start to investigate it. These are diversions from the main task, which is to study what is literally at hand.

A third position maintains that trying to construct a comprehensive theory of human behavior is a task worth pursuing. Much work has already been done that could contribute to creating such a framework, especially when existing theories are freed from their dogmatic contexts. Comparative studies, both synchronic and diachronic, offer an empirically based strategy for systematically assessing the appropriateness of specific types of explanations (Trigger 2003a). Until recently, the significance of such theories was all too often determined on the basis of limited case studies or *ad hoc* explanations supported by anecdotal evidence. If archaeologists are to help to construct a comprehensive theoretical framework, they must take account of cross-cultural regularities and idiosyncracies that relate not only to the ecological and sociopolitical spheres but also to belief systems. They must address the biological proclivities of human beings, the emergent properties of cultural systems, what is needed to survive in a world that exists independently of human volition, and the complex ways in which all of these factors interact. Only an explicitly emergentist approach is appropriate for this task (Bunge 2003).

A comprehensive theory of human behavior might provide a common framework in relation to which archaeologists could acknowledge, negotiate, and continue to attempt to resolve their theoretical disagreements. Although it is highly unlikely that such an endeavor would ever result in total agreement, it might provide stronger and more efficacious incentives to achieve a reasoned reconciliation of divergent viewpoints than does direct theoretical confrontation. Even partial success in creating a broadly accepted corpus of theory would facilitate the more informed selection of frames of reference to guide research on specific problems (Binford 2001). Such a framework also would reduce the need for archaeologists repeatedly to renegotiate the same problems, as if nothing had been accomplished. It thus would eliminate much useless reinventing of the wheel (Trigger 2003d).

Assessing the relative value of different propositions requires determining how well specific theoretical propositions correspond with empirical evidence, including archaeological evidence. Constructing a general theoretical framework requires ascertaining in what contexts particular sorts of explanations are useful and integrating these approaches. Archaeologists must strive to establish under what conditions and to what extent learned behavior is likely to predominate over individual innovation and how innovations do and do not become established in society. What combinations of factors are functionally likely, possible, or impossible? Under what circumstances does natural selection favor certain behavioral traits or types of sociocultural systems over others and what effect does such selection have on general patterns of cultural development? What sorts of behavior reflect drives or thought patterns that are innate to humans and to what extent can such drives and patterns be manipulated by cultural and social factors? To what extent must long-term processes be understood separately from short-term ones, as Fernand Braudel (1972) proposes, or are such trajectories, as evolutionary biologists believe, outcomes of the same processes that bring about short-term change?

Even without creating a formal theoretical framework, it seems that sufficient evidence already exists to permit archaeologists to evaluate in a general fashion the usefulness of various developments that are occurring in archaeological and anthropological theory. It seems unproductive for archaeologists to assume dogmatically either that behavior is determined by ideas or that ideas are merely passive facilitators of behavior. Most archaeologists have long agreed that, as a result of biological evolution, all human behavior is conceptually – and, hence, culturally – mediated. As we have already noted, Childe (1949, 1956b) embraced the idea that the world humans adapt to is not the world as it really is but the world as specific groups of humans believe it to be. Nevertheless, as a materialist, Childe also believed that, in order to endure, every view of the world had to accord to a significant degree with the world as it actually was. Thus, archaeologists and other social scientists face two challenges: understanding how people adjust to the real world and how they understand that world. These problems are focused on behavior and perception respectively. In engaging with these problems, archaeologists are addressing the two fundamental didactic missions of anthropology: demonstrating the intelligence and rationality of all peoples and celebrating their cultural creativity and diversity.

Ecological archaeologists, applying the concepts of energy flow, least effort, and optimal foraging to archaeological data can demonstrate that prehistoric hunter-gatherers had a sound knowledge of their environment and were able to devise strategies that exploited that environment in a nearly optimal manner. The Cree people of northern Quebec traditionally preferred to hunt caribou, which gave them approximately a twenty-five-fold caloric return on the energy that was required to kill the animals. They also knew the next most appropriate hunting practices if caribou or other types of game were not available. They also clearly understood that in prehistoric times they could never have survived by trapping only foxes, which yield a lower caloric return than is required to hunt them (Feit 1978; A. Tanner 1979). Demonstrating rationality of this sort is a matter of no small importance. It confirms the ability of specific prehistoric peoples to analyze the environment and exploit it in highly effective ways. In richer environments a number of subsistence patterns may work almost equally well, allowing cultural choice to play a greater role in influencing what strategies were adopted.

Effective subsistence patterns do not signify, however, that a hunter-gatherer society's understanding of the environment was based on the same concepts as those used by Western cultural ecologists. Hunter-gatherers do not calculate their subsistence behavior in terms of energy expenditures and gains measured in calories. In many traditional societies, knowledge of the environment and the impact that humans have on it is encoded in religious beliefs. We know from ethnographic studies that the Cree believe that all animals are rational beings like humans, but that each species has a different nature. Humans cannot kill animals but, when a hunter has established the right relations with animal spirits, animals will sacrifice their own lives to support humans. Thus, relations with what we regard as the natural world are not seen as based on knowledge of the environment, hunting skills, and calculations of caloric returns. They are based on the kinds of relations individual hunters have with animal spirits.

Robert Boyd and Peter Richerson (1985) have demonstrated that long-term transmissions of knowledge of this sort in the form of cultural traditions are better adapted to serve individual and collective needs than are individual calculations. Individual calculations are sometimes required to respond to changing conditions, but they tend to be *ad hoc* and are often poorly thought through. Over time the repeated use of ideas by large numbers of individuals tends to favor the positive selection and improvement of their more effective attributes and to ensure that innovations serve collective as well as individual goals. The transmission of Cree ecological knowledge in the form of religious concepts and ritual also enhanced the chances of its survival. Traditional knowledge is not necessarily, or even typically, a collection of antiquated and dysfunctional beliefs from the past, as E. B. Tylor maintained. Among the Cree, it provides a means for encoding and preserving information that is essential for their survival. It was agreed that their understanding of how their environment worked and how a living might be extracted from it was far more detailed and precise than that of the Western cultural ecologists who worked with them in the 1970s. Much wrangling between processual and postprocessual archaeologists might have been avoided had early processual archaeologists, in accordance with their claim to be behaviorists, accepted that what they were discussing using archaeological evidence was whether people in prehistoric societies had behaved rationally in terms of their subsistence activities rather than what specific concepts were guiding their behavior.

In recent years, some postprocessual archaeologists have retreated from their claims that they can reconstruct beliefs from archaeological evidence alone. They stress instead the utility of predispositions, habits, intentions, and other learned but often unconscious tendencies as explanations of patterning in the archaeological record (Gosden 1994). They argue that these psychological states may be more important determinants of human behavior than are explicit beliefs, as well as easier to infer intuitively from archaeological data alone. Invariably, however, these interpretations remain the archaeologist's speculations about the mental states that might have produced, or been produced by, a particular patterning of material culture that is preserved in the archaeological record.

Beliefs about hunting, recorded by anthropologists from living Cree hunters, present detailed information about the specific ideas that relate these hunters to their game. These ideas are novel in the sense that they differ from anything a social scientist coming from a modern industrial society might have imagined about them. They provide a basis for understanding in detail the specific cultural mediation associated with Cree subsistence behavior. It would be no more possible for an archaeologist to reconstruct these beliefs from archaeological data alone than it would be for an archaeologist to reconstruct the specific vocabulary and grammar of the language spoken by a prehistoric group using only material culture as evidence; something that no archaeologist or linguist, except perhaps Nikolay Marr, has ever claimed is possible. Even if a behavioral generalization existed to the effect that in all hunter-gatherer societies hunting practices are mediated by religious beliefs, it would be impossible to reconstruct the culturally specific content of such beliefs.

Yet historical archaeologists, equipped with ethnographic knowledge of Cree beliefs, might be able to associate some of them with archaeological evidence of special treatment accorded to the bones of specific animal species. In this way, it might be possible to infer the possible time depth of specific practices and to identify some archaeological evidence concerning the possible antiquity of some or all of the traditional belief system of Cree hunters. Archaeologists also could use ecological studies to trace stability and changes in Cree hunting practices and how they were or were not affected by environmental changes and the development of the fur trade with Europeans. Working from a historically documented context, archaeologists could hope to gain insights into how the patterning of archaeological data relating to Cree hunting was influenced by the culturally specific ideas that guided this activity. In the absence of such data, they would be limited to studying Cree behavior and calculating to what extent it was guided by accurate knowledge of the environment and how that environment might be exploited. This case study suggests that what archaeologists can do in contexts in which detailed textual information is and is not available is very different. These differences are likely to persist regardless of what theoretical developments occur. Because of this, I suggest that the distinction between historical and prehistoric archaeology will probably remain the most important one in archaeology for a long time.

It is possible that the production of further behavioral generalizations and their application to understanding data relating to specific societies will expand the ability of archaeologists to learn more about the cultural as well as the societal aspects of prehistoric groups. Yet what is already known about the nature of cross-cultural regularities and idiosyncracies suggests that the impact of such research is likely to be limited. Although it is the duty of archaeologists to do all they can to expand knowledge of the past, one of the most important items on the theoretical agenda of archaeology should be to consider realistically in what theoretical domains their discipline can hope to make significant contributions to the social sciences and in what problem areas it cannot. Archaeology clearly has a unique role to play in studying the full scope of human history and providing a general historical framework into which the findings of other social science disciplines can be fitted. The study of material culture has much to contribute to understanding various categories of human behavior and, where data in verbal form are also available, to a better understanding of how human beliefs and habits relate to material culture. Determining what archaeologists can and cannot hope to accomplish may help to increase the productivity of archaeological research by assisting archaeologists to avoid cultivating theories and pursuing approaches that ultimately prove to be unproductive and offer little that is of value in return for their work.

CHAPTER 10

The Relevance of Archaeology

The test of any good idea in archaeology, whatever its source, is whether it helps archaeologists look for things in the archaeological record that they might otherwise overlook or underrate.

JOHN E. TERRELL, "Archaeological Inference and Ethnographic Analogies" (2003), p. 74

In this concluding chapter, I will review some general theoretical challenges facing archaeology and consider how archaeologists might respond more effectively to these problems in the future. I also will discuss briefly the special roles that archaeology can play within the social sciences and in modern society.

The Challenge of Relativism

Because archaeology deals with complex phenomena and is not an experimental discipline, it is particularly vulnerable to what is accepted as true being whatever seems to be most reasonable to archaeologists, both individually and collectively. Archaeologists may establish sound correlations, weed out logical inconsistencies, and demonstrate that accepted interpretations do not accord with new data. Yet this historical survey reveals that, even if archaeology has grown considerably more resistant to subjectivity as its database and techniques for studying these data have expanded, interpretations are still subtly influenced by social, personal, and disciplinary perceptions of reality that often preclude an awareness of the full range of alternative explanations that require testing. In many cases, neither sufficient data nor strong enough correlations among the variables being examined are available to counteract these biases.

As archaeologists have grown more aware of the complexity of what they have to explain, they also have become more interested in learning how and to what extent their experience of the present influences their interpretations of the past. Even positivists, such as Lewis Binford, have long accepted that the social milieu affects the questions that archaeologists ask. Others, more open to a relativist perspective, see the milieu in which they live as affecting both the problems archaeologists choose to address and the answers they are predisposed to regard as reasonable. It is easy to illustrate that throughout the world the interpretation of archaeological evidence has been influenced by social, economic, and political considerations. These interpretations consciously or unconsciously support the political and economic interests of those who fund archaeological research, by either reinforcing or defending the ideological postures associated with them. Archaeological interpretations are colored by gender prejudices, ethnic concerns, political control of research and publishing, generational and personal conflicts among researchers, and the personal idiosyncracies of charismatic archaeologists. They are also influenced by the analytical models that are offered by the physical, biological, and to a still greater degree the social sciences.

Most interpretations are not straightforward reflections of such influences but versions of the past created by archaeologists trying under specific historical circumstances to promote or defend preferred social interests. Racial doctrines can be used to promote national unity or to justify colonial aggression. Strong religious beliefs can be held responsible for retarding technological progress or hailed as a major factor promoting cultural development. The options that are selected reflect the specific interests existing in modern societies and how individual archaeologists understand and relate to those interests. Such considerations not only play a major role in shaping variations in archaeological practice but also shift in response to changing social conditions.

At worst, these considerations could mean that there is no past to study, not only in the undeniable positivist sense that what we interpret is merely "the marks of the past in the present" but also in accord with Collingwood's more profound definition of history as a discipline in which one relives the past in one's own mind. This observation implies that there is no way in which an archaeologist or historian can verifiably reconstruct the past as it actually was. Yet Ernst Gellner (1985: 134) points out that most archaeologists believe that "the past was once present, as *the present*, and it was real." All but the most extreme relativists are convinced that the things people did in the past really happened and that their having happened has played a significant role in shaping the archaeological record that we study. The past therefore had a reality of its own that is independent of the reconstructions and explanations that archaeologists may give of it. Moreover, because the archaeological record, as a product of the past, has been shaped by forces that are independent of our own beliefs, the evidence that it provides at least potentially can act as a constraint on archaeologists' imaginations. To that extent, the study of the past has different goals from writing a work of fiction. One of the most important of these goals must be to recover knowledge of what has been forgotten. Yet the crucial questions remain unanswered: How far can archaeologists go in acquiring objective knowledge of the past and how certain can they be of the accuracy of what they believe they know about that past, given the propensity of value judgments to color their interpretations?

In recent years, many archaeologists have shifted from a naive positivism to a more far-reaching acceptance of relativism than at any time in the past. Alison Wylie (1985b: 73) points out that even "the most straightforward observational experience is actively structured by the observer and acquires significance as evidence . . . only under theory- and 'paradigm'-specific interpretation." Before past human behavior is explained, it must be inferred from material remains that in turn acquire status as data as a result of theory-influenced and, hence, at least partly subjective processes of classification. Hence both when classifying material remains and even more when interpreting human behavior, archaeologists are dealing with something quite different from the objective facts postulated by those historians who continue to follow the precepts of the von Ranke school (Patrik 1985). Such historians distinguish between a relatively stable core of factual data about the past, which is deemed to be objective and to expand incrementally as new documents are studied, and the interpretation of these data, which is highly subjective and can differ radically from one historian to another. The question that archaeologists face is therefore whether they must accept the position of the extreme relativists or some containment of relativism is possible. The desire to gain deeper insight into this problem has been the chief factor encouraging a growing interest in the history of archaeology.

The Development of Archaeology

The development of archaeological understanding cannot be reduced to any single pattern described in Chapter 1. A number of genetic models capture important aspects of a complexity that defies total encapsulation by any one model. These models provide complementary insights into the development of archaeological thought.

Contrary to the expectation of extreme relativists, the development of archaeological understanding displays a considerable amount of directionality, although not enough to support a unilinear, positivist view of that development, such as that embraced by Gordon Willey and Jeremy Sabloff in *A History of American Archaeology* (1974). Archaeological findings about what human beings have done in the past have irreversibly altered our understanding of human origins and development, at least for people who are prepared to abide by scientific canons of reasoning. Before the nineteenth century, evolutionary schemes of human development were entertained alongside creationist and degenerationist views and various cyclical speculations. Each of these scenarios was a possible description of human history, but there was no scientific evidence that would allow scholars to determine which of these theories offered the most likely explanation of human origins and cultural development. Since then, archaeological data have presented solid evidence, which indicates that human beings evolved from higher primate stock, most likely in Africa. There is considerable disagreement about the significance of morphological variations among early hominids and which of them were the direct ancestors of modern human beings. Yet it is clear that throughout most of their history human beings and their hominid ancestors subsisted by eating wild plants and animals. It also seems likely that scavenging and killing small game preceded the hunting of large animals.

By late Lower Palaeolithic times, hominids had spread from tropical regions at least into colder temperate climates and by the Middle and Upper Palaeolithic periods some human beings had adapted to living in periglacial conditions. Prior to 40,000 years ago, human groups had made their way across a narrow stretch of ocean into Australia–New Guinea and by at least 11,000 years ago they had spread throughout the New World from Bering Strait to Tierra del Fuego. By the end of the last Ice Age, if not earlier, denser and more sedentary food-collecting populations had developed in richer natural environments in many parts of the world. Intensive food collecting was supplemented by food production, which gradually became the principal source of nourishment in many regions of the Old and New Worlds. It has, however, become evident that the more sedentary collecting societies, such as those that were encountered on the west coast of Canada in the nineteenth century, have more in common, demographically and in terms of social and political organization, with sedentary tribal agricultural societies than they do with big-game hunters (Testart 1982; Price and Brown 1985). This observation has provided a new basis for interpreting the evidence concerning "Mesolithic" societies in the Old World and "Archaic" ones in the Americas, which in the past seemed anomalous and difficult to understand. There is no suggestion of historical connections between many of the major zones in which plant and animal domestication occurred and steadily increasing archaeological evidence of continuities within various regions suggests that domestication was a process that happened independently in many places. The same can be said about the first civilizations, which evolved as some tribal agricultural societies became transformed into hierarchical, class-based ones, dominated by small elites who used part of the surplus wealth they controlled to produce monumental architecture and works of art that served, among other things, as status symbols.

It is also clear that not all societies evolved through this sequence. Some remained hunter-gatherers into modern times, whereas others abandoned agriculture and took up big-game hunting when new technologies made hunting and gathering a more productive option, as happened on the Great Plains of North America in the eighteenth century, or when environmental change or loss of productive lands diminished the viability of agriculture. As some cultures grew more complex, relations between neighboring societies of different sizes and with dissimilar economies became more common. Under certain ecological conditions, more complex societies were able to dominate and absorb less complex neighboring ones, but in other situations pastoral or hunter-gatherer societies succeeded in maintaining their autonomy into modern times. This selective process explains how more complex societies gradually replaced simpler ones over large areas of the world, with pastoral and hunter-gatherer societies remaining dominant only in areas unsuitable for agriculture. The ability of more complex societies to dominate at least some weaker and less complex ones also explains why the transition from hunting and gathering to sedentary life to civilization is the dominant pattern in human history.

Although much remains to be learned about the timing and precise nature of cultural stability and change in various parts of the world in prehistoric times, the general picture outlined above is sustained by an immense and growing corpus of evidence collected and analyzed by an ever increasing number of archaeologists. This does not mean that in the future archaeologists may not discover earlier intensive collecting or agricultural societies than those currently known, new early civilizations, or even unsuspected cultural connections between different parts of the world. Yet, for over a century, the general picture of what happened in prehistoric times that has been derived from archaeological discoveries has been refined rather than overturned. The same cannot be said of either detailed or general explanations of why these things happened. Moreover, although the broad outline of prehistory presented in modern textbooks may not differ enormously from some of the speculative evolutionary reconstructions of the nineteenth or even the eighteenth centuries, it does differ in being based on archaeological evidence that is replete with circumstantial detail, both about the nature of individual cultures and about specific sequences of change. These data elaborate what is known about both particular developmental sequences and the general pattern of prehistory. The cumulative development of archaeological knowledge indicates that erroneous interpretations of what happened in the past can be detected as a result of the discovery of new archaeological evidence, which contradicts previous conclusions; an awareness of new theories of human behavior, which provide fresh insights into the meaning of archaeological data; and the development of more reliable means for inferring human behavior and beliefs from archaeological data.

An alternative approach, and the one that has been used to trace the history of archaeological theory in this volume, sees various theoretical perspectives, each of which addresses different sorts of questions, as coexisting but varying in relative importance over time and in different places. This approach seems best suited for examining the empirical content of different perspectives relating to archaeological analysis and for studying how they and their relations to one

534

another have changed over time. The first coherently formulated perspective was historical archaeology, which developed, initially as classical archaeology, in Europe in the eighteenth century and has persisted in recognizable form until the present. It focused on studying the epigraphy, art, and architecture of ancient civilizations in order to enhance knowledge of the elite cultures of those societies that was originally derived from surviving texts. This approach was deeply influenced by European humanism, especially as formulated by the philosopher Johann Herder. Prehistoric archaeology came into being in Scandinavia in the early nineteenth century and almost from the beginning exhibited three complementary interests, in the evolution of culture (evolutionary archaeology), the culture-history of specific regions (culture-historical archaeology), and how people had lived in the past (functional-processual archaeology). Evolutionary archaeology developed as Palaeolithic archaeology between 1860 and 1880, whereas culture-historical archaeology flourished preeminently between 1880 and 1960. Functional-processual archaeology began to receive increasing attention around the beginning of the twentieth century and after 1960 dominated much of the theoretical work in archaeology, first with a behavioral (processual) emphasis and then with a cultural (postprocessual) one.

It has been widely assumed that the growth of functional-processual archaeology at the expense of culture-historical archaeology was a linear process in which the construction of cultural chronologies was superseded by efforts to explain the archaeological record in terms of human behavior. This scenario also might account for the major shift, brought about by the adoption of elements of processual and postprocessual archaeology, which is currently transforming the older historical archaeologies into practices that more closely resemble prehistoric archaeology. Yet the pursuit of functional-processual archaeology has reciprocally necessitated the elaboration and refinement of cultural chronologies as the result of an increasing need to distinguish ever briefer intervals of time in the archaeological record. The result of this development appears to be the breaking down of the distinction between culture-historical and functional-processual archaeology. This is accompanied by a similar erosion of the distinction between evolutionary and culture-historical archaeology that results from the repudiation of the artificial dichotomy between historical and evolutionary change. In place of these older archaeologies, a new programmatic distinction appears to be emerging between historical and prehistoric archaeology, based on what can be accomplished in interpreting archaeological evidence when written texts, oral traditions, and cultural homologies are and are not available. The overall pattern suggests that a variety of different approaches to doing archaeology had to be elaborated separately, but possibly for the most part in no particular order, before they could be used together.

An approach based on theoretical perspectives is complemented by the detailed examination of what theoretical concepts have guided the development of archaeological research in particular countries or regions. In these studies, a considerable degree of idiosyncratic variation becomes evident. Yet, once again, it appears that, ideally, archaeology everywhere is characterized by a broad set of topics that must be investigated if the fullest possible range of information about human behavior and human history is to be recovered. Still, today, different kinds of data are studied selectively by archaeologists working in different localities and even on different periods in particular localities. The order in which different modes of analysis are adopted seems to be highly variable, reflecting the differing values, political orientations, and academic allegiances of local archaeologists. Yet, as archaeological research develops, it becomes increasingly evident that dogmatic selectivity about low-level generalizations and middle-level theory is unproductive, even if archaeologists disagree about the ultimate use that is to be made of their data. As a result, in the absence of dogmatic ideological controls, archaeologists in any particular region will adopt an ever more inclusive range of analytical concerns, as far as these are economically supportable.

This suggests that an inclusive corpus of methods for inferring human behavior ultimately will constitute the ideal, if not the reality, of archaeological research everywhere. The principal factor encouraging the realization of that goal is the spread of information about how other groups of archaeologists are doing things, largely promoted by a spirit of emulation. Opposing such dissemination are isolation, the inertia associated with habitual behavior, and national pride, which together or separately encourage the maintenance of local traditions of archaeological research. It was local practices of this sort that in the late nineteenth century the anthropologists and archaeologists at the Smithsonian Institution attempted to crush with their campaign against the Davenport Academy and that David Clarke (1973) more recently sought to replace with an international "scientific" archaeology. The successful creation of more generally agreed standards of archaeological performance seems to result from long-term, multilateral interaction among individual archaeologists rather than from new ideas being summarily imposed on the discipline by a small number of proselytizing gurus.

Theoretical approaches also exhibit cyclical tendencies. An interest in cultural evolution revived in British and American archaeology beginning in the 1930s, after several decades when evolutionism was ignored in favor of a culture-historical approach. Stuart Piggott (1950) noted a more long-term alternation of rationalist and romantic approaches to doing archaeology that dates back to the eighteenth century. Evolutionary archaeology was an expression of rationalism and culture-historical archaeology of romanticism. Only recently have archaeologists begun to consider whether these two approaches are in reality contradictory or complementary.

Laura Nader (2001) suggests that shifts in theoretical orientations are regularly accompanied by significant levels of collective amnesia, as a result of which abandoned, but potentially useful, concepts must be reinvented at a later date. This creates a situation in which, as a result of self-imposed mutual isolation, rival approaches tend to inhibit, rather than encourage, progress. The recent efforts by Darwinian archaeologists to examine culture-historical theory as it applies to archaeology and to redeploy useful culture-historical concepts in the context of their own selectionist synthesis are commendable examples of a systematic attempt to counteract such amnesia. Evolving analytical techniques also appear to have some capacity to counteract the negative effects of these cyclical trends. The influence of such techniques is exemplified by the impact that the Baconian approach, championed by the Royal Society of London, had on improving the practice of antiquarianism in England in the eighteenth century.

The external pressures that it is claimed were exerted on archaeological theory and practice by Michel Foucault's successive epistemes often were moderated by local traditions of interpreting archaeological data that persisted despite hypothesized major shifts in overall intellectual orientations (Trigger 1978b; Chippindale 1983). Critically studying how specific archaeological concepts and understandings have developed makes it easier to avoid accepting such beliefs as being natural and unquestionable (Moro Abadía and González Morales 2003). Finally, Kuhn's concept of paradigms seems invalidated by his insistence on their incommensurability. Although archaeologists who subscribe to any one school of interpretation may have little sympathy for, and less than a deep understanding of, rival approaches, they rarely fail to understand the basic ideas of their opponents.

Relations with Other Social Sciences

There also has been considerable disagreement about how archaeologists should relate to the other social sciences in their efforts to explain human behavior. Classical archaeologists and those who work as Egyptologists and Assyriologists mostly identify themselves as humanists, whereas prehistoric archaeologists have cultivated close associations with either history or anthropology. In general, in Europe, ties have been closest with anthropology during brief periods of evolutionary interest in cross-cultural regularities and with history the rest of the time, when cultural (including culture-historical) interests have been in the ascendant. In North America, the interests of prehistoric archaeologists in evolutionary and cultural approaches have followed similar shifts within anthropology.

In Europe, prehistoric archaeology has tended to be institutionalized either as an independent discipline or in history departments; in North America it is usually located in anthropology departments. Unfortunately, archaeologists constitute a minority of teaching staff in most anthropology departments and the technical training of archaeology students tends to be slighted in favor of training in general anthropological theory. Hodder and Hutson (2003: 242–6) have recently argued that archaeology should be an independent discipline in which archaeologists are free to forge the links with those disciplines that best enable them to explain archaeological data. Such an arrangement, it is claimed, also would make it easier for archaeologists to create the kinds of theories relating to material culture that are needed to infer behavior and ideas from archaeological data.

Yet, regardless of the institutional settings in which they work, individual archaeologists can never become intimately familiar with all the sources of knowledge that are needed to interpret their findings.

That would require links not only with all the social sciences but also with psychology and neuroscience, in addition to maintaining long-standing technical linkages with the physical and biological sciences. In general, archaeologists share more interests in high-level theory with anthropologists than with any other social scientists. For various reasons, anthropologists, unlike political scientists, economists, and sociologists, have not specialized in studying a particular sort of human behavior. Instead, they continue to investigate every aspect of non-industrial societies, employing perspectives that range from cultural evolution to highly postmodern cultural studies. As historical archaeologists in particular develop an increasing interest in human cognition and behavior, archaeology and anthropology are coming to share a growing number of theoretical and substantive interests that are focused on, but not limited to, the study of material culture.

Whatever institutional arrangements exist for archaeology, close ties between anthropologists and archaeologists are essential for the provision of both middle-ranging and high-level theory. The sustained theoretical productivity of prehistoric archaeology in the United States since the 1920s as a result of its close institutional ties to anthropology, the important role played by French Marxist anthropology in the development of postprocessual archaeology in Britain, and the many contributions by archaeologists at Cambridge University, where archaeology and anthropology have been associated more closely than in many other European universities, contrast with the much slower and more diffuse production of high-level theory where the two disciplines are less closely aligned.

Archaeology, for its part, is the leading source of information about long-term change and the only discipline that can construct a comprehensive historical framework into which the findings of socio-cultural anthropology and the other social sciences can be pigeon-holed, mainly as studies of the accommodation of human beings to the development of the modern world system. Once again, however, the interests of anthropologists and archaeologists match more closely than do those of archaeologists and any other social scientists. It therefore seems preferable for archaeologists who have established effective working relations with anthropologists to strive to improve those relations rather than to replace them with new and probably less productive ones (Trigger 1989c).

Coping with Subjectivity

Over the years, archaeological interpretation has been progressively facilitated by the development of new methods of dating, such as by measuring the ratios of carbon and potassium-argon isotopes, the more precise identification of plant and animal remains, and trace-element analysis, all of which employ techniques developed by the physical and biological sciences (for the limitations and complexities of some interpretations based on trace-element analysis, see Gill [1987]). The introduction of computers also has permitted the analysis of much larger amounts of archaeological data than ever before. This innovation has enhanced the ability of archaeologists to search for patterning in their data and to formulate and test hypotheses using ever-increasing amounts of data. Although the development of such techniques depends on the internal dynamics of the physical and biological sciences, and their adoption by archaeologists demonstrably is influenced by the goals, resources, knowledge, and personalities of different researchers, it seems likely that, given enough time, any significant new technique of this sort will be employed by archaeologists around the world. Likewise, although the recovery and classification of archaeological data are also influenced by the interests of different groups of archaeologists, over time there has been a growing understanding of the extent and significance of the formal variation that occurs in the archaeological record.

Archaeological evidence also intervenes at every level of interpretation to at least partially constrain and limit what it is possible to believe about the past. Contrary to what some innovators allege, in their desire to portray all previous phases in the development of archaeology as primitive and unscientific, archaeologists have long been aware of the need to question accepted interpretations of archaeological data. They have also utilized new evidence in an attempt to gain a more objective understanding of the past and, at least since the eighteenth century, have sought to devise tests that relate to proposals concerning the behavioral significance of archaeological data. For as long as this sort of verification has been attempted, archaeologists have been engaged in scientific studies.

There is evidence, as we have already noted, that the ongoing collection and analysis of archaeological data have resulted in a more robust understanding of prehistory as well as of the human behavior and other forces that have shaped that history. This makes possible the growing confidence with which archaeologists are able to distinguish between their own interpretations of what happened in prehistoric times and alternative popular beliefs that lack a scientifically acceptable factual basis (J. White 1974). The inability of sober archaeological accounts of the past to satisfy many popular expectations also attests to the ideological importance of what archaeologists are accomplishing. One example of opposition to a scientific understanding of the past is the persistent and widespread resistance to the idea that more advanced cultures have developed as a result of internal processes that can be understood in scientific terms. Speculative thinkers have long sought to trace the origin of known civilizations back to mysterious beginnings on lost continents, such as Atlantis and Mu, whereas in the early twentieth century hyperdiffusionists derived agriculture and civilization from Egypt or Mesopotamia, where they were alleged to have evolved as the result of a historical accident. Since 1945, faced with the threat of nuclear annihilation, in developed countries increasing numbers of insecure and secularly oriented members of the educated middle classes have taken comfort in the belief that intelligent beings from another planet have been benevolently guiding human development and will save humanity, or some chosen remnant of it, from some ultimate catastrophe (J. Cole 1980; Feder 1984, 1990; Eve and Harrold 1986). These salvationists, who increasingly draw Atlantis and ancient Egypt into their historical constructions, look in vain to archaeology to provide evidence of interplanetary contacts that will support their arguments.

It is not extraordinary that in the eighteenth century, when knowledge of the archaeological record was almost nonexistent, even a scholar such as William Stukeley, who was capable of carrying out sound antiquarian research, should have been attracted to what we now regard as the extravagant and unsubstantiated fantasies of the degenerationist school, as they related to the druids. By the 1920s, the hyperdiffusionist view of human history, although promoted by reputable ethnologists and physical anthropologists, was overwhelmingly rejected by archaeologists because it did not correspond with the archaeological record as it even by then was understood for various parts of the world. Hyperdiffusionist influences were limited to explaining restricted archaeological phenomena, such as the megalithic monuments of western Europe.

Extraterrestrial salvationism was born and remains an amateur fad with semireligious connotations. Despite its assertions to the contrary, its always tentative explanations of isolated archaeological finds do not provide a satisfactory alternative interpretation of the archaeological record (von Daniken 1969, 1971). Extreme relativists, such as Barnes and Feyerabend, may imply that the views of the past held by professional archaeologists and believers in extraterrestrial salvationism are cultural alternatives and that philosophers and historians of science have no basis for distinguishing between them in terms of their correctness or scientific status. Archaeologists cannot, of course, rule out the possibility that extraterrestrial visitors have influenced the course of human development to some degree, any more than biologists can exclude the existence somewhere on earth of a herd of purple unicorns. Yet, clumsy, inadequate, and uncertain as our present scientific understandings of cultural change may be, they account for what is observed in the archaeological record in both its totality and its individual features, while extraterrestrial salvationism keeps alive only by making speculative and always inconclusive claims about isolated phenomena. It is surely folly, given the available evidence, to claim equivalent status for these two approaches.

Archaeologists also have demonstrated their capacity to alter their interpretations in order to account better for growing bodies of archaeological data (Gallay 1986: 288–95). In the early part of the twentieth century, diffusion was invoked to explain evidence of change in the archaeological record that did not accord with earlier racist views that North American Indians were incapable of cultural change. Yet diffusion by itself implied a continuing belief in a lack of creativity among these peoples. The New Archaeology not only accounted for internal transformations in archaeological cultures that were becoming increasingly evident as more detailed archaeological research was carried out, but, in order to explain these changes, archaeologists were compelled to invoke internal responses that un-self-consciously eliminated the last vestiges of the view that indigenous North Americans were inherently less creative than were Europeans. The influence of less hostile public stereotypes of indigenous people in bringing about these changes should not be underestimated, but neither should the constraint of the archaeological record (Trigger 1980b).

It is the amateur fringe that continues to explain the prehistory of the Americas in terms of Libyan, Carthaginian, Scandinavian, Black African, and Asian visitors and thus denigrates, presumably unwittingly, the indigenous peoples of the Western Hemisphere by attributing major elements of their cultural heritage to others (Fell 1976, 1982; for an anthropological explanation of the material referred to in the second book, see Vastokas and Vastokas 1973). In so doing, these amateurs rely exclusively on diffusionist canons of archaeological interpretation that long ago were discovered to be inadequate by professional archaeologists. Archaeologists do not deny the importance of diffusion. Nor do they deny that some pastoralists and agriculturalists have become hunter-gatherers in the course of human history. Yet these happenings are now viewed in a broader context, in which other processes, such as ecological adaptation and internal cultural change, are occurring. Simultaneously, an increasingly detailed archaeological record offers growing resistance to faddish and unbalanced explanations of what happened in the past.

Yet, despite such progress, archaeology can never escape from the influences of the social milieus in which it is practiced. Subjective factors clearly continue to influence the interpretation of archaeological data. They are not merely a visible contaminant that can be removed through the rigorous application of scientific method, as more zealous positivists maintain. Archaeologists continue to produce interpretations of the archaeological record that promote national, ethnic, and other ideological agendas. At the same time, new political issues, such as environmental protection, neoconservative economic policies, and fighting terrorism, impress themselves on the minds of archaeologists and influence their understanding of the modern world and of the significance of archaeological findings. There is no reason to believe that archaeologists are more objective today than they were at any time in the past.

Often biases are unconscious, but sometimes they are not. Sometimes they lead to a deeper, lasting understanding of the archaeological record, although this happens rarely when archaeological findings are purposefully misused for propaganda purposes. The deliberate invention or misrepresentation of archaeological data for political ends – as may have happened with respect to the events leading, with loss of human life, to Hindu rioters demolishing the historic

Babri Mosque in Ayodhya, India in 1992 (J. Shaw 2000; Ratnagar 2004) – should entail the mandatory decertification of archaeologists who engage in such unethical practices and be classified as a serious criminal offense at both the national and international levels if it results in civil disturbances or harm to individuals. By contrast, the deployment of archaeological evidence to help disfavored minority groups to understand their pasts in a more objective and complete manner is an activity to be applauded.

In recent decades, archaeologists have become more aware of the deleterious influences that nationalism, colonialism, and gender bias exert on their interpretations of archaeological data and many have been trying to counteract such influences. Yet, at the same time, new demands and restrictions are being imposed on archaeologists by the state and by various sectors of society. In many countries, much archaeological research is being sponsored to stimulate tourism and archaeologists are required to excavate and reconstruct sites in accordance with policies formulated by governments and travel experts who are seeking to attract more tourists and to stimulate the economy (Silberman 1995: 258–61). Cultural resource management experts set standards that dictate which sites can or cannot be dug, what sorts of data are to be collected, and how finds are to be studied and reported (Shennan 2002: 9–10). Indigenous peoples in some areas are gaining power to control prehistoric archaeological research and to license archaeological surveys and excavations. Often they seek archaeological confirmation of their current beliefs about the past or support for land claims. Although it is important that local people should play a significant role in the study of their own past, serious problems arise when any group exercising economic or political control attempts to dictate the conclusions that archaeologists must draw from their research. At the same time that they reach out to all possible groups, archaeologists must resist threats to their personal and professional integrity, regardless of who makes them.

There is, however, a need to empower indigenous groups to guard and protect their cultural heritage, especially as the theft and illegal trade of antiquities increase around the world (Brodie et al. 2001; Kristiansen 2004b). Such empowerment must include training indigenous people to become fully qualified professional archaeologists and providing impoverished indigenous groups with the economic resources that they require to conserve their heritage. Only in this way can the last vestiges of colonialism be purged from archaeology. Cultural heritage should be legally recognized as the dual possession of the descendants of the people who created it and of all humanity, to whose cultural diversity and creativity it attests. It should be illegal to exploit economically, damage, or willfully destroy such heritage, and wherever possible the descendants of its creators should be its custodians on behalf of humanity as a whole. Although this formulation, which embodies many of the universalist ideas of the Enlightenment, will not please those relativists who would maintain that every group should be free to do what it wants with its own heritage, it reflects the reality of the modern world, in which the whole of humanity is becoming inextricably interrelated (A. Hall 2003).

Even without overt social and political pressures, there has always been a temptation for archaeologists to leap to conclusions in the absence of sufficient data or of adequate analysis and proper methods of interpretation. This occurs at every level of archaeological research, although it is perhaps at the highest level, the explanation of behavior, that the most daring leaps have been made. Many archaeologists are eager to draw far-reaching conclusions about the past from their findings, even if this requires them to infer specific forms of behavior without adequate linking arguments and to employ poorly tested explanations of human behavior. Especially if interpretations correspond with common sense and the beliefs of the investigator, archaeologists may be quite unaware of the inadequacies of their work. In the past, toleration for this type of laxness resulted to a large degree from a small number of researchers trying to cope with large and intractable problems. In pioneering efforts to collect data and reconstruct a broad picture of the past many of the requirements for doing sound archaeological research were ignored.

Finally, high-level theories exert their own nefarious influences on archaeological interpretation. To some degree, such theories are like languages. It is believed to be possible to express any idea in any natural language, although the difficulty with which a particular concept may be conveyed will vary greatly from one language to another, depending on its syntax and the content of its lexicon. Moreover, a message can depart only a short distance from conventional understandings and established norms before it loses intelligibility and relevance to the receiver, however capable the person delivering it may be at transmitting novel ideas through periphrases and detailed explanations. In the same manner, the difficulty of conceiving of a satisfactory explanation for a particular form of human behavior will vary according to the general theory that is espoused. In due course, growing problems in using a particular general theory to explain human behavior may lead social scientists, including archaeologists, to abandon that theory on the ground that it is inefficient by comparison with some alternative one. In this way, the constraints of evidence can exert a selective influence over general theories. Alternatively, subjective factors may lead social scientists to continue using a particular high-level theory long after its inefficiency has been demonstrated. Such theories often are modified and upgraded in opportunistic ways to try to adapt them to new circumstances. Only rarely are high-level theories definitively abandoned.

In recent years, archaeologists have been attempting in various ways to counteract the effects of unseen biases and inadequate research designs. By becoming more aware of how theories influence their research, they seek to reduce the impact that unexamined preconceptions have on their findings. Although these efforts are not always successful, simply discovering that certain beliefs may influence interpretations in specific ways can lessen the chances that such concepts will distort findings. Studying the history of archaeology, by enhancing an awareness of the theories that archaeologists used in the past and what happened when these theories were employed to interpret archaeological data, not only makes archaeologists more aware of the biases that were built into such concepts but also lessens the chances of their reinventing of the wheel. Other techniques also are being employed to counter bias in the course of doing research. Asking questions and formulating theories from as many standpoints as possible is seen as a way to broaden the range of perspectives that archaeologists can bring to bear on the study of any particular issue. Independent arrays of data with their appropriate analytical methods are also being used to investigate specific problems, with the expectation that concurrent results will reinforce the likelihood that the conclusion each approach reaches is valid. In this way, the database for studying the past is expanded to include physical anthropology, linguistics, and other nonarchaeological approaches. At the same time, the contextual approach is being applied systematically. Although neither archaeologists nor archaeological theory are free from bias, using these and other approaches is resulting in insights into the behavioral and cultural significance of archaeological data that can better withstand the discovery of new evidence and the development of new theoretical perspectives.

These developments at least partly explain why the views that modern archaeologists have concerning how societies evolved are radically different not only from the divinely ordered world of the ancient Sumerians but also from the creationist views that dominated European society 200 years ago. Evolutionary archaeology developed not as a neutral search for truth but in radical opposition to religious ideas that no longer accounted adequately for geological and biological evidence. The findings of archaeology, however subjectively interpreted, have altered our perception of the general course of human history, of our relation to nature, and of our own nature in ways that are irreversible without the total abandonment of the scientific method. Archaeology is itself a product of social and economic change, but what it has led us to believe about the past is more than a fanciful projection of contemporary social concerns into the past. Neither separate from society nor merely a reflection of it, archaeology has a role to play in a rational dialogue about the nature of humanity, which a better understanding of the relations between archaeological practice and its social context will facilitate. It has been claimed that, by helping to expand our temporal and spatial frames of reference, archaeology has irreversibly altered "the range and quality of human thought" (C. Becker 1938: 25).

Yet the struggle to establish these views is far from over. Religious fundamentalists, who make up a large portion of the population of the United States, still support creationism. Archaeologists who believe that the findings of their discipline represent a more accurate view of human history than do religious fantasies cannot accept extreme relativist pronouncements that archaeological and creationist views offer equally valid interpretations of the past. Instead, they are challenged to rescue the study of the past from an aggressive miasma of atavistic speculation.

The fact that archaeology can provide a growing number of insights into what has happened in the past suggests that it may constitute an increasingly effective basis for understanding social change. That in turn indicates that over time it also may serve as an increasingly effective guide for future development, not by providing technocratic knowledge to social planners but by helping citizens to make more informed choices with respect to public policy. In a world that, as a result of increasingly powerful technologies, has become too dangerous and is changing too quickly for humanity to rely to any considerable extent on trial and error, knowledge derived from archaeology may be important for human survival. If archaeology is to serve that purpose, archaeologists must strive against heavy odds to see the past and the human behavior that produced it as each was, not as they or anyone else for their own reasons wish them to have been.

BIBLIOGRAPHICAL ESSAY

Studying the History of Archaeology

Since the late 1980s, there has been an explosion of books and papers dealing with the history of archaeology. As a result, it is no longer possible to provide readers with a detailed guide to this literature. Only general trends can be delineated, with relevant examples. When considering the history of the discipline, it is worth recalling that probably as many as 90 percent of all archaeologists who have ever lived are alive today (Christenson 1989b: 163).

Some of the increasing production of histories of archaeology may result from growing competition for funding among schools and research groups (Croissant 2000: 205). A more general explanation is that the history of archaeology has assumed a more central role in the practice of archaeology as the result of a declining belief in culture-free explanations of human behavior. A historical approach also provides a basis for examining important epistemological issues from a perspective that is already familiar to many archaeologists. Whatever the motives for such studies, disciplinary histories have come to play a major role in the evaluation of archaeological knowledge and the history of archaeology is now recognized as constituting a significant branch or subfield of archaeology (J. Reid 1991).

Growing concerns with problems of method and theory relating to the history of archaeology resulted in a conference on these topics held at Southern Illinois University in May 1987. The proceedings were published by the organizer Andrew Christenson as *Tracing Archaeology's Past* (1989a), the first book to consider how to study the history of archaeology. The same year, a committee on the History of Archaeology was established within the Society for American Archaeology. Its goals were to identify, preserve, and make more accessible old field notes, films, photographs, letters, and oral histories relating to the history of archaeology. The following year, a series of symposia on the history of archaeology was initiated that has alternated annually between the meetings of the Society for American Archaeology and the American Anthropological Association. Papers read at these symposia have been published by Reyman (1992), Kehoe and Emmerichs (1999), Browman and Williams (2002), and Fowler and Wilcox (2003). In 1991, Douglas Givens established the *Bulletin of the History of Archaeology*, the first periodical dedicated to this subject. Two encyclopedias have been published, one devoted to the history of classical archaeology (De Grummond 1996) and the other to the history of archaeology in general (Murray 1999a, 2001a). Papers are also devoted to enumerating, analyzing, and critiquing histories of archaeology (Trigger 1985a, 1994a; Givens 1992b; Murray 1999b) and to theorizing such studies (Croissant 2000). A promising series of books dealing with the history of archaeology has been launched by Nathan Schlanger and Alain Schnapp (2005–).

Histories of archaeology have been written for many purposes: to entertain readers; to commemorate important archaeologists, finds, and research projects; and to instruct students, draw attention to neglected data, justify specific programs or ideas, reveal biases, disparage the research or conclusions of rival archaeologists, encourage reflection about the goals of archaeology, and try to make archaeology more objective.

Most histories of archaeology have been written by archaeologists. Some of these have been disciplinary elders reflecting on the past, but over the years a growing number of active archaeologists have devoted a substantial amount of their time to studying the history of their discipline. For the most part, archaeologists have had to train themselves in historiographic methods, including techniques of archival research. Some of these histories reveal their authors' lack of knowledge of historiographic methods. Their naiveté offers little resistance to the natural tendencies of archaeologists to view their discipline's history presentistically and from a parochial viewpoint. Yet, many other archaeologists, such as D. K. Grayson (1983), D. J. Meltzer (1983), and M. Bowden (1991), have demonstrated high levels of proficiency in their research.

Only a small number of historians and historians of science have been attracted to studying the history of archaeology. These include C. M. Hinsley (1981, 1985), S. Mendyk (1989), R. T. Ridley (1992), A. B. Ferguson (1993), S. L. Marchand (1996), and B. Kuklick (1996). Although some of these historians have made distinguished contributions to the history of archaeology, their relations with archaeologists who study that history tend to remain elusive. This is wholly unlike the close ties that have developed between archaeologists and philosophers of science who study archaeology. Some historians of science appear to believe that only they are qualified to write histories of archaeology (Croissant 2000: 203).

Yet, even if it were true that "insiders" tend to be unduly presentistic and self-justifying and to overemphasize the coherence, uniformity, and unilinearity of the history of archaeology, whereas "outsiders" are better equipped to understand its contextuality and subjective qualities, archaeologists know from experience more about how archaeology works than do historians. Writing the history of any scientific discipline requires familiarity with two separate fields. On the one hand, substantive knowledge is required of the discipline being studied; on the other, knowledge is needed of historical methodology, including ideas about disciplinary formation, as well as a sound understanding of the history of Western culture, in the context of which archaeology as we know it has arisen. Only rarely do individual scholars achieve parity in their understanding of both disciplines. Much could be gained from cooperation among professional historians, historians of science, and archaeologists who are studying the history of archaeology and neither archaeologists nor historians ought to claim a monopoly in this endeavor. Yet, despite their lack of cooperation, the history of archaeology has matured in recent years, in the sense that understanding the development of archaeology has grown both more diversified and more contested.

Some of the first histories of archaeology were written for didactic purposes. The physicist Joseph Henry, who was the first secretary of the Smithsonian Institution, sought to purge archaeology of useless speculation and encourage factual research. He commissioned Samuel Haven, the librarian of the American Antiquarian Society, to review and expose the inadequacies of previous studies of American prehistory in a work titled *Archaeology of the United States* (1856). Henry also published accounts of recent developments in archaeology in the *Annual Report of the Smithsonian Institution*, which was widely distributed in North America. The most influential of these papers was "General views on archaeology" by the Swiss geologist and archaeologist Adolf Morlot (1861). That paper, which summarized major developments in the study of European prehistory over the previous fifty years, did much to encourage the adoption of a more scientific approach to doing archaeological research in North America.

For the next century, however, most histories of archaeology were chronicles of discovery that recounted by whom and under what circumstances the most spectacular archaeological finds had been made. One of the most popular and enduring of these works, despite its superficiality, was *Gods, Graves and Scholars* by C. W. Ceram (pseudonym for Kurt Marek) (1951). Seton Lloyd's *Foundations in the Dust* (1947; 2nd ed. 1981) offered a more richly contextualized account of

Mesopotamian archaeology, while Geoffrey Bibby (1956) and Michael Hoffman (1979) provided histories of archaeological research on prehistoric Europe and Egypt that also informed readers about what that research had discovered concerning the past. Brian Fagan's best-selling *The Rape of the Nile* (1975) is evidence of the continuing popularity of this genre. Recent general histories of archaeology for nonspecialists include those by W. H. Stiebing Jr. (1993) and Paul Bahn (1996). In popular histories of archaeology, little attention is paid to the work of archaeologists such as Gordon Childe or Grahame Clark, who, although they made no spectacular discoveries of archaeological data, played a major role in shaping a professional understanding of how archaeological data should be interpreted.

German archaeologists have long taken great care to document the history of research relating to every topic and site they investigate. They do this because they accord great importance to ensuring continuity in research and believe that their interpretations should take account of all available work that is relevant to a topic. Hence chronicles of prior investigations are vital for establishing the credibility of their research. At the same time, they have, until recently, generally avoided analyzing the intellectual and social histories of their discipline.

The modern analytical study of the history of archaeology began in England in the late 1930s, in the context of a growing awareness of generational differences among professional archaeologists, which led some younger ones to try to understand what was happening to their discipline. These early intellectual histories of archaeology were strongly influenced by publications such as Christopher Hussey's *The Picturesque* (1927) and Kenneth Clark's *The Gothic Revival* (1928), which sought to relate changes in literary and artistic fashions to shifts in the broader history of ideas. Stanley Casson's *The Discovery of Man* (1939) was written to justify an already moribund evolutionary anthropology and archaeology that he saw as a product of intellectual freedom resulting from Europe's Age of Discovery. The main importance of this book was that it indicated that an intellectual history of archaeology was possible and worthwhile. Brief sketches of the early development of prehistoric archaeology were published around the same time by P. Shorr (1935), H. J. E. Peake (1940), and V. G. Childe (1953).

The general study of the history of archaeology was guided for several decades by Glyn Daniel. His paper *The Three Ages* (1943) launched research that culminated in his *A Hundred Years of Archaeology* (1950; 2nd ed. 1975), which traced the development of archaeology in Britain and western Europe. Although Daniel maintained that archaeology had changed gradually and adventitiously, his overall theme was the early development of evolutionary archaeology and its eventual replacement by a culture-historical approach, which Daniel clearly favored and regarded as essential to keep archaeology from reverting to an object-oriented antiquarianism. His later works, dealing primarily with western European archaeology, include Daniel (1967) and (1981a).

In 1956, Mikhail Miller, an undistinguished provincial émigré archaeologist who had fled the Soviet Union during World War II, published a polemical, Cold War history of Russian and Soviet archaeology and in 1964 the French archaeologist Annette Laming-Emperaire produced *Origines de l'archéologie préhistorique en France*, which traced the development of prehistoric archaeology in that country from the medieval period to the late nineteenth century. Her book was distinguished by a careful examination of how structures of teaching and research, professional associations, and journals both reflected and shaped the development of French archaeology.

Glyn Daniel actively encouraged the writing of regional and national histories of archaeology. *A History of American Archaeology* (1974; 2nd ed. 1980; 3rd ed. 1993) by Gordon Willey and Jeremy Sabloff, Ole Klindt-Jensen's *A History of Scandinavian Archaeology* (1975), and Ignacio Bernal's *A History of Mexican Archaeology* (1980) all first appeared in his "World of Archaeology" series. Willey and Sabloff provided a historical legitimation of processual archaeology, while criticizing what they regarded as its theoretical shortcomings. Klindt-Jensen and Bernal followed Daniel in demonstrating parallels between western European intellectual fashions and what was happening in archaeology in their respective countries.

In the United States, the analytical study of the history of archaeology had resumed with Walter Taylor's (1948) undiplomatic and unwelcomed critique of what he regarded as the theoretical inadequacies and methodological shortcomings that had characterized the work of the previous generation of American archaeologists. This was followed by Douglas Schwartz's *Conceptions of Kentucky Prehistory* (1967), James Fitting's (1973) multiauthored study of the development of archaeology in different regions of North America, and a short general account by S. Gorenstein (1977). These studies, as well as Willey and Sabloff's history, divided the history of archaeology into a series of periods, each with its own characteristics and clearly differentiated from earlier and later periods by marked alterations in archaeological practice (Schuyler 1971). Sometimes these changes were explicitly identified as examples of Kuhn's paradigm shifts (Sterud 1973).

The study of the history of archaeology on a worldwide basis was further stimulated by an international conference on the history of archaeology held, under the sponsorship of the International Union of Prehistoric and Protohistoric Sciences, at Aarhus, Denmark, in 1978 (Daniel 1981b); by a series of papers on "Regional Traditions of Archaeological Research" published in *World Archaeology* (Trigger and Glover 1981, 1982); and by further papers in a Festschrift for Glyn Daniel (J. D. Evans et al. 1981: 11–70). Since the early 1980s, many monographs and collections of papers have been published that study the development of archaeology in different regions: Mexico (Vázquez León 1996, 2003), Latin America (Politis and Alberti 1999), the United States (Patterson 1995; Kehoe 1998), various regions of the United States (P. J. Watson 1990; J. Johnson 1993; O'Brien 1996a; Janetski 1997b; Fowler 2000; Rolingson 2001; Snead 2001; Tushingham et al. 2002), Canada (Smith and Mitchell 1998), Australia (Horton 1991), sub-Saharan Africa (Robertshaw 1990), the Middle East (Silberman 1982, 1989; Meskell 1998), India (Chakrabarti 1988, 1997, 2003), central Europe (Sklenář 1983), Denmark (Fischer and Kristiansen 2002), and Italy (Guidi 1988: a general history of archaeology with special sections devoted to Italy). Eve Gran-Aymerich (1998) has chronicled the work done by French archaeologists not only in France but in other parts of the world, especially North Africa and the Middle East. Alice Kehoe's (1998) study of the history of archaeology in the United States is notable for its irreverence and staunch defense of Boasian culture-historical archaeology.

Growing interest in ethnicity and nationalism, beginning in the late 1980s as a result of the disintegration of the Soviet Union and the growth of the European Union, stimulated the production of a series of collective works dealing with the long-term impact that ethnicity and nationalism had on archaeology in Europe and other parts of the world. Books published include Kohl and Fawcett (1995), Díaz-Andreu and Champion (1996a), Graves-Brown et al. (1996), and Crooke (2000). In addition, collections of papers dealing with regional archaeologies have appeared periodically in the journal *Antiquity*, for example, Cleere (1993). Many of these works are strongly externalist, examining how specific social, political, economic, and ethnic factors have influenced the practice of archaeology.

In recent years, Spanish archaeologists have shown much interest in the history of archaeology in their country; for a brief discussion and bibliography, see M. Díaz-Andreu (2003). Some German archaeologists also have become interested in critically examining the history of archaeology in Germany, especially the nationalist tendencies of some archaeologists and their relations with National Socialism (Härke 2000a; Leube and Hegewisch 2002).

Three general studies appeared beginning in the late 1980s. The first edition of *A History of Archaeological Thought* (Trigger 1989a) sought to trace the development of archaeological theory at a global level, although most emphasis was on Europe, the United States, and the Soviet Union. Attention was paid not only to the social and intellectual contexts in which archaeological thought had developed but also to the spread of ideas and the circumstances that promoted their perpetuation and elaboration. The main developments were conceptualized in terms of theoretical movements rather than successive stages or regional traditions. Jaroslav Malina and Zdenek Vašíček's *Archaeology Yesterday and Today* (1990) sought to contextualize the development of archaeology in relation to the growth of other sciences and the humanities. They maintained that there could be no history of archaeology without a history of science in general. Alain Schnapp's *The Discovery of the Past* (1997, French original 1993) detailed the development of an interest in the material remains of the past from earliest times to the nineteenth century.

An already existing interest in relations between archaeology and its social, political, and economic context was accentuated by the development of postprocessual archaeology and by the founding of the World Archaeological Congress in 1986 (Ucko 1987). The result was an intensification of efforts to reveal biases in "hegemonic" interpretations of the past and to enable repressed groups to reclaim their cultural heritage (Lowenthal 1985; Cleere 1989; Gathercole and Lowenthal 1989; Layton 1989a, 1989b; Stone and MacKenzie 1990; Bond and Gillam 1994; Schmidt and Patterson 1995; Tunbridge and Ashworth 1996; Bender 1998; Watkins 2003). These endeavors produced numerous historical studies that assigned a preponderant role to social and cultural factors in shaping archaeological discourse (e.g., Hodder 1991a; Ucko 1995a), but they have not yet resulted in a general history of archaeology, perhaps because of postprocessual archaeologists' widespread antipathy toward "grand narratives." The most ambitious product inspired by this approach has been Peter Ucko's "Encounters with Ancient Egypt," an eight-volume collection of papers of widely varying quality that examine the long-term reciprocal relations between the study of ancient Egypt and its varied social, economic, and political contexts. At least four of these volumes relate directly to the history of archaeology: R. Matthews and C. Roemer (2003), J. Tait (2003), D. Jeffreys (2003), and P. J. Ucko and T. Champion (2003).

Most recently, the desire of Darwinian archaeologists to incorporate major aspects of American culture-historical archaeology into their own selectionist general theory has resulted in the production of a large number of books and papers dealing with the history of American prehistoric archaeology during the twentieth century. Although these works serve a specific intellectual agenda, as do all histories of archaeology, they have made extremely important contributions to understanding the development of American archaeology. The major general historical works produced by this group are M. J. O'Brien, *Paradigms of the Past: The Story of Missouri Archaeology* (1996a), R. L. Lyman, M. J. O'Brien, and R. C. Dunnell, *The Rise and Fall of Culture History* (1997a), and, with a behavioral archaeologist, M. J. O'Brien, R. L. Lyman, and M. B. Schiffer, *Archaeology as a Process* (2005). Equally important specialized studies and biographies produced by this group will be noted later.

In addition to prehistoric archaeology, other branches of archaeology have produced their own histories. These works generally seek to define the changing institutional structures of a particular branch of archaeology, determine how it resembled and differed from other branches over time, and discuss problems it may currently be encountering. Recent general studies of classical archaeology include A. M. Snodgrass (1987), M. Shanks (1996), and S. L. Dyson (1998). Egyptological archaeology has been surveyed by J. Wilson (1964) and D. M. Reid (2002) and biblical archaeology by P. R. S. Moorey (1991) and W. G. Dever (2003). The history of Maya archaeology has been examined by J. A. Sabloff (1990) and in C. W. Golden and G. Borgstede (2004), and the impact on it of the decipherment of the Maya script has been analyzed by M. D. Coe (1992). A. Andrén (1998) has surveyed historical archaeology in global perspective. The development of medieval archaeology is covered by Gerrard (2003). Histories of colonial and industrial archaeology have not yet received monographic treatment but are examined in papers in Murray (2001a). Historical sketches are also frequently included in books dealing with issues of theory and method related to these branches. Other histories deal with archaeological methods, such as aerial photography (Deuel 1973), chronology (R. Taylor 1987; O'Brien and Lyman 1999a; Nash 1999, 2000a; Truncer 2003), marine archaeology (J. Taylor 1966), salvage archaeology (Baldwin 1996), and settlement archaeology (Billman and Feinman 1999). Although early histories traced the development of new analytical techniques and their application to archaeology, more recent ones, such as S. E. Nash's *It's About Time* (2000a) are paying more attention to the ways in which the values and aspirations of archaeologists have shaped the reception and use of techniques that originated in other disciplines.

A growing number of historical studies examine specific archaeological projects, controversies, and transitions. Much of the key research that is expanding an understanding of the history of archaeology is of this sort. Examples of such work include T. Kendrick's (1950) interpretation of the development of antiquarianism in Tudor England as a triumph of Renaissance over medieval thought; Robert Silverberg's (1968) study of how the concept of the Moundbuilders both reflected and reinforced prejudice against aboriginal Americans during the nineteenth century; C. Chippindale's (1983) examination of changing interpretations of Stonehenge; D. Grayson's (1983) clarification of key debates establishing the great antiquity of human beings in Europe; D. Meltzer's (1983) detailed analysis of nineteenth-century controversies about the earliest human inhabitants of the New World; B. Gräslund's (1987) study of the role played by typology in the early development of Scandinavian archaeology; I. Jenkin's (1992) examination of the reasons for changing collecting and display policies in the British Museum between 1800 and 1939; R. T. Ridley's (1992) study of the methodological innovations associated with French excavations carried out during the Napoleonic occupation of Rome; S. L. Marchand's (1996) detailed examination of the impact of philhellenism on German archaeology from 1750 to 1970; N. Abu El-Haj's (2001) documentation of how archaeology can be used to transform landscapes politically, and T. C. Patterson's (2003) study of the impact of Marxism on archaeological interpretation in the United States during the twentieth century.

Biographies focus on the role played by the individual in archaeology. Written for most of the same purposes as more general histories of archaeology, they are important for understanding the history of the discipline. Although conventional biographies of archaeologists seek mainly to chronicle the social life, personal contacts, and discoveries of their subjects (J. Hawkes 1982; Winstone 1990), others that contextualize the work of archaeologists shed important light on the history of archaeology (I. Graham 2002). Most of them make available archival materials that are important for understanding disciplinary history. Among the most valuable contextualized biographies are those by S. Piggott (1950; 2nd ed. 1985) on William Stukeley; R. Woodbury (1973) and D. Givens (1992a) on Alfred Kidder; M. Hunter (1975) on John Aubrey; C. C. Parslow (1995) on Karl Weber (which also contributes to the general understanding of eighteenth-century classical archaeology); M. J. O'Brien and R. L. Lyman (1998) on James

Ford; H. Grünert (2002) on Gustav Kossinna; and R. L. Lyman and M. J. O'Brien (2003) on W. C. McKern and the Midwestern Taxonomic Method. Less well known is the historian Gerald Killan's (1983) insightful biography of the nineteenth-century Canadian archaeologist David Boyle. At least five books on the life and work of Gordon Childe (McNairn 1980; Trigger 1980a; S. Green 1981; Gathercole et al. 1995; Lech and Stepniowski 1999 – with English abstracts) as well as numerous papers reflect the enormous and continuing fascination with this archaeologist. A growing interest in feminism is reflected by M. Allesbrook's (1992) biography of Harriet Boyd Hawes, Char Solomon's (2002) biography of Tatiana Proskouriakoff, and S. L. Dyson's (2004) biography of Eugénie Strong as well as by collections of papers examining the careers of female archaeologists edited by C. Claassen (1994), M. Díaz-Andreu and M. L. S. Sørensen (1998), N. M. White et al. (1999), and part of A. Kehoe and M. B. Emmerichs (1999). Chapman (1998) considers how M. Gimbutas's life experiences influenced her understanding of the past. Gordon Willey (1988) published a series of short biographies of deceased archaeologists he had known and T. Murray (1999a) contains biographies of fifty-eight distinguished archaeologists, only a few of whom are still alive.

Autobiographies tend to be sources for studying the history of archaeology rather than contributions to it. R. S. MacNeish's (1978) account of his career contains many observations about the development of American archaeology that blur this distinction. G. R. Willey (1974a), G. Daniel and C. Chippindale (1989), and S. South (1998) are collections of autobiographical essays that various senior archaeologists were invited to write. These essays contain, in addition to their purely biographical component, many valuable observations about the development of archaeology.

Less attention has been paid to the history of archaeological institutions. Major studies of national institutions have been published by Joan Evans (1956), A. S. Bell (1981), and C. M. Hinsley Jr. (1981), the latter being a magisterial account of the anthropological work of the Smithsonian Institution before 1910. Berta Stjernquist (2005) has written a history of the Historical Museum in Lund, Sweden. Susan Allen (2002) presents a history of the Archaeological Institute of America. The role of amateur archaeological societies in nineteenth-century England is among the topics considered by S. Piggott (1976), K. Hudson (1981), and P. Levine (1986). M. McKusick (1970, 1991) has traced a celebrated conflict between the Smithsonian Institution and a local amateur scientific society in the United States concerning the authenticity of some finds made in the nineteenth century. P. Fagette (1996) and E. Lyon (1996) examine the impact of government funding on the practice of American archaeology in the 1930s. B. Kuklick (1996) and M. Balter (2005) study the histories of specific archaeological research projects. Balter (2005) and M. J. O'Brien, R. L. Lyman, and M. B. Schiffer (2005) have adopted a network approach, which examines the relations between cooperating and competing individuals and institutions.

Anthologies of significant papers dealing with the history of archaeology are especially valuable for students. Useful popular compilations include J. Hawkes (1963) and, for the New World, Deuel (1967). R. F. Heizer (1959) reprints a set of papers of enduring methodological importance, including translations of originals published in foreign languages. Anthologies dealing with major interpretative issues have been edited by Heizer (1962a) and G. Daniel (1967). C. S. Larsen (1985) presents papers on what were claimed to be "Palaeolithic" remains in North America written in the nineteenth century and B. Trigger (1986a) a collection dealing with North American studies of coastal shell mounds from the same period. R. L. Lyman, M. J. O'Brien, and R. C. Dunnell (1997b) reprint major theoretical papers published by American culture-historical archaeologists. A. Fischer and K. Kristiansen (2002) have translated into English many papers relating to the history of Danish archaeology.

Finally, there are a growing number of studies of "counter archaeologies" or "fantastic archaeologies" that offer alternatives to the interpretations of professional archaeologists. Many of these studies have a historical component: R. Wauchope (1962), J. P. White (1974), C. Cazeau and S. Scott (1979), J. A. Sabloff (1982), K. L. Feder (1984, 1990), W. H. Stiebing Jr. (1984), and S. Williams (1991).

General discussions of internalist and externalist approaches to the study of disciplinary histories include Basalla (1968), Morrell (1981), Lelas (1985), Tamarkin (1986), and Shapin (1992).

I am opposed to presentistic explanations of the history of archaeology in the sense that I hold that past developments must be understood in relation to the context in which they occurred, not measured against what we presently believe about the past. I am not, however, persuaded that it is possible for historians of archaeology totally to forget the present state of archaeology or that knowledge of the present does not sometimes provide useful strategic guidance to historians. In a summary history such as this one, it is impossible to discuss many examples of seemingly fruitful competing trends in archaeological research or numerous dead ends. This may give a false impression of unilinearity in the development of archaeology. Yet, I have sought to combat this impression by drawing attention to some important dead ends, by considering how archaeology might have developed differently in specific instances, and by investigating variations in the development of archaeology in different parts of the world. I have also, however, drawn attention to theoretical and methodological innovations that appear to have irreversibly altered the practice of archaeology and that produce something resembling a unilinear trend in the development of the discipline. I am convinced that archaeology is capable of answering many diverse questions about human behavior and history, provided that it develops appropriate theories and means to address them. Creating such theories is, however, comparable to assembling a large jigsaw puzzle. There are thousands of different sequences in which the pieces can be put together but, in the long run, the same overall picture must emerge. As a result, the history of archaeology displays directionality, even though it does not exhibit unilinearity.

Classical and Other Text-Based Archaeologies

The most comprehensive study of the origins of antiquarian research is Schnapp (1997). For an older evolutionary sequence of conceptualizations of the past, see Childe (1956b).

Ancient Egyptian and Mesopotamian historiography is discussed by Van Seters (1983), Redford (1986), Baines (1989), and Jonker (1995), and in Tait (2003), as well as more generally by Butterfield (1981). Classical, medieval, and early modern views of the past are surveyed within the context of broader anthropological concerns by Casson (1939), Hodgen (1964), and Slotkin (1965). Classical views are examined in greater detail by Wace (1949), Shrimpton (1992), Antonaccio (1995), Alcock, Cherry, and Elsner (2001), Alcock (2002), Boardman (2002), and Press (2003). Medieval views of history are discussed by Sandford (1944) and medieval western European relations with the surviving monuments of antiquity by Peacock (1979) and Greenhalgh (1989). Toulmin and Goodfield (1966) and Rossi (1985) examine early modern challenges to biblical chronologies and the changing philosophy of history since the medieval period.

The most comprehensive guide to the history of classical archaeology is *An Encyclopedia of the History of Classical Archaeology*, edited by De Grummond (1996). Lowenthal (1985) discusses changing modern attitudes toward classical antiquity. MacKendrick (1960) surveys modern archaeology in Italy and Stoneman (1987) its early development in Greece. Weiss (1969), Jacks (1993), and Barkan (1999) trace the Italian Renaissance's discovery of classical antiquity, and Rowe (1965) discusses the Renaissance as it relates to anthropology. Parslow (1995), Ridley (1992), and Bignamini (2004) trace successive phases in the development of excavation techniques at classical sites in Italy into the early nineteenth century. For views on collecting, excavation, and other ethical issues relating to the practice of archaeology in the eighteenth century, see Ramage (1990, 1992). Marchand (1996) provides a brilliantly researched analysis of classical archaeology in Germany from the late eighteenth to the mid-twentieth century. Her book also constitutes a model of how the history of archaeology should be written. Gran-Aymerich (1998) traces the development of classical archaeology in France, and Dyson (1989, 1998) examines its development in the United States. Morris (1994a) and Shanks (1996) view it from an international perspective. Bruford (1975), Jenkyns (1980), and F. Turner (1981) investigate attitudes toward ancient Greece in the nineteenth century. M. Bernal (1987) discusses (too one-sidedly) the emphasis that was placed beginning in the nineteenth century on the autochthonous nature of Greek culture. Bodnar (1960) provides a biography of Cyriacus of Ancona; Leppmann (1970) of Winckelmann; Allesbrook (1992) of Hawes; and Dyson (2004) of Eugénie Strong. R. Chamberlin (1983), Jenkins (1992), and Yalouri (2001) discuss European attitudes toward classical heritage. For the extension of classical archaeology to investigate the protohistory of the Mediterranean region, see McDonald and Thomas (1990).

The histories of Egyptology and Assyriology have been chronicled in many popular works. A selective bibliography listing numerous older contributions is found in Daniel (1975: 401–3). Among the more informative general histories of the archaeology of ancient Egypt are Greener (1966) and Fagan (1975). One of the most illuminating accounts of archaeological activities during the nineteenth century, which also conveys the spirit of such research, is Amelia Edwards's *Egypt and its Monuments: Pharaohs, Fellahs and Explorers* (1891). Wortham (1971) examines British studies of ancient Egypt between 1549 and 1906. J. Wilson (1964) and N. Thomas (1995, 1996) present histories of American archaeological research in Egypt. Greek and Roman views about ancient Egypt are discussed in Matthews and Roemer (2003). Medieval Arab interests are examined by El Daly (2004) and early modern European views are analyzed by Yates (1964), Wortham (1971), Irwin (1980), Curl (1982), Iversen (1993), and Rossi (1985). More recent popular engagements with ancient Egypt are examined by Carrott (1978) and by papers in Jeffries (2003) and MacDonald and Rice (2003). Mitchell (1988) discusses European colonialism in Egypt. The impact of colonialism on Egyptology is analyzed by J. Thompson (1992), D. Reid (1997, 2002), Ridley (1998), Wood (1998), and Mayes (2003). Petrie's career is chronicled by Drower (1985) and Frankfort's contributions are evaluated by Wengrow (1999). Lloyd (1947, 1981) chronicles the history of Assyriology, M. Larsen (1996) examines the development of Assyriology in the 1840s and 1850s, and B. Kuklick (1996) investigates American archaeological research in Iraq between 1880 and 1930.

G. Wang (1985) provides a brief but very useful summary of traditional Chinese historiography. Rudolf (1962–1963), Chêng (1963: 1–7), Li (1977: 3–13), Chang (1981), and Schnapp (1997: 74–9) trace the development of antiquarian studies in China, as do Hoffman (1974), Ikawa-Smith (1982, 2001), and Bleed (1986) for Japan. For information about the concept of time in East Asia, see Vinsrygg (1986) and G. Barnes (1990a).

Antiquarianism without Texts

The development of antiquarian research in Europe north of the Alps is surveyed as part of more general histories by Daniel (1950), Laming-Emperaire (1964), Klindt-Jensen (1975), Sklenář (1983), and Schnapp (1997); and for America by Willey and Sabloff (1993) and Browman and Williams (2002). Many studies have examined the early development of antiquarianism in Britain. The best synthesis of this work is Piggott (1989; see also Moir 1958). Readers should be on the lookout for important future publications on this topic by Tim Murray, especially in his forthcoming comprehensive study, *A History of Prehistoric Archaeology in England*. The historiography of the late medieval and early modern periods has been studied by Walters (1934), Kendrick (1950), and L. Fox (1956). L. Clark (1961), Lynch and Lynch (1968), Marsden (1974, 1984), Piggott (1976, 1978), and Schnapp (1997) survey the development of a scientific approach to prehistoric archaeology before 1800. Aubrey's archaeological manuscripts have been reproduced by Fowles (1980, 1982) and Stukeley's manuscript on Stonehenge by Burl and Mortimer (2005). Laming-Emperaire (1964) and Laurent (1999) survey the development of antiquarianism and prehistoric archaeology in France.

The recognition of prehistoric stone tools as being of human manufacture and the role played by the Three-Age theory in the study of prehistory before 1800 have been examined by Heizer (1962b), Daniel (1963a, 1976), Rodden (1981), and Goodrum (2002). Biographical studies that are particularly valuable for illuminating the development of antiquarianism include Piggott (1950, 1985) on Stukeley, Hunter (1975) on Aubrey, R. H. Cunnington (1975) on William Cunnington, and G. Parry (1995) on various English antiquaries of the seventeenth century. Sweet (2004) examines British antiquaries of the eighteenth century. For a useful critique of Piggott's interpretation of Stukeley's career, see Ucko et al. (1991). These works do not confirm Crawford's (1932) mechanistic attribution of a leading role in the development of antiquarian research to increasing numbers of finds resulting from industrial development, although such development later assisted the work of Boucher de Perthes. Pomian (1990) provides a study of the collecting of antiquities between 1500 and 1800.

Among numerous works examining the early attitudes of Europeans toward indigenous peoples, especially those of the New World, are Fairchild (1928), G. Boas (1948), H. Jones (1964), Huddleston (1967), Chiappelli (1976), and MacCormack (1995). Spanish views are discussed by Hanke (1959), Keen (1971), and Pagden (1982), and English and French ones by Pearce (1965), Jaenen (1976), Berkhofer (1978), Vaughan (1979, 1982), Sheehan (1980), and Kupperman (1980). These views partially explain the slowness with which antiquarianism developed in the New World.

For studies of the Enlightenment, see Hampson (1982), Beiser (1992), and Im Hof (1994). The Scottish Enlightenment is discussed by Bryson (1945) and Schneider (1967), and in Herman's (2001) popular but useful history. A critical, but one-sided, analysis of Enlightenment thought is provided by Vyverberg (1989). L. Furst (1969), Beiser (1992), and Dumont (1994) provide background on eighteenth-century romanticism and Barnard (1965, 2003) and Zammito (2002) discuss the ideas of the German philosopher Johann Herder. Tully (1989) traces ideas regarding progress from 1789 to 1989.

The Beginnings of Prehistoric Archaeology

The general understanding of the early development of prehistoric archaeology in Scandinavia is being radically transformed, especially for readers of English, by the research of Peter Rowley-Conwy. His findings have been very influential for revising the first half of this chapter. Hopefully, the results of his investigations will be published in full in the near future. Gräslund (1974, for an English summary see 1976; 1987) examines in detail the development of an understanding of prehistoric chronology in Scandinavia. For other studies dealing with the early development of Scandinavian archaeology, see Morlot (1861, reprinted in Trigger 1986a), Bibby (1956), Klindt-Jensen (1975, 1976),

Kristiansen (1985), and Fischer and Kristiansen (2002). Although much has been written about the role played by Christian Thomsen in the development of prehistoric archaeology, most accounts overemphasize his application of the Three-Age concept and fail to deal adequately with his methodological innovations (e.g., Klindt-Jensen 1975: 49–57). Specialized studies of his work include Heizer (1962b), Daniel (1976), Gräslund (1981), Rodden (1981), Rowley-Conwy (1984), and Paddayya (1993). Sven Nilsson is discussed by Hegardt (1999). The origin of the concept of hunter-gatherers is discussed in Pluciennik (2002). The earliest use of the concept of prehistory as both adjective and noun is considered by Clermont and Smith (1990) and Welinder (1991). The development of the concept of the Mesolithic has been examined by Rowley-Conwy (1996). Weiss (1969) and McKay (1976) discuss numismatics and its relation to archaeology. For the beginnings of prehistoric archaeology in Scotland, see A. Bell (1981), Trigger (1992), Kehoe (1998), and Hulse (1999). Morlot (1861), Childe (1955), and Kaeser (2001, 2004a, 2004b) discuss analogous developments in Switzerland. The idea of progress and its use for understanding the past during the nineteenth century is surveyed by Burrow (1966), Bowler (1989), and Sanderson (1990); Herbert Spencer's sociological work is examined by Peel (1971). For more on J. W. Dawson, see Sheets-Pyenson (1996).

The developments in uniformitarian geology that provided a necessary background for the emergence of Palaeolithic archaeology are chronicled in Zittel (1901), Geikie (1905), Gillispie (1951), Chorley et al. (1964), Davies (1969), Schneer (1969), and Porter (1977). Similar developments in evolutionary biology are covered by Irvine (1955), Wendt (1955), Barnett (1958), Eiseley (1958), Haber (1959), and J. Greene (1959).

Groenen (1994) offers a detailed, analytical history of Palaeolithic archaeology focused mainly on developments in France. The establishment of a scientific understanding of human antiquity has been masterfully researched by Gruber (1965) and Grayson (1983). Grayson's definitive treatment should be consulted for numerous primary and secondary references. The study of prehistory in England before the development of Palaeolithic archaeology is surveyed in Levine (1986), Van Riper (1993), M. Morse (1999), and T. Murray (2001b). The development of Palaeolithic archaeology in France and England is analyzed by Laming-Emperaire (1964), Van Riper (1993), Chazan (1995), and Gran-Aymerich (1998). Sackett (1981, 1991, 2000) examines later developments and, in particular, the influence of Mortillet. Warren and

Rose (1994) discuss Pengelly's excavation techniques. Grayson follows French usage in equating the development of Palaeolithic archaeology with the beginnings of prehistoric archaeology and excluding Scandinavian archaeology on the ground that it addressed mainly protohistoric times (defined as beginning everywhere at the time writing was first developed in the Middle East ca. 3000 BC). This terminological difference should not obscure the close similarity between Grayson's position and my own.

The development of prehistoric archaeology in the United States has been described by Willey and Sabloff (1993: 21–64). The Moundbuilder controversy is examined magisterially by Silverberg (1968) and the work of Squier and Davis is evaluated by Welch (1998). Anthropology in the United States during the nineteenth century is discussed by Bieder (1986). Squier's archaeological work is examined by Tax (1975) and the influence of Joseph Henry by Washburn (1967). American shell-mound excavations are discussed by Christenson (1985) and Trigger (1986a). R. Evans (2004) examines the appropriation of Mexican prehistory as part of the United States' cultural heritage. Interesting parallels can be noted with the appropriation of the ancient civilizations of the Middle East by European scholars. Early research on the Maya is surveyed by Brunhouse (1973). Desmond and Messenger (1988) examine in detail the careers of two nineteenth-century Maya antiquaries.

The use of the terms antiquary and archaeologist to distinguish an amateur from a professional dedicated to studying the material remains of the past correlates roughly (and probably accidentally) with the first use of the term scientist in 1833. Schnapp (2002) discusses similarities and differences between antiquaries and archaeologists.

Evolutionary Archaeology

Little has been published in recent times about John Lubbock's archaeological and ethnological writings. This dearth is incommensurate with his importance as a promoter of Darwinian thought in archaeology. His standard biographies remain Hutchinson (1914) and Duff (1924). Tim Murray (1989) discusses his role in preserving ancient monuments.

The debate between polygenists and monogenists is examined in its British context by Stocking (1973) and in its American one by Stanton (1960). The impact of Darwinian evolutionism on racial thinking and the disagreements between Darwin and Wallace concerning the evolutionary status of "primitive" human groups are examined by Eiseley

(1958). Street (1975) presents popular British stereotypes of Africans between 1858 and 1920 and Nederveen Pieterse (1992) analyzes images of Africa and Africans in Western popular culture.

Nineteenth-century prehistoric archaeology in the United States is included in this section because it was primarily shaped, as was American anthropology as a whole, by the colonial encounter between dramatically expanding Euro-American settlement and the indigenous peoples of central and western North America. General discussions of racial behavior in the nineteenth century that are relevant for under-standing archaeological practice in colonial settings are provided by M. Harris (1968a), Stocking (1968, 1982), S. J. Gould (1981), Stepan (1982), and Bieder (1986). The development of biological anthropology and of racial views concerning the North American Indians has been studied by Glass et al. (1959), Glacken (1967), and Horsman (1975, 1981). Conn (1998) examines the role of museums in the United States from 1876 to 1926. Willey and Sabloff (1993: 38–64) trace the development of North American archaeology during the middle and late nineteenth centuries and Silverberg (1968) chronicles the demise of the Moundbuilder myth. Patterson (1991) considers the nature of pre-professional archaeology in the United States. Hinsley (1981) examines the role played by the Smithsonian Institution in the professionalization of indigenous American studies, including archaeology. He also examines social factors influencing the development of archaeology at the Peabody Museum of Archaeology and Ethnology (Hinsley 1985), as does Appel (1992). McKusick (1970, 1991) offers a case study of the competition to interpret prehistoric archaeological data between amateur and professional archaeologists in the United States and Meltzer (1983) analyzes the very active role played by archaeologists employed by the United States federal government in nineteenth-century "Early Man" controversies. Kehoe (1998) discusses the importance of Daniel Wilson's work for nineteenth-century American archaeology. Trigger (1980b, 1985b, 1986b) examines the role of racism at this time. Max Uhle's varied contributions are discussed by Rowe (1954) and Menzel (1977).

The history of Australian archaeology is documented by Horton (1991), Moser (1995a), T. Murray (2001c), and in a broader anthropological context Griffiths (1996). Aspects of it are treated more briefly by McCarthy (1959), Megaw (1966), Mulvaney (1969, 1981), R. Jones (1979), Murray and White (1981), and McBryde (1986). Developments since the middle of the twentieth century, with an emphasis on relations between archaeology and Australian politics, are examined in collections of papers edited by Gathercole et al. (1995) and Bonyhady and Griffiths (1996). The most accessible accounts of the development of New Zealand archaeology are Sorrenson (1977), Davidson (1979), Gathercole (1981), Sutton (1985), and H. Allen (2001). Gathercole provides references to a number of other early studies in New Zealand anthropological newsletters. Historical issues relating to hunter-gatherer archaeology in isolated parts of the world are discussed by Gamble (1992), Bowler (1992), T. Murray (1992), R. Jones (1992), Mazel (1992), and Borrero (1992).

The most comprehensive study of the history of African archaeology has been edited by Robertshaw (1990). Fagan (1981) and Posnansky (1982) each provide a brief survey of the history of sub-Saharan archaeology and M. Hall (1984), Schrire et al. (1986), T. Shaw (1991), and Schlanger (2002, 2003) discuss the development of prehistoric archaeology in South Africa. Chanaiwa (1973), Garlake (1973, 1983), and H. Kuklick (1991b) chronicle and discuss archaeological investigations at Great Zimbabwe and other stone ruins in south-central Africa and the prolonged controversies that have surrounded these sites. Works dealing with cultural contacts between Egypt and the rest of Africa include O'Connor (1993), Trigger (1994b), Celenko (1996), and O'Connor and Reid (2003). MacGaffey (1966) documents the impact of racist stereotypes on African ethnological studies. M. Bernal (1987, 2001) polemically discusses controversies concerning the role played by ancient Egyptian civilization in African and world history; for alternative views see Lefkowitz and Rogers (1996). Critiques of archaeological research in Africa include Ki-Zerbo (1981), Andah (1985, 1995), Schrire (1995), N. Shepherd (2002b), and papers in Schmidt and McIntosh (1996).

Comments relating to colonial and postcolonial archaeology in various parts of the world are found in D. Miller (1980) and in papers published in Ucko (1995a) and Schmidt and Patterson (1995).

Culture-Historical Archaeology

Culture-historical archaeology is currently of great interest to archaeologists and historians of archaeology. These include not only Darwinian archaeologists, who seek to incorporate selected aspects of culture-historical archaeology into their own approach, but also postprocessualists and other archaeologists who are curious about what processual archaeology replaced. This curiosity appears to have been stimulated by a final rejection of the hegemonic claims of processual archaeology.

For discussions of Ratzel, see Wanklyn (1961), J. D. Hunter (1983), W. D. Smith (1991: 140–61), and Zimmerman (2001: 202–5).

H. Kuklick (1991a) considers the role played by diffusion in British anthropology. M. Harris (1968a: 373–92) and Trigger (1978a: 54–74) discuss the development of diffusionism in anthropology and archaeology; W. Adams et al. (1978) trace the separate employment of the concepts of migration and diffusion to explain culture change; Daniel (1963a: 104–27) discusses hyper-diffusionism; and Rouse (1958, 1986), Härke (1998), and Burmeister (2000) the archaeological analysis of migrations. Elkin and Macintosh (1974) have edited a study of the career of Grafton Elliot Smith.

Despite his undeniable importance, no substantial biography of Montelius is available, although a conference was held to celebrate the 150th anniversary of his birth (Åström 1995). Gräslund (1974, 1976, 1987) offers the most detailed analysis of Montelius's assumptions, methods, and contributions to the study of European prehistory, while Klindt-Jensen (1975: 84–93) sets his work into its Scandinavian context. Renfrew (1973a) critiques Montelius's diffusionist assumptions.

Kroeber and Kluckhohn (1952) document the origins and history of the anthropological concept of culture. Although no equally detailed study of the development of the concept of the archaeological culture is available, Meinander (1981) and Díaz-Andreu (1996a) ably summarize what is known about its origins. The development of this concept in Europe and America is compared in Trigger (1978a: 75–95). I am most grateful to Peter Rowley-Conwy for tracing at my request the early use of the term "culture" by Scandinavian archaeologists.

Recent discussions of nationalism are provided by Gellner (1983), Hobsbawm (1990), and B. Anderson (1991). Weber (1976) examines the promotion of national unity in France and Dumont (1994) compares French and German ideas of collective identity. Kohl (1998) discusses the relation between nationalism and archaeology. For an examination of the connections between ideas of ethnicity and racism, see E. Barkan (1992).

Unfortunately, no detailed evaluation of the important contributions of Kossinna to the development of archaeology has been published in English. Grünert's (2002) massive biography provides important and hitherto unavailable information about Kossinna's life and career, but it does not supply the detailed summaries of Kossinna's publications that are necessary to understand the development of his ideas. Schwerin von Krosigk (1982) discusses in detail Kossinna's methods and theories with special reference to his papers that were until recently deposited at the Christian-Albrechts University in Kiel. Klejn (1974) summarizes Kossinna's views and evaluates them in a judicious fashion. All these works are available only in German. The best discussion of Kossinna's work in English is Klejn (1999a). For Virchow's work in archaeology, see Ottaway (1973) and, for the context of German archaeology and anthropology in which Virchow and his followers worked, Fetten (2000) and Zimmerman (2001). German nationalism is discussed by Kohn (1960) and in a broader European context by Poliakov (1974). Thomas Huxley's (1896: 271–328) essay "The Aryan Question and Prehistoric Man" provides valuable insights into how scholars viewed European prehistory at the end of the nineteenth century.

A general account of Childe's archaeological ideas is presented in Trigger (1980a), some aspects of which are modified and updated in later works (Trigger 1984b, 1986c). Childe's specific contributions to culture-historical archaeology are discussed in Trigger (1980a: 32–55). S. Green (1981) chronicles his family background, life, and career; McNairn (1980) and Patterson and Orser (2004) reproduce and comment on extracts from his writings; and Gathercole et al. (1995) examine Childe's political activities in Australia. Specialized discussions and evaluations of his work are found in Piggott (1958), Ravetz (1959), J. Allen (1967, 1981), Gathercole (1971, 1976, 1982), Grahame Clark (1976), Trigger (1982b), Tringham (1983), Veit (1984), Ridgway (1985), Sherratt (1989), K. Greene (1999), and Bakker (2001). For a discussion of Polish influence on Childe's understanding of the concept of the archaeological culture, compare Barford (2002: 177–8) and Lech (2002: 212–17). An important evaluation of Childe's contributions to archaeology is found in a set of papers presented at the Institute of Archaeology in 1992 (D. Harris 1994). Familiarity with Myres (1911) is essential to understand many specific aspects of Childe's culture-historical approach to European prehistory.

Since the 1990s, there has been a strong interest in historical studies that relate the practice of culture-historical archaeology to issues of nationalism and identity (Kane 2003). In some of these studies, the role of archaeology in nationalist movements has been brought into sharper focus by employing analytical techniques derived from material culture studies. Collections of papers dealing with national traditions of archaeology across Europe are found in Díaz-Andreu and Champion (1996a), Graves-Brown et al. (1996), and Galaty and Watkinson (2004), and for Europe since 1960 in Hodder (1991a). For a similar treatment of archaeology in eastern Europe, see Cleere (1993) and for southeastern Europe and the Middle East Meskell (1998). More broadly ranging collections of papers are found in Ucko (1995a) and Kohl and

Fawcett (1995). The latter publication also critiques the political and academic shortcomings of nationalist archaeology. Excellent accounts of the development of local variants of culture-historical archaeology also are found in the entries for many single countries in T. Murray (2001a).

In recent years, there has at last been growing interest in studying the history of German archaeology. For major collections of papers, see Härke (2000a) and Steuer (2001), as well as Leube and Hegewisch (2002), the latter dealing specifically with archaeology during the Nazi period. Important single papers include Klejn (1977), McCann (1989), Veit (1989), Arnold (1990), Härke (1991, 1995, 2000b), Kossack (1992), Arnold and Hassmann (1995), Wiwjorra (1996), Junker (1998), Hassmann (2000), Wolfram (2000), Maischberger (2002), Eickhoff (2005), and Halle (2005).

Culture-historical archaeology in France is chronicled by Gran-Aymerich (1998) and its relevance to French national identity is discussed by Audouze and Leroi-Gourhan (1981), Dietler (1994, 1998), M. Heffernan (1994), Chazan (1995), Fleury-Ilett (1996), Laurent (1999), Legendre (1999), and Demoule (1999). Guidi (1987) provides a brief history of Italian archaeology in English. Important aspects of the development of Dutch archaeology are discussed by Bazelmans et al. (1997) and Bakker (2001) and the history of Spanish archaeology is surveyed in a collection of papers edited by Mora and Díaz-Andreu (1997). For a history of Polish archaeology, see Lech (1999). Binétruy (1994) has published a biography of Joseph Dechélette and Brodrick (1963), Skrotzky (1964), Strauss (1992), and C. Cohen (1999) discuss Henri Breuil. Information about Dorothy Garrod is provided by G. Clark (1999), P. J. Smith et al. (1997), and P. J. Smith (2000). The most detailed account of Caton Thompson's career is her autobiography (Caton Thompson 1983).

The history of archaeology in East Asia is examined in a series of papers published by Malone and Kaner (1999). Chinese archaeology is discussed by R. Pearson (1977), Li (1977), K. C. Chang (1981, 2002), W. Watson (1981), Olsen (1987), An (1989), Chen (1989), Falkenhausen (1993, 1995, 1999), T. Wang (1997), and Liu and Chen (2001); Evasdottir (2004) offers an interesting account of how Chinese archaeologists conduct research. Japanese archaeology is examined by Ikawa-Smith (1982, 1995), Tanaka (1984), Bleed (1986, 1989), Fawcett (1986, 1995), Habu (1989, 2004), G. Barnes (1990b), Habu and Fawcett (1999), and Mizoguchi (2002, 2004); South Asian archaeology by Chakrabarti (1981, 1982, 1988, 1997, 2001, 2003), Thapar (1984),

Hassan (1995), Coningham and Lewer (2000), Ratnagar (2004), and Singh (2004); and Middle Eastern archaeology by Masry (1981), D. M. Reid (1985, 1997, 2002), Bahrani (1998), Hassan (1998), Wood (1998), Abdi (2001), Bernbeck and Pollock (2004), Bernhardsson (2005), and Erciyas (2005). A vast and growing literature, some of it highly polemical, is focused on Israeli archaeology. A representative sampling includes: Bar-Yosef and Mazar (1982), Paine (1983, 1994), Hanbury-Tenison (1986), Shay (1989), Silberman (1989, 1993), Moorey (1991), Ben-Yehuda (1995, 2002), Silberman and Small (1997), Abu El-Haj (2001), Dever (2001a, 2001b, 2003), Finkelstein and Silberman (2001), Hallote and Joffe (2002), and Kletter (2006). For colonial archaeology in Palestine, see Silberman (1982, 1991) and T. Davis (2004).

The history of archaeology in sub-Saharan Africa in the late colonial and postcolonial periods is examined by Fagan (1981), Posnansky (1982), M. Hall (1984), Nzewunwa (1984), Schrire (1995), Schlanger (2002, 2003), and N. Shepherd (2002a, 2002b). Robertshaw (1990) contains many excellent papers dealing with the transition from colonial to national archaeologies. On the relation of sub-Saharan African archaeology to the study of African history during this same time span, see D. McCall (1964), Ki-Zerbo (1981), Ehret and Posnansky (1982), and Andah (1995).

Archaeology in Latin American countries is surveyed in Politis and Alberti (1999); see also Burger (1989), Funari (1997), Politis (2003), and Politis and Pérez-Gollán (2004). The history of Mexican archaeology during the culture-historical period is examined by I. Bernal (1980, 1983), Lorenzo (1981, 1984), Cabrero (1993), and Vázquez León (1996; 2nd ed. 2003). Maya archaeology is covered by Brunhouse (1975), Hammond (1983), Marcus (1983b, 2003), Black (1990), and Sabloff (1990); Brazilian archaeology by Barreto (1998), Goes Neves (1998), and Funari (1999a, 2001).

Major contributions dealing with the development of archaeological methods in the context of culture-historical archaeology are reprinted in Heizer (1959); those relating to stratigraphy are found on pages 222–343 and those relating to seriation (including the innovative studies of Petrie and Kroeber) on pages 376–448. On the career of Schliemann, see Calder and Cobet (1990), Herrmann (1990), and Turner (1990). Pitt Rivers's contributions to the development of excavation techniques are examined by Bowden (1991), Wheeler's by J. Hawkes (1982), and Kenyon's by Moorey (1979). For more on Pitt Rivers, see M. Thompson (1977), R. Bradley (1983), and W. R. Chapman (1984, 1985, 1989). The development of excavation techniques in

Germany is discussed by Kossack (1992) and their spread to Britain by C. Evans (1989). For parallel developments in the United States, see Fagette (1996) and Lyon (1996).

Adams and Adams (1991) and W. Adams (2001) provide general discussions of the development of classification in archaeology. Although little specific has been published, except by Gräslund (1987), about the development of systems of artifact and cultural classification in Europe, I have been able to summarize only in broad outline the vast primary and secondary literature relating to those topics for United States archaeology. In recent years, several Darwinian archaeologists have produced outstanding in-depth studies of the analytical contributions of early-twentieth-century culture-historical archaeologists in the United States. The most general and important of these works are Lyman, O'Brien, and Dunnell, *The Rise and Fall of Culture History* (1997a), and its accompanying anthology of key methodological and theoretical papers written by culture-historical archaeologists (1997b). Also of major importance are an analytical biography of James A. Ford (O'Brien and Lyman 1998) and a definitive study of the Midwestern Taxonomic Method (Lyman and O'Brien 2003). Other works by this group include O'Brien's (1996a) history of Missouri archaeology, as well as papers dealing with the development of stratigraphic excavations (Lyman and O'Brien 1999) and the direct historical approach (Lyman and O'Brien 2001). Outside this group, Browman and Givens (1996) have discussed early stratified excavations in the United States, Kehoe (1990) and Fisher (1997) have commented on the Midwestern Taxonomic Method, Woodbury (1973) and Givens (1992a) have published biographies of Kidder, and Pinsky (1992a, 1992b) has examined the relation between culture-historical archaeological practice and Boasian anthropology.

The most accessible general survey of Collingwood's career and ideas is his autobiography (Collingwood 1939). Studies of him from a philosophical perspective include W. M. Johnston (1967) and Mink (1969). For an insightful analysis of Hawkes's "ladder" of inference, see C. Evans (1998).

Early Functional-Processual Archaeology

Fewer historical studies have been published dealing with early functional-processual archaeology than might have been expected. This may reflect the reluctance of many processual archaeologists and their postprocessual critics to recognize the early beginnings of many of their respective ideas.

The early development of environmental approaches in Scandinavia, central Europe, and England is discussed by Morlot (1861), Daniel (1975: 302–8), Bibby (1956), G. Wright (1971), Klindt-Jensen (1975), Goudie (1976), Moberg (1981), and Kristiansen (2002). Deuel (1973) discusses the impact of aerial photography on environmental research in archaeology. Spate (1968) discusses environmental possibilism.

M. Harris (1968a: 464–567) traces the early development of social anthropology. H. Kuklick (1991a) examines the replacement of culture-historical anthropology by social anthropology in Britain. Some important essays on the development of social anthropology are found in Stocking (1984). Information about Durkheim is provided by Alpert (1939), Duvignaud (1965), and T. Parsons (1968).

Childe's contributions to functional-processual archaeology are examined in the main studies of his life and works listed in the previous section. H. Orenstein (1954) discusses his evolutionary theorizing, K. Greene (1999) his use of the concept of "revolution," and L. Klejn (1994b) Childe's relations with Soviet archaeologists.

Studying the history of Soviet archaeology presents special difficulties. Anything published in the Soviet Union while the Communist Party was in power was subject to political censorship, whereas works produced in the West, especially during the Cold War, were sometimes extremely polemical and frequently ill-informed. Since the collapse of the Soviet Union, revisionist studies of the history of Soviet archaeology have begun to appear, some of them based on careful archival research. However, much research remains to be done on the history of archaeology during the Soviet period. Because I do not read Russian, I have been unable to use as effectively as I would wish Genings's (1982) monograph on the history of Soviet archaeology. Klejn's (1993a) major study of Soviet archaeology is available in Spanish (Klejn 1993b) and German (1997) translations. Leo Klejn informs me that the German edition contains more information than the Spanish and Russian ones. This book contains much biographical material relating to Soviet archaeologists.

The most detailed history of Russian and early Soviet archaeology available in English remains M. Miller (1956). It is, however, a highly polemical work written by an émigré archaeologist during the Cold War and is held in low regard by modern Russian historians of archaeology. It must be used with extreme caution as must works based largely on it (e.g., Trigger 1984c). Periodizations of the development of Russian and Soviet archaeology have been proposed by Miller (1956), Gening (1982), Soffer (1985), Dolitsky (1985), and Klejn (1993a, 2001b).

The understanding of archaeology in the Soviet Union before the imposition of Marxist orthodoxy, beginning in 1928, is being revolutionized by the archival research of Nadezhda Platonova. She is revealing the distorted nature of later Soviet accounts of this period, beginning in 1929 with Ravdonikas's officially-mandated denunciation of "old archaeology." Various Western studies of scientific research and cultural policy in the Soviet Union in the 1920s and 1930s help to contextualize the creation of Soviet archaeology: G. Fischer (1967), L. Graham (1967), S. Cohen (1973), S. Fitzpatrick (1974), Shapiro (1982), and T. O'Connor (1983).

Gening (1982) presents a comprehensive, albeit conventional, history of Soviet archaeology from the mid-1920s to the mid-1930s, together with brief biographies of the major figures in Soviet archaeology at this time. Archaeology in the Soviet Union in the 1930s and 1940s is discussed in English by Golomshtok (1933), Tallgren (1936), Grahame Clark (1936), Field and Prostov (1937), Artsikhovskii and Brussov (1958), Avdiyev (1945), and in a series of papers by Childe (1940b, 1942b, 1942c, 1942d, 1942e, 1943, 1945b, 1952). Major translated Soviet archaeological writings of the early post-war period include rival Soviet (1959) and British (1961) versions of Mongait's *Archaeology in the U.S.S.R.*, M. Thompson's (1967) selected papers on the medieval excavations at Novgorod, S. Semenov (1964) on use-wear analysis, and various syntheses of Siberian archaeological research: Rudenko (1961, 1970), Michael (1962, 1964), Okladnikov (1965, 1970), and Chernetsov and Moszyńska (1974). Useful information is also contained in entries to the *Great Soviet Encyclopedia*, especially Artsikhovsky's (1973) essay on "Archaeology." Surveys of work done during this period are provided by Field and Price (1949), Combier (1959), Chard (1961, 1963, 1969), Debetz (1961), Frumkin (1962), Boriskovsky (1965), and Klein (1966). Polemical literature includes M. Thompson (1965) and Klejn (1969, 1970). Extracts from Mongait's notorious "The Crisis in Bourgeois Archaeology" are translated in M. Miller (1956: 147–52). A review of Tallgren's archaeological work, including his contacts with Soviet archaeologists, is provided by Kokkonen (1985).

Examinations of Soviet archaeology in the post-Stalin period include Klejn (1973a, 1973b, 1977), Levitt (1979), Ranov and Davis (1979), R. Davis (1983), Tringham (1983), Soffer (1983, 1985), Dolitsky (1985), and Kolpakov and Vishnyatsky (1990). Bulkin et al. (1982) provide a brief history of Soviet archaeology produced in the late 1970s. Soviet archaeological publications of the post-Stalin period that are translated into English include Dolukhanov (1979), Klejn (1982), and a volume of papers on central Asia in the Bronze Age (Kohl 1981a).

574

Translations of selected papers by Soviet archaeologists appeared regularly in the American journal *Soviet Anthropology and Archeology*.

Changing Soviet applications of Marxist concepts to the social sciences are reviewed by Danilova (1971) and by Petrova-Averkieva and others in Gellner (1980). Soviet scholarly views about "primitive" societies are analyzed by Howe (1976, 1980) and Bloch (1985). Discussions of the concept of culture by Soviet archaeologists are examined by Bulkin et al. (1982), Klejn (1982), and R. Davis (1983).

Works in English dealing with the history of Soviet archaeology written since the collapse of the Soviet Union include Dolukhanov (1995), Shnirelman (1995, 1996, 2001), Chernykh (1995), Kohl and Tsetskhladze (1995), and Klejn (2001b), the latter as part of a brief history of Russian and Soviet archaeology.

B. Fagan (2001) has published an attractive, popular book-length intellectual biography of Grahame Clark that contains admirable summaries of all Clark's important writings. Rowley-Conwy (1999) offers an insightful analysis of Clark's career and P. J. Smith (1997) provides valuable accounts of Clark's early research and publications and of his role in the establishment of the Prehistoric Society (Smith 1999). Clark authored a brief intellectual autobiography (Clark 1974) and a critique of his own work at Star Carr (Clark 1972). He also set his life and work into its Cambridge University context and reprinted his major papers on economic topics (Clark 1989a, 1989b). Sieveking (1976) and R. Chapman (1979) assess Clark's influence on the work of David Clarke and some of his other students. For an assessment of Eric Higgs's work, see Bailey (1999).

Willey and Sabloff (1993) and Dunnell (1986) provide a detailed chronicle of the development of a functionalist approach in United States' archaeology from the mid-1930s. They do not, however, explicitly trace the origins of this approach in the American archaeology of the late nineteenth and early twentieth centuries, as do W. Taylor (1948: 73–80) and Trigger (1978c). J. Bennett (1943) and W. Taylor (1948) provide contemporary accounts of the growth of a functionalist approach in the 1940s. Little has been written about Walter Taylor in recent years apart from an interesting character sketch by Reyman (1999). M. Harris (1968a: 393–463) describes and evaluates the culture and personality approach in Boasian anthropology. The development of the ecological approach in American archaeology is described autobiographically by Braidwood (1974) and MacNeish (1974, 1978) and the early development of settlement archaeology is documented by Trigger (1967) and Willey (1974b). Trigger (1984d) considers some of the early weaknesses of this approach as well as its relation to the

New Archaeology. Billman and Feinman (1999) evaluate settlement-pattern archaeology from the perspective of fifty years.

For the origins of radiocarbon dating and its application to archaeology, see Libby (1955), Renfrew (1973a), R. E. Taylor (1985, 1987), Bowman (1990), R. E. Taylor et al. (1992), and Marlowe (1999).

Processualism and Postprocessualism

The broader perspective offered by the passage of time and by more recent developments in archaeology permits a more contextualized understanding of the history of processual archaeology than was presented in the original edition of this book. The most valuable study of the history of American processual archaeology published in the past fifteen years is O'Brien, Lyman, and Schiffer's *Archaeology as a Process* (2005), a work inspired by David Hull's *Science as a Process* (1988). *Archaeology as a Process* is based on the principle that one cannot hope to understand the history of science without knowing about the personalities, alliances, and rivalries of the people involved. It thus presents a richly detailed account of processual archaeology. Other recent general histories of American archaeology that discuss both processual and postprocessual archaeology are Patterson's (1995) social history, Kehoe's (1998) critical history, and the third edition of Willey and Sabloff's (1993) history of American archaeology. Also of major importance is Patterson's (2003) study of the impact of Marxism on American archaeology both before and after the inception of New Archaeology, a work that can profitably be read in conjunction with R. McGuire (1992) and Kolakowski's (1978a, 1978b, 1978c) critical survey of the entire history of Marxist thought. These histories of American archaeology provide alternative perspectives that complement my intellectual history. Apart from these works, few studies of the history of processual and postprocessual archaeology transcend mere polemic.

M. Harris (1968a: 634–87) discusses the development of neoevolutionism. Major anthropological works that cast doubt on the value of this approach in the 1970s and early 1980s include Fried (1975), Sahlins (1976), and Wolf (1982); see also Wallerstein (1974) for a more nuanced view of sociocultural development.

Gamble (1999) surveys Binford's life and works. Important supplementary information can be found in interviews of Binford conducted by P. Sabloff (1988) and D. Van Reybrouck (2001). What appear to be totally contradictory claims about his early intellectual orientation appear in Preston (1995: 81) and Kehoe (1998: 118–21). Binford (1972:

1–14) details his rebellion against the culture-historical approach, specifically the variant of the Midwestern Taxonomic Method that he encountered in the person of J. B. Griffin at the University of Michigan in the 1950s. His early writings are reprinted in Binford (1972). The widely shared disenchantment of young archaeologists with culture-historical archaeology in the 1950s is noted in Trigger (1984d: 368–9). Although there is disagreement about who first used the term "New Archaeology" to denote the earliest manifestations of processual archaeology, it appears to be derived from the title of Caldwell's (1959) paper "The New American Archaeology." The term New Archaeology had been applied to culture-historical archaeology long before (Wissler 1917). Deetz is sometimes considered to be an independent pioneer of New Archaeology (Willey and Sabloff 1980: 209). The spread of New Archaeology into American historical archaeology is chronicled by South (1977a, 1977b).

Many of the most important early papers exemplifying the New Archaeology can be found in S. and L. Binford (1968), Leone (1972), Clarke (1972a), Redman (1973), and Renfrew (1973b). The first textbook treatment of New Archaeology was P. J. Watson et al. (1971; 2nd ed. 1984), although New Archaeology's impact on American archaeology was already evident in the second edition of Hole and Heizer's (1969) influential general textbook of archaeology. A widely read popularization of new scientific techniques was published by David Wilson (1975).

David Clarke's career is evaluated by Fletcher (1999). Clarke's main writings are found in Clarke (1968, 1979). His contributions are surveyed and evaluated by students and colleagues in Clarke (1979) and, more recently, in a collection of papers published in *Antiquity* (Malone and Stoddart 1998). Renfrew's early essays are reprinted in Renfrew (1979, 1984).

The most substantial polemic directed against New Archaeology was written by the French classical archaeologist Courbin (1988), who in a Rankean fashion equated archaeology with the recovery of archaeological data. His book mainly succeeds in documenting the lack of theoretical sophistication and the narrow-mindedness of at least one distinguished culture-historical archaeologist. Brief but equally pugnacious defenses of culture-historical archaeology include J. Hawkes (1968), A. Hogarth (1972), and Daniel (1975: 370–4). All these polemics are by Europeans. In the United States, such works are notable by their absence. Ringing endorsements by older American archaeologists are almost equally rare, the notable exception being by P. Martin (1971). Critical evaluations of aspects of the general program of processual archaeology were offered by Bayard (1969), R. Watson (1972), Sabloff et al. (1973), Dumond (1977), Trigger (1978a: 2–18), P. Larson (1979), Gándara (1980, 1981), and Gibbon (1984). Criticism of Binford's advocacy of primary reliance on a deductive approach was made, among others, by C. Morgan (1973, 1978), Read and LeBlanc (1978), M. Salmon (1982), Kelley and Hanen (1988), Gibbon (1989), and Wylie (1989b, 2002). The antihistoricism of American processual archaeology was opposed on technical grounds by Sabloff and Willey (1967) and on philosophical and strategic grounds by Trigger ([1970] 1978a: 19–36; [1973] 1978a: 37–52). Although philosophical realism was promoted as providing a more satisfactory epistemological basis for archaeological research (Bhaskar 1978; Harré 1970, 1972; Harré and Madden 1975; Gibbon 1989), Binford (1986, 1987a) continued to offer an energetic defense of positivism.

Important studies relating to ethnoarchaeology include Kleindienst and Watson (1956), Jochim (1976), Yellen (1977), Binford (1978), R. Gould (1978a, 1980), Tringham (1978), Kramer (1979, 1982), P. J. Watson (1979), Hodder (1982b), Tooker (1982), Hayden and Cannon (1984), and Kent (1984, 1987). Pinsky (1992a) provides a detailed study of the use of ethnographic data by processual archaeologists. Ingersoll et al. (1977), Coles (1979), and Hayden (1979) discuss experimental archaeology.

On the employment of statistics and other forms of mathematical analysis in processual archaeology, see Hodson et al. (1971), Steiger (1971), Doran and Hodson (1975), Hodder and Orton (1976), D. Thomas (1976, 1978), Cowgill (1977), Hodder (1978b), and Sabloff (1981). Discussions of General Systems Theory can be found in Wiener (1961), Buckley (1968), Bertalanffy (1969), F. Emery (1969), and Laszlo (1972a, 1972b, 1972c). Saunders (1980) offers a general review of catastrophe theory. Discussions of the unique properties of archaeological data and how such data can be made relevant to the social sciences include Clarke (1973), Schiffer (1976), Binford (1977, 1981, 1983a, 1983b, 1984), and Bulkin et al. (1982).

The most comprehensive survey of theoretical trends in American archaeology during the 1970s and early to mid-1980s is the volume edited by Meltzer et al. (1986), especially the papers published in it by Dunnell, Jennings, Knudson, Leone, and P. J. Watson; see also Lamberg-Karlovsky (1989). Other surveys include Willey and Sabloff (1980: 248–64), Dunnell (1979, 1980b, 1981, 1982a, 1983, 1984, 1985), Kohl (1981b, 1984), Wylie (1982, 1985a, 1985c), Gibbon (1984), Trigger (1984e), Yengoyan (1985), Patterson (1986b), Leone et al. (1987), and Earle and Preucel (1987). Gibbon (1984), Trigger (1984e), and Gallay (1986) discuss trends in archaeology resulting from the declining influence of evolutionism and cultural ecology. Flannery (1982) distances himself from many of the methodological concerns of New Archaeology. Renfrew (1980) and Wiseman (1980a, 1980b) discuss the changing relations between humanistic and social science approaches as a result of processualism.

The most detailed survey of postprocessual archaeology is by Hodder and Hutson (2003); it is an updated version of Hodder (1986, 1991d). Many alternative approaches to understanding this complex subject are possible (e.g., Patterson 1990). The polemical exchanges both between processual and postprocessual archaeologists and among postprocessual archaeologists center to a considerable degree on whether the ideas of processual and postprocessual archaeology are complementary or mutually exclusive and to what extent postprocessual archaeology does or does not represent a single school of thought (R. Chapman 2003: 13–15). Early attempts to define postprocessual archaeology include Hodder (1985), Leone (1986), Earle and Preucel (1987), Patterson (1989), Watson and Fotiadis (1990), and Preucel (1995). Although postprocessualists emphasize the diversity of their various positions, they are all idealist in orientation and their heterogeneity is not greater than that found among materialist archaeologists.

Major works marking the development of postprocessual archaeology include Hodder (1982c, 1986, 1992, 1999, 2001, 2003a), Miller and Tilley (1984), Shanks and Tilley (1987a, 1987b), Tilley (1990a, 1993), Hodder et al. (1995), Karlsson (1998), and J. Thomas (1996). Brück (2005) provides an overview of the use of the phenomenological approach by archaeologists. Examinations of the confrontation between processual and postprocessual archaeologists are found in collections of papers edited by Preucel (1991), Yoffee and Sherratt (1993), and Preucel and Hodder (1996). Balter (2005) provides a detailed account of Hodder's life and work. Bintliff (1993) presented what turned out to be a premature obituary of postprocessual archaeology in which he argued that cognitive-processual archaeology represents an ideal "pragmatic merger" of the processual and postprocessual approaches. For what knowledgeable British archaeologists have believed at different times their colleagues should know about anthropology, compare Orme (1981), Hodder (1982a), and C. Gosden (1999).

Bintliff (1984), in the spirit of postprocessualism, offers an interesting study of the impact of early-twentieth-century aesthetic concepts on A. Evans's reconstructions of Minoan mural paintings. Joyce (2002) discusses the role of narrative in archaeological interpretation. Mithen

(2003) provides an example of the responsible use of a narrative device incorporating fiction to popularize archaeological findings; Ferris (1999) similarly uses fictional scenarios to illustrate the significance of alternative interpretations of the same archaeological evidence.

For a survey of theoretical developments in European archaeology between 1960 and 1990, see Hodder (1991a). The impact of processual and postprocessual archaeology in Latin America is discussed by Politis and Alberti (1999) and in India by Paddayya (1983, 1990), S. Singh (1985), Boivin and Fuller (2002), Fuller and Boivin (2002), and Chakrabarti (2003).

Pragmatic Synthesis

Very little historical research has been published regarding the development of archaeology since 1990. The polemical literature is noted in Chapter 9.

Hegmon (2003) provides a critical survey of the present state of North American archaeology, although she does not go on to consider how the synthesis of current approaches that she calls for can be achieved. Peregrine (2000) offers an interesting discussion of what has been happening to processual archaeology. Schiffer (2000a) and many other American archaeologists stress the need for theoretical synthesis to replace confrontation. In Europe, Kristiansen (2004a) considers the implications of the broader range of high-level theories that archaeologists are currently employing and calls for a critical synthesis of epistemologically incompatible approaches, in particular of those that seek to dichotomize biological and cultural explanations. Politis (2003) surveys crucial theoretical developments in Latin American archaeology and R. Chapman (2003) provides a valuable account of recent Marxist archaeology in Spain. Hodder (1999) and Hodder and Hutson (2003) examine the current state of postprocessual archaeology. Balter's (2005) biography of Hodder and account of the work being done at the site of Çatalhöyük also assesses recent developments in postprocessual archaeology.

Numerous collections of papers document the current state of archaeological theory, among them Holtorf and Karlsson (2000), Schiffer (2000a), Hodder (2001), Biehl et al. (2002), VanPool and VanPool (2003), Bintliff (2004), and Meskell and Preucel (2004).

Individually authored works that are especially relevant for understanding various current developments in archaeological theory include Hodder (1999, 2003a), A. Jones (2002), Shennan (2002), Renfrew and Bahn (2004), and J. Thomas (2004). Kristiansen and

Larsson (2005), in their study of Bronze Age Europe, offer the most extensive, empirically-based effort to transcend the dichotomy between processual and postprocessual, or social and cultural, approaches as well as a new treatment of cultural diffusion. They view their approach as marking the beginning of a "new Culture History." While I lack the specialized knowledge needed to evaluate many of their specific arguments, this work clearly exemplifies the more holistic theoretical approaches that are becoming popular in archaeology.

REFERENCES

Abbott, C. C. 1881. *Primitive Industry*. Salem, MA, G. A. Bates.

Abdi, K. 2001. Nationalism, politics, and the development of archaeology in Iran. *American Journal of Archaeology* 105: 51–76.

Abercromby, J. 1902. The oldest Bronze-Age ceramic type in Britain: its probable origin in Central Europe. *Journal of the Royal Anthropological Institute* 32: 373–97.

   1912. *A Study of the Bronze Age Pottery of Great Britain and Ireland and its Associated Grave-Goods*. 2 vols., Oxford, Oxford University Press.

Aberle, D. F., A. K. Cohen, A. K. Davis, M.-J. Levy Jr, and F. X. Sutton. 1950. The functional prerequisites of a society. *Ethics* 60: 100–1.

Abramowicz, A. 1981. Sponte nascitur ollae . . . In G. Daniel, 1981b, pp. 146–9.

Abu El-Haj, N. 2001. *Facts on the Ground: Archaeological Practice and Territorial Self-fashioning in Israeli Society*. Chicago, IL, University of Chicago Press.

Adams, R. McC. 1965. *Land Behind Baghdad*. Chicago, IL, University of Chicago Press.

   1966. *The Evolution of Urban Society: Early Mesopotamia and Prehispanic Mexico*. Chicago, IL, Aldine.

   1974. Anthropological perspectives on ancient trade. *Current Anthropology* 15: 239–58.

   1981. *Heartland of Cities*. Chicago, IL, University of Chicago Press.

Adams, R. McC. and H. J. Nissen. 1972. *The Uruk Countryside*. Chicago, IL, University of Chicago Press.

Adams, W. Y. 2001. Classification. In T. Murray 2001a, pp. 336–53.

Adams, W. Y. and E. W. Adams. 1991. *Archaeological Typology and Practical Reality: A Dialectical Approach to Artifact Classification and Sorting*. Cambridge, Cambridge University Press.

Adams, W. Y., D. P. Van Gerven, and R. S. Levy. 1978. The retreat from migrationism. *Annual Review of Anthropology* 7: 483–532.

Alcock, S. E. 2002. *Archaeologies of the Greek Past: Landscape, Monuments, and Memories*. Cambridge, Cambridge University Press.

Alcock, S. E., J. F. Cherry, and J. Elsner. 2001. eds. *Pausanias: Travel and Memory in Roman Greece*. Oxford, Oxford University Press.

Alden, J. R. 1982. Trade and politics in proto-Elamite Iran. *Current Anthropology* 23: 613–40.

References

Alexander, J. and A. Mohammed. 1982. Frontier theory and the Neolithic period in Nubia. In *Nubian Studies*, ed. by J. M. Plumley pp. 34–40. Warminster, UK, Aris and Phillips.

Allen, H. 2001. New Zealand: prehistoric archaeology. In T. Murray, 2001a, pp. 938–50.

Allen, J. 1967. Aspects of Vere Gordon Childe. *Labour History* 12: 52–9.

    1981. Perspectives of a sentimental journey: V. Gordon Childe in Australia 1917–1921. *Australian Archaeology* 12: 1–11.

Allen, J. P. 1999. A monument of Khaemwaset honoring Imhotep. In *Gold of Praise: Studies on Ancient Egypt in Honor of Edward F. Wente*, ed. by E. Teeter and J. A. Larson, pp. 1–10. Chicago, IL, Oriental Institute.

Allen, S. H. 2002. *Excavating Our Past: Perspectives on the History of the Archaeological Institute of America*. Boston, MA, Archaeological Institute of America.

Allesbrook, M. 1992. *Born to Rebel: The Life of Harriet Boyd Hawes*. Oxford, Oxbow.

Allison, P. M. 2001. Using the material and written sources: turn of the millennium approaches to Roman domestic space. *American Journal of Archaeology* 105: 181–208.

    2003. *Pompeian Households: An Analysis of the Material Culture*. Los Angeles, CA, UCLA, Costen Institute of Archaeology.

Alpert, H. 1939. *Emile Durkheim and his Sociology*. New York, Columbia University Press.

Alters, B. J. and C. E. Nelson. 2002. Perspective: teaching evolution in higher education. *Evolution* 56: 1891–1901.

An, Z. 1989. Chinese archaeology: past and present. *Archaeological Review from Cambridge* 8(1): 12–18.

Andah, B. W. 1985. *No Past! No Present! No Future! Anthropological Education and African Revolution*. (inaugural lecture). Ibadan, Department of Archaeology and Anthropology, University of Ibadan.

    1995. European encumbrances to the development of relevant theory in African archaeology. In P. J. Ucko, 1995a, pp. 96–109.

Anderson, B. 1991. *Imagined Communities: Reflections on the Origin and Spread of Nationalism*. London, Verso.

Andersson, J. G. 1934. *Children of the Yellow Earth*. London, Kegan Paul.

Andrén, A. 1998. *Between Artifacts and Texts: Historical Archaeology in Global Perspective*. New York, Plenum.

Andresen, J. M., B. F. Byrd, M. D. Elson, R. H. McGuire, R. M. Mendoza, E. Staski, and J. P. White. 1981. The deer hunters: Star Carr reconsidered. *World Archaeology* 13: 31–46.

Andriolo, K. R. 1979. Kulturkreislehre and the Austrian mind. *Man* 14: 133–44.

Anthony, D. W. 1990. Migration in archeology: the baby and the bathwater. *American Anthropologist* 92: 895–914.

    1995. Nazi and ecofeminist prehistories: ideology and empiricism in Indo-European archaeology. In P. L. Kohl and C. Fawcett, pp. 82–96.

References

Antonaccio, C. M. 1995. *An Archaeology of Ancestors: Tomb Cult and Hero Cult in Early Greece*. Lanham, MD, Rowman and Littlefield.

Appel, T. A. 1992. A scientific career in the age of character: Jeffries Wyman and natural history at Harvard. In *Science at Harvard University: Historical Perspectives*, ed. by C. A. Elliott and M. W. Rossiter, pp. 96–120. Bethlehem, PA, Lehigh University Press.

Arkell, A. J. 1961. *A History of the Sudan from the Earliest Times to 1821*. 2nd edn. London, Athlone Press.

Arnold, B. 1990. The past as propaganda: totalitarian archaeology in Nazi Germany. *Antiquity* 64: 464–78.

Arnold, B. and H. Hassmann. 1995. Archaeology in Nazi Germany: the legacy of the Faustian bargain. In P. L. Kohl and C. Fawcett, pp. 70–81.

Artsikhovsky, A. V. 1973. Archaeology. *Great Soviet Encyclopedia* 2: 245–50. New York, Macmillan.

Artsikhovskii, A. V. and A. Y. Brussov. 1958. On the task of the journal "Soviet Archaeology." *American Antiquity* 23: 349–52.

Ascher, R. 1961. Analogy in archaeological interpretation. *Southwestern Journal of Anthropology* 16: 317–25.

Ashmore, W. 2002. Decisions and dispositions: socializing spatial archaeology. *American Anthropologist* 104: 1172–83.

   2004. Social archaeologies of landscape. In L. Meskell and R. W. Preucel, pp. 255–71.

Ashmore, W. and B. Knapp. 1999. eds. *Archaeologies of Landscape: Contemporary Perspectives*. Oxford, Blackwell.

Åström, P. 1995. *Oscar Montelius, 150 Years*. Stockholm, Alquist and Wiksell.

Atwater, C. 1820. Description of the antiquities discovered in the State of Ohio and other western states. *Archaeologia Americana: Transactions and Collections of the American Antiquarian Society* 1: 105–267.

Audouze, F. and A. Leroi-Gourhan. 1981. France: a continental insularity. *World Archaeology* 13: 170–89.

Audouze, F. and N. Schlanger. 2004. eds. *Autour de l'homme: Contexte et actualité d'André Leroi-Gourhan*. Antibes, Editions APDCA.

Avdiyev, V. 1945. Achievements of Soviet archaeology. *American Journal of Archaeology* 49: 221–5.

Aveni, A. F. 1981. Archaeoastronomy. *Advances in Archaeological Method and Theory* 4: 1–77.

Bachofen, J. J. 1861. *Das Mutterrecht*. Stuttgart, Krais und Hoffman.

Bahn, P. G. 1978. The "unacceptable face" of the Western European Upper Palaeolithic. *Antiquity* 52: 183–92.

   1996. ed. *The Cambridge Illustrated History of Archaeology*. Cambridge, Cambridge University Press.

Bahrani, Z. 1998. Conjuring Mesopotamia: imaginative geography and a world past. In Meskell, pp. 159–74.

Bailey, G. 1999. Eric Higgs 1908–1976. In T. Murray 1999a, pp. 531–65.

Baines, J. 1989. Ancient Egyptian concepts and uses of the past. In *Who Needs the Past?* ed. by R. Layton, pp. 131–49. London, Unwin Hyman.

References

Baker, F. and J. Thomas. 1990. eds. *Writing the Past in the Present*. Lampeter, UK, St. David's University College.

Bakker, J. A. 2001. Childe, Van Giffen, and Dutch archaeology until 1970. In *Patina: Essays Presented to Jay Jordan Butler*, ed. by W. H. Metz, B. L. van Beek, and H. Steegstra, Groningen, Metz et al., pp. 49–74.

Baldwin, G. C. 1996. *Race Against Time: The Story of Salvage Archaeology*. New York, Putnam.

Balfour, M. D. 1979. *Stonehenge and Its Mysteries*. New York, Scribner.

Balter, M. 2005. *The Goddess and the Bull; Çatalhöyük: An Archaeological Journey to the Dawn of Civilization*. New York, Free Press.

Bamforth, D. B. 2002. Evidence and metaphor in evolutionary archaeology. *American Antiquity* 67: 435–52.

Bapty, I. and T. Yates. 1990. eds. *Archaeology After Structuralism: Post-Structuralism and the Practice of Archaeology*. London, Routledge.

Barford, P. M. 2002. Reflections on J. Lech's vision of the history of "Polish" archaeology. *Archaeologia Polona* 40: 171–84.

    2004. Polish archaeology and Marxism: just a passing phase? In L. Vishnyatsky et al., pp. 182–97.

Barkan, E. 1992. *The Retreat of Scientific Racism: Changing Concepts of Race in Britain and the United States between the World Wars*. Cambridge, Cambridge University Press.

Barkan, L. 1999. *Unearthing the Past: Archaeology and Aesthetics in the Making of Renaissance Culture*. New Haven, CT, Yale University Press.

Barker, G. 1999. ed. *Companion Encyclopedia of Archaeology*. 2 vols. London, Routledge.

Barley, M. W. 1977. ed. *European Towns: Their Archaeology and Early History*. New York, Academic Press.

Barnard, F. M. 1965. *Herder's Social and Political Thought: From Enlightenment to Nationalism*. Oxford, Oxford University Press.

    2003. *Herder on Nationality, Humanity, and History*. Montreal, McGill-Queen's University Press.

Barnes, A. S. 1939. The differences between natural and human flaking on prehistoric flint implements. *American Anthropologist* 41: 99–112.

Barnes, B. 1974. *Scientific Knowledge and Sociological Theory*. London, Routledge and Kegan Paul.

    1977. *Interests and the Growth of Knowledge*. London, Routledge and Kegan Paul.

Barnes, G. L. 1990a. The "idea of prehistory" in Japan. *Antiquity* 64: 929–40.

    1990b. The origins of bureaucratic archaeology in Japan. *Journal of the Hong Kong Archaeological Society* 12: 183–96.

    1993. *China, Korea, and Japan: The Rise of Civilization in East Asia*. London, Thames and Hudson.

Barnett, S. A. 1958. ed. *A Century of Darwin*. Cambridge, MA, Harvard University Press.

References

Barreto, C. 1998. Brazilian archaeology from a Brazilian perspective. *Antiquity* 72: 573–81.

Barrett, J. 1994. *Fragments from Antiquity: An Archaeology of Social Life in Britain, 2900–1200 B. C.* Oxford, Blackwell.

Barth, F. 1969. ed. *Ethnic Groups and Boundaries: The Social Organization of Culture Difference.* Boston, MA, Little, Brown.

Barton, C. M. and G. A. Clark. 1997. eds. *Rediscovering Darwin: Evolutionary Theory and Archeological Explanation.* Washington, DC, Archeological Papers of the American Anthropological Association 7.

Bar-Yosef, O. and A. Mazar. 1982. Israeli archaeology. *World Archaeology* 13: 310–25.

Basalla, G. 1968. ed. *The Rise of Modern Science; External or Internal Factors?* Lexington, MA, Heath.

Baté, L. F. 1977. *Arqueología y materialismo histórico.* México, DF, Ediciones de Cultura Popular.

  1978. *Sociedad, formación económicosocial y cultura.* México, DF, Ediciones de Cultura Popular.

  1998. *El proceso de investigación en arqueología.* Barcelona, Editorial Crítica.

Bauer, H. H. 1992. *Scientific Literacy and the Myth of the Scientific Method.* Urbana, University of Illinois Press.

Bayard, D. T. 1969. Science, theory, and reality in the "New Archaeology." *American Antiquity* 34: 376–84.

Bazelmans, J., J. Kolen, and H. T. Waterbolk. 1997. On the natural history of the peasant landscape: an archaeological dialogue with Tjalling Waterbolk. *Archaeological Dialogues* 4: 71–101.

Beard, M. 2001. "Pausanias in petticoats," or *The Blue Jane.* In S. E. Alcock, J. F. Cherry, and J. Elsner, pp. 224–39.

Beardsley, R. K., P. Holder, A. D. Krieger, B. J. Meggers, J. B. Rinaldo, and P. Kutsche. 1956. Functional and evolutionary implications of community patterning. Menasha, WI, Society for American Archaeology, *Memoir* 11: 129–57.

Beauchamp, W. M. 1900. *Aboriginal Occupation of New York.* Albany, Bulletin of the New York State Museum, 7 (32).

Becker, C. L. 1938. What is historiography? *American Historical Review* 44: 20–8.

Becker, M. J. 1979. Priests, peasants, and ceremonial centers: the intellectual history of a model. In *Maya Archaeology and Ethnohistory*, ed. by N. Hammond and G. R. Willey, pp. 3–20. Austin, University of Texas Press.

Beiser, F. C. 1992. *Enlightenment, Revolution, and Romanticism: The Genesis of Modern German Political Thought, 1790–1800.* Cambridge, MA, Harvard University Press.

Bell, A. S. 1981. ed. *The Scottish Antiquarian Tradition.* Edinburgh, John Donald.

References

Bell, J. A. 1994. Interpretation and testability in theories about prehistoric thinking. In A. C. Renfrew and E. B. W. Zubrow, pp. 15–21.

Bellhouse, D. R. and W. D. Finlayson. 1979. An empirical study of probability sampling designs. *Canadian Journal of Archaeology* 3: 105–23.

Bellwood, P. and A. C. Renfrew. 2003. eds. *Examining the Farming/Language Dispersal Hypothesis.* Cambridge, McDonald Institute for Archaeological Research, Monograph.

Bender, B. 1993. ed. *Landscape: Politics and Perspectives.* Oxford, Berg.

  1998. *Stonehenge: Making Space.* Oxford, Berg.

Bender, B., S. Hamilton, and C. Tilley. 1997. Leskernick: stone worlds; alternative narratives; nested landscapes. *Proceedings of the Prehistoric Society* 63: 147–78.

Benedict, R. 1934. *Patterns of Culture.* Boston, Houghton Mifflin.

Benjamin, W. 1969. *Illuminations.* New York, Schocken.

Bennett, J. W. 1943. Recent developments in the functional interpretation of archaeological data. *American Antiquity* 9: 208–19.

  1944. Middle American influences on cultures of the southeastern United States. *Acta Americana* 2: 25–50.

Bennett, W. C. 1945. Interpretations of Andean archaeology. *Transactions of the New York Academy of Sciences*, series 2, vol. 7: 95–9.

Bent, J. T. 1892. *The Ruined Cities of Mashonaland.* London, Longmans, Green.

Benvenisti, M. 2000. *Sacred Landscape: The Buried History of the Holy Land Since 1948.* Berkeley, University of California Press.

Ben-Yehuda, N. 1995. *The Masada Myth: Collective Memory and Mythmaking in Israel.* Madison, University of Wisconsin Press.

  2002. *Sacrificing Truth: Archaeology and the Myth of Masada.* Amherst, NY, Humanity Books.

Berkhofer, R. F. Jr. 1978. *The White Man's Indian: Images of the American Indian from Columbus to the Present.* New York, Knopf.

Berlinski, D. 1976. *On Systems Analysis.* Cambridge, MA, M.I.T. Press.

Bernal, I. 1980. *A History of Mexican Archaeology.* London, Thames and Hudson.

  1983. The effect of settlement pattern studies on the archaeology of Central Mexico. In *Prehistoric Settlement Patterns: Essays in Honor of Gordon R. Willey*, ed. by E. Z. Vogt and R. M. Leventhal, pp. 389–98. Albuquerque, University of New Mexico Press.

Bernal, M. 1987. *Black Athena: The Afroasiatic Roots of Classical Civilization*, vol. 1, *The Fabrication of Ancient Greece, 1785–1985.* London, Free Association Books.

  2001. *Black Athena Writes Back: Martin Bernal Responds to his Critics.* Durham, NC, Duke University Press.

Bernbeck, R. and S. Pollock. 2004. The political economy of archaeological practice and the production of heritage in the Middle East. In L. Meskell and R. W. Preucel, pp. 335–52.

References

Bernhardsson, M. T. 2005. *Reclaiming a Plundered Past: Archaeology and Nation Building in Modern Iraq.* Austin, University of Texas Press.

Bertalanffy, L. von. 1969. *General System Theory.* New York, Braziller.

Best, E. 1916. Maori and Maruiwi. *Transactions of the New Zealand Institute* 48: 435–47.

Bhaskar, R. 1978. *A Realist Theory of Science.* 2nd edn. Atlantic Highlands, NJ, Humanities Press.

Bibby, G. 1956. *The Testimony of the Spade.* New York, Knopf.

Bieder, R. E. 1975. Albert Gallatin and the survival of Enlightenment thought in nineteenth-century American anthropology. In *Toward a Science of Man: Essays in the History of Anthropology,* ed. by T. H. H. Thoresen, pp. 91–8. The Hague, Mouton.

1986. *Science Encounters the Indian, 1820–1880: The Early Years of American Ethnology.* Norman, University of Oklahoma Press.

Biehl, P. F., A. Gramsch, and A. Marciniak. 2002. eds. *Archäologien Europas: Geschichte, Methoden und Theorien/Archaeologies of Europe: History, Methods and Theories.* Münster, Waxmann.

Bietak, M. 1979. The present state of Egyptian archaeology. *Journal of Egyptian Archaeology* 65: 156–60.

Bignamini, I. 2004. ed. *Archives and Excavations: Essays on the History of Archaeological Excavations in Rome and Southern Italy from the Renaissance to the Nineteenth Century.* Archaeological Monographs of the British School at Rome 14. London, British School at Rome.

Billman, B. R. and G. M. Feinman. 1999. eds. *Settlement Pattern Studies in the Americas: Fifty Years since Viru.* Washington, DC, Smithsonian Institution Press.

Binétruy, M.-S. 1994. Itinéraires de Joseph Déchelette. Lyon, LUGD.

Binford, L. R. 1962. Archaeology as anthropology. *American Antiquity* 28: 217–25.

1965. Archaeological systematics and the study of culture process. *American Antiquity* 31: 203–10.

1967a. Smudge pits and hide smoking: the use of analogy in archaeological reasoning. *American Antiquity* 32: 1–12.

1967b. Comment. *Current Anthropology* 8: 234–5.

1968a. Some comments on historical versus processual archaeology. *Southwestern Journal of Anthropology* 24: 267–75.

1968b. Archeological perspectives. In S. R. and L. R. Binford, pp. 5–32.

1971. Mortuary practices: their study and their potential. In J. A. Brown, pp. 6–29.

1972. *An Archaeological Perspective.* New York, Seminar Press.

1977. ed. *For Theory Building in Archaeology.* New York, Academic Press.

1978. *Nunamiut Ethnoarchaeology.* New York, Academic Press.

1980. Willow smoke and dogs' tails: hunter-gatherer settlement systems and archaeological site formation. *American Antiquity* 45: 4–20.

1981. *Bones: Ancient Men and Modern Myths.* New York, Academic Press.

References

1983a. *Working at Archaeology*. New York, Academic Press.

1983b. *In Pursuit of the Past*. London, Thames and Hudson.

1984. *Faunal Remains from Klasies River Mouth*. New York, Academic Press.

1986. In pursuit of the future. In D. J. Meltzer et al., pp. 459–79.

1987a. Data, relativism and archaeological science. *Man* 22: 391–404.

1987b. Research ambiguity: frames of reference and site structure. In S. Kent, pp. 449–512.

2001. *Constructing Frames of Reference: An Analytical Method for Archaeological Theory Building Using Ethnographic and Environmental Data Sets*. Berkeley, University of California Press.

Binford, L. R. and S. R. Binford. 1966. A preliminary analysis of functional variability in the Mousterian of the Levallois facies. *American Anthropologist* 68 (2, 2): 238–95.

Binford, L. R. and J. A. Sabloff. 1982. Paradigms, systematics, and archaeology. *Journal of Anthropological Research* 38: 137–53.

Binford, L. R. and N. M. Stone. 1986. Zhoukoudian: a closer look. *Current Anthropology* 27: 453–75.

Binford, S. R. and L. R. Binford. 1968. eds. *New Perspectives in Archeology*. Chicago, IL, Aldine.

Bintliff, J. L. 1984. Structuralism and myth in Minoan studies. *Antiquity* 58: 33–8.

1991. ed. *The Annales School and Archaeology*. Leicester, UK, Leicester University Press.

1993. Why Indiana Jones is smarter than the post-processualists. *Norwegian Archaeological Review* 26: 91–100.

2004. ed. *A Companion to Archaeology*. Oxford, Blackwell.

Bird, A. 2000. *Thomas Kuhn*. Princeton, NJ, Princeton University Press.

Bird-David, N. 1990. The giving environment: another perspective on the economic system of gatherer-hunters. *Current Anthropology* 31: 189–96.

Bisson, M. S. 2000. Nineteenth century tools for twenty-first century archaeology? Why the Middle Paleolithic typology of François Bordes must be replaced. *Journal of Archaeological Method and Theory* 7: 1–48.

Black, J. L. 1986. *G.-F. Müller and the Imperial Russian Academy*. Montreal, McGill-Queen's University Press.

Black, S. L. 1990. The Carnegie Uaxactun Project and the development of Maya archaeology. *Ancient Mesoamerica* 1: 257–76.

Blakeslee, D. J. 1987. John Rowzée Peyton and the myth of the Mound Builders. *American Antiquity* 52: 784–92.

Blanton, R. E. 1978. *Monte Albán: Settlement Patterns at the Ancient Zapotec Capital*. New York, Academic Press.

Blanton, R. E., S. A. Kowalewski, G. Feinman, and J. Appel. 1981. *Ancient Mesoamerica: A Comparison of Change in Three Regions*. Cambridge, Cambridge University Press.

References

Bleed, P. 1986. Almost archaeology: early archaeological interest in Japan. In *Windows on the Japanese Past: Studies in Archaeology and Prehistory*, ed. by R. Pearson, G. L. Barnes, and K. L. Hutterer, pp. 57–67. Ann Arbor, MI, Center for Japanese Studies, University of Michigan.

1989. Foreign archaeologists in Japan: strategies for exploitation. *Archaeological Review from Cambridge* 8(1): 19–26.

Bloch, M. 1985. *Marxism and Anthropology*. Oxford, Oxford University Press.

Boardman, J. 2002. *The Archaeology of Nostalgia: How the Greeks Re-created their Mythical Past*. London, Thames and Hudson.

Boas, F. 1887. Museums of ethnology and their classification. *Science* 9: 587–9.

1940. *Race, Language and Culture*. New York, Macmillan.

Boas, F. et al. 1909. eds. *Putnam Anniversary Volume: Anthropological Essays Presented to Frederic W. Putnam in Honor of his 70th Birthday*. New York, Stechert.

Boas, G. 1948. *Essays on Primitivism and Related Ideas in the Middle Ages*. Baltimore, MD, Johns Hopkins Press.

Bodnar, E. W. 1960. *Cyriacus of Ancona and Athens*. Bruxelles, Latomus.

Böhner, K. 1981. Ludwig Lindenschmit and the Three Age system. In G. Daniel, 1981b, pp. 120–6.

Boivin, N. and D. Q. Fuller. 2002. Looking for post-processual theory in South Asian archaeology. In S. Settar and R. Korisettar, pp. 191–215.

Bond, G. C. and A. Gillam. 1994. eds. *Social Construction of the Past: Representation as Power*. London, Routledge.

Bonyhady, T. and T. Griffiths. 1996. eds. *Prehistory to Politics: John Mulvaney, The Humanities and the Public Intellectual*. Melbourne, Melbourne University Press.

Boone, J. L. and E. A. Smith. 1998. Is it evolution yet? A critique of evolutionary archaeology. *Current Anthropology* 39: S141–S173.

Bordes, F. H. 1953. Essai de classification des industries "moustériennes." *Bulletin de la Société Préhistorique Française* 50: 457–66.

1972. *A Tale of Two Caves*. New York, Harper and Row.

Boriskovsky, P. J. 1965. A propos des récents progrès des études paléolithiques en U.R.S.S. *L'Anthropologie* 69: 5–30.

Borrero, L. A. 1992. Pristine archaeologists and the settlement of southern South America. *Antiquity* 66: 768–70.

Boserup, E. 1965. *The Conditions of Agricultural Growth*. London, Allen and Unwin.

Boule, M. 1905. L'origine des éoliths. *L'Anthropologie* 16: 257–67.

Bourdieu, P. 1977. *Outline of a Theory of Practice*. Cambridge, Cambridge University Press.

1980. *Questions de sociologie*. Paris, Les Editions de Minuit.

Bowden, M. 1991. *Pitt Rivers: The Life and Archaeological Work of Lieutenant-General Augustus Henry Lane Fox Pitt Rivers*. Cambridge, Cambridge University Press.

References

Bowler, P. J. 1989. *The Invention of Progress: The Victorians and the Past.* Oxford, Blackwell.

1992. From "savage" to "primitive": Victorian evolutionism and the interpretation of marginalized peoples. *Antiquity* 66: 721–9.

Bowman, S. 1990. *Radiocarbon Dating.* Berkeley, University of California Press.

Boyd, R. and P. J. Richerson. 1985. *Culture and the Evolutionary Process.* Chicago, IL, University of Chicago Press.

Boyer, P. 1994. *The Naturalness of Religious Ideas: A Cognitive Theory of Religion.* Berkeley, University of California Press.

1996. What makes anthropomorphism natural: intuitive ontology and cultural representations. *Journal of the Royal Anthropological Institute* 2: 83–97.

Boyle, D. 1904. Who made the effigy stone pipes. *Archaeological Report for Ontario, 1903*, pp. 27–35, 48–56.

Bradley, J. W. 1987. *Evolution of the Onondaga Iroquois: Accommodating Change, 1500–1655.* Syracuse, NY, Syracuse University Press.

Bradley, R. 1983. Archaeology, evolution and the public good: the intellectual development of General Pitt Rivers. *Archaeological Journal* 140: 1–9.

1984. *The Social Foundations of Prehistoric Britain.* London, Longman.

1993. *Altering the Earth: The Origins of Monuments in Continental Europe.* Edinburgh, Society of Antiquaries of Scotland, Monograph Series 8.

1998. *The Significance of Monuments: On the Shaping of Human Experience in Neolithic and Bronze Age Europe.* London, Routledge.

2000. *An Archaeology of Natural Places.* London, Routledge.

2002. *The Past in Prehistoric Societies.* London, Routledge.

2003. The translation of time. In R. M. Van Dyke and S. E. Alcock, pp. 221–7.

Braidwood, R. J. 1974. The Iraq Jarmo Project. In G. R. Willey, 1974a, pp. 59–83.

1981. Archaeological retrospect 2. *Antiquity* 55: 19–26.

Braithwaite, M. 1984. Ritual and prestige in the prehistory of Wessex c. 2,200–1,400 BC: a new dimension to the archaeological evidence. In D. Miller and C. Tilley, pp. 93–110.

Brasser, T. J. C. 1971. Group identification along a moving frontier. *Verhandlungen des XXXVIII Internationalen Amerikanistenkongresses* (Munich) 2: 261–5.

Braudel, F. 1972. *The Mediterranean and the Mediterranean World in the Age of Philip II.* 2 vols. London, Fontana.

Braun, D. P. 1983. Pots as tools. In J. A. Moore and A. S. Keene, pp. 107–34.

Bray, T. L. and T. W. Killion. 1994. eds. *Reckoning With the Dead: The Larsen Bay Repatriation and the Smithsonian Institution.* Washington, DC, Smithsonian Institution Press.

References

Breasted, J. H. 1912. *Development of Religion and Thought in Ancient Egypt.* New York, Scribner.

Brodie, N., J. Doole, and C. Renfrew. 2001. eds. *Trade in Illicit Antiquities: The Destruction of the World's Archaeological Heritage.* Cambridge, McDonald Institute for Archaeological Research.

Brodrick, A. H. 1963. *Father of Prehistory: The Abbé Henri Breuil, His Life and Times.* New York, Morrow.

Bronowski, J. 1971. Symposium on technology and social criticism: Introduction – technology and culture in evolution. *Philosophy of the Social Sciences* 1: 195–206.

Bronson, B. 1972. Farm labor and the evolution of food production. In B. Spooner, pp. 190–218.

Brose, D. S. 1973. The northeastern United States. In J. E. Fitting, pp. 84–115.

Brothwell, D. R. and E. S. Higgs. 1963. eds. *Science in Archaeology.* London, Thames and Hudson.

Broughton, J. M. and J. F. O'Connell. 1999. On evolutionary ecology, selectionist archaeology, and behavioral archaeology. *American Antiquity* 64: 153–65.

Browman, D. L. 2002. The Peabody Museum, Frederic W. Putnam, and the rise of US anthropology, 1866–1903. *American Anthropologist* 104: 508–19.

Browman, D. L. and D. R. Givens. 1996. Stratigraphic excavation: the first "new archaeology". *American Anthropologist* 98: 80–95.

Browman, D. L. and S. Williams. 2002. eds. *New Perspectives on the Origins of Americanist Archaeology.* Tuscaloosa, University of Alabama Press.

Brown, D. E. 1988. *Hierarchy, History, and Human Nature.* Tucson, University of Arizona Press.

Brown, I. W. 1993. William Bartram and the direct historical approach. In *Archaeology of Eastern North America: Papers in Honor of Stephen Williams,* pp. 277–82. Jackson, Mississippi Department of Archives and History, Archaeological Report 25.

Brown, J. A. 1971. ed. *Approaches to the Social Dimensions of Mortuary Practices.* Washington, DC, Society for American Archaeology, Memoir no. 25.

Brown, J. A. and S. Struever. 1973. The organization of archaeological research: an Illinois example. In C. L. Redman, pp. 261–80.

Brown, K. S. 1994. Seeing stars: character and identity in the landscapes of modern Macedonia. *Antiquity* 68: 784–96.

Brown, S. 2001. Iran. In T. Murray, 2001a, pp. 674–82.

Brück, J. 2005. Experiencing the past? The development of a phenomenological archaeology in British prehistory. *Archaeological Dialogues* 12: 45–72.

Bruford, W. H. 1975. *The German Tradition of Self-Cultivation.* Cambridge, Cambridge University Press.

Brunhouse, R. L. 1973. *In Search of the Maya: The First Archaeologists.* Albuquerque, University of New Mexico Press.

References

1975. *Sylvanus G. Morley and the World of the Ancient Mayas*. Norman: University of Oklahoma Press.

Bruwer, A. J. 1965. *Zimbabwe, Rhodesia's Ancient Greatness*. Johannesburg, Keartland.

Bryson, G. 1945. *Man and Society: The Scottish Inquiry of the Eighteenth Century*. Princeton, NJ, Princeton University Press.

Buckley, W. F. 1968. ed. *Modern Systems Research for the Behavioral Scientist: A Sourcebook*. Chicago, IL, Aldine.

Bulkin, V. A., L. S. Klejn, and G. S. Lebedev. 1982. Attainments and problems of Soviet archaeology. *World Archaeology* 13: 272–95.

Bulleid, A. H. and H. St. George Gray. 1911, 1917. *The Glastonbury Lake Village: A Full Description of the Excavations and the Relics Discovered, 1892–1907*. 2 vols. Glastonbury, UK, Glastonbury Antiquarian Society.

Bunge, M. 1979. *A World of Systems*. Dordrecht, D. Reidel.

1996. *Finding Philosophy in Social Science*. New Haven, CT, Yale University Press.

1997. Mechanism and explanation. *Philosophy of the Social Sciences* 27: 410–65.

2003. *Emergence and Convergence: Qualitative Novelty and the Unity of Knowledge*. Toronto, University of Toronto Press.

Burger, R. L. 1989. An overview of Peruvian archaeology (1976–1986). *Annual Review of Anthropology* 18: 37–69.

Burkitt, M. C. 1921. *Prehistory: A Study of Early Cultures in Europe and the Mediterranean Basin*. Cambridge, Cambridge University Press.

1928. *South Africa's Past in Stone and Paint*. Cambridge, Cambridge University Press.

Burl, A. and N. Mortimer. 2005. eds. *Stukeley's "Stonehenge": An Unpublished Manuscript, 1721–1724*. New Haven, CT, Yale University Press.

Burling, R. 1962. Maximization theories and the study of economic anthropology. *American Anthropologist* 64: 802–21.

Burmeister, S. 2000. Archaeology and migration. *Current Anthropology* 41: 539–67.

Burrow, J. W. 1966. *Evolution and Society: A Study in Victorian Social Theory*. Cambridge, Cambridge University Press.

Butterfield, H. 1981. *The Origins of History*. New York, Basic Books.

Butterworth, B. 1999. *What Counts: How Every Brain is Hardwired for Math*. New York, Free Press.

Butzer, K. W. 1976. *Early Hydraulic Civilization in Egypt*. Chicago, IL, University of Chicago Press.

Byers, A. M. 1999. Intentionality, symbolic pragmatics, and material culture: revisiting Binford's view of the Old Copper Complex. *American Antiquity* 64: 265–87.

2004. *The Ohio Hopewell Episode: Paradigm Lost and Paradigm Gained*. Akron, OH, The University of Akron Press.

Byrne, D. 1993. The Past of Others: Archaeological Heritage Management in Thailand and Australia. Ph.D. diss., Canberra, Department of Anthropology, Australian National University.

Cabrero, G., M. T. 1993. ed. *II Coloquio Pedro Bosh-Gimpera*. México, DF, Universidad Nacional Autónoma de México, Instituto de Investigaciones Anthropológicas.

Calder, W. M. and J. Cobet. 1990. *Heinrich Schliemann nach Hundert Jahren*. Frankfurt, Klostermann.

Caldwell, J. R. 1958. *Trend and Tradition in the Prehistory of the Eastern United States*. Menasha, WI, American Anthropological Association, Memoir no. 88.

1959. The new American archeology. *Science* 129: 303–7.

1964. Interaction spheres in prehistory. In *Hopewellian Studies*, ed. by J. R. Caldwell and R. L. Hall, pp. 133–43. Springfield, Illinois State Museum Scientific Papers no. 12.

Cancian, F. 1966. Maximization as norm, strategy, and theory: a comment on programmatic statements in economic anthropology. *American Anthropologist* 68: 465–70.

Cannon, A. 1989. The historical dimension in mortuary expressions of status and sentiment. *Current Anthropology* 30: 437–58.

Cannon, G. 1990. *The Life and Mind of Oriental Jones: Sir William Jones, the Father of Modern Linguistics*. Cambridge, Cambridge University Press.

Carr, E. H. 1967. *What is History?* New York, Vintage.

Carrasco, D. 1982. *Quetzalcoatl and the Irony of Empire*. Chicago, IL, University of Chicago Press.

Carrithers, M. 1992. *Why Humans Have Cultures: Explaining Anthropology and Social Diversity*. Oxford, Oxford University Press.

Carrott, R. G. 1978. *The Egyptian Revival: Its Sources, Monuments, and Meaning, 1808–1858*. Berkeley, University of California Press.

Carson, R. L. 1962. *Silent Spring*. Boston, Houghton Mifflin.

Casson, S. 1921. The Dorian invasions reviewed in the light of new evidence. *Antiquarian Journal* 1: 198–224.

1939. *The Discovery of Man*. London, Hamish Hamilton.

Caton Thompson, G. 1931. *The Zimbabwe Culture*. Oxford, Oxford University Press.

1983. *Mixed Memoirs*. Gateshead, UK, Paradigm Press.

Cauvin, J. 2000. *The Birth of the Gods and the Origins of Agriculture*. Cambridge, Cambridge University Press.

Cazeau, C. and S. Scott. 1979. *Explaining the Unknown: Great Mysteries Reexamined*. New York, Da Capo Press.

Celenko, T. 1996. *Egypt in Africa*. Indianapolis, IN, Indianapolis Museum of Art.

Ceram, C. W. 1951. *Gods, Graves, and Scholars: The Study of Archaeology*. New York, Knopf.

Césaire, A. 1955. *Discourse on Colonialism*. New York, Monthly Review Press.

Chakrabarti, D. K. 1981. Indian archaeology: the first phase, 1784–1861. In G. Daniel, 1981b, pp. 169–85.

1982. The development of archaeology in the Indian subcontinent. *World Archaeology* 13: 326–44.

1988. *A History of Indian Archaeology: From the Beginning to 1947.* New Delhi, Munshiram Manoharlal.

1997. *Colonial Indology: Sociopolitics of the Ancient Indian Past.* New Delhi, Munshiram Manoharlal.

2001. South Asia. In T. Murray, 2001a, pp. 1183–94.

2003. *Archaeology in the Third World: A History of Indian Archaeology since 1947.* New Delhi, D. K. Printworld.

Chamberlin, R. 1983. *Loot! The Heritage of Plunder.* London, Thames and Hudson.

Chamberlin, T. C. 1890. The method of multiple working hypotheses. *Science* 15(366): 92–6. Reprinted in *Science* 148(1965): 745–59.

Chambers, R. 1844. *Vestiges of the Natural History of Creation.* London, John Churchill.

Champion, T. 1991. Theoretical archaeology in Britain. In I. Hodder, 1991a, pp. 129–60.

1996. Three nations or one? Britain and the national use of the past. In M. Díaz-Andreu and T. Champion, 1996a, pp. 119–45.

Chanaiwa, D. 1973. *The Zimbabwe Controversy: A Case of Colonial Historiography.* Syracuse, NY, Syracuse University, Program of East African Studies.

Chang, K. C. 1963. *The Archaeology of Ancient China.* New Haven, CT, Yale University Press.

1981. Archaeology and Chinese historiography. *World Archaeology* 13: 156–69.

1986. *The Archaeology of Ancient China.* 4th ed. New Haven, CT, Yale University Press.

2002. Reflections on Chinese archaeology in the second half of the twentieth century. *Journal of East Asian Archaeology* 3: 5–13.

Chapman, J. 1998. The impact of modern invasions and migrations on archaeological explanation: a biographical sketch of Marija Gimbutas. In M. Díaz-Andreu and M. L. S. Sørensen, pp. 295–314.

Chapman, R. 1979. "Analytical Archaeology" and after – Introduction. In D. L. Clarke, pp. 109–43.

2003. *Archaeologies of Complexity.* London, Routledge.

Chapman, W. R. 1984. Pitt Rivers and his collection, 1874–1883: the chronicle of a gift horse. In *The General's Gift – A Celebration of the Pitt Rivers Museum Centenary,* ed. by B. A. L. Cranstone and S. Seidenberg. Journal of the Anthropological Society of Oxford, Occasional Paper 3: 6–25.

1985. Arranging ethnology: A. H. L. F. Pitt Rivers and the typological tradition. G. W. Stocking, Jr, pp. 15–48.

1989. The organizational context in the history of archaeology: Pitt Rivers and other British archaeologists in the 1860s. *Antiquaries Journal* 69: 23–42.

Chard, C. S. 1961. New developments in Siberian archaeology. *Asian Perspectives* 5: 118–26.

1963. Soviet scholarship on the prehistory of Asiatic Russia. *Slavic Review* 22: 538–46.

1969. Archaeology in the Soviet Union. *Science* 163: 774–9.

Chazan, M. 1995. Concepts of time and the development of Palaeolithic chronology. *American Anthropologist* 97: 457–67.

Chen, C. 1989. Chinese archaeology and the West. *Archaeological Review from Cambridge* 8(1): 27–35.

Chêng, T.-K. 1963. *Archaeology in China*, vol. 3, *Chou China*. Cambridge, Heffer.

Chernetsov, V. N. and W. Moszyńska. 1974. *Prehistory of Western Siberia*. Montreal, McGill-Queen's University Press.

Chernykh, E. N. 1995. Postscript: Russian archaeology after the collapse of the USSR – infrastructural crisis and the resurgence of old and new nationalisms. In P. L. Kohl and C. Fawcett, pp. 139–48.

Chiappelli, F. 1976. *First Images of America: The Impact of the New World on the Old*. Berkeley and Los Angeles, University of California Press.

Childe, V. G. 1925a. *The Dawn of European Civilization*. London, Kegan Paul.

1925b. National art in the Stone Age. *Nature* 116: 195–7.

1926. *The Aryans: A Study of Indo-European Origins*. London, Kegan Paul.

1928. *The Most Ancient East: The Oriental Prelude to European Prehistory*. London, Kegan Paul.

1929. *The Danube in Prehistory*. Oxford, Oxford University Press.

1930. *The Bronze Age*. Cambridge, Cambridge University Press.

1931. *Skara Brae: A Pictish Village in Orkney*. London, Kegan Paul.

1932. Chronology of prehistoric Europe: a review. *Antiquity* 6: 206–12.

1933a. Is prehistory practical? *Antiquity* 7: 410–18.

1933b. Races, peoples and cultures in prehistoric Europe. *History* 18: 193–203.

1934. *New Light on the Most Ancient East: The Oriental Prelude to European Prehistory*. London, Kegan Paul.

1935a. *The Prehistory of Scotland*. London, Kegan Paul.

1935b. Changing methods and aims in prehistory. *Proceedings of the Prehistoric Society* 1: 1–15.

1936. *Man Makes Himself*. London, Watts (pages cited from 4th edn, 1965).

1939. *The Dawn of European Civilization*. 3rd edn. London, Kegan Paul.

1940a. *Prehistoric Communities of the British Isles*. London, Chambers.

1940b. Archaeology in the U.S.S.R. *Nature* 145: 110–11.

References

1942a. *What Happened in History.* Harmondsworth, UK, Penguin (pages cited from 1st American edn, 1946).

1942b. Prehistory in the U.S.S.R. I. Palaeolithic and Mesolithic, A: Caucasus and Crimea. *Man* 42: 98–100.

1942c. Prehistory in the U.S.S.R. I. Palaeolithic and Mesolithic, B.: The Russian Plain. *Man* 42: 100–3.

1942d. Prehistory in the U.S.S.R. II. The Copper Age in South Russia. *Man* 42: 130–6.

1942e. The significance of Soviet archaeology. *Labour Monthly* 24: 341–3.

1942f. The chambered cairns of Rousay. *Antiquaries Journal* 22: 139–42.

1943. Archaeology in the U.S.S.R. The forest zone. *Man* 43: 4–9.

1944a. *Progress and Archaeology.* London, Watts.

1944b. The future of archaeology. *Man* 44: 18–19.

1945a. Directional changes in funerary practices during 50,000 years. *Man* 45: 13–19.

1945b. Archaeology and anthropology [in the USSR]. *Nature* 156: 224–5.

1946a. *Scotland before the Scots.* London, Methuen.

1946b. Archaeology and anthropology. *Southwestern Journal of Anthropology* 2: 243–51.

1947. *History.* London, Cobbett.

1949. *Social Worlds of Knowledge.* London, Oxford University Press.

1950a. *Prehistoric Migrations in Europe.* Oslo, Aschehaug.

1950b. Cave man's buildings. *Antiquity* 24: 4–11.

1951. *Social Evolution.* New York, Schuman.

1952. Archaeological organization in the USSR. *Anglo-Soviet Journal* 13(3): 23–6.

1953. The constitution of archaeology as a science. In *Science, Medicine and History,* ed. by E. A. Underwood, pp. 3–15. Oxford, Oxford University Press.

1954. Prehistory. In *The European Inheritance,* ed. by E. Barker, G. Clark, and P. Vaucher, pp. 3–155. Oxford, Oxford University Press.

1955. The significance of lake dwellings in the history of prehistory. *Sibrium* 2(2): 87–91.

1956a. *Piecing Together the Past: The Interpretation of Archaeological Data.* London, Routledge & Kegan Paul.

1956b. *Society and Knowledge: The Growth of Human Traditions.* New York, Harper.

1958a. *The Prehistory of European Society.* Harmondsworth, UK, Penguin.

1958b. Retrospect. *Antiquity* 32: 69–74.

1958c. Valediction. *Bulletin of the Institute of Archaeology.* University of London 1: 1–8.

Childe, V. G. and M. C. Burkitt. 1932. A chronological table of prehistory. *Antiquity* 6: 185–205.

Chilton, E. S. 1999. ed. *Material Meanings: Critical Approaches to the Interpretation of Material Culture.* Salt Lake City, University of Utah Press.

References

Chinchilla Mazariegos, O. 1998. Archaeology and nationalism in Guatemala at the time of independence. *Antiquity* 72: 376–86.

Chippindale, C. 1983. *Stonehenge Complete*. London, Thames and Hudson.

  1993. Ambition, deference, discrepancy, consumption: the intellectual background to a post-processual archaeology. In N. Yoffee and A. Sherratt, pp. 27–36.

Chorley, R. J., A. J. Dunn, and R. P. Beckinsale. 1964. *The History of the Study of Landforms or the Development of Geomorphology*, vol. 1, *Geomorphology before Davis*. London, Methuen.

Chorley, R. J. and P. Haggett. 1967. eds. *Models in Geography*. London, Methuen.

Choy, M. 1960. Le Revolución Neolítica en los orígenes de la civilización Americana. In R. Matos Mendieta, *Antiguo Peru, espacio y tiempo*, pp. 149–97. Lima, Librería Juan Mejía Baca.

Chrisomalis, S. and B. G. Trigger. 2004. Reconstructing prehistoric ethnicity: problems and possibilities. In *A Passion for the Past: Papers in Honour of James F. Pendergast*, ed. by J. V. Wright and J.-L. Pilon, pp. 419–33. Gatineau, Quebec, Canadian Museum of Civilization, Mercury Series, Archaeological Paper 164.

Christenson, A. L. 1985. The identification and study of Indian shell middens in eastern North America: 1643–1861. *North American Archaeologist* 6: 227–44.

  1989a. ed. *Tracing Archaeology's Past: The Historiography of Archaeology*. Carbondale, Southern Illinois University Press.

  1989b. The past is still alive: the immediacy problem and writing the history of archaeology. In A. L. Christenson, 1989a, pp. 162–68.

Claassen, C. 1994. ed. *Women in Archaeology*. Philadelphia, University of Pennsylvania Press.

Clark, G. A. 2003. American archaeology's uncertain future. In S. D. Gillespie and D. L. Nichols, 2003, pp. 51–67.

Clark, J. G. D. (Grahame). 1932. *The Mesolithic Age in Britain*. Cambridge, Cambridge University Press.

  1936. Russian archaeology: the other side of the picture. *Proceedings of the Prehistoric Society* 2: 248–9.

  1939. *Archaeology and Society*. London, Methuen.

  1940. *Prehistoric England*. London, Batsford.

  1942. Bees in antiquity. *Antiquity* 16: 208–15.

  1945. Man and nature in prehistory, with special reference to Neolithic settlement in northern Europe. *Conference on the Problems and Prospects of European Archaeology*, pp. 20–28. London, Institute of Archaeology, Occasional Paper 6.

  1952. *Prehistoric Europe: The Economic Basis*. London, Methuen.

  1953. The economic approach to prehistory: Albert Reckitt Archaeological Lecture, 1953. *Proceedings of the British Academy* 39: 215–38.

  1954. *Excavations at Star Carr*. Cambridge, Cambridge University Press.

  1957. *Archaeology and Society*. 3rd edn. London, Methuen.

1961. *World Prehistory: An Outline.* Cambridge, Cambridge University Press.

1966. The invasion hypothesis in British archaeology. *Antiquity* 40: 172–89.

1969. *World Prehistory: A New Outline.* Cambridge, Cambridge University Press.

1972. *Star Carr: A Case Study in Bioarchaeology.* Reading, MA, Addison-Wesley Modular Publications, McCaleb Module no. 10.

1974. Prehistory Europe: the economic basis. In Willey, 1974a, pp. 31–57.

1975. *The Earlier Stone Age Settlement of Scandinavia.* Cambridge, Cambridge University Press.

1976. Prehistory since Childe. *Bulletin of the Institute of Archaeology, University of London* 13: 1–21.

1977. *World Prehistory in New Perspective.* Cambridge, Cambridge University Press.

1989a. *Prehistory at Cambridge and Beyond.* Cambridge, Cambridge University Press.

1989b. *Economic Prehistory: Papers on Archaeology.* Cambridge, Cambridge University Press.

1999. Dorothy Garrod 1892–1968. In T. Murray, 1999a, pp. 401–12.

Clark, K. M. 1928. *The Gothic Revival: An Essay in the History of Taste.* London, Constable. 3rd edn. 1962. London, Murray.

Clark, L. K. 1961. *Pioneers of Prehistory in England.* London, Sheed and Ward.

Clarke, D. L. 1968. *Analytical Archaeology.* London, Methuen.

1970. *Beaker Pottery of Great Britain and Ireland.* 2 vols. Cambridge, Cambridge University Press.

1972a. ed. *Models in Archaeology.* London, Methuen.

1972b. A provisional model of an Iron Age society and its settlement system. In D. L. Clarke, 1972a, pp. 801–69.

1973. Archaeology: the loss of innocence. *Antiquity* 47: 6–18.

1977a. ed. *Spatial Archaeology.* London, Academic Press.

1977b. Spatial information in archaeology. In D. L. Clarke, 1977a, pp. 1–32.

1979. *Analytical Archaeologist.* New York, Academic Press.

Cleere, H. 1984. ed. *Approaches to Archaeological Heritage.* Cambridge, Cambridge University Press.

1989. ed. *Archaeological Heritage Management in the Modern World.* London, Unwin Hyman.

1993. ed. Central European archaeology in transition. *Antiquity* 67: 121–56.

Clermont, N. and P. E. L. Smith. 1990. Prehistoric, prehistory, prehistorian . . . who invented the terms? *Antiquity* 64: 97–102.

Clifford, J. 1988. *The Predicament of Culture: Twentieth-Century Ethnography, Literature, and Art.* Cambridge, MA, Harvard University Press.

Coe, M. D. 1992. *Breaking the Maya Code.* London, Thames and Hudson.

Cohen, C. 1999. Abbé Henri Breuil 1877–1961. In T. Murray, 1999a, pp. 301–12.

References

Cohen, M. N. 1977. *The Food Crisis in Prehistory*. New Haven, CT, Yale University Press.

Cohen, M. N. and G. J. Armelagos. 1984. eds. *Paleopathology at the Origins of Agriculture*. New York, Academic Press.

Cohen, S. F. 1973. *Bukharin and the Bolshevik Revolution: A Political Biography*. New York, Knopf.

Cole, F.-C. and T. Deuel. 1937. *Rediscovering Illinois*. Chicago, IL, University of Chicago Press.

Cole, J. R. 1980. Cult archaeology and unscientific method and theory. *Advances in Archaeological Method and Theory* 3: 1–33.

Coles, J. 1979. *Experimental Archaeology*. London, Academic Press.

Coles, J., A. Goodall, and A. Minnitt. 1992. *Arthur Bulleid and the Glastonbury Lake Village, 1892–1992*. Taunton, UK, Somerset Levels Project, Somerset County Council Museums Service.

Collingwood, R. G. 1930. *The Archaeology of Roman Britain*. London, Methuen.

  1939. *An Autobiography*. Oxford, Oxford University Press.

  1946. *The Idea of History*. Oxford, Oxford University Press.

Collis, J. 1996. Celts and politics. In P. Graves-Brown et al., pp. 167–78.

Colton, H. S. 1932. *A Survey of Prehistoric Sites in the Region of Flagstaff, Arizona*. Washington, DC, Smithsonian Institution, Bureau of American Ethnology, Bulletin 104.

Colton, H. S. and L. L. Hargrave. 1937. *Handbook of Northern Arizona Pottery Wares*. Flagstaff, Museum of Northern Arizona, Bulletin no. 11.

Combier, J. 1959. Recherches sur l'âge de la Pierre en U.R.S.S. *L'Anthropologie* 63: 160–74.

Coningham, R. and N. Lewer. 2000. eds. Archaeology and identity in South Asia: interpretations and consequences. *Antiquity* 74: 664–712.

Conkey, M. W. and J. D. Spector. 1984. Archaeology and the study of gender. *Advances in Archaeological Method and Theory* 7: 1–38.

Conkey, M. W. and R. Tringham. 1995. Archaeology and the goddess: exploring the contours of feminist archaeology. In *Feminisms in the Academy*, ed. by D. C. Stanton and A. J. Stewart, pp. 199–247. Ann Arbor, University of Michigan Press.

Conn, S. 1998. *Museums and American Intellectual Life, 1876–1926*. Chicago, IL, University of Chicago Press.

Conroy, G. C. 1990. *Primate Evolution*. New York, Norton.

Cook, S. 1966. The obsolete "anti-market" mentality: a critique of the substantive approach to economic anthropology. *American Anthropologist* 68: 323–45.

Cooney, G. 1995. Theory and practice in Irish archaeology. In P. J. Ucko, 1995a, pp. 263–77.

  1996. Building the future on the past: archaeology and the construction of national identity in Ireland. In M. Díaz-Andreu and T. Champion, 1996a, pp. 146–63.

References

Corbey, R. and W. Roebroeks. 2001. eds. *Studying Human Origins: Disciplinary History and Epistemology*. Amsterdam, University of Amsterdam Press.

Cordell, L. S. and F. Plog. 1979. Escaping the confines of normative thought: a reevaluation of Puebloan prehistory. *American Antiquity* 44: 405–29.

Costopoulos, A. 2002. Playful agents, inexorable process: elements of a coherent theory of iteration in anthropological simulation. *Archeologia e Calcolatori* 13: 259–65.

Coudart, A. 1999. André Leroi-Gourhan 1911–1986. In T. Murray, 1999a, pp. 653–64.

Courbin, P. 1988. *What is Archaeology? An Essay on the Nature of Archaeological Research*. Chicago, IL, University of Chicago Press.

Cowgill, G. L. 1975. On causes and consequences of ancient and modern population changes. *American Anthropologist* 77: 505–25.

1977. The trouble with significance tests and what we can do about it. *American Antiquity* 42: 350–68.

2000. "Rationality" and contexts in agency theory. In M.-A. Dobres and J. E. Robb, pp. 51–60.

Coye, N. 1997. *La préhistoire en parole et en acte: Méthodes et enjeux de la pratique archéologique (1830–1950)*. Paris, L'Harmattan.

Crawford, O. G. S. 1912. The distribution of Early Bronze Age settlements in Britain. *Geographical Journal* 40: 299–303.

1921. *Man and his Past*. London, Oxford University Press.

1923. Air survey and archaeology. *Geographical Journal* 61: 342–60.

1932. The dialectical process in the history of science. *Sociological Review* 24: 165–73.

Crawford, O. G. S. and A. Keiller. 1928. *Wessex from the Air*. Oxford, Oxford University Press.

Creel, H. G. 1937. *The Birth of China: A Study of the Formative Period of Chinese Civilization*. New York, Raynal and Hitchcock.

Croissant, J. L. 2000. Narrating archaeology: a historiography and notes toward a sociology of archaeological knowledge. In S. E. Nash, 2000a, pp. 186–206.

Cronin, C. 1962. An analysis of pottery design elements indicating possible relationships between three decorated types. *Fieldiana Anthropology* 53: 105–14.

Crooke, E. M. 2000. *Politics, Archaeology, and the Creation of a National Museum in Ireland: An Expression of National Life*. Dublin, Irish Academic Press.

Crumley, C. L. 1976. Toward a locational definition of state systems of settlement. *American Anthropologist* 78: 59–73.

Culbert, T. P. 1973. ed. *The Classic Maya Collapse*. Albuquerque, University of New Mexico Press.

Cunliffe, B. 1974. *Iron Age Communities in Britain*. London, Routledge and Kegan Paul.

References

Cunnington, R. H. 1975. *From Antiquary to Archaeologist*. Princes Risborough, UK, Shire Publications.

Curl, J. S. 1982. *The Egyptian Revival: An Introductory Study of a Recurring Theme in the History of Taste*. London, George Allen and Unwin.

Cushing, F. H. 1886. A study of Pueblo pottery as illustrative of Zuñi culture growth. Washington, DC, *Bureau of American Ethnology, Annual Report* 4: 467–521.

d'Agostino, B. 1991. The Italian perspective on theoretical archaeology. In I. Hodder, 1991a, pp. 52–64.

Dall, W. H. 1877. On succession in the shell-heaps of the Aleutian Islands. Washington, DC, *United States Geological and Geographic Survey, Contributions to North American Ethnology* 1: 41–91.

Dalton, G. 1961. Economic theory and primitive society. *American Anthropologist* 63: 1–25.

Daniel, G. E. 1943. *The Three Ages: An Essay on Archaeological Method*. Cambridge, Cambridge University Press.

  1950. *A Hundred Years of Archaeology*. London, Duckworth.

  1958. Editorial. *Antiquity* 32: 65–8.

  1963a. *The Idea of Prehistory*. Cleveland, OH, World.

  1963b. The personality of Wales. In *Culture and Environment: Essays in Honour of Sir Cyril Fox*, ed. by I. Ll. Foster and L. Alcock, pp. 7–23. London, Routledge and Kegan Paul.

  1967. *The Origins and Growth of Archaeology*. Harmondsworth, UK, Penguin.

  1975. *A Hundred and Fifty Years of Archaeology*. 2nd edn. London, Duckworth.

  1976. Stone, bronze and iron. In J. V. S. Megaw, pp. 35–42.

  1981a. *A Short History of Archaeology*. London, Thames and Hudson.

  1981b. ed. *Towards a History of Archaeology*. London, Thames and Hudson.

Daniel, G. E. and C. Chippindale. 1989. eds. *The Pastmasters: Eleven Modern Pioneers of Archaeology*. London, Thames and Hudson.

Daniel, G. E. and C. Renfrew. 1988. *The Idea of Prehistory*. 2nd edn. Edinburgh, Edinburgh University Press.

Daniels, S. G. H. 1972. Research design models. In D. Clarke, 1972a, pp. 201–29.

Danilova, L. V. 1971. Controversial problems of the theory of precapitalist societies. *Soviet Anthropology and Archeology* 9: 269–328.

Dark, K. R. 1995. *Theoretical Archaeology*. Ithaca, NY, Cornell University Press.

Darnton, R. 1984. *The Great Cat Massacre and Other Episodes in French Cultural History*. New York, Basic Books.

Davidson, J. M. 1979. New Zealand. In J. D. Jennings, pp. 222–48.

Davies, G. L. 1969. *The Earth in Decay: A History of British Geomorphology, 1578–1878*. New York, American Elsevier.

Davis, R. S. 1983. Theoretical issues in contemporary Soviet Paleolithic archaeology. *Annual Review of Anthropology* 12: 403–28.

Davis, T. W. 2004. *Shifting Sands: The Rise and Fall of Biblical Archaeology*. Oxford, Oxford University Press.

Dawkins, W. B. 1874. *Cave Hunting: Researches on the Evidence of Caves Respecting the Early Inhabitants of Europe*. London, Macmillan.

Dawson, J. W. 1888. *Fossil Men and their Modern Representatives*. 3rd edn. London, Hodder and Stoughton(1st edn 1880, Montreal, Dawson Brothers).

1901. *Fifty Years of Work in Canada, Scientific and Educational*. London, Ballantyne, Hanson.

Debetz, G. F. 1961. The social life of early Paleolithic man as seen through the work of the Soviet anthropologists. In *Social Life of Early Man*, ed. by S. L. Washburn, pp. 137–49. Chicago, IL, Aldine.

Deetz, J. J. F. 1965. *The Dynamics of Stylistic Change in Arikara Ceramics*. Urbana, University of Illinois Press.

1968. Late man in North America: archeology of European Americans. In B. J. Meggers, pp. 121–30.

1977. *In Small Things Forgotten*. Garden City, NY, Anchor.

De Grummond, N. T. 1996. ed. *An Encyclopedia of the History of Classical Archaeology*. 2 vols. London, Fitzroy Dearborn.

De Laet, S. J. 1957. *Archaeology and its Problems*. New York, Macmillan.

Delâge, D. 1985. *Le pays renversé: Amérindiens et européens en Amérique du nord-est 1600–1664*. Montreal, Boréal Express.

Deloria, V., Jr. 1995. *Red Earth, White Lies: The Foremost American Indian Activist Exposes the Myth of Scientific Fact, and the Truth of his People's Oral Tradition*. New York, Scribner.

Demoule, J.-P. 1999. Ethnicity, culture and identity: French archaeologists and historians. *Antiquity* 73: 190–98.

Denbow, J. R. 1984. Prehistoric herders and foragers of the Kalahari: the evidence for 1500 years of interaction. In C. Schrire, pp. 175–93.

Dennell, R. 1990. Progressive gradualism, imperialism and academic fashion: Lower Paleolithic archaeology in the 20th century. *Antiquity* 64: 549–58.

Dennett, D. C. 2003. *Freedom Evolves*. New York, Viking.

Desmond, A. J. 1982. *Archetypes and Ancestors: Palaeontology in Victorian London 1850–1875*. London, Blond and Briggs.

1989. *The Politics of Evolution: Morphology, Medicine, and Reform in Radical London*. Chicago, IL, University of Chicago Press.

Desmond, A. J. and J. Moore. 1992. *Darwin*. Harmondsworth, UK, Penguin Books.

Desmond, L. G. and P. M. Messenger. 1988. *A Dream of Maya: Augustus and Alice LePlongeon in Nineteenth-Century Yucatan*. Albuquerque: University of New Mexico Press.

Deuel, L. 1967. *Conquistadors Without Swords: Archaeologists in the Americas*. New York, St. Martin's Press.

1973. *Flights into Yesterday: The Story of Aerial Archaeology*. Harmondsworth, UK, Penguin.

Dever, W. G. 2001a. Syro-Palestinian and biblical archaeology. In T. Murray, 2001a, pp. 1244–53.

2001b. Israel. In T. Murray, 2001a, pp. 715–21.

2003. *Who Were the Early Israelites and Where Did They Come From?* Grand Rapids, MI, William B. Eerdmans.

Devon, Earl of. 1873. Inaugural address to the annual meeting held at Exeter, 1873. *Archaeological Journal* 30: 205–10.

Diamond, J. M. 1997. *Guns, Germs, and Steel: The Fates of Human Societies*. New York, Norton.

Diamond, S. 1974. *In Search of the Primitive: A Critique of Civilization*. New Brunswick, NJ, Transaction Books.

Díaz-Andreu, M. 1993. Theory and ideology in archaeology: Spanish archaeology under the Franco régime. *Antiquity* 67: 74–82.

1996a. Constructing identities through culture: the past in the forging of Europe. In P. Graves-Brown et al., pp. 48–61.

1996b. Islamic archaeology and the origin of the Spanish nation. In M. Díaz-Andreu and T. Champion, pp. 68–89.

1997. Nationalism, ethnicity and archaeology – the archaeological study of Iberians through the looking glass. *Journal of Mediterranean Studies* 7: 155–68.

2003. Review of F. Garcia et al., *58 anys i 7 dies: Correspondència de Pere Bosch Gimpera a Lluís Pericot (1919–1974)*. *Bulletin of the History of Archaeology* 13(2): 15–17.

2004. Britain and the other: the archaeology of imperialism. In *History, Nationhood and the Question of Britain*, ed. by H. Brocklehurst and R. Phillips, pp. 227–41. New York, Palgrave Macmillan.

Díaz-Andreu, M. and T. Champion. 1996a. eds. *Nationalism and Archaeology in Europe*. London, UCL Press.

1996b. Nationalism and archaeology in Europe: an introduction. In M. Díaz-Andreu and T. Champion, 1996a, pp. 1–23.

Díaz-Andreu, M. and M. L. S. Sørensen. 1998. eds. *Excavating Women: A History of Women in European Archaeology*. London, Routledge.

Diehl, R. A. 1983. *Tula: The Toltec Capital of Ancient Mexico*. London, Thames and Hudson.

Dietler, M. 1994. "Our ancestors the Gauls": archaeology, ethnic nationalism, and the manipulation of ethnic identity in modern Europe. *American Anthropologist* 96: 584–605.

1998. A tale of three sites: the monumentalization of Celtic oppida and the politics of collective memory and identity. *World Archaeology* 30: 72–89.

Diop, C. A. 1974. *The African Origin of Civilization: Myth or Reality*. Westport, CT, Lawrence Hill.

Dixon, R. B. 1913. Some aspects of North American archeology. *American Anthropologist* 15: 549–77.

1928. *The Building of Cultures.* New York, Scribner's.

Dobres, M.-A. and J. E. Robb. 2000. eds. *Agency in Archaeology.* New York, Routledge.

Dodson, A. 1988. Egypt's first antiquarians? *Antiquity* 62: 513–7.

Dolitsky, A. B. 1985. Siberian Paleolithic archaeology: approaches and analytic methods. *Current Anthropology* 26: 361–78.

Dolukhanov, P. M. 1979. *Ecology and Economy in Neolithic Eastern Europe.* London, Duckworth.

1995. Archaeology in Russia and its impact on archaeological theory. In P. J. Ucko, 1995a, pp. 327–42.

Dommasnes, L. H. 1992. Two decades of women in prehistory and in archaeology in Norway: a review. *Norwegian Archaeological Review* 25: 1–14.

Donald, M. 1991. *Origins of the Modern Mind: Three Stages in the Evolution of Culture and Cognition.* Cambridge, MA, Harvard University Press.

Dongoske, K. E., M. Aldenderfer, and K. Doehner. 2000. *Working Together: Native Americans and Archaeologists.* Washington, DC, Society for American Archaeology.

Donnan, C. B. 1976. *Moche Art and Iconography.* Los Angeles, CA, UCLA, Latin American Center Publications.

Doran, J. E. and F. R. Hodson. 1975. *Mathematics and Computers in Archaeology.* Edinburgh, Edinburgh University Press.

Dragadze, T. 1980. The place of "ethnos" theory in Soviet anthropology. In E. Gellner, pp. 161–70.

Dray, W. 1957. *Laws and Explanation in History.* Oxford, Oxford University Press.

Drower, M. S. 1985. *Flinders Petrie: A Life in Archaeology.* London, Gollancz.

Duff, A. G. 1924. *The Life-Work of Lord Avebury (Sir John Lubbock) 1834–1913.* London, Watts.

Duff, R. S. 1950. *The Moa-Hunter Period of Maori Culture.* Wellington, Government Printer.

Duke, P. 1991. *Points in Time: Structure and Event in a Late Northern Plains Hunting Society.* Niwot, University Press of Colorado.

1995. Working through theoretical tensions in contemporary archaeology: a practical attempt from southwestern Colorado. *Journal of Archaeological Method and Theory* 2: 201–29.

Dumond, D. E. 1977. Science in archaeology: the saints go marching in. *American Antiquity* 42: 330–49.

Dumont, L. 1994. *German Ideology: From France to Germany and Back.* Chicago, IL, University of Chicago Press.

Dunnell, R. C. 1970. Seriation method and its evaluation. *American Antiquity* 35: 305–19.

1971. *Systematics in Prehistory.* New York, Free Press.

1978. Style and function: a fundamental dichotomy. *American Antiquity* 43: 192–202.

1979. Trends in current Americanist archaeology. *American Journal of Archaeology* 83: 437–49.

References

1980a. Evolutionary theory and archaeology. *Advances in Archaeological Method and Theory* 3: 35–99.

1980b. Americanist archaeology: the 1979 contribution. *American Journal of Archaeology* 84: 463–78.

1981. Americanist archaeology: the 1980 literature. *American Journal of Archaeology* 85: 429–45.

1982a. Americanist archaeological literature: 1981. *American Journal of Archaeology* 86: 509–29.

1982b. Science, social science, and common sense: the agonizing dilemma of modern archaeology. *Journal of Anthropological Research* 38: 1–25.

1983. A review of the Americanist archaeological literature for 1982. *American Journal of Archaeology* 87: 521–44.

1984. The Americanist literature for 1983: a year of contrasts and challenges. *American Journal of Archaeology* 88: 489–513.

1985. Americanist archaeology in 1984. *American Journal of Archaeology* 89: 585–611.

1986. Five decades of American archaeology. In D. J. Meltzer et al., pp. 23–49.

2001. United States of America, prehistoric archaeology. In T. Murray, 2001a, pp. 1289–1307.

Durkheim, E. 1893. *De la division du travail social.* Paris, Alcan.

1895. *Les Règles de la méthode sociologique.* Paris, Alcan.

1897. *Le Suicide.* Paris, Alcan.

1912. *Les Formes élémentaires de la vie religieuse.* Paris, Alcan.

Duvignaud, J. 1965. *Durkheim: sa vie, son oeuvre.* Paris, Presses Universitaires de France.

Dymond, D. P. 1974. *Archaeology and History: A Plea for Reconciliation.* London, Thames and Hudson.

Dyson, S. L. 1989. The role of ideology and institutions in shaping classical archaeology in the nineteenth and twentieth centuries. In A. L. Christenson, 1989a, pp. 127–35.

1993. From new to new age archaeology: archaeological theory and classical archaeology: a 1990's perspective. *American Journal of Archaeology* 97: 195–206.

1998. *Ancient Marbles to American Shores: Classical Archaeology in the United States.* Philadelphia, University of Pennsylvania Press.

2004. *Eugénie Sellers Strong: Portrait of an Archaeologist.* London, Duckworth.

Earl, G. W. 1863. On the shell-mounds of Province Wellesley, in the Malay Peninsula. *Transactions of the Ethnological Society of London* 2: 119–29.

Earle, T. K. and R. W. Preucel. 1987. Processual archaeology and the radical critique. *Current Anthropology* 28: 501–38.

Echo-Hawk, R. C. 2000. Ancient history in the New World: integrating oral traditions and the archaeological record in deep time. *American Antiquity* 65: 267–90.

References

Edwards, A. A. B. 1891. *Egypt and its Monuments: Pharaohs, Fellahs and Explorers*. New York, Harper.

Edwards, D. N. 2003. Ancient Egypt in the Sudanese Middle Nile: a case of mistaken identity. In D. O'Connor and A. Reid, pp. 137–50.

Edwards, I. E. S. 1985. *The Pyramids of Egypt*. Revised edn. Harmondsworth, UK, Penguin.

Eggan, F. R. 1966. *The American Indian*. London, Weidenfeld and Nicolson.

Eggers, H. J. 1950. Das problem der ethnischen Deuten in der Frühgeschichte. In *Ur- und Frühgeschichte als historische Wissenschaft (Festschrift E. Wahle)*, ed. by H. Kirchner, pp. 49–59. Heidelberg, Winter Universitätsverlag.

Ehret, C. and M. Posnansky. 1982. eds. *The Archaeological and Linguistic Reconstruction of African History*. Berkeley, University of California Press.

Ehrlich, P. R. 1968. *The Population Bomb*. New York, Ballantine.

Eickhoff, M. 2005. German archaeology and National Socialism: some historiographical remarks. *Archaeological Dialogues* 12: 73–90.

Eiseley, L. C. 1958. *Darwin's Century: Evolution and the Man Who Discovered It*. Garden City, NY, Doubleday.

Eisenstadt, S. N. 1986. ed. *Origins and Diversity of Axial Age Civilizations*. Albany, State University of New York Press.

Ekholm, K. and J. Friedman. 1979. "Capital" imperialism and exploitation in ancient world systems. In *Power and Propaganda: A Symposium on Ancient Empires*, ed. by M. T. Larsen, pp. 41–58. Copenhagen, Akademisk Forlag.

El Daly, O. 2004. *Egyptology: The Missing Millennium, Ancient Egypt in Medieval Arabic Writings*. London, UCL Press.

Eldredge, N. 1982. La macroévolution. *La Recherche* 13 (133): 616–26.

Eliade, M. 1954. *The Myth of the Eternal Return*. New York, Pantheon Books.

Elisseeff, D. 1986. *China: Treasures and Splendors*. Paris, Les Editions Arthaud.

Elkin, A. P. and N. W. G. Macintosh. 1974. eds. *Grafton Elliot Smith: The Man and his Work*. Sydney, Sydney University Press.

Ellegård, A. 1981. Stone Age science in Britain? *Current Anthropology* 22: 99–125.

Elliot Smith, G. see G. E. Smith.

Embree, L. 1992. ed. *Metaarchaeology: Reflections by Archaeologists and Philosophers*. Dordrecht, Kluwer.

Emery, F. E. 1969. ed. *Systems Thinking*. New York, Penguin.

Emery, W. B. 1961. *Archaic Egypt*. Harmondsworth, UK, Penguin.

Engelstad, E. 1991. Feminist theory and post-processual archaeology. In D. Walde and N. Willows, pp. 116–120.

Erciyas, D. B. 2005. Ethnic identity and archaeology in the Black Sea region of Turkey. *Antiquity* 79: 179–90.

Erman, A. 1894. *Life in Ancient Egypt*. London, Macmillan.

Evans, A. J. 1890. On a late-Celtic urn-field at Aylesford, Kent. *Archaeologia* 52: 315–88.

  1896. The "Eastern Question" in anthropology. *Proceedings of the British Association for the Advancement of Science, 1896*, 906–22.

Evans, C. 1989. Archaeology and modern times: Bersu's Woodbury 1938 and 1939. *Antiquity* 63: 436–50.

  1995. Archaeology against the state: roots of internationalism. In P. J. Ucko, 1995a, pp. 312–26.

  1998. Historicism, chronology and straw men: situating Hawkes' "ladder of inference." *Antiquity* 72: 398–404.

  1999. Christopher Hawkes 1905–1992. In T. Murray, 1999a, pp. 461–79.

Evans, Joan. 1956. *A History of the Society of Antiquaries*. London, The Society of Antiquaries.

Evans, John. 1864. *The Coins of the Ancient Britons*. London, B. Quaritch.

  1872. *The Ancient Stone Implements, Weapons, and Ornaments, of Great Britain*. London, Longmans, Green.

  1881. *The Ancient Bronze Implements, Weapons, and Ornaments, of Great Britain and Ireland*. London, Longmans, Green.

Evans, J. D., B. Cunliffe, and C. Renfrew. 1981. eds. *Antiquity and Man: Essays in Honour of Glyn Daniel*. London, Thames and Hudson.

Evans, R. T. 2004. *Romancing the Maya: Mexican Antiquity in the American Imagination, 1820–1915*. Austin, University of Texas Press.

Evans-Pritchard, E. E. 1940. *The Nuer*. Oxford, Oxford University Press.

  1949. *The Sanusi of Cyrenaica*. Oxford, Oxford University Press.

  1962. Anthropology and history. In *Essays in Social Anthropology*, by E. E. Evans-Pritchard, pp. 46–65. London, Faber.

Evasdottir, E. E. S. 2004. *Obedient Autonomy: Chinese Intellectuals and the Achievement of Orderly Life*. Vancouver, BC, UBC Press.

Eve, R. A. and F. B. Harrold. 1986. Creationism, cult archaeology, and other pseudoscientific beliefs. *Youth and Society* 17: 396–421.

Fabião, C. 1996. Archaeology and nationalism: the Portuguese case. In M. Díaz-Andreu and T. Champion, 1996a, pp. 90–107.

Fagan, B. M. 1975. *The Rape of the Nile: Tomb Robbers, Tourists, and Archaeologists in Egypt*. New York, Charles Scribner's.

  1981. Two hundred and four years of African archaeology. In J. D. Evans et al., pp. 42–51.

  2001. *Grahame Clark: An Intellectual Life of an Archaeologist*. Boulder, CO, Westview Press.

Fagette, P. 1996. *Digging for Dollars: American Archaeology and the New Deal*. Albuquerque, University of New Mexico Press.

Fairbanks, C. H. 1942. The taxonomic position of Stalling's Island, Georgia. *American Antiquity* 7: 223–31.

Fairchild, H. N. 1928. *The Noble Savage: A Study in Romantic Naturalism*. New York, Columbia University Press.

References

Falkenhausen, L. von. 1993. On the historiographical orientation of Chinese archaeology. *Antiquity* 67: 839–49.

1995. The regionalist paradigm in Chinese archaeology. In P. L. Kohl and C. Fawcett, pp. 198–217.

1999. Su Bingqi 1909–1997. In T. Murray, 1999a, pp. 591–9.

Fawcett, C. 1986. The politics of assimilation in Japanese archaeology. *Archaeological Review from Cambridge* 5(1): 43–57.

1995. Nationalism and postwar Japanese archaeology. In P. L. Kohl and C. Fawcett, 232–46.

Feder, K. L. 1984. Irrationality and popular archaeology. *American Antiquity* 49: 525–41.

1990. *Frauds, Myths, and Mysteries: Science and Pseudoscience in Archaeology.* Mountain View, CA, Mayfield Publishing.

Fedigan, L. M. 1986. The changing role of women in models of human evolution. *Annual Review of Anthropology* 15: 25–66.

Feit, H. 1978. Waswanipi Realities and Adaptations: Resource Management and Cognitive Structure. PhD dissertation, Montreal, McGill University.

Fell, B. 1976. *America B.C.: Ancient Settlers in the New World.* New York, Quadrangle.

1982. *Bronze Age America.* Boston, MA, Little, Brown.

Ferguson, A. B. 1993. *Utter Antiquity: Perceptions of Prehistory in Renaissance England.* Durham, NC, Duke University Press.

Ferguson, T. J. 2003. Anthropological archaeology conducted by tribes: traditional cultural properties and cultural affiliation. In S. D. Gillespie and D. L. Nichols, pp. 137–44.

Ferris, N. 1999. Telling tales: interpretive trends in southern Ontario Late Woodland archaeology. *Ontario Archaeology* 68: 1–62.

Fetten, F. G. 2000. Archaeology and anthropology in Germany before 1945. In H. Härke, 2000a, pp. 140–79.

Fewkes, J. W. 1896. The prehistoric culture of Tusayan. *American Anthropologist* 9: 151–73.

Feyerabend, P. K. 1975. *Against Method: Outline of an Anarchistic Theory of Knowledge.* London, NLB.

Field, H. and K. Price. 1949. Recent archaeological discoveries in the Soviet Union. *Southwestern Journal of Anthropology* 5: 17–27.

Field, H. and E. Prostov. 1937. Archaeology in the Soviet Union. *American Anthropologist* 39: 457–90.

Finkelstein, I. and N. A. Silberman. 2001. *The Bible Unearthed: Archaeology's New Vision of Ancient Israel and the Origin of its Sacred Texts.* New York, Free Press.

Finley, M. I. 1975. *The Use and Abuse of History.* London, Chatto and Windus.

Fischer, A. and K. Kristiansen. 2002. eds. *The Neolithisation of Denmark: 150 Years of Debate.* Sheffield, UK, J. R. Collis.

Fischer, G. 1967. ed. *Science and Ideology in Soviet Society.* New York, Atherton Press.

References

Fischer, U. 1987. Zur Ratio der prähistorischen Archäologie. *Germania* 65: 175–95.

Fish, S. K. and S. A. Kowalewski. 1990. eds. *The Archaeology of Regions: A Case for Full-Coverage Survey.* Washington, DC, Smithsonian Institution Press.

Fisher, A. K. 1997. Origins of the Midwestern Taxonomic Method. *Mid-Continental Journal of Archaeology* 22: 117–22.

Fitting, J. E. 1973. ed. *The Development of North American Archaeology.* Garden City, NY, Anchor Books.

Fitzpatrick, A. P. 1996. "Celtic" Iron Age Europe: the theoretical basis. In P. Graves-Brown et al., 1996, pp. 238–55.

Fitzpatrick, S. 1974. Cultural revolution in Russia 1928–32. *Journal of Contemporary History* 9: 33–51.

Flannery, K. V. 1965. The ecology of early food production in Mesopotamia. *Science* 147: 1247–55.

1966. The postglacial "readaptation" as viewed from Mesoamerica. *American Antiquity* 31: 800–5.

1967. Culture history v. culture process: a debate in American archaeology. *Scientific American* 217(2): 119–22.

1968. Archeological systems theory and early Mesoamerica. In B. J. Meggers, pp. 67–87.

1972. The cultural evolution of civilizations. *Annual Review of Ecology and Systematics* 3: 399–426.

1973. Archaeology with a capital S. In C. L. Redman, pp. 47–53.

1976. ed. *The Early Mesoamerican Village.* New York, Academic Press.

1982. The golden Marshalltown: a parable for the archaeology of the 1980s. *American Anthropologist* 84: 265–78.

1983. Archaeology and ethnology in the context of divergent evolution. In K. V. Flannery and J. Marcus, pp. 361–2.

1986. A visit to the master. In *Guilá Naquitz: Archaic Foraging and Early Agriculture in Oaxaca, Mexico,* ed. by Kent Flannery, pp. 511–19. Orlando, FL, Academic Press.

Flannery, K. V. and J. Marcus. 1983. eds. *The Cloud People: Divergent Evolution of the Zapotec and Mixtec Civilizations.* New York, Academic Press.

1993. Cognitive archaeology. *Cambridge Archaeological Journal* 3: 260–70.

Fleck, L. 1979. *Genesis and Development of a Scientific Fact.* Chicago, IL, University of Chicago Press.

Fletcher, R. 1977. Settlement studies (micro and semi-micro). In D. L. Clarke, 1977a, pp. 47–162.

1995. *The Limits of Settlement Growth: A Theoretical Outline.* Cambridge, Cambridge University Press.

1999. David Clarke 1938–1976. In T. Murray, 1999a, pp. 855–68.

Fleure, H. J. and W. E. Whitehouse. 1916. Early distribution and valleyward movement of population in south Britain. *Archaeologia Cambrensis* 16: 101–40.

References

Fleury-Ilett, B. 1996. The identity of France: archetypes in Iron Age studies. In P. Graves-Brown et al., pp. 196–208.

Flood, J. 1983. *Archaeology of the Dreamtime*. Sydney, Collins.

Ford, J. A. 1936. *Analysis of Indian Village Site Collections from Louisiana and Mississippi*. New Orleans, Louisiana State Geological Survey, Department of Conservation, Anthropological Study no. 2.

   1938. A chronological method applicable to the Southeast. *American Antiquity* 3: 260–4.

Ford, J. A. and G. R. Willey. 1941. An interpretation of the prehistory of the eastern United States. *American Anthropologist* 43: 325–63.

Ford, R. I. 1973. Archeology serving humanity. In C. L. Redman, pp. 83–93.

Forge, A. 1972. Normative factors in the settlement size of Neolithic cultivators (New Guinea). In *Man, Settlement and Urbanism*, ed. by P. J. Ucko, R. Tringham and G. W. Dimbleby, pp. 363–76. London, Duckworth.

Fossey, J. M. 1988. *Topography and Population of Ancient Boiotia*. Chicago, IL, Ares.

Foucault, M. 1970. *The Order of Things: An Archaeology of the Human Sciences*. London, Tavistock.

   1972. *The Archaeology of Knowledge*. New York, Pantheon.

Fowler, D. D. 1987. Uses of the past: archaeology in the service of the state. *American Antiquity* 52: 229–48.

   2000. *A Laboratory for Anthropology: Science and Romanticism in the American Southwest, 1846–1930*. Albuquerque, University of New Mexico Press.

Fowler, D. D. and D. R. Wilcox. 2003. eds. *Philadelphia and the Development of Americanist Archaeology*. Tuscaloosa: University of Alabama Press.

Fowles, J. 1980, 1982. ed. *John Aubrey's Monumenta Britannica*, annotated by R. Legg. Sherborne, UK, Dorset Publishing Company.

Fox, C. 1923. *The Archaeology of the Cambridge Region*. Cambridge, Cambridge University Press.

   1932. *The Personality of Britain*. Cardiff, UK, National Museum of Wales.

Fox, E. 2001. *Sacred Geography: A Tale of Murder and Archaeology in the Holy Land*. New York, Henry Holt.

Fox, L. 1956. ed. *English Historical Scholarship in the Sixteenth and Seventeenth Centuries*. London, Oxford University Press.

Francis, D. and T. Morantz. 1983. *Partners in Furs: A History of the Fur Trade in Eastern James Bay, 1600–1870*. Montreal, McGill-Queen's University Press.

Frankfort, H. 1948. *Kingship and the Gods: A Study of Ancient Near Eastern Religion as the Integration of Society and Nature*. Chicago, IL, University of Chicago Press.

Fraser, S. M. 1998. The public forum and the space between: the materiality of social strategy in the Irish Neolithic. *Proceedings of the Prehistoric Society* 64: 203–24.

2004. Metaphorical journeys: landscape, monuments, and the body in a Scottish Neolithic. *Proceedings of the Prehistoric Society* 70: 129–51.

Freidel, D. A., L. Schele, and J. Parker. 1993. *Maya Cosmos: Three Thousand Years on the Shaman's Path.* New York, William Morrow.

Frick, W. 1934. The teaching of history and prehistory in Germany. *Nature* 133: 298–9.

Fried, M. H. 1967. *The Evolution of Political Society.* New York, Random House.

1975. *The Notion of Tribe.* Menlo Park, CA, Cummings.

Friedman, J. and M. J. Rowlands. 1978a. eds. *The Evolution of Social Systems.* London, Duckworth.

Friedman, J. and M. J. Rowlands. 1978b. Notes towards an epigenetic model of the evolution of "civilization." In J. Friedman and M. J. Rowlands, 1978a, pp. 201–76.

Fritz, J. M. 1973. Relevance, archeology, and subsistence theory. In C. L. Redman, pp. 59–82.

Frumkin, G. 1962. Archaeology in Soviet Central Asia and its ideological background. *Central Asian Review* 10: 334–42.

Fuller, D. Q. and N. Boivin. 2002. Beyond description and diffusion: a history of processual theory in the archaeology of South Asia. In S. Settar and R. Korisettar, pp. 159–90.

Fuller, P. 1980. *Beyond the Crisis in Art.* London, Writers and Readers.

Funari, P. 1997. Archaeology, history, and historical archaeology in South America. *International Journal of Historical Archaeology* 1: 189–206.

1999a. Brazilian archaeology: a reappraisal. In G. G. Politis and B. Alberti, pp. 17–37.

1999b. Historical archaeology from a world perspective. In P. Funari, M. Hall, and S. Jones, pp. 37–66.

2001. Brazil. In T. Murray, 2001a, pp. 180–93.

Funari, P., M. Hall, and S. Jones. 1999. eds. *Historical Archaeology: Back from the Edge.* London, Routledge.

Furst, L. 1969. *Romanticism in Historical Perspective.* Oxford, Oxford University Press.

Galaty, M. L. and C. Watkinson. 2004. eds. *Archaeology Under Dictatorship.* New York, Kluwer.

Gallay, A. 1986. *L'Archéologie demain.* Paris, Belfond.

1989. Logicism: a French view of archaeological theory founded in computational perspective. *Antiquity* 63: 27–39.

Gamble, C. 1992. Archaeology, history and the uttermost ends of the earth – Tasmania, Tierra del Fuego and the Cape. *Antiquity* 66: 712–20.

1999. Lewis Binford b. 1929. In T. Murray, 1999a, pp. 811–34.

Gamio, M. 1916. *Forjando Patria (Pro Nacionalismo).* México, DF, Porrúa Hermanos.

Gándara, M. 1980. La vieja "Nueva Arqueología" (primera parte). *Boletín de Antropología Americana* 2: 7–45.

1981. La vieja "Nueva Arqueología" (segunda parte). *Boletín de Antropología Americana* 3: 7–70.

Gardin, J.-C. 1965. On a possible interpretation of componential analysis in archeology. *American Anthropologist* 67(5), pt. 2: 9–22.

1967. Methods for the descriptive analysis of archaeological materials. *American Antiquity* 32: 13–30.

1980. *Archaeological Constructs: An Aspect of Theoretical Archaeology.* Cambridge, Cambridge University Press.

1992. Semiotic trends in archaeology. In J.-C. Gardin and C. S. Peebles, pp. 87–104.

2004. Current progress in theoretical archaeology. In L. Vishnyatsky et al., pp. 87–99.

Gardin, J.-C. and C. S. Peebles. 1992. eds. *Representations in Archaeology.* Bloomington, Indiana University Press.

Garlake, P. S. 1973. *Great Zimbabwe.* London, Thames and Hudson.

1983. Prehistory and ideology in Zimbabwe. In *Past and Present in Zimbabwe*, ed. by J. D. Y. Peet and T. Ranger, pp. 1–19. Manchester, UK, Manchester University Press.

1984. Ken Mufuka and Great Zimbabwe. *Antiquity* 58: 121–3.

Gathercole, P. 1971. "Patterns in prehistory": an examination of the later thinking of V. Gordon Childe. *World Archaeology* 3: 225–32.

1976. Childe the "outsider." *RAIN* 17: 5–6.

1981. New Zealand prehistory before 1950. In Glyn Daniel, 1981b, pp. 159–68.

1982. Gordon Childe: man or myth? *Antiquity* 56: 195–8.

1984. A consideration of ideology. In M. Spriggs, 1984a, pp. 149–54.

Gathercole, P., T. H. Irving and G. Melleuish. 1995. eds. *Childe and Australia: Archaeology, Politics, and Ideas.* St. Lucia, University of Queensland Press.

Gathercole, P. and D. Lowenthal. 1989. eds. *The Politics of the Past.* London, Unwin Hyman.

Gayre, R. 1972. *The Origin of Zimbabwean Civilisation.* Salisbury, Southern Rhodesia, Galaxie Press.

Gazzaniga, M. S. 1992. *Nature's Mind: The Biological Roots of Thinking, Emotions, Sexuality, Language, and Intelligence.* New York, Basic Books.

1998. *The Mind's Past.* Berkeley, University of California Press.

Geary, P. 1986. Sacred commodities: the circulation of medieval relics. In *The Social Life of Things: Commodities in Cultural Perspective*, ed. by A. Appadurai, pp. 169–91. Cambridge, Cambridge University Press.

Geertz, C. 1965. The impact of the concept of culture on the concept of man. In *New Views of the Nature of Man*, ed. by J. R. Platt, pp. 93–118. Chicago, IL, University of Chicago Press.

1973. *The Interpretation of Cultures: Selected Essays.* New York, Basic Books.

Geikie, A. 1905. *The Founders of Geology.* 2nd edn. London, Macmillan.

References

Gellner, E. 1980. ed. *Soviet and Western Anthropology*. London, Duckworth.
1983. *Nations and Nationalism*. Ithaca, NY, Cornell University Press.
1985. *Relativism and the Social Sciences*. Cambridge, Cambridge University Press.

Gening, V. F. 1982. *Ocherki po Istorii Sovetskoy Arkheologii*. Kiev, Naukova Dumka.

Geras, N. 1983. Marx and Human Nature: Refutation of a Legend. London, Verso.

Gero, J. M. 1983. Gender bias in archaeology: a cross-cultural perspective. In J. M. Gero, D. M. Lacy and M. L. Blakey, pp. 51–7.

Gero, J. M. and M. W. Conkey. 1991. eds. *Engendering Archaeology: Women and Prehistory*. Oxford, Blackwell.

Gero, J. M., D. M. Lacy, and M. L. Blakey. 1983. eds. *The Socio-Politics of Archaeology*. Amherst, University of Massachusetts, Department of Anthropology, Research Report no. 23.

Gerrard, C. 2003. *Medieval Archaeology: Understanding Traditions and Contemporary Approaches*. London, Routledge.

Gibbon, G. E. 1984. *Anthropological Archaeology*. New York, Columbia University Press.
1985. Classical and anthropological archaeology: a coming rapprochement? In *Contributions to Aegean Archaeology*, ed. by N. C. Wilkie and W. D. E. Coulson, pp. 283–94. Minneapolis, University of Minnesota Press.
1989. *Explanation in Archaeology*. Oxford, Blackwell.

Giddens, A. 1984. *The Constitution of Society: Outline of the Theory of Structuration*. Berkeley, University of California Press.

Gilchrist, R. 1994. *Gender and Material Culture: The Archaeology of Religious Women*. London, Routledge.
1999. *Gender and Archaeology: Contesting the Past*. London, Routledge.

Gill, D. W. J. 1987. Metru.Menece: an Etruscan painted inscription on a mid 5th-century BC red-figure cup from Populonia. *Antiquity* 61: 82–7.

Gillespie, S. D. and D. L. Nichols. 2003. eds. *Archaeology is Anthropology*. Washington, DC, Archeological Papers of the American Anthropological Association 13.

Gillispie, C. C. 1951. *Genesis and Geology: A Study in the Relations of Scientific Thought, Natural Theology, and Social Opinion in Great Britain, 1790–1850*. Cambridge, MA, Harvard University Press.

Gilman, A. 1976. Bronze Age dynamics in southeast Spain. *Dialectical Anthropology* 1: 307–19.
1981. The development of social stratification in Bronze Age Europe. *Current Anthropology* 22: 1–23.

Gimbutas, M. 1982. *The Goddesses and Gods of Old Europe, 6500–3500 BC: Myths and Cult Images*. London, Thames and Hudson.

Givens, D. R. 1992a. *Alfred Vincent Kidder and the Development of Americanist Archaeology*. Albuquerque, University of New Mexico Press.

1992b. The role of biography in writing the history of archaeology. In J. E. Reyman, pp. 51–66.

Gjessing, G. 1968. The social responsibility of the social scientist. *Current Anthropology* 9: 397–402.

Glacken, C. J. 1967. *Traces on the Rhodian Shore: Nature and Culture in Western Thought from Ancient Times to the End of the Eighteenth Century*. Berkeley and Los Angeles, University of California Press.

Gladwin, W. and H. S. Gladwin. 1930. *A Method for the Designation of Southwestern Pottery Types*. Globe, AZ, Medallion Papers no. 7.

1934. *A Method for Designation of Cultures and their Variations*. Globe, AZ, Medallion Papers no. 15.

Glass, H. B., O. Temkin, and W. L. Straus Jr. 1959. eds. *Forerunners of Darwin, 1745–1859*. Baltimore, MD, Johns Hopkins University Press.

Glassie, H. H. 1975. *Folk Housing in Middle Virginia: A Structural Analysis of Historic Artifacts*. Knoxville, University of Tennessee Press.

Gledhill, J. 1984. The transformation of Asiatic formations: the case of late prehispanic Mesoamerica. In M. Spriggs, 1984a, pp. 135–48.

Gobineau, J.-A., comte de. 1853–5. *Essai sur l'inégalité des races humaines*. 4 vols. Paris, Didot.

Godelier, M. 1986. *The Mental and the Material: Thought, Economy and Society*. London, Verso.

Godwin, H. 1933. British Maglemose harpoon sites. *Antiquity* 7: 36–48.

Goes Neves, E. 1998. Twenty years of Amazonian archaeology in Brazil (1977–1997). *Antiquity* 72: 625–32.

Goffman, E. 1963. *Behavior in Public Places: Notes on the Social Organization of Gatherings*. New York, Free Press.

Golden, C. W. and G. Borgstede. 2004. eds. *Continuities and Changes in Maya Archaeology: Perspectives at the Millennium*. London, Routledge.

Golomshtok, E. 1933. Anthropological activities in Soviet Russia. *American Anthropologist* 35: 301–27.

Gomaà, F. 1973. *Chaemwese, Sohn Ramses' II und Hoherpriester von Memphis*. Wiesbaden, Harrassowitz.

González Marcén, P. and R. Risch. 1990. Archaeology and historical materialism: outsider's reflections on theoretical discussions in British archaeology. In F. Baker and J. Thomas, pp. 94–104.

Goodenough, E. R. 1953–68. *Jewish Symbols in the Greco-Roman Period*. 13 vols. New York, Pantheon Books.

Goodrum, M. R. 2002. The meaning of ceraunia: archaeology, natural history and the interpretation of prehistoric stone artefacts in the eighteenth century. *British Journal of the History of Science* 35: 255–69.

Goodwin, A. J. H. and C. Van Riet Lowe. 1929. *The Stone Age Cultures of South Africa*. Cape Town, Annals of the South African Museum no. 27.

Gopal, L. 1985. Foreword. In Trigger 1985c, pp. i–vi.

Gopnik, M. 1997. ed. *The Inheritance and Innateness of Grammars*. Oxford, Oxford University Press.

Gordon, R. J. 1992. *The Bushman Myth: The Making of a Namibian Underclass.* Boulder, CO, Westview Press.

Gorenstein, S. 1977. History of American archaeology. In *Perspectives on Anthropology, 1976,* ed. by A. F. C. Wallace, pp. 86–115. Washington, DC, American Anthropological Association, Special Publication 10.

Gorodzov, V. A. 1933. The typological method in archaeology. *American Anthropologist* 35: 95–102.

Gosden, C. 1994. *Social Being and Time.* Oxford, Blackwell.

  1999. *Anthropology and Archaeology: A Changing Relationship.* London, Routledge.

  2004. *Archaeology and Colonialism: Cultural Contact from 5000 BC to the Present.* Cambridge, Cambridge University Press.

Goudie, A. 1976. Geography and prehistory. *Journal of Historical Geography* 2: 197–205.

Gould, R. A. 1978a. ed. *Explorations in Ethnoarchaeology.* Albuquerque, University of New Mexico Press.

  1978b. Beyond analogy in ethnoarchaeology. In R. A. Gould, 1978a, pp. 249–93.

  1980. *Living Archaeology.* Cambridge, Cambridge University Press.

Gould, R. A. and M. B. Schiffer. 1981. eds. *Modern Material Culture: The Archaeology of Us.* New York, Academic Press.

Gould, S. J. 1980. *The Panda's Thumb: More Reflections in Natural History.* New York, Norton.

  1981. *The Mismeasure of Man.* New York, Norton.

Gould, S. J. and N. Eldredge. 1977. Punctuated equilibria: the tempo and mode of evolution reconsidered. *Paleobiology* 3: 115–51.

  1993. Punctuated equilibrium comes of age. *Nature* 366: 223–7.

Gradmann, R. 1906. Beziehung zwischen Pflanzengeographie und Siedlungsgeschichte. *Geographische Zeitschrift* 12: 305–25.

Graham, I. 2002. *Alfred Maudslay and the Maya: A Biography.* Norman, University of Oklahoma Press.

Graham, L. R. 1967. *The Soviet Academy of Sciences and the Communist Party, 1927–1932.* Princeton, NJ, Princeton University Press.

Graham-Campbell, J. and D. Kidd. 1980. *The Vikings.* London, British Museum Publications.

Gramsci, A. 1992. *Prison Notebooks.* New York, Columbia University Press.

Gran-Aymerich, E. 1998. *Naissance de l'archéologie moderne, 1798–1945.* Paris, CNRS Editions.

Grant, G. 1965. *Lament for a Nation: The Defeat of Canadian Nationalism.* Toronto, McClelland and Stewart.

Grant, M. 1916. *The Passing of the Great Race; or, the Racial Basis of European History.* New York, Scribner's.

Gräslund, B. 1974. *Relativ Datering: Om Kronologisk Metod i Nordisk Arkeologi.* Uppsala, TOR no. 16.

1976. Relative chronology: dating methods in Scandinavian archaeology. *Norwegian Archaeological Review* 9: 69–126.

1981. The background to C. J. Thomsen's Three-Age system. In G. Daniel, 1981b, pp. 45–50.

1987. *The Birth of Prehistoric Chronology*. Cambridge, Cambridge University Press.

Graves, M. W. and C. Erkelens. 1991. Who's in control? Method and theory in Hawaiian archaeology. *Asian Perspectives* 30: 1–17.

Graves-Brown, P., S. Jones, and C. Gamble. 1996. eds. *Cultural Identity and Archaeology: The Construction of European Communities*. London, Routledge.

Grayson, D. K. 1983. *The Establishment of Human Antiquity*. New York, Academic Press.

1986. Eoliths, archaeological ambiguity, and the generation of "middle range" research. In D. J. Meltzer et al., pp. 77–133.

Green, S. 1981. *Prehistorian: A Biography of V. Gordon Childe*. Bradford-on-Avon, UK, Moonraker Press.

Greene, J. C. 1959. *The Death of Adam*. Ames, Iowa State University Press.

Greene, K. 1999. V. Gordon Childe and the vocabulary of revolutionary change. *Antiquity* 73: 97–109.

Greener, L. 1966. *The Discovery of Egypt*. London, Cassell.

Greenhalgh, M. 1989. *The Survival of Roman Antiquities in the Middle Ages*. London, Duckworth.

Griffin, J. B. 1980. The Mesoamerican-southeastern U.S. connection. *Early Man* 2(3): 12–18.

Griffiths, T. 1996. *Hunters and Collectors: The Antiquarian Imagination in Australia*. Cambridge, Cambridge University Press.

Groenen, M. 1994. *Pour une histoire de la préhistoire: le Paléolithique*. Grenoble, J. Millon.

Gruber, J. W. 1965. Brixham Cave and the antiquity of man. In *Context and Meaning in Cultural Anthropology*, ed. by M. E. Spiro, pp. 373–402. New York, Free Press.

Grünert, H. 2002. Gustaf Kossinna (1858–1931), Vom Germanisten zum Prähistoriker: Ein Wissenschaftler im Kaiserreich und in der Weimarer Republik. Rahden / Westfalen, Leidorf.

Guest, E. 1883. *Origines Celticae (a Fragment)*, ed. by W. Stubbs and C. Deedes. London, Macmillan.

Guidi, A. 1987. The development of prehistoric archaeology in Italy: a short review. *Acta Archaeologica* 58: 237–47.

1988. *Storia della Paletnologia*. Rome, Editori Laterza.

1996. Nationalism without a nation: the Italian case. In M. Díaz-Andreu and T. Champion, 1996a, pp. 108–18.

Gutting, G. 1989. *Michel Foucault's Archaeology of Scientific Reason*. Cambridge, Cambridge University Press.

Haber, F. C. 1959. *The Age of the World: Moses to Darwin*. Baltimore, MD, Johns Hopkins University Press.

References

Habermas, J. 1971. *Knowledge and Human Interests*. Boston, MA, Beacon Press.

1975. *Legitimation Crisis*. Boston, MA, Beacon Press.

Habu, J. 1989. Contemporary Japanese archaeology and society. *Archaeological Review from Cambridge* 8(1): 36–45.

2004. *Ancient Jomon of Japan*. Cambridge, Cambridge University Press.

Habu, J. and C. Fawcett. 1999. Jomon archaeology and the representation of Japanese origins. *Antiquity* 73: 587–93.

Hall, A. J. 2003. *The American Empire and the Fourth World*. Montreal, McGill-Queen's University Press.

Hall, J. 1986. *Powers and Liberties: The Causes and Consequences of the Rise of the West*. Harmondsworth, UK, Penguin.

Hall, M. 1984. The burden of tribalism: the social context of southern African Iron Age studies. *American Antiquity* 49: 455–67.

Hall, R. N. 1909. *Prehistoric Rhodesia*. London, Unwin.

Hall, R. N. and W. G. Neal. 1902. *The Ancient Ruins of Rhodesia*. London, Methuen.

Halle, U. 2005. Archaeology in the Third Reich, academic scholarship and the rise of the "lunatic fringe." *Archaeological Dialogues* 12: 91–102.

Hallote, R. S. and A. H. Joffe. 2002. The politics of Israeli archaeology: between "nationalism" and "science" in the age of the second republic. *Israel Studies* 7(3): 84–116.

Hallowell, A. I. 1960. The beginnings of anthropology in America. In *Selected Papers from the American Anthropologist 1880–1920*, ed. by F. de Laguna, pp. 1–90. Evanston, IL, Row, Peterson and Company.

Hallpike, C. R. 1979. *The Foundations of Primitive Thought*. Oxford, Oxford University Press.

1986. *The Principles of Social Evolution*. Oxford, Oxford University Press.

Hamann, B. 2002. The social life of pre-sunrise things: indigenous Mesoamerican archaeology. *Current Anthropology* 43: 351–82.

Hamell, G. 1983. Trading in metaphors: the magic of beads. In *Proceedings of the 1982 Glass Trade Bead Conference*, ed. by C. F. Hayes, III, pp. 5–28. Rochester, NY, Rochester Museum and Science Center, Research Records no. 16.

Hamilakis, Y., M. Pluciennik, and S. Tarlow. 2002. eds. *Thinking through the Body: Archaeologies of Corporeality*. New York, Plenum.

Hammond, N. 1983. Lords of the jungle: a prosopography of Maya archaeology. In *Civilization in the Ancient Americas*, ed. by R. M. Leventhal and A. L. Kolata, pp. 3–32. Albuquerque, University of New Mexico Press.

Hampson, N. 1982. *The Enlightenment*. Harmondsworth, UK, Penguin.

Hanbury-Tenison, J. 1986. Hegel in prehistory. *Antiquity* 60: 108–14.

Handsman, R. G. 1981. Early capitalism and the Center Village of Canaan, Connecticut: a study of transformations and separations. *Artifacts* 9(3): 1–22.

Hanen, M. and J. Kelley. 1992. Gender and archaeological knowledge. In L. Embree, pp. 195–225.

References

Hanke, L. 1959. *Aristotle and the American Indians*. Chicago, IL, Regnery.

Harding, R. 2003. Archaeology and religious landscapes in India: a case study. *Bulletin of the History of Archaeology* 13(2): 4–8.

Härke, H. 1991. All quiet on the Western Front? Paradigms, methods and approaches in West German archaeology. In Ian Hodder, 1991a, pp. 187–222.

1995. "The Hun is a methodical chap": reflections on the German tradition of pre- and proto-history. In P. J. Ucko, 1995a, pp. 46–60.

1998. Archaeologists and migrations: a problem of attitude. *Current Anthropology* 39: 19–45.

2000a. ed. *Archaeology, Ideology and Society: The German Experience*. Frankfurt am Main, Peter Lang.

2000b. The German experience. In H. Härke, 2000a, pp. 12–39.

2000c. Social analysis of mortuary evidence in German protohistoric archaeology. *Journal of Anthropological Archaeology* 19: 369–84.

Harré, R. 1970. *The Principles of Scientific Thinking*. Chicago, IL, University of Chicago Press.

1972. *The Philosophies of Science: An Introductory Survey*. Oxford, Oxford University Press.

Harré, R. and E. H. Madden. 1975. *Causal Powers: A Theory of Natural Necessity*. Oxford, Blackwell.

Harrington, J. C. 1955. Archeology as an auxiliary science to American history. *American Anthropologist* 57: 1121–1130.

Harrington, M. R. 1924. *An Ancient Village Site of the Shinnecock Indians*. New York, Anthropological Papers of the American Museum of Natural History, no. 22, pt. 5.

Harris, D. R. 1994. ed. *The Archaeology of V. Gordon Childe: Contemporary Perspectives*. London, UCL Press.

Harris, M. 1968a. *The Rise of Anthropological Theory*. New York, Crowell.

1968b. Comments. In S. R. and L. R. Binford, 1968, pp. 359–61.

1974. *Cows, Pigs, Wars and Witches*. New York, Random House.

1977. *Cannibals and Kings: The Origins of Cultures*. New York, Random House.

1979. *Cultural Materialism: The Struggle for a Science of Culture*. New York, Random House.

1981. *America Now: The Anthropology of a Changing Culture*. New York, Simon and Schuster.

Harrison, R. J. 1980. *The Beaker Folk: Copper Age Archaeology in Western Europe*. London, Thames and Hudson.

Hart, J. P. and J. E. Terrell. 2002. eds. *Darwin and Archaeology: A Handbook of Key Concepts*. Westport, CT, Bergin and Garvey.

Harvey, D. 1989. *The Condition of Postmodernity*. Oxford, Blackwell.

Hassan, F. A. 1995. The World Archaeological Congress in India: politicizing the past. *Antiquity* 69: 874–7.

1998. Memorabilia: archaeological materiality and national identity in Egypt. In L. Meskell, pp. 200–16.

Hassmann, H. 2000. Archaeology in the "Third Reich." In H. Härke, 2000a, pp. 65–139.

Haven, S. 1856. *Archaeology of the United States*. Washington, DC, Smithsonian Contributions to Knowledge, no. 8(2).

1864. Report of the librarian. *Proceedings of the American Antiquarian Society*, April 1864: 30–52.

Haverfield, F. J. 1912. *The Romanization of Roman Britain*. 2nd edn. Oxford, Oxford University Press.

Hawkes, C. F. 1954. Archeological theory and method: some suggestions from the Old World. *American Anthropologist* 56: 155–68.

Hawkes, J. 1963. ed. *The World of the Past*. 2 vols. New York, Knopf.

1968. The proper study of mankind. *Antiquity* 42: 255–62.

1982. *Mortimer Wheeler: Adventurer in Archaeology*. London, Weidenfeld and Nicolson.

Hayden, B. 1979. ed. *Lithic Use-Wear Analysis*. New York, Academic Press.

Hayden, B. and A. Cannon. 1984. *The Structure of Material Systems: Ethnoarchaeology in the Maya Highlands*. Washington, DC, Society for American Archaeology, Paper no. 3.

Heffernan, M. J. 1994. A state scholarship: the political geography of French international science during the nineteenth century. *Transactions of the Institute of British Geographers* 19: 21–45.

Heffernan, T. F. 1988. *Wood Quay: The Clash over Dublin's Viking Past*. Austin, University of Texas Press.

Hegardt, J. 1999. Sven Nilsson. In T. Murray, 1999a, pp. 65–78.

2001. Sweden. In T. Murray, 2001a, pp. 1224–36.

Hegmon, M. 2003. Setting theoretical egos aside: issues and theory in North American archaeology. *American Antiquity* 68: 213–43.

Heizer, R. F. 1959. ed. *The Archaeologist at Work: A Source Book in Archaeological Method and Interpretation*. New York, Harper and Row.

1962a. ed. *Man's Discovery of his Past: Literary Landmarks in Archaeology*. Englewood Cliffs, NJ, Prentice-Hall.

1962b. The background of Thomsen's Three-Age system. *Technology and Culture* 3: 259–66.

Held, D. 1980. *Introduction to Critical Theory: Horkheimer to Habermas*. Berkeley, University of California Press.

Hellmich, M. 1923. *Die Besiedlung Schlesiens in vor- und frühgeschichtlicher Zeit*. Breslau, Preuss und Jünger.

Hempel, C. G. 1942. The function of general laws in history. *The Journal of Philosophy* 39: 35–48.

1962. Deductive-nomological vs. statistical explanation. In *Scientific Explanation, Space, and Time*, ed. by H. Feigl and G. Maxwell, pp. 98–169. Minneapolis, University of Minnesota Press.

1965. *Aspects of Scientific Explanation*. New York, Free Press.

1966. *Philosophy of Natural Science*. Englewood Cliffs, NJ, Prentice-Hall.

Hempel, C. G. and P. Oppenheim. 1948. Studies in the logic of explanation. *Philosophy of Science* 15: 135–75.

References

Herman, A. 2001. *How the Scots Invented the Modern World*. New York, Crown.

Herold, J. C. 1962. *Bonaparte in Egypt*. New York, Harper and Row.

Herrmann, J. 1990. *Heinrich Schliemann: Wegbereiter einer neuen Wissenschaft*. Berlin, Akademie-Verlag.

Herzfeld, M. 1992. Metapatterns: archaeology and the uses of evidential scarcity. In J.-C. Gardin and C. S. Peebles, pp. 66–86.

Hewett, E. L. 1906. *Antiquities of the Jemez Plateau, New Mexico*. Washington, DC, Bureau of American Ethnology, Bulletin no. 32.

Hides, S. 1996. The genealogy of material culture and cultural identity. In P. Graves-Brown et al., 1996, pp. 25–47.

Higgs, E. S. 1968. Archaeology – where now? *Mankind* 6: 617–20.

   1972. ed. *Papers in Economic Prehistory*. Cambridge, Cambridge University Press.

   1975. ed. *Palaeoeconomy*. Cambridge, Cambridge University Press.

Hill, J. N. 1968. Broken K Pueblo: patterns of form and function. In S. R. and L. R. Binford, pp. 103–42.

   1970. *Broken K Pueblo: Prehistoric Social Organization in the American Southwest*. Tucson, University of Arizona Press.

Hinsley, C. M., Jr. 1981. *Savages and Scientists: The Smithsonian Institution and the Development of American Anthropology 1846–1910*. Washington, DC, Smithsonian Institution Press.

   1985. From shell-heaps to stelae: early anthropology at the Peabody Museum. In G. W. Stocking, Jr, pp. 49–74.

   1999. Frederic Ward Putnam. In T. Murray, 1999a, pp. 141–54.

Hobsbawm, E. J. 1964. ed. *Karl Marx, Pre-Capitalist Economic Formations*. London, Lawrence and Wishart.

   1990. *Nations and Nationalism since 1780: Programme, Myth, Reality*. Cambridge, Cambridge University Press.

Hodder, I. 1978a. ed. *The Spatial Organisation of Culture*. London, Duckworth.

   1978b. ed. *Simulation Studies in Archaeology*. Cambridge, Cambridge University Press.

   1982a. *The Present Past: An Introduction to Anthropology for Archaeologists*. London, Batsford.

   1982b. *Symbols in Action: Ethnoarchaeological Studies of Material Culture*. Cambridge, Cambridge University Press.

   1982c. ed. *Symbolic and Structural Archaeology*. Cambridge, Cambridge University Press.

   1984a. Burials, houses, women and men in the European Neolithic. In D. Miller and C. Tilley, 1984a, pp. 51–68.

   1984b. Archaeology in 1984. *Antiquity* 58: 25–32.

   1985. Postprocessual archaeology. *Advances in Archaeological Method and Theory* 8: 1–26.

   1986. *Reading the Past: Current Approaches to Interpretation in Archaeology*. Cambridge, Cambridge University Press.

1987a. ed. *Archaeology as Long-term History*. Cambridge, Cambridge University Press.

1987b. *The Archaeology of Contextual Meanings*. Cambridge, Cambridge University Press.

1988. Material culture texts and social change: a theoretical discussion and some archaeological examples. *Proceedings of the Prehistoric Society* 54: 67–75.

1990. *The Domestication of Europe: Structure and Contingency in Neolithic Societies*. Oxford, Blackwell.

1991a. ed. *Archaeological Theory in Europe: The Last Three Decades*. London, Routledge.

1991b. Preface. In I. Hodder, 1991a, pp. vii–xi.

1991c. Interpretive archaeology and its role. *American Antiquity* 56: 7–18.

1991d. *Reading the Past: Current Approaches to Interpretation in Archaeology*. 2nd ed. Cambridge, Cambridge University Press.

1992. ed. *Theory and Practice in Archaeology*. London, Routledge.

1999. *The Archaeological Process: An Introduction*. Oxford, Blackwell.

2001a. ed. *Archaeological Theory Today*. Cambridge, UK, Polity Press.

2001b. Introduction: a review of contemporary theoretical debates in archaeology. In I. Hodder, 2001a, pp. 1–13.

2003a. *Archaeology Beyond Dialogue*. Salt Lake City, University of Utah Press.

2003b. Archaeology as a discontinuous domain. In T. L. VanPool and C. S. VanPool, pp. 5–9.

Hodder, I. et al. 1995. eds. *Interpreting Archaeology: Finding Meaning in the Past*. London, Routledge.

Hodder, I. and M. Hassall. 1971. The non-random spacing of Romano-British walled towns. *Man* 6: 391–407.

Hodder, I. and S. Hutson. 2003. *Reading the Past: Current Approaches to Interpretation in Archaeology*. Cambridge, Cambridge University Press.

Hodder, I. and C. Orton. 1976. *Spatial Analysis in Archaeology*. Cambridge, Cambridge University Press.

Hodgen, M. T. 1964. *Early Anthropology in the Sixteenth and Seventeenth Centuries*. Philadelphia, University of Pennsylvania Press.

Hodson, F. R., D. G. Kendall, and P. Tăutu. 1971. eds. *Mathematics in the Archaeological and Historical Sciences*. Edinburgh, Edinburgh University Press.

Hoebel, E. A. 1949. *Man in the Primitive World*. New York, McGraw-Hill.

Hoffman, M. A. 1974. The rise of antiquarianism in Japan and Western Europe. *Arctic Anthropology* 11, supplement: 182–8.

1979. *Egypt before the Pharaohs: The Prehistoric Foundations of Egyptian Civilization*. New York, Knopf.

Hogarth, A. C. 1972. Common sense in archaeology. *Antiquity* 46: 301–4.

Hogarth, D. G. 1899. ed. *Authority and Archaeology, Sacred and Profane*. London, John Murray.

References

Hole, F. and R. F. Heizer. 1969. *An Introduction to Prehistoric Archaeology.* 2nd edn. New York, Holt, Rinehart and Winston.

Holmes, T. R. 1907. *Ancient Britain and the Invasions of Julius Caesar.* Oxford, Oxford University Press.

Holmes, W. H. 1903. Aboriginal pottery of the eastern United States. Washington, DC, *Bureau of American Ethnology, Annual Report* 20: 1–237.

1914. Areas of American culture characterization tentatively outlined as an aid in the study of the antiquities. *American Anthropologist* 16: 413–46.

Holtorf, C. 2002. Notes on the life history of a pot sherd. *Journal of Material Culture* 7: 49–71.

Holtorf, C. and H. Karlsson. 2000. eds. *Philosophy and Archaeological Practice: Perspectives for the 21st Century.* Göteborg, Bricoleur Press.

Hood, D. 1964. *Davidson Black: A Biography.* Toronto, University of Toronto Press.

Hooton, E. A. 1938. *Apes, Men, and Morons.* London, Allen and Unwin.

Horsman, R. 1975. Scientific racism and the American Indian in the mid-nineteenth century. *American Quarterly* 27: 152–68.

1981. *Race and Manifest Destiny: The Origins of American Racial Anglo-Saxonism.* Cambridge, MA, Harvard University Press.

Horton, D. 1991. *Recovering the Tracks: The Story of Australian Archaeology.* Canberra, Aboriginal Studies Press.

Howe, J. E. 1976. Pre-agricultural society in Soviet theory and method. *Arctic Anthropology* 13: 84–115.

1980. The Soviet Theories of Primitive History: Forty Years of Speculation on the Origins and Evolution of People and Society. PhD thesis, Seattle, University of Washington.

Huddleston, L. E. 1967. *Origins of the American Indians: European Concepts, 1492–1729.* Austin, University of Texas Press.

Hudson, K. 1981. *A Social History of Archaeology: The British Experience.* London, Macmillan.

Hull, D. L. 1988. *Science as a Process: An Evolutionary Account of the Social and Conceptual Development of Science.* Chicago, IL, University of Chicago Press.

Hulse, E. 1999. ed. *Thinking with Both Hands: Sir Daniel Wilson in the Old World and The New.* Toronto, University of Toronto Press.

Hunt, L. 1989. Introduction: history, culture, and text. In *The New Cultural History: Essays,* ed. by L. Hunt, pp. 1–22. Berkeley, University of California Press.

Hunt, T. L., C. P. Lipo, and S. L. Sterling. 2001. eds. *Posing Questions for a Scientific Archaeology.* Westport, CT, Bergin and Garvey.

Hunter, J. 1983. *Perspective on Ratzel's Political Geography.* Lanham, MD, University Press of America.

Hunter, M. 1975. *John Aubrey and the Realm of Learning.* London, Duckworth.

References

Huntington, R. and P. Metcalf. 1979. *Celebrations of Death*. Cambridge, Cambridge University Press.

Hurt, T. D. and G. F. M. Rakita. 2001. eds. *Style and Function: Conceptual Issues in Evolutionary Archaeology*. Westport, CT, Bergin and Garvey.

Hussey, C. 1927. *The Picturesque: Studies in a Point of View*. New York, Putnam's.

Hutchinson, H. G. 1914. *Life of Sir John Lubbock, Lord Avebury*. 2 vols. London, Macmillan.

Huxley, T. H. 1896. *Man's Place in Nature and Other Anthropological Essays*. New York, Appleton.

Iggers, G. G. and J. M. Powell. 1990. eds. *Leopold von Ranke and the Shaping of the Historical Discipline*. Syracuse, NY, Syracuse University Press.

Ihering, H. von. 1895. A civilisacão prehistorica do Brasil meridional. São Paulo, *Revista do Museu Paulista* 1: 34–159.

Ikawa-Smith, F. 1982. Co-traditions in Japanese archaeology. *World Archaeology* 13: 296–309.

    1995. The Jomon, the Ainu, and the Okinawans: the changing politics of ethic identity in Japanese archeology. In *Communicating with Japan: An Interdisciplinary Anthology*, ed. by D. J. Dicks, pp. 43–56. Montreal, Concordia University.

    2001. Japan. In T. Murray, 2001a, pp. 734–44.

Im Hoff, U. 1994. *The Enlightenment*. Oxford, Blackwell.

Ingersoll, D., J. Yellen, and W. Macdonald. 1977. eds. *Experimental Archaeology*. New York, Columbia University Press.

Ingold, T. 1996. Hunting and gathering as ways of perceiving the environment. In *Redefining Nature: Ecology, Culture and Domestication*, ed. by R. Ellen and K. Fukui, pp. 117–55. Oxford, Berg.

Irvine, W. 1955. *Apes, Angels, and Victorians*. New York, McGraw-Hill.

Irwin, J. T. 1980. *American Hieroglyphs: The Symbol of the Egyptian Hieroglyphs in the American Renaissance*. New Haven, CT, Yale University Press.

Isaac, R. 1982. *The Transformation of Virginia, 1740–1790*. Chapel Hill, University of North Carolina Press.

Isaacs, J. 1980. ed. *Australian Dreaming: 40,000 Years of Aboriginal History*. Sydney, Lansdowne Press.

Iversen, E. 1993. *The Myth of Egypt and its Hieroglyphs in European Tradition*. Princeton, NJ, Princeton University Press.

Jacks, P. 1993. *The Antiquarian and the Myth of Antiquity: The Origins of Rome in Renaissance Thought*. Cambridge, Cambridge University Press.

Jacob-Friesen, K. H. 1928. *Grundfragen der Urgeschichtsforschung: Stand und Kritik der Forschung über Rassen, Völker und Kulturen in urgeschichtlicher Zeit*. Hannover, Helwing.

Jacobs, J. 2000. German unification and East German archaeology. In H. Härke, 2000a, pp. 339–52.

References

Jacobson, J. 1979. Recent developments in South Asian prehistory and proto-history. *Annual Review of Anthropology* 8: 467–502.

Jaenen, C. 1976. *Friend and Foe: Aspects of French-Amerindian Cultural Contact in the Sixteenth and Seventeenth Centuries.* Toronto, McClelland and Stewart.

Jahnkuhn, H. 1977. *Einführung in die Siedlungsarchäologie.* Berlin, de Gruyter.

Jairazbhoy, R. A. 1974, 1976. *The Old World Origins of American Civilization.* 2 vols. Totawa, NJ, Rowman and Littlefield.

Janetski, J. C. 1997a. Fremont hunting and resource intensification in the eastern Great Basin. *Journal of Archaeological Science* 24: 1075–88.

  1997b. 150 years of Utah archaeology. *Utah Historical Quarterly* 65: 101–33.

Jarman, M. R., G. N. Bailey, and H. N. Jarman. 1982. eds. *Early European Agriculture: Its Foundations and Development.* Cambridge, Cambridge University Press.

Jaspers, K. 1953. *The Origin and Goal of History.* New Haven, CT, Yale University Press.

Jeffreys, D. 2003. ed. *Views of Ancient Egypt since Napoleon Bonaparte: Imperialism, Colonialism and Modern Appropriations.* London, UCL Press.

Jencks, C. 1986. *What is Postmodernism?* New York, St. Martin's Press.

Jenkins, I. 1992. *Archaeologists and Aesthetes in the Sculpture Galleries of the British Museum, 1800–1939.* London, British Museum Press.

Jenkyns, R. 1980. *The Victorians and Ancient Greece.* Cambridge, MA, Harvard University Press.

Jenness, D. 1932. Fifty years of archaeology in Canada. *Royal Society of Canada, Fifty Years Retrospect, Anniversary Volume, 1882–1932,* pp. 71–6. Toronto, Ryerson Press.

Jennings, J. D. 1979. ed. *The Prehistory of Polynesia.* Cambridge, MA, Harvard University Press.

Jochim, M. A. 1976. *Hunter-Gatherer Subsistence and Settlement: A Predictive Model.* New York, Academic Press.

Johnson, G. A. 1978. Information sources and the development of decision-making organizations. In *Social Archeology,* ed. by C. L. Redman et al., pp. 87–112. New York, Academic Press.

  1981. Monitoring complex system integration and boundary phenomena with settlement size data. In *Archaeological Approaches to the Study of Complexity,* ed. by S. E. van der Leeuw, pp. 143–88. Amsterdam, Van Giffen Institute.

Johnson, J. K. 1993. ed. *The Development of Southeastern Archaeology.* Tuscaloosa, University of Alabama Press.

Johnson, L. L. 1978. A history of flint-knapping experimentation, 1838–1976. *Current Anthropology* 19: 337–72.

Johnson, M. H. 1989. Conceptions of agency in archaeological interpretation. *Journal of Anthropological Archaeology* 8: 189–211.

References

1996. *An Archaeology of Capitalism*. Oxford, Blackwell.

1999. *Archaeological Theory: An Introduction*. Oxford, Blackwell.

Johnson, S. 1970. *Johnson's Journey to the Western Islands of Scotland*, ed. by R. W. Chapman. Oxford, Oxford University Press.

Johnston, W. M. 1967. *The Formative Years of R. G. Collingwood*. The Hague, Martinus Nijhoff.

Jones, A. 2002. *Archaeological Theory and Scientific Practice*. Cambridge, Cambridge University Press.

Jones, H. M. 1964. *O Strange New World: American Culture, The Formative Years*. New York, Viking Press.

Jones, R. 1979. The fifth continent: problems concerning the human colonization of Australia. *Annual Review of Anthropology* 8: 445–66.

1992. Philosophical time travellers. *Antiquity* 66: 744–57.

Jones, S. 1997. *The Archaeology of Ethnicity: Constructing Identities in the Past and Present*. London, Routledge.

Jonker, G. 1995. *The Topography of Remembrance: The Dead, Tradition and Collective Memory in Mesopotamia*. Leiden, Brill.

Joyce, R. A. 2002. *The Languages of Archaeology: Dialogue, Narrative, and Writing*. Oxford, Blackwell.

2003. Concrete memories: fragments of the past in the Classic Maya present (500–1000 AD). In R. M. Van Dyke and S. E. Alcock, pp. 104–25.

2004. Embodied subjectivity: gender, femininity, masculinity, sexuality. In L. Meskell and R. W. Preucel, pp. 82–95.

Junker, K. 1998. Research under dictatorship: the German Archaeological Institute 1929–1945. *Antiquity* 72: 282–92.

Kaeser, M.-A. 2001. Switzerland. In T. Murray, 2001a, pp. 1236–44.

2002. On the international roots of prehistory. *Antiquity* 76: 170–77.

2004a. *L'Univers du préhistorien: science, foi et politique dans l'oeuvre et la vie d'Edouard Desor, 1811–1882*. Paris: L'Harmattan.

2004b. *Les Lacustres: archéologie et mythe national*. Lausanne, Presses Polytechniques et Universitaires Romandes.

Kaiser, T. 1995. Archaeology and ideology in southeast Europe. In P. L. Kohl and C. Fawcett, pp. 99–119.

Kaiser, W. 1957. Zur inneren Chronologie der Naqadakultur. *Archaeologia Geographica* 6: 69–77.

Kane, S. 2003. ed. *The Politics of Archaeology and Identity in a Global Context*. Boston, MA, Archaeological Institute of America.

Karlsson, H. 1998. *Re-thinking Archaeology*. Gotarc Series B, 8. Göteborg, Göteborg University, Department of Archaeology.

Keen, B. 1971. *The Aztec Image in Western Thought*. New Brunswick, NJ, Rutgers University Press.

Kehoe, A. B. 1990. The monumental Midwestern Taxonomic Method. In *The Woodland Tradition in the Western Great Lakes*, ed. by G. Gibbon, pp. 31–36. Minneapolis, University of Minnesota Publications in Anthropology 4.

1998. *The Land of Prehistory: A Critical History of American Archaeology.* New York, Routledge.

Kehoe, A. B. and M. B. Emmerichs. 1999. eds. *Assembling the Past: Studies in the Professionalization of Archaeology.* Albuquerque, University of New Mexico Press.

Kelley, J. H. and M. P. Hanen. 1988. *Archaeology and the Methodology of Science.* Albuquerque, University of New Mexico Press.

Kelly, R. L. 1995. *The Foraging Spectrum: Diversity in Hunter-Gatherer Lifeways.* Washington, DC, Smithsonian Institution Press.

2000. Elements of a behavioral ecological paradigm for the study of prehistoric hunter-gatherers. In M. B. Schiffer, 2000a, pp. 63–78.

Kendall, D. G. 1969. Some problems and methods in statistical archaeology. *World Archaeology* 1: 68–76.

1971. Seriation from abundance matrices. In F. R. Hodson, D. G. Kendall, and P. Tăutu, pp. 215–52.

Kendrick, T. D. 1950. *British Antiquity.* London, Methuen.

Kent, S. 1984. *Analyzing Activity Areas: An Ethnoarchaeological Study of the Use of Space.* Albuquerque: University of New Mexico Press.

1987. ed. *Method and Theory for Activity Area Research: An Ethnoarchaeological Approach.* New York, Columbia University Press.

Keur, D. L. 1941. *Big Bead Mesa.* Menasha, WI, Society for American Archaeology, Memoir 1.

Kidder, A. V. 1924. *An Introduction to the Study of Southwestern Archaeology.* New Haven, CT, Papers of the Southwestern Expedition, Phillips Academy, no. 1.

1935. *Year Book*, no. 34. Washington, DC, Carnegie Foundation.

1962. *An Introduction to the Study of Southwestern Archaeology, with an Introduction, "Southwestern Archaeology Today," by Irving Rouse.* New Haven, CT, Yale University Press.

Killan, G. 1983. *David Boyle: From Artisan to Archaeologist.* Toronto, University of Toronto Press.

Kingsley, M. H. 1897. *Travels in West Africa: Congo Français, Corisco and Cameroons.* London, Macmillan.

Kirch, P. V. and M. D. Sahlins. 1992. *Anahulu: The Anthropology of History in the Kingdom of Hawaii.* 2 vols. Chicago, IL, University of Chicago Press.

Ki-Zerbo, J. 1981. ed. *General History of Africa*, vol. I, *Methodology and African Prehistory.* Berkeley and Los Angeles, University of California Press.

Klein, R. G. 1966. Chellean and Acheulean on the territory of the Soviet Union: a critical review of the evidence as presented in the literature. *American Anthropologist* 68(2), pt. 2: 1–45.

Kleindienst, M. R. and P. J. Watson. 1956. "Action archaeology": the archaeological inventory of a living community. *Anthropology Tomorrow* 5: 75–8.

References

Klejn, L. S. 1969. Characteristic methods in the current critique of Marxism in archeology. *Soviet Anthropology and Archeology* 7(4): 41–53.

1970. Archaeology in Britain: a Marxist view. *Antiquity* 44: 296–303.

1973a. Marxism, the systemic approach, and archaeology. In Renfrew 1973b, pp. 691–710.

1973b. On major aspects of the interrelationship of archaeology and ethnology. *Current Anthropology* 14: 311–20.

1974. Kossinna im Abstand von vierzig Jahren. *Jahresschrift für mitteldeutsche Vorgeschichte* 58: 7–55.

1977. A panorama of theoretical archaeology. *Current Anthropology* 18: 1–42.

1982. *Archaeological Typology*. Oxford, BAR, International Series, no. 153.

1990. Theoretical archaeology in the making: a survey of books published in the West in 1974–1979. *Fennoscandia Archaeologica* 7: 3–15.

1991. A Russian lesson for theoretical archaeology: a reply. *Fennoscandia Archaeologica* 8: 67–71.

1993a. *Fenomen Sovetskoy Arkheologii*. St. Petersburg, Farn.

1993b. *La Arqueología Soviética: Historia y Teoría de una Escuela Desconocida*. Barcelona, Editoria Crítica.

1994a. Overcoming national romanticism in archaeology. *Fennoscandia Archaeologica* 11: 87–8.

1994b. Childe and Soviet archaeology: a romance. In D. R. Harris, pp. 75–99.

1997. *Das Phänomen der sowjetischen Archäologie*. Frankfurt am Main, Peter Lang.

1999a. Gustaf Kossinna 1858–1931. In T. Murray, 1999a, pp. 233–46.

1999b. Vasiliy Alekeyevich Gorodcov. In T. Murray, 1999a, pp. 247–62.

2001a. Metaarchaeology. *Acta Archaeologica* 27: 1–149.

2001b. Russia. In T. Murray, 2001a, pp. 1127–45.

Klemm, G. F. 1843–52. *Allgemeine Cultur-Geschichte der Menschheit*. 10 vols. Leipzig, Teubner.

1854–1855. *Allgemeine Kulturwissenschaft*. Leipzig, J. A. Romberg.

Kletter, R. 2006. *Just Past? The Making of Israeli Archaeology*. London, Equinox.

Klindt-Jensen, O. 1975. *A History of Scandinavian Archaeology*. London, Thames and Hudson.

1976. The influence of ethnography on early Scandinavian archaeology. In J. V. S. Megaw, pp. 43–8.

Kluckhohn, C. 1940. The conceptual structure in Middle American studies. In *The Maya and their Neighbors*, ed. by C. L. Hay et al., pp. 41–51. New York, Appleton-Century.

Knapp, A. B. 1988. Ideology, archaeology and polity. *Man* 23: 133–63.

1992. ed. *Archaeology, Annales, and Ethnohistory*. Cambridge, Cambridge University Press.

References

Knorr-Cetina, K. D. 1981. *The Manufacture of Knowledge: An Essay on the Constructivist and Contextual Nature of Science.* Oxford, Pergamon.

Koepping, K.-P. 1983. *Adolf Bastian and the Psychic Unity of Mankind: The Foundations of Anthropology in Nineteenth Century Germany.* St. Lucia, University of Queensland Press.

Kohl, P. L. 1975. The archaeology of trade. *Dialectical Anthropology* 1: 43–50.

1978. The balance of trade in southwestern Asia in the mid-third millennium B.C. *Current Anthropology* 19: 463–92.

1979. The "world economy" of West Asia in the third millennium B.C. In *South Asian Archaeology 1977*, ed. by M. Taddei, vol. 1, pp. 55–85. Naples, Istituto Universitario Orientale, Seminario di Studi Asiatici.

1981a. ed. *The Bronze Age Civilization of Central Asia: Recent Soviet Discoveries.* Armonk, NY, Sharpe.

1981b. Materialist approaches in prehistory. *Annual Review of Anthropology* 10: 89–118.

1984. Force, history and the evolutionist paradigm. In M. Spriggs, 1984a, pp. 127–34.

1987. The ancient economy, transferable technologies, and the Bronze Age world system: a view from the northwestern frontier of the ancient Near East. In *Centre and Periphery in the Ancient World*, ed. by M. J. Rowlands and M. T. Larsen, pp. 13–24. Cambridge, Cambridge University Press.

1993. Limits to a post-processual archaeology (or, the dangers of a new scholasticism). In N. Yoffee and A. Sherratt, pp. 13–19.

1998. Nationalism and archaeology: on the construction of nations and the reconstructions of the remote past. *Annual Review of Anthropology* 27: 223–46.

Kohl, P. L. and C. Fawcett. 1995. eds. *Nationalism, Politics, and the Practice of Archaeology.* Cambridge, Cambridge University Press.

Kohl, P. L. and J. A. Pérez Gollán. 2002. Religion, politics, and prehistory: reassessing the lingering legacy of Oswald Menghin. *Current Anthropology* 43: 561–610.

Kohl, P. L. and G. R. Tsetskhladze. 1995. Nationalism, politics, and the practice of archaeology in the Caucasus. In P. L. Kohl and C. Fawcett, pp. 149–74.

Kohn, H. 1960. *The Mind of Germany.* New York, Scribner's.

Kokkonen, J. 1985. Aarne Michaël Tallgren and Eurasia Septentrionalis Antiqua. *Fennoscandia Archaeologica* 2: 3–10.

Kolakowski, L. 1976. *La Philosophie positiviste.* Paris, Denoël.

1978a. *Main Currents of Marxism*, vol. 1, *The Founders.* Oxford, Oxford University Press.

1978b. *Main Currents of Marxism*, vol. 2, *The Golden Age.* Oxford, Oxford University Press.

1978c. *Main Currents of Marxism*, vol. 3, *The Breakdown.* Oxford, Oxford University Press.

References

Kolpakov, E. M. and L. B. Vishnyatsky. 1990. Current theoretical discussion in Soviet archaeology: an essay. *Fennoscandia Archaeologica* 7: 17–25.

Kossack, G. 1992. Prehistoric archaeology in Germany: its history and current situation. *Norwegian Archaeological Review* 25: 73–109.

Kossinna, G. 1911. *Die Herkunft der Germanen*. Leipzig, Kabitzsch.

1926–1927. *Ursprung und Verbreitung der Germanen in Vor- und Frühgeschichtlicher Zeit*. 2 vols. Berlin, Lichterfelde.

Kosso, P. 2001. *Knowing the Past: Philosophical Issues of History and Archaeology*. Amherst, NY, Humanity Books.

Kotsakis, K. 1991. The powerful past: theoretical trends in Greek archaeology. In I. Hodder, 1991a, pp. 65–90.

Kramer, C. 1979. ed. *Ethnoarchaeology: Implications of Ethnography for Archaeology*. New York, Columbia University Press.

1982. *Village Ethnoarchaeology: Rural Iran in Archaeological Perspective*. New York, Academic Press.

Kristiansen, K. 1981. A social history of Danish archaeology (1805–1975). In G. Daniel, 1981b, pp. 20–44.

1984. Ideology and material culture: an archaeological perspective. In M. Spriggs, 1984a, pp. 72–100.

1985. A short history of Danish archaeology: an analytical perspective. In *Archaeological Formation Processes*, ed. by K. Kristiansen, pp. 12–34. Copenhagen, Nationalmusset.

1993. "The strength of the past and its great might"; an essay on the use of the past. *Journal of European Archaeology* 1: 3–32.

1996. European origins – "civilisation" and "barbarism." In P. Graves-Brown et al., 1996, pp. 138–44.

2002. The birth of ecological archaeology in Denmark: history and research environments 1850–2000. In A. Fischer and K. Kristiansen, pp. 11–31.

2004a. Genes versus agents: a discussion of the widening theoretical gap in archaeology (with comments). *Archaeological Dialogues* 11: 77–132.

2004b. Who owns the past? reflections on roles and responsibilities. In L. Vishnyatsky et al., pp. 79–86.

Kristiansen, K. and T. B. Larsson. 2005. *The Rise of Bronze Age Society: Travels, Transmissions and Transformations*. Cambridge, Cambridge University Press.

Kroeber, A. L. 1909. The archaeology of California. In F. Boas et al., pp. 1–42.

1916. Zuñi potsherds. New York, *Anthropological Papers of the American Museum of Natural History* 18(1): 7–37.

1952. *The Nature of Culture*. Chicago, IL, University of Chicago Press.

1953. ed. *Anthropology Today*. Chicago, IL, University of Chicago Press.

Kroeber, A. L. and C. Kluckhohn. 1952. *Culture – A Critical Review of Concepts and Definitions*. Cambridge, MA, Harvard University, Papers of the Peabody Museum of American Archaeology and Ethnology no. 47.

Kroker, A. 1984. *Technology and the Canadian Mind: Innis/McLuhan/Grant*. Montreal, New World Perspectives.

References

Kruglov, A. P. and G. V. Podgayetsky. 1935. *Rodovoe Obshchestvo Stepei Vostochnoi Evropy*. Leningrad, Izvestiia GAIMK no. 119.

Kubler, G. 1962. *The Shape of Time: Remarks on the History of Things*. New Haven, CT, Yale University Press.

Kuhn, T. S. 1962. *The Structure of Scientific Revolutions*. Chicago, IL, University of Chicago Press.

1970. *The Structure of Scientific Revolutions*. 2nd edn. Chicago, IL, University of Chicago Press.

1977. *The Essential Tension: Selected Studies in Scientific Tradition and Change*. Chicago, IL, University of Chicago Press.

Kuklick, B. 1996. *Puritans in Babylon: The Ancient Near East and American Intellectual Life, 1880–1930*. Princeton, NJ, Princeton University Press.

Kuklick, H. 1991a. *The Savage Within: The Social History of British Anthropology, 1885–1945*. Cambridge, Cambridge University Press.

1991b. Contested monuments: the politics of archaeology in southern Africa. In *Colonial Situations: Essays on the Contextualization of Ethnographic Knowledge* (*History of Anthropology* 7), ed. by G. W. Stocking Jr, pp. 135–69. Madison, University of Wisconsin Press.

Kupperman, K. O. 1980. *Settling with the Indians: The Meeting of English and Indian Cultures in America, 1580–1640*. Totowa, NJ, Rowman and Littlefield.

Kus, S. 1984. The spirit and its burden: archaeology and symbolic activity. In M. Spriggs, 1984a, pp. 101–7.

1992. Toward an archaeology of body and soul. In J.-C. Gardin and C. S. Peebles, pp. 168–77.

2000. Ideas are like burgeoning grains on a young rice stalk: some ideas on theory in anthropological archaeology. In M. B. Schiffer, 2000a, pp. 156–72.

Kushner, G. 1970. A consideration of some processual designs for archaeology as anthropology. *American Antiquity* 35: 125–32.

Lacovara, P. 1981. The Hearst excavations at Deir-el-Ballas: the eighteenth dynasty town. In *Studies in Ancient Egypt, the Aegean, and the Sudan*, ed. by W. K. Simpson and W. M. Davis, pp. 120–4. Boston, MA, Museum of Fine Arts.

Lakoff, G. 1987. *Women, Fire, and Dangerous Things: What Categories Reveal about the Mind*. Chicago, IL, University of Chicago Press.

Lakoff, G. and M. Johnson. 1980. *Metaphors We Live By*. Chicago, IL, University of Chicago Press.

Lal, M. 1984. *Settlement History and Rise of Civilization in Ganga-Yamuna Doab*. Delhi, B. R. Publishing.

Lamberg-Karlovsky, C. C. 1975. Third millennium modes of exchange and modes of production. In J. A. Sabloff and C. C. Lamberg-Karlovsky, pp. 341–68.

1981. Afterword. In Kohl, 1981a, pp. 386–97.

1985. The Near Eastern "breakout" and the Mesopotamian social contract. *Symbols*, spring issue, 8–11, 23–4.

1989. ed. *Archaeological Thought in America*. Cambridge, Cambridge University Press.

Laming-Emperaire, A. 1962. *La signification de l'art rupestre paléolithique*. Paris, Picard.

1964. *Origines de l'archéologie préhistorique en France, des superstitions médiévales à la découverte de l'homme fossile*. Paris, Picard.

Lampeter Archaeological Workshop. 1997. Relativism, objectivity and the politics of the past. *Archaeological Dialogues* 4: 164–84.

Landau, M. 1991. *Narratives of Human Evolution*. New Haven, CT, Yale University Press.

Laplace, G. 1964. Essai de typologie systématique. *Annali dell' Universita di Ferrara* 15: 1–85.

Larsen, C. S. 1985. ed. *The Antiquity and Origin of Native North Americans*. New York, Garland.

Larsen, M. T. 1996. *The Conquest of Assyria: Excavations in an Antique Land, 1840–60*. London, Routledge.

Larson, P. A., Jr. 1979. Archaeology and science: surviving the preparadigmatic crisis. *Current Anthropology* 20: 230–1.

Laszlo, E. 1972a. *Introduction to Systems Philosophy*. New York, Gordon and Breach.

1972b. ed. *The Relevance of General Systems Theory*. New York, Braziller.

1972c. *The Systems View of the World*. New York, Braziller.

Latham, R. G. and A. W. Franks. 1856. eds. *Horae Ferales; or Studies in the Archaeology of the Northern Nations, by the late John M. Kemble*. London, Lovell, Reeve.

Latour, B. and S. Woolgar. 1979. *Laboratory Life: The Social Construction of Scientific Facts*. Beverly Hills, CA, Sage.

Laudan, L. 1990. *Science and Relativism: Some Key Controversies in the Philosophy of Science*. Chicago, IL, University of Chicago Press.

Laufer, B. 1913. Remarks. *American Anthropologist* 15: 573–7.

Laurent, O. 1999. The origins of French archaeology. *Antiquity* 73: 176–83.

Layton, R. 1989a. ed. *Conflict in the Archaeology of Living Traditions*. London, Unwin Hyman.

1989b. ed. *Who Needs the Past? Indigenous Values and Archaeology*. London, Unwin Hyman.

Leach, E. R. 1970. *Lévi-Strauss*. London, Fontana/Collins.

1973. Concluding address. In C. Renfrew, 1973b, pp. 761–71.

Leakey, L. S. B. 1931. *The Stone Age Cultures of Kenya Colony*. Cambridge, Cambridge University Press.

Leakey, M. 1984. *Disclosing the Past*. New York, Doubleday.

Lech, J. 1999. *Between Captivity and Freedom: Polish Archaeology in the 20th Century*. Warsaw, Arwil.

2002. On Polish archaeology in the 20th century: remarks and polemic. *Archaeologia Polona* 40: 185–252.

Lech, J. and F. M. Stepniowski. eds. 1999. *V. Gordon Childe i Archaeologia w XX wieku*. Warsaw, Wydawnictwo Naukowe PWM.

References

Lee, R. B. 1990. Primitive communism and the origin of social inequality. In S. Upham, pp. 225–46.

Lee, R. B. and I. DeVore. 1968. eds. *Man the Hunter*. Chicago, IL, Aldine.

Leeds, E. T. 1913. *The Archaeology of Anglo-Saxon Settlements*. Oxford, Clarendon Press.

Lefkowitz, M. R. and G. M. Rogers. 1996. eds. *Black Athena Revisited*. Chapel Hill, University of North Carolina Press.

Legendre, J.-P. 1999. Archaeology and ideological propaganda in annexed Alsace (1940–1944). *Antiquity* 73: 184–90.

Lelas, S. 1985. Typology of internal and external factors in the development of knowledge. *Ratio* 27: 67–81.

Leonard, R. D. 2001. Evolutionary archaeology. In I. Hodder, 2001a, pp. 65–97.

Leonard, R. D. and G. T. Jones. 1987. Elements of an inclusive evolutionary model for archaeology. *Journal of Anthropological Archaeology* 6: 199–219.

Leone, M. P. 1972. ed. *Contemporary Archaeology*. Carbondale, Southern Illinois University Press.

1981. Archaeology's relationship to the present and the past. In R. Gould and M. Schiffer, pp. 5–14.

1982. Some opinions about recovering mind. *American Antiquity* 47: 742–60.

1984. Interpreting ideology in historical archaeology: using the rules of perspective in the William Paca Garden in Annapolis, Maryland. In D. Miller and C. Tilley, 1984a, pp. 25–35.

1986. Symbolic, structural, and critical archaeology. In D. J. Meltzer et al., pp. 415–38.

2005. *The Archaeology of Liberty in an American Capital: Excavations in Annapolis*. Berkeley, University of California Press.

Leone, M. P. and P. B. Potter, Jr. 1988. eds. *The Recovery of Meaning: Historical Archaeology in the Eastern United States*. Washington, DC, Smithsonian Institution Press.

Leone, M. P., P. B. Potter Jr and P. A. Shackel. 1987. Toward a critical archaeology. *Current Anthropology* 28: 283–302.

Leppmann, W. 1970. *Winckelmann*. New York, Knopf.

Lepsius, C. R. 1880. *Nubische Grammatik, mit einer Einleitung über die Völker und Sprachen Afrikas*. Berlin, Hertz.

Leroi-Gourhan, A. 1964. *Les religions de la préhistoire*. Paris, Presses Universitaires de France.

1993. *Gesture and Speech*. Boston, MA, M.I.T. Press.

Leube, A. and M. Hegewisch. 2002. eds. *Prähistorie und Nationalsozialismus: die mittel- und osteuropäische Ur- und Frühgeschictsforschung in den Jahren 1933–1945*. Heidelberg, Synchron.

Levi, P. 1979. *Pausanias: Guide to Greece*. 2 vols. Harmondsworth, UK, Penguin.

References

Levine, P. 1986. *The Amateur and the Professional: Antiquarians, Historians and Archaeologists in Victorian England, 1838–1886*. Cambridge, Cambridge University Press.

Levitt, J. 1979. A review of experimental traceological research in the USSR. In B. Hayden, pp. 27–38.

Lewis, T. M. N. and M. Kneberg. 1941. *The Prehistory of the Chickamauga Basin in Tennessee*. Knoxville, Tennessee Anthropology Papers, no. 1.

Lewis-Williams, J. D. 2002. *The Mind in the Cave: Consciousness and the Origins of Art*. London, Thames and Hudson.

Lewis-Williams, J. D. and T. A. Dowson. 1988. The signs of all times: entoptic phenomena in Upper Palaeolithic art. *Current Anthropology* 29: 201–45.

Li, Chi. 1977. *Anyang*. Seattle, University of Washington Press.

Libby, W. F. 1955. *Radiocarbon Dating*. 2nd edn. Chicago, IL, University of Chicago Press.

Ligi, P. 1993. National romanticism in archaeology: the paradigm of Slavonic colonization in north-west Russia. *Fennoscandia Archaeologica* 10: 31–9.

Lillios, K. T. 1995. Nationalism and Copper Age research in Portugal during the Salazar regime (1932–1974). In P. L. Kohl and C. Fawcett, pp. 57–69.

Linebaugh, D. W. 2005. *The Man Who Found Thoreau: Roland W. Robbins and the Rise of Historical Archaeology in America*. Durham, University of New Hampshire Press.

Linton, R. 1944. North American cooking pots. *American Antiquity* 9: 369–80.

Lissarrague, F. 1990. *Aesthetics of the Greek Banquet: Images of Wine and Ritual*. Princeton, NJ, Princeton University Press.

Little, B. J. 1994. People with history: an update on historical archaeology in the United States. *Journal of Archaeological Method and Theory* 1: 5–40.

Liu, L. and X. Chen. 2001. China. In T. Murray, 2001a, pp. 315–33.

Lloyd, S. H. 1947. *Foundations in the Dust: A Story of Mesopotamian Exploration*. Oxford, Oxford University Press (2nd edn, London, Thames and Hudson, 1981).

Locke, J. [1690] 1952. *The Second Treatise of Government*, ed. by Thomas P. Peardon. New York, Liberal Arts Press.

Longacre, W. A. 1968. Some aspects of prehistoric society in east-central Arizona. In S. R. and L. R. Binford, pp. 89–102.

 1970. *Archaeology as Anthropology: A Case Study*. Tucson, University of Arizona Press.

Longacre, W. A. and J. M. Skibo. 1994. eds. *Kalinga Ethnoarchaeology: Expanding Archaeological Method and Theory*. Washington, DC, Smithsonian Institution Press.

Loprieno, A. 2003. Views of the past in Egypt during the first millennium BC. In J. Tait, 2003, pp. 139–54.

Lord, B. 1974. *The History of Painting in Canada: Toward a People's Art*. Toronto, NC Press.

References

Lorenzo, J. L. 1981. Archaeology south of the Rio Grande. *World Archaeology* 13: 190–208.

1984. Mexico. In H. Cleere, pp. 89–100.

Lorenzo, J. L., A. P. Elias, and J. G. Barcena. 1976. *Hacia una Arqueología Social: Reunión de Teotihuacán*. México, DF, Instituto Nacional de Antropología e Historia.

Low, B. S. 2000. *Why Sex Matters: A Darwinian Look at Human Behavior*. Princeton, NJ, Princeton University Press.

Lowenthal, D. 1985. *The Past is a Foreign Country*. Cambridge, Cambridge University Press.

Lowther, G. R. 1962. Epistemology and archaeological theory. *Current Anthropology* 3: 495–509.

Lubbock, John [Lord Avebury]. 1865. *Pre-historic Times, as Illustrated by Ancient Remains, and the Manners and Customs of Modern Savages*. London, Williams and Norgate.

1869. *Pre-historic Times*. 2nd edn. London, Williams and Norgate.

1870. *The Origin of Civilisation and the Primitive Condition of Man*. London, Longmans, Green.

Lucas, A. 1926. *Ancient Egyptian Materials*. London, Arnold.

Lumbreras, L. 1974. *La Arqueología como Ciencia Social*. Lima, Ediciones Histar.

Lustig, J. 1997. ed. *Anthropology and Egyptology: A Developing Dialogue*. Sheffield, UK, Sheffield Academic Press.

Lyell, C. 1863. *The Geological Evidences of the Antiquity of Man, with Remarks on Theories of the Origin of Species by Variation*. London, Murray.

Lyman, R. L. and M. J. O'Brien. 1998. The goals of evolutionary archaeology: history and explanation. *Current Anthropology* 39: 615–52.

1999. Americanist stratigraphic excavation and the measurement of culture change. *Journal of Archaeological Method and Theory* 6: 55–108.

2001. The direct historical approach, analogical reasoning, and theory in Americanist archaeology. *Journal of Archaeological Method and Theory* 8: 303–42.

2003. *W. C. McKern and the Midwestern Taxonomic Method*. Tuscaloosa, University of Alabama Press.

Lyman, R. L., M. J. O'Brien, and R. C. Dunnell. 1997a. *The Rise and Fall of Culture History*. New York, Plenum.

1997b. eds. *Americanist Culture History: Fundamentals of Time, Space, and Form*. New York, Plenum.

Lynch, B. D. and T. F. Lynch. 1968. The beginnings of a scientific approach to prehistoric archaeology in 17th and 18th century Britain. *Southwestern Journal of Anthropology* 24: 33–65.

Lynott, M. J. and A. Wylie. 1995. eds. *Ethics in American Archaeology: Challenges for the 1990s*. Washington, DC, Society for American Archaeology.

Lyon, E. A. 1996. *A New Deal for Southeastern Archaeology*. Tuscaloosa, University of Alabama Press.

References

Lyotard, J.-F. 1984. *The Postmodern Condition: A Report on Knowledge.* Minneapolis, University of Minnesota Press.

McBryde, I. 1985. ed. *Who Owns the Past?* Melbourne, Oxford University Press.

1986. Australia's once and future archaeology. *Archaeology in Oceania* 21: 13–28.

McCall, D. F. 1964. *Africa in Time-Perspective.* Boston, MA, Boston University Press.

McCann, W. J. 1989. "Volk und Germanentum": the presentation of the past in Nazi Germany. In P. Gathercole and D. Lowenthal, pp. 74–88.

McCarthy, F. D. 1959. Methods and scope of Australian archaeology. *Mankind* 5: 297–316.

McDonald, W. A. 1966. Some suggestions on directions and a modest proposal. *Hesperia* 35: 413–18.

McDonald, W. A. and C. G. Thomas. 1990. *Progress into the Past: The Rediscovey of Mycenaean Civilization.* 2nd ed. Bloomington, Indiana University Press.

McGregor, J. C. 1941. *Southwestern Archaeology.* New York, Wiley.

McGuire, J. D. 1899. Pipes and smoking customs of the American aborigines, based on material in the U.S. National Museum. Washington, DC, *United States National Museum, Annual Report, 1897,* pt. 1: 351–645.

McGuire, R. H. 1983. Breaking down cultural complexity: inequality and heterogeneity. *Advances in Archaeological Method and Theory* 6: 91–142.

1992a. *A Marxist Archaeology.* San Diego, CA, Academic Press.

1992b. Archaeology and the First Americans. *American Anthropologist* 94: 816–36.

1993. Archaeology and Marxism. *Archaeological Method and Theory* 5: 101–57.

2004. Contested pasts: archaeology and Native Americans. In L. Meskell and R. W. Preucel, pp. 374–95.

McGuire, R. H. and R. Paynter. 1991. eds. *The Archaeology of Inequality.* Oxford, Blackwell.

McGuire, R. H. and P. Reckner. 2002. The unromantic West: labor, capital and struggle. *Historical Archaeology* 36: 44–58.

2003. Building a working-class archaeology: the Colorado Coal Field War project. *Industrial Archaeology Review* 25: 83–95.

McIntosh, R. J. 2001. Africa, francophone. In T. Murray, 2001a, pp. 21–35.

McKay, A. G. 1976. Archaeology and the creative imagination. In *Symposium on New Perspectives in Canadian Archaeology,* ed. by A. G. McKay, pp. 227–34. Ottawa, Royal Society of Canada, Symposium 15.

McKern, W. C. 1937. An hypothesis for the Asiatic origin of the Woodland culture pattern. *American Antiquity* 3: 138–43.

1939. The Midwestern Taxonomic Method as an aid to archaeological culture study. *American Antiquity* 4: 301–13.

McKusick, M. 1970. *The Davenport Conspiracy.* Iowa City, University of Iowa.

1991. *The Davenport Conspiracy Revisited*. Ames, Iowa State University Press.

McLennan, J. F. 1865. *Primitive Marriage*. Edinburgh, Adam and Charles Black.

McNairn, B. 1980. *Method and Theory of V. Gordon Childe*. Edinburgh, Edinburgh University Press.

McNeill, W. H. 1986. *Mythistory and Other Essays*. Chicago, IL, University of Chicago Press.

McNitt, F. 1990. *Richard Wetherill-Anasazi: Pioneer Explorer of Southwestern Ruins*. Albuquerque, University of New Mexico Press.

MacCormack, C. P. and M. Strathern. 1980. eds. *Nature, Culture and Gender*. Cambridge, Cambridge University Press.

MacCormack, S. 1995. Limits of understanding: perceptions of Greco-Roman and Amerindian paganism in early modern Europe. In *America in European Consciousness 1493–1750*, ed. by K. O. Kupperman, pp. 79–129. Chapel Hill, University of North Carolina Press.

1991. *Religion in the Andes: Vision and Imagination in Early Colonial Peru*. Princeton, NJ, Princeton University Press.

MacDonald, S. and M. Rice. 2003. eds. *Consuming Ancient Egypt*. London, UCL Press.

MacGaffey, W. 1966. Concepts of race in the historiography of northeast Africa. *Journal of African History* 7: 1–17.

MacKendrick, P. 1960. *The Mute Stones Speak: The Story of Archaeology in Italy*. New York, St. Martin's Press.

MacNeish, R. S. 1952. *Iroquois Pottery Types: A Technique for the Study of Iroquois Prehistory*. Ottawa, National Museum of Canada, Bulletin no. 124.

1974. Reflections on my search for the beginnings of agriculture in Mexico. In G. R. Willey, 1974a, pp. 205–34.

1978. *The Science of Archaeology?* North Scituate, MA, Duxbury Press.

1992. *The Origins of Agriculture and Settled Life*. Norman, University of Oklahoma Press.

MacWhite, E. 1956. On the interpretation of archeological evidence in historical and sociological terms. *American Anthropologist* 58: 3–25.

Maischberger, M. 2002. German archaeology during the Third Reich, 1933–45: a case study based on archival evidence. *Antiquity* 76: 209–18.

Majewski, T. 2003. Historical archaeology and disciplinary exegesis. In S. D. Gillespie and D. L. Nichols, pp. 77–84.

Makkay, J. 1991. Gordon Childe (1892–1957) and Hungary: a centenary tribute. *The New Hungarian Quarterly* 32: 107–14.

Malina, J. and Z. Vašíček. 1990. *Archaeology Yesterday and Today: The Development of Archaeology in the Sciences and Humanities*. Cambridge, Cambridge University Press.

Malinowski, B. 1922. *Argonauts of the Western Pacific*. New York, E. P. Dutton.

1945. *The Dynamics of Culture Change: An Inquiry into Race Relations in Africa.* New Haven, CT, Yale University Press.

Mallows, W. 1985. *The Mystery of the Great Zimbabwe.* London, Robert Hale.

Malmer, M. P. 1963. Metodproblem inom järnålderns Konsthistoria (with English summary). Lund, Acta Archaeologica Lundensia, series altera, 3.

Malone, C. and S. Kaner. 1999. eds. Heritage and archaeology in the Far East. *Antiquity* 73: 585–629.

Malone, C. and S. Stoddart. 1998. eds. David Clarke's "Archaeology: the loss of innocence" (1973) 25 years after. *Antiquity* 72: 676–702.

Malthus, T. 1798. *An Essay on the Principle of Population.* London, J. Johnson.

Marchak, M. P. 1991. *The Integrated Circus: The New Right and the Restructuring of Global Markets.* Montreal, McGill-Queen's University Press.

Marchand, S. L. 1996. *Down from Olympus: Archaeology and Philhellenism in Germany, 1750–1970.* Princeton, NJ, Princeton University Press.

Marcus, J. 1983a. A synthesis of the cultural evolution of the Zapotec and Mixtec. In K. V. Flannery and J. Marcus, pp. 355–60.

1983b. Lowland Maya archaeology at the crossroads. *American Antiquity* 48: 454–88.

1992. *Mesoamerican Writing Systems: Propaganda, Myth, and History in Four Ancient Civilizations.* Princeton, NJ, Princeton University Press.

2003. Recent advances in Maya archaeology. *Journal of Archaeological Research* 11: 71–148.

Marcuse, H. 1964. *One Dimensional Man.* London, Routledge and Kegan Paul.

Mariátegui, J. C. 1952. *Siete ensayos de interpretación de la realidad Peruana.* Lima, Biblioteca Amauta.

Marlowe, G. 1999. Year one: radiocarbon dating and American archaeology, 1947–1948. *American Antiquity* 64: 9–32.

Marsden, B. M. 1974. *The Early Barrow-Diggers.* Park Ridge, UK, Noyes Press.

1984. *Pioneers of Prehistory: Leaders and Landmarks in English Archaeology (1500–1900).* Ormskirk, UK, Hesketh.

Marshall, Y. 2002. ed. Community archaeology. *World Archaeology* 34, 2.

Martin, P. S. 1971. The revolution in archaeology. *American Antiquity* 36: 1–8.

Martin, P. S., C. Lloyd, and A. Spoehr. 1938. Archaeological work in the Ackmen-Lowry area, southwestern Colorado, 1937. Chicago, IL, *Field Museum of Natural History, Anthropological Series* 23: 217–304.

Martin, P. S. and F. Plog. 1973. *The Archaeology of Arizona.* Garden City, NY, Natural History Press.

Martin, P. S., G. I. Quimby, and D. Collier. 1947. *Indians Before Columbus.* Chicago, IL, University of Chicago Press.

References

Martin, P. S. and J. Rinaldo. 1939. Modified Basket Maker sites, Ackmen-Lowry area, southwestern Colorado, 1938. Chicago, IL, *Field Museum of Natural History, Anthropological Series* 23: 305–499.

Marvin, U. B. 1973. *Continental Drift: The Evolution of a Concept.* Washington, DC, Smithsonian Institution Press.

Marx, K. 1906. *Capital: A Critique of Political Economy.* New York, The Modern Library, Random House.

Marx, K. and F. Engels. 1962. *Selected Works in Two Volumes.* Moscow, Foreign Languages Publishing House.

1964. *On Religion.* New York, Schocken.

Mason, O. T. 1895. *The Origins of Invention.* New York, Scribner.

1896. Influence of environment upon human industries or arts. Washington, DC, *Annual Report of the Smithsonian Institution for 1895*: 639–65.

Mason, R. J. 2000. Archaeology and Native American oral traditions. *American Antiquity* 65: 239–66.

Masry, A. H. 1981. Traditions of archaeological research in the Near East. *World Archaeology* 13: 222–39.

Masterman, M. 1970. The nature of a paradigm. In *Criticism and the Growth of Knowledge*, ed. by I. Lakatos and A. Musgrave, pp. 59–89. Cambridge, Cambridge University Press.

Matos Moctezuma, E. 1984. The templo mayor of Tenochtitlan: economics and ideology. In *Ritual Human Sacrifice in Mesoamerica*, ed. by E. H. Boone, pp. 133–64. Washington, DC, Dumbarton Oaks.

Matthews, R. and C. Roemer, 2003. eds. *Ancient Perspectives on Egypt.* London, UCL Press.

Mayes, S. 2003. *The Great Belzoni: The Circus Strongman Who Discovered Egypt's Ancient Treasures.* New York, Tauris Parke.

Mazel, A. D. 1992. Changing fortunes: 150 years of San hunter-gatherer history in the Natal Drakensberg, South Africa. *Antiquity* 66: 758–67.

Meacham, W. 1977. Continuity and local evolution in the Neolithic of South China: a non-nuclear approach. *Current Anthropology* 18: 419–40.

Meeks, D. and C. Favard-Meeks. 1996. *Daily Life of the Egyptian Gods.* Ithaca, NY, Cornell University Press.

Megaw, J. V. S. 1966. Australian archaeology: how far have we progressed? *Mankind* 6: 306–12.

1976. ed. *To Illustrate the Monuments: Essays on Archaeology Presented to Stuart Piggott.* London, Thames and Hudson.

Megaw, R. and J. V. S. Megaw. 1989. *Celtic Art: From Its Beginnings to the Book of Kells.* London, Thames and Hudson.

Meggers, B. J. 1955. The coming of age of American archeology. In *New Interpretations of Aboriginal American Culture History*, ed. by M. T. Newman, pp. 116–29. Washington, DC, Anthropological Society of Washington.

1960. The law of cultural evolution as a practical research tool. In *Essays in the Science of Culture*, ed. by G. E. Dole and R. L. Carneiro, pp. 302–16. New York, Crowell.

1968. ed. *Anthropological Archeology in the Americas.* Washington, DC, Anthropological Society of Washington.

Meillassoux, C. 1981. *Maidens, Meal and Money: Capitalism and the Domestic Economy.* Cambridge, Cambridge University Press.

Meinander, C. F. 1981. The concept of culture in European archaeological literature. In G. Daniel, 1981b, pp. 100–11.

Meltzer, D. J. 1979. Paradigms and the nature of change in American archaeology. *American Antiquity* 44: 644–57.

1983. The antiquity of man and the development of American archaeology. *Advances in Archaeological Method and Theory* 6: 1–51.

1999. William Henry Holmes 1846–1933. In T. Murray, 1999a, pp. 175–91.

Meltzer, D. J., D. D. Fowler, and J. A. Sabloff. 1986. eds. *American Archaeology Past and Future: A Celebration of the Society for American Archaeology 1935–1985.* Washington, DC, Smithsonian Institution Press.

Mendyk, S. A. E. 1989. *"Speculum Britanniae": Regional Study, Antiquarianism, and Science in Britain to 1700.* Toronto, University of Toronto Press.

Menzel, D. 1977. *The Archaeology of Ancient Peru and the Work of Max Uhle.* Berkeley, University of California, R. H. Lowie Museum of Anthropology.

Meskell, L. M. 1996. The somatisation of archaeology: discourses, institutions, corporeality. *Norwegian Archaeological Review* 29: 1–16.

1998. ed. *Archaeology Under Fire: Nationalism, Politics and Heritage in the Eastern Mediterranean and Middle East.* London, Routledge.

1999. *Archaeologies of Social Life: Age, Sex, Class et cetera in Ancient Egypt.* Oxford, Blackwell.

2002. The intersections of identity and politics in archaeology. *Annual Review of Anthropology* 31: 279–301.

Meskell, L. and R. W. Preucel. 2004. eds. *A Companion to Social Archaeology.* Oxford, Blackwell.

Meyer, E. 1884–1902. *Geschichte des Alterthums.* 5 vols. Stuttgart, J. G. Cotta.

Michael, H. N. 1962. ed. *Studies in Siberian Ethnogenesis.* Toronto, University of Toronto Press.

1964. *The Archaeology and Geomorphology of Northern Asia: Selected Works.* Toronto, University of Toronto Press.

Miller, D. 1980. Archaeology and development. *Current Anthropology* 21: 709–26.

1984. Modernism and suburbia as material ideology. In D. Miller and C. Tilley, pp. 37–49.

1985. *Artefacts as Categories: A Study of Ceramic Variability in Central India.* Cambridge, Cambridge University Press.

Miller, D., M. Rowlands, and C. Tilley. 1989a. eds. *Domination and Resistance.* London, Unwin Hyman.

1989b. Introduction. In D. Miller, M. Rowlands, and C. Tilley, 1989a, pp. 1–26.

References

Miller, D. and C. Tilley. 1984a. eds. *Ideology, Power and Prehistory*. Cambridge, Cambridge University Press.

1984b. Ideology, power and long-term social change. In D. Miller and C. Tilley, 1984a, pp. 147–52.

Miller, M. O. 1956. *Archaeology in the U.S.S.R*. London, Atlantic Press.

Millon, R., R. B. Drewitt, and G. L. Cowgill. 1973. *Urbanization at Teotihuacán, Mexico*, vol. 1, *The Teotihuacán Map*. Austin, University of Texas Press.

Mills, W. C. 1902. Excavations of the Adena Mound. *Ohio Archaeological and Historical Quarterly* 10: 452–79.

Mink, L. O. 1969. *Mind, History, and Dialectic: The Philosophy of R. G. Collingwood*. Bloomington, Indiana University Press.

Mitchell, T. 1988. *Colonising Egypt*. New York, Cambridge University Press.

Mithen, S. J. 1990. *Thoughtful Foragers: A Study of Prehistoric Decision Making*. Cambridge, Cambridge University Press.

1993. Simulating mammoth hunting and extinction: implications for the Late Pleistocene of the Central Russian Plain. In *Hunting and Animal Exploitation in the Later Palaeolithic and Mesolithic of Eurasia*, ed. by G. L. Peterkin, H. Bricker, and P. Mellars, pp. 163–78. Tucson, AZ, Archeological Papers of the American Anthropological Association 4.

1996. *The Prehistory of the Mind: A Search for the Origins of Art, Religion and Science*. London, Thames and Hudson.

2003. *After the Ice: A Global Human History*, 20,000–5000 BC. London, Weidenfeld and Nicolson.

Mizoguchi, K. 2002. *An Archaeological History of Japan*, 30,000 B.C. to A.D. 700. Philadelphia, University of Pennsylvania Press.

2004. Identity, modernity, and archaeology: the case of Japan. In L. Meskell and R. W. Preucel, pp. 396–414.

Moberg, C.-A. 1976. *Introduction à l'archéologie*. Paris, Maspero.

1981. From artefacts to timetables to maps (to mankind?): regional traditions in archaeological research in Scandinavia. *World Archaeology* 13: 209–21.

Moir, E. 1958. The English Antiquaries. *History Today* 8: 781–92.

Molino, J. 1992. Archaeology and symbol systems. In J.-C. Gardin and C. S. Peebles, pp. 15–29.

Momigliano, A. 1966. Ancient history and the antiquarian. In *Studies in Historiography* by A. Momigliano, pp. 1–39. London, Weidenfeld and Nicolson.

Mongait, A. L. 1959. *Archaeology in the U.S.S.R*. Moscow, Foreign Languages Publishing House.

1961. *Archaeology in the USSR*. trans. by M. W. Thompson. Harmondsworth, UK, Penguin.

Monks, G. G. 1981. Seasonality studies. *Advances in Archaeological Method and Theory* 4: 177–240.

Montané, J. C. 1980. *Marxismo y Arqueología*. México, Ediciones de Cultura Popular.

References

Montelius, O. 1885. *Om tidsbestämning inom bronsåldern med särskildt afseende på Skandinavien*. Stockholm, Vitterhets Historie och Antikvitets Akademien, Handlingar 30, ny, följd, 10.

1899. *Der Orient und Europa*. Stockholm, Königl. Akademie der schönen Wissenschaften, Geschichte und Alterthumskunde.

1903. *Die typologische Methode: Die älteren Kulturperioden im Orient und in Europa*, vol. 1. Stockholm, Selbstverlag.

Moore, C. B. 1892. Certain shell heaps of the St. John's River, Florida, hitherto unexplored. *American Naturalist* 26: 912–22.

Moore, J. A. and A. S. Keene. 1983. *Archaeological Hammers and Theories*. New York, Academic Press.

Moorehead, W. K. 1909. A study of primitive culture in Ohio. In F. Boas et al., pp. 137–50.

1910. *The Stone Age in North America*. 2 vols. Boston, MA, Houghton Mifflin.

Moorey, P. R. S. 1979. Kathleen Kenyon and Palestinian archaeology. *Palestine Exploration Quarterly* (January–June): 3–10.

1991. *A Century of Biblical Archaeology*. Cambridge, UK, Lutterworth Press.

Mora, G. and M. Díaz-Andreu. 1997. eds. *La Cristalización del Pasado: Génesis y Desarrollo del Marco Institucional de la Arqueología en España*. Málaga, Servicio de Publicationes de la Universidad de Málaga.

Moret, A. and G. Davy. 1926. *From Tribe to Empire: Social Organization among Primitives and in the Ancient East*. London, Kegan Paul.

Morgan, C. G. 1973. Archaeology and explanation. *World Archaeology* 4: 259–76.

1978. Comment on D. W. Read and S. A. LeBlanc, "Descriptive statements, covering laws, and theories in archaeology." *Current Anthropology* 19: 325–6.

Morgan, L. H. 1877. *Ancient Society*. New York, Holt.

1881. *Houses and House-life of the American Aborigines*. Washington, DC, Contribution to North American Ethnology 4, U.S. Geological and Geographical Survey of the Rocky Mountain Region.

Morlot, A. 1861. General views on archaeology. Washington, DC, *Annual Report of the Smithsonian Institution for 1860*: 284–343.

Moro Abadía, O. 2002. Towards a definition of time in archaeology: French prehistoric archaeology (1850–1900). *Papers from the Institute of Archaeology* 13: 51–63.

Moro Abadía, O. and M. R. González Morales. 2003. L'art bourgeois de la fin du XIXe siècle face à l'art mobilier Paléolithique. *L'anthropologie* 107: 455–70.

2004. Towards a genealogy of the concept of "paleolithic mobiliary art." *Journal of Anthropological Research* 60: 321–39.

Morrell, J. B. 1981. "Externalism" and "Internalism." In *Dictionary of the History of Science*, ed. by W. F. Bynum, E. J. Browne, and R. Porter, pp. 145–46, 211. London, Macmillan.

References

Morris, I. 1987. *Burial and Ancient Society: The Rise of the Greek City-State.* Cambridge, Cambridge University Press.

1994a. ed. *Classical Greece: Ancient Histories and Modern Archaeologies.* Cambridge, Cambridge University Press.

1994b. Archaeologies of Greece. In I. Morris, 1994a, pp. 8–47.

2000. *Archaeology as Cultural History.* Oxford, Blackwell.

Morse, E. S. 1879. Traces of an early race in Japan. *Popular Science Monthly* 14: 257–66.

Morse, M. A. 1999. Craniology and the adoption of the Three-Age System in Britain. *Proceedings of the Prehistoric Society* 65: 1–16.

Mortillet, G. de. 1883. *Le préhistorique: antiquité de l'homme.* Paris, C. Reinwald.

1897. *Formation de la nation française.* Paris, Alcan.

Morton, S. G. 1839. *Crania Americana.* Philadelphia, PA, Dobson.

1844. *Crania Aegyptiaca.* Philadelphia, PA, Penington.

Moser, S. 1992. The visual language of archaeology: a case study of the Neanderthals. *Antiquity* 66: 831–44.

1995a. *Archaeology and its Disciplinary Culture: The Professionalization of Australian Prehistoric Archaeology.* PhD dissertation, Sydney, University of Sydney.

1995b. The "aboriginalization" of Australian archaeology: the contribution of the Australian Institute of Aboriginal Studies to the indigenous transformation of the discipline. In P. J. Ucko, 1995a, pp. 150–77.

Much, M. 1907. *Die Trugspiegelung orientalischer Kultur in den vorgeschichtlichen Zeitaltern nord- und mittel-Europas.* Jena, Costenoble.

Mufuka, K. 1983. *Dzimbahwe Life and Politics in the Golden Age, 1100–1500 AD.* Harare, Harare Publishing House.

Mulvaney, D. J. 1969. *The Prehistory of Australia.* London, Thames and Hudson.

1981. Gum leaves on the Golden Bough: Australia's Palaeolithic survivals discovered. In J. D. Evans et al. pp. 52–64.

Mulvaney, D. J. and J. P. White. 1987. eds. *Australians to 1788.* Broadway, NSW, Fairfax, Syme and Weldon.

Murdock, G. P. 1949. *Social Structure.* New York, Macmillan.

Murdock, G. P., C. S. Ford, A. E. Hudson, R. Kennedy, L. W. Simmons, and J. H. Whiting. 1938. *Outline of Cultural Materials.* New Haven, CT, Yale University, Institute of Human Relations.

Murray, P. 1980. Discard location: the ethnographic data. *American Antiquity* 45: 490–502.

Murray, T. 1989. The history, philosophy and sociology of archaeology: the case of the Ancient Monuments Protection Act (1882). In *Critical Traditions in Contemporary Archaeology: Essays in the Philosophy, History, and Socio-Politics of Archaeology,* ed. by V. Pinsky and A. Wylie, pp. 55–67. Cambridge, Cambridge University Press.

1992. Tasmania and the constitution of "the dawn of humanity." *Antiquity* 66: 730–43.

1999a. ed. *Encyclopedia of Archaeology: The Great Archaeologists.* 2 vols. Santa Barbara, CA, ABC-CLIO.

1999b. Epilogue: the art of archaeological biography. In T. Murray, 1999a, pp. 869–83.

2001a. ed. *Encyclopedia of Archaeology: History and Discoveries.* 3 vols. Santa Barbara, CA, ABC-CLIO.

2001b. Britain, prehistoric archaeology. In T. Murray, 2001a, pp. 199–217.

2001c. Australia, prehistoric. In T. Murray, 2001a, pp. 121–27.

2004a. ed. *The Archaeology of Contact in Settler Societies.* Cambridge, Cambridge University Press.

2004b. Archbishop Ussher and archaeological time. In L. Vishnyatsky et al., pp. 204–15.

Murray, T. and J. P. White. 1981. Cambridge in the bush? Archaeology in Australia and New Guinea. *World Archaeology* 13: 255–63.

Myhre, B. 1991. Theory in Scandinavian archaeology since 1960: a view from Norway. In I. Hodder, 1991a, pp. 161–86.

Myres, J. L. 1911. *The Dawn of History.* London, Williams and Norgate.

1923a. Primitive man, in geological time. In *Cambridge Ancient History,* vol. 1, ed. by J. B. Bury, S. A. Cook, and F. E. Adcock, pp. 1–56. Cambridge, Cambridge University Press.

1923b. Neolithic and Bronze Age cultures. Ibid., pp. 57–111.

Nader, L. 2001. Anthropology! distinguished lecture – 2000. *American Anthropologist* 103: 609–20.

Nagel, E. 1961. *The Structure of Science: Problems in the Logic of Scientific Explanation.* New York, Harcourt, Brace and World.

Nash, S. E. 1999. *Time, Trees, and Prehistory: Tree-Ring Dating and the Development of North American Archaeology, 1914–1950.* Salt Lake City, University of Utah Press.

2000a. ed. *It's About Time: A History of Archaeological Dating in North America.* Salt Lake City, University of Utah Press.

2000b. Just a matter of time? North American archaeological dating in the twenty-first century. In Nash, 2000a, pp. 208–10.

Nederveen Pieterse, J. 1992. *White on Black: Images of Africa and Blacks in Western Popular Culture.* New Haven, CT, Yale University Press.

Neff, H. 2000. On evolutionary ecology and evolutionary archaeology: some common ground? *Current Anthropology* 41: 427–29.

Nelson, M. C., S. M. Nelson, and A. Wylie. 1994. eds. *Equity Issues for Women in Archeology.* Washington, DC, Archeological Papers of the American Anthropological Association 5.

Nelson, N. C. 1916. Chronology of the Tano ruins, New Mexico. *American Anthropologist* 18: 159–80.

Nelson, S. M. 1997. *Gender in Archaeology: Analyzing Power and Prestige.* Walnut Creek, CA, AltaMira.

Nicholas, G. P. and T. D. Andrews. 1997. eds. *At a Crossroads: Archaeology and First Peoples in Canada*. Burnaby, BC, Simon Fraser University, Archaeology Press, Publication 24.

Nicholson, H. B. 1976. ed. *Origins of Religious Art and Iconography in Preclassic Mesoamerica*. Los Angeles, UCLA, Latin American Center Publications.

Nilsson, S. 1868. *The Primitive Inhabitants of Scandinavia*. 3rd edn, trans. by J. Lubbock. London, Longmans, Green.

Noble, D. F. 1977. *America by Design: Science, Technology, and the Rise of Corporate Capitalism*. New York, Knopf.

Nott, J. C. and G. R. Gliddon. 1854. *Types of Mankind*. Philadelphia, PA, Lippincott, Grambo.

Nzewunwa, N. 1984. Nigeria. In H. Cleere, pp. 101–8.

O'Brien, M. J. 1996a. *Paradigms of the Past: The Story of Missouri Archaeology*. Columbia, University of Missouri Press.

   1996b. ed. *Evolutionary Archaeology: Theory and Application*. Salt Lake City, University of Utah Press.

   2005. Evolutionism and North America's archaeological record. *World Archaeology* 37: 26–45.

O'Brien, M. J. and T. D. Holland. 1990. Variation, selection, and the archaeological record. *Archaeological Method and Theory* 2: 31–79.

O'Brien, M. J. and R. D. Leonard. 2001. Style and function: an introduction. In T. D. Hurt and G. Rakita, pp. 1–23.

O'Brien, M. J. and R. L. Lyman. 1998. *James A. Ford and the Growth of Americanist Archaeology*. Columbia, University of Missouri Press.

   1999a. *Seriation, Stratigraphy, and Index Fossils: The Backbone of Archaeological Dating*. New York, Kluwer Academic/Plenum.

   1999b. The Bureau of American Ethnology and its legacy to southeastern archaeology. *Journal of the Southwest* 41: 407–40.

   2000. eds. *Applying Evolutionary Archaeology: A Systematic Approach*. New York, Plenum.

O'Brien, M. J., R. L. Lyman, and R. D. Leonard. 1998. Basic incompatibilities between evolutionary and behavioral archaeology. *American Antiquity* 63: 485–98.

O'Brien, M. J., R. L. Lyman, and M. B. Schiffer. 2005. *Archaeology as a Process: Processualism and Its Progeny*. Salt Lake City, University of Utah Press.

O'Connor, D. 1993. *Ancient Nubia: Egypt's Rival in Africa*. Philadelphia, University of Pennsylvania, The University Museum.

O'Connor, D. and A. Reid. 2003. eds. *Ancient Egypt in Africa*. London, UCL Press.

O'Connor, T. E. 1983. *The Politics of Soviet Culture, Anatolii Lunacharskii*. Ann Arbor, MI, University Microfilms International Research Press.

Odell, G. H. 2001. Research problems R us. *American Antiquity* 66: 679–85.

Odum, E. P. 1953. *Fundamentals of Ecology*. Philadelphia, PA, Saunders.

Okladnikov, A. P. 1965. *The Soviet Far East in Antiquity*. Toronto, University of Toronto Press.

1970. *Yakutia Before Its Incorporation into the Russian State*. Montreal, McGill-Queen's University Press.

O'Laverty, J. 1857. Relative antiquity of stone and bronze weapons. *Ulster Journal of Archaeology* 5: 122–7.

Oldfield, E. 1852. Introductory address. *Archaeological Journal* 9: 1–6.

Oliveira, V. and S. O. Jorge. 1995. Theoretical underpinnings of Portuguese archaeology in the twentieth century. In P. J. Ucko, 1995a, pp. 251–62.

Olsen, B. 1990. Roland Barthes: from sign to text. In Tilley, 1990a, pp. 163–205.

Olsen, J. W. 1987. The practice of archaeology in China today. *Antiquity* 61: 282–90.

Orenstein, H. 1954. The evolutionary theory of V. Gordon Childe. *Southwestern Journal of Anthropology* 10: 200–14.

Orme, B. 1973. Archaeology and ethnology. In Renfrew, 1973b, pp. 481–92.

1981. *Anthropology for Archaeologists: An Introduction*. London, Duckworth.

Orser, C. E., Jr. 1996. *A Historical Archaeology of the Modern World*. New York, Plenum.

2004. *Historical Archaeology*. 2nd ed. Upper Saddle River, NJ, Pearson Prentice Hall.

Ortman, S. G. 2000. Conceptual metaphor in the archaeological record: methods and an example from the American Southwest. *American Antiquity* 65: 613–45.

Orton, C. 1980. *Mathematics in Archaeology*. London, Collins.

O'Shea, J. M. 1984. *Mortuary Variability: An Archaeological Investigation*. New York, Academic Press.

Osgood, C. B. 1951. Culture: its empirical and non-empirical character. *Southwestern Journal of Anthropology* 7: 202–14.

Ottaway, J. H. 1973. Rudolf Virchow: an appreciation. *Antiquity* 47: 101–8.

Owen, A. L. 1962. *The Famous Druids: A Survey of Three Centuries of English Literature on the Druids*. Oxford, Oxford University Press.

Paddayya, K. 1980. On the threshold: a review article on the latest developments in method and theory in archaeology. *Bulletin of the Deccan College Research Institute* 39: 117–34.

1982. Ecological archaeology and the ecology of archaeology: the archaeologist's viewpoint. *Bulletin of the Deccan College Research Institute* 41: 130–50.

1983. Myths about the New Archaeology. *Saeculum* 34: 70–104.

1986. The epistemology of archaeology: a postscript to the New Archaeology. *Bulletin of the Deccan College Postgraduate and Research Institute* 45: 89–115.

1990. *The New Archaeology and Aftermath: A View from Outside the Anglo-Saxon World*. Pune, Ravish.

1993. C. J. Thomsen and the Three Age system. *Man and Environment* 18: 129–40.

Pagden, A. 1982. *The Fall of Natural Man*. Cambridge, Cambridge University Press.

Paine, R. 1983. Israel and totemic time? *Royal Anthropological Institute News* 59: 19–22.

1994. Masada: a history of a memory. *History and Anthropology* 6: 371–409.

Pande, G. C. 1985. *An Approach to Indian Culture and Civilization*. Varanasi, Banaras Hindu University, Monograph of the Department of Ancient Indian History, Culture and Archaeology no. 15.

Panofsky, E. 1960. *Renaissance and Renascences in Western Art*. Stockholm, Almquist and Wiksell.

Parker, A. C. 1907. *Excavations in an Erie Indian Village and Burial Site at Ripley, Chautauqua County, New York*. Albany, New York State Museum, Bulletin no. 117.

1916. The origin of the Iroquois as suggested by their archeology. *American Anthropologist* 18: 479–507.

1920. *The Archaeological History of New York*. Albany, New York State Museum, Bulletins nos. 235–8.

Parker Pearson, M. 1982. Mortuary practices, society and ideology: an ethnoarchaeological study. In I. Hodder, 1982c, pp. 99–113.

1984. Social change, ideology and the archaeological record. In M. Spriggs, 1984a, pp. 59–71.

1999. *The Archaeology of Death and Burial*. Stroud, UK, Sutton Publishing.

Parry, G. 1995. *The Trophies of Time: English Antiquarians of the Seventeenth Century*. Oxford, Oxford University Press.

1999. John Aubrey 1626–1697. In T. Murray, 1999a, pp. 15–37.

Parslow, C. C. 1995. *Rediscovering Antiquity: Karl Weber and the Excavation of Herculaneum, Pompeii, and Stabiae*. Cambridge, Cambridge University Press.

Parsons, T. 1968. Durkheim, Emile. In D. L. Sills, vol. 4, pp. 311–20.

Patrik, L. E. 1985. Is there an archaeological record? *Advances in Archaeological Method and Theory* 8: 27–62.

Patterson, T. C. 1983. The historical development of a coastal Andean social formation in central Peru: 6000 to 500 B.C. In *Investigations of the Andean Past*, ed. by D. Sandweiss, pp. 21–37. Ithaca, NY, Cornell University, Latin American Studies Program.

1986a. The last sixty years: toward a social history of Americanist archeology in the United States. *American Anthropologist* 88: 7–26.

1986b. Some postwar theoretical trends in U.S. archeology. *Culture* 6: 43–54.

1989. History and the post-processual archaeologies. *Man* 24: 555–66.

1990. Some theoretical tensions within and between the processual and postprocessual archaeologies. *Journal of Anthropological Archaeology* 9: 189–200.

1991. Who did archaeology in the United States before there were archaeologists and why? Preprofessional archaeologies of the nineteenth century. In R. W. Preucel, pp. 242–50.

1994. Social archaeology in Latin America: an appreciation. *American Antiquity* 59: 531–7.

1995. *Toward a Social History of Archaeology in the United States*. Fort Worth, TX, Harcourt Brace.

1997. *Inventing Western Civilization*. New York, Monthly Review Press.

1999. The political economy of archaeology in the United States. *Annual Review of Anthropology* 28: 155–74.

2003. *Marx's Ghost: Conversations with Archaeologists*. Oxford, Berg.

Patterson, T. C. and C. E. Orser Jr. 2004. eds. *Foundations of Social Archaeology: Selected Writings of V. Gordon Childe*. Walnut Creek, CA, AltaMira Press.

Pauketat, T. R. 2003. Materiality and the immaterial in historical-processual archaeology. In T. L. and C. S. VanPool, pp. 41–53.

Peace, W. J. 1988. Vere Gordon Childe and American anthropology. *Journal of Anthropological Research* 44: 417–33.

1993. Leslie White and evolutionary theory. *Dialectical Anthropology* 18: 123–51.

Peacock, D. P. S. 1997. Charlemagne's black stones: the re-use of Roman columns in early medieval Europe. *Antiquity* 71: 709–15.

Peake, H. J. E. 1922. *The Bronze Age and the Celtic World*. London, Benn.

1940. The study of prehistoric times. *Journal of the Royal Anthropological Institute* 70: 103–46.

Peake, H. J. E. and H. J. Fleure. 1927. *The Corridors of Time*, vol. 3, *Peasants and Potters*. Oxford, Oxford University Press.

Pearce, R. H. 1965. *Savagism and Civilization: A Study of the Indian and the American Mind*. Baltimore, MD, Johns Hopkins University Press.

Pearson, R. J. 1977. The social aims of Chinese archaeology. *Antiquity* 51: 8–10.

Peel, J. D. 1971. *Herbert Spencer: The Evolution of a Sociologist*. London, Heinemann Educational.

Peregrine, P. 2000. A tale of two archaeologies. *Ethnohistory* 47: 249–56.

Perry, W. J. 1923. *The Children of the Sun*. London, Methuen.

1924. *The Growth of Civilization*. London, Methuen.

Petrie, W. M. F. 1901. *Diospolis Parva*. London, Egypt Exploration Fund.

1911. *The Revolutions of Civilisation*. London, Harper.

1939. *The Making of Egypt*. London, Sheldon.

Petrova-Averkieva, Yu. 1980. Historicism in Soviet ethnographic science. In E. Gellner, pp. 19–27.

Phillips, P. 1955. American archaeology and general anthropological theory. *Southwestern Journal of Anthropology* 11: 246–50.

Phillips, P. and G. R. Willey. 1953. Method and theory in American archeology: an operational basis for culture-historical integration. *American Anthropologist* 55: 615–33.

References

Piggott, S. 1935. Stukeley, Avebury and the druids. *Antiquity* 9: 22–32.

1950. *William Stukeley: An Eighteenth-Century Antiquary.* Oxford, Oxford University Press.

1958. Vere Gordon Childe, 1892–1957. *Proceedings of the British Academy* 44: 305–12.

1959. *Approach to Archaeology.* Cambridge, MA, Harvard University Press.

1968. *The Druids.* London, Thames and Hudson.

1976. *Ruins in a Landscape: Essays in Antiquarianism.* Edinburgh, Edinburgh University Press.

1978. *Antiquity Depicted: Aspects of Archaeological Illustration.* London, Thames and Hudson.

1983. *The Earliest Wheeled Transport: From the Atlantic Coast to the Caspian Sea.* London, Thames and Hudson.

1985. *William Stukeley: An Eighteenth-Century Antiquary,* rev. edn. London, Thames and Hudson.

1989. *Ancient Britons and the Antiquarian Imagination: Ideas from the Renaissance to the Regency.* London, Thames and Hudson.

Pinker, S. 2002. *The Blank Slate: The Modern Denial of Human Nature.* New York, Viking Press.

Pinsky, V. 1992a. Anthropology and the New Archaeology: A Critical Study of Disciplinary Change in American Archaeology. PhD dissertation, Department of Archaeology, Cambridge University.

1992b. Archaeology, politics, and boundary formation: the Boas censure (1919) and the development of American archaeology during the inter-war years. In J. E. Reyman, pp. 161–89.

Pitt-Rivers, A. H. L.-F. 1906. *The Evolution of Culture and Other Essays.* Oxford, Oxford University Press.

Plog, F. 1982. Can the centuries-long experience of the Hohokam . . . be ignored? *Early Man* 4(4): 24–5.

Plog, S. 1980. *Stylistic Variation in Prehistoric Ceramics: Design Analysis in the American Southwest.* Cambridge, Cambridge University Press.

Pluciennik, M. 2002. The invention of hunter-gatherers in seventeenth-century Europe. *Archaeological Dialogues* 9: 98–151.

Polanyi, K. 1944. *The Great Transformation.* New York, Farrar and Rinehart.

1966. *Dahomey and the Slave Trade: An Analysis of an Archaic Economy.* Seattle, University of Washington Press.

Polanyi, K., C. M. Arensberg, and H. W. Pearson. 1957. *Trade and Market in the Early Empires.* Glencoe, IL, Free Press.

Poliakov, L. 1974. *The Aryan Myth: A History of Racist and Nationalist Ideas in Europe.* New York, Basic Books.

Politis, G. G. 2003. The theoretical landscape and the methodological development of archaeology in Latin America. *American Antiquity* 68: 245–72.

Politis, G. G. and B. Alberti. 1999. eds. *Archaeology in Latin America.* London, Routledge.

References

Politis, G. G. and J. A. Pérez Gollán. 2004. Latin American archaeology: from colonialism to globalization. In L. Meskell and R. W. Preucel, 2004, pp. 353–73.

Pomian, K. 1990. *Collectors and Curiosities: Paris and Venice 1500–1800.* London, Polity Press.

Popper, K. R. 1959. *The Logic of Scientific Discovery.* London, Hutchinson.

Porter, R. 1977. *The Making of Geology: Earth Science in Britain 1660–1815.* Cambridge, Cambridge University Press.

Posnansky, M. 1976. Archaeology as a university discipline – Ghana, 1967–71. *Proceedings of the Panafrican Congress of Prehistory*, pp. 329–31.

   1982. African archaeology comes of age. *World Archaeology* 13: 345–58.

Possehl, G. L. 2002. *The Indus Civilization: A Contemporary Perspective.* Walnut Creek, CA, AltaMira Press.

Prescott, W. H. 1843. *History of the Conquest of Mexico.* New York, Harper.

   1847. *History of the Conquest of Peru.* New York, Harper and Brothers.

Press, G. A. 2003. *The Development of the Idea of History in Antiquity.* Montreal, McGill-Queen's University Press.

Preston, D. 1995. The mystery of Sandia Cave. *The New Yorker*, June 12, pp. 66–83.

Preucel, R. W. 1991. ed. *Processual and Postprocessual Archaeologies: Multiple Ways of Knowing the Past.* Carbondale, Southern Illinois University at Carbondale, Center for Archaeological Investigations, Occasional Paper 10.

   1995. The postprocessual condition. *Journal of Archaeological Research* 3:147–75.

Preucel, R. W. and M. S. Chesson. 1994. Blue corn girls: a herstory of three early women archaeologists at Tecolote, New Mexico. In C. Claassen, pp. 67–84.

Preucel, R. W. and I. Hodder. 1996. eds. *Contemporary Archaeology in Theory: A Reader.* Oxford, Blackwell.

Price, B. J. 1977. Shifts in production and organization: a cluster-interaction model. *Current Anthropology* 18: 209–33.

Price, D. 1993. *Threatening Anthropology: McCarthyism and the FBI's Surveillance of Activist Anthropologists.* Durham, NC, Duke University Press.

Price, N. S. 2001. ed. *The Archaeology of Shamanism.* London, Routledge.

Price, T. D. and J. A. Brown. 1985. eds. *Prehistoric Hunter-Gatherers: The Emergence of Cultural Complexity.* New York, Academic Press.

Prichard, J. C. 1813. *Researches into the Physical History of Man.* London, John and Arthur Arch.

Priest, J. 1833. *American Antiquities, and Discoveries in the West.* Albany, NY, Hoffman and White.

Pumpelly, R. 1908. ed. *Explorations in Turkestan.* 2 vols. Washington, DC, Carnegie Institution.

References

Puodžiūnas, G. and A. Girininkas. 1996. Nationalism doubly oppressed: archaeology and nationalism in Lithuania. In M. Díaz-Andreu and T. Champion, 1996a, pp. 243–55.

Raab, L. M. and A. C. Goodyear. 1984. Middle-range theory in archaeology: a critical review of origins and applications. *American Antiquity* 49: 255–68.

Radcliffe-Brown, A. R. 1922. *The Andaman Islanders.* Cambridge, Cambridge University Press.

Raglan, F. R. R. S. 1939. *How Came Civilization?* London, Methuen.

Ramage, N. 1990. Sir William Hamilton as collector, exporter, and dealer: the acquisition and dispersal of his collections. *American Journal of Archaeology* 94: 469–80.

1992. Goods, graves, and scholars: 18th-century archaeologists in Britain and Italy. *American Journal of Archaeology* 96: 653–61.

Ramsden, P. G. 1977. *A Refinement of Some Aspects of Huron Ceramic Analysis.* Ottawa, Archaeological Survey of Canada, Mercury Series no. 63.

1996. The current state of Huron archaeology. *Northeast Archaeology* 51: 101–12.

Randall-MacIver, D. 1906. *Mediaeval Rhodesia.* London, Macmillan.

Randall-MacIver, D. and C. L. Woolley. 1909. *Areika.* Philadelphia, University of Pennsylvania, University Museum.

Ranov, V. A. and R. S. Davis. 1979. Toward a new outline of the Soviet Central Asian Paleolithic. *Current Anthropology* 20: 249–70.

Rappaport, R. A. 1968. *Pigs for the Ancestors: Ritual in the Ecology of a New Guinea People.* New Haven, CT, Yale University Press.

Rathje, W. L. 1974. The Garbage Project: a new way of looking at the problems of archaeology. *Archaeology* 27: 236–41.

1975. The last tango in Mayapán: a tentative trajectory of production-distribution systems. In J. A. Sabloff and C. C. Lamberg-Karlovsky, pp. 409–48.

Ratnagar, S. 2004. Archaeology at the heart of a political confrontation: the case of Ayodhya. *Current Anthropology* 45: 239–59.

Ratzel, F. 1882–1891. *Anthropogeographie.* Stuttgart, Engelhorn.

1896–1898. *The History of Mankind.* trans. by A. J. Butler. 3 vols. London, Macmillan.

Rautman, A. E. 2000. ed. *Reading the Body: Representations and Remains in the Archaeological Record.* Philadelphia, University of Pennsylvania Press.

Ravetz, A. 1959. Notes on the work of V. Gordon Childe. *The New Reasoner* 10: 55–66.

Read, D. W. and S. A. LeBlanc. 1978. Descriptive statements, covering laws, and theories in archaeology. *Current Anthropology* 19: 307–35.

Redfield, R. 1953. *The Primitive World and Its Transformations.* Ithaca, NY, Cornell University Press.

Redford, D. B. 1986. *Pharaonic King-Lists, Annals and Day Books: A Contribution to the Study of the Egyptian Sense of History.* Mississauga, ON, Benben Publications.

Redman, C. L. 1973. ed. *Research and Theory in Current Archeology*. New York, Wiley.

1986. *Qsar es-Seghir: An Archaeological View of Medieval Life*. New York, Academic Press.

1991. In defense of the seventies – the adolescence of New Archeology. *American Anthropologist* 93: 295–307.

Redman, C. L. et al. 1978. eds. *Social Archeology: Beyond Subsistence and Dating*. New York, Academic Press.

Reid, A. 2003. Ancient Egypt and the source of the Nile. In D. O'Connor and A. Reid, pp. 55–76.

Reid, D. M. 1985. Indigenous Egyptology: the decolonization of a profession. *Journal of the American Oriental Society* 105: 233–46.

1997. Nationalizing the Pharaonic past: Egyptology, imperialism, and Egyptian nationalism, 1922–1952. In *Rethinking Nationalism in the Arab Middle East*, ed. by J. Jankowski and I. Gershoni, pp. 35–69. New York, Columbia University Press.

2002. *Whose Pharaohs? Archaeology, Museums, and Egyptian National Identity from Napoleon to World War I*. Berkeley, University of California Press.

Reid, J. J. 1991. On the history of archaeology and archaeologists. *American Antiquity* 56: 195–6.

Reid, J. J., W. L. Rathje, and M. B. Schiffer. 1974. Expanding archaeology. *American Antiquity* 39: 125–6.

Reinach, S. 1893. *Le Mirage oriental*. Paris, G. Masson.

1903. L'Art et la magie: à propos des peintures et des gravures de l'âge du renne. *L'Anthropologie* 14: 257–66.

Reisner, G. A. 1910. *The Archaeological Survey of Nubia, Report for 1907–1908*. 2 vols. Cairo, National Printing Department.

1923a. *Excavations at Kerma, I–III*. Boston, MA, Harvard African Studies 5.

1923b. *Excavations at Kerma, IV–V*. Boston, MA, Harvard African Studies 6.

Renfrew, A. C. 1972. *The Emergence of Civilisation: The Cyclades and the Aegean in the Third Millennium B.C.* London, Methuen.

1973a. *Before Civilization: The Radiocarbon Revolution and Prehistoric Europe*. London, Cape.

1973b. ed. *The Explanation of Culture Change: Models in Prehistory*. London, Duckworth.

1973c. Wessex as a social question. *Antiquity* 47: 221–5.

1973d. *Social Archaeology* (inaugural lecture). Southampton, The University.

1975. Trade as action at a distance: questions of integration and communication. In J. A. Sabloff and C. C. Lamberg-Karlovsky, pp. 3–59.

1978a. Trajectory discontinuity and morphogenesis. *American Antiquity* 43: 203–22.

References

1978b. Space, time and polity. In J. Friedman and M. J. Rowlands, 1978a, pp. 89–112.

1979. *Problems in European Prehistory.* Cambridge, Cambridge University Press.

1980. The great tradition versus the great divide: archaeology as anthropology? *American Journal of Archaeology* 84: 287–98.

1982a. Explanation revisited. In *Theory and Explanation in Archaeology*, ed. by A. C. Renfrew, M. J. Rowlands, and B. A. Segraves, pp. 5–23. New York, Academic Press.

1982b. *Towards an Archaeology of Mind* (inaugural lecture). Cambridge, Cambridge University Press.

1984. *Approaches to Social Archaeology.* Edinburgh, Edinburgh University Press.

1988. *Archaeology and Language: The Puzzle of Indo-European Origins.* New York, Cambridge University Press.

1992. Archaeology, genetics and linguistic diversity. *Man* 27: 445–78.

Renfrew, A. C. and P. Bahn. 2004. *Archaeology: Theories, Methods and Practice.* 4th edn. London, Thames and Hudson.

Renfrew, A. C. and J. F. Cherry. 1986. eds. *Peer Polity Interaction and Socio-Political Change.* Cambridge, Cambridge University Press.

Renfrew, A. C. and K. L. Cooke. 1979. eds. *Transformations: Mathematical Approaches to Culture Change.* New York, Academic Press.

Renfrew, A. C., J. E. Dixon and J. R. Cann. 1968. Further analysis of Near Eastern obsidians. *Proceedings of the Prehistoric Society* 34: 319–31.

Renfrew, A. C. and C. Scarre. 1998. eds. *Cognition and Material Culture: The Archaeology of Symbolic Storage.* Cambridge, McDonald Institute for Archaeological Research.

Renfrew, A. C. and S. Shennan. 1982. eds. *Ranking, Resource and Exchange: Aspects of the Archaeology of Early European Society.* Cambridge, Cambridge University Press.

Renfrew, A. C. and E. B. W. Zubrow. 1994. eds. *The Ancient Mind: Elements of Cognitive Archaeology.* Cambridge, Cambridge University Press.

Reyman, J. E. 1992. ed. *Rediscovering our Past: Essays on the History of American Archaeology.* Aldershot, UK, Avebury.

1999. Walter W. Taylor 1913–1997. In T. Murray, 1999a, pp. 681–700.

Ribes, R. 1966. Pièces de la période archaïque trouvées vers 1700 dans la region de Bécancour. *Cahiers d'archéologie québecoise* 2(1): 22–34.

Ridgway, D. 1985. V. Gordon Childe a venticinque anni dalla morte. In *Studi di Paletnologia in Onore di Salvatore M. Puglisi*, ed. by M. Liverani, A. Palmieri, and R. Peroni, pp. 3–11. Rome, Università di Roma.

Ridley, R. T. 1992. *The Eagle and the Spade: Archaeology in Rome during the Napoleonic Era, 1809–1814.* Cambridge, Cambridge University Press.

1998. *Napoleon's Proconsul in Egypt: The Life and Times of Bernardino Drovetti.* London, Rubicon.

References

Rindos, D. 1984. *The Origins of Agriculture: An Evolutionary Perspective*. New York, Academic Press.

1989. Undirected variation and the Darwinian explanation of culture change. *Archaeological Method and Theory* 1: 1–45.

Ritchie, W. A. 1944. *The Pre-Iroquoian Occupations of New York State*. Rochester, NY, Rochester Museum of Arts and Sciences Memoir no. 1.

1965. *The Archaeology of New York State*. Garden City, NY, Natural History Press.

Ritchie, W. A. and R. E. Funk. 1973. *Aboriginal Settlement Patterns in the Northeast*. Albany, New York State Museum and Science Service, Memoir no. 20.

Rivers, W. H. R. 1914. *The History of Melanesian Society*. Cambridge, Cambridge University Press.

Robb, J. E. 1998. The archaeology of symbols. *Annual Review of Anthropology* 27: 329–46.

Roberts, C. 1996. *The Logic of Historical Explanation*. University Park, Pennsylvania State University Press.

Robertshaw, P. T. 1990. ed. *A History of African Archaeology*. London, James Currey.

Rodden, J. 1981. The development of the Three Age System: archaeology's first paradigm. In G. Daniel, 1981b, pp. 51–68.

Rolingson, M. A. 2001. ed. *Historical Perspectives on Midsouth Archeology*. Fayetteville, Arkansas Archeological Survey.

Roscoe, P. 2002. Culture. In J. P. Hart and J. E. Terrell, pp. 107–24.

Rose, M. A. 1991. *The Post-Modern and the Post-Industrial: A Critical Analysis*. Cambridge, Cambridge University Press.

Rosenau, P. M. 1992. *Post-Modernism and the Social Sciences: Insights, Inroads, and Intrusions*. Princeton, NJ, Princeton University Press.

Rossi, P. 1985. *The Dark Abyss of Time: The History of the Earth and the History of Nations from Hooke to Vico*. Chicago, IL, University of Chicago Press.

Rouse, I. B. 1939. *Prehistory in Haiti: A Study in Method*. New Haven, CT, Yale University Publications in Anthropology no. 21.

1953. The strategy of culture history. In A. L. Kroeber, pp. 57–76.

1958. The inference of migrations from anthropological evidence. In *Migrations in New World Culture History*, ed. by R. H. Thompson, pp. 63–8. Tucson, University of Arizona, Social Science Bulletin no. 27.

1965. The place of "peoples" in prehistoric research. *Journal of the Royal Anthropological Institute* 95: 1–15.

1972. *Introduction to Prehistory*. New York, McGraw-Hill.

1986. *Migrations in Prehistory: Inferring Population Movement from Cultural Remains*. New Haven, CT, Yale University Press.

Rowe, J. H. 1954. *Max Uhle, 1856–1944: A Memoir of the Father of Peruvian Archaeology*. Berkeley, University of California Press.

1965. The renaissance foundations of anthropology. *American Anthropologist* 67: 1–20.

Rowlands, M. J. 1984a. Objectivity and subjectivity in archaeology. In M. Spriggs, 1984a, pp. 108–13.

1984b. Conceptualizing the European Bronze and Early Iron Ages. In *European Social Evolution: Archaeological Perspectives*, ed. by J. Bintliff, pp. 147–56. Bradford, UK, University of Bradford.

Rowley-Conwy, P. 1984. C. J. Thomsen and the Three Age system: a contemporary document. *Antiquity* 58: 129–31.

1996. Why didn't Westropp's "Mesolithic" catch on in 1872? *Antiquity* 70: 940–44.

1999. Sir Grahame Clark 1907–1995. In T. Murray, 1999a, pp. 507–29.

Rudenko, S. I. 1961. *The Ancient Culture of the Bering Sea and the Eskimo Problem*. Toronto, University of Toronto Press.

1970. *Frozen Tombs of Siberia: The Pazyryk Burials of Iron Age Horsemen*. Berkeley, University of California Press.

Rudolph, R. C. 1962–1963. Preliminary notes on Sung archaeology. *Journal of Asian Studies* 22: 169–77.

Ruiz, A. and F. Nocete. 1990. The dialectic of the past and the present in the construction of a scientific archaeology. In F. Baker and J. Thomas, pp. 105–11.

Ruiz, A., A. Sanchez, and J. P. Bellon. 2002. The history of Iberian archaeology: one archaeology for two Spains. *Antiquity* 76: 184–90.

Ruiz Zapatero, G. 1996. Celts and Iberians: ideological manipulations in Spanish archaeology. In P. Graves-Brown et al., pp. 179–95.

Ruppel, T., J. Neuwirth, M. P. Leone, and G.-M. Fry. 2003. Hidden in view: African spiritual spaces in North American landscapes. *Antiquity* 77: 321–35.

Rushton, J. P. 1995. *Race, Evolution, and Behavior: A Life History Perspective*. New Brunswick, NJ, Transaction Publishers.

Sabloff, J. A. 1981. ed. *Simulations in Archaeology*. Albuquerque, University of New Mexico Press.

1982. ed. *Archaeology: Myth and Reality: Readings from Scientific American*. San Francisco, CA, W. H. Freeman.

1990. *The New Archaeology and the Ancient Maya*. New York, Scientific American Library.

Sabloff, J. A., T. W. Beale, and A. M. Kurland Jr. 1973. Recent developments in archaeology. *Annals of the American Academy of Political and Social Science* 408: 103–18.

Sabloff, J. A. and C. C. Lamberg-Karlovsky. 1975. eds. *Ancient Civilization and Trade*. Albuquerque, University of New Mexico Press.

Sabloff, J. A. and G. R. Willey. 1967. The collapse of Maya civilization in the southern lowlands: a consideration of history and process. *Southwestern Journal of Anthropology* 23: 311–36.

Sabloff, P. L. W. 1998. *Conversations with Lew Binford*. Norman, University of Oklahoma Press.

Sackett, J. R. 1981. From de Mortillet to Bordes: a century of French Palaeolithic research. In G. Daniel, 1981b, pp. 85–99.

1991. Straight archaeology French style: the phylogenetic paradigm in historic perspective. In *Perspectives on the Past: Theoretical Biases in Mediterranean Hunter-Gatherer Research*, ed. by G. A. Clark, pp. 109–39. Philadelphia, University of Pennsylvania Press.

2000. Human antiquity and the Old Stone Age: the nineteenth century background to paleoanthropology. *Evolutionary Anthropology* 9(1): 37–49.

Sahlins, M. D. 1958. *Social Stratification in Polynesia*. Seattle, University of Washington Press.

1968. *Tribesmen*. Englewood Cliffs, NJ, Prentice-Hall.

1972. *Stone Age Economics*. Chicago, IL, Aldine.

1976a. *Culture and Practical Reason*. Chicago, IL, University of Chicago Press.

1976b. *The Use and Abuse of Biology: An Anthropological Critique of Sociobiology*. Ann Arbor, University of Michigan Press.

Sahlins, M. D. and E. R. Service. 1960. eds. *Evolution and Culture*. Ann Arbor, University of Michigan Press.

Said, E. W. 1978. *Orientalism*. New York, Pantheon.

Saitta, D. J. 1983. The poverty of philosophy in archaeology. In J. A. Moore and A. S. Keene, pp. 299–304.

1992. Radical archaeology and middle-range methodology. *Antiquity* 66: 886–97.

Salmon, M. H. 1982. *Philosophy and Archaeology*. New York, Academic Press.

Salmon, M. H. and W. C. Salmon. 1979. Alternative models of scientific explanation. *American Anthropologist* 81: 61–74.

Salmon, W. C. 1967. *The Foundations of Scientific Inference*. Pittsburgh, PA, University of Pittsburgh Press.

1984. *Scientific Explanation and the Causal Structure of the World*. Princeton, NJ, Princeton University Press.

1992. Explanation in archaeology: an update. In L. Embree, pp. 243–53.

Salmon, W. C., R. C. Jeffrey, and J. Greeno. 1971. *Statistical Explanation and Statistical Relevance*. Pittsburgh, PA, Pittsburgh University Press.

Salzman, P. C. 2000. *Black Tents of Baluchistan*. Washington, DC, Smithsonian Institution Press.

Sanders, W. T., J. R. Parsons, and R. S. Santley. 1979. *The Basin of Mexico: Ecological Processes in the Evolution of a Civilization*. New York, Academic Press.

Sanders, W. T. and B. J. Price. 1968. *Mesoamerica: The Evolution of a Civilization*. New York, Random House.

Sanderson, S. K. 1990. *Social Evolutionism: A Critical History*. Oxford, Blackwell.

Sanford, E. M. 1944. The study of ancient history in the middle ages. *Journal of the History of Ideas* 5: 21–43.

Sanoja, M. and I. Vargas. 1978. *Antiguas formaciones y modos de producción Venezolanos*. Caracas, Monte Avila Editores.

References

Sapir, E. 1916. *Time Perspective in Aboriginal American Culture: A Study in Method*. Ottawa, Geological Survey of Canada, Memoir 90.

  1921. *Language: An Introduction to the Study of Speech*. New York, Harcourt, Brace.

Sartre, J.-P. 1971–1972. *L'idiot de la famille: Gustave Flaubert de 1821–1857*. 3 vols. Paris, Gallimard.

Sauer, E. W. 2004. ed. *Archaeology and Ancient History: Breaking Down the Boundaries*. London, Routledge.

Saunders, P. T. 1980. *An Introduction to Catastrophe Theory*. Cambridge, Cambridge University Press.

Saxe, A. A. 1970. Social Dimensions of Mortuary Practices. PhD dissertation, Department of Anthropology, University of Michigan.

Scham, S. A. 2001. The archaeology of the disenfranchised. *Journal of Archaeological Method and Theory* 8: 183–213.

Schiffer, M. B. 1972. Archaeological context and systemic context. *American Antiquity* 37: 156–65.

  1976. *Behavioral Archeology*. New York, Academic Press.

  1978–1985. ed. *Advances in Archaeological Method and Theory*, vols. 1–8. New York, Academic Press.

  1995. *Behavioral Archaeology: First Principles*. Salt Lake City, University of Utah Press.

  1996. Some relationships between behavioral and evolutionary archaeologies. *American Antiquity* 61: 643–62.

  2000a. ed. *Social Theory in Archaeology*. Salt Lake City, University of Utah Press.

  2000b. Social theory in archaeology: building bridges. In M. B. Schiffer, 2000a, pp. 1–13.

Schlanger, N. 2002. Making the past for South Africa's future: the prehistory of Field-Marshal Smuts (1920s–1940s). *Antiquity* 76: 200–9.

  2003. The Burkitt affair revisited: colonial implications and identity politics in early South African prehistoric research. *Archaeological Dialogues* 10: 5–55.

Schlanger, N. and A. Schnapp. 2005–. eds. *Histories of Archaeology* (series). Oxford, Berghahn Books.

Schliz, A. 1906. Der schnurkeramische Kulturkreis und seine Stellung zu der anderen neolithischen Kulturformen in Sudwestdeutschland. *Zeitschrift für Ethnologie* 38: 312–45.

Schmidt, P. R. and R. J. McIntosh. 1996. eds. *Plundering Africa's Past*. Bloomington, Indiana University Press.

Schmidt, P. R. and T. C. Patterson. 1995. eds. *Making Alternative Histories: The Practice of Archaeology and History in Non-Western Settings*. Santa Fe, NM, School of American Research Press.

Schnapp, A. 1993. La Conquête du passé: aux origines de l'archéologie. Paris, Editions Carré.

  1997. *The Discovery of the Past: The Origins of Archaeology*. London, British Museum Press.

2002. Between antiquarians and archaeologists – continuities and ruptures. *Antiquity* 76: 134–40.

Schnapp, A. and K. Kristiansen. 1999. Discovering the past. In G. Barker, pp. 3–47.

Schneer, C. J. 1969. ed. *Toward a History of Geology*. Cambridge, MA, M.I.T. Press.

Schneider, L. 1967. ed. *The Scottish Moralists on Human Nature and Society*. Chicago, IL, University of Chicago Press.

Schofield, J. F. 1948. *Primitive Pottery: An Introduction to South African Ceramics, Prehistoric and Protohistoric*. Cape Town, South African Archaeological Society, Handbook Series no. 3.

Schrire, C. 1980. An inquiry into the evolutionary status and apparent identity of San hunter-gatherers. *Human Ecology* 8: 9–32.

1984. ed. *Past and Present in Hunter Gatherer Studies*. New York, Academic Press.

1995. *Digging through Darkness: Chronicles of an Archaeologist*. Charlottesville, University Press of Virginia.

Schrire, C., J. Deacon, M. Hall, and D. Lewis-Williams. 1986. Burkitt's milestone. *Antiquity* 60: 123–31.

Schuyler, R. L. 1971. The history of American archaeology: an examination of procedure. *American Antiquity* 36: 383–409.

1978. ed. *Historical Archaeology: A Guide to Substantive and Theoretical Contributions*. New York, Baywood Publishers.

2001. Historical archaeology. In T. Murray, 2001a, pp. 623–30.

Schwartz, D. W. 1967. *Conceptions of Kentucky Prehistory: A Case Study in the History of Archeology*. Lexington, University of Kentucky Press.

1981. The foundations of northern Rio Grande archaeology. *Archaeological Society of New Mexico, Anthropological Papers* 6: 251–73.

Schwerin von Krosigk, H. 1982. *Gustav Kossinna: Der Nachlass – Versuch einer Analyse*. Neumünster, Karl Wachholtz.

Scott, J. 2003. *The Pleasures of Antiquity: British Collectors of Greece and Rome*. New Haven, CT, Yale University Press.

Searle, J. R. 1983. *Intentionality: An Essay in the Philosophy of Mind*. Cambridge, Cambridge University Press.

Seligman, C. G. 1930. *Races of Africa*. London, Butterworth.

Semenov, S. A. 1964. *Prehistoric Technology*. London, Cory, Adams and Mackay.

Semenov, Yu. I. 1980. The theory of socio-economic formations and world history. In E. Gellner, pp. 29–58.

Service, E. R. 1962. *Primitive Social Organization*. New York, Random House.
1975. *Origins of the State and Civilization*. New York, Norton.

Settar, S. and R. Korisettar. 2002. eds. *Archaeology and Historiography: History, Theory and Method* (*Indian Archaeology in Retrospect*, vol. 4). New Delhi, Manohar.

Shackel, P. A. 1996. *Culture Change and the New Technology: An Archaeology of the Early American Industrial Era*. New York, Plenum.

Shanks, M. 1996. *Classical Archaeology of Greece: Experiences of the Discipline.* London, Routledge.

Shanks, M. and C. Tilley. 1982. Ideology, symbolic power and ritual communication: a reinterpretation of Neolithic mortuary practices. In I. Hodder, 1982c, pp. 129–54.

   1987a. *Re-Constructing Archaeology: Theory and Practice.* Cambridge, Cambridge University Press. 2nd edn. 1993.

   1987b. *Social Theory and Archaeology.* Cambridge, UK, Polity Press.

   1989. Archaeology into the 1990s. *Norwegian Archaeological Review* 22: 1–54.

Shapin, S. 1992. Disciplining and bounding: the history and sociology of science as seen through the externalism-internalism debate. *History of Science* 30: 333–69.

Shapiro, J. 1982. *A History of the Communist Academy, 1918–1936.* Ann Arbor, MI, University Microfilms International.

Shaw, J. 2000. Ayodhya's sacred landscape: ritual memory, politics and archaeological "fact." *Antiquity* 74: 693–700.

Shaw, T. 1991. Goodwin's graft, Burkitt's craft. *Antiquity* 65: 579–80.

Shay, T. 1989. Israeli archaeology – ideology and practice. *Antiquity* 63: 768–72.

Sheehan, B. W. 1980. *Savagism and Civility: Indians and Englishmen in Colonial Virginia.* New York, Cambridge University Press.

Sheehy, J. 1980. *The Rediscovery of Ireland's Past: The Celtic Revival, 1830–1930.* London, Thames and Hudson.

Sheets-Pyenson, S. 1996. *John William Dawson: Faith, Hope, and Science.* Montreal, McGill-Queen's University Press.

Shennan, S. J. 1989a. ed. *Archaeological Approaches to Cultural Identity.* London, Unwin Hyman.

   1989b. Introduction. In S. J. Shennan 1989a, pp. 1–32.

   2002. *Genes, Memes and Human History: Darwinian Archaeology and Culture History.* London, Thames and Hudson.

Shennan, S. J. and J. R. Wilkinson. 2001. Ceramic style change and neutral evolution: a case study from Neolithic Europe. *American Antiquity* 66: 577–93.

Shepherd, L. 1993. *Lifting the Veil: The Feminine Face of Science.* Boston, MA, Shambhala.

Shepherd, N. 2002a. Disciplining archaeology: the invention of South African prehistory, 1923–1953. *Kronos* 28: 127–45.

   2002b. The politics of archaeology in Africa. *Annual Review of Anthropology* 31: 189–209.

Sherratt, A. G. 1979. Problems in European prehistory. In D. L. Clarke, pp. 193–206.

   1989. V. Gordon Childe: archaeology and intellectual history. *Past and Present* 125: 151–85.

   1993. The relativity of theory. In N. Yoffee and A. Sherratt, pp. 119–30.

1996. "Settlement patterns" or "landscape studies"? reconciling reason and romance. *Archaeological Dialogues* 3: 140–59.

Sherratt, Y. 2006. *Continental Philosophy of Social Science: Hermeneutics, Genealogy, and Critical Theory, from Greece to the Twenty-First Century.* Cambridge, Cambridge University Press.

Shetrone, H. C. 1920. The culture problem in Ohio archaeology. *American Anthropologist* 22: 144–72.

Shnirelman, V. A. 1995. From internationalism to nationalism: forgotten pages of Soviet archaeology in the 1930s and 1940s. In P. L. Kohl and C. Fawcett, pp. 120–38.

1996. The faces of nationalist archaeology in Russia. In M. Díaz-Andreu and T. Champion, 1996a, pp. 218–42.

1999. Passions about Arkaim: Russian nationalism, the Aryans, and the politics of archaeology. *Inner Asia* 1: 267–82.

2001. *The Value of the Past: Myths, Identity and Politics in Transcaucasia.* Osaka, National Museum of Ethnology, Senri Ethnological Studies 57.

Shorr, P. 1935. The genesis of prehistorical research. *Isis* 23: 425–43.

Shrimpton, G. S. 1992. *History and Memory in Ancient Greece.* Montreal, McGill-Queen's University Press.

Sielmann, B. 1971. Zur Interpretationsmöglichkeit ökologischer Befunde im Neolithikum Mitteleuropas. *Germania* 49: 231–38.

Sieveking, G. 1976. Progress in economic and social archaeology. In *Problems in Economic and Social Archaeology*, ed. by G. Sieveking, I. H. Longworth, and K. E. Wilson, pp. xv–xxvi. London, Duckworth.

Silberman, N. A. 1982. *Digging for God and Country.* New York, Knopf.

1989. *Between Past and Present: Archaeology, Ideology, and Nationalism in the Modern Middle East.* New York, Henry Holt.

1991. Desolation and restoration: the impact of a biblical concept on Near Eastern archaeology. *Biblical Archaeologist*, June, 76–87.

1993. *A Prophet from Amongst You: The Life of Yigael Yadin.* Reading, MA, Addison-Wesley.

1995. Promised lands and chosen peoples: the politics and poetics of archaeological narrative. In P. L. Kohl and C. Fawcett, pp. 249–62.

Silberman, N. A. and D. Small. 1997. eds. *The Archaeology of Israel: Constructing the Past, Interpreting the Present.* Sheffield, UK, Sheffield Academic Press.

Sills, D. L. 1968. ed. *International Encyclopedia of the Social Sciences.* 19 vols. New York, Macmillan.

Silverberg, R. 1968. *Mound Builders of Ancient America.* Greenwich, CT, New York Graphic Society.

Singh, S. 1985. *Models, Paradigms and the New Archaeology.* Varanasi, Banaras Hindu University, Department of Ancient Indian History, Culture and Archaeology.

Singh, U. 2004. *The Discovery of Ancient India: Early Archaeologists and the Beginnings of Archaeology.* Delhi, Permanent Black.

Skibo, J. M. and G. M. Feinman. 1999. eds. *Pottery and People: A Dynamic Interaction*. Salt Lake City, University of Utah Press.

Skibo, J. M., W. H. Walker, and A. E. Nielsen. 1995. eds. *Expanding Archaeology*. Salt Lake City, University of Utah Press.

Skinner, H. D. 1921. Culture areas in New Zealand. *Journal of the Polynesian Society* 30: 71–8.

Sklenář, K. 1983. *Archaeology in Central Europe: The First 500 Years*. Leicester, UK, Leicester University Press.

Skrotzky, N. 1964. *L'abbé Breuil*. Paris, Editions Seghers.

Slapšak, B. and P. Novaković. 1996. Is there national archaeology without nationalism? Archaeological tradition in Slovenia. In M. Díaz-Andreu and T. Champion, 1996a, pp. 256–93.

Slobodin, R. 1978. *W. H. R. Rivers*. New York, Columbia University Press.

Slotkin, J. S. 1965. ed. *Readings in Early Anthropology*. New York, Viking Fund Publications in Anthropology no. 40.

Smith, A. T. 2003. *The Political Landscape: Constellations of Authority in Early Complex Polities*. Berkeley, University of California Press.

Smith, B. D. 1978. ed. *Mississippian Settlement Patterns*. New York, Academic Press.

Smith, G. E. 1911. *The Ancient Egyptians and their Influence upon the Civilization of Europe*. New York, Harper.

1915. *The Migrations of Early Culture*. London, Longmans.

1928. *In the Beginning: The Origin of Civilization*. London, G. Howe.

1933. *The Diffusion of Culture*. London, Watts.

Smith, H. I. 1910. *The Prehistoric Ethnology of a Kentucky Site*. New York, Anthropological Papers of the American Museum of Natural History no. 6, pt. 2.

Smith, M. A. 1955. The limits of inference. *Archaeological Newsletter* 6: 3–7.

Smith, M. L. 2003. ed. *The Social Construction of Ancient Cities*. Washington, DC, Smithsonian Institution Press.

Smith, P. E. L. and T. C. Young Jr. 1972. The evolution of early agriculture and culture in Greater Mesopotamia: a trial model. In B. Spooner, pp. 1–59.

Smith, P. J. 1997. Grahame Clark's new archaeology: the Fenland Research Committee and Cambridge prehistory in the 1930s. *Antiquity* 71: 11–30.

1999. "The coup": how did the Prehistoric Society of East Anglia become the Prehistoric Society? *Proceedings of the Prehistoric Society* 65: 465–70.

2000. Dorothy Garrod, first woman Professor at Cambridge. *Antiquity* 74: 131–6.

Smith, P. J., J. Callander, P. G. Bahn, and G. Pincon. 1997. Dorothy Garrod in words and pictures. *Antiquity* 71: 288–99.

References

Smith, P. J. and D. Mitchell. 1998. eds. *Bringing Back the Past: Historical Perspectives on Canadian Archaeology*. Ottawa, Canadian Museum of Civilization, Archaeological Survey of Canada, Mercury Series, 158.

Smith, S. P. 1913, 1915. *The Lore of the Whare Wananga*. Wellington, The Polynesian Society.

Smith, S. T. 2003. *Wretched Kush: Ethnic Identities and Boundaries in Egypt's Nubian Empire*. London, Routledge.

Smith, W. D. 1991. *Politics and the Sciences of Culture in Germany, 1840–1920*. New York, Oxford University Press.

Smolla, G. 1964. Analogien und Polaritäten. In *Studien aus Alteuropa (Tackenberg-Festschrift)*, ed. by R. von Uslar and K. J. Narr, vol. 1, pp. 30–35. Cologne, Böhlau.

Snead, J. E. 2001. *Ruins and Rivals: The Making of Southwest Archaeology*. Tucson, University of Arizona Press.

Snodgrass, A. M. 1964. *Early Greek Armour and Weapons*. Edinburgh, Edinburgh University Press.

1980. *Archaic Greece: The Age of Experiment*. London, Dent.

1985. The New Archaeology and the classical archaeologist. *American Journal of Archaeology* 89: 31–7.

1987. *An Archaeology of Greece: The Present State and Future Scope of a Discipline*. Berkeley, University of California Press.

Snow, D. R. 2002. Individuals. In J. P. Hart and J. E. Terrell, pp. 161–81.

Soffer, O. 1983. Politics of the Paleolithic in the USSR: a case of paradigms lost. In J. M. Gero, D. M. Lacy, and M. L. Blakey, pp. 91–105.

1985. *The Upper Paleolithic of the Central Russian Plain*. New York, Academic Press.

Sollas, W. J. 1911. *Ancient Hunters and their Modern Representatives*. London, Macmillan. 2nd edn 1924.

Solli, B. 1996. Narratives of Veøy: on the poetics and scientifics of archaeology. In P. Graves-Brown et al., pp. 209–27.

Solomon, C. 2002. *Tatiana Proskouriakoff: Interpreting the Ancient Maya*. Norman, University of Oklahoma Press.

Sørensen, M. L. S. 1996. The fall of a nation, the birth of a subject: the national use of archaeology in nineteenth-century Denmark. In M. Díaz-Andreu and T. Champion, 1996a, pp. 24–47.

1999. Mats P. Malmer b. 1921. In T. Murray, 1999a, pp. 775–89.

Sorrenson, M. P. K. 1977. The whence of the Maori: some nineteenth century exercises in scientific method. *Journal of the Polynesian Society* 86: 449–78.

South, S. A. 1977a. *Method and Theory in Historical Archaeology*. New York, Academic Press.

1977b. ed. *Research Strategies in Historical Archaeology*. New York, Academic Press.

1998. *Pioneers in Historical Archaeology: Breaking New Ground*. New York, Plenum.

References

Spate, O. H. K. 1968. Environmentalism. In D. L. Sills, vol. 5, pp. 93–7.

Spaulding, A. C. 1946. Northeastern archaeology and general trends in the northern forest zone. In *Man in Northeastern North America*, ed. by F. Johnson, pp. 143–67. Andover, MA, Robert S. Peabody Foundation for Archaeology, Papers no. 3.

  1953. Statistical techniques for the discovery of artifact types. *American Antiquity* 18: 305–13.

  1960. The dimensions of archaeology. In *Essays in the Science of Culture in Honor of Leslie A. White*, ed. by G. E. Dole and R. L. Carneiro, pp. 437–56. New York, Crowell.

  1968. Explanation in archeology. In S. R. Binford and L. R. Binford, pp. 33–9.

Spector, J. 1993. *What this Awl Means: Feminist Archaeology at a Wahpeton Dakota Village*. St. Paul, Minnesota Historical Society Press.

Speer, A. 1970. *Inside the Third Reich: Memoirs by Albert Speer*. New York, Macmillan.

Spencer, W. B. 1901. *Guide to the Australian Ethnographical Collection in the National Museum of Victoria*. Melbourne, Government Printer.

Spencer, W. B. and F. J. Gillen. 1899. *The Native Tribes of Central Australia*. London, Macmillan.

Spier, L. 1917. *An Outline for a Chronology of Zuñi Ruins*. New York, Anthropological Papers of the American Museum of Natural History no. 18, pt. 3.

Spinden, H. J. 1928. *Ancient Civilizations of Mexico and Central America*. New York, American Museum of Natural History Handbook Series no. 3.

Spooner, B. 1972. ed. *Population Growth: Anthropological Implications*. Cambridge, MA, M.I.T. Press.

Spriggs, M. 1984a. ed. *Marxist Perspectives in Archaeology*. Cambridge, Cambridge University Press.

  1984b. Another way of telling: Marxist perspectives in archaeology. In M. Spriggs, 1984a, pp. 1–9.

Squier, E. G. and E. H. Davis. 1848. *Ancient Monuments of the Mississippi Valley*. Washington, DC, Smithsonian Contributions to Knowledge no. 1.

Stanton, W. 1960. *The Leopard's Spots: Scientific Attitudes toward Race in America, 1815–59*. Chicago, IL, University of Chicago Press.

Steiger, W. L. 1971. Analytical archaeology? *Mankind* 8: 67–70.

Stepan, N. 1982. *The Idea of Race in Science: Great Britain 1800–1900*. Hamden, CT, Archon Books.

Sterud, E. L. 1973. A paradigmatic view of prehistory. In A. C. Renfrew, 1973b, pp. 3–17.

Steuer, H. 2001. ed. *Eine hervorragend nationale Wissenschaft: Deutsche Prähistoriker zwischen 1900 und 1995*. Ergänzungbände zum Reallexikon der Germanischen Altertumskunde 29. Berlin, W. de Gruyter.

References

Stevenson, D. 1988. *Origins of Freemasonry*. Cambridge, Cambridge University Press.

Steward, J. H. 1937a. *Ancient Caves of the Great Salt Lake Region*. Washington, DC, Bureau of American Ethnology, Bulletin no. 116.

    1937b. Ecological aspects of southwestern society. *Anthropos* 32: 87–104.

    1953. Evolution and process. In A. L. Kroeber, pp. 313–26.

    1955. *Theory of Culture Change*. Urbana, University of Illinois Press.

    1968. Cultural ecology. In D. L. Sills, 4: 337–44.

Steward, J. H. and F. M. Setzler. 1938. Function and configuration in archaeology. *American Antiquity* 4: 4–10.

Stiebing, W. H., Jr. 1984. *Ancient Astronauts, Cosmic Collisions and other Popular Theories about Man's Past*. Buffalo, NY, Prometheus Books.

    1993. *Uncovering the Past: A History of Archaeology*. Buffalo, NY, Prometheus Books.

Stjernquist, B. 2005. *The Historical Museum and Archaeological Research at Lund University 1805–2005*. Lund, Papers of the Historical Museum, University of Lund, 1.

Stocking, G. W., Jr. 1968. *Race, Culture, and Evolution: Essays in the History of Anthropology*. New York, Free Press.

    1973. From chronology to ethnology: James Cowles Prichard and British anthropology 1800–1850. In J. C. Prichard, *Researches into the Physical History of Man*, ed. by G. W. Stocking Jr, pp. ix–cx. Chicago, IL, University of Chicago Press.

    1982. *Race, Culture, and Evolution: Essays in the History of Anthropology*. 2nd edn. Chicago, IL, University of Chicago Press.

    1984. ed. *Functionalism Historicized: Essays on British Social Anthropology (History of Anthropology 2)*. Madison, University of Wisconsin Press.

    1985. ed. *Objects and Others: Essays on Museums and Material Culture (History of Anthropology 3)*. Madison, University of Wisconsin Press.

    1987. *Victorian Anthropology*. New York, Free Press.

Stoczkowski, Wiktor. 2002. *Explaining Human Origins: Myth, Imagination and Conjecture*. Cambridge, Cambridge University Press.

Stone, P. and R. MacKenzie. 1990. *The Excluded Past: Archaeology in Education*. London, Unwin Hyman.

Stoneman, R. 1987. *Land of Lost Gods: The Search for Classical Greece*. Norman, University of Oklahoma Press.

Stow, G. W. and G. M. Theal. 1905. *The Native Races of South Africa*. London, Sonnenschein.

Strauss, L. G. 1992. L'abbé Henri Breuil: archaeologist. *Bulletin of the History of Archaeology* 2(1): 5–9.

Street, B. V. 1975. *The Savage in Literature: Representations of "Primitive" Society in English Fiction, 1858–1920*. London, Routledge and Kegan Paul.

Stringer, C. and C. Gamble. 1993. *In Search of the Neanderthals: Solving the Puzzle of Human Origins*. London, Thames and Hudson.

References

Strong, W. D. 1935. *An Introduction to Nebraska Archeology*. Washington, DC, Smithsonian Miscellaneous Collections no. 93 (10).

1936. Anthropological theory and archaeological fact. In *Essays in Anthropology Presented to A. L. Kroeber*, ed. by R. H. Lowie, pp. 359–70. Berkeley, University of California Press.

1951. Cultural resemblances in nuclear America: parallelisms or diffusion? In *The Civilizations of Ancient America: Selected Papers of the IXIXth International Congress of Americanists*, ed. by Sol Tax, pp. 271–9. Chicago, IL, University of Chicago Press.

Struever, S. 1968. Problems, methods and organization: a disparity in the growth of archeology. In B. J. Meggers, pp. 131–51.

Sumner, W. M. 1990. Full-coverage regional archaeological survey in the Near East: an example from Iran. In S. K. Fish and S. A. Kowalewski, pp. 87–115.

Sutton, D. G. 1985. The whence of the Moriori. *New Zealand Journal of History* 19: 3–13.

Swartz, B. K., Jr. 1967. A logical sequence of archaeological objectives. *American Antiquity* 32: 487–97.

Swayze, N. 1960. *The Man Hunters*. Toronto, Clarke, Irwin.

Sweet, R. 2004. *Antiquaries: The Discovery of the Past in Eighteenth-Century Britain*. London, Palgrave Macmillan.

Swidler, N., K. E. Dongoske, R. Anyon, and A. S. Downer. 1997. eds. *Native Americans and Archaeologists: Stepping Stones to Common Ground*. Walnut Creek, CA, AltaMira Press.

Tabío, E. and E. Rey. 1966. *Prehistoria de Cuba*. La Habana, Academia de Ciencias de Cuba.

Tainter, J. A. 1988. *The Collapse of Complex Societies*. Cambridge, Cambridge University Press.

Tait, J. 2003. ed. *"Never Had the Like Occurred": Egypt's View of its Past*. London, UCL Press.

Tallgren, A. M. 1936. Archaeological studies in Soviet Russia. *Eurasia Septentrionalis Antiqua* 10: 129–70.

1937. The method of prehistoric archaeology. *Antiquity* 11: 152–61.

Tamarkin, B. 1986. Naturalized philosophy of science, history of science and the internal/external debate. *Proceedings of the Biennial Meeting of the Philosophy of Science Association*, 1986(1): 258–68.

Tanaka, M. 1984. Japan. In H. Cleere, pp. 82–8.

Tanner, A. 1979. *Bringing Home Animals: Religious Ideology and Mode of Production of the Mistassini Cree Hunters*. St. John's, Memorial University of Newfoundland, Institute of Social and Economic Research, Social and Economic Studies 23.

Tanner, N. M. 1981. *On Becoming Human*. Cambridge, Cambridge University Press.

Tansley, A. G. 1935. The use and abuse of vegetation concepts and terms. *Ecology* 16: 284–307.

References

Tardits, C. 1981. ed. *Contribution de la recherche ethnologique à l'histoire des civilisations du Cameroun*. 2 vols. Paris, Editions du CNRS.

Tax, T. G. 1975. E. George Squier and the mounds, 1845–1850. In *Toward a Science of Man: Essays in the History of Anthropology*, ed. by T. H. H. Thoresen, pp. 99–124. The Hague, Mouton.

Taylor, J. 1966. ed. *Marine Archaeology: Developments during Sixty Years in the Mediterranean*. New York, Crowell.

Taylor, R. E. 1985. The beginnings of radiocarbon dating in *American Antiquity*: a historical perspective. *American Antiquity* 50: 309–25.

　1987. *Radiocarbon Dating: An Archaeological Perspective*. San Diego, CA, Academic Press.

Taylor, R. E., A. Long, and R. S. Kra. 1992. eds. *Radiocarbon After Four Decades: An Interdisciplinary Perspective*. New York, Springer.

Taylor, W. W. 1948. *A Study of Archeology*. Menasha, WI, American Anthropological Association Memoir 69. (Pages cited from the 1967 reprint, Carbondale, Southern Illinois University Press.)

　1972. Old wine and new skins: a contemporary parable. In M. P. Leone, pp. 28–33.

Teltser, P. A. 1995. ed. *Evolutionary Archaeology: Methodological Issues*. Tucson, University of Arizona Press.

Terrell, J. E. 2003. Archaeological inference and ethnographic analogies: rethinking the "Lapita cultural complex." In S. D. Gillespie and D. L. Nichols, 2003, pp. 69–76.

Testart, A. 1982. *Les chasseurs-cueilleurs ou l'origine des inégalités*. Paris, Société d'Ethnographie, Mémoire no. 26.

Teviotdale, D. 1932. The material culture of the moa-hunters in Murihiku. *Journal of the Polynesian Society* 41: 81–120.

Textor, R. B. 1967. *A Cross-Cultural Summary*. New Haven, CT, HRAF Press.

Thapar, B. K. 1984. India. In H. Cleere, pp. 63–72.

Thom, R. 1975. *Structural Stability and Morphogenesis*. Reading, MA, Benjamin.

Thomas, C. 1894. *Report on the Mound Explorations of the Bureau of Ethnology*. Washington, DC, Bureau of American Ethnology, Annual Report, 12: 3–742.

　1898. *Introduction to the Study of North American Archaeology*. Cincinnati, OH, Clarke.

Thomas, D. H. 1972. A computer simulation model of Great Basin Shoshonean subsistence and settlement patterns. In D. L. Clarke, 1972a, pp. 671–704.

　1974. An archaeological perspective on Shoshonean bands. *American Anthropologist* 76: 11–23.

　1976. *Figuring Anthropology: First Principles of Probability and Statistics*. New York, Holt, Rinehart and Winston.

　1978. The awful truth about statistics in archaeology. *American Antiquity* 43: 231–44.

2000. *Skull Wars: Kennewick Man, Archaeology, and the Battle for Native American Identity*. New York, Basic Books.

Thomas, J. 1996. *Time, Culture, and Identity: An Interpretative Archaeology*. New York, Routledge.

2000. Reconfiguring the social, reconfiguring the material. In M. B. Schiffer, 2000a, pp. 143–55.

2001. Archaeologies of place and landscape. In I. Hodder, 2001a, pp. 165–86.

2004. *Archaeology and Modernity*. London, Routledge.

Thomas, N. 1995. ed. *The American Discovery of Ancient Egypt*. Los Angeles, CA, Los Angeles County Museum of Art.

1996. ed. *The American Discovery of Ancient Egypt: Essays*. Los Angeles, CA, Los Angeles County Museum of Art.

Thompson, J. 1992. *Sir Gardner Wilkinson and his Circle*. Austin, University of Texas Press.

Thompson, M. W. 1965. Marxism and culture. *Antiquity* 39: 108–16.

1967. *Novgorod the Great*. London, Evelyn, Adams and Mackay.

1977. *General Pitt-Rivers: Evolution and Archaeology in the Nineteenth Century*. Bradford-on-Avon, UK, Moonraker Press.

Thomson, D. F. 1939. The seasonal factor in human culture. *Proceedings of the Prehistoric Society* 5: 209–21.

Thomson, G. 1949. Review of V. G. Childe, *History*. *The Modern Quarterly* N. S. 4: 266–9.

Thruston, G. P. 1890. *The Antiquities of Tennessee*. Cincinnati, OH, Clarke.

Thwaites, R. G. 1896–1901. *The Jesuit Relations and Allied Documents*. 73 vols. Cleveland, OH, Burrows Brothers.

Tilley, C. Y. 1984. Ideology and the legitimation of power in the Middle Neolithic of southern Sweden. In D. Miller and C. Tilley, 1984a, pp. 111–46.

1990a. ed. *Reading Material Culture: Structuralism, Hermeneutics and Post-Structuralism*. Oxford, Blackwell.

1990b. Michel Foucault: towards an archaeology of archaeology. In C. Tilley, 1990a, pp. 281–347.

1993. ed. *Interpretative Archaeology*. Oxford, Berg.

1994. *A Phenomenology of Landscape: Places, Paths and Monuments*. Oxford, Berg.

1999. *Metaphor and Material Culture*. Oxford, Blackwell.

Toffler, A. 1970. *Future Shock*. New York, Random House.

Tooker, E. 1982. ed. *Ethnography by Archaeologists*. Washington, DC, The American Ethnological Society.

Tosi, M. 1984. The notion of craft specialization and its representation in the archaeological record of early states in the Turanian Basin. In M. Spriggs, 1984a, pp. 22–52.

Toulmin, S. E. 1970. Does the distinction between normal and revolutionary science hold water? In *Criticism and the Growth of Knowledge*, ed. by I.

Lakatos and A. Musgrave, pp. 39–47. Cambridge, Cambridge University Press.

Toulmin, S. E. and J. Goodfield. 1966. *The Discovery of Time*. New York, Harper and Row.

Treaty 7 Elders and Tribal Council with W. Hildebrant, S. Carter, and D. First Rider. 1996. *The True Spirit and Original Intent of Treaty 7*. Montreal, McGill-Queen's University Press.

Treherne, P. 1995. The warrior's beauty: the masculine body and self-identity in Bronze-Age Europe. *Journal of European Archaeology* 3: 105–44.

Trevelyan, G. M. 1952. *Illustrated English Social History*, vol. 4, *The Nineteenth Century*. London, Longmans, Green.

"Trevelyan." 1857. Letters on Irish antiquities by a Cornish man. *Ulster Journal of Archaeology* 5: 150–2, 185–7, 336–42.

Trevor-Roper, H. R. 1966. *The Rise of Christian Europe*. 2nd edn. London, Thames and Hudson.

Trigger, B. G. 1965. *History and Settlement in Lower Nubia*. New Haven, CT, Yale University Publications in Anthropology no. 69.

1966. Sir John William Dawson: a faithful anthropologist. *Anthropologica* 8: 351–9.

1967. Settlement Archaeology – its goals and promise. *American Antiquity* 32: 149–60.

1968a. *Beyond History: The Methods of Prehistory*. New York, Holt, Rinehart and Winston.

1968b. The determinants of settlement patterns. In *Settlement Archaeology*, ed. by K. C. Chang, pp. 53–78. Palo Alto, CA, National Press.

1968c. Major concepts of archaeology in historical perspective. *Man* 3: 527–41.

1969. The personality of the Sudan. In *East African History*, ed. by D. F. McCall, N. R. Bennett, and J. Butler, pp. 74–106. New York, Praeger.

1976. *Nubia under the Pharaohs*. London, Thames and Hudson.

1978a. *Time and Traditions: Essays in Archaeological Interpretation*. Edinburgh, Edinburgh University Press.

1978b. The strategy of Iroquoian prehistory. In *Archaeological Essays in Honor of Irving B. Rouse*, ed. by R. C. Dunnell and E. S. Hall Jr, pp. 275–310. The Hague, Mouton.

1978c. William J. Wintemberg: Iroquoian archaeologist. In *Essays in Northeastern Anthropology in Memory of Marian E. White*, ed. by W. E. Engelbrecht and D. K. Grayson, pp. 5–21. Rindge, Occasional Publications in Northeastern Anthropology no. 5.

1980a. *Gordon Childe: Revolutions in Archaeology*. London, Thames and Hudson.

1980b. Archaeology and the image of the American Indian. *American Antiquity* 45: 662–76.

1981a. Anglo-American archaeology. *World Archaeology* 13: 138–55.

1981b. Archaeology and the ethnographic present. *Anthropologica* 23: 3–17.

1982a. Archaeological analysis and concepts of causality. *Culture* 2(2): 31–42.

1982b. If Childe were alive today. *University of London, Bulletin of the Institute of Archaeology* 19: 1–20.

1984a. Alternative archaeologies: nationalist, colonialist, imperialist. *Man* 19: 355–70.

1984b. Childe and Soviet archaeology. *Australian Archaeology* 18: 1–16.

1984c. Marxism and archaeology. In *On Marxian Perspectives in Anthropology*, ed. by J. Maquet and N. Daniels, pp. 59–97. Malibu, CA, Undena.

1984d. History and Settlement in Lower Nubia in the perspective of fifteen years. In *Meroitistische Forschungen 1980*, ed. by F. Hintze. *Meroitica* 7: 367–80.

1984e. Archaeology at the crossroads: what's new? *Annual Review of Anthropology* 13: 275–300.

1985a. Writing the history of archaeology: a survey of trends. In G. W. Stocking Jr, pp. 218–35.

1985b. The past as power: anthropology and the North American Indian. In I. McBryde, pp. 11–40.

1985c. *Archaeology as Historical Science*. Varanasi, Banaras Hindu University, Department of Ancient Indian History, Culture and Archaeology, Monograph no. 14.

1986a. ed. *Native Shell Mounds of North America: Early Studies*. New York, Garland.

1986b. Prehistoric archaeology and American society. In D. J. Meltzer et al., pp. 187–215.

1986c. The role of technology in V. Gordon Childe's archaeology. *Norwegian Archaeological Review* 19: 1–14.

1989a. *A History of Archaeological Thought*. Cambridge, Cambridge University Press.

1989b. Hyperrelativism, responsibility, and the social sciences. *Canadian Review of Sociology and Anthropology* 26: 776–97.

1989c. Archaeology and anthropology: current and future relations. *Canadian Journal of Archaeology* 13: 1–11.

1990. Maintaining economic equality in opposition to complexity: an Iroquoian case study. In S. Upham, pp. 119–45.

1992. Daniel Wilson and the Scottish Enlightenment. *Proceedings of the Society of Antiquaries of Scotland* 122: 55–75.

1993. Marxism in contemporary Western archaeology. *Archaeological Method and Theory* 5: 159–200.

1994a. The coming of age of the history of archaeology. *Journal of Archaeological Research* 2: 113–36.

1994b. Paradigms in Sudanese archaeology. *International Journal of African Historical Studies* 27: 323–45.

1995. Expanding middle-range theory. *Antiquity* 69: 449–58.

1998a. *Sociocultural Evolution: Calculation and Contingency.* Oxford, Blackwell.

1998b. Archaeology and epistemology: dialoguing across the Darwinian chasm. *American Journal of Archaeology* 102: 1–34.

2003a. *Understanding Early Civilizations: A Comparative Study.* Cambridge, Cambridge University Press.

2003b. *Artifacts and Ideas: Essays in Archaeology.* New Brunswich, NJ, Transaction Publishers.

2003c. All people are [not] good. *Anthropologica* 45(1): 39–44.

2003d. *Archaeological Theory: The Big Picture.* Grace Elizabeth Shallit Memorial Lecture Series. Provo, UT, Department of Anthropology, Brigham Young University.

Trigger, B. G. and I. Glover. 1981–82. eds. Regional Traditions of Archaeological Research, I, II. *World Archaeology* 13(2); 13(3).

Tringham, R. 1978. Experimentation, ethnoarchaeology, and the leapfrogs in archaeological methodology. In R. A. Gould, 1978a, pp. 169–99.

1983. V. Gordon Childe 25 years after: his relevance for the archaeology of the eighties. *Journal of Field Archaeology* 10: 85–100.

1991. Households with faces: the challenge of gender in prehistoric architectural remains. In J. Gero and M. Conkey, pp. 93–131.

Trinkaus, E. and P. Shipman. 1993. *The Neanderthals: Changing the Image of Mankind.* New York, Knopf.

Truncer, J. 2003. ed. *Picking the Lock of Time: Developing Chronology in American Archaeology.* Gainesville, University Press of Florida.

Tully, J. 1989. Progress and skepticism 1789–1989. Ottawa, *Transactions of the Royal Society of Canada* 5: 22–33.

Tunbridge, J. E. and G. J. Ashworth. 1996. *Dissonant Heritage: The Management of the Past as a Resource in Conflict.* Chichester, UK, Wiley.

Turner, D. 1990. Heinrich Schliemann: the man behind the masks. *Archaeology* 43(6): 36–42.

Turner, F. M. 1981. *The Greek Heritage in Victorian Britain.* New Haven, CT, Yale University Press.

Turner, V. 1967. *The Forest of Symbols: Aspects of Ndembu Ritual.* Ithaca, NY, Cornell University Press.

1975. *Revelation and Divination in Ndembu Ritual.* Ithaca, NY, Cornell University Press.

Tushingham, S., J. Hill, and C. H. McNutt. 2002. *Histories of Southeastern Archaeology.* Tuscaloosa, University of Alabama Press.

Tylor, E. B. 1865. *Researches into the Early History of Mankind and the Development of Civilization.* London, John Murray.

1871. *Primitive Culture.* London, John Murray.

Ucko, P. J. 1983. Australian academic archaeology: aboriginal transformation of its aims and practices. *Australian Archaeology* 16: 11–26.

1987. *Academic Freedom and Apartheid: The Story of the World Archaeological Congress.* London, Duckworth.

1989a. Foreward. In D. Miller, M. Rowlands, and C. Tilley, 1989a, pp. ix–xiv.

1989b. Foreward. In P. Gathercole and D. Lowenthal, 1990, pp. ix–xxi.

1995a. ed. *Theory in Archaeology: A World Perspective*. London, Routledge.

1995b. Introduction: archaeological interpretation in a world context. In P. J. Ucko, 1995a, pp. 1–27.

Ucko, P. J. and T. Champion. 2003. eds. *The Wisdom of Egypt: Changing Visions through the Ages*. London, UCL Press.

Ucko, P. J., M. Hunter, A. J. Clark, and A. David. 1991. *Avebury Reconsidered: From the 1660s to the 1990s*. London, Unwin Hyman.

Ucko, P. J. and A. Rosenfeld. 1967. *Palaeolithic Cave Art*. London, Weidenfeld and Nicolson.

Uhle, M. 1907. The Emeryville shellmound. Berkeley, *University of California Publications in American Archaeology and Ethnology* 7: 1–107.

Upham, S. 1990. ed. *The Evolution of Political Systems: Sociopolitics in Small-Scale Sedentary Societies*. Cambridge, Cambridge University Press.

van der Leeuw, S. and J. McGlade. 1997. eds. *Time, Process and Structural Transformation in Archaeology*. London, Routledge.

Van Dyke, R. M. and S. E. Alcock. 2003. eds. *Archaeologies of Memory*. Oxford, Blackwell.

VanPool, C. S. and T. L. VanPool. 1999. The scientific nature of postprocessualism. *American Antiquity* 64: 33–53.

VanPool, T. L. and C. S. VanPool. 2003. eds. *Essential Tensions in Archaeological Method and Theory*. Salt Lake City, University of Utah Press.

Van Reybrouck, D. 2001. Howling wolf: the archaeology of Lewis Binford. *Archaeological Dialogues* 8: 70–85.

Van Riper, A. B. 1993. *Men Among the Mammoths: Victorian Science and the Discovery of Human Prehistory*. Chicago, IL, University of Chicago Press.

Van Sertima, I. 1977. *They Came Before Columbus: The African Presence in Ancient America*. New York, Random House.

Van Seters, J. 1983. *In Search of History: Historiography in the Ancient World and the Origins of Biblical History*. New Haven, CT, Yale University Press.

Vansina, J. 1985. *Oral Tradition as History*. Madison, University of Wisconsin Press.

Vastokas, J. M. and R. K. Vastokas. 1973. *Sacred Art of the Algonkians: A Study of the Peterborough Petroglyphs*. Peterborough, ON, Mansard Press.

Vaughan, A. T. 1979. *New England Frontier: Puritans and Indians, 1620–1675*. 2nd edn. New York, Norton.

1982. From white man to red skin: changing Anglo-American perceptions of the American Indian. *American Historical Review* 87: 917–53.

References

Vázquez León, L. 1996. *El Leviatán Arqueológico: Antropología de una Tradición Científica en México*. Leiden, Research School CNWS. 2nd edn. Mexico, DF, CIESAS, 2003.

Vázquez Varela, J. M. and R. Risch. 1991. Theory in Spanish archaeology since 1960. In I. Hodder, 1991a, pp. 25–51.

Veit, U. 1984. Gustaf Kossinna und V. Gordon Childe: Ansätze zu einer theoretischen Grundlegung der Vorgeschichte. *Saeculum* 35: 326–64.

1989. Ethnic concepts in German prehistory: a case study on the relationship between cultural identity and archaeological objectivity. In S. J. Shennan, 1989a, pp. 35–56.

2001. German prehistoric archaeology. In T. Murray, 2001a, pp. 576–85.

Vidal de la Blache, P. 1952. *Principles of Human Geography*. London, Constable.

Vinsrygg, S. 1986. Time in archaeological thought: China and the West. In *Time, Science, and Society in China and the West (Study of Time, 6)*, ed. by J. T. Fraser, N. Lawrence and F. C. Haber, pp. 225–40. Amherst, University of Massachusetts Press.

Vishnyatsky, L. B., A. A. Kovalev, and O. A. Scheglova. 2004. eds. *The Archaeologist: Detective and Thinker*. St. Petersburg, St. Petersburg University Press.

Vishnyatsky, L. B. et al. 1992. Review of B. Trigger, *A History of Archaeological Thought*. *Rossyskaya Arkheologiya* 3: 251–62.

Vita-Finzi, C. and E. S. Higgs. 1970. Prehistoric economy in the Mount Carmel area of Palestine: site catchment analysis. *Proceedings of the Prehistoric Society* 36: 1–37.

von Daniken, E. 1969. *Chariots of the Gods?* New York, Putnam's.

1971. *Gods from Outer Space*. New York, Putnam's.

von Gernet, A. D. 1985. *Analysis of Intrasite Artifact Spatial Distributions: The Draper Site Smoking Pipes*. London, ON, Museum of Indian Archaeology Research Report no. 16.

1993. The construction of prehistoric ideation: exploring the universality-idiosyncrasy continuum. *Cambridge Archaeological Journal* 3: 67–81.

von Gernet, A. and P. Timmins. 1987. Pipes and parakeets: constructing meaning in an Early Iroquoian context. In I. Hodder, 1987a, pp. 31–42.

von Haast, J. 1871. Moas and moa hunters. *Transactions of the New Zealand Institute* 4: 66–107.

1874. Researches and excavations carried out in and near the Moa-bone Point Cave, Sumner Road in the year 1874. *Transactions of the New Zealand Institute* 7: 54–85.

Vyverberg, H. 1989. *Human Nature, Cultural Diversity and the French Enlightenment*. Oxford, Oxford University Press.

Wace, A. J. B. 1949. The Greeks and Romans as archaeologists. *Société royale d'archéologie d'Alexandrie, Bulletin* 38: 21–35.

Wahle, E. 1915. Urwald und offenes Land in ihrer Bedeutung für die Kulturentwicklung. *Archiv für Anthropologie* N.S. 13: 404–13.

References

1921. Die Besiedelung Südwestdeutschlands in vorrömischer Zeit nach ihren natürlichen Grundlagen. *Bericht der Römisch-germanischen* Kommission 12. Frankfurt, Baer.

1941. *Zur ethnischen Deutung frühgeschichtlicher Kulturprovinzen: Grenzen der frühgeschichtlichen Erkenntnis 1*. Heidelberg, Sitzungsberichte der Heidelberger Akademie der Wissenschaften, Philologisch-historische Klasse, Jahrgang 1940/41, 2 Abhandlung.

Walde, D. and N. Willows. 1991. eds. *The Archaeology of Gender*. Calgary, Archaeological Association of the University of Calgary.

Walker, M. 2003. The Ludlow Massacre: labor struggle and historical memory in southern Colorado. *Historical Archaeology* 37: 66–80.

Walker, S. T. 1883. The aborigines of Florida. Washington, DC, *Annual Report of the Smithsonian Institution for 1881*: 677–80.

Wallace, A. F. C. 1950. A possible technique for recognizing psychological characteristics of the ancient Maya from an analysis of their art. *The American Imago* 7: 239–58.

1999. *Jefferson and the Indians: The Tragic Fate of the First Americans*. Cambridge, MA, Harvard University Press.

Wallerstein, I. 1974. *The Modern World-System*, vol. 1. New York, Academic Press.

Walters, H. B. 1934. *The English Antiquaries of the Sixteenth, Seventeenth and Eighteenth Centuries*. London, Walters.

Wang, Gungwu. 1985. Loving the ancient in China. In I. McBryde, pp. 175–95.

Wang, Tao. 1997. Establishing the Chinese archaeological school: Su Bingqi and contemporary Chinese archaeology. *Antiquity* 71: 31–6.

Wanklyn, H. G. 1961. *Friedrich Ratzel: A Biographical Memoir and Bibliography*. Cambridge, Cambridge University Press.

Waring, A. J., Jr and P. Holder. 1945. A prehistoric ceremonial complex in the southeastern United States. *American Anthropologist* 47: 1–34.

Warren, C. N. and S. Rose. 1994. William Pengelly's Techniques of Archaeological Excavation. Torquay, UK, Torquay Natural History Society, Publication 5.

Warren, S. H. 1905. On the origin of "eolithic" flints by natural causes, especially by the foundering of drifts. *Journal of the Royal Anthropological Institute* 35: 337–64.

Washburn, W. E. 1967. Joseph Henry's conception of the purpose of the Smithsonian Institution. In *A Cabinet of Curiosities*, ed. by W. M. Whitehill, pp. 106–66. Charlottesville, University Press of Virginia.

Watkins, J. E. 2000. *Indigenous Archaeology: American Indian Values and Scientific Practice*. Walnut Creek, CA, AltaMira Press.

2003. Beyond the margin: American Indians, First Nations, and archaeology in North America. *American Antiquity* 68: 273–85.

Watson, J. B. 1925. *Behaviorism*. New York, Norton.

References

Watson, P. J. 1979. *Archaeological Ethnography in Western Iran.* Viking Fund Publications in Anthropology no. 57. Tucson, University of Arizona Press.

1986. Archaeological interpretation, 1985. In J. Meltzer et al., pp. 439–57.

1990. Trend and tradition in southeastern archaeology. *Southeastern Archaeology* 9(1): 43–54.

Watson, P. J. and M. Fotiadis. 1990. The razor's edge: symbolic-structuralist archeology and the expansion of archeological inference. *American Anthropologist* 92: 613–29.

Watson, P. J., S. A. LeBlanc, and C. L. Redman. 1971. *Explanation in Archeology: An Explicitly Scientific Approach.* New York, Columbia University Press.

1984. *Archeological Explanation: The Scientific Method in Archeology.* New York, Columbia University Press.

Watson, R. A. 1972. The "New Archaeology" of the 1960s. *Antiquity* 46: 210–15.

Watson, W. 1981. The progress of archaeology in China. In J. D. Evans et al., pp. 65–70.

Wauchope, R. 1962. *Lost Tribes and Sunken Continents: Myth and Method in the Study of American Indians.* Chicago, IL, University of Chicago Press.

1965. Alfred Vincent Kidder, 1885–1963. *American Antiquity* 31: 149–71.

Webb, W. S. and W. D. Funkhouser. 1928. *Ancient Life in Kentucky.* Frankfurt, Kentucky Geological Survey.

Weber, E. J. 1976. *Peasants into Frenchmen: The Modernization of Rural France, 1870–1914.* Stanford, CA, Stanford University Press.

Wedel, W. R. 1938. *The Direct-Historical Approach in Pawnee Archeology.* Washington, DC, Smithsonian Miscellaneous Collections no. 97(7).

1941. *Environment and Native Subsistence Economies in the Central Great Plains.* Washington, DC, Smithsonian Miscellaneous Collections no. 101(3).

Weeks, K. 1979. ed. *Egyptology and the Social Sciences: Five Studies.* Cairo, American University in Cairo Press.

Weiss, R. 1969. *The Renaissance Discovery of Classical Antiquity.* Oxford, Blackwell.

Welch, P. D. 1998. *Ancient Monuments of the Mississippi Valley* by E. G. Squier and E. H. Davis: the first classic of US archaeology. *Antiquity* 72: 921–7.

Welinder, S. 1991. The word förhistorisk, "prehistoric," in Swedish. *Antiquity* 65: 295–6.

Wells, P. S. 1984. *Farms, Villages, and Cities: Commerce and Urban Origins in Late Prehistoric Europe.* Ithaca, NY, Cornell University Press.

Wendt, H. 1955. *In Search of Adam.* Boston, MA, Houghton Mifflin.

Wengrow, D. 1999. The intellectual adventures of Henri Frankfort: a missing chapter in the history of archaeological thought. *American Journal of Archaeology* 103: 597–613.

2003. Landscapes of knowledge, idioms of power: the African foundations of ancient Egyptian civilization reconsidered. In D. O'Connor and A. Reid, pp. 121–35.

Wenke, R. J. 1981. Explaining the evolution of cultural complexity: a review. *Advances in Archaeological Method and Theory* 4: 79–127.

Whallon, R., Jr. 1968. Investigations of late prehistoric social organization in New York State. In S. R. and L. R. Binford, pp. 223–44.

1982. Comments on "explanation." In A. C. Renfrew and S. Shennan, pp. 155–8.

Wheeler, R. E. M. 1954. *Archaeology from the Earth*. Oxford, Oxford University Press.

White, J. P. 1974. *The Past is Human*. Sydney, Angus and Robertson.

White, J. P. and J. F. O'Connell. 1982. *A Prehistory of Australia, New Guinea and Sahul*. Sydney, Academic Press.

White, L. A. 1945. "Diffusion vs. evolution": an anti-evolutionist fallacy. *American Anthropologist* 47: 339–56.

1949. *The Science of Culture*. New York, Farrar, Straus.

1959. *The Evolution of Culture*. New York, McGraw-Hill.

1975. *The Concept of Cultural Systems*. New York, Columbia University Press.

White, N. M., L. P. Sullivan, and R. A. Marrinan. 1999. eds. *Grit-Tempered: Early Women Archaeologists in the Southeastern United States*. Gainesville, University Press of Florida.

White, R. 1993. Introduction. In A. Leroi-Gourhan, pp. xiii–xxii.

Whiteley, P. M. 2002. Archaeology and oral tradition: the scientific importance of dialogue. *American Antiquity* 60: 405–15.

Whitley, D. S. and J. D. Keyser. 2003. Faith in the past: debating an archaeology of religion. *Antiquity* 77: 385–93.

Wiener, N. 1961. *Cybernetics*. 2nd edn. Cambridge, MA, M.I.T. Press.

Wilcox, D. R. and W. B. Masse. 1981. eds. *The Protohistoric Period in the North American Southwest, AD 1450–1700*. Tempe, Arizona State University, Anthropological Research Paper no. 24.

Wilcox, D. J. 1987. *The Measure of Times Past: Pre-Newtonian Chronologies and the Rhetoric of Relative Time*. Chicago, IL, University of Chicago Press.

Wilk, R. R. 1985. The ancient Maya and the political present. *Journal of Anthropological Research* 41: 307–26.

Wilkinson, J. G. 1837. *Manners and Customs of the Ancient Egyptians*. 6 vols. London, John Murray.

Willett, F. 1967. *Ife in the History of West African Sculpture*. London, Thames and Hudson.

Willey, G. R. 1948. A functional analysis of "horizon styles" in Peruvian archaeology. In *A Reappraisal of Peruvian Archaeology*, ed. by W. C. Bennett, pp. 8–15. Menasha, WI, Society for American Archaeology Memoir 4.

1953. *Prehistoric Settlement Patterns in the Virú Valley, Peru*. Washington, DC, Bureau of American Ethnology, Bulletin no. 155.

1956. ed. *Prehistoric Settlement Patterns in the New World*. New York, Viking Fund Publications in Anthropology no. 23.

1966. *An Introduction to American Archaeology*, vol. 1, *North and Middle America*. Englewood Cliffs, NJ, Prentice-Hall.

1971. *An Introduction to American Archaeology*, vol. 2, *South America*. Englewood Cliffs, NJ, Prentice-Hall.

1974a. ed. *Archaeological Researches in Retrospect*. Cambridge, MA, Winthrop.

1974b. The Virú Valley settlement pattern study. In G. R. Willey, 1974a, pp. 147–76.

1985. Ancient Chinese-New World and Near Eastern ideological traditions: some observations. *Symbols*, spring issue, 14–17, 22–3.

1988. *Portraits in American Archaeology: Remembrances of Some Distinguished Americanists*. Albuquerque, University of New Mexico Press.

Willey, G. R., W. R. Bullard Jr, J. B. Glass, and J. C. Gifford. 1965. *Prehistoric Maya Settlements in the Belize Valley*. Cambridge, MA, Papers of the Peabody Museum of Archaeology and Ethnology no. 54.

Willey, G. R. and P. Phillips. 1955. Method and theory in American archeology, II: historical-developmental interpretation. *American Anthropologist* 57: 723–819.

1958. *Method and Theory in American Archaeology*. Chicago, IL, University of Chicago Press.

Willey, G. R. and J. A. Sabloff. 1974. *A History of American Archaeology*. London, Thames and Hudson.

1980. *A History of American Archaeology*. 2nd edn. San Francisco, CA, Freeman.

1993. *A History of American Archaeology*. 3rd edn. New York, Freeman.

Williams, H. 2003. ed. *Archaeologies of Remembrance: Death and Memory in Past Societies*. New York, Kluwer Academic.

Williams, S. 1991. *Fantastic Archaeology: The Wild Side of North American Prehistory*. Philadelphia, University of Pennsylvania Press.

Wilmsen, E. N. and J. R. Denbow. 1990. Paradigmatic history of San-speaking peoples and current attempts at revision. *Current Anthropology* 31: 489–525.

Wilson, D. 1851. *The Archaeology and Prehistoric Annals of Scotland*. Edinburgh, Sutherland and Knox.

1862. *Prehistoric Man: Researches into the Origin of Civilisation in the Old and the New World*. London, Macmillan.

1876. *Prehistoric Man*. 3rd edn. London, Macmillan.

Wilson, D. 1975. *Atoms of Time Past*. London, Allen Lane.

Wilson, D. M. 1976. ed. *The Archaeology of Anglo-Saxon England*. London, Methuen.

References

Wilson, E. O. 1975. *Sociobiology: The New Synthesis*. Cambridge, MA, Harvard University Press.

Wilson, J. A. 1964. *Signs and Wonders upon Pharaoh*. Chicago, IL, University of Chicago Press.

Winstone, H. V. F. 1990. *Woolley of Ur: The Life of Sir Leonard Woolley*. London, Secker and Warburg.

Wiseman, J. 1980a. Archaeology in the future: an evolving discipline. *American Journal of Archaeology* 84: 279–85.

1980b. Archaeology as archaeology. *Journal of Field Archaeology* 7: 149–51.

1983. Conflicts in archaeology: education and practice. *Journal of Field Archaeology* 10: 1–9.

Wissler, C. 1914. Material cultures of the North American Indians. *American Anthropologist* 16: 447–505.

1917. The new archaeology. *American Museum Journal* 17: 100–1.

Wittfogel, K. A. 1957. *Oriental Despotism: A Comparative Study of Total Power*. New Haven, CT, Yale University Press.

Wiwjorra, I. 1996. German archaeology and its relation to nationalism and racism. In M. Díaz-Andreu and T. Champion, 1996a, pp. 164–88.

Wobst, H. M. 1974. Boundary conditions for Paleolithic social systems: a simulation approach. *American Antiquity* 39: 147–78.

1978. The archaeo-ethnology of hunter-gatherers or the tyranny of the ethnographic record in archaeology. *American Antiquity* 43: 303–9.

Wolf, E. R. 1982. *Europe and the People without History*. Berkeley, University of California Press.

Wolfram, S. 2000. "Vorsprung durch Technik" or "Kossinna Syndrome"? Archaeological theory and social context in post-war West Germany. In H. Härke 2000a, pp. 180–201.

Wood, E. M. 2000. Capitalism or enlightenment? *History of Political Thought* 21: 405–26.

Wood, M. 1998. The use of the Pharaonic past in modern Egyptian nationalism. *Journal of the American Research Center in Egypt* 35: 179–96.

Woodbury, R. B. 1973. *Alfred V. Kidder*. New York, Columbia University Press.

Woodman, P. C. 1995. Who possesses Tara? Politics in archaeology in Ireland. In P. J. Ucko 1995a, pp. 278–97.

Woolley, C. L. 1950. *Ur of the Chaldees*. Harmondsworth, UK, Penguin (1st edn 1929).

Worsaae, J. J. A. 1849. *The Primeval Antiquities of Denmark*, trans. By W. J. Thoms. London, Parker.

Wortham, J. D. 1971. *British Egyptology, 1549–1906*. Newton Abbott, UK, David and Charles.

Wotzka, H. P. 1997. Massstabsprobleme bei der ethnischen Deutung neolithischer "Kulturen." *Das Altertum* 43: 163–76.

References

Wright, G. A. 1971. Origins of food production in southwestern Asia: a survey of ideas. *Current Anthropology* 12: 447–77.

Wright, R. P. 1996. ed. *Gender and Archaeology*. Philadelphia, University of Pennsylvania Press.

Wylie, M. A. 1982. Epistemological issues raised by a structuralist archaeology. In I. Hodder, 1982c, pp. 39–46.

　1985a. The reaction against analogy. *Advances in Archaeological Method and Theory* 8: 63–111.

　1985b. Facts of the record and facts of the past: Mandelbaum on the anatomy of history "proper." *International Studies in Philosophy* 17: 71–85.

　1985c. Putting Shakertown back together: critical theory in archaeology. *Journal of Anthropological Archaeology* 4: 133–47.

　1989a. Archaeological cables and tacking: the implications of practice for Bernstein's "Options beyond objectivism and rationalism." *Philosophy of the Social Sciences* 19: 1–18.

　1989b. The interpretive dilemma. In *Critical Traditions in Contemporary Archaeology*, ed. by V. Pinsky and A. Wylie, pp. 18–27. Cambridge, Cambridge University Press.

　1992. The interplay of evidential constraints and political interests: recent archaeological research on gender. *American Antiquity* 57: 15–35.

　1993. A proliferation of new archaeologies: "Beyond objectivism and relativism." In N. Yoffee and A. Sherratt, pp. 20–26.

　1996. The constitution of archaeological evidence: gender politics and science. In *The Disunity of Science: Boundaries, Contexts, and Power*, ed. by P. Galison and D. J. Stump, pp. 311–43. Stanford, CA, Stanford University Press.

　1997. The engendering of archaeology: refiguring feminist science studies. *Osiris* 12: 80–99.

　2000. Questions of evidence, legitimacy, and the (dis)unity of science. *American Antiquity* 65: 227–37.

　2002. *Thinking from Things: Essays in the Philosophy of Archaeology*. Berkeley, University of California Press.

Wyman, J. 1875. *Fresh-Water Shell Mounds of the St. John's River, Florida*. Salem, MA, Memoirs of the Peabody Academy of Science no. 4.

Yalouri, E. 2001. *The Acropolis: Global Fame, Local Claim*. Oxford, Berg.

Yates, F. A. 1964. *Giordano Bruno and the Hermetic Tradition*. Chicago, IL, University of Chicago Press.

Yellen, J. E. 1977. *Archaeological Approaches to the Present: Models for Reconstructing the Past*. New York, Academic Press.

Yellowhorn, E. C. 2002. Awakening Internalist Archaeology in the Aboriginal World. PhD dissertation, Montreal, Department of Anthropology, McGill University.

Yelton, J. K. 1989. A comment on John Rowzée Peyton and the Mound Builders: the elevation of a nineteenth-century fraud to a twentieth-century myth. *American Antiquity* 54: 161–5.

References

Yengoyan, A. A. 1985. Digging for symbols: the archaeology of everyday material culture. *Proceedings of the Prehistoric Society* 51: 329–34.

Yentsch, A. 1991. The symbolic division of pottery: sex-related attributes of English and Anglo-American household pots. In R. H. McGuire and R. Paynter, 1991, pp. 192–230.

Yoffee, N. 1999. Robert McCormick Adams b. 1926. In T. Murray, 1999a, pp. 791–810.

   2005. *Myths of the Archaic State: Evolution of the Earliest Cities, States, and Civilizations*. Cambridge, Cambridge University Press.

Yoffee, N. and G. L. Cowgill. 1988. eds. *The Collapse of Ancient States and Civilizations*. Tucson, University of Arizona Press.

Yoffee, N. and A. Sherratt. 1993. eds. *Archaeological Theory: Who Sets the Agenda?* Cambridge, Cambridge University Press.

Zammito, J. H. 2002. *Kant, Herder, and the Birth of Anthropology*. Chicago, IL, University of Chicago Press.

Ziadeh, G. 1995. Ethno-history and "reverse chronology" at Ti'innik, a Palestinian village. *Antiquity* 69: 999–1008.

Zimmerman, A. 2001. *Anthropology and Antihumanism in Imperial Germany*. Chicago, IL, University of Chicago Press.

Zittel, K. A. von. 1901. *History of Geology and Palaeontology to the End of the Nineteenth Century*. London, Scott.

Zvelebil, M. 1996. Farmers our ancestors and the identity of Europe. In P. Graves-Brown et al., pp. 145–66.

INDEX

Abbott, Charles C., 186
Abdi, K., 571
Abercromby, John, 223
aborigines (Australia): and concept of
  dream-time, 41; and cross-cultural studies of
  hunter-gatherers, 441; and Darwinian
  evolutionism, 170; and evolutionary
  archaeology, 189–93, 209; and studies of
  seasonality, 358; and totemism in cave art,
  155. *See also* indigenous peoples
Abu El-Haj, Nadia, 13, 557, 571
Abydos (Egypt), 502
Academia Sinica (Beijing), 267
Académie Celtique, 213
Achaemenian dynasty (Persia), 272
Achulean handaxes, 139, *140f*, 150, 308
Acosta, José de, 115–16
Adams, Barbara, 502
Adams, E. W., 572
Adams, Robert McC., 352–3, 379, 402, 413
Adams, William Y., 298, 568, 572
adaptive systems, cultures as, 398
Adena culture (U.S.), 159–63
Adorno, Theodor, 445
aerial photography, 317, 556, 573
Africa: decolonization since 1960s and changes
  in archaeology of, 275–6; postprocessual
  archaeology and Hodder's research in,
  452–3; and racism in evolutionary
  archaeology, 195–207; resources on
  development of archaeology in, 554, 567,
  571. *See also* Great Zimbabwe; South Africa
African-Americans, and historical archaeology,
  515
African burial ground site (New York), 515
Afrikaaners, 197, 203
Agassiz, Louis, 169
agency, and postprocessual archaeology,
  468–70
Agricola, Georgius, 93
agriculture: development of in Africa, 206; and
  economic approaches to
  functional-processual archaeology, 323; and
  environmental functional-processualism,
  318–9; and hunter-gatherers, 533, 534; and
  New Archaeology, 411; oasis theory of, 12,
  317. *See also* irrigation systems
Alberti, B., 571, 580
Alberti, Leon Battista, 54

Albright, William F., 272, 375
Alcock, S. E., 560
Aldrovandi, Ulisse, 93
Alexander VI, Pope, 55
Algonquian speaking peoples, 183, 285, 475
Allen, H., 567
Allen, J., 569
Allen, Susan, 558
Allesbrook, M., 558, 561
Alpert, H., 573
Altamira (Spain), 155
alternative interpretations, and multiple
  working hypotheses, 514–15
Althusser, Louis, 444, 467, 469
Amarna (Egypt), 502
American Anthropological Association, 393,
  449, 549–50
American Antiquarian Society, 161
American Philosophical Society, 161
American Revolution, and Enlightenment, 177
An, Z., 570
analogies: and Clark on ethnography, 357; and
  direct historical approach, 511, 516; and New
  Archaeology, 416–17; and theory in
  culture-historical archaeology, 307–8. *See also*
  ethnography; homologies
analytical theory, 432
Anau (Turkmenistan), 234, 317
Andah, Bassy, 275, 511, 567, 571
Andersen, Knud, 358
Anderson, B., 568
Andersson, J. G., 265, 266
Andrén, A., 556
androcentrism, and gender archaeology, 459
animals. *See* domestication; extinct mammals;
  faunal remains; fossils; zooarchaeology
Annales School, 478
Annapolis (Maryland), 515
anthologies, of papers on history of
  archaeology, 559
anthropology: cultural evolution in American
  of 1950s and 1960s, 387; and
  culture-historical archaeology in Germany,
  235; diffusionism and Viennese school of,
  219; and education of prehistoric
  archaeologists, 22; and future of
  archaeology, 538–9. *See also* cultural
  anthropology; ethnography; ethnology;
  physical anthropology;

Index

Index

Aztecs, 42, 116, 178, 179

Babylon, 44, 70, 72
Bachofen, Johann, 154
Bacon, Francis, 26, 97
Bagford, John, 139
Bahn, Paul, 552, 580
Bahrani, Z., 571
Bailey, G., 575
Baines, J., 560
Bakker, J. A., 569, 570
Balter, Michael, 16, 559, 579, 580
Bandelier, Adolf, 280
Bandinelli, Baccio, 55
Bantu, and Great Zimbabwe, 199, 201
Barford, P. M., 569
Barkan, E., 568
Barkan, L., 560–1
Barnard, F. M., 563
Barnes, A. S., 152
Barnes, Barry, 18, 468, 542
Barnes, G., 562, 570
Barnett, S. A., 564
Barreto, C., 571
Barrett, John, 472
barrows (England), 113
Barth, Frederick, 309
Barthélemy, Jean-Jacques, 70
Barton, Benjamin, 159
Bartram, William, 117–18, 159, 184
Bar Yosef, O., 571
Basalla, G., 559
Basketmaker cultures (U.S.), 280, 281–2
Bastian, Adolf, 154, 218, 219, 235
Baté, Luis, 496
Batres, Leopoldo, 276
Bayard, D. T., 578
Bazelmans, J., 570
"Beaker folk," 223
Beard, Mary, 65–6
Beardsley, Richard, 380
Beauchamp, Joseph de, 70
Beazley, John, 65–6
Becker, C., 547
behavior and behaviorism: and abandonment of dysfunctional patterns, 488; archaeological interpretation and changing theories of, 24; and biological archaeology, 491–5; and cognitive archaeology, 491; and cultural evolutionism in American anthropology, 387; and diversification of processual archaeology, 425; high-level theory and comprehensive theory of, 523; material culture and goals of archaeology, 506–508; and New Archaeology, 394, 400, 402, 415, 417–18; and postprocessual archaeology in Europe, 481–2; rationalist versus romantic views of, 11; subjectivity and explanations of, 545; and universal generalizations, 37. See also behavioral correlations; cognition
behavioral archaeology, 426–8, 497. See also biological archaeology

behavioral correlations, and middle-ranging theory, 509–10, 512, 516
Beiser, F. C., 563
Belgae, 223
beliefs: future of archaeology and popular, 541; and historical archaeology, 505; and postprocessual archaeology, 450; and processual archaeology, 424. See also ideology; religion
Bell, A. S., 558, 564
Bel-Shalti-Nannar (Iraq), 44
Belzoni, Giovanni, 68
Benedict, Ruth, 365, 370
Benjamin, Walter, 18
Benjamin of Tudela, Rabbi, 70
Bennett, John W., 367, 575
Bent, J. Theodore, 197, 198f
Ben-Yehuda, N., 571
Berkhofer, R. F., Jr., 563
Bernal, Ignacio, 553, 571
Bernal, M., 561, 567
Bernbeck, R., 571
Bernier, François, 169
Berr, Henri, 256
Bersu, Gerhard, 300
Bertalanffy, Ludwig von, 419, 578
Best, Elsdon, 193–4
Bianchini, Francesco, 56
Bibby, Geoffrey, 552, 563, 573
Bible: and antiquity of humanity, 142–3, 168; and culture-historical archaeology in Palestine and Israel, 272, 274; and early European views of Indians, 115; and Egyptology, 68; and evolutionary archaeology in Africa, 197; and medieval view of history, 50–1; and Middle Eastern archaeologists, 158; and Montelius's interpretation of European prehistory, 228; and stone tools, 93, 95; and text-aided archaeology in Israel, 503–504; and traditional chronology, 137, 138
biblical archaeology, 556
bibliographical resources: and antiquarianism, 562–3; and classical and text-based archaeologies, 560–2; and culture-historical archaeology, 567–72; and evolutionary archaeology, 565–7; and functional-processual archaeology, 572–6; and pragmatic synthesis, 580–1; and prehistoric archaeology, 563–5; and processual and postprocessual archaeology, 576–80; and study of history of archaeology, 549–60
Bieder, R. E., 565, 566
Biehl, P. F., 580
Bietak, Manfred, 502
big-game hunting societies, 412, 533. See also hunting practices
Bignamini, I., 561
Billman, B. R., 576
binary oppositions, and postprocessual archaeology, 463, 465, 511

683

Index

Index

Index

Index

Index

Index

Index

Index

Index

Index

Leeds, E. T., 214
Lefkowitz, M. R., 567
Legendre, J.–P., 570
Legrand d'Aussy, Pierre, 110
Leibniz, Gottfried, 90
Leland, John, 85
Lelas, S., 559
Leman, Thomas, 113
Le Moustier site (France), 148–9
Lenin, V. I., 326, 327
Leone, Mark, 393, 428–9, 460, 577, 578, 579
Leppmann, W., 561
Lepsius, Karl, 68, 202
Leroi-Gourhan, André, 307, 463–4, 466, 476, 478, 492, 570
Le Roy, Julien-David, 60
Leroy, Loys, 99
Leube, A., 570
levels, in settlement patterns, 379
Levine, P., 558, 564
Lévi-Strauss, Claude, 463, 465, 467, 479, 511
Levitt, J., 574
Lewer, N., 571
Lewis-Williams, J. D., 476
Lhwyd, Edward, 94
Libby, Willard F., 382, 576
Li Ji (Li Chi), 76, 265, 266, 562, 570
linearization, as evolutionary mechanism, 424
Linnaean-style system, for classifying pottery, 298
Linnaeus, Carolus, 169
Linton, Ralph, 375
Lissarrague, François, 505
literature, revival of German in 18th century, 214. *See also* autobiographies; bibliographical resources; biographies; Gothic literature
lithic debitage, analysis of, 300. *See also* stone tools
Lithic period, and culture-historical archaeology in U.S., 289
Lithuania, 250
Liu, L., 570
Lloyd, Seton, 551–2, 562
localities, and culture-historical archaeology in U.S., 289
local nationalism, and ethnicity in Soviet Union, 339
Locke, John, 116
logicism, 479–80
Lombard kings (Italy), 48
London Society of Antiquaries, 84
Long, Edward, 169
Longacre, William A., 393, 403, 405
Longshan culture (China), 266
Lorenzo, J. L., 571
Lowenthal, D., 560
Lowie, Robert, 365
low-level generalizations, 31–2, 36
Lubbock, John, 147–8, 171–6, 177, 189, 208, 565
Lucretius Carus, Titus, 104
Lu Dalin, 74

Ludlow Massacre site (Colorado), 515
Lumbreras, Luis, 496
Lyell, Charles, 144–5, 146, 157
Lyman, R. Lee, 15–16, 180, 556, 557, 558, 559, 572, 576, 576
Lynch, B. D. & T. F., 562
Lyon, E., 559, 572
Lyttelton, Bishop Charles, 94

McBryde, Isabel, 566
McCall, D. F., 571
McCann, W. J., 570
McCarthy, Fred D., 191, 566
McCarthy, Joseph, 396
McCulloh, James, 159
McDonald, William, 501, 561
McGregor, John C., 284
McGuire, J. D., 181, 187
McGuire, Randall, 495, 576
McIntosh, R. J., 567
McKay, A. G., 564
McKern, William C., 283, 284, 558
McKusick, M., 558, 566
McLennan, John, 154
McNairn, B., 569
McNeill, William, 4
MacCormack, S., 563
MacDonald, S., 561
Macedonia, 249
MacEnery, Rev. John, 141, 142
MacGaffey, W., 567
Macintosh, N. W. G., 568
MacKendrick, P., 560
Mackinder, H. J., 317
MacNeish, Richard S., 373, 558, 575
Macpherson, James, 112
MacWhite, Eóin, 308, 310
Madison, Rev. James, 159
Magdalenian culture (France), 255
Maglemosian culture (Denmark), 238, 353
Mahr, Adolph, 253
Mahudel, Nicolas, 105
Maischberger, M., 570
Majewski, Erazm, 239
Major, Johann, 90
Malina, Jaroslav, 10, 555
Malinowski, Bronislaw, 319–20, 321, 365
Mallows, Wilfrid, 200
Malmer, Mats, 479
Malone, C., 570
Malthus, Thomas, 36
mammoths, 142, 143
Mammoth and Wooly Rhinoceros Age, 148
Man Makes Himself (Childe, 1936), 345–6
Maori, 193–5
Mao Zedong, 266
Marchand, S. L., 550, 557, 561
Marcus, Joyce, 424, 503, 514, 571
Marcuse, Herbert, 18, 445
Marek, Kurt (C. W. Ceram), 551
Mariátegui, José, 496
Mariette, Auguste, 69

Index

Index

Index

National Bureau of Cultural Relics (China), 266–7

National Institute of Anthropology and History (Mexico), 277

nationalism: and antiquarianism in France, 89; and Australian prehistory, 192; and beginnings of prehistoric archaeology, 133, 136; bibliographical resources on, 554, 568, 569–70; and culture-historical archaeology in India, 270–1; and development of culture-historical archaeology in Europe, 248–61, 300; and early interest in ethnicity, 212; emergence of African, 205; and Kossinna on ancient Germans, 236, 240; and romanticism, 112; and Scandinavian archaeology, 214; and Zimbabwe, 200. *See also* patriotism

National Museum of Ireland, 253

National Polytechnical School (Mexico), 277

National Science Foundation (U.S.), 373, 407

Native Americans. See North American indigenous peoples

natural selection: and antiquity of humanity, 146–7; and biological archaeology, 495; and evolutionary archaeology, 173–4, 175, 176, 487; and processual archaeology, 429; and racism, 170; and role of induction and deduction in scientific theory, 36–7

nature, distinction between culture and, 465–6

Nazi party (Germany), 240–1, 487, 570

Neal, W. G., 199

Neanderthals, 170, 255, 403

Nederveen Pieterse, J., 566

Nelson, Nels C., 280, 281, 295

Neo-Confucianism, 76

neoconservatism, 260, 543

neoevolutionism, 386–92, 395, 396, 410, 436, 437, 449, 576

Neo-Marxism, 34, 445, 449

neoracism, 495

Netherlands, 99, 478, 570

networks, and settlement archaeology, 377

neuroscience, and binary oppositions, 463

New Archaeology: bibliographical resources on, 577; and conjunctive approach to functional-processual archaeology, 371–2; in England, 433–6; processualism and early, 392–418; and role of institutions, 16; and views of North American indigenous peoples, 542. *See also* processual archaeology

"new classical archaeology," 501

"new Culture History," 581

New Economic Policy (Soviet Union), 327, 328

New Guinea, and lake dwellings, 134

Newton, Charles, 66

Newton, Isaac, 97, 106, 351

New World, and study of past in colonial settings, 114–18

New Zealand, 193–5, 567

Niebuhr, Barthold, 62

Nigeria, 205, 275

Nihon Shoki (Chronicles of Japan), 76

Nilsson, Sven, 12, 129–30, 315, 564

Nineveh, 70, 71*f*

Nippur (Iraq), 72

nomothetic generalizations, and New Archaeology, 408, 409

non-cultural formation processes (N-transforms), 427–8

Nordenskiold, Gustaf, 280

Normans, and English national identity, 214

North American indigenous peoples: and beginnings of prehistoric archaeology in U.S., 158–64; and culture-historical archaeology in U.S., 286, 288–9; and diffusion, 542; early European theories on origins of, 114–18, 177, 563; evolutionary archaeology in U.S. and views of, 183–5, 188–9, 566; and New Archaeology, 409–10; political activism by and postprocessual archaeology, 458; and polygenic theories of human origins, 169. *See also* Algonquian speaking peoples; Cree; Creek Indians; Moundbuilders; Pueblo Indians; Shoshone; Siouan speaking peoples; Zuñi sites

Norway, 234, 250. *See also* Scandinavia and Scandinavian archaeology

Nott, Josiah C., 169

November Uprising of 1830 (Poland), 250

Novgorod (Russia), 251–2

Nubia, and Egyptology, 68, 380, 505, 513

numismatics, 564

Nunamiut Eskimos (Alaska), 405–406, 417, 418*f*

Nünningh, J. H., 90

Nyerup, Rasmus, 119, 123

Nzewunwa, N., 571

oasis theory, of origin of food production, 12, 317

Obermaier, Hugo, 255, 280

Obermeilen (Switzerland), 134

objectivity, problem of in history of archaeology, 1–5. *See also* subjectivity

O'Brien, Michael, 15–16, 180, 556, 557, 558, 559, 572, 576

"occurrence seriation," 294–5, 297

O'Connor, David, 502, 567

O'Connor, T., 574

Odell, George, 440

Oklandnikov, A. P., 574

Oldovai Gorge (Kenya), 204–5

Olmec culture (Mexico), 42

Olsen, J. W., 570

Olympia (Greece), 63

On the Origin of Species (Darwin, 1859), 104, 146–7

Opovo site (Yugoslavia), 471

optimal foraging theory, 419

oral traditions: and historical interpretation, 510, 517; and New Zealand archaeology, 194, 195 *See also* folklore; myths

Orenstein, H., 573

Index

orientalism, 73
Orme, Bryony, 11, 579
Orser, C. E., Jr., 569
Ortelius, Abraham, 86
Ortman, Scott, 475–6
Orton, C., 578
Ossian (Celtic bard), 112
Ottaway, J. H., 569
Ottoman Empire, 255
Outline of Cultural Materials (Murdock et al., 1938), 369

Paddayya, K., 564, 580
Pagden, A., 563
Pahlavi, Mohammad Reza, 272
Paine, R., 571
palaeobotany, 361
palaeoeconomy, 361
paleoethnography, 371
palaeoethnological archaeology, in Soviet Union, 327–8, 330
Palaeo-Indian sites (U.S.), 279
palaeolithic archaeology: and African colonial archaeology, 203–5; and antiquity of humanity, 138–9; and beginnings of prehistoric archaeology, 147–56; bibliographical resources on, 564–5; and culture-historical archaeology, 255, 267; and disciplinary specialization, 15; and migration of hominids, 532–3; and radiocarbon dating, 384; and Soviet archaeology, 335, 341
palaeontology, 138–9, 141, 149, 519
palaeopsychology, 371, 401
Palestine, 272–5, 571
Pan-Russian Conference for Archaeology and Ethnography, 330
paradigms, and Kuhn's model of scientific practice, 6–9, 538, 553
Paris Exposition of 1867, 155
Parker, A. C., 362
Parker Pearson, Michael, 450, 451
Parry, G., 563
Parslow, C. C., 557
Parsons, J. R., 402
Parsons, T., 573
past: classical archaeology and interest in, 40–8, 560; Enlightenment and evolutionary view of, 97–105; history and reconstruction of, 530; medieval view of, 49–52; study of in colonial settings, 114–18
patriotism: and antiquarianism in northern Europe, 82; and early interest in ethnicity, 211; and Kossinna on ancient Germans, 236; and prehistoric archaeology in Denmark, 121; and Slavic archaeology, 340. *See also* nationalism
Patterson, Thomas C., 449, 495, 557, 566, 567, 569, 576, 578, 579
Pauketat, Timothy, 497
Paul II, Pope, 55
Pausanias (Greece), 46

Peabody Museum of Archaeology and Ethnology (Harvard University), 566
Peacock, D. P. S., 560
Peake, Harold J. E., 12, 242, 318–19, 325, 552
Pearce, R. H., 563
Pearson, R. J., 570
Pecos Conference (1927), 282
Pecos Pueblo (New Mexico), 280–1
Peel, J. D., 564
"peer polity" interaction, 438
Peiresc, Nicolas Fabri de, 89
Pengelly, William, 146, 565
Peregrine, P., 580
Pérez Gollán, J. A., 571
Pergamon (Greece), 64
Péringuey, Louis, 203
Perry, W. J., 220, 319
Persepolis (Iran), 70
Persian Empire, 70, 229, 272
Peru: and culture-historical archaeology, 276; and early functional-processual archaeology, 366, 375; Marxism and social archaeology in, 496; prehistoric archaeology of, 177–8; Spanish colonialism and destruction of archaeological monuments, 116–17. *See also* Inka; Latin America
Peter the Great, Czar, 91
Petrarch, 53
Petrie, W. M. F., 3, 24, 69, 158, 221–2, 291, *292f, 294–5, 296f,* 297, 562
Petrova-Averkieva, Yu, 575
phases, and Midwestern Taxonomic Method, 283, 284, 289
phenomenology, and postprocessual archaeology, 472–3, 474, 579
Phidias (Greece), 57
Phillips, Philip, 289, 307, 308, 390, 401, 409
philosophy: and Enlightenment, 99; and processual archaeology, 400–401, 578; and theory of culture-historical archaeology, 303–6. *See also* epistemology; idealism; materialism; positivism; rationalism
Phoenician alphabet, 70
physical anthropology, and Soviet archaeology, 338
physical sciences, and technical developments in archaeological interpretation, 23, 540
Picard, Casimir, 143
Piggott, Stuart, 10–11, 305–6, 307, 499, 537, 557, 558, 562, 563, 569
Pigorini, Luigi, 250
Pinsky, V., 572, 578
Pitt Rivers, Augustus Lane Fox, 291, 293–5, 300, 571
plants. *See* agriculture; floral remains; forest change; pollen analysis; vegetation zones
Platonova, Nadezhda, 574
Plekhanov, G. V., 334
Pliny the Elder, 46
Plog, Fred, 393, 408, 429
Pluciennik, M., 564
Podgayetsky, G. P., 330, 336, 348

Index

Poland: and culture-historical archaeology since 1990s, 489, 490; nationalism and archaeology in, 215, 250, 256; resources on development of archaeology in, 570
Polanyi, Karl, 432
Poliakov, L., 569
"political archaeology," 409
politics: aborigines and Australian, 192; and biological explanations of human behavior, 494; Childe and racism, 248; Cold War and functional-processual archaeology in U.S., 373, 396; and culture-historical archaeology in Japan, 263, 264; and culture-historical archaeology in Mexico, 277; and ideas about the past, 41–2; Indian activism and postprocessual archaeology in U.S., 458; influence of on archaeology, 3–4; and interpretation of archaeological data, 250–1; and Israeli archaeology, 274; and Kossinna's misuse of archaeological data, 236–7, 240–1; and postprocessual archaeology, 470–1; and poststructuralism, 467; and protest movements in U.S. of 1950s and 1960s, 410–11; and social context of archaeology, 530, 543–4, 555. *See also* conservatism; government; nationalism; patriotism
Politis, G. G., 496, 571, 580
pollen analysis, 316
Pollock, S., 571
polygenesis, and origins of human beings, 168–9, 565
Polynesians, 193–4, 195, 436, 514
polythetic definition, of archaeological cultures, 300
Pomian, K., 563
Pompeii, 58, 60, 63, 427
Pontoppidan, Erik, 95, 110
Popper, Karl, 27
popular culture, images of Africans in, 566
population: and colonial archaeology in U.S., 183; and development of civilization, 129–30, 324–5, 411
Porter, R., 564
Portugal, 253
positivism: and Binford's influence on New Archaeology, 400; and cultural evolutionism in American anthropology, 387; and epistemology in history of archaeology, 2; and postprocessual archaeology, 452; and processual archaeology, 29, 30, 578; and social context, 17, 530
Posnansky, M., 567, 571
Possehl, Gregory, 485–6
possibilism, and cultural change, 319. *See also* environmental possibilism
Post, E. J. Lennart von, 316
Postclassic period, and culture-historical archaeology in U.S., 289
postdepositional human activities, 427–8, 432
postmodernism, and postprocessual archaeology, 446–8, 449. *See also* radical postmodernism

postmold patterns, 300
postprocessual archaeology: bibliographical resources on, 555, 576–80; and biological explanations of human behavior, 494; and classical archaeology, 501–502; and competing theoretical approaches in post-2000 era, 485–6; as conscious alternative to processual archaeology, 444–78; and cultural archaeology, 495; and Egyptology, 502; in Europe, 478–80; and high-level theory, 521–2; and historical archaeology, 517; and ideas as principal determinants of behavior, 8; psychological states and determinants of human behavior, 526; and scientific theory, 29–30; and text-aided archaeology, 504–505
poststructuralism, and postprocessual archaeology, 467–8, 469
pottery types, and cultural history of American Southwest, 281, 295–9. *See also* ceramics
Powell, John Wesley, 184, 185, 187
practical applications, emphasis on in New Archaeology, 408–409. *See also* empiricism
practice theory, 469–70
Praxiteles (Greece), 57
preclass societies, and postprocessual archaeology, 445
predepositional theory, 431–2
prediction, and explanation in New Archaeology, 400–401
prehistorians, and archaeologists, 307, 354
prehistoric anthropology, and culture-historical archaeology in Germany, 235
prehistoric archaeology: and antiquarianism, 80, 110; beginnings of, 121–65, 535; bibliographical resources on, 563–5; and culture-historical archaeology, 216; and ethnology, 166; and historical or text-aided archaeology, 498–505, 517, 527; and Maya, 503; recognition of stone tools and development of, 92–7. *See also* prehistory
Prehistoric England (Clark, 1940), 357
Prehistoric Europe: The Economic Basis (Clark, 1952), 358, 360
Prehistoric Man (Wilson, 1876), 178
Prehistoric Society, 575
Pre-historic Times (Lubbock, 1865), 171–2, 175
prehistory: broad outline of trends in, 532–4; and culture-historical archaeology, 307; Mortillet's epochs of, 150, 151f; use of term, 133, 564; and psychological anthropology, 401; and world archaeology, 383. *See also* prehistorians; prehistoric archaeology; world archaeology
Prescott, William H., 178
presentism, in histories of science and archaeology, 26, 559–60
preservation, of material culture, 355
Press, G. A., 560
Preston, D., 576
Prestwich, Joseph, 146
Preucel, R. W., 578, 579, 580

702

Index

Prichard, James Cowles, 169–70
Priest, Josiah, 160
processual archaeology: bibliographical resources on, 576–80; Canada and combination with culture-historical archaeology, 312; and competing theoretical approaches in post-2000 era, 485–6; definition of, 314; diversification of, 418–44; and early New Archaeology, 392–418; in Europe, 478–80; and historical archaeology, 499; and indigenous peoples, 458; in Israel, 274; and Kuhn's idea of scientific revolutions, 7–8; and materialism, 349; and neoevolutionism, 386–92; and positivist epistemology, 29; and prehistoric archaeology, 517; and Soviet archaeology, 489; and universal generalizations, 37. *See also* functional-processual archaeology; postprocessual archaeology
"processual-plus" archaeology, 497
production, and Marxist archaeology, 331–2, 334, 496
professionalization: and classical archaeology, 64–5; and evolutionary archaeology in U.S., 187–8; and prehistoric archaeology in Germany, 235
progress, concept of, 98, 101–102, 346, 446
promotion, as evolutionary mechanism, 424
propaganda, and misinterpretation of archaeological data, 543–4
Proskouriakoff, Tatiana, 558
Prostov, E., 574
Protestant Reformation, 82
Prussia, and classical studies, 61–2
psychic unity, 100–102, 154, 167, 491
psychological anthropology, 365, 371, 401
psychology: and behaviorism, 387; and Binford on understanding of prehistory, 401–402
public interest: in controversies concerning archaeological finds, 3; in Japanese history, 264–5; in literature on history of archaeology, 551–2; in pre-Islamic history in Middle East, 271
public policy, and future of archaeology, 548. *See also* government
Pueblo Indians, 183, 280, 475–6
Pumpelly, Raphael, 12, 234, 317
punctuated equilibrium, 413
Puritans, in Massachusetts, 115
Putnam, Frederic W., 180, 186, 187, 188
Puycournian Epoch, 150

Qing Dynasty (China), 74–5
Quimby, G. I., 288, 363

race and racism: and biological explanations of human behavior, 494, 495; and colonialism, 556; and culture-historical archaeology, 236–7, 248; and diffusionism, 217; in Egyptology and Assyriology, 73; and

Euro-American views of Indians, 159, 160; and evolutionary archaeology, 167–71, 189, 195–207, 565–6, 567. *See also* ethnicity
Radcliffe-Brown, E. R., 319–20, 321, 365
radical postmodernism, 447
radiocarbon dating, 382–4, 576
Raglan, Lord, 220
Raleigh, Walter, 97
Ramage, N., 561
Ramsden, P. G., 504
Randall-MacIver, David, 199
random intrasite sampling, 402
Ranov, V. A., 574
Raphael, 54
Rappaport, Roy, 424
Rathje, William, 393, 426
rationalism: and antiquarianism, 110; Binford and New Archaeology, 395; and ecological archaeology, 525; and Enlightenment, 98; and logicism, 480; and romantic approaches to archaeology, 537; and views of human behavior, 11
Ratnagar, S., 571
Ratzel, Friedrich, 218–19, 233, 279, 567
Ravdonikas, V. I., 329f, 330, 334, 338, 574
Ravetz, A., 569
Rawlinson, Henry, 70
Raynal, Guillaume-Thomas, 178
Read, D. W., 578
realism: and epistemology of science, 30; and processual archaeology, 578
Redfield, Robert, 366
Redford, D. B., 560
Redman, Charles L., 393, 419, 425, 577
refuse disposal, patterns of, 426, 427
regional catastrophism, 141
regional cultural chronologies, and culture-historical archaeology in U.S., 285–6, 288
regional diversity, in history of archaeology, 12–15, 536
regional surveys, and New Archaeology, 402
regions, and culture-historical archaeology in U.S., 289
Reid, A., 567
Reid, D. M., 556, 562, 571
Reid, Thomas, 99
Reinach, Salomon, 229
Reindeer Age, 148, 150
Reisner, George, 69, 203, 280
relative dating, and prehistoric archaeology, 121–9, 135
relativism: and biological explanations of human behavior, 494; continuing challenge of, 529–31; and cultural construction of gender, 516; and postmodernism, 446, 447; and postprocessual archaeology, 468, 470, 477; and scientific theory, 28; and social context of archaeology, 18–19, 40; use of term, 2–3. *See also* cultural relativism

Index

religion: and antiquarianism, 77, 120; and archaeology in Palestine and Israel, 273, 274; and biological archaeology, 492–4; and development of archaeology in Japan, 76, 263; and fundamentalism in contemporary U.S., 547; and interest in past, 44–5; and Montelius's interpretation of European prehistory, 228; and postprocessual archaeology, 450; and sacrifices as behavioral correlations, 509; and transmission of Cree ecological knowledge, 525. *See also* Bible; creationism; deism; Hinduism; Roman Catholic Church

Renaissance: and antiquarianism, 52–61; bibliographical resources on, 561; and Egyptology, 67

Renfrew, Colin, 259–60, 383–4, 393, 413, 425, 433–6, 501, 568, 576, 577, 579, 580

rescue archaeology, 301, 303, 444

retrieval theory, 432

revisionist studies, of Soviet archaeology, 573

revolution: and Childe's influence on archaeology, 247, 324–5, 573; Kuhn's model of scientific, 6–9. *See also* cultural revolution; French Revolution

Rey, Estrella, 496

Rey, Pierre-Philippe, 444

Reyman, J. E., 550, 575

Rhode, Andreas & Christian, 90

Rhodes, Cecil, 197

Rhodesia Ancient Ruins Limited, 197, 199

Rice, M., 561

Rich, Claudius, 70

Richerson, Peter, 525

Ridgeway, William, 66

Ridgway, D., 569

Ridley, R. T., 550, 557, 561, 562

Rigollot, Marcel-Jérôme, 144, 146

Rindos, David, 429–30

Ripley site (New York), 362

Ritchie, William, 363

ritual, and postprocessual archaeology, 451

Rivers, W. H. R., 219–20

Robenhausen (Switzerland), 134

Robertshaw, P. T., 567, 571

Robertson, William, 99, 103, 178

Robinson, Keith, 201

Rodden, J., 562, 564

Roemer, C., 555, 561

Rogers, G. M., 567

Roman Catholic Church, 49–52, 115

Roman Empire: and culture-historical archaeology, 216; and evolutionary view of cultural development, 104; French interest in, 213; and interest in past, 46–7; and medieval view of history, 48–9; and Renaissance antiquarianism, 53–4, 56, 57, 60. *See also* Pompeii

Romanesque architecture, 49

Roman-German Boundary Commission, 300

Roman-Germanic Central Museum, 216

romanticism: and antiquarianism, 110–14; and rationalist approaches to archaeology, 537; and views of human behavior, 11

Rose, M. A., 565

Rosellini, Ippolito, 68

Rosetta Stone, 68

Rosicrucianism, 68

Rossi, P., 560, 561

Rous, John, 84

Rouse, Irving B., 289, 299, 363–4, 415, 568

Rousseau, Jean-Jacques, 111, 174

Rowe, J. H., 561, 566

Rowlands, Rev. Henry, 118

Rowlands, M. J., 307, 452

Rowley-Conwy, Peter, 354, 563, 564, 568, 575

Royal Geographical Society, 197

Royal Museum of Ethnology (Berlin), 154

Royal Society of London, 106, 107, 112, 146, 537

Rudbeck, Olof, 88

Rudenko, S. I., 328, 574

Rudolph, R. C., 562

Ruskin, John, 217

Rushton, J. P., 495

Russia: and antiquarianism, 91–2; and classical archaeology, 64; and culture-historical archaeology since 1990s, 490; and development of archaeology in late 19th century, 230–2; and environmental functional-processualism, 316–17. *See also* Soviet Union

Russian Academy for the History of Material Culture (RAIMK), 326

Russian Academy of Sciences, 91

Russian Archaeology Society, 231

Rygh, Olof, 234

Sabloff, Jeremy A., 5, 282–3, 364, 532, 553, 556, 559, 562, 565, 566, 571, 575, 576, 578

Sabloff, P., 576

Sackett, James, 142, 564

Sahlins, Marshall D., 389, 436, 441, 449, 469, 494, 576

Saint-Simon, Henri de, 320

Saitta, Dean, 509

Salazar, António, 253

Salmon, Merrilee H., 440, 492, 578

Salmon, W. C., 440

salvage archaeology, 340, 556

Samothrace (Greece), 63

sampling strategies, and New Archaeology, 402, *404f*

San (South Africa), 417, 441

San Cristóbal Pueblo site (New Mexico), 280, 295

Sanders, William T., 380, 402

Sanderson, S. K., 564

Sandford, E. M., 560

San Juan baskets (southwestern U.S.), 370

San Miguel Amantla (Mexico), 277

Sanoja, Mario, 496

Santley, R. S., 402

Index

Index

Index

theory: and culture-historical archaeology, 303–11; definition of scientific, 28; and generalizations, 30–8; literature on current status of, 580–1; and New Archaeology, 415. *See also* high-level theory; middle-range theory

thermodynamic systems, and cultural evolution, 388

Thom, René, 413

Thomas, C. G., 561

Thomas, Cyrus, 180, 181, 183, 185, 201

Thomas, D., 578

Thomas, Isaiah, 161

Thomas, Julian, 470, 472, 579, 580

Thomas, N., 561

Thompson, J., 562

Thompson, M., 571, 574

Thomsen, Christian, 7, 22, 121–9, 132, 135, 137, 233–4, 564

Thomson, Donald, 309, 357–8

Thomson, George, 347

Thorlacius, Skuli, 105

Three-Age concept, 104–105, 123, 128, 132, 562, 564

Thruston, G. P., 279

Thucydides, 46

Thule culture (Canada), 308

Tiahuanaco horizon (Peru), 366

Tilley, Christopher, 19, 450–2, 464, 466, 467–9, 470, 472, 579

time, culturally variable concepts of, 41

Timmins, Peter, 476

Tindale, Norman, 191

Tiye, Queen (Egypt), 44

Tokugawa period, 76

Tokyo National Museum, 262

Tolstov, S. P., 341, 342

Tooker, E., 578

Tószeg (Hungary), 242

Toulmin, Stephen, 10, 560

tourism: and culture-historical archaeology in Mexico, 277–8; and future of archaeology, 544; and Pharaonic heritage in Egypt, 271; and prehistoric archaeology in Switzerland, 135

Tournal, Paul, 141, 142

Tracing Archaeology's Past (Christenson, 1989), 549

trade: functional-processual archaeology and definition and context of, 324; and Montelius's chronology for European prehistory, 227–8

Tradescant, John, 85

Tret'yakov, P. N., 330, 336, 341

Trevor-Roper, H. R., 205

Trigger, Bruce, 12, 380, 555, 559, 563, 564, 565, 566, 567, 568, 569, 575–6, 577, 578–9

Tringham, Ruth, 471, 569, 574, 578

Tripolje culture (Russia), 231, 234

Trois-Rivières (Quebec), 117

Troy, Schliemann's excavation of, 291

Tsetskhladze, G. R., 575

Tsuboi Shogoro, 262

Tularosa black-on-white pottery, 298

Turgot, Marie-Robert-Jacques, baron de l'Aulne, 99, 101, 103

Turkmenia, and Soviet archaeology, 342

Turner, D., 571

Turner, F., 561

Twyne, John, 85, 93

Tylor, Edward B., 154, 233, 525

typological method, and Montelian synthesis of European prehistory, 224–32

Ucko, Peter, 25, 467–8, 555, 563, 567, 569

Uhle, Max, 180, 280, 566

Ulkestrup (Denmark), 358

Umehara Suezi, 263

Únětice culture (Czech Republic), 234

uniformitarianism, 29, 144–5, 259, 416, 564

unilinear evolutionism, 153, 173, 184, 208–9, 338, 341, 346

unilinear views, of history of archaeology, 10, 559–60

United States: and beginnings of prehistoric archaeology, 158–64; and contemporary beliefs on evolution, 52; cultural resource management and rescue archaeology in, 444; and culture-historical archaeology, 278–90, 301, 303, 368; and early functional-processual archaeology, 361–7, 380, 382; and early New Archaeology, 392–418; evolutionary archaeology in, 177–89; and future of archaeology, 539, 547; and link between prehistoric archaeology and ethnology, 166; and Marxism, 449–50; neoevolutionism and processualism in, 386–92; and postprocessual archaeology, 448–9, 456–62, 477–8; radiocarbon dating and prehistory of, 384; resources on development of archaeology in, 553, 554, 556, 559, 561, 565, 566, 572, 575–6, 577, 578–9. *See also* North American indigenous peoples

universal laws, on human nature, 37, 491–5, 516–17

universities: and archaeology courses in Africa, 206; and future of archaeology, 538–9; Kossinna's followers in German, 240; and professionalization of archaeology in U.S., 187; and Soviet archaeology, 327

University of Chicago, 393

University of Melbourne, 191

University of Michigan, 393

University of Minnesota, 501

University of Moscow, 327

University of Petrograd, 327

University of Sydney, 191

Uppsala (Sweden), 88

Ur (Iraq), 70, 72, 158

urbanism: and Childe on development of civilization, 324–5; and Maya ceremonial centers, 513

Urgeschichte (history of beginnings), 80

Index